W9-BOH-142

EGYPT

EGYPT

Mona Russell

 ABC-CLIO

Santa Barbara, California • Denver, Colorado • Oxford, England

Library of Congress Cataloging-in-Publication Data

Russell, Mona.
  Egypt / Mona Russell.
     p. cm. — (Middle East in focus)
  Includes bibliographical references and index.
  ISBN 978-1-59884-233-3 (hardcopy : alk. paper) — ISBN 978-1-59884-234-0 (e-book)
1. Egypt. I. Title.
  DT46.R87 2013
  962—dc23   2012020948

ISBN: 978-1-59884-233-3
EISBN: 978-1-59884-234-0

17 16 15 14 13   1 2 3 4 5

This book is also available on the World Wide Web as an eBook.
Visit www.abc-clio.com for details.

ABC-CLIO, LLC
130 Cremona Drive, P.O. Box 1911
Santa Barbara, California 93116-1911

This book is printed on acid-free paper ∞

Manufactured in the United States of America

Copyright Acknowledgments

Image found on chapter opening pages:

Detail from coffin of Nespawershepi, chief scribe of the Temple of Amun. Osiris, Isis, Horus and the beast that devoured the hearts of the dead that failed to balance against the feather of truth. Country of Origin: Egypt. Culture: Ancient Egyptian. Date/Period: 21st dynasty, c. 984 BC. Place of Origin: Western Thebes. Material Size: painted wood. (Werner Forman Archive/ Fitzwilliam Museum, Cambridge Location: 39.)

To Hailey & Jasmine

Contents

About the Author and Contributors

Mona Russell is an associate professor of modern Middle East history at East Carolina University, specializing in the history of women and gender in Egypt. She has published a number of articles, chapters, and a translation on this topic, as well as her monograph *Creating the New Egyptian Woman: Consumerism, Education, and National Identity, 1863–1922.* Her upcoming project is a textbook on Women and Gender in the Modern Middle East.

Pamela Allegretto-Diiulio, PhD, is an assistant professor of English literature and composition at Argosy University. Her book *Naguib Mahfous: A Western and Eastern Cage of Female Entrapment* was published in 2007, and she is a reviewer for the *International Journal for Applied Educational Studies.* She has a special interest in Egyptian literature, authors, poets, and publishers.

Ramsey M. Awwad earned a BBA in economics and finance at the American University of Kuwait. He is a research analyst at KIPCO Asset Management (KAMCO) in Kuwait City.

Jelena Bogdanović (PhD Princeton University) is an assistant professor at Iowa State University. She specializes in architectural history of Byzantine, Slavic, Western European, and Islamic cultures. Her contributions have been published in *Byzantinoslavica, Byzantinische Zeitschrift, Hilandarski Zbornik, Serbian Studies, Annales d'Esthétique, The Encyclopaedia of the Hellenic World* (2008), *The Oxford Dictionary of the Middle Ages* (2010), *Spatial Icons. Performativity in Byzantium and*

Medieval Russia (Moscow, 2011), *Dionysius the Areopagite between Orthodoxy and Heresy* (Newcastle, 2011), and *Approaches to Byzantine Architecture and Its Decoration* (Ashgate, 2012).

Karen Culcasi is an assistant professor of geography in the Department of Geology and Geography at West Virginia University. She completed her doctoral degree at Syracuse University in 2008. Employing critical geopolitical and cartographic lenses, Karen's research examines both Western and Arab geographical imaginings of the Middle East and the Arab world. Her recent publications include articles in *Political Geography*, *Antipode*, *The Geographical Review*, and *Aether: The Journal of Media Geography*. Karen has recently received a grant to pursue a new research project on Palestinian Refugees in Jordan.

Patrick Herman is an MA candidate in the Program for Maritime Studies at East Carolina University. His interests include modern European history, navies in the age of sail, and the maritime history of the Pacific Northwest. He is currently working on a project to document and explore the cultural relevance of the historic ferry MV *Kalakala*.

Aly Mansour is an associate professor of management at the American University of Kuwait in the newly founded College of Business and Economics. He has been the vice president of the Association for Egyptian-American Scholars since 2010. After graduating from the American University in Cairo in 1975, he worked as a diplomat with the Egyptian Foreign service for almost 20 years, during which time he obtained his master's and doctorate degrees at the George Washington University. Since the 1990s, Dr. Mansour has presented several papers concerning the enhancement of the economy and higher education in Egypt.

Note on Transliteration

This work is aimed at the nonexpert. All names appear without diacritical marks with one standard spelling; uniformity and consistency has been the goal, but undoubtedly some errors remain. Words, such as infitah and jihad, that have been incorporated into the jargon of the profession remain without diacriticals and unitalicized. Where appropriate, certain words and proper names have been rendered for their pronunciation in Egyptian dialect, for example, Kefaya and Zamalek. Other Arabic terms have a simple transliteration without markings for long vowels.

Acknowledgments

This book is the product of working in the field of Egyptian history for many years, and the opportunity came at the time of my father's death in 2008. It gave me a chance to fill a void in my life with love and passion, just as a young man from Wisconsin did when he met a beautiful Egyptian graduate student and married her in 1959. Being only half-Egyptian meant (in my household) that Arabic was not spoken in the home and it was something I had to do on my own. My unique roots influenced the direction of my studies, which were enhanced when I did a year of intensive language study on CASA fellowship in Cairo (1991–1992). During this time I gained fluency in colloquial Egyptian dialect. Not only being able to read documents and newspapers, but speaking with ordinary Egyptians in daily life added a new dimension to my life and my research. From these conversations in taxi cabs, the National Library, health clubs, homes, restaurants, and stores, from my Egyptian mentor the late Raouf Abbas directing me to sources to the waiter suggesting specials of the day, I began to learn more and more about life from Egyptians, who are extraordinarily helpful, solicitous, and engaging.

Some of the most endearing friendships of my lifetime have been made as a result of my research on Egypt. The friends made during my CASA fellowship, during my ARCE grants, 1994–1995 and 2002, as well as the summers of 2008 and 2009 not only sustained my separation from my nuclear family, but provided me with some of the most valuable professional contacts of my lifetime. Through this network of friends I have met countless other friends as a result of my participation in the Middle East Studies Association of North America. The continuing high quality of its Egypt panels has greatly contributed to the success of this volume. The generation or so of students that have completed dissertations since I finished mine have raised the bar and continued the path first broken by my mentors, Judith Tucker, Amira Sonbol, and Peter Gran, and their generation. The list of friends and people whose work I admire is so lengthy that I fear leaving someone's name out. Examining the bibliography of each chapter will be useful for seeing the names of many young, promising scholars, as well as those established in the field. The only exception to the no-name rule is my long-time friend Lisa Pollard, who entered the archives and libraries of Cairo at the same time as myself and has remained close ever since. My own work on advertising and the press has colored this volume. References to advertising, cartoons, and caricatures, generally refer to my own primary source research.

The contributors to this volume have done a tremendous job, and their work speaks for itself. I am grateful to East Carolina University (ECU) in general, as well as the Harriot College of Arts and Sciences and the School of Art and Design in particular for their generous support and for putting me in touch with Jelena Bogdanović, who contributed the chapter on art. She, in turn, has received nurturing support from the colleagues in her department, and valuable time from her graduate assistants. Her presence at ECU will be greatly missed. I am appreciative of the semester of release time that I received when I first began the project, as well as the start-up funds that allowed me to travel to Egypt in the summers of 2008 and 2009. I am particularly grateful for the help I received from my graduate assistant Adam Stoddard in the fall of 2008. He compiled most of the holiday chart, provided information on associations, and helped me locate some of the contributors. He even offered some of his personal photographs. My graduate assistant Patrick Herman in 2012 edited and coauthored the economy chapter.

Finally, I would like to thank my family both near and far. My extended family in Egypt hosted me for endless Friday lunches, festive birthday gatherings, beautiful weddings, memorable passings and commemorations, and countless visits. Being part of my mother's family gave me a vista into Egyptian family life that most Americans never see, and they provided me with love and support while I was away from home. Furthermore, my mother's good nature and many friendships, as well as the sheer size of her family allowed me entrance into circles of society that would make most scholars envious. My nuclear family also deserves its share of praise for putting up with Mom's absence and frustration over her many deadlines. I could not ask for a better team than Pete, Hailey, and Jasmine Boyer. My daughters Hailey and Jasmine, as well as my niece Camille Russell, accompanied me on a trip to Upper Egypt in the summer of 2009, as well as revisiting many museums and sights in and around Cairo, which reawakened my fondness for ancient Egyptian history, seeing it through the eyes of the young. The girls helped with photography and morale during the sweltering heat of Upper Egypt in June. We were also blessed with a remarkable tour guide, Amr, who helped this modern historian navigate her way through ancient Egypt.

Mona L. Russell, April 2012

CHAPTER 1

Geography

Karen Culcasi

INTRODUCTION

Egypt has existed as a place of continuous civilization for thousands of years. Its long and famed history has earned the country an indisputable place in the geographical imaginations of people across the globe, as well as on world maps. Though the boundaries and geographical extent of Egypt have shifted over its long history (see Chapter 2), what has remained the most formative aspect of its geography and history is the Nile River. Cutting through a vast desert landscape, the Nile River has been the "lifeline" of Egypt since its earliest civilizations. Indeed, after the Greek historian Herodotus traveled through Egypt in the fifth century BCE, he wrote that Egypt was the "gift of the Nile." A second formative geographical feature is its position at the crossroads of Africa, Europe, and Asia. Located in the northeastern corner of the African continent, myriad peoples and armies have traveled and settled throughout Egypt for thousands of years. Today, Egypt's geographical positioning in the Middle East has made it a key player in world and regional geopolitics, particularly in the Palestinian–Arab–Israeli conflict.

The modern country is officially known as the Arab Republic of Egypt, but in Arabic it is generally referred to as "*Miṣr.*" Egypt's capital city of Cairo sits on the banks of the Nile in the northern portion of the country. Internally, Egypt is divided in 29 administrative units, or governorates. Each governorate has a central city, a governor, and many of them have further subdivisions. The irregular patchwork of Egypt's governorates is highly reflective of the country's population distribution. There is a clustering of governorates around the Nile River and the Nile Delta where the majority of Egypt's population is found. Compared to the desert regions

1

Egypt Today. (ABC-CLIO)

of Egypt, the governorates around the Nile River have a smaller land area, but a greater population. For example, Cairo, the sixth governorate, is only 83 square miles, but it is home to approximately 7,786,640 people. While in southwestern Egypt, the 17th governorate of New Valley is nearly 145,369 square miles, but has a population of only 187,256. The total land area of Egypt is approximately 386,662 square miles (1,001,450 square kilometers), which is an area smaller than the state of Alaska, but significantly larger than Texas. The Mediterranean Sea forms most of Egypt's northern boundary, while the Red Sea constitutes much of its eastern boundary. Its western border with Libya is 693 miles (1,115 kilometers) long, while to the south it shares a 791 mile (1,273 kilometers) political border with Sudan. On Egypt's Sinai Peninsula, it shares a 7 mile (11 kilometers) land boundary with the Gaza Strip and almost 159 miles (255 kilometers) with Israel. Several of Egypt's international boundaries are considered geopolitical "hotspots," but perhaps most contentious are the borders it shares with Israel and the Gaza Strip (see "Geopolitics" subsequently).

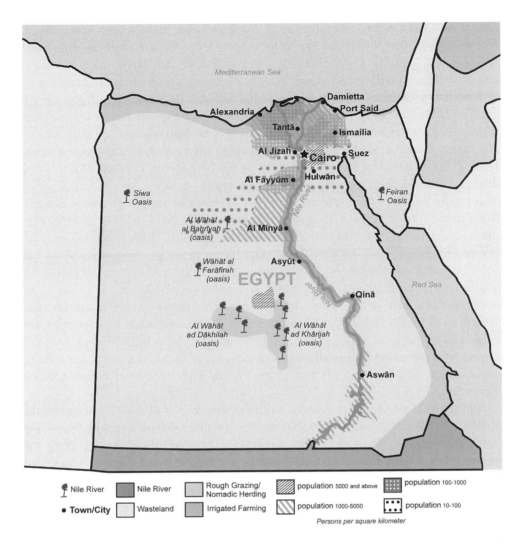

Egypt: Land Use and population density. (ABC-CLIO)

PHYSICAL LANDSCAPES

From the fertile, emerald green Nile Valley and its Delta to the expansive desert that surrounds it, Egypt's physical geography is one of stark contrasts. Defined in great part by the Nile and the desert, there are four distinct physical landscapes of Egypt—the Nile Valley and Delta, the vast Western Desert, the rugged Eastern Desert, and the mountainous Sinai Peninsula.

Egypt is located entirely within the expansive Sahara Desert of North Africa. In this arid and inhospitable environment, the Nile has provided the water and fertile soils that have sustained large and thriving civilizations over thousands of years. Thus, the Nile Valley and its Delta is where nearly all of Egypt's arable land, its major cities, and its population are located (as well as most of ancient Egypt's relics). At 4,184 miles (6,695 kilometers), the Nile is the longest river in the world. The sources of the Nile River are to the south in the East African Highlands of Ethiopia and Uganda. From these highlands, the Blue Nile River flows westward and the White Nile River flows northward to converge (known as the confluence) in Khartoum, Sudan. From Khartoum the single Nile River then flows northward to transverse the entire north–south length of Egypt. It passes through the capital of Cairo and then branches off into several distributaries, which eventually empty into the Mediterranean Sea through an expansive, fan-shaped delta. Built up by continuous sedimentation from the Nile River, the Nile Delta is one of the world's largest river deltas (at approximately 8,495 square miles), and has historically been a population and agricultural center of Egypt. There are literally thousands of agricultural settlements throughout the delta, as well as large textile manufacturing cities. Mahalla al-Kubra and Shubra al-Khayma, two textile-producing giants, have become large population centers for workers since the (re)creation of local industry close to the site of cotton production. Mansura, in addition to its agricultural and commercial significance, is home to the site of an important crusader battle, where tourists can still visit ruins. Other commercial centers in the delta, for example, Zagazig and Tanta, are home to spiritual festivals, celebrating local saints (see Chapters 5 and 6). Alexandria, Egypt's second largest city, is located at the northwestern extreme of the delta (see subsequently), while on the northeastern extreme is Port Said, where the Suez Canal's Mediterranean port is located.

Egypt's Eastern Desert extends from the eastern banks of the Nile River to the Red Sea. Rocky plateaus and rugged mountains dominate this region, creating a harsh environment. However, there has been substantial development along the coastal fringe of the Eastern Desert, which is an area renowned for its white sand beaches and world-class scuba diving. The small port city of Suez is located in this region. At the southern terminus of the Suez Canal, this geostrategic city is a place of international transit, but it has also been a geopolitical hot spot (see "Geopolitics" subsequently).

To the west of the Nile is the expansive Western Desert, which constitutes more than two-thirds of Egypt's total land area. There are two distinct physical landscapes in this region. The first is the rocky plateaus of the southeast, and the second is the sand dunes to the northwest. Stretching from the Libyan border to the southeast plateaus, the Great Sand Sea contains some of the world's tallest sand dunes. Within this vast and harsh desert there are several natural depressions in which fresh water is available. These scattered oases have helped sustain life and livelihoods in the desert for centuries. For example, the town of Siwa near the Libyan border is a lush oasis replete with date and olive groves, and has seen continuous settlement since around the 10th century BCE.

The Sinai Peninsula is the triangular-shaped "land bridge" of northeastern Egypt that connects the African and Asian continents. For centuries, various peoples, pilgrims, and armies have both traveled through and occasionally settled there. Its physical landscape is dry and dominated by rugged mountains. On the eastern side of the peninsula is the Gulf of Aqaba, which shares its coastline with Israel,

Siwa Oasis. (AP Photo/Annedore Smith)

Jordan, Saudi Arabia, and Egypt. On the western side of the peninsula is the Gulf of Suez, and to the north of the Gulf of Suez is the internationally geostrategic Suez Canal. Both the Gulf of Aqaba and the Gulf of Suez are the arms of the Red Sea, which extend northward to the Mediterranean Sea. Like the Red Sea coast of the Eastern Desert, sun- and surf-related tourism has developed along the coasts of the Sinai Peninsula. For example, Sharm el-Sheikh, Dahab, and Taba are all popular resort towns for Egyptian and foreign tourists alike. Mount Saint Catherine (Jebel Catherine) is located on the Sinai Peninsula. At 8,650 feet (2,637 meters), this is the tallest mountain in Egypt. Adjacent to Mount Saint Catherine is the celebrated and holy Mount Sinai (also known as Jebel Musa, Mount Moses, Mount Musa, or Mount Horeb). According to the Bible, Moses received the Ten Commandments on this mountain. The holy sites of the Burning Bush and Saint Catherine's Monastery (which is the oldest operating Christian monastery in the world) are located at the foot of Mount Sinai, making this place a popular destination for many believers of the "Abrahamic" religions.

Climatically, nearly all of Egypt is a desert. The official Koppen climatic classification system categorizes Egypt as a "hot desert climate," meaning that it has hot dry summers and warm dry winters. Annual rainfall in Egypt ranges from 0 to 14 inches (0 to 35 centimeters) and the average daily temperature is above 64.4 degrees F (18 degrees C). Of course, there are climatic variations throughout the country. In the town of Aswan, in the southern portion of the country, summer daytime high temperatures generally exceed 100 degrees F (40 degrees C) and rainfall is often nonexistent throughout the entire year. Cairo's summer high temperatures typically average around 95 degrees F (35 degrees C), and the city only receives rainfall during the winter months of November through February (less than 0.2 inches or 4 millimeters per month). Located on the Mediterranean Sea, the city of Alexandria is a bit cooler and wetter than most of Egypt.

Because Egypt is primarily a desert, there are no forests in the country. There are, however, a variety of orchards and groves scattered throughout the country. Along the Nile, papyrus, lotus, and jasmine are common plants. This valley is also where Egypt's agricultural sector thrives. Cotton, wheat, and corn are among Egypt's most common agricultural products, though there are many other crops grown for both domestic consumption and foreign trade. Wildlife is rather sparse in Egypt, but there are Nile crocodiles, camels, and abundant bird species, while the coral reefs along the Sinai Peninsula are renowned for supporting diverse fish species.

Egypt's natural resources are numerous. Egypt has oil (petroleum) and natural gas reserves in areas along both coasts of the Gulf of Suez, as well as in the Western Desert and the Mediterranean basin. In 1995, Egypt reached its peak oil production at 992,000 barrels per day (bpd). Compared with Saudi Arabia, for example, which in March 2009 produced well over 8 million bpd, Egypt's oil production is quite modest. Egypt's gas reserves, however, are more bountiful, and estimated to be the largest in the eastern Mediterranean. Egypt contains and excavates other natural resources such as gold, phosphates, and manganese and iron ore.

Like every country across the globe, Egypt is experiencing a variety of environmental problems. Perhaps the most critical concern is that of water scarcity. Though the Nile is the longest river in the world and it does provide Egypt with a wealth of water for irrigation, industry, and human consumption, the average annual flow of the Nile is lower than 32 other rivers across the globe. With global climate change and growing populations, arid climates such as that of Egypt are likely to experience more severe water shortages and desertification (the encroachment of the desert on arable land). Arable ground constitutes only 2.92 percent of all land in Egypt, thus the threat of desertification is a palpable concern for Egypt's economy and its food security. Water is also a scarce resource in Egypt's neighboring countries. Though the sources of the Nile are to the south of Egypt in the East African Highlands, Egypt controls and uses the majority of the river's waters. Unsurprisingly, the control of the Nile and its tributaries has been a contentious political issue throughout the entire Nile River water basin. Disagreements and nonviolent disputes between Egypt, Sudan, and Ethiopia have erupted over control of the Nile River. Such disputes have the potential of escalating as global climate change will likely make this water-scarce area of the world even drier.

The long-term impacts of development projects such as the booming tourist industry, the manufacturing sector, and the Aswan High Dam have caused numerous environmental concerns. Air quality is an enormously devastating problem in Egypt, and particularly in Cairo. The largest city not only in Egypt, but also in the entire African continent and the Arab World (which includes Arabic-speaking countries throughout North Africa and Southwest Asia), Cairo's air quality has

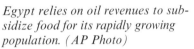

Egypt relies on oil revenues to subsidize food for its rapidly growing population. (AP Photo)

ASWAN HIGH DAM

The Nile River and its annual floods have been a central feature of Egypt's long history. Management of the Nile River's annual floods has been attempted throughout Egypt's past, but not until the late 19th century were large-scale dams constructed. The construction of these dams, and particularly the Aswan High Dam, has had several important and positive effects on Egypt. Completed in 1970, the Aswan High Dam has facilitated increased control of irrigation and crop production. It also generates clean hydroelectric power for the country. The Dam has even become a tourist attraction.

---

been ranked among the unhealthiest in the world. Air pollution not only affects the health of people, but it also threatens the continued preservation of many of Egypt's ancient relics and monuments. In the Mediterranean and Red Seas, offshore pollution due to oil production, agricultural runoff, and industrial waste is a concern. Formed in 1997, Egypt's Ministry of State for Environmental Affairs is cognizant of environmental issues and has made some attempts to reduce pollution and protect natural resources. In conjunction with the U.S. Agency for

---

REPERCUSSION OF THE ASWAN HIGH DAM

Although the dam has helped to control floods and produce energy, several concerns have emerged. Some of the rich soils that have been naturally deposited along the banks of the Nile River and in the Mediterranean for thousands of years are now being trapped in either the dam or in massive reservoir (known as Lake Nasser) to its south. There has been much concern over the long-term effects of the loss of this fertile soil on agriculture and aquatic wildlife, as well as concerns about the build-up of salts (salinization) along the Nile. Culturally, the building of the Aswan High Dam created international alarm over the inundation of several ancient Egyptian sites. UNESCO (United Nations Educational, Scientific, and Cultural Organization) intervened to help relocate many ancient relics such as Abu Simbel, but nevertheless, some were flooded and remain under water. The damming of the Nile also displaced approximately 100,000 Nubians who still consider the flooding of their land as an egregious offence by the Egyptian government.

International Development (USAID), there have been several initiatives to improve air quality and preserve Egypt's antiquities. Further, there are now several national parks and protected areas throughout Egypt, a number of them concentrated on the Sinai Peninsula.

STATE FORMATION

Egypt has been an independent state since 1952, but it has existed as a geographical entity since 3200 BCE. During its long history, the geographical size of Egypt has shifted greatly. Under the New Kingdom (approximately 1600 to 1000 BCE), Egypt's borders reached as far as modern-day Israel (and the occupied territories) and Lebanon. However, Egypt has been under nearly continuous foreign domination since the sixth century BCE, when Egypt fell to the Persian Empire.

European influence in Egypt began to grow at the end of the 18th century. However, Egypt was not geostrategically crucial to European powers until the Suez Canal opened in 1869. Located in the northeastern corner of the Sinai Peninsula, this 107-mile-long canal created a seafaring route through the Europe–Asia–Africa landmass by connecting the Mediterranean Sea to the Gulf of Suez, which ultimately connected the Atlantic and Indian Oceans. Before the opening of the canal, traveling from Europe to Asia meant circumventing the entire continent of Africa. For the British, the canal was an "imperial lifeline," meaning that they could access their "Crown Jewel" of India in less time and with less expense. A seafaring voyage from London to Bombay via the Cape of Good Hope (the tip of southern Africa) was 10,800 nautical miles, whereas the same trip via the Suez Canal was only 6,300 nautical miles. With a perceived need to secure its geostrategic position along the canal, in 1882 British military forces invaded Egypt. With this occupation, the United Kingdom had established itself as the de facto colonial power of Egypt (see Chapter 2).

During the peace negotiations that followed World War I, Egyptian nationalists fought to secure Egypt's freedom from the British. In 1922, after several years of upheavals and negotiations, the British declared Egypt an independent monarchy. However, Egypt's independence was merely nominal. The British were unwilling to grant Egypt complete independence greatly because they wanted to maintain control over the Suez Canal.

In 1952, a bloodless coup dubbed the Free Officers Revolution overthrew both the British and the Egyptian monarchy. Though it was not until 1956 that the British were entirely removed from Egypt (see "Geopolitics" subsequently), this revolutionary event signaled the beginning of Egypt's independence from foreign rule, as well as a drastic shift in the politics and governance of the country. Gamal Abd al-Nasser, a leader of the revolution, became president of Egypt in 1954. Nasser was a charismatic leader whose political agenda merged anti-imperialist, socialist, and nationalist ideologies. He strongly supported and cultivated the rise of Arab nationalism—a movement that sought to unite Arabic-speaking people across the Arab World—and soon became the undisputed leader of the Arab World. The Arab nationalist movement reached its pinnacle in 1958 when Egypt and Syria united to form the United Arab Republic. The unification of these two separate countries created one noncontiguous Arab country (the state of Israel wedged in between). Though the United Arab Republic broke apart less than three years later, during this short period of time, the political map of the world changed.

HUMAN LANDSCAPES

Egypt is a country of diverse peoples and cultures, yet there are several traits or identities that help to unify Egyptians. Most Egyptians speak Arabic and about 92 percent of Egypt's population identify themselves as Arab. However, much of what it means to be Egyptian is simply to live in Egypt. Therefore, Egyptians include the Arab ethnic majority as well as other ethnic groups such as Nubians from the southern portion of Egypt, Berbers from around Alexandria, and ethnic Armenians and Greeks in Cairo. Although considered Arab, other minority groups in Egypt include the semi-nomadic Bedouin people of the Sinai Peninsula and the Christian Copts. Religion plays an important part of the identity of most Egyptians (see Chapter 5). Approximately 90 percent of Egyptians are Sunni Muslim and 10 percent are Christian. Though a minority today, the Christian Copts are considered to be the ancestors of ancient Egyptians. When the Arab-Islamic conquest of the seventh century reached Egypt, the Copts eventually adopted the Arabic language, but they resisted conversion to Islam (see Chapter 6). It is also important to note that even though many Americans or "Westerners" consider Egypt to be a part of the "Middle East," that is a term created by "Westerners" and it has very little significance to people living in Egypt (as well as the rest of the Middle East).

With a population of approximately 83,082,869, Egypt is the most populous country in both the Middle East and the Arab World. Egypt's growth rate is relatively high, at just over 1.6 percent (the United States' growth rate is slightly less than 1 percent). As mentioned earlier, the population of Egypt is concentrated along Nile Valley and its delta, where nearly all of Egypt's rural communities and cities are located. About 43 percent of the Egyptians live in cities, and this trend toward urban living (urbanization) is increasing at about 1.8 percent a year.

Cairo, or *al-Qahira* in Arabic, is the capital city of Egypt. Located along the east bank of the Nile River, its metropolitan population in 2003 was 10.8 million (New York City was 18.3 million). Cairo is the largest city in the Arab World, the Middle East, and the entire African continent. The area where Cairo is located today was settled in the early first century. The ancient cities of Memphis and al-Fustat were located just outside modern-day Cairo. In 969, the Fatimid Empire (909–1171) named the burgeoning city "al-Qahira" and declared the city its capital. Since the Fatimid era, Cairo has been considered a cultural, educational, and political center. Often referred to as the "city of a thousand minarets," Cairo is famous for its Islamic architecture, its old souk (marketplace) Khan al-Khanili, and its celebrated Egyptian Museum. Alexandria, or *al-Iskandariyya* in Arabic, is located on the Mediterranean Sea to the western extreme of the Nile Delta. It is the second largest city in Egypt, but it boasts Egypt's largest and most important port. Alexander the Great founded Alexandria in 332 BCE and soon afterward it became the capital of the Ptolemaic Empire (305 to 30 BCE). Today, Alexandria houses a renovated version of the famous Library of Alexandria, the largest library of the ancient world, and contains many relics from the Ptolemaic Empire.

The beauty of Corniche in Alexandria has captivated visitors since its creation in the fourth century BCE. (Courtesy of Mona Russell)

Both Cairo and Alexandria are popular destinations for domestic and international tourists, but Egypt's tourist industry is far from limited to these two major cities. Indeed, the ancient sites that are scattered throughout the entire country have drawn tourists to Egypt for centuries. Only about 15 miles southwest of Cairo in the city Giza are the famed Great Pyramids and the Sphinx. Just a bit south of Giza are the step pyramids of Saqqara. In southern Egypt, there are numerous ancient sites around the towns of Luxor, Aswan, and Abu Simbel. As mentioned earlier, Egypt has been building its reputation as a sun and a surf destination. Many areas along the Mediterranean Sea, the Red Sea, the Gulf of Suez, and the Gulf of Aqaba have renowned beaches and coral reefs. Though a major sector of Egypt's economy, the growth of Egypt's tourist industry has sparked concerns over environmental and cultural degradation.

GEOPOLITICS

Since its independence (1952), Egypt has played a significant role in regional geopolitics. During most of the Cold War, Egypt's president Gamal Abd al-Nasser maintained a close relationship with the Soviet bloc (see Chapter 2), thus distancing himself from the United States and NATO (North Atlantic Treaty Organization) allies. Built during the height of the Cold War, the construction of the Aswan High Dam became a geopolitical issue. In 1955, Egypt engaged in talks with the United States, the United Kingdom, and the Soviet Union about financial support for building the dam. After months of negotiations, the United States and the United Kingdom withdrew their offers to fund the dam, greatly because they saw Egypt moving closer to an alliance with the Soviet Union. Nasser responded to the United States' and United Kingdom's withdrawal of funds by taking control and nationalizing the Suez Canal from the British (who had maintained control of the canal even after the 1952 Revolution). His move to control the canal, and collect its revenues, initiated what became known as the 1956 Suez Crisis. After the Suez Crisis had settled, all remaining British troops were forced out of Egypt and the Egyptian government was in control of the canal for the first time since its construction. However, the canal's revenues were not large enough to fully finance the building of the Aswan High Dam. Therefore, in 1958, the Egyptian government accepted funds from the Soviet Union to build the dam. Throughout the Cold War years of the 1960s and most of the 1970s, the positive and healthy relationship between Egypt and the Soviet Union facilitated extremely poor politics between Egypt and the United States.

Not until Nasser's sudden death in 1970 and the presidency of Anwar Sadat did Egypt's relationship with the United States improve. Indeed, since the late 1970s, the relationship between Egypt and the United States has been one of alliance and support. Since 1979, Egypt has been the second largest recipient of U.S. monetary aid, second only to Israel. The Egypt–U.S. alliance has maintained strength well after the fall of the Soviet Union greatly because of Egypt's geostrategic and geopolitical relations with other Middle Eastern states, and most particularly its northeastern neighbor of Israel.

Soviet-Egyptian Friendship Monument celebrates the relationship between Egypt and the Soviet Union at the time the Aswan High Dam was built. It is now a tourist destination in Upper Egypt. (iStockPhoto/© Sandra vom Stein)

Egypt, like its Arab neighbors, did not recognize Israel when it declared its statehood in 1948. Though violent conflicts between Egypt and Israel began in 1948, it was not until the Six Day War of 1967 that major territorial changes would occur. After Israel's swift attack and defeat of Arab forces in the 1967 war, Israel occupied huge extents of Arab territory that include the Golan Heights, the West Bank, the Gaza Strip, and the Sinai Peninsula.

After the devastating losses of 1967, the once strong Arab national movement weakened. Nevertheless, in 1973, a coalition of Arab forces led by Egypt and Syria

---

THE GAZA STRIP

The Gaza Strip, captured by Israel in the 1967 War, shares a seven-mile-long border with Egypt. Between 1967 and 2005, Israel was responsible for the border crossing, and after 2005 the Palestinian Authority became responsible. Palestinians living in Gaza have relied on unrestricted access to Egypt in order to obtain many everyday life-sustaining items—such as gasoline, food, and medical supplies. However, as Israel tightened sanctions and blockades to the Gaza Strip over the last several decades and particularly since 2005, access to these goods has become critical.

attacked Israel in attempt to recapture both lost territory and lost pride. Though the Arab forces were defeated in the 1973 war (also known as the Ramadan or Yom Kippur War), they did reclaim some pride for mounting an attack on a much more powerful country.

The 1973 war eventually led to peace negotiations between Israel and Egypt. The United States–brokered 1979 Israel–Egypt Peace Treaty declared that in return for Egypt recognizing Israel's existence, Israel would withdraw its troops from the Sinai Peninsula. While this agreement returned the Sinai to Egypt and established peace between these two belligerent countries, it fundamentally altered Egypt's geopolitical relations with its Arab allies. Egypt's Arab neighbors, as well as many Egyptians, perceived the Egyptian government's peace treaty with Israel as a gross violation and betrayal of Arab unity. The Arab League, the official multinational organization of Arab states, even revoked Egypt's membership in 1979. In general, relations between Egypt and its Arab neighbors have been greatly remedied, and Egypt was readmitted to the Arab League in 1989. Considered by some people as a broker of peace and others as a traitor, the role that Egypt has and will continue to play in the ongoing Palestinian–Arab–Israeli conflict is significant.

During times of geopolitical conflict, Egypt has exercised control of two internationally traveled waterways—the Suez Canal and the Straits of Tiran. As discussed earlier, the Suez Canal is of vital importance to ships wishing to travel from the Mediterranean Sea or Atlantic Ocean to the Red Sea or Indian Ocean. The Strait of Tiran, on the southeastern tip of the Sinai Peninsula, links the Gulf of Aqaba to the Red Sea and then to the Indian Ocean. The strait is of direct geopolitical importance to Israel, Jordan, Saudi Arabia, and Egypt, which all have boundaries and ports north of the strait on the Gulf of Aqaba. Yet the strait itself is within the territorial seas of only of Saudi Arabia and Egypt, and though there has been some dispute between these two countries over control of the strait, Egypt has asserted its dominance over the waterway.

EGYPT'S CONTINUING ROLE IN GAZA

In June 2007, Egypt closed the border between Gaza and Egypt after HAMAS—a political organization that Israel, the United States, and the European Union have labeled a terrorist organization—came to power in Gaza. The closing of the border caused increased stress and deprivation in Gaza and eventually culminated in the literal tearing down of the border. In January 2008, Gazans tore down fences and bulldozed barriers in order to enter into Egypt and obtain goods. The Egyptian government was in a difficult geopolitical position, attempting to balance demands from its Arab allies to aid the Gazans and from the United States and Israel to secure its border. Ultimately, Egypt allowed impoverished Gazans into Egypt for a short amount of time before reclosing the border (see also Chapter 7). Finally, in June of 2010 Egypt reopened the border.

During the first Arab–Israeli war of 1948–1949, Egypt restricted the passage of Israeli ships, as well as non-Israeli ships traveling to or from Israel, through both the canal and the strait. After the war, the Egyptian government maintained this policy against Israel. The prohibition of Israeli ships through the canal directly affected trade to and from Israeli's main port of Haifa. The restrictions placed on the strait limited Israeli access to its port of Eilat, which is the country's second most viable port. Unsurprisingly, Israel refuted Egypt's restrictions on their ships, and Egypt responded with opposing rationales that justified their limitations on Israeli vessels. The restrictions on Israelis ships and cargo were detrimental to the Israeli economy, and a major reason that Israel joined France and the United Kingdom in the 1956 Suez War.

Control over this important waterway has been an important aspect of Egypt's recent history. The Suez Crisis and War began in 1956 after Nasser's nationalization of the Suez Canal. The United States intervened in the crisis and negotiated a settlement that required the withdrawal of all foreign troops from Egypt, and in return, Egypt was obligated to allow unfettered passage of all ships through its waterways. Though the 1956 Suez Crisis was a military defeat for Egypt, it was a significant political and economic success. For the first time since its construction, Egypt fully controlled the Suez Canal and no foreign powers remained on its land. And for Israel, the 1956 Crisis resulted in the opening and safe passage of its ships through both the strait and the canal.

In May 1967, Nasser became aware of the pending Israeli attack and began his own preparations, which included closing the Suez Canal and the Strait of Tiran to Israeli ships (and to ships en route to Israel that might have contained military or strategic materials). Shortly afterward, Israel attacked not only Egypt but also Jordan and Syria, beginning the Six Day War of 1967. With Israel's clear dominance in the war, the strait was soon reopened to Israeli vessels. The Suez Canal, however, was in the frontline of the war and therefore it remained closed to all transit. Not until 1975, when a peace agreement between Israel and Egypt seemed viable, did the Canal reopen. Since the 1979 Israel–Egypt Peace Treaty, safe passage of all ships has been assured at the Strait of Tiran and the Suez Canal.

To the south of Egypt, there is another unsettled geopolitical issue. The examination of most political maps of Egypt will reveal that it has two different borders with Sudan. One line is the straight political boundary along the 22nd parallel, which was established by the British in 1899. The other line is the administrative boundary of 1902, which was negotiated between Egyptian and Sudanese officials. The area between these two lines, known as the Hala'ib Triangle, is populated by a people who have much stronger connections with Sudan than they have with Egypt. Thus, the 1902 boundary was drawn in order to recognize Sudan's administrative control of the population of the Hala'ib Triangle, whilst maintaining Egypt's ultimate control and sovereignty of the area. Since the early 20th century, this area has been a point of contention between these two countries, and tensions have heightened as speculation grows about the likelihood of natural resource being discovered in the area, as the scarcity of water in the region become more acute, and as Islamic factions have gained some movement in the region. Fortunately, the conflicts over the Hala'ib region have not been violent.

With the toppling of the Mubarak regime in 2011, there has been a lapse in security in general, and borders in particular. There have been complaints of lawlessness in the Sinai and the usual disruptions from Gaza in the East to refugees and instability from the civil war in Libya to the West. Even after the fall of Qaddafi, in March of 2012, Libya closed the Salloum crossing, the largest, due to continuing problems with the smuggling of weapons and drugs from Libya (and Sudan) into Egypt, making their way as far as the Gaza Strip.

CONCLUSION

Understanding the human and physical geography of Egypt helps to understand the country's history, culture, economics, and politics, all of which are intimately intertwined. The Nile River is understandably the most famed aspect of Egypt's geography. Not only is it the world's longest river, but it has also helped to support a population of people from ancient times to today. Egypt's location at the crossroads of Asia, Africa, and Europe has placed the country at the center stage of regional and global interactions for centuries. Indeed, this geostrategic position has placed Egypt at the center of the ongoing Palestinian–Arab–Israeli conflict.

GENERAL REFERENCES

Anderson, E. *The Middle East: Geography and Geopolitics.* New York: Routledge, 2000.

Drysdale, A., and G. Blake. *The Middle East and North Africa, a Political Geography.* New York: Oxford University Press, 1985.

Held, C. *Middle East Patterns: Places, People, and Politics.* Boulder, CO: Westview Press, 2005.

Stewart, D. *The Middle East Today: Political, Geographical and Cultural Perspectives.* New York: Routledge, 2009.

Tessler, M. *A History of the Israel–Palestinian Conflict.* Bloomington, IN: Indiana University, 1994.

Specific References Used for Statistic Data

Boyd, A., and J. Comentez. *An Atlas of World Affairs.* 11th ed. New York: Routledge, 2007.

Bradshaw, M., G. White, J. Dymond, and E. Chacko. *Essentials of World Regional Geography.* 8th ed. New York: McGraw-Hill, 2008.

CIA *The World Factbook*, data retrieved on March 5, 2009, and May 14, 2009. https://www.cia.gov/library/publications/the-world-factbook/geos/eg.html#Geo

CRS (Congressional Research Service) Report for Congress, "Foreign Aid: An Introductory Overview of U.S. Programs and Policy," January 19, 2005.

Dempsey, M. *Atlas of the Arab World.* New York: Facts on File Publications, 1983.

Parks, P. *Aswan High Dam.* Farmington Hills, MI: Cengage Gale, 2003.

World Bank. World Development Indicators, 2007.

CHAPTER 2

History

CHRONOLOGY

ca. 3100 BCE—Unification of Upper and Lower Egypt

ca. 2686 BCE—Beginning of Third Dynasty and of Old Kingdom—beginning of pyramid construction

ca. 2181 BCE—End of Old Kingdom and beginning of First Intermediate Period—period of chaos and political disorder

ca. 2055 BCE—Beginning of Middle Kingdom—recovery and greater stability

ca. 1640 BCE—Second Intermediate Period—Hyksos invasion

ca. 1557 BCE—Beginning of New Kingdom—rebuilding Egyptian Empire; tombs of Valley of Kings constructed

ca. 1200 BCE—Attack and repulsion of the Sea Peoples

ca. 1069 BCE—Third Intermediate Period

ca. 715 BCE—Late Period

670 BCE—Conquest by Assyria

525 BCE—Persian (Achaemenid) conquest

332–331 BCE—Alexander the Great invades and ends Persian rule over Egypt

323 BCE—Death of Alexander and beginning of Ptolemaic dynasty

30 BCE—Egypt becomes a Roman province

306–337—Reign of Constantine, Christianity becomes legal religion of empire, and empire is divided—Eastern half becomes Byzantine Empire

451—Coptic Monophysitism rejected by Council of Chaldean

619—Persian (Sassanid) Conquest of Egypt

629—Egypt returned to Byzantine rule

639—Beginning of Islamic conquest under Amr ibn al-As

661—Establishment of the Umayyad Dynasty

868—Beginning of the Tulunid Dynasty

934—Ikhshids receive power after Tulunids die out

969—Fatimids conquer Egypt and found al-Qahira (Cairo) as capital

1099—Capture of Jerusalem by Crusaders

1171—Salah al-Din al-Ayyubi takes control from Fatimid dynasty to found Ayyubid dynasty

1187—Battle of Hittin Salah al-Din captures Jerusalem from Crusaders

1248–1249—Louis IX launches seventh crusade against Egypt; penultimate Ayyubid ruler dies of natural causes.

1250—Shajarat al-Durr named co-ruler with Mamluk Aybak, thus beginning Baḥri Mamluk era of Egyptian history

1260—Mamluk victory at Ayn Jalut

1382—Beginning of the Burgi (Citadel) Mamluks

1513—Portuguese defeat Mamluk Navy

1517—Egypt becomes an Ottoman province

1760—Ali Bey al-Kabir becomes *Shaykh al-Balad*

1773—Assassination of Ali Bey al-Kabir

1798—French invasion

1799—Discovery of the Rosetta Stone by French officer

1801—Anglo-Ottoman forces arrive in Egypt; French withdrawal; Rosetta Stone taken by British

1805–1848—Reign of Muhammad Ali

1811—Muhammad Ali's massacre of Mamluks

1848—Death of Ibrahim Pasha, regent for Muhammad Ali

1848–1854—Reign of Abbas Pasha

1849—Death of Muhammad Ali

1854–1863—Reign of Said Pasha

1863–1879—Reign of Khedive Ismail

1869—Opening of the Suez Canal

1875—Egypt bankrupt; Ismail sells Egyptian shares of the Suez Canal Company to the British

1876—British and French create Creation of Public Debt Commission

1877—Abolition of the slave trade in the Ottoman Empire and Egypt (second attempt)

1879—Ismail ends Dual Financial Control and is deposed by the Ottoman sultan at the behest of European creditors

1879–1882—Urabi Revolt

1879–1892—Reign of Khedive Tawfiq

1881—Mahdi Revolt in the Sudan

1882–1914—British occupation and informal protectorate

1892–1914—Reign of Khedive Abbas II

1906—Taba incident; Dinshaway incident

1907—Lord Cromer retires as high commissioner; death of Mustafa Kamil; Saad Zaghlul becomes Minister of Education

1914—Outbreak of World War I; Abbas II deposed; Egypt becomes a formal British protectorate

1914–1917—Reign of (Sultan) Husayn Kamil

1917–1936—Reign of Sultan, later King, Fuad I

1919–1922—A period of strikes and demonstrations commonly referred to as the 1919 Revolution

1920—Founding of Bank Miṣr

1922—Egypt achieves partial independence from the British; discovery of the King Tut tomb

1922–1952—Egypt's "liberal" era, ruled by a constitutional monarchy

1927—Death of Saad Zaghlul

1928—Founding of Muslim Brotherhood

1936—Anglo-Egyptian Treaty removes British points of control

1936–1952—Reign of King Faruq

1938—Grand Royal wedding of King Faruq and Safinaz Zulficar (Farida)

1942—British surround Abdin palace with tanks and force prime-ministerial choice (Wafd) on King Faruq

1945—Arab League established with Cairo as headquarters

1948—First Arab–Israeli War; King Faruq divorces Farida; Prime Minister Nuqrashi Pasha assassinated by Muslim Brotherhood

1949—Armistice with Israel signed; assassination of Hasan al-Banna, founder of Muslim Brotherhood

1951—Tensions mount in Suez Canal zone between Muslim Brotherhood and British troops, Egyptian police unwilling and/or unable to act against the Brotherhood; Parliament abrogates 1936 Treaty

1952—British attack of police barracks in Ismailia; burning of Cairo; Egyptian Revolution

1953—Political parties abolished; creation of Liberation Rally; Anglo-Egyptian agreement on Sudan

1954—Anglo-Egyptian Suez Pact negotiating British withdrawal and usage of Suez Canal and base; Lavon Affair uncovered; assassination attempt on Nasser resulting in a victory in his power struggle over Gen. Neguib and harsh retribution against Muslim Brotherhood.

1955—Gaza Raid; Czech Arms deal; Bandung Conference of Non-Aligned States; creation of Baghdad Pact

1956—Suez Crisis; Sudanese Independence

1957—Eisenhower Doctrine announced; Israeli withdrawal from Sinai

1958—Coup in Iraq; American invasion of Lebanon; renewal of anti-Communist measures in Egypt as tensions ease with United States

1958–1961—Union with Syria (Creation of United Arab Republic)

1961—Nasser creates his own Arab Socialism after Syria breaks from United Arab Republic (UAR)

1962—Creation of The National Charter; revolution in Yemen and Nasser aids revolutionaries

1964—Provisional Constitution; creation of Palestine Liberation Organization by Nasser; communists released from prison

1966—Sayyid Qutb, philosopher of the Muslims Brotherhood executed by the Nasserist government, thus making him a "martyr" for future followers; Israelis raid Samu, Jordan; Arab Socialist Union (ASU) official assassinated and persecution of old elites renewed

1967—Nasser withdraws United Nations Emergency Forces (UNEF) and closes the Straits of Tiran to Israeli shipping; Israeli preemptively strikes occupying, Gaza, West Bank, Golan Heights, Arab Jerusalem, and the Sinai; UN Security Council adopts Resolution 242, thereby offering the first "land for peace" plan; Khartoum Resolution

1968—Widespread student and worker demonstrations; widespread visions of the Virgin Mary over a Coptic Church by people of all faiths

1969—War of Attrition announced

1970—Ceasefire accepted; Black September in Jordan leading to Cairo Summit, after which Nasser dies; Sadat succeeds Nasser

1971 May 15—Correction; permanent constitution adopted; purge of Nasserist opposition, Pope Shenouda III becomes Patriarch of the Coptic Church

1972—Massive expulsion of Soviet advisors and military personnel

1973—War of the Crossing (October or Yom Kippur War)

1974—Sinai I disengagement; announcement of Infitah

1975—Sinai II disengagement

1976—Multiple platforms created within ASU in preparation for a multiparty system

1977—Bread riots ensue as Egypt ends subsidies on basic foodstuffs; Sadat visits Jerusalem

1978—Egyptian delegation visits Israeli delegation facilitated by President Carter at Camp David

1979—Camp David Accords signed; Egypt's relations with Arab world fragmented due to recognition of Israel; Arab League temporarily removed from Cairo

1980—Diplomatic relations established with Israel; Law of Shame

1981—Assassination of Sadat; succession of Mubarak

1982—Israeli withdrawal from Sinai complete aside from Taba

1986—Security police riots

1988—Israel returns Taba to Egypt after international arbitration

1989—Egypt returned to Arab fold and suspension from Arab League ended

1991—Egypt participates in Desert Storm

1992–1997—Having witnessed damage to tourism industry caused by recent Gulf War, radical Islamists see a target to weaken government power

1994—Government cracks down on radical Islamic groups

1995—Prof. Nasr Abu Zayd, author of controversial works on Quranic interpretation, granted full professorship at Cairo University; Cairo Court of Appeals divorced him from his wife on the grounds of apostasy; Prof. Abu Zayd then fled to Europe after assassination threats from Islamic Jihad; internet first made available to the public in Egypt

1996—Economic liberalization accelerated

1997—Tourist massacre at Luxor

1999—Truce between Islamic radicals and the government; alliance between Ayman al-Zawahiri (an Egyptian) and Osama bin Laden

2000—After a decade of sectarian violence in Upper Egypt, the Virgin Mary begins to appear over a Church in Assiut and multi-faith groups appear for healing

2001—Publication of lurid photographs of an alleged Coptic monk having sex with parishioners in one of the holiest sites in Egypt heighten tensions between Muslims and Copts that have been brewing over past two decades; 9/11 attacks on the World Trade Center in the United States; raid of the Queen Boat

2002—President Mubarak announces January 7 as a National holiday to create a unified spirit between the country's Muslims and Christians; Gamal Mubarak, son of the President becomes General Secretary of the Policy Committee of the ruling National Democratic Party (NDP), the third highest position in the party

2003—The United States invades Iraq; Egypt demands the return of the Rosetta Stone

2004—"Gamal's Cabinet" put in place with cabinet reshuffling—after his position as General Secretary of Steering Committee of NDP

2005—First presidential election in Egypt held through multiple candidacy rather than referendum; Israel withdraws from Gaza; Egyptian director of antiquities negotiates for a loan and eventual return of Egypt's Rosetta Stone; British send Egypt a replica of the Rosetta Stone

2005–2006—Converging evidence supports truth of reports regarding Egypt's involvement in the outsourcing of the torture of U.S. prisoners, despite disclaimers by both governments

2006—Israel invades Lebanon

2007—Egyptian mummy bone (cat) found in Joan of Arc's tomb; Egypt decides to copyright pyramids, sphinx, and so on to fund upkeep of historic sites

2008—Egyptian newspaper editor Ibrahim Eissa jailed for printing rumors about the condition of Mubarak's health; Civil Rights activist Saad Eddin Ibrahim sentenced to two years' imprisonment for "defaming" country

2009—Israel invades Gaza

2010—Nasr Abu Zayd dies in Egypt (of natural causes); Egypt opens Rafah border to Gaza after Israeli flotilla incident

2011—Egyptian Revolution, Mubarak removed from power and Emergency law challenged

2012—Death of Pope Shenouda

Editor's Note: The focus of the historical section is on the medieval and modern periods, that is, the era after the rise of Islam. Thus, the ancient period will be highly abbreviated, focusing on themes that will facilitate an understanding of later periods. As for the modern period, discussions of domestic policy and government may be abbreviated as they will be the focus of Chapter 3.

ANCIENT EGYPT

Egypt is the mother of the world.

—Egyptian saying of unknown origin.

Egypt is the gift of the Nile.

—Herodotus

Predynastic and Old Kingdom

These two statements taken together inform our understanding of Egypt's history and how Egyptians view their position in world history. The Nile River (see Chapter 1) has shaped the Egyptian lives for thousands of years. The river's annual flooding in late summer or early fall helped assure the surplus needed to create great civilizations. One area of contention among scholars is the extent to which Egyptian civilization was linked to neighboring regions in Africa and the further implications for Western civilization as expounded by the highly controversial "Black Athena" thesis put forth by Afrocentrists. While mainstream academia has largely dismissed this theory as first expounded in the 1970s, more recently scientists and anthropologists have found genetic evidence supporting some of the most important claims. According to Dr. Richard Leakey, all modern men, regardless of race, emerged from the same part of Africa, and it is likely that Egypt's Old Kingdom was influenced by older civilizations in present-day Kenya and the Sudan.

Organizing Egypt's history is a monumental task, and even in ancient times it was necessary to develop organizational conventions. During the Ptolemaic period in the third century BCE, the historian Manetho created a classification system that we still use today to categorize the various kingdoms and dynasties: Old, Middle, and New Kingdoms with intermediate, preliminary, and late periods. Furthermore, since much of the dating is guess work, we use ca. to represent circa (approximately) where no exact date is known.

Predynastic Egypt emerged as various spheres of settlements where surplus developed and along with it, technology, specialization of function occupationally, social stratification (including monarchs), and the development of commemorative arts. With kingship came competing kings, and ultimately there were two large kingdoms one in the south and one in the north. Around 3100 BCE King Narmer united the two wearing the double crowns, the red of the north and the white of the south.

The unification of Egypt was understood by the people in the myth of kingship told in the story of Osiris, who was married to his sister Isis. Osiris was the first great leader, and his brother Seth murdered Osiris in a jealous rage. Besot with grief, Isis found the remains, tried to restore his life, and in doing so became pregnant with their son Horus, who later defeated the evil Seth. Although Osiris recovered only long enough to impregnate Isis, he did become God of the underworld, where he would evaluate souls of the deceased. According to one variation of the myth, Seth actually kills him again, shreds his remains, dumps them in the Nile, and Isis pieces them back together with cloth, creating the prototypical mummy. It is their son Horus, however, who represents temporal rule and kingship by punishing Seth.

The king, or pharaoh ("big house"), of ancient Egypt had a tremendous amount of power. Egypt was a tributary state based on taxation and the pharaoh could utilize its resources. Notions of private property as they exist in the West today did not exist in ancient Egypt. Pharaoh had the right to allocate and appropriate all resources under his jurisdiction, as well as to utilize the labor of men living within his borders (corvée). This type of work was necessary for vast irrigation and public works projects that maintained the state. The centralization that began in ancient Egypt would allow peasants to collectively gain knowledge and wisdom about the land and the river that would allow them to serve a variety of rulers from a host of foreign lands in the centuries to come. In turn, the king provided people a source of comfort and

CONSANGUINE MARRIAGE PATTERNS

While most cultures find incest distasteful today, ancient Egyptian royalty practiced it widely. It was accepted by the population because they deemed their rulers superior. The pharaohs were often polygamous, marrying more than one wife and having consorts. The royal blood ran through the female line. The existence of numerous family branches could lead to political fragmentation, outside alliances, and other types of problems that consanguine marriage could potentially solve. Most marriages were not among full-blooded brothers and sisters, but half-siblings. When the Ptolemies came to rule Egypt, they adopted pharaonic practice with respect to worship of the ruler and the practice of sibling marriage. Their marriages were distinctive, because they tended to be among full-blooded brothers and sisters. The most infamous among the Ptolemies for this practice was Ptolemy VIII (ca. 182–116 BCE), who married his sister Cleopatra II, who had previously been married to their brother Ptolemy VI. Without divorcing her, he then married his niece, Cleopatra III.

justice, since his subjects believed that he was bestowed with gifts that enabled him rule as a god and mediate the worship of other gods.

First Intermediate Period, Middle Kingdom, and Second Intermediate Period

Around the capable leadership of Mentuhotep II (ca. 2055 BCE), the country achieved reunification placing the capital city at Thebes, near present-day Luxor in Upper Egypt. During his half-century tenure, he carried out large numbers of public works projects that helped to bring about a sense of unity in the country. Other competent rulers tended to focus on building both centers of worship and irrigation, for example, Amenemhet III (ca. 1831–1786 BCE).

The Middle Kingdom ended with the invasion of the Hyksos of Western Asia (ca. 1640). Egyptian literature of the second intermediate period describes these outsiders, who brought new technologies, for example, chariot, curved sword, armor, the compound bow. Egyptians eventually perfected these weapons and used them against the Hyksos. Foreign invasion raised the idea of expansion, and Egypt moved south into Nubia and westward into Asia.

New Kingdom and Third Intermediate Period

Recentralization emerged under the New Kingdom (ca. 1557 BCE) with Thebes as its glorious capital. Thebes would remain the center of gravity for worship; however, administratively it posed problems. Memphis, not far from the current capital of Egypt at the base of the delta, would prove to be a more strategic location from which to rule Upper and Lower Egypt. A vizier for both districts would report directly to the capital and be responsible for the bureaucratic, military, religious, and judicial administration of his region.

An important aspect of leadership and worship was the building of the temple complexes at Thebes. Worship of the god associated with Thebes, Amun, merged with the worship of the all important god of the sun, Ra, to form Amun-Ra, and leaders established fabulous monuments to commemorate his worship, along with other significant gods. It is not surprising that a civilization so tied to agricultural cycles and fertility would place such an emphasis on the sun. Among the more spectacular ruins still in existence today is the temple complex at Karnak with its sphinx lined boulevard and numerous temples within it.

One of the noteworthy breaks with tradition in the New Kingdom came with the reign of Amenhotep IV (ca. 1352–1336 BCE), who changed his name to Akhenaton ("he who acts for Aton") to reflect his radical new philosophy, belief in one god (Aton). He moved the capital to Akheteton "horizon of Aton" (Amarna) in Middle Egypt to demonstrate his break with Memphis and Thebes. Akhenaton may seem inordinately "advanced" for his monotheism, but by the same token, his beliefs were at odds with the majority of his subjects. Interestingly enough, there was some

The Avenue of Sphinxes was once a thoroughfare for processions between the Luxor and Karnak temples. (Courtesy of Mona Russell)

continuity, perhaps to attract believers. The symbol for Aton was the sun's disc, for he was the one god from whom all life radiated. The legacy of Akhenaton was quickly eradicated by his son (or most likely his son's advisors), since we know that his son died at a young age and is famous for leaving behind the only un-raided tomb in the Valley of the Kings, Tutankhamun, who was actually born Tutankhaton.

Before the close of the New Kingdom, there would be both great leadership and challenges from the outside during the reign of Ramsis II (ca. 1279–1213 BCE). During his enormously long tenure, he undertook incredible building programs in the Valley of the Kings, much of which was simply to bury the enormous family, and he extended his building program around the country. He faced a huge military threat in the Levant from the Anatolian Hittites with whom he achieved a coexistence through diplomacy and by marrying the daughter of this former enemy.

Shortly thereafter (ca. 1200 BCE) Egypt faced another challenge, the invasion of the Sea Peoples, not a disciplined, organized army but masses of people of uncertain origin that had already overrun Anatolia, destroying the Hittites. Some scholars speculate that perhaps they were victims of an unknown natural disaster, who now made their way toward Egypt, both over land and by sea. Although Egypt survived the attack, Asia was severely impacted as were trade routes in the Levant from which Egypt received goods it did not produce itself, for example, wood. These events initiated a steady decline. The third intermediate period begins ca. 1069 after the reign of Ramses XI, the last king for whom a tomb was cut in the Valley of the Kings.

Late Period: Rise of Foreign Domination

Egypt's late period begins with the emergence of a new dynasty in 715 BCE on the eve of the Assyrian invasion. Egypt was not ready to meet the challenge of the Assyrians, who had advanced weapons and organization. At this time Egypt was beset by a number of problems including a religious establishment that had grown unwieldy in power, an army that contained legions of foreign elements from the West (what is present-day Libya), and a general disregard for temple complexes both by ordinary tomb-raiders and by government officials. The Assyrian campaign came in several waves, but was completed ca. 670 BCE. Eventually a common enemy, the Chaldeans of Babylon, emerged. Then, the Egyptians fought alongside the Assyrians, but the Assyrian empire dissolved in 612 BCE.

By the sixth century BCE, Egypt was no longer the jewel of the East. Another great empire had arisen under Cyrus the Great of Persia (present-day Iran). Under Cyrus's son, Cambyses (r. 525–522 BCE) Egypt was invaded in 525 BCE. Egypt would no longer be the ruler, but a component of a huge empire that extended from India in the East through Persia and Mesopotamia, into Anatolia and Greater Syria. Aside from scattered uprisings and one-fourth century dynasty, there would be no other Egyptian ruling Egypt until the 20th century.

HELLENIC, ROMAN, AND COPTIC

Ptolemaic and Roman Rule

By the fourth century BCE another major player emerged to challenge Persian domination in the Old World: the Greek-speaking Macedonians. Philip II of Macedon (d. 336 BCE) began an empire that his son Alexander "The Great" multiplied by many times. Alexander invaded Egypt in 332 BCE beginning a process that would ultimately end Persian rule in Egypt. He was a syncretic ruler who was able to blend with and adapt to the belief system of the conquered land. Egyptians, long tired of the Persians, alternately viewed him as Horus or the son of Amun-Ra, which Alexander readily accepted; and he in turn consulted the oracle of Amun, viewing this God as the Egyptian equivalent of Zeus. He started work on an incredible new capital city, named after him, Alexandria. Alexander left Egypt to conquer the rest of the Persian Empire, and died in 323 BCE. Alexander's boyhood friend and general Ptolemy successfully emerged from the power struggle that ensued following the conqueror's departure, and he founded the dynasty that bears his name. Like Alexander, the Ptolemies blended aspects of Egyptian worship with their beliefs in a way that buttressed their own rule (see Chapter 5).

Ptolemaic Egypt bears striking contrasts. On the one hand, it is known for its remarkable level of culture and civilization. A highly efficient bureaucratic state monopolized technology that utilized Egypt's vast agricultural surplus to its maximum potential. The use of the *saqqiya*, as it is known in Egypt, or Archimedes screw, as it is known in the West, replaced the old *shaduf*, or counterweighted bucket as the primary means of irrigation. Nevertheless, the Ptolemies granted privilege to a small Greek-speaking elite, and native Egyptians, as well as Jews, did not have equal rights. One of two groups of Egyptians that had some status was the priestly elite who was recruited to support their rule, especially when times were bad.

Rival Alexandrian successor states existed elsewhere in the Middle East, and fighting between those states and among branches of families within those states meant that by the second century BCE the Ptolemaic dynasty was but a remnant of what it once was in its heyday during the reign of its first three rulers, despite the incredible surplus generated by Egyptian wheat. The Romans saw the infighting and took advantage of the weakened situation in the Middle East. The rest is a story that Hollywood could only make up in detail. Cleopatra VII (ca. 69–30 BCE) had undoubtedly heard of the trials and tribulations that her father Ptolemy XII had suffered early in his rule as an illegitimate child and a pawn of Roman politics. She was only a teenager when her father died in 51 BCE, and she became a coruler with her younger brother Ptolemy XIII (ca. 62–47 BCE). At the same time that she was trying to achieve some measure of authority over her brother, the Roman sphere of politics had moved into Egypt with its vying warrior-politicians using the region as a base of operations. Among the Romans in Egypt were the legendary Julius Caesar and Marc Antony, both of whom fathered children with Cleopatra, and helped her in her struggle against her brother, who died in battle in 47 BCE, although they

The shaduf was the traditional method of irrigation in Egypt. (Library of Congress)

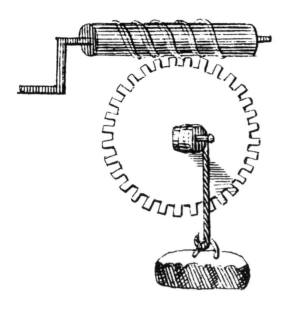

Archimedes' screw, invented by the Greek mathematician of the same name (3rd century BCE), greatly improved irrigation in Egypt. (iStockPhoto/© Classix)

initially installed another younger brother, Ptolemy XIV, as coruler. After Caesar's death in 44 BCE, Cleopatra no longer had to put up with Ptolemy XIV, whom she executed; and she made Caesar's infant son, Caesarion, her coruler. She married Marc Antony living out Hellenistic-Egyptian mythology in grand style as the incarnates of Dionysus and Isis, much to the dismay of Romans and Egyptians. The forces of Octavian (Caesar's nephew) defeated those of Marc Antony in 31 BCE, although Antony had already received a false report about Cleopatra's suicide causing him to take his own life. Not wanting to submit to Octavian, Cleopatra committed suicide in 30 BCE. With these events, so begins Roman rule in Egypt.

The famed Roman Empire pulled Egypt again into the orbit of a large prosperous empire, which brought both advantages and disadvantages to its subject class. First, the Romans did maintain the class structure as it existed. Native Egyptians and Jews generally did not hold positions of power, which went to the Greek-speaking

JULIAN CALENDAR

The 12-month calendar that we use today is actually a legacy of the ancient Egyptians and efforts of Julius Caesar after his visit to Egypt. He consulted with the astronomer Sosigenes of Alexandria, who had created the 365-day year, divided among 12 months, with an additional day every four years. The Julian calendar has been replaced by the Gregorian calendar, created in the late 16th century, to account for an overabundance of leap-year days; however, most Orthodox churches still use the Julian calendar.

elite, although one major departure was increased private land ownership. Greek remained the language of administration in the country. Egyptian wheat became an integral part of the Roman Empire. While the Ptolemies and the pharaohs had heavily taxed their peasants, consumption had largely remained internal. Under the Romans, commercial activity and manufacturing expanded. The city of Alexandria continued in its pivotal position, where Greeks and Jews played important roles.

In the third century CE, a series of foreign incursions, heavy tax burdens, tomb raiding, high rates of brigandage, and peasant flight were both symptoms and causes of Roman imperial decay. Finally, at the end of the third century, the emperor Diocletian began a series of reforms. The state sold off its remaining estates to large, wealthy landholders, who treated peasants even worse than the state. The era of reform would continue under Constantine (306–307 CE), who shifted the imperial capital of the empire East, to Constantinople (present-day Istanbul) and utilized Christianity as the new social glue to hold the hold Roman Empire together, thus opening a new chapter in Egypt's history. This eastern portion of the empire, which would outlast the Western empire, would be known as the Byzantine Empire after the fall of the western portion in 476.

Coptic Egypt

Egypt was a center of Christian culture and learning in the Middle East. Its exposure to Persian dualism and to Judaism meant that Egyptians were not unfamiliar with other forms of faith. According to legend, St. Mark (d. 68 CE) brought Christianity to Egypt in the first century. But exactly when or how Christianity took root in Egypt is more difficult to determine. As the fifth century wore on the imperial capital waffled between doctrinal orthodoxy and freedom of belief for this province that was so important in feeding the empire. Ultimately, the Council of Chalcedon in 451 decided the question, and the Coptic Orthodox Church emerged as a separate church (see Chapter 5). Egypt remained within the empire; however, the last years of Byzantine rule were characterized by frequent clashes and invasions, even occupation, by the neighboring Persian Empire. Weakness of the two ancient empires and the bitterness associated with their rule allowed the Arabs access to Egypt in much the same way that Alexander had nine centuries earlier.

DERIVATION OF EGYPT

The words Copt and Egypt are both related to the ancient Egyptian word, *hikaptah*, or house of the spirit of Ptah. Ptah in Egyptian mythology represents the primordial earth. In Greek it translates as *Aigyptos*. After the Arab invasion in the seventh century CE, the Arabs referred to Egypt as *dar al-qibt*, home of the Copts, pronounced in Egyptian dialect of Arabic as *dar al-ibt*.

MEDIEVAL EGYPT

Islamic Conquest and Umayyad Rule

The Arab expansion grew out of the Wars of Apostasy on the Arabian Peninsula in the months after Muhammad's death in 632 (see Chapter 5). Some tribes refused to pay their *zakat* (alms) to the central treasury, and the first caliph Abu Bakr (r. 632–634) sent an army to put down the rebellious tribes. Afterward, the army continued up and out of the peninsula in what would be known as the Arab expansion or the Islamic conquest. Under the second successor, Umar (r. 634–644), an army of about 8,000 under the capable leadership of Amr ibn al-As made its way into Egypt in 639, thus ending Byzantine rule. People frequently are under the misperception that there was "conversion of the sword" when in fact it was in the interest of the rulers to have a marked distinction between themselves and the population, in terms of ethnicity and religion. The Arabs found paganism repugnant, but this had long been eradicated in Egypt, and the conquerors promised to respect the people, their system of worship, and their property as long as taxes were paid, which included ordinary (land) taxes, a head tax for non-Muslims, and an extra tax when the Nile reached 24 feet, indicating a good harvest.

The Byzantines were not able to rally against the Arabs internally or externally. The death of Heraclius in 641 and a state of struggle in Byzantium, along with the Coptic clergy's acceptance of the new rulers meant that there would be no nucleus around which a viable opposition could rally. Amr Ibn al-As's competent governorship after years of misrule must have been a welcome change. For years stories circulated about the brutal Arabs burning the library at Alexandria, but most likely these are apocryphal since the complex had suffered many devastations and riots during Roman and Byzantine times. These stories circulated conveniently some 600 years later at a time when religious tensions were high for other reasons (the Crusades—see subsequently). Indeed, both Umar and Amr made sure that the Arab armies did not confiscate land, and the governor himself was forbidden from owning a permanent home. The capital moved away from Alexandria back toward the base of the delta, but not at Memphis. The Arabs created their own tent village, al-Fustat, where they laid down their garrison and the first mosque, which still exists, built over the spot where Amr had his tent and was later renovated to hold up to 5,000 students.

The Arabs had little experience with running an agricultural tributary state, and this is where the collective Egyptian experience and the wisdom of the Arabs in listening to their subjects came to the fore. The military were people who knew about herding, grazing, and raiding, whereas the leadership, that is, those from the Quraysh (tribe of the Prophet), knew about long-distance trade. Thus, the particulars of Egyptian administration as it had been done for centuries, both with respect to agricultural technique and bureaucratic style, required knowledge that was specifically Egyptian in nature. In fact, Greek and Coptic (written in Greek script) remained the languages of administration for nearly seven decades. Amr appointed a marshal to keep order with control over the army and various militias and a *qadi* to instill justice. Before the creation of a body of Islamic law, the application of justice was done using the

SAVING THE MOSQUE OF AMR IBN AL-AS AND OTHER IMPORTANT MONUMENTS

After the building of the Aswan High Dam, the Nile shifted its course, and groundwater rose in monuments around Fustat, where the oldest mosque in Africa resides, as well as nearby Old Cairo, where important Coptic, Jewish, and ancient Roman sites exist. Some of these buildings had literally withstood millennia until the groundwater started rising. In 1978 a USAID project that was looking at greater Cairo began to take a special interest in a project that would drain the water from the Mosque of Amr, St. George's Church, the Synagogue of Ben Ezra, and other important locations in the area, although much of the actual work did not begin until 2000. Egypt also suffered an earthquake in 1992 after which many of its important monuments required additional restoration. Creating drainage solutions that would not damage the ancient buildings has been a modern engineering feat.

Although it has been restored, rebuilt, and revitalized many times, the Amr ibn al-As Mosque is the oldest mosque in Africa. (iStockPhoto/© Rui Santos)

customary law of region, and again local knowledge was central to this process. The caliphal government appointed the treasurer to insure faithful collection of taxes from Muslims (*zakat*) and the various taxes from the subject population. At this time, the Muslims were not allowed to own land, therefore the only tax for which they were responsible was the mandatory alms.

For the Copts and the Jews of Egypt there was a marked change. While they were still second-class citizens by 21st-century standards, by medieval standards the quality of their lives had improved remarkably. Most Westerners today would find the laws regarding dress, hairstyle, and the barring of horseback riding offensive to our sensibilities, but relatively speaking, there was now much greater freedom of worship and action. While they had to pay the additional head tax, known as the *jizya*, they would never have to serve in the army and they would be free to follow their own community's norms with respect to matters of personal status, for example, marriage, inheritance, and divorce. The Arab army would provide protection that kept roads and waterways safe for trade, providing Egypt with a surplus that would generate another era of great civilization.

The competent Amr was recalled to the Arabian Peninsula by the third Caliph Uthman (r. 644–656), who preferred to replace some of the administrators in the provinces with his own kinsmen. Although Uthman is one of the *rashidun*, or Orthodox, caliphs generally beloved by Muslims, his tenure generated quite a few hostilities due to growing pains of the empire, some of his policies, and perhaps because he was from the infamous Umayyad clan that had given Prophet Muhammad so much trouble during his lifetime. Egypt and what is present-day Iraq were both seed-beds of anti-Uthman activity among the garrisons. Before the anti-Uthman activities could take place, the Byzantines took advantage of Amr's departure to lay siege to Alexandria, and Arab forces fought the Byzantines back out of Egypt in 645–646. It may be this success that caused Uthman's half-brother Abdullah, the governor, to carry out an expansionist policy in Nubia in 652, which met with mixed results. The region was not subdued, but did agree to pay a tribute in slaves.

Troops arrived from garrisons in Egypt, Kufa, and Basra to complain about government policy at the same time that the Meccan aristocracy was bringing forth new leadership. Angry mobs surrounded Uthman's house, and he was assassinated by a group led by a faction of the Meccan elite and supported by the unhappy soldiers from the provinces. The first Civil War in Islam erupted, which would ultimately create the first schism in Islam, that is, the Sunni–Shiite divide, and it would usher in the Umayyad dynasty in 661.

Mu'awiya (r. 661–680) had been a fellow kinsmen of Uthman and had served as a governor in Syria, prior to the war. He shifted the political center of gravity north and made Damascus the new capital of the Arab Empire. He had been a late convert to Islam, but since he was from a prominent family, he had been given a high position as part of the negotiations prior to Muhammad's death. Due to his intelligence, diplomacy, and skill he was able to maneuver that position to his own advantage. Mu'awiya had created an alliance with Amr Ibn al-As during the civil war, and then regranted him governorship of Egypt when the war was over. Nevertheless, Amr by then was 87 years old, and he died a wealthy man at the age of 90 in 664.

In the years that followed Egypt underwent tremendous change. Egyptians gathered around Fustat interested in the power and wealth of the conquerors and began to convert to the new religion; and conversely, Arabs used to a nomadic pattern of existence settled in Egypt, not just as an army, but eventually taking land and intermarrying with the population. What were temporary tent dwellings in Fustat turned into permanent buildings. Shortly after the turn of the eighth century, Arabic finally became the language of administration. There were Coptic families in Egypt for whom government administration ran as deeply as family memory; however, that distinction would be erased if the new language was not adopted. Over the course of the next six centuries the Coptic language would become all but extinct, except among Coptic clergy.

Even as the Arabs settled, Egyptians began converting, and Arabic became the official language, the class structure under the Umayyads remained the same. The premise on which the system was built was that all Arabs (male and female) were Muslims who were in the army held positions of power over the non-Muslim, tax-paying majority. As time passed, the army recruited new converts, for example, the zealous Berber tribes of North Africa. Others settled and married into the population. Furthermore, new converts felt they should not be taxed at the rate of non-Muslims.

While the Umayyads always had these structural problems, during times of plenty and expanding borders, for example, the North African and Iberian campaigns, taxation remained at sustainable levels. Once the taxes were raised in the mid-720s by more than 10 percent, frictions between Copts and the Arabs, as well as converts and Arabs, continued simmering with an occasional boil until the Abbasid Revolution in the mid-eighth century, sapping the Egyptian garrison of its strength and highlighting the ineffective Umayyad leadership.

Abbasid Revolution

At the other end of the Umayyad empire a movement had taken place among converts, rallying around a figure who traced his lineage back to the Prophet's uncle Abbas, hence the name Abbasids, who would eventually replace the Umayyads and create a new social structure whereby an Islamic element would replace the Arab element and new taxes would be equally applied to all subjects; however, non-Muslims would still pay the *jizya* and Muslims would still pay *zakat* (see Chapter 5). By 750 the Umayyads had been swept from power in Damascus, and the Abbasids would create a new capital, further from Egypt, at Baghdad. The Abbasid Revolution served reunify and consolidate the Islamic empire restoring and revitalizing networks of trade. Where the Umayyads had made war with the Byzantines a pastime, the Abbasids preferred to focus on the large free-trade zone in their domain. Abbasid politics would eventually impact how Egyptian administration ran. Most historians consider the reign of Harun al-Rashid (r. 786–809) the apogee of centralized Abbasid power and civilization. Harun al-Rashid divided his empire among his sons, giving the Persian portion to his son (of Persian descent) Mamun and the actual caliphate and Arab portion to his son of aristocratic Arab descent Amin, ultimately creating civil war, which Mamun (r. 813–833) won. In the years that followed, however, caliphs had to reward generals and supporters with military land grants.

Harun al-Rashid's third son Mutasim (r. 833–844) had a Turkish slave mother, and he began to recruit large numbers of Turkish slaves as his personal elite bodyguards. It is this group of individuals who rose to prominence throughout the empire. In 834 Egypt was granted as an *iqta'*, or military land grant, that allowed the holder to collect taxes and remit a certain portion back to the central treasury. Obviously a great deal of leeway existed in a wealthy province, for example, Egypt, for the collector could be heavy-handed and stingy in his remissions, thus becoming quite wealthy in the process. Making Egypt an *iqṭa'* helped to foster an already existing notion of identity, and the policies of independent-minded governors, along with the collective wisdom of Egyptian peasants on whom Egypt's surplus rests, would create the conditions for an Egyptian national identity in the future.

One of the more successful Turkish governors of Egypt was Ahmad ibn Tulun (r. 868–884), who established a pattern of leadership that others would follow. He created a new neighborhood or town near Fustat, called al-Qatai, or "the districts," referring to the placement of different divisions of his military by ethnicity in the new city. He created a grand mosque, which still stands, providing a place for education and the dispensation of welfare. He improved irrigation and taxation, thus making the country function more efficiently, including the building of a canal to feed drinking water to Egypt's second most important city, Alexandria. Ibn Tulun increased Egypt's revenue by expanding its borders; he pushed into Syria up to the Byzantine frontier. This maneuver gave him enough power to display his authority in another act of Islamic sovereignty: minting coins in his name, although the Caliph's name still appeared on the coins as well. His success did not go unnoticed in Baghdad, indeed it was at times a source of conflict. When he died, he left behind a large number of ships, sons, and pack animals, along with 10 million dinars. Egypt was in such good condition that his governorship became hereditary. Unfortunately, his sons lacked his knack for government. The chroniclers' tales of his first successor, Kharamawayh, are something in between a soap opera and an X-rated Vegas act, involving eunuchs, harem women, drunkenness, and the murder Kharamawayh himself. How this individual who managed to betroth his daughter to the Abbasid caliph and start his rule with expanded borders and a full treasury could then sink so low is a bit baffling. The last of the Tulunids was defeated in 905 when the caliph sent a force to Qatai and brought the city to the ground, except for the mosque.

For another three decades Baghdad haphazardly sent various Turkish military commanders and utilized a direct form of control rather than *iqṭa'*. The situation was difficult and taxes were high. To keep order and collect those taxes commanders brought their own armies. Additionally there might be occasional incursions from regiments of North African troops. The most stable aspect of people's life was the religious establishment and the justice provided through the rule of law. The *shari'a* was now fully developed into a body of jurisprudence in four schools of law, three of which were practiced in Egypt: Shafii, Hanafi, and Maliki. Having a system of checks and balances in place did not mean that offenders (including oppressive governors) were undeterred, but the most grievous offences were challenged and punished.

Muhammad Ibn Tughg "al-Ikhshid" (r. 934–946), originally governor of Damascus, earned the title "leader" from the Caliph al-Radi, who sent him to Egypt to restore order. As capable administrators were often prone to doing, he controlled not only Egypt but also Syria and the Hejaz (western strip of the Arabian Peninsula where the Holy cities of Mecca and Medina are situated) during his 11-year rule. He remained on solid ground with the caliphate, even as the Turkish guard monopolized control of the office, killing and replacing caliphs at will. In 947 his office became hereditary; but since his sons were young, their tutor, a eunocized Nubian slave,

Kafur, ruled the dynasty. Kafur was a great lover of arts, poetry, and literature; he showered great wealth on his court, despite the fact that Egypt was in the midst of a series of rather difficult problems of both man-made and natural varieties: low Niles, famines, rebellions, invasions, fire, and naval assault. Kafur dealt with the multiplicity of problems as best he could through public works; however, taxes were extremely high. Kafur died in 968, and there was not an Ikhshid who was up to the challenge of reorganizing Egyptian affairs.

The Fatimids and Ayyubids

By the time of Kafur's death, some three centuries after the Arab conquest, major changes had taken place in Egyptian society. The process of Arabization and Islamization of the majority of the population had taken place. There was (and still is) a Coptic presence in Egypt, but the descendents of the Arab conquerors had settled and intermarried with the population and over time more of the population converted to Islam. Islam throughout the Abbasid Empire and beyond did not remain unified. The fundamental break in Islam between Sunnis and Shiites stems from the difference in belief over where religious authority lies, and who should have been the first successor to Muhammad. Simply put, Sunnis believe that religious authority stems from a consensus of religious scholars, and that the trajectory of Islamic history happened the way that it did (and should have) because it was part of God's greater plan. Shiites believe that religious authority stems from divine, charismatic leadership emanating from the bloodline of the Prophet Muhammad and that Ali, his cousin and son-in-law, should have been the first caliph. Within Shiism, there are splits as to how that divine leadership flows. The Fatimids (from Fatima the Prophet's daughter and wife of Ali) were a dynasty of Sevener or Ismaili Shiites that

---

TWELVER SHIISM VERSUS SEVENERS OR ISMAILI SHIISM

The majority of Muslims in the world today are Sunnis (about 85 percent) and of those remaining the majority are twelver Shiites. They believe in leadership flowing from the bloodline of the prophet that ends in the martyrdom of the 11th imam Hasan al-Askari (d. 874), followed by the disappearance of his son, the 12th imam, whom they believe is in occult. Occult is a form of hiding in which the imam can return at any time to usher in a day of judgment. Ismaili Shiites follow the same line of imams up to the sixth imam, Jafar al-Sadiq (d. 765); however, twelvers departed from standard practice by accepting a younger son and seveners accepted Ismail (who actually may have predeceased his father). Given oppression by Abbasid caliphs, disappearances, and hiding, early death among Shiite leaders was not uncommon. Ismailis believe that Ismail's son Muhammad also went into occult. Today, Nizari Muslims, followers of the Aga Khan, are the spiritual descendents of the Fatimids.

emerged in 10th-century North Africa and easily moved into Egypt in 969. They had attacked Egypt several times unsuccessfully under the Ikhshids, but now there was no one to stop them. Despite the propagandizing and missionary efforts of the Fatimid movement previously, the rulers did not jeopardize this valuable asset (Egypt) for the sake of their belief system.

Following the basic formula for successful rule, the Fatimids started work on a new city, al-Qahira, next to Fustat. The first ruler al-Muiz li Din Allah al-Fatimi worked hard to insure the trust of the Egyptians, who had been suffering during the last years of Ikhshid rule. Still operating from his base in North Africa, he sent grain to feed the hungry, planned public works to provide labor and create efficient administration, and ordered work on an incredible new mosque complex al-Azhar (see Chapter 5), which in and of itself was a monumental public works project involving large numbers of craftsmen and artists. He followed an expansionist foreign policy into Syria and the Hejaz. Finally, four years after the conquest, Muiz arrived in Cairo. He set out on a program of fiscal and bureaucratic reform. Things were running so much better under the Fatimids that the commercial center of gravity in the Islamic world pulled away from Baghdad and swung toward Egypt.

Fatimid rule brought some notable administrative and military changes to Egypt. Having come from North Africa, the Fatimids brought with them large numbers of Berber troops. While non-Muslims had largely been excluded from the military, now most members of the population were also now excluded from the military establishment, and the presence of a foreign military elite had become a longstanding theme in Egyptian history. Even looking at just the Islamic portion of history, there were the Arabs, then the Turks, and now the Berbers. As Fatimid rule wore on, wily Fatimid caliphs—who usurped the title from the Sunnis in Baghdad who used it simultaneously—would use the various groups of troops against one another, Berber versus Turk versus Sudanese, who were later recruited. Only the Fatimid elite, the military and ruling establishment lived in Cairo, some 18,000 in the glorious new

CAIRO, EGYPT, MIṢR

The superstitious Fatimids named the capital city al-Qahira. At the most auspicious moment, building was to be signaled by the ringing of a bell. A bird let off the signal early and forced the astrologers to figure out what planet was in its ascendancy, which happened to be Mars, al-Qahir, which comes from the same Arabic root as victory, making Cairo, the "City Victorious." The Fatimids meant for Cairo to be a segregated city, just as Fustat and Qatai had been, nevertheless, all of these territories were in proximity to one another. Although the Ptolemies and Romans used Alexandria and Thebes as capitals, for much of Egypt's long history the most important capitals have been at the base of the delta. The Arabic word for Egypt is *Miṣr* pronounced *Maṣr* in colloquial Egyptian dialect, which literally means civilization. Egyptians use the same word *Maṣr* to refer to both Cairo and to Egypt.

BERBERS

The Berbers are a tribal people who live in North Africa. Unlike most of the subject people who experienced the Islamic conquest, some were early converts, perhaps owing to their similar form of organization and beliefs. They were readily organized into armies and garrisons, and they became important components in many campaigns including the Umayyad campaign into Spain in 711. Nevertheless, the Berbers became quickly alienated with Umayyad rule because of unequal treatment based upon race. They became involved in a variety of heterodox religious movements that appealed to their sense of egalitarianism, including *kharijism,* which claims that any adult male can be caliph, establishing a number of North African dynasties. They were also important components of the Fatimid army. Responding to what they deemed as flaws in mainstream religious practice, Berbers established a number of puritanical Sunni dynasties in North Africa and Spain: Almoravids (1040–1147), Almohads (1121–1269). There were also Berbers who were relatively late converts to Islam.

city. Egyptians were allowed access through the city's southern gate to provision the capital and provide services, exiting at night. Similarly, theoretically, at night, the troops were supposed to stay out of Fustat, where ordinary folks lived. Over the 200 years of Fatimid rule, the Egyptian chronicles are filled with stories of the various ethnicities of troops fighting one another and attacking the people of Fustat.

The Fatimids are known, with a few notable exceptions, as tolerant rulers. Despite the fact that they were now the minority, Copts achieved high positions in administration. The Jewish community, which had not been a significant force in Egyptian life since a revolt in Roman times, prospered again, and there were also Jews who even attained ministerial posts. Previously, the Jewish community had been centered in Alexandria, and now the Jewish community was based in Fustat, centered around the Ben Ezra Synagogue, which was a great center of learning (see Chapter 5).

The great exception to Fatimid tolerance came in the form of al-Hakim (r. 996–1020), who was also a symptom of the beginning of Fatimid decline. al-Hakim's quirky eccentricities caused great unhappiness in the population that took to rioting, burning, and various forms of protest in Fustat. al-Hakim would then let loose his Sudanese troops on the crowds. Tensions among the troops were rising because of perceived Sudanese favoritism, as well as unhappiness among the Turkish troops about al-Hakim's vizier's proclamations regarding his divinity. Not everything from al-Hakim's rule was a disaster; he reconstructed the canal feeding clean water to Alexandria at a cost of 15, 0000 dinars, and he built Bayt al-Hikma, or the House of Wisdom, as a great center of learning, which even had facilities for women. One powerful and strong-willed woman, al-Hakim's sister Sitt al-Mulk, most likely engineered his murder. He went out one night for one of his donkey rides never to return in 1021, and she benefited materially by serving as regent for the young caliph

AL-HAKIM

al-Hakim was only a child of 11 when he became caliph, therefore rule fell into the hands of his tutor, a man he later grew to resent and executed. His next right-hand man, Darazi, was a bit of a sycophant, a yes-man who told him that he was the incarnate of a godhead and that his subjects should worship him. al-Hakim passed bizarre legislation including sumptuary laws highlighting the distinctions between religious communities; he carried out forced conversions; and he ordered the Church of the Holy Sepulchre destroyed in 1009. He did not think women should go out of their homes, therefore he forbade cobblers from making their shoes. He was a man of great simplicity and austerity, and thus he poured wine and honey into the Nile River. He could not stand the rival form of Islam, therefore he forbade the eating of *mulukhiyya* (see Chapter 6), an Egyptian favorite, but rumored also to be a favorite of the founder of the Umayyad dynasty.

al-Zahir. After a few years of famine and low Niles, Sitt al-Mulk working with al-Zahir restored order although problems with factionalism in the army continued.

al-Mustansir (r. 1035–1094) succeeded al-Zahir the same year that Sitt al-Mulk died, and she was still wielding a heavy hand in government up until her last days. The reckless infighting of the various regiments, as well as the despoliation and partition of the country was horrific. The Sudanese troops held the land in Upper Egypt, closest to their native lands, the Berbers held the rich agricultural lands of the delta, and the Turks held the administrative nucleus of the capital. At the same time, however, visitors to Egypt, for example, Nasiri Khusraw, who traveled in the middle of the 11th century, marveled at the brick construction, sewage systems, commercial networks, criminal justice, and "sky scrapers," not only in Cairo but also in Fustat. By the end of Mustansir's reign much of these cities would be destroyed due to rioting, fires, and pillaging after a period of misery caused by low Niles and famine in the mid-1060s.

The Fatimids were beginning to lose grip on their far-flung empire, which prior to including Egypt had gone as far as Italy. In 1071 Sicily was lost, much of Syria was slipping away, and the government was not even effectively collecting taxes on the Egyptian homeland. The Sunni Seljuq Turks posed an eminent threat to the East as they controlled the caliphate in Baghdad; however, the assassination of the enterprising vizier Nizam al-Mulk in 1092 postponed an impending invasion of Egypt. Within the Fatimid royal family schisms broke out, and one disgruntled family member joined the infamous Assassins sect in Syria. Thus, at the end of the 11th century, the contest for Syria between the Fatmids, the Seljuq Turks, and the wildcard factor of the Assassins continued to play itself out; this was when the Crusaders arrived.

The professed European reason for mounting the Crusades was to recapture the Holy Land, but historians have found that there were numerous other "push" factors including swelling populations and an outlet for lesser noble discontent. It conveniently fit into patterns of pilgrimage, crusade, and piety that were familiar in Western Christendom at the time. The Crusaders took Fatimid Jerusalem in 1099, massacring most of its population, including Christians. The great misperception about the Crusades is that it was the Muslims against the Christians because there were factions fighting factions within and among both religions. Indeed, the Fatimids initially welcomed the Crusaders as a counterbalance to Seljuq power and hegemony (before they took Jerusalem). Reading firsthand Muslim and Christian accounts from the period is rather enlightening for seeing how these alliances worked. The most exploited and harmed group were native Christians who were viewed as traitors by Muslims and as non-Christians by the invaders.

As the Crusaders carved up principalities in Syria for themselves they looked rapaciously toward weakened and wealthy Egypt. The factionalized Fatimid army, its ever-warring viziers, and lackluster leadership managed to repel a number of invasions that took place between 1117 and 1163, mostly due to circumstances rather than great military finesse; however, they were forced into paying tribute to the Crusaders. Fatimid holdings were eventually restricted to Egypt proper. When Amalric of the Latin Kingdom of Jerusalem invaded Egypt in 1164, drastic measures had to be taken. Shiite Fatimids allied with the only other power broker in existence, Sunni Nur al-Din al-Zangi, who had consolidated Muslim power in Syria. Nur al-Din responded to the "Frankish" (as all non-native Christians were known) threat by sending one of his most capable generals, a Kurd by the name of Shirkuh to Egypt.

In 1169 Shirkuh, accompanied by his nephew, Salah al-Din al-Ayyubi, arrived in Egypt and killed the incompetent Fatimid vizier so that he himself could take the position. The situation, like most of the Crusades, was quite complicated. In Egypt a small faction of the population supported the Crusaders, some factions supported Nur al-Din, but most of the population just suffered. Some were determined that if the Crusaders won there would be nothing left to win and burned large portions of Fustat. At any rate, Shirkuh died, and Salah al-Din assumed his role as vizier. When the Fatimid caliph died in 1171, Salah al-Din was already formally in charge of all aspects of military and the government. He pronounced himself Sultan, a title of political leadership, and he returned Egypt officially to Sunni orthodoxy by saying the name of the Abbasid caliph in Friday prayers, something that had not been done since the Fatimid invasion. This marks the beginning of the Ayyubid dynasty.

Thematically and predictably Salah al-Din, or Saladin, as he is better known carried out policies of successful Egyptian leaders. He waged an expansionist foreign policy against the Crusaders and even challenged the authority of his previous overlord Nur al-Din. He ousted the Crusaders from Jerusalem in 1187 at the Battle of Hittin, relegating the Crusader presence to a few small states, and in doing so displaying great feats of magnanimity, chivalry, and generosity earning a great reputation in the West. The Ayyubid Empire stretched from Mosul in the East, to Yemen in the South across Greater Syria through Egypt in the West. His large family helped in provincial government, as well as fielding positions for which Saladin was not prepared, for example, fiscal administration.

Internally he rebuilt centers of Sunni learning and scholarship that had fallen by the wayside under the heterodox Fatimids. He built an incredible citadel, fortified city walls, constructed an aquaduct to bring clean water to the capital, and re-dug the old canal connecting the Nile and the Red Sea. He opened the capital city that had formerly been the domain of the ruling establishment to the general population. With respect to trade, he fostered the development of the Red Sea spice trade encouraging Muslim traders, seeing Christian Crusaders as a threat economically. When Saladin died in 1193, his successors generally continued his policies of public works, strategic commerce, and support of education.

In the early 13th century, the Islamic world was besieged by two sets of threats, one old and one new: the Crusaders and the Mongols. As for the latter, far from Egypt just East of the Abbasid Caliphate the Khwarezmian Sultanate, as well as other smaller Muslim rulers, fell with the first wave of the Mongol invasions under Genghis Khan (d. 1227). Of more immediate concern to Egypt was the fifth Crusade, striking directly at Damietta, the Crusaders having made an alliance with Seljuq Turks of Rum. The combined Frisean and Genoese fleets took Damietta. In what can only be described as extreme greed, ignorance, or both, the Crusaders refused the new Ayyubid Sultan, al-Kamil's offer of Jerusalem for Damietta, for they wanted everything and it seemed within reach. al-Kamil was desperate since his father had just died in the midst of the siege. Nevertheless, the invaders were not ready to face the rising waters of the Nile and had to retreat before "taking everything." When al-Kamil was faced with negotiations again in 1229, he was better prepared to deal with the situation. He avoided conflict altogether.

The penultimate Ayyubid ruler, al-Salih (al-Kamil's son), was more of a fighter than a diplomat, and he began recruiting an army of *mamluks*, Turkic slaves primarily from central Asia to serve as his elite army. He housed these *mamluks* in barracks on the island of Roda, therefore they are known as *bahri mamluks*, literally "sea mamluks," because Egyptians consider the Nile as vast as a sea. It would be this crack fighting force of dependable soldiers who would repel the Seventh Crusade, initiated by Louis IX of France. The latter's strategy was to use Egypt as a base of operations to then launch another offensive on the Holy Land. The Crusaders arrived at Mansura, led by the king himself. This was an age of chivalry, and both al-Salih and Louis were in command of their armies. The situation became complicated when al-Salih died of natural causes. What happened next is an amazing segment in the history of women and slavery in Egypt. His consort Shajarat al-Durr, who was one among many, but clearly his favorite, played a key role in concealing the death of the king so that the morale of the army would not be shaken at this critical moment. Her desire was to make sure that his son by another woman could return from his provincial post before the news broke. She appointed a key mamluk Fakhr al-Din to command the army and ran the government with the assistance of a eunuch. As intense fighting continued in early 1250 and Fakhr al-Din lost his life, Louis was taken captive and the French were forced to pay a large ransom by the time that Turanshah returned home to take his father's place on the throne. The leading mamluks named her *Sultana*, after they murdered Turanshah, who did not show them or Shajarat al-Durr the proper respect. He had shown preference to his provincial mamluks over the Cairene *bahri mamluks*. Some sources indicate Shajarat al-Durr's complicity in the murder, and seemingly she did have the motivation and the means. She had gained ultimate power and wielded it utilizing Islamic means, minting coins in her name and having her name said in Friday prayers. The Abbasid caliph was not amused (she had actually been his property previously and had been a gift to al-Salih) and the caliph offered to send a man to fill the position, angry at seeing a woman doing the job. Having ruled 80 days on her own, she married Aybak, another mamluk general, inviting him to serve as co-ruler. Still having some power and authority, she forced Aybak to divorce his first wife, Umm Ali, before marrying her. The marriage of Shajarat-Durr to Aybak effectively marks the beginning of mamluk rule in Egypt, although she co-ruled with him for seven years.

The Mamluks

Originally purchased just for various rulers, the mamluk system centered on households headed by manumitted slaves (mamluks), who perpetuated the system by purchasing young male slaves. Initially, they were from Central Asia, the Russian Urals, and Circassia. Generally speaking, Turkic dialects were the spoken language of this group. Having been separated from parents and home from such a tender age, the boys developed strong attachments to the household and its patriarch, as well as their "brothers," "uncles," and "cousins." In the household a boy would be converted to Islam, learn some basic Arabic, but mostly he learned equestrian skills, martial arts, and other talents that would facilitate a military career. When he reached puberty, he would be manumitted and allowed to start his own household that would be allied to that of his patriarch. The outward sign of his physical and political maturity was manifested in the growth of his beard, which could not be grown until manumission. Manumitted slaves were provided with land to support themselves.

The mamluk system did not overwhelm itself due to mamluk infighting, as well as external warfare and conflict. Because they were urban and foreign they were more susceptible to disease, thus when the plague arrived in 1347, they died in much

---

THE ASSASSINATION OF SHAJARAT AL-DURR

Accounts indicate that the co-rule of Shajarat al-Durr and Aybak went smoothly for seven years, but then various versions of the story claim that she was either unhappy with her husband's fiscal management, or alternately that she was unhappy about his impending marriage to a Turkish princess. Several versions of the assassination story exist with some having the wife carrying out the act, whereas in others she uses assassins or a eunuch to kill her husband. Ali, and his mother (Umm Ali), the spurned (first) wife of Aybak, led her retinue of women in a beating with wooden bath clogs. Shajarat al-Durr's bloody body was thrown into the moat and left for days before being collected and buried in the mausoleum that she had built for herself several years earlier. The famous Egyptian dessert Umm Ali (see Chapter 6) was made by the woman who led the group in her beating, as a celebration of Shajarat al-Durr's death.

larger numbers than the general population. The *baḥri mamluks* generally followed a system whereby one mamluk was the Sultan or holder of power, whereas the *burgi mamluks* (Citadel mamluks) had a more decentralized system of rule. Another principle rule, but not always followed, was that mamluks did not enlist their sons in the ranks of the mamluks. In other words, mamluks perhaps felt their own sons too "sissified" for the system. When one died, his lands were assigned to his fictive sons not his blood sons, who were often given government posts or married into to the prominent families representing the religious establishment or long-distance trade. Mamluk households were supported by tax farms, which allowed the mamluks to ruthlessly exploit the peasantry. They maintained their distance literally and figuratively from the population by the privilege of riding on horseback and the distinction of their Turkish language.

By 1257 the only viable power brokers in Egypt were the mamluks, and they rallied around Qutuz, one of Aybak's trusted generals. For a brief period of time, they winked at the authority of a shadow sultan, a young son of Aybak, but with the Mongol threat on the horizon such hollow gestures were not necessary. Hülegü, grandson of the infamous Genghis Khan, began marching eastward in 1255, on the orders of his brother Möngke, now the great Khan, who wanted the destruction of all Muslim states. By 1258, the Abbasid caliphate had fallen, and Hülegü sent strident warnings by envoy to the mamluks to simply hand over power or else, citing the path of destruction that had been left in his wake. Qutuz responded in kind by quartering the envoys and hanging them from the southern gate of the city, Bab Zuweila. So intimidating were the Mongols that even the Latin Kingdom offered to contribute forces, but Qutuz refused. The mamluks routed the Mongols at the Battle of Ain Jalut (Northern Palestine) in 1260 with a most heroic display by Baibars, a mamluk general. The victory is significant because it made the people, not only in Egypt, but also in Syria, feel safe from the Mongol threat that heretofore had seemed unstoppable. While the mamluks might have been an alien, foreign elite, they provided protection—first against the later Crusaders, but more importantly against the Mongol hordes.

Once the threat was gone, mamluk factionalism set in. Qutuz had not properly rewarded those mamluks who had served well in recent battles, and for this offense he paid with his life. In mamluk politics the most powerful cream rises to the top, in this case Baibars (r. 1260–1277), the hero of Ain Jalut. Baibars' exploits were of such epic proportion that they have been recounted in story and song and retold by countless generations of Egyptians. Following the pattern of good rule, he maintained the expanded borders that included Syria where he continuously ate away at remaining Crusader holdings at Antioch (1268) and the Krak des Chevaliers fortress (1271); he carried out numerous public works projects, including an improved postal service; built schools and mosques; and created strategic alliances, which kept his borders safe (Byzantines) and kept a supply of young mamluks streaming into Egypt (Golden Horde Mongols). As a grand gesture to his subjects, he restored a shadow Abbasid caliphate in Cairo, by which he gave shelter to an escaped member of the Abbasid family whose descendents would still be in Egypt at the time of the Ottoman conquest. This measure provided legitimacy to mamluk rule. He continued and built on the established policy of convening, creating, and protecting the annual

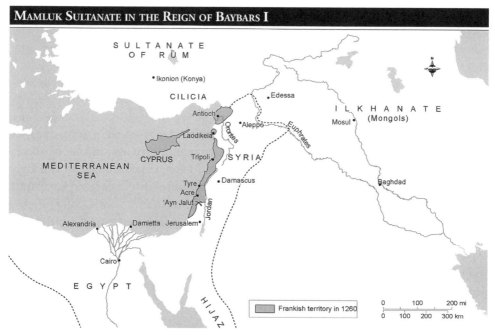

MAMLUK SULTANATE IN THE REIGN OF BAYBARS I

SULTANATE OF RŪM

• Ikonion (Konya)

CILICIA

• Edessa

Antioch

I L K H A N A T E
(Mongols)

• Aleppo

Mosul •

Laodikeia

Orotes

Euphrates

CYPRUS

Tripoli

S Y R I A

MEDITERRANEAN
SEA

• Damascus

Baghdad

Tyre

Acre

'Ayn Jalut

Jordan

Alexandria

Damietta

Jerusalem •

Cairo •

E G Y P T

H I J A Z

Frankish territory in 1260

0   100   200 mi
0 100 200 300 km

Mamluk Sultanate in the reign of Baybars I. (ABC-CLIO)

caravan to the holy cities of Mecca and Medina at the time of the annual pilgrimage. Even the great Baibars was not immune to the nastiness of mamluk politics; he allegedly died from poison that he prepared for someone else. He wanted political rule to fall to his son, but not being there to protect his interests; and since his son really had no special talent for ruling, the job went to Qalawun (r. 1279–1290), one of Baibars' generals, whose daughter had been married to Baibars' son. Most likely Baibars had created this marriage alliance for the purpose of assisting his son after his death, not ending his son's rule.

Qalawun was an extraordinary ruler whose good works can still be seen in Cairo today. He built a huge complex that contained his mosque and tomb, a school, and a hospital, which is still in existence today. With respect to foreign affairs, he maintained Baibars' aggressive Syrian policy, continuing to push the last Crusader holdings, Tripoli falling in 1289, and Acre on the brink of collapse just before Qalawun's death in 1290. He continued to play one Mongol faction against another. He allied with the Golden Horde, which continued to supply slaves. Egypt's enemy remained the menacing Il-Khanids, who continued to occupy Eastern lands and maintain an alliance with Christian states. It is right at the end of Qalawun's reign that Pope Niccola IV began a series of sanctions against the mamluks, aimed at debilitating their war-making capabilities, for example, obtaining iron, wood, and slaves. Other Western powers would continue this policy with greater and lesser success up until the Ottoman conquest. Nevertheless, the papacy also traded in "forgiveness" for trading in forbidden goods with the enemy. Mamluk success necessitated those items that Egypt did not have internally.

Like others before him Qalawun tried to assure hereditary succession for his dynasty, which in one sense was successful, but in another was evidence that the real power lay with the military, which could reject a sultan in favor of his brother or some other relative at any moment. Real mamluks by the very definition of the term were those who had been purchased in the system not born into it. One of Qalawun's sons even tried to balance the power of the *bahri mamluks*, by bringing in new mamluks from Circassia and housing them at the Citadel, the *burgi mamluks*. This action did not wash well with the *bahris*; but despite these power struggles, the age generally is remembered by historians, of the mamluk and contemporary age, as one of abundance and well-being. Nevertheless, the Il-Khanid Mongols continued to threaten the country. The period was also marked by a flourishing of arts (see Chapter 6) and an expansion of trade. The "trickle down" effect was evident in the early *bahri* period by a lack of popular riots or sectarian strife.

Problems began around the early 14th century. Even the best of rulers cannot handle the whims of the Nile, and low Niles are generally followed by periods of famine and disease. In bad times people usually look to minorities as scapegoats, and a wave of anti-Christian riots broke out in the country in the 1321. Destruction of private property, looting of sacred buildings, and enforcement of sumptuary laws characterized this era of persecution that ended in more conversions to Islam.

al-Nasir Muhammad's (d. 1341) lengthy rule represents the highpoint of bahri mamluk rule. He instituted a program of building public works, such as the Mosque of al-Nasir Muhammad which still stands today. (Courtesy of Mona Russell)

Stability returned with better economic times, wise guidance, and fiscal responsibility that followed under the leadership of al-Nasir Muhammad, a son of Qalawun's who ruled intermittently between 1309 and 1341. Successful rulers make irrigation a priority, and not surprisingly he refurbished the canal bringing fresh water to Alexandria. This stability would not last due to the arrival of the Black Death in Egypt in 1347, which continued to recur in regular cycles (on average every nine years) all the way into the 19th century. As it did on the other side of the Mediterranean, the plague in Egypt carried a significant portion of the population. Scholars estimate that Egypt lost about one-third of its population and that it did not regain this population until the Ottoman period.

Sultan Hasan, builder of the great mosque bearing his name, was at the reins of government when the crisis struck; in fact, he built the colossal structure from confiscated (unclaimed) estate money and recycled pyramid stone. Meanwhile, land taxes, collected by the *iqta'* system had declined significantly. Even though the numbers of mamluks had also declined, state expenses and the costs of war had not, which made the mamluks ever more predatory in their search for income. Hasan fell at the hands of one of his own mamluks in 1361. In the meantime, yet another Crusader, Peter I of Lusignan of Cyprus, literally hit Alexandria and ran in 1365, burning, plundering, and taking prisoners, before the mamluks could even respond. *Bahri mamluk* infighting continued until the Qalawun dynasty came to an end and the Circassian *burgi mamluk*, Barquq imposed his will on the country in 1382.

Sultan Hasan Mosque. This fourteenth-century mosque near the Citadel contains an egg-shaped dome, as well as more typical mamluk architectural styles, e.g. the pointed arch. (Courtesy of Mona Russell)

The *burgi mamluks*, mostly of Circassian and Greek origin, were dealt a much different set of cards: a country wracked by disease, famine, brigandage, a decreased tax base in the post-plague era and in a time of war when Western Christendom was making it more difficult to obtain the commodities necessary for making war. Furthermore, the mamluks were not ones to adopt the rapidly changing technologies of war. Power depended on maintaining a hegemonic bloc of alliances among the great mamluk households. Between 1382 and 1517 nearly two dozen sultans came to power, but only six ruled over a combined total of more than 100 years. In other words, the good sultans were really good, but many were just marginal leaders.

Another major threat to Egypt came in the late 14th century when yet another Mongol scourge swept across Asia, this time in the form of Timur the Lame (Tamerlane) (r. 1380–1405), a former Chagatai vassal who rose up against his overlord and began expanding territories using infamous Mongol techniques and adding his own style, for example, pyramid of skulls; his descendents would eventually found the Mughal empire in India. Egypt at first allied with the Ottomans, another rising power in Asia, but when Timur managed to capture the Ottoman Sultan Bayezid I, the mamluks paid tribute to Timur and avoided conflict.

Fighting between and among mamluks in Egypt and Syria was a problem in the early 1400s. Traditionally, stable rule in Egypt had typically followed an expansionist foreign policy, which was the case under Barsbay (r. 1422–1438). He expanded Red Sea spice trade interests moving further into the Indian Ocean, which reinforced Egypt's control of the Hejaz, and he removed the Crusader presence at Cyprus, placing it under mamluk occupation.

The other notable *burgi* Sultan is Qaitbey (r. 1468–1496). He utilized his three-decade rule to consolidate power in Egypt and Syria and is most famous for his magnificent public works and building projects, including a spectacular fort that still stands in Alexandria, built on the ruins of Ptolemy's Pharos Lighthouse, most likely

---

WHO ARE THE OTTOMAN TURKS?

The Ottomans were one of many groups of Turks in Anatolia in the 13th century, and at that time they were not very powerful. The Seljuq Turks of Rum (1077–1307) granted them a small province in the northwest in 1280 on which they continued to build until they had a massive empire, long after their original masters were no longer a force. Some historians theorize that they were among the groups of Turks that came during the pivotal battle of Manzikert (1071), whereas others place them there long after the battle. Expansion into the Balkans began in the reign of Murad I (r. 1359–1389), the conquest of Constantinople under Muhammad I in 1453, and the conquest of the Middle East during the reign of Selim the Grim (r. 1512–1520). The Ottoman Empire lasted until just after World War I.

recycling some of the stones, as well as his spectacular mausoleum complex in Cairo that also contains a *madrasa* (see Chapter 5). Although his rule was generally characterized by economic prosperity, he was challenged by the rise of the Portuguese, who were already making their way down the coastline of Africa in search of a new route to the spices and would succeed in 1498. Egypt suffered a particularly nasty bout of plague in 1492, which took Cairene inhabitants by the thousands daily. A bovine disorder followed that of the humans, causing even more tragedy, since they were the main beast of burden in the fields. Additionally, cattle disorders brought down the price of meat and raised the prices of cooking butter, cheese, and milk, all of which was bad for the common man.

Qaitbey's successor, after some struggle for power, was Qansuh al-Ghuri (r. 1501–1516) who was not one to think out of the box, but rather to tax the peasantry senselessly, particularly since the Ottomans were posing a land threat and the Portuguese a naval assault on commercial territories: the lucrative spice trade. Egypt never had been a producer of the items needed to make war, therefore new monies were needed—taxes collected in advance, custom duties raised, and charitable endowments confiscated. Yet another rising power, the Safavids of Persia, offered to ally with the mamluks against the Ottomans, but al-Ghuri felt it unnecessary. After the Safavid defeat at the Battle of Chaldiran in 1514, which opened up mamluk Syria for the Ottomans, it was clear that this was a mistake. The Ottomans were a truly a gunpowder empire, while the mamluks used it only to defend fortresses, boats, and positions. They prided themselves on the "manly" art of warfare and guns were too sissy for them. They did not require artistry, skill, and precision. The Ottomans under Selim the Grim did not split hairs over masculinity and warfare; they simply took Damascus. Meanwhile al-Ghuri, a septuagenarian, hoped Selim would be content to remain on the other side of the Sinai. Despite their superior weaponry, the Ottomans used their favorite trick, bribing the second in command, which proved quite effective.

OTTOMAN EGYPT

Direct Rule and Mamluk Resurgence

Like all foreign rulers before them, the Ottomans could not rule Egypt without some assistance from both the people who had administered the territory before them (mamluks) and the collective knowledge of the peasantry who understood how to farm and irrigate what would become the most lucrative province of the Ottoman Empire, which was at its height in the 16th century. Khair al-Din governed Egypt until his death in 1522, while the Ottomans were still consolidating their rule. This process lasted until about 1525, when Sulayman the Magnificent (r. 1520–1566) reorganized its administration. Meanwhile, rowdy mamluks had been executed or fled to Upper Egypt, but those willing to work within the system were incorporated into Ottoman janissary regiments because they had the local knowledge that Sulayman needed; in fact he had used them in his expedition against Rhodes in 1522. A visit by Sulayman's grand vizier in 1525 laid out the pattern for Ottoman

ISLAMIC SLAVERY: OTTOMAN JANISSARIES

The Ottomans used a human tax (*devşirme*) on some of the Christian minorities in their Balkan provinces. Boys between the ages of about 8 and 12 would be assembled in Balkan towns, often with the assistance of local officials or even parish priests. The boys would be taken to the Ottoman capital and tested where the smartest 10 percent would be sent to the palace school alongside the sons of the sultan, intended for a career in the bureaucracy. Reminiscent of the mamluks, the remainder would be converted to Islam, given training in military arts, and ultimately destined for the Ottoman infantry, the Janissaries. While these individuals were technically the property of the sultan, they were also part of the ruling establishment. The existence of this tax defied the notion of protected Christian communities. The Ottomans skirted this issue by citing the (relatively) late conversion of these communities to Christianity.

government, establishing a viceroy, with a *divan* (council) to meet regularly; and Egypt was divided into administrative districts, some of which would even be governed by tribal elites in Upper Egypt.

Technically, all land was owned by the Ottoman state. Initially the Ottomans used a form of direct tax collection, but ultimately they found it easier by the early 1600s to use a tax farming system, known as *iltizam*. The *multazim* bought the rights to collect the taxes, but he or she was responsible for the irrigation works and general upkeep of the lands under his or her control. It was in the *multazim's* interest to develop agricultural land and maintain canals, ditches, and the like, in order to increase his or her profit. These individuals simply guaranteed a specific return to the state. The peasant had usage rights to the land such that a person would farm the same land as his ancestors, but this differed from both the *multazim's* rights and the state's rights. The Ottomans gave great autonomy to Egypt as long as the central treasury received appropriate tax money, as well as food to feed the capital. Nevertheless, no single entity owned the Nile or any other single body of water, so the state also had a vested interest in maintaining water works and making sure that peasants utilized all fertile agricultural lands. Bureaucrats (not *multazims*) could be accountable with their lives for allowing rich land to lie fallow. A large percentage of *multazims* were mamluks. Sulayman used the three-decade long rule of Qaitbey as a reference for his procedures, citing it frequently in his roadmap to Egyptian administration (Mikhail 2008).

Although Egypt was no longer the center of an empire, it was a strategic location in administering Ottoman territories via the Red Sea along the Hejaz and commercially in the competition with emerging Christian powers in the Indian Ocean trade. Having conquered the holy cities of Mecca and Medina, the Ottomans no longer needed to keep the shadow Abbasid caliphate in Cairo. They now became the protectors of the holy cities, although the Sultan would not claim the title caliph until the 19th century.

The first six decades of Ottoman rule ran fairly smoothly; however, beginning in 1586, the first in a series of rebellions that marked Egyptian defiance of Ottoman authority occurred. A number of the major problems actually began outside Egypt itself but articulated with Ottoman rule of the province. The first was the growing impact of the global climate change on other parts of the Empire, which made Ottoman dependency on Egyptian grain and stability all the more important. Thus the second problem became all the more troublesome, namely, devaluation of the salary of Ottoman Janissaries, the infantry, in the face of New World silver, the repercussions of which were being felt worldwide.

The Ottomans relied on mamluk regiments to deal with these problems. The mamluks continued to perpetuate themselves; however, in the Ottoman age they had diversified slightly, and now some came from Bosnia and Greece. Soon the mamluks were rewoven into all facets of the ruling fabric taking important posts, for example, *amir al-ḥajj,* the leader of the caravan to Mecca, and chief financial administrator by the mid-17th century.

By this point as well, the mamluks could unseat any unpopular Ottoman governor sent from Istanbul, the latter generally serving a year's term. With the death of Ridwan Bey al-Fiqara in 1656, the leading mamluk of the age, the Ottomans were able to recapture some centralized authority due to mamluk infighting that followed. This Ottoman reassertion of power was brief. After the Great Insurrection of 1711, a turf war involving various regiments stationed in Egypt, the mamluks reasserted their primacy, in a period known as the beylicate in which they had more power than the central administration's garrison or any of its representatives.

The Beylicate

By this point, the Janissaries had also developed some local ties. Given that their salaries had become so devalued, what started as a predatory relationship with the artisans and craftsmen of Egypt evolved into a much more symbiotic relationship as the Janissaries married into these families, enlisted in guilds, and entered their children into the rosters of the Janissary regiments.

Despite all this infighting, Egypt's economy was growing. Returning to the sphere of a large empire, and with it a large centralized state, committed to the protection of commercial networks meant a great boon to Egypt's long-distance traders. During Ottoman times coffee became the new item of long-distance trade and the local sugar industry boomed. Egyptian wheat and textiles continued to prosper. Coffee, which originated in Ethiopia and spread through the Middle East in the five to six centuries before the Ottoman conquest, was well suited to the needs of long-distance trade. It traveled well, did not spoil easily, and it became extremely popular among Sufis, Muslim mystics, for its stimulant effect.

Merchants used their wealth to sponsor charitable endowments, which themselves could generate enormous incomes that could then be put back into the community. For example, a merchant could create a hostel to house other merchants and store commodities, the income of which would then be used to sponsor charitable works, such as soup kitchens, schools, fountains, and so on. These endeavors were not always selfless projects, as many times they were simply tax shelters that enabled merchants to shield their wealth from the state and the predations of income-sniffing mamluks and Janissaries. One could name a relative as a beneficiary before the ultimate charitable diversion of these funds. Even truly charitable endowments were often done for the sole means of demonstrating that someone had achieved status.

In the 18th century, there was extreme prosperity, characterized by an increased trade with France, which was in need of raw materials for its incipient industries, as well as wheat. While trade with the French generally helped Egypt, at least initially, it later brought problems, especially when the French introduced New World coffee that replaced mocha from the Hejaz. Additionally, the French began to copy Egyptian textiles so that they could reproduce them more cheaply. Old turf wars between the central administration and local players, as well as among local players, led to one very clever mamluk rising to the top by playing the game in a new way. In the meanwhile, all the vicious war-making meant that *multazims* had to sell their tax farms in order to fund these military adventures, and there was a veritable land grab in the 18th century. The groups that had the assets to pay for these tax farms were long-distance traders (*tujjar*), members of the religious establishments, and women, many of whom turned their *iltizams* into charitable endowments (*waqfs*) to avoid the predations of various tax-collecting agencies.

The clever mamluk was Ali Bey al-Kabir (the Great) (r. 1760–1773), also known as *bulut kapan*, Turkish for cloud catcher because of his sky-high ideas. First, he decided that the old mamluk system was cumbersome and that it would take too long to raise an army to maturity, so he simply bought an army of mercenaries. He even utilized new military technologies that other mamluks had been shy to adopt and perfect. He had to replace all government officials with his own, including the tribal chieftains in Upper Egypt. He had already gotten rid of the Ottoman viceroy and named himself *Shaykh al-Balad*, a title that had existed among the mamluks themselves but now received official recognition. Like other successful rulers he dominated Egypt's economic resources and engaged in an expansionist foreign policy. He carried out policies that had worked for previously successful rulers, but he looked toward new means for solving fiscal crises and greater autonomy from the Ottoman overlord. He moved into Syria and the Hejaz, and he replaced custom officials with new ones that helped him innovate and make the most of the markets in his newly conquered territories. The Ottomans were not going to allow this upstart with his "head in the clouds" to take not only Egypt but also other lucrative and symbolic provinces, so they played the game they played well, namely bribery. What had worked best about the mamluk system was its loyalty, based on fictive kinship. Since Ali Bey's army was composed of mercenaries, the Ottomans did not have to overcome this stumbling block. They were able to bribe his second in command and assassinate him.

After the overthrow of Ali Bey al-Kabir, politically, socially, culturally, and economically, Egypt began to suffer intensely. The economic changes, with respect to shifting trade patterns that had damaged Red Sea trade, continued, mocha coffee continued to lose its value, and Egyptian textiles were slowly being replaced by European ones. In the absence of a charismatic figure, like Ali Bey, various factions and oligarchies of mamluks ruled, but no single power or authority existed as it had under his rule.

Add to these man-made problems those of the environment. Although we usually think of the cycle of problems starting with low Niles, followed by famine, and plague, a new historian of the environment Alan Mikhail has asserted that the real pattern actually begins with the flood before the low Nile, which brings the rats in proximity to humans and flood waters ravaging stored supplies of grain in cities. Thus, when a period of low Niles impacts the agricultural harvests for a period of time, the food supply for the entire country is in jeopardy. This cycle began in 1790 with the plague striking in 1791 and a series of disasters following (2008). The Egyptian chronicles of the day are filled with tales of people eating their own dead, in addition to dead animals unfit for human consumption. The peasants fled the land in search of the grain stored in the cities, but these supplies were long gone, and the lands were left untilled. The French, long suffering from shortages of their own and at the tail end of their revolution, took the opportunity to invade Egypt and take advantage of its many resources.

The French Invasion

Under the leadership of Napoleon Bonaparte, the French army invaded Egypt in 1798. The largely outnumbered mamluks made the mistake of crossing the Nile to meet the French with their superior weapons at the Battle of the Pyramids. No longer could the mamluks claim to be the protectors against foreign invasion, a title they claimed since the 13th century. Napoleon came with a team of explorers and scientists ready to probe Egypt in all of its dimensions. Using what we would now call psychological warfare, Napoleon distributed leaflets published in Arabic proclaiming that he was actually a Muslim who was going to deliver the Egyptians from the "foreign" mamluks and restore Egypt back to its rightful sovereign, the Sultan. Egyptian chronicler al-Jabarti writing his account of the spectacle did not find him to be genuine, and he described the occupying forces to be rude, crass, and vulgar. Nevertheless, the French believed that men of the religious establishment, that is, those who were literate, were the ones that could be harnessed to the yoke of French leadership. They demonstrated French technology, scientific experiments, and all manner of incentives to bring them on board since they were the bridge to the people of Egypt.

Although Napoleon claimed to be restoring Egypt to the Ottoman Sultan, Selim III (r. 1789–1806), the Sultan did not buy his story and sought the assistance of the British in dislodging the French forces from Egypt. By this point Napoleon had returned to France to achieve greater fame. French forces in Egypt, now expanded to Syria, were suffering from diseases ranging from the plague to intestinal disorders. A combined Anglo-Ottoman force pushed the French out in 1801, but this left a vacuum and several factions vying for power. The French had not given up hope. The Ottomans wanted the opportunity to restore this lucrative province to centralized control. The mamluks, who utilized the age-old trick of hiding in Upper Egypt, were laying in wait to return to power. The British recognized the chance to gain a foothold in Egypt and looked for a group of pliable mamluks through whom they could rule. Out of this mess, an unlikely candidate rose to the task of reorganizing Egypt, the second in command of an auxiliary Albanian mercenary contingent. Even after the first in command died, no one would have imagined that Muhammad Ali, the commander of this obscure regiment, would rise to such heights.

MODERN EGYPT

Age of Muhammad Ali

Prior to his military career, Muhammad Ali's roots were in Kavala (Macedonia) from a merchant family, and he metaphorically "sold" himself to Egypt's long-distance traders and leading religious scholars (*'ulama*) as someone who could restore order to the country. The *'ulama* went to the Ottoman Sultan and petitioned for him to be their viceroy (governor) in 1805. Sultan Selim III (r. 1789–1807) was facing multiple internal and external crises of his own and felt that he had nothing to lose by giving Muhammad Ali a chance; if he failed then he was no worse off than before, and if indeed he restored order, then Selim had the profits of a lucrative province to gain. Neither man had any way of knowing that Muhammad Ali's dynasty would outlive Selim's by three decades.

Muhammad Ali's first six years of rule were spent consolidating his power. The viceroy did not consider himself an Egyptian, and while he desired greater autonomy for and hereditary control of Egypt, he recognized his position as a vassal of the Ottoman state. Though many historians credit him with founding modern Egypt, it was not necessarily his intent to do so, and it certainly was not for the sake of the Egyptians. Some of the changes that Egypt had experienced were already underway in the 18th century, in terms of the economy. Many of the policies that Muhammad Ali supported were continuation of policies enacted by the French colonial state, for example, quarantine, seizure of property, and coercion of labor. Nevertheless, the entrance of Egyptians into the army, bureaucracy, and educational system would have a long-term impact on national identity and would shape modern Egyptian history.

After 1811, Muhammad Ali set out on an aggressive program of economic and military expansion, buttressed by a growing central government of technology-savvy officials. The year 1811 is significant because it marks the year that the Sultan Mahmud II (r. 1808–1839) asked the viceroy to put down a puritanical Wahhabi threat emanating from the Nejd (Eastern peninsula) that threatened the holy cities in the Hejaz. Muhammad Ali called for a banquet at the Citadel to commemorate the investiture of his son Tusun Pasha to lead these forces. He took the opportunity to invite the last remaining mamluk opposition to the festivities. Several dozen of his strongest opponents and their retainers attended. Muhammad Ali had calculatedly whittled down the numbers of his enemies by allowing them to fight each other off during the first years of his reign. Over the course of the evening, he ransacked their homes, divesting them of their portable wealth, and when the mamluks were exiting the narrow passageway from the Citadel, Albanian sharpshooters assassinated them. Thus marks the beginning of Muhammad Ali's new era of rule. A number of mamluks were wise enough not to accept the invitation and fled to Upper Egypt where Muhammad Ali's son Ibrahim pursued them relentlessly.

To carry out Muhammad Ali's expansionist policies, he needed an army. Initially, he utilized the Albanian mercenaries who arrived with him, as well as his own mamluks. His first thought was to invade Sudan (1820) and utilize it as a source of gold and slaves. Although the expedition was successful, neither of the other ideas "panned" out. The slaves did not fare well in the Egyptian environment, and he did not find much gold. His eldest son Ibrahim, the commander of his armed forces, suggested using native Egyptians in the army. Since the time of the expansion in the seventh century, Islamic empires had provided the military, which subject-producers supported through taxation. Now Egyptians would be responsible for their own defense, albeit under the command of a Turkish-speaking officer corps. The Ottoman sultan called on Egyptian troops for a number of campaigns, including the previously discussed campaign in the Hejaz and future ones in the Mediterranean, but there were also unsolicited ones, for example, the one in Sudan and the one in Syria (beginning 1831) that put the viceroy marching distance from the imperial capital. Egyptians were not particularly happy about serving in Ibrahim's army, and apparently they went to great lengths to avoid conscription, for example, whole-scale abandonment of villages, fighting conscription officers, and disfiguring their bodies. One European traveler claims to have seen a brigade formed entirely of men with one eye, missing teeth, or cut fingers; but the problem was more commonly addressed by imprisoning offenders, sending them on public works projects, and/or conscripting their relatives to send the message not to continue these futile tactics.

One of the things that Ibrahim's army needed was arms, and Muhammad Ali was a mercantilist who aimed toward self-sufficiency. The big downfall of the mamluks had been their inability first to use and then to produce arms of their own, which meant that they were constantly in search of new sources of income to buy them from abroad. Thus, Muhammad Ali wanted to create his own industries to fill this gap, and he needed both the schools (see Chapter 5) and the industries necessary to do so. Another industry he saw as a natural fit for Egypt was textiles, and he introduced long-staple cotton to Egypt in 1821, where it could be utilized along with other indigenous fibers, for example, flax and linen.

With respect to the economy, Muhammad Ali turned Egypt into a one-man monopoly whereby he was the single buyer and seller of all goods. He dismantled the tax-farming system in Egypt and created private property, distributing land to his family and to rural Egyptian notables, who cemented their loyalty by sending their sons to his new schools, the recruiting ground for his expanding bureaucracy. The Egyptian peasant used to the rhythm and cycle of the Nile and the seasons was now told what to grow, when to grow it, and how much the state was willing to pay for it. Conscription for the army or for massive public works projects, like the Mahmudiyya canal, took men away from their homes in droves. While irrigation projects had been characteristic of Egyptian public life for literally thousands of years, the means of quantifying and harnessing that manpower were taking on new proportions. The Mahmudiyya canal (1817–1820) was the latest incarnation of the canal connecting

Cairo and Alexandria to bring potable drinking water; however, this was literally to be "another Nile," and it necessitated the labor of some 300,000 to 350,000 workers at a time when Egypt's population was somewhere between 4.5 and 5 million. Even more startling, and perhaps baffling, is the estimated number of deaths: 12,000–100,000. The quantifying capabilities of the state grew; initially it only cared about counting male workers who could be levied for such projects or conscripted in the army, classified by age, religion, and health status. By the time of Muhammad Ali's retirement in 1848, the census had become far more sophisticated, enumerating all citizens, male and female, young and old, free and enslaved, as well as foreign residents. New graduates of engineering and surveying schools conducted cadastral surveys and mapped the land to fully understand its potential (Mikhail 2008).

The state under Muhammad Ali also took greater control of its land by administering Egypt's charitable endowments (*waqfs*), which accounted for up to 20 percent of the arable land. The religious establishment, which had great autonomy due to its role as administrators of these lands, as well as tax farmers, lost any autonomy that it previously had. These individuals now became salaried workers of the state, wishing perhaps that they had not petitioned Selim III to take Muhammad Ali as viceroy. In the years to come as the Ottoman state changed legal codes, the area over which they had purview declined to simply personal status issues, as the state apparatus grew and new bureaucracies and schools replaced them.

In many ways Muhammad Ali's reforms were predecessors of changes that would come later for the Ottomans during the *tanzimat* era of reform (1839–1876). The Ottomans both relied on and were wary of their vassal in Egypt. The fiasco of Greek

Mosque of Muhammad Ali within the Citadel originally built by Saladin. (Dreamstime.com)

TANZIMAT REFORMS

The *tanzimat* reforms began in 1839 with a decree making all Ottoman citizens regardless of religion or ethnicity equal before the law, with respect to taxation, access to education, government jobs, and availability for conscription. This decree was reformulated in 1856 to reestablish equality of all citizens. This "reorganization" of the empire changed the way Islamic empires had been run since the seventh century. Nevertheless, the Quran remained the source of inspiration for the Sultan, who would officially adopt the title of caliph in the 19th century.

---

independence (beginning 1821) highlighted the ineffectiveness of Ottoman troops, the superiority of Muhammad Ali's troops, and the failure of Ottoman diplomacy, which literally sunk the Ottoman-Egyptian fleet at Navarino in 1827 and led to the conflict in Morea. The Mediterranean experience left a bitter taste in Muhammad Ali's mouth, which he then used to rebuild his fleet and occupy Syria, beginning in late 1831. Like other successful Egyptian leaders he held Syria and the Hejaz, giving him markets for his goods. The British saw an aggressive competitor in Muhammad Ali in their favored industry (textiles), and they encouraged the Ottoman sultan to ratify the Treaty of Balta Liman, which dismantled Egypt's monopolies. This treaty in combination with previous trading agreements, known as Capitulations, meant that Egyptian textiles (and other industries) would not be able to compete with European ones. Within two years, the British forced Egypt out of the Hejaz and coastal Syria; however, Muhammad Ali was given hereditary control of Egypt, following the Ottoman pattern of succession of eldest male, granted in the Treaty of London (1840). During the last years of his reign, many of his greatest accomplishments faded, and Egypt turned into a supplier of raw cotton for the United Kingdom.

Ibrahim, Abbas, and Said: The Beginnings of a Dynasty

The logical successor to Muhammad Ali would have been Ibrahim, the commander in chief of his armed forces and eldest son, who actually spoke Arabic, the language of the people. In fact, when Muhammad Ali first fell ill Ibrahim did serve as regent. The 1840s were a time when cures were often as bad as ailments, and the viceroy's dysentery was treated with silver nitrate, leaving him incapacitated in 1848. Indeed, Ibrahim would have liked to not only secure the post of viceroy but also change the policy from the eldest male in the family to primogeniture through his line, but he had tuberculosis and lacked a good relationship with Istanbul. Ibrahim predeceased his father; the combination of his disease, champagne, equestrian feats, and a new concubine took their toll on the nearly 60-year-old battle-worn soldier. The next oldest male was Muhammad Ali's grandson, Abbas (r. 1848–1854), son of Tusun, born during his campaign and occupation of the Hejaz.

Abbas was cut from the Ottoman mold. He got rid of foreign advisors and relocated Egyptian ones he did not like. Similar to Ibrahim he wanted to establish primogeniture for his line, and he took the first step by marrying his son Ilhami to Sultan Abdül Mejid's daughter. Not surprisingly, Turkish remained the most significant language of the government. He did improve the transportation and communication networks in Egypt with a new railway line and a new road linking Cairo and Suez. His desire to please the capital naturally made him concerned about productivity and agricultural efficiency. Schools, armies, navies, and industries were all considered a waste of money, except for a small army that he used for personal displays of dominance. Western historians have given Abbas a bleak report card because of the reversal of a number of popular policies. In recent years some historians have called for a review of his tenure, at least from the Egyptian and Ottoman perspectives, to see if this assessment truly holds water (Toledano 1990). What cannot be denied is that he was assassinated by two slaves in his retinue in 1854, which also meant that his dreams of fulfilling primogeniture for his line were never carried to fruition.

Given the pattern of multiple women bearing children over a period of years, it is not surprising that an uncle would succeed his nephew, and this was the case with Muhammad Ali's son Said (r. 1854–1863), succeeding his older nephew Abbas. While Said was more worldly and Francophile than Abbas, he was not particularly enamored of educating the masses. Like Abbas he continued working on Egypt's railway and began work on the telegraph networks. He is most notorious in Egyptian history for negotiating the deal for the Suez Canal.

The Suez Canal placed the viceroy in personal debt, which the state inherited on his death, and tens of thousands of Egyptians perished in the digging of the canal. Another noteworthy cause for Said was his effort to end the slave trade; however, since Egypt lacked effective control over the areas from which they were coming, it did not have a great impact. What did have greater significance was the Ottoman Land Code of 1858 passed during his reign, which allowed both Egyptians and

---

SUEZ CANAL: ALL FOR A PLATE OF PASTA?

Said Pasha was the fourth son of Muhammad Ali, born in 1822 after his father was already in position of power, unlike his older brothers. As a child Said was chubby, aggravating his military-minded father. Muhammad Ali put him on an endless regime of diets, exercises, and military drills including running around the Alexandria palace walls, climbing boat masts in the harbor, and just plain starving the boy. To cope with these difficulties Said had made friends with the folks at the French consulate nearby who occasionally slipped him a plate of pasta. He was especially close to the vice-consul who took him riding and helped him with his French. Years later after he became viceroy, Ferdinand de Lesseps, his old friend from the French consulate and an engineer approached him regarding a project to build a canal connecting the Mediterranean and Red Seas.

SUEZ CANAL: GOOD IDEA OR BAD IDEA FOR EGYPT

While the Suez Canal project itself was a magnificent idea, the terms upon which they were laid were horrific for Egypt. The country would be forced to purchase any unsold shares in the Suez Canal Company (about $40 million in 1860), Egypt would provide the labor, and Egypt would provide the technology. Subscriptions did not sell well, and masses of peasants went to dig the canal—20,000 at a time, mostly by hand. The forced labor conditions, the lack of proper tools, and the unsustainable diets meant that tens of thousands of Egyptians died. Only after international arbitration, which was not particularly arbitrary since it was done by Napoleon III, compelled Egypt to buy dredging equipment to speed up the process of digging. The project, which had begun in 1859, was not completed until 1869, six years after Said's death.

---

foreigners to buy and sell land within the empire. Although Muhammad Ali had distributed land that had been reorganized according to the state's needs, the new land code gave landowners specific rights and allowed foreigners to come to Egypt and invest. Large numbers of foreigners, particularly from southern Europe, arrived in Egypt to take advantage of the new laws.

By mid-century the royal family had become fixtures in public life, and their appearance at school openings, ribbon-cuttings, and groundbreaking events punctuated the life of the country. One such event was the inauguration of a new railway line that spanned the Nile over a swing bridge. A terrible accident took place whereby the heir apparent and a number of other princes perished in the crash, thus always casting gloom on Ismail Pasha (r. 1863–1879), who chose not to attend the festivities that day with Ahmad Rifaat.

Ismail the Magnificent

Ismail was the son of Ibrahim Pasha, and his father insisted that he learn Arabic as part of his extensive curriculum. Ismail also spent time studying in Vienna and Paris where he perfected his French. Registers in the *Période Ismail* archives indicate that he subscribed to 50 European newspapers for the palace. Many historians remember Ismail as a ruler who wanted to turn Egypt into a European nation, and thus it is ironic that he is the one who helped to cement the processes that forged a national identity. To say that Ismail wanted to turn all of Egypt into Europe is a misconception. In reality there are only a few bits and pieces of the country that he wanted to Europeanize; the remainder would stay as it had for centuries—the source of Egypt's surplus.

Ismail began utilizing Arabic as a language for government, and he revitalized the educational system by restoring closed schools and opening new ones, including a primary school for girls (see Chapter 5). He built on Egypt's economic infrastructure by expanding railroad and telegraph lines, as well as by improving ports and roads. The Suez Canal opened during the reign of Ismail. His reforms were aimed at modernizing Cairo and key cities in the delta, as well as linking sites of production and consumption. Thus, the national identity that was emerging among his bureaucrats and in the educational system did not necessarily extend to the entire country.

Another key event occurred during the reign of Ismail: the abolition of the slave trade in 1877. Over the course of the 19th century, sources for male slaves slowly diminished as the Russian empire expanded into those areas that had previously been held by allies who traded in mamluks. Furthermore, with the rise to power of Muhammad Ali and the creation of a national army, the need for mamluks declined. Still prominent in government by mid-century, manumitted mamluks eventually retired, died, or migrated. Their positions in the growing government bureaucracy were gradually filled by graduates from Egypt's modernized schools. European advisors and government bureaucrats, who had visited or studied in Europe, created a curriculum that forged a national identity. The new school system helped bridge the gap between the old Turkish-speaking elite and the newer Arabophone Egyptian elite. With respect to the African slave trade, Ismail had greater success than Said because of the expansion of the Egyptian army and use of that army to move further in the Sudan.

The trade in female slaves continued, however. In fact, Ismail was the beneficiary of that trade. His mother and the mother of the Ottoman Sultan Abdül Aziz were sisters (both concubines), and thus he had a connection to the Ottoman court that no other viceroy had—they were cousins. In 1866, he was able to secure a new title for his post, Khedive (Persian for ruler), and he secured primogeniture for his line, which was no easy feat given the hard feelings from Ahmad Rifaat's branch of the family. Ismail quickly dealt with all of these problems by creating a grand-slam month-long wedding event in 1873 in which he married his heir apparent Tawfiq to Amina, the daughter of Ilhami Pasha and Abdül Mejid, and then three of his other children, each in week-long festivities, some of which were aimed at dealing with the rift with the short-shrifted branch of his own family.

During the reign of Ismail, new cultural institutions formed to create a more unified elite. Ismail sponsored a vibrant press culture that debated changes in Egyptian society. He opened museums, libraries, a national opera house, and a geographic society to promote Egyptian culture in Egypt and in colonized portions of East Africa. Although Ismail's vision of Egyptian culture was extremely West-oriented, ultimately these institutions did promote an Egyptian identity that adopted Western technology but retained core values with respect to religion and morals.

Ismail continued his predecessors' policies of expanding transportation and communication networks, and he purchased the postal service that had been operating as a private concession. Thus, the changes that were taking place in Cairo had the potential of reaching other parts of the country, but Egypt was divided along an axis of regions of consumption and regions of production, the latter of which did not have access to the same education, culture, technology, or commodities.

The reign of Ismail is highly debated among historians. Those who see him as enlightened will enumerate the miles of railroad track and telegraph cable laid, the number of schools opened, the curricular advances made therein, the remaking of Cairo along Parisian lines, and the establishment of great cultural institutions as his legacy. Soldiers, diplomats, and merchants who enjoyed his company rave about his intellect and foresight. His detractors point out that he spent money on an extraordinary scale, and that he was a bit of an eccentric imbecile collecting odd items, for example, toy trains. Finances were good early in his reign due to the high price of cotton owing to shortages worldwide because of the on-going Civil War in the United States. The records of the *Période Ismail* indicate his love of luxury foods, fine clothing, and expensive tobacco. Ismail, his 14 consorts, and their children did everything extravagantly. Thus, when Egypt's finances were in peril in the mid-1870s, drastic measures had to be taken.

Ismail sold Egypt's shares in the Suez Canal Company to the British government, which did not have the money either, without the backing of the famous Rothschild family. Ismail was collecting taxes in advance to pay current debts, and the large foreign community in Egypt was exerting its will in new ways, leading to the creation of a new court system (see Chapter 3). By 1876 Egypt was bankrupt and a Public Debt Administration was created by Egypt's four leading European creditors. Two controllers, one British and one French, would oversee Egypt's finances. By 1879, Egypt's budget was still not balanced, and the Europeans wanted a European-controlled cabinet. In the meantime, budget cuts had a negative impact on army officers, soldiers, and civil servants who demanded to be paid. Ismail dismissed the Dual Control, and consequently, European bondholders requested that the Ottoman Sultan (Abdül Hamid II), no longer a cousin, depose him in favor of his son Tawfiq (r. 1879–1892).

British Occupation: The Veiled Protectorate

Ismail's program of reform, the increasing power of European creditors at the end of his rule, and Tawfiq's European-protected reign brought to the fore a national movement sponsored by a party calling itself the Nationalist Party. This movement combined large landowners who wanted a greater say in government affairs, urban bureaucrats and professionals who wanted government accountability, and Egyptians in the army who wanted parity with the Turkish-speaking officer corps. Only a handful had risen to the officer corps, and many soldiers were being pensioned off due to budgetary cuts before they could rise through the ranks. It was the army issue that created the impetus for the movement, whose rallying cry was "Egypt for the Egyptians!"

There were other reasons that such a slogan had resonance: the large numbers of foreigners in residence since the reign of Said and the lack of judicial protection for Egyptians due to Capitulations and the extraterritorial rights granted to foreigners. The Mixed Courts provided some relief, but not enough. Moneylenders often had steep rates, as high as 20 percent a month. Peasant lands were seized for nonpayment.

Under pressure to do something, Tawfiq appointed Sharif Pasha premier and asked him to start work on a constitution, but then got cold feet and instead deported one of the greatest political advocates, Jamal al-Din al-Afghani, and dismissed Sharif in favor of a more conservative candidate. The army was at the forefront of the opposition, led by one of the few Egyptian officers who had risen to the rank of Colonel, Ahmad Urabi. In January 1881 he delivered a petition to Tawfiq in the name of the people demanding a constitution, an increase in the size of the army, and a change in government. As the epic story goes, Urabi rode to Abdin palace accompanied by 2,500 men while the Khedive was accompanied by the British Controller, and they got into a shouting match during which Tawfiq announced "I am the Khedive of this country and will do as I please," to which Urabi responded, "We are not slaves, and never more shall we be inherited!" Despite his alleged show of power, Tawfiq had to make concessions to the rebels: compromise figure Sharif Pasha returned to government, plans for a constitution put in place, the army increased by recalling pensioned soldiers, and Urabi was appointed minister of war, thus making him responsible for public security.

The Khedive was setting Urabi up for failure by making him responsible for security, particularly as tensions flared. A nationalist press emerged with Abdullah Nadim as its spokesman. He cleverly wrote in a combination of both classic and colloquial Arabic such that his fiery speeches would be understood when read aloud. On the other side, European bondholders still demanded payments, and Egypt was still behind. Tawfiq ignored his government assuming that the Ottomans or the British would intervene, and the large number of foreign frigates off the Alexandrian coast was an indication that this might take place. There were also rumors that he might be overthrown in favor of another son of Muhammad Ali. Thus, a spark between a donkey boy and his drunken European client sent waves of antiforeign violence throughout Alexandria in the summer of 1882. The vacationing Khedive jumped aboard a British frigate, and the British used their guns to "temporarily" restore

---

JAMAL AL-DIN AL-AFGHANI (1838–1897)

Although his nomenclature indicates birth in Afghanistan, most likely Jamal al-Din al-Afghani, born Muhammad ibn Safdar, was actually born in Persia and wanted to mask his Shiite origins. He is probably the most influential pan-Islamic activist of the 19th century, and he was a major force in Egyptian, Ottoman, and Persian politics. Afghani was in Egypt during the reign of Ismail and was expelled for his political views in 1868. He returned to Egypt a few years later where he taught both formally and informally, attracting followers including Muhammad Abdu, Qasim Amin, Yacub Sannu', and Abdullah Nadim. Afghani's disciples ranged from secular nationalists to Islamic reformers. The idea behind the latter was to update Islam in keeping with changes in the modern world. Afghani encouraged his followers to publish and disseminate their ideas. Interestingly enough, prior to his ascension to the throne, even Prince Tawfiq joined a secret society led by al-Afghani, which is perhaps why he would consider him a threat later.

order. The last British troops did not leave Egypt until 1956. The arrival of the British and their extended occupation helped advance the cause of nationalism beyond the upper classes.

Sir Evelyn Baring, better known as Lord Cromer, arrived in Egypt to serve as High Commissioner. He had already done a stint as Controller, so he was quite familiar with Egypt and its finances. His family owned a significant portion of the Egyptian debt, therefore he had a great deal of self interest in bringing Egyptian finances back to solvency (Marsot 1968). Some of the greatest cuts came in education. Cromer believed that Egyptians should pay their own way, at least while the country was in debt. British engineers looked at ways to make the country more productive—by improving irrigation, which would lead to more surplus, more revenue, and less debt. By now the United Kingdom owned Egypt's shares in the Suez Canal, and its geostrategic importance was all-encompassing (see Chapter 1).

Not everything ran smoothly in the occupation. Egypt and the United Kingdom were faced with the complicated matter of the Sudanese Mahdist revolt in 1885, and even the talents of Maj. Gen. Charles "Chinese" Gordan could not handle the situation. His assassination (1885) helped cement British public opinion that the British should remain in Egypt. The British could reach no agreement with the rebels, nor could they subdue them. The situation remained as such until 1898 when the British reconquered the territory and gave it a new status—joint condominium rule with the Egyptians.

As for the Egyptian peasantry, their lot continued to worsen. Although other projects of this nature had existed, for example, under the Fatimids, the first modern Aswan Dam helped to change the nature of land and land tenure in Upper Egypt. The British began construction of the dam in 1889, but it was not completed until 1902 (see Chapter 1). Reclaiming this land was particularly important for the state for diversifying the economy. The lands of the delta were much better suited to growing cotton. and by expanding land under cultivation and making sure that sugar was grown on that land, the Egyptian state would not be so intimately tied to the fluctuations of the cotton market. French capitalists eagerly seized the opportunity to start sugar plantations in the south. The only people not happy about growing sugar in the south were Egyptian peasants, who refused to grow sugar and rebelled against foreign control of their lands (Derr 2009).

The British found an easy and malleable ruler in Tawfiq. However, when he died unexpectedly in 1892, Lord Cromer was shocked to confront his teenage son, Abbas II (r. 1892–1914), whom he found to be "very Egyptian," despite the fact that he had not a drop of Egyptian blood. He was the son of Amina and Tawfiq. Given the marriage within the family, his namesake was both his great grandfather and a great uncle, and he had a bit of Ottoman blood. Cromer found his "Egyptianness" in his attitude, his outlook, his ability to speak Arabic, and his connection to his people. His Egyptianness was perhaps an "otherness" because he was not schooled in the British school system. His training was at the Theresianum in Vienna, and his advisors were mostly Austrians and Germans. In his own memoirs, Abbas II identifies himself as an Egyptian ruler, depicts his reign as a watershed moment in Egyptian nationalism, and prides himself on his Arabic language skills.

During the early years of the occupation, the British heavily censored the once-lively Egyptian press. By 1892 these restrictions had been lifted, and the press re-emerged as an important factor in Egyptian political life. The use of the term political life is deliberate because in the absence of functioning political parties, the various newspapers served as platforms for rulers, factions, and foreign interests in Egypt. The vision presented by the political press was not unified. Many journalists in Egypt were Syrian Christians. They tended to speak in terms of an "Eastern" identity, which united Muslims, Christians, and Jews, as well as relocated Syrians and native Egyptians. These views were even present in advertising, encouraging Egyptians to patronize "Eastern" establishments rather than "foreign-owned" ones. Other secular Egyptians looked back toward Egypt's ancient glory rather than its more recent Islamic past. Still other newspapers were pan-Islamic in orientation, seeking to unite Muslims in Ottoman lands and beyond. By the turn of the century, there were journals for women and children. Even more than the occupation itself, the issue of education and the need for reform were the single most important issues of the day.

As was the case in many parts of the world, law students and lawyers espoused a nationalism rooted in expelling foreign powers, a notion supported by Egyptians of all classes. The most famous of these individuals was Mustafa Kamil, the founder of the (re-created) Nationalist Party. Kamil's death at the age of 33 in 1907 led to the splintering of his party into various nationalist groupings, of which some favored working with the Abbas II, some preferred to maintain ties with the Ottoman state, some favored pan-Islamism, and some even desired working either with the British or with the French. Abbas II and Mustafa Kamil had been allies early in his reign, but grew apart over a highly publicized court battle that was a metaphor for many of the changes taking place in Egyptian society. The elite often moved ahead of Egyptian public opinion.

MARRIAGE OF SHAYKH ALI YUSIF

Born in Upper Egypt, Ali Yusif worked his way up to an education at al-Azhar. In 1889, he began the newspaper *al-Mu'ayyad* with backing from the government. Many newspapers were owned by Syrian Christians, so a newspaper edited by a Muslim Egyptian represented a departure. He had ties to those expressing anti-British views, namely, Mustafa Kamil. When Abbas II came to power in 1892, his paper became the mouthpiece for the palace position, which was in harmony with the Nationalist Party position until Yusif married the daughter of Egypt's highest ranking Muslim dignitary Shaykh Sadat. According to Islamic tradition, marriage is supposed to be between two equals, although if a man had married a [lesser] unequal woman, in all likelihood no one would have batted an eyelash. Yusif's case went before a Sharia court which voided his marriage, but the Khedive backed Yusif in higher courts against the wishes of Kamil and Egyptian public opinion. In 1904, Kamil publicly broke with the palace.

The occupation still represented a huge thorn in Egypt's side, and Egyptians were willing to settle scores in favor of the Ottomans over the British, even at the Egyptian expense, as evidenced in the Taba affair (1906). The Sinai was an important buffer for the all-important artery of the United Kingdom, the Suez Canal, and a dispute over a new Ottoman garrison highlighted these conflicting interests (see Chapter 1). The new fortress was technically west of the official line, and the British sent a naval show of force to threaten the Ottomans. Most Egyptians supported the Ottoman position because (1) it was anti-British; (2) it was pan-Islamic; and (3) at the time Taba had nothing to offer Egypt, unlike it would in the 1980s when the issue would arise again. Only a small faction of extreme territorial nationalists demanded all the land. The Taba incident was followed by another chapter in the annals of the occupation that no Egyptian will ever forget.

A group of Britons had gone pigeon hunting in the Nile delta village of Dinshaway. The peasants found this particularly offensive because they kept the birds and used the droppings for fertilizer. When the Brits returned the following year, in 1906, an altercation ensued, one British officer died, and the Egyptians were blamed. The British set up a special tribunal and charged more than 50 villagers with the death of the British officer. The penalties were particularly harsh, ranging from hangings and floggings to hard labor. Egyptians of all classes were outraged over the severity of the sentences. The ensuing hostility against the British occupation even led to the resignation of Lord Cromer, who had been Egypt's High Commissioner since 1882. The word Dinshaway is a "hot-button" word in Egyptian history, and like the "Alamo" in American history it brings passion, nationalist sentiment, and anger to people who never experienced it.

The Taba affair, the Dinshaway incident, and an economic downturn in 1907 all helped fuel the burgeoning nationalist press as it grew ever more critical of the British occupation. A more coherent vision of nationalism was presented by mainstream newspapers, as well as the women's press, which promoted the nuclear family as the building block of the nation. The abolition of slavery and intermarriage between the old and new elites supported this view of the family. Rather than power emanating from a single (or several) fortress-like home (as it had been in mamluk times), it was diffused among middle- and upper-class Egyptian homes with vested interests in the well-being of the state. Curriculum and textbooks in state-sponsored, missionary, private, and foreign community schools encouraged students to create homes and families that were worthy of self-rule. A major justification of the occupation was the "different" nature of Egypt, and thus nationalists felt they had to prove they were worthy of the task of self-rule (Pollard, Russell).

World War I, the Protectorate, and the 1919 Revolution

The period between 1882 and the outbreak of World War I is referred to as the "veiled protectorate" because the British had no formal control over Egypt. The occupation was meant to be temporary. With the outbreak of World War I and the critical need to maintain strategic positions in the Mediterranean, as well as control of the Suez Canal, the British formally turned Egypt into a protectorate. The British perceived Abbas I to be a lover of all things Austro-Hungarian and German, and they resented his Ottoman blood and his general popularity among the Egyptian populace. Thus, they decided he needed to be overthrown. The fact that he was conveniently vacationing in Turkey when the war broke out made it even easier. They replaced him with an aging son of Ismail, his uncle Husayn Kamil (r. 1914–1917), who at first rejected the offer. The job received a name change—Sultan—making Egypt's ruler on par with the Ottoman Sultan, at least in title. In reality, the British held all the power. Meanwhile, many Egyptians responded enthusiastically to the Ottoman sultan's call for jihad against the British and the French. Furthermore, the war environment meant that Egyptians ran short of staple items that foreigners acquired more easily. The shortages cut across class lines, which again encouraged a nationalism calling for the expulsion of the British.

At the close of the war, a delegation (*wafd*) of Egyptian nationalists went to the residence of the British High Commissioner, Sir Reginald Wingate, to ask permission to attend the Versailles peace conference (January 1919). Saad Zaghlul, leader of the Wafd Party, had been encouraged by Wilson's 14 points. The British rejected Egypt's request, and by March 1919, wide-scale rioting in Egypt occurred among all classes. Elite men and women supporting the Wafd Party wanted their protests to appear civilized, yet at the same time they portrayed themselves as speaking for all classes. Workers, peasants, and other ordinary Egyptians undertook more spontaneous action in the streets and in the countryside. Demonstrations, the arrest and deportation of leaders, and celebrations marking the return of such leaders characterized the period between 1919 and 1922, the 1919 Revolution, after which Egypt gained its partial independence. The British retained control of defense, communications, minority affairs, and the Sudan. In theory, Egypt would be a constitutional monarchy with Fuad (r. 1917–1936), a brother of Husayn Kamil, renamed as king. Egypt would now become a battleground between the British, the monarchy, and political parties.

The Liberal Era

Egypt's king Fuad represented a step back in terms of connection with the people. He was a non-Arabic-speaking autocrat who saw the new era as a return to the old era of Egyptian autonomy without being tied to the Ottomans (see Chapter 3). The era just after independence was one of giddy optimism and patriotism. The flag chosen by nationalists was Nile green with a crescent and three stars, representing each of Egypt's religious communities: Muslims, Christians, and Jews. One of the most significant nationalist accomplishments of the 1920s was the creation of Bank Misr, a financial group to sponsor Egyptian-owned industries, the most important of which was textiles (see Chapter 4). By the 1930s its success was evident in the advertising of various Bank Misr interests in a wide range of publications. Nevertheless, most of Egypt's industries remained foreign-owned, and Egypt's bourgeoisie preferred to invest in land or real estate.

A façade of parliamentary democracy existed; Egypt's political parties represented the interests of a small minority (see Chapter 3). Two percent of Egypt's population

A KING FIT FOR THE TABLOIDS

Fuad was a boy when his father was exiled and he never properly learned Arabic. He returned to Egypt and married his cousin Chivekiar in order to have some measure of financial stability. Prince Fuad enjoyed spending his wife's money gambling and going to various sporting and men's clubs, which Princess Chivekiar's brother, Prince Seif el-Din found to be offensive. He waylaid Fuad at the Muhammad Ali club and shot him several times. Fortunately, for Fuad, a doctor was at the club and was able to remove all but one bullet from his throat; however, it left him with an uncontrollable bark. Obviously, while he was just a prince it was a source of great amusement to bystanders. When he became king no one laughed—royal protocol dictated its official nonexistence. Fuad divorced Chivekiar in 1898.

owned about half of its land. In fact, the richest of the rich (the top half of 1 percent) owned 35 percent of the land, another 5 percent owned 30 percent, and 94 percent of the people owned the remaining 35 percent. Fuad passed away in April 1936, and his only son Faruq (r. 1936–1952) was brought back home from boarding school in the United Kingdom, and the country held great hope for the new king. Fuad had made sure that Faruq did not make the same mistake that he had made. He learned Arabic, and for all his faults, Faruq enjoyed visits and being a "man of the people," making jokes and mixing with the crowds (albeit briefly).His storybook wedding to Safinaz Zulficar, Farida, the first royal wedding in Egypt since pharaonic times, cemented his relationship with the public.

WHATEVER HAPPENED TO THE CRIMINAL PRINCE, HIS ASSETS, AND HIS SISTER

The Khedive Abbas I did not like the idea of a royal doing hard labor. By 1901, Prince Seif el-Din found himself booked on a one-way boat to an asylum in United Kingdom. He had no way of knowing that Abbas would be deposed in 1914 or that his victim's brother and his victim would be the next rulers. His substantial assets were left behind. In 1927 the income alone generated more than 119,000 Egyptian pounds. That year he escaped from United Kingdom to Turkey to attempt to claim his sizeable fortune in Egypt through the Mixed Courts as a Turkish citizen, then through the religious courts, attempting to bribe politicians. King Fuad used the press to his advantage highlighting the dealings of unscrupulous lawyer-politicians. As for Princess Chivekiar (d. 1947), she went on to marry four more times and was known in Cairo as the supreme party giver, in addition to being a great patron of the charitable and feminist organizations.

QUEEN NAZLI, FROM RICHES TO RAGS

Fuad married again in 1919, the beautiful Nazli Sabri, daughter of the Minister of Agriculture and descendent of the legendary French mercenary, Suleiman Pasha. Fuad kept Nazli secluded when women were becoming more active politically. When he died, she blossomed with freedom and even served as regent. She came into her own in middle age with a number of scandalous affairs, including her son's tutor. Some speculate that she may have had an affair with her Coptic secretary Riad Ghali before her daughter Fathia became enamored of him. Faruq did not accept this relationship and the trio, Nazli, Fathia, and Ghali fled to the United States in the late 1940s, where the Queen and the Princess would later convert to Roman Catholicism. The three became downwardly mobile, and Ghali murdered Fathia in 1976. Nazli pawned her royal jewels, did odd jobs, lived in a small apartment in Westwood (Los Angeles), and lived off the charity of the Iranian royal family until her death in 1978.

On January 20, 1938, youthful King Faruq of Egypt and beautiful Safinaz Zulficar were married in a traditional ceremony in the Royal Palace, after which the Queen was renamed "Farida" in accordance with her late father in-law's preference for the letter "F." (AP Photo)

The worldwide depression had not been kind to Egypt, with its overdependence on a single crop. Peasant landlessness was a major problem. The wealthy managed to squeeze small holdings into their own, and the poor were forced to work the land of others. Wages by the 1930s dropped precipitously as prices for basic goods, for example, clothing and food, rose. Egypt was finding it difficult to grow enough food to feed itself. Too much land was dedicated to the growing of cotton. Parliament would not allow peasant labor to organize; in fact, there was little urban labor organization. Many more peasants fled to the cities in search of work. Some were pleasantly surprised to find an organization to help them: the Muslim Brotherhood. Other parties on the extreme left and right formed, but the conditions were not yet ripe for revolution. Indeed, by the time of Faruq's wedding in 1938, there were some signs of improvement. The Capitulations were ended in 1937, and provisions made for the dissolution of the Mixed Courts over a period of 13 years (see Chapter 3).

Faruq garnered public respect by going to Friday prayers at al-Azhar and other major mosques, demonstrating his piety. He even grew a beard, the traditional sign of political maturity in Islam, since his advisors had given him the notion that he might become caliph. The office had been vacant since 1924 when Atatürk abolished the caliphate. He received such widespread coverage that a short piece in *Time* magazine appeared in January 1939 describing the "sporty" young king taking time away from his hectic schedule to "[don] the robes of an imam" to the "thunderous applause of his audience" including army officers and foreign dignitaries. Faruq never achieved this goal. The complexities of World War II and his fading public image rapidly diminished his chances for this opportunity.

In the waning days of Fuad's tenure and in the regency of the queen mother and Faruq's tutor, Wafd politicians negotiated the Anglo-Egyptian Treaty of 1936 with the British, removing the remaining points of control, placing foreign policy, communications, defense, and minority affairs in Egyptian hands; however, the British still allowed themselves leeway, particularly where the canal and war were concerned. What had been meaningless detail then became trouble when war was on the horizon and larger numbers of British troops were arriving and making use of Egypt's resources. A class of war profiteers arose, a network so blatant and extensive that even years after the war ended, the "war profiteer" still appeared as a popular character in cartoons. Egypt became a major center of production and distribution for the war, providing sugar, alcohol, cigarettes, cotton, soap, shoes, glass, cement, and furniture for the British.

Egyptians were not of a unified mind-set on the war. Most did not support the British position wholeheartedly. At the same time, many were suspicious of Italian imperialism that was ever-expanding on Egypt's borders. A few saw Germany as a counterbalance to the British. The British suspected the king of having pro-German leanings, and after Rommel's successes, there could be no room for error; they needed to have a prime minister they could trust. In February 1942, the British sent tanks to surround Abdin palace to force the king to accept their viewpoint, a Wafd candidate. It was a humiliating defeat for Faruq, who never displayed courageous, masculine leadership again. Where charisma and piety marked his early years, the next few years were more likely to find him with his "party" cabinet at a club on the

EGYPT IN WWII

Egypt and Egyptian dissident groups were a source of great interest for Italy's Mussolini, who used his base in Libya to launch incursions into Egypt (September 1940) and make contacts there. Egypt, which had a sizeable Italian community, had already detained the male Italian population and seized their assets, leaving Italian women impoverished. The Italian advance did not go well, and legendary German General Erwin Rommel's Afrika Korps came in early 1941 to reinforce the Italians. The major battle site in Egypt was El-Alamein, less than 75 miles west of Alexandria and only 150 miles northwest of the capital. A German victory in Egypt would compromise Britain's geostrategic possession, the Suez Canal. Fighting continued periodically throughout 1942, and by November the Allies had defeated the Germans in what some military historians believe was one of the two defining victories of the war, the other being Stalingrad.

pyramid strip, making passes at other men's women. While he did not drink anything but orangeade during these escapades, he made a habit of late-night clubbing when the country needed a strong leader. The emasculating scene at the palace seemed to cause him to lose his will to rule effectively, and he shaved the beard.

Faruq began to clamp down on all opposition movements, including the Muslim Brotherhood and the Communist Party, both of which expanded their ranks in the 1940s. Where these groups had been in formative, organizational stages in the 1930s, by the 1940s they were ready to take action. The latter was growing ever more critical of elite politicians and the inequity of the social system in Egypt that led to the hyperdevelopment of some aspects of the economy and complete neglect of others, all at the expense of the peasantry and urban poor. The Muslim Brotherhood, in addition to its concerns about the social ills within Egypt, was concerned about the growing problem in Palestine, which Egypt's politicians had been warned to ignore during treaty negotiations. By the end of the war, internal dissension in Egypt was steadily increasing.

The creation of the United Nations, the promulgation of an Atlantic Charter, and the creation of an Arab League in 1945 set the stage for another situation like the 1919 Revolution. Egyptians felt that the promises that had been made, that there were ideals of freedom and democracy, did not exist in reality, especially with the cloud of the British still looming on the horizon. A series of student and popular demonstrations broke out in 1945–1946. The police opened a draw bridge on rioters at one of these protests, and a number of students were killed.

In 1947, Faruq convened a meeting of Arab heads of state to discuss the UN partition plan for Palestine and agreed to commit Egyptian forces to forestall the implementation of the partition plan and the creation of the Jewish state. When the British mandate ended in May 1948, the first Arab–Israeli war went disastrously for Egyptian forces, particularly since the king's "party" cabinet had arranged for the arms deal. The defective arms, old Belgian World War II surplus, were more dangerous to the

UN PARTITION OF PALESTINE

The UN Special Committee on Palestine (UNSCOP) was the 11th such commission studying "what-to-do-about-Palestine" since the conclusion of World War I, and it decided on partition as a solution. The plan divided the mandate according to where the majority of Arabs and Jews were currently living, and it gave the Jews 5,500 square miles and the Arabs, 4,500; however, much of the extra acreage for the Jews was in the desert. Nevertheless, Jews owned no more than 12 percent of the arable land. Arabs comprised 99 percent of the proposed Arab state, whereas the Jews comprised only 55 percent of the proposed Jewish state. Thus, the Arabs, inside and outside of Palestine, felt that the partition plan was unfair. Israel declared statehood when the British mandate ended on May 15, 1948, and five surrounding Arab states invaded (Egypt, Iraq, Jordan, Lebanon, and Syria). Israel was able to gain significantly from the war, achieving a state comprising about 78 percent of the mandate.

user than the target. The Egyptian army captured portions of Gaza, but they were then besieged at Faluja. During the months spent here, the soldiers used the time talking among themselves about conditions in Egypt, and one officer (Nasser) even occasionally chatted across enemy lines, seeking advice on how to get rid of the British.

The years 1948 and 1949 were particularly bad for Egypt and the monarchy. First, there was the disastrous Arab–Israeli war that ended with Egypt's occupation of the Gaza Strip, but it did not end with any official peace, just a ceasefire. Second, Faruq's marriage to Queen Farida was ending in divorce. He could not tolerate her producing only female heirs, and the infidelities on both sides, particularly his, were enormous. Just 10 years earlier the wedding had been the public relations event of the century. Topping it off, it appeared as though his sister Fawzia's marriage to the Shah of Iran, that he arranged, was also permanently ended. Political violence and assassinations were at a peak. The premier, Nuqrashi Pasha, suppressed the Muslim Brotherhood in December 1948, and a few weeks later he was assassinated. By early 1949, Hasan al-Banna was assassinated, most likely by someone in government.

The Americans urged King Faruq to take drastic action, something on the order of a New Deal or White Revolution, but the king was slow to act. He felt that he had American support because of his staunch anti-Communist stance. To redistribute wealth would be too difficult. While he held a significant portion of royal lands, most were distributed among the rest of his family, and it would not be easy to take those back and give them to the peasantry.

Elections in 1950 brought a new Wafd government back to power, and in 1951 Mustafa al-Nahhas abrogated the 1936 treaty as a means of getting the British out of the canal zone. Young Egypt, the Muslim Brothers, and others began attacking the British in Ismailiyya, while Egyptian workers in British camps went on strike. The police, who were expected to keep order in the area, sympathized with the guerillas and generally did nothing to stop these activities. The British retaliated by taking

MARRIAGE TO NARRIMAN

Narriman Sadek was a 16-year-old teenager engaged to somebody else when the divorced King set eyes on her in 1951. Numerous stories circulate about how she and the king ended up in the same jewelry store for a "chance" meeting. Regardless, he managed to convince her to break her engagement, receive special training in protocol in Europe, go on a diet, and get married all on quite short order. The trousseau for Farida had cost some $30,000, whereas that of Narriman cost $250,000. He still got popular press from the marriage because he was marrying an "Egyptian" girl, a commoner. After their wedding in May of 1951 the two left on a three-month honeymoon cruise, which coincided with Ramadan, but it did not stop the couple from excesses in eating, spending, and gambling. At the end of the trip, the new bride was showing signs of pregnancy.

control of all the major arteries leading to the port cities and the Suez customs house, that is, they were hoping to starve out the enemy. On January 25, 1952, the British attacked the police barracks in Ismailiyya as punishment for the complicity in the events. The Wafdist minister of the interior, Fuad Serageldin, encouraged the police to fight back.

The anger over this event spilled over into Cairo in an event known as Black Saturday. On January 26, 1952, while the clueless King Faruq was celebrating the birth of his heir apparent with 600 officers and assorted members of his family, the city literally burned around him. A great deal is unknown about the causes of the Cairo fire and what specifically was planned for particular demonstrations. The literal spark that started the fire occurred when several groups of demonstrators converged. Students from Fuad I University and al-Azhar, who were joined by some police, continued to move through downtown picking up more people as they went. They had a nasty confrontation with the folks at the outdoor terrace of Badia Masabni's Casino, which ended in thrown furniture, petrol, and flames. The downtown district—the exclusive clubs, cinemas, theatres, tony boutiques, fancy restaurants—became the target for and symbol of social inequity, foreign interests, and the unending occupation. Not only did the demonstrators attack these hallmarks, but also the workers inside them looted the very stores where they made their livelihoods. The army was too slow to respond and did too little once it was called into action.

Revolution

During the first Arab–Israeli war, amidst the siege of Faluja, a group of officers had formed the Free Officers Movement to discuss and develop ideas about Egypt's future. These ideas, up until Black Saturday, were largely theoretical, but the movement's leader Gamal Abd al-Naṣr (Nasser) decided that the moment was propitious to act. He put a popular general, Mohamed Neguib, as a figurehead, and carried out the revolution in July 1952. The Americans were well aware of the revolution and eased the transition by helping King Faruq abdicate safely. The nearly bloodless revolution took place in the summer when most officials, Egyptian or British, were vacationing in Alexandria. Nasser and the Free Officers simply moved into all the important government facilities and proclaimed the revolution. For the first time since pharaonic times, Egypt would again be ruled by an Egyptian—whether this would mean democracy or a return of the pharaoh would be another issue.

The new regime quickly passed populist legislation that would garner support, including land redistribution, educational expansion, abolition of political parties, and suspension of the 1923 constitution. The wealthy landowning class to some degree danced around this restriction by dividing land among all members of the family, male and female, and marrying within the family. Certainly lands were lost, but elites found strategies for maintaining land fortunes. For the Egyptian peasant, these changes created great hope and inspiration.

Nasser wanted to create an alliance with the United States that would provide him with the arms to become a significant regional power. The goals of the revolution were modernization and independence from foreign powers, which American arms would provide him. The Eisenhower administration seemed willing to give Nasser the assistance he needed. Secretary of State Dulles made a trip in the spring of 1953, during which he assured Nasser of the administration's intention to have a more even-handed approach to foreign policy vis-à-vis the Arab states. Both men agreed that getting the British out of the canal zone was the precondition for any further moves, and the Suez Pact was signed in July 1954, providing for the withdrawal of British troops by June 1956.

There was a major point of contention between the perspectives of the two men. Nasser wanted independence, and Dulles saw Egypt as a key player in a regional defense plan that would include the United Kingdom, namely the Baghdad Pact (February 1955). Nasser would never be able to sign a regional defense plan that included the "soon-to-be" former occupying power, and thus Dulles refused to give him arms. Dulles also saw Nasser as the logical regional broker for an Arab–Israeli peace. Attaching strings to regional peace and not putting the Palestinians at the forefront were two major mistakes. Nasser was the man to be negotiating these changes since Gen. Neguib had been pushed aside in October 1954 after an assassination attempt on Nasser (see Chapter 3). While unlikely that Neguib was involved, it was a convenient pretext for moving him out of office.

Since the army was the backbone of Nasser's regime, he needed arms to sustain support, particularly after Israel's raid of the Gaza Strip in February 1955. Nasser continued to plead for U.S. arms, but began to look elsewhere. While attending the Bandung Conference of nonaligned states in the spring of 1955, Zhou En-Lai of China suggested the Soviet Union, and Nasser found his long-awaited arms, more discreetly negotiated through Czechoslovakia. It was worth more than $300 million and would improve Egyptian aircraft strength by 100 percent and tank strength by 50 percent, to be paid on easy terms with Egyptian commodities, cotton and rice. Dulles was furious; his first reaction was to "strangle" Egypt economically, but then he did a 180-degree turn and offered assistance, in conjunction with the World Bank, in building the Aswan High Dam in December 1955.

Relations between Egypt and the United States, as well as Egypt and the conservative Arab states, declined in the winter and spring of 1956. In June, Dulles retracted the U.S. offer to build the Aswan High Dam; thus in a high stakes poker game Nasser nationalized the Suez Canal the following month. This action strained Egyptian relations with the West, and the United States froze Egyptian assets in the United States and ended various aid programs to Egypt including the PL 480 wheat program that provided food assistance. Meanwhile, the Israelis, who viewed this action and the arms deal as intolerable, collaborated with the British and the French to attack Egypt in the fall of 1956. Eisenhower was unaware of the actions of his allies while he was in the midst of his reelection campaign and Secretary of State Dulles was in Walter Reed hospital.

Despite the fact that Egypt was the "loser" in the Suez War, Nasser became immensely popular throughout the entire Arab world, indeed throughout much of the Third World, for standing up to the British and the French. Eisenhower responded quickly to chastise his allies, forcing the British and French out more quickly than the Israelis; however, Egypt was not necessarily his friend. To counter the loss of the old imperial powers in the region, he proclaimed the Eisenhower Doctrine, which would allow the executive branch of government to use economic and military incentives to fight international communism in the region. The doctrine was phrased vaguely enough so that it could meet any number of enemies, communist or otherwise in the region, and its application (or nonapplication) in the two years that followed demonstrated that Nasserism—Arab nationalism as practiced by Nasser (Jordan, 1957)—and protection of U.S. interests in the region (Lebanon, 1958) were more significant factors than communism itself (Syria).

PL 480 WHEAT: FOOD FOR THOUGHT

This American aid program was created after World War II to deal with the grain surpluses produced by American farmers and to keep prices high, while offering humanitarian aid wherever needed. During the Suez Crisis, the United States cut off all aid programs. In the wake of the Iraqi Revolution in 1958, Eisenhower reoriented his Middle East policy and resumed the PL 480 aid. The aid continued to flow under Kennedy; however, relations strained on both sides over foreign policy decisions in the region. Johnson used wheat as a weapon, which Egypt lost in the era building up to the 1967 war. Even in the 1960s Egypt was still a net exporter of food. Wheat started flowing back to Egypt again under Sadat, and by the 1980s, Egypt became a net food importer. Egypt received $2.6 million in PL 480 aid in 1974 and by 1981, $287 million. By the 1990s Egypt received 7 million tons of wheat annually, compared to 2 million tons in the 1960s.

SUEZ CRISIS OR OPERATION KADESH OR TRIPARTITE INVASION (OCTOBER 29 TO NOVEMBER 7, 1956)

Israel never at peace with Egypt after the first Arab–Israeli war, suffering from shipping blockades and enduring raids from the Gaza strip, conspired with Britain and France to attack Egypt before Nasser could absorb the large cache of arms he had just acquired from the Soviet bloc. The plan was for Israel to strike first, Britain and France to call for a cease fire from the combatants, and then when Egypt would not "obey," to strike, allowing the old imperialists to retake the newly nationalized canal. Israel's strike displayed the leadership talents of Moshe Dayan, as well as one rogue paratrooper commander, Ariel Sharon, who defied orders and engaged in what Dayan would later call an "unnecessary" battle at Mitla Pass. The United Nations forced Britain and France out of Egypt by December, but it would take until March 1957 for the withdrawal of Israeli troops. Afterwards the United Nations Emergency Forces (UNEF) served as a peacekeeping force in the Sinai until the 1967 war.

Nasser utilized many of the same strategies as other successful Egyptian rulers; however, he was not necessarily successful in deploying them. After his "victory" at Suez, he created a short-lived federation with Syria as the United Arab Republic (1958–1961). The expansion into Syria was less about seeking markets and more about dealing with the regional balance of power and trying to lessen Soviet influence—

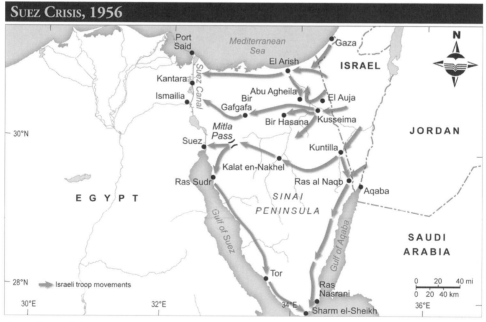

Suez Crisis (ABC-CLIO)

even when the Americans could not. Nevertheless, Nasser's regime ushered in a brutal, authoritarian dictatorship. Arab socialism simply replaced the old bourgeoisie with the state (See Chapter 3). Nasser was never able to dominate the Hejaz, although Yemen did briefly join his union. Ironically, when Yemen became a republic in 1962, Nasser joined the rebels in what would become his own personal Vietnam. As part of the Arab Cold War, he had to support the young cadre of officers and intellectuals against the medieval imamate.

There were even parts of the historic Egyptian empire that Nasser lost. The issue of the Sudan had long been an ambiguous and difficult one involving the United Kingdom as well. Despite Nasser's diplomacy, the Sudanese opted for independence in 1956. The Sudanese felt much the same way about Egypt that Egypt felt about the United Kingdom.

Other successful rulers have demonstrated toleration and discouraged sectarianism in Egypt; Nasser's record is mixed at best. He created some legislation aimed at annihilating difference, for example, getting rid of the Sharia courts and placing them within the civil court system in 1956. The Jews of Egypt survived the first Arab–Israeli War in 1948; however, the Suez Crisis and the nationalizations that followed forcefully demonstrated that Egypt's Jewry would not be part of the national family. There was one notorious case of Egyptian Jews spying for Israel prior to the Suez Pact (Lavon Affair), but Egyptian Jews had shown themselves to be strong nationalists. Like the large landowners, Nasser considered them enemies of the state, and their assets could be seized for the greater good, particularly as Nasser turned inward in the late 1950s and early 1960s and began a strong program of Arab Socialism (see Chapter 3). Other minority groups—many of whom considered themselves Egyptian—suffered as well, for example, Greeks and Italians. Even native Egyptians suffered under Nasser's authoritarian state. His secret police, the *mukhabarat*, were legendary for their ruthless tactics and Nasser for his paranoia. Nasser, like Muhammad Ali, used the state as a tool for structuring and controlling the population (see Chapter 3). He used similar tools to administer the Gaza Strip. Nasser created the Palestine Liberation Organization (PLO) in 1964 as an umbrella organization—a watchdog—for all the Palestinian groups that were under his purview.

By the mid-1960s, the regional conflict had grown quite hot. The disputes over water, which were nearly as vicious as those over land, had resulted in states creating simultaneous water diversion projects along the Jordan River. Among the first acts of Palestinian aggression against Israel were those against these water projects, the guerrillas often coming from Syria. Israel tended to punish Jordan because (1) it was easier and (2) it did not involve a Soviet client, but sent the same message. Antagonisms between Arab rulers were also high. In May 1967 King Hussein taunted Nasser into removing the UNEF troops from the Sinai who had been there as peacekeepers since the Suez War of 1956. Nasser's removal of these troops and his closing of the Straits of Tiran to Israeli shipping, based on faulty Soviet intelligence, led to Israel making its legendary preemptory strike in June 1967 against Egypt, Syria, and Jordan, creating the political geography of the Middle East that still, aside from the return of the Sinai, exists today. The remaining years of Nasser's presidency until his death

EGYPT AND THE JUNE WAR

Many scholars "blame" Nasser for his removal of the UNEF peacekeeping troops from the Sinai in May of 1967 and his subsequent blockade of Israeli shipping in the Straits of Tiran, citing them as being the proximate causes of the preemptory Israeli strike in June 1967. More recent studies shed light on other issues, for example, the regional competition for water resources and their relationship to long-term peace, the rivalry among Arab heads of state, rising Palestinian nationalism, and the growing border struggle between Israel and Soviet-backed Syria. Another factor was the internal power bid by Nasser's chief of staff Amir, who hoped an Egyptian victory might facilitate this effort (see Chapter 3). As a result of this devastating war, Egypt lost about 70 percent of its aircraft, approximately 2,000 men in fighting and 10,000 in retreat; the Suez Canal was littered with sunken ships and closed indefinitely, and the Sinai Peninsula lost temporarily.

in 1970 were marked by his continued struggle with Israel in a War of Attrition and a struggle to maintain power internally (see Chapter 3).

Sadat and Infitah

In Egypt, Anwar Sadat's reputation is not nearly what it is in the West or in Israel. Egyptians remember him for the wealth, the personal aggrandizement of his office, and the lack of a lasting peace with Israel that involved the Palestinians. Sadat's first concern was for Egypt, and Egypt's economy was in ruins. The state socialist programs had overwhelmingly burdened the state without giving much in return. He wanted a reorientation of foreign policy toward the United States, and he needed to get the attention of a Vietnam-mired United States back to the Middle East. In July 1972, he dismissed Soviet military personnel and advisors—many of whom actually flew planes and missions for the Egyptians and numbered as many as 20,000. This grand gesture received no attention. Internally, Sadat was confronted with fighting both Nasserists and Communists (see Chapter 3). Given Sadat's use of Islamists to balance his enemies, it is not surprising that sectarian conflict increased (see Chapter 7).

With respect to foreign policy, Sadat continually promised a war with Israel, one that neither the Israelis nor the Arabs ever thought would come. Thus, when he actually planned an attack with Hafez al-Assad of Syria for October 1973, the Israeli leadership was stunned. Egypt was spending incredible sums on a war machine, the Suez Canal remained closed, and the peace process was stalled; it was a gamble worth taking. The boost to Egyptian morale of crossing the Bar-Lev line, Israeli fortifications on the Eastern side of the Suez Canal, was so great that Egyptians still consider this war a victory, despite the fact that a massive airlift of U.S. aid (approximately 22,000 tons) allowed the Israelis to fight back. The lasting Arab victory came with

OPEC's oil embargo to the United States and the Netherlands, the Western distribution point for oil, which caused the price of oil to quadruple in a matter of days.

Sadat's strategy worked. The Middle East came back to the U.S. radar screen, along with the Egyptian–Israeli portion of the peace process. Secretary of State Kissinger believed the problems of peace to be so intractable that one needed to work around the periphery in order to get the process moving, and in doing so, he established the Sinai I (1974) and Sinai II (1975) disengagements, which allowed Sadat to reopen the canal.

Successful Egyptian leaders have generally tried to stimulate economic growth or create massive public works projects. While Sadat's new policy—infitah policy—stimulated change and generated growth, that growth was felt by only a small segment of the population. The outcome of infitah economics was the rise of a new super wealthy class, or in some cases the reemergence of a super wealthy class, while the poor remained poor and segments of the middle class actually declined.

Sadat's turnaround allowed Egypt to become the second-largest recipient of U.S. aid, after Israel, and by 1977 the United States and other agencies, such as World Bank and IMF, began to pressure the country to end subsidies on basic goods on which its citizens depend, like bread, flour, rice, and cooking oil. The result was bread riots ending in hundreds of deaths. In the future the government would resort to greater subterfuge, for example, smaller loaves of bread rather than dramatic price increases.

More openness also referred to the political climate, a topic that will be treated in depth in Chapter 3. Sadat continued this radical era of change in 1977 with his historic trip to Jerusalem where he addressed the Knesset, the Israeli parliament, declaring that he wanted peace with Israel. This grand gesture started the Egyptian–Israeli peace process that culminated in the Camp David Accords of 1979, which returned the Sinai back to Egypt. Many Egyptians did not agree with this maneuver, and the Arab world was shocked. The Arab League responded by moving its headquarters out of Egypt and temporarily kicking Egypt out. Relations with Israel normalized. While a few small delegations of Egyptian intellectuals went to Israel, much larger groups of Israelis came to Egypt. Embassies opened in both countries.

Despite Sadat's new "open" political system, he continuously undermined its meaning. The Law of Shame, passed in 1980, made it illegal to criticize anything that offends the "dignity of the state." The era of repression culminated in the mass wave of arrests that took place in the summer of 1981 when more than 1,500 people representing beliefs across the political spectrum were incarcerated.

On October 6, 1981, Sadat went to the annual parade in celebration of the War of the Crossing, and a gunman, an Islamist radical, whose brother had been incarcerated over the summer, jumped out of his armored vehicle and sprayed Sadat with bullets. Khalid al-Islambuli reportedly said, "I have killed Pharaoh!," before succumbing to bullet fire himself.

The Mubarak Years

Just as people underestimated Sadat, so too did people underestimate the obscure pilot, who worked his way up to chairmanship of the National Democratic Party (see

Chapter 3). While not judging him by the standards of democracy and human rights, where he most certainly would fall short, Hosni Mubarak displayed a number of characteristics of successful Egyptian rule. With respect to foreign policy, he was able to regain connections to the Arab world after Sadat's break, while still maintaining the peace with Israel. The need for inter-Arab cooperation as a result of the Iran–Iraq war provided the impetus for Egypt to return back to the Arab fold, followed by the first Gulf War in which Egypt participated in the American led coalition. The Arab League returned to Cairo. Egypt's population was literally divided into half over this decision. Participation in the war provided Egypt with material compensation, including cancelation of its military debt to the United States. While relations with Israel have been "normal" and Mubarak was constantly at the forefront of delegations of peace with other neighbors, he did not refrain from pulling his ambassador at moments of crisis, for example, after the Sabra and Shatila massacres of 1982 or the Hebron massacre of 1994. Mubarak's peace with Israel allowed him to escape criticism for security issues for which he was responsible. The 2009 Israeli invasion of Gaza was based on the pretext that Gaza missiles were being used against Israel. Iran received the brunt of the blame for sending the missiles, while the porous Gaza border seemed to get little attention.

Since the beginning of the U.S. war on terror in the post-9/11 era, the unflinching policy of U.S. support has been more difficult to justify to his populace. Where there were many Egyptians who condemned Saddam Hussein in 1991, a decade later most Egyptians viewed him as a victim of U.S. imperialism. The invasion of Iraq brought massive demonstrations to the streets of Cairo. The level of anti-Americanism has grown in recent years.

After the first Gulf War, Islamists saw the devastation that the drop in tourism caused the economy, and they saw a means to lash out at the state. From 1992 to 1997 strikes against foreigners in Egypt coincided with sectarian violence in Egypt generally. The climax of the violence came with the attack in Luxor in 1997, after which the government and the Islamists reached a modus vivendi; however, the second Gulf War intensified the situation until the period of the 2011 Revolution.

Internally, Mubarak's strategy was to use external targets—Israel, the gay community, or other perceived "deviants"—allowing Egyptians to vent their frustrations while the real problems festered: social inequality, lack of housing, poor economy, need for food imports, and so on.

Like other successful rulers, Mubarak directed his administration to carry out a major irrigation project, but this one was on a scale like no other. The Toshka project would literally create a New Nile Valley emanating from Lake Nasser from a pumping station at Toshka Bay where it would move through a series of canals to the Western desert, bringing nearly 600,000 acres into cultivation. This project was estimated to increase Egypt's arable land by 10 percent and provide land for potentially 3 million citizens. The food produced by the new land would reduce Egypt's dependency on imports and create surplus. The project, started in 2005, was originally slated for completion in 2020. The workers of the South Valley Agricultural Development Company and the Ramses Agricultural Services Company in Toshka were among the many workers who rose in protest during the 2011 Egyptian Revolution, and in particular called into question graft by the company's president Seoudi Eleiwa. Since that time some evidence has come to light that a member of the Saudi royal family has heavily invested in this project, calling into question its nationalist credentials. Furthermore, Toshka has met only 10 percent of its goals, with none of the new cities, factories, schools, or hospitals built. Even produce from the project has been exported to companies that have invested. Egyptians remain divided over the notion of mega-projects that appear to be quick-fixes, like Toshka and the Aswan High Dam, or more rudimentary solutions will solve Egypt's woes. It remains to be seen how the newly elected Egyptian government will handle the project (Hope 2012).

REFERENCES

Bell, H. Idris. *Egypt from Alexander the Great to the Arab Conquest: A Study in the Diffusion and Decay of Hellenism.* Westport, CT: Greenwood Press, 1977 (1946).

Brewer, Douglas, and Emily Teeter. *Egypt & the Egyptians.* Cambridge: Cambridge University Press, 2007 (second edition).

Butler, Alfred. *The Arab Conquest of Egypt.* London: Darf Publishers, 1988.

Derr, Jennifer. "The Development of the Egyptian Sugar Industry: Geography, Authority, and Community in Southern Egypt." Ph.D. Dissertation, Stanford University, 2009.

Fahmy, Khalid. *All the Pasha's Men: Mehmed Ali, His Army, and the Making of Modern Egypt.* Cambridge: Cambridge University Press, 1997.

Fassone, Alessia, and Enrico Ferraris. *Egypt: Pharaonic Period.* Translated by Jay Hyams. Dictionaries of Civilization Series. Berkeley, CA: University of California Press, 2007.

Hanna, Nelly. "Egypt in the Fatimid, Ayyubid, and Mamluk Eras." Proceedings of the First, Second, and Third International Colloquium [*sic*] Organized at the Katholieke Universiteit Leuven in May 1992, 1993 and 1994. Published in *Journal of the American Oriental Society* 118 (4) (1998).

Hanna, Nelly, and Raouf Abbas, eds. *Society and Economy in Egypt and the Eastern Mediterranean, 1600–1900: Essays in Honor of André Raymond.* Cairo: AUC Press, 2005.

Hope, Bradley. "Egypt's New Nile Valley: Grand Plan Gone Bad." *The National*, April 22, 2012.

Hunter, F. Robert. *Egypt under the Khedives, 1805–1879: From Household Government to Modern Bureaucracy.* Pittsburgh, PA: University of Pittsburgh, 1984.

al-Jabarti, 'Abd al-Rahman. *Chronicle of the French Occupation: Napoleon in Egypt.* Translated by Shmuel Moreh. Princeton, NJ: Markus Wiener, 1993.

Leakey, Richard. "On the Origins and Future of Humanity." Voyages of Discovery Lecture Series, ECU, October 10, 2008.

Marsot, Afaf Lutfi al-Sayyid. *Egypt and Cromer: A Study in Anglo-Egyptian Relations.* London: Murray, 1968.

Marsot, Afaf Lutfi al-Sayyid. *Egypt's Liberal Experiment, 1922–1936.* Berkeley, CA: University of California Press, 1978.

Marsot, Afaf Lutfi al-Sayyid. *Egypt in the Reign of Muhammad Ali.* Cambridge: Cambridge University Press, 1984.

Mikhail, Alan. "The Nature of Ottoman Egypt: Irrigation, Environment, and Bureaucracy, in the Long Eighteenth Century." Ph.D. Dissertation. University of California, Berkeley, 2008.

Pollard, Lisa. *Nurturing the Nation: The Family Politics of Modernizing, Colonizing, and Liberating Egypt, 1805–1923.* Berkeley, CA: University of California Press, 2005.

Sabra, Adam Abdelhamid. *Poverty and Charity in Medieval Islam: Mamluk Egypt, 1250–1517.* Cambridge: Cambridge University Press, 2001.

Toledano, Ehud. *State and Society in Mid-Nineteenth Century Egypt.* Cambridge: Cambridge University Press, 1990.

Government and Politics

We had a real constitution, real political parties, and a king that cared about us.

—Retired officer, born three years before
the Egyptian revolution.

They hate him like they hate a disease.

—Random Egyptian queried at JFK airport by an
eager tourist wondering how Egyptians
really feel about Mubarak.

INDEPENDENCE AND EGYPT'S
LIBERAL ERA: 1922–1952

Nostalgia

In the past 15 or 20 years, the era between Egyptian independence and Egypt's revolution, dubbed as the "liberal era," has received a great deal of attention both by the popular media as well as by historians, journalists, and writers leading to a major reassessment of the period in the hearts and minds of Egyptians. While some have romanticized the age by giving it this positive-sounding name, the monarchy generally has received low marks during these decades. Recently, new books about Fuad, Faruq, Nazli, and members of the inner circle of the palace have been written in Arabic as well as in English and French shedding new light on the period. The

TABLE 3.1

	Former Government at a Glance	Transitional Power Structure after 2011
Type	Republic	Republic
Legislature	Bicameral, consisting of a largely consultative upper house with 264 seats, of which one-third are appointed by the president and two-third are elected (*majlis al-shura*), whose members serve staggered six-year terms and the People's Assembly (*majlis al-sha'b*), which traditionally had consisted of 454 seats of which the president appoints 10 seats and the remainder are elected for five-year terms. 50% of seats restricted for workers and peasants. In 2009 the number of seats increased to 518, with 64 seats reserved for women	Still bicameral. *Majlis al-Shura* increase by 6 seats, 2 appointed 4 elected. People's Assembly seats reduced from recently increased 518 to 508 (498 elected and 10 appointed). The process is different with one-third of candidates for PA chosen by majority ballot and two-third by party list. Restrictions on seats for workers and farmers remain; however new legislation holding women's seats removed.
Constitution	September 11, 1971, amended May 22, 1980, May 25, 2005, and March 26, 2007	Articles 76, 77, 88, 93, 139. 148, 179, and 189 amended in March 2011, mainly dealing with elections, the presidency, and executive power.
Head of State	(Mohamed) Hosni Mubarak from October 14, 1981 to February 11, 2011. Prior to 2005 election was by referendum, and since then constitution was amended for multicandidate elections by popular vote. Six-year term with no term limits.	*De facto* head of state until elections in 2012 is Field Marshal Mohamed Hussein Tantawi, head of SCAF.
Head of Government	Prime Minister Ahmed Mohamed Nazif from July 9, 2004 to January 29, 2011	Essam Sharaf takes post in March 2011 and steps down in December after clashes with SCAF over executive authority, replaced by Kamal Ganzouri.
Cabinet	Appointed by President	Until elections presidential elections, run by SCAF
Suffrage	Universal and (allegedly) compulsory from age 18.	Voters now use national ID cards instead of voting cards making enfranchisement easier. High election commission in charge of polling instead of Ministry of Interior.
Judiciary	Independent, based upon an amalgam of Islamic and Western law codes; highest court is Supreme Constitutional Court	Still independent.

Data from CIA *The World Factbook,* al-Jazeera, and Jadaliyya.

late Prince Hassan Hassan published his own family album, which although not a political tract, gives a human and multidimensional face to the royal family. Where once it was unthinkable to speak or even think of Faruq as "a nice guy," the 2007 Ramadan miniseries on the life of *al-Malik Faruq* (*King Faruq*) in 30 segments created a true pro-monarchy frenzy in which those who never lived through this period of history are now eager to defend its king. They feel the royal family, in general, and Faruq, in particular, have been maliciously maligned by the Free Officers who profited from the revolution. Indeed, segments of the Egyptian population now feel that Faruq's philandering, the faulty arms deal, and other negative aspects of Faruq's reign were all created by his detractors to ease the way for the revolution, and they hearken back romantically to a period that never existed. Long before the miniseries, a phony (Ahmad) Fuad II roamed the streets of Cairo quite literally receiving the royal treatment because he looked exactly like the former king (Faruq)—which was precisely the giveaway to his farce—Ahmad Fuad does not resemble his father.

Why do Egyptians feel this way? In the midst of severe economic crises, lack of democracy, and the fundamental need for more basic civil and human rights, people nostalgically look back to the period before the revolution. For those individuals whose lifetimes actually span the 20th century, they remember a time with less pollution, less crowding, and better schools. They remember the notion of a functioning political system where governments changed and opposition parties existed. Before the fall of Mubarak, after the 1952 revolution, although elections occurred regularly,

Muhammad Neguib (second from right), Gamal Abdel Nasser (third from right), and Anwar Sadat (fourth from left) with other Free Officers in 1952. The Free Officers carried out the 1952 Revolution. (AFP/Getty Images)

the head of state changed only with the death of the previous head of state. As Mubarak aged and his health declined, his son Gamal was being groomed for the presidency (see Chapter 7); Egyptians greeted the liberal era with great nostalgia. Although parties were initially outlawed after the 1952 revolution, the former regime exerted extreme force over its opposition imprisoning those who spoke out not only against the government, but simply for democracy. While there is optimism that the 2011 revolution will bring change, it has not occurred yet.

The Liberal Experiment and Triangular Politics

As discussed in Chapter 2, Egypt received its independence in 1922, but the British retained four points of control. Egypt's nationalists, the large landowners who had opposed the British occupation, were now Egypt's politicians. Nevertheless, these were mostly men who benefited tangibly from an economic relationship with their former occupiers, who still remained in the Suez Canal zone. In 1923 these men created Egypt's first constitution, influenced as well by the autocratic King Fuad and the British. The compromise document was an amalgam of the Belgian and Prussian constitutions. King Fuad was fond of the aspects of the Prussian constitution that gave the monarch a great deal of authority including the right to call and dismiss parliament, the right to choose the prime minister, and the right to appoint two-fifths of the senators. The parliament would have a bicameral legislature in which the remainder of the representatives would be elected. Parliament would be able to bring down the cabinet with a vote of no confidence; however, in practice, this never happened due to the previously mentioned authority of the monarch. The reality of power was a triangle in which the British sat at the top arbitrating battles between the king and the political parties, the latter of which represented the interests of Egypt's large landowners. The vast majority of Egypt's population did not have a say in politics. Women could not vote, elections were frequently rigged, and peasants were often compelled (materially or physically) to vote for the candidate of their landlord.

The most powerful political party of the liberal era was the Wafd party, the party of Saad Zaghlul. This party emerged from the group of individuals who had wanted to attend the Versailles Peace conference after World War I, only to be rebuked by the British High Commissioner in Egypt. According to Afaf Marsot, any legitimate election could easily be won by the Wafd because they were the only party that had large-scale popular backing. Zaghlul's ability to speak in the idiom of the people and his peasant (albeit rich) roots enabled him to connect with the majority of Egypt's citizens. Zaghlul passed away in 1927, leaving the party in the hands of Mustafa al-Nahhas. Although al-Nahhas had accompanied Zaghlul in exile, the latter cast a long shadow that would be difficult to fill. Nevertheless, the Wafd remained popular. It should be emphasized, however, that despite its ability to connect with the masses the Wafd was still a party of large, landowning men. After Zaghlul's death, some of his followers broke with the Wafd and formed the Saadist party, feeling that the Wafdists were not upholding his principles.

Most of the parties of the liberal period did not vary that much in tone or tenor, but rather they clustered around the charismatic person(s) who led the party. The liberal constitutionalists centered around Adli Yakan and Abd al-Khalaq Tharwat, both of whom had been one-time supporters of the Wafd; but broke with Zaghlul and took a softer line with both the British and the monarchy. This party was the largest party after the Wafd. Another monarchist (at least with respect to Fuad), Ismail Sidqi (d. 1950), a lawyer and a politician, founded the (mis)named People's Party. His support for the monarchy waned as he became highly critical of Faruq's behavior, which lost Sidqi a state-sponsored funeral. King Fuad even set up his own Union Party to battle the politicians, utilizing religious students and his control over appointments to al-Azhar to maneuver this party against his opponents. It allowed the monarchy to have an authentic flavor with the masses in the face of the secular politicians. Remnants of the old Nationalist Party still existed (see Chapter 2), which represented a distinct voice of anti-British fervor that the other groups lacked. The other parties had sound reason for maintaining a dialogue with the British, namely the removal of the four points of control, accomplished by the Wafd in the Anglo-Egyptian Treaty of 1936 (see Chapter 2). King Fuad had been an instigator of the treaty; however, he died before its signing in December.

During the 1930s and 1940s party politics moved into a more radical phase. By the terms of the Anglo-Egyptian Treaty, Egypt was now in charge of its own foreign policy, and with the death of Fuad the country had a handsome, young king who could actually speak the language of the people. Nevertheless, the 1930s was a time of global depression, extremist politics, and economic despair in Egypt. In this climate, new parties and organizations formed; these groupings were not necessarily allowed access to participate in the political process, but some had widespread popular support. The Muslim Brotherhood, founded by an Egyptian school teacher in 1928, attracted many followers in the 1930s and 1940s. Hasan al-Banna started the organization in Ismailia, one of the Suez Canal zone cities, where tensions between Egyptians and the British ran high. Within four years, the headquarters moved to Cairo, where al-Banna founded charitable organizations, workshops, and a newspaper all of which furthered his message of Islamic purification and the creation of an Islamic state in Egypt. Additionally, he was a proponent of the Arab cause in Palestine, long before the politicians and many of the mainstream papers began covering the issue. It should be noted that nearly all radical Muslim organizations today can trace their lineage to either the Egyptian Muslim Brotherhood or the Pakistani Islamic Bloc.

Another party formed in the wake of 1930s despair was Young Egypt founded by Ahmad Husayn in 1933. He modeled the group along the lines of parties in Italy and Germany with slogans meant to unify Muslim and Copt alike: "God, Fatherland, the King" and "Egypt above all." The party's doctrine decried foreign influence and rallied around a militant brand of Egyptian nationalism. Its fascistic bands of young men with Green Shirts were copied by other parties, notably the Blue Shirts of the Wafd. Violent tactics characterized its early years including an assassination attempt on Wafdist prime minister al-Nahhas in 1937. After World War II and fascism's political demise, it played on local capital by adopting Islamic Socialist principles as well as a new name (the Islamic Socialist party). By 1951 it had elected a member to parliament. Although never a particularly powerful player, this party at times enjoyed the support of the monarchy; however, just as often, it was a critic. In addition, the party served as a vocal opponent of the Muslim Brotherhood. In the prerevolutionary era it was perhaps most (in)famous for instigating some of the demonstrations on Black Saturday (see Chapter 2) leading to the burning of Cairo on January 26, 1952.

The Communist Party in Egypt, like Young Egypt, found backing during a time of economic and political crisis. Although first formed in 1923, the Communist Party did not garner much support until the 1940s when students at the Lycée Français du Caire and university students began to join the movement in large numbers. Ironically, some of the wealthiest members of society belonged to the Communist Party, and minority groups, such as Jews and foreigners formed a disproportionate number of its members. Women were actively involved, which led its opponents to circulate wild rumors about sexual opportunism among its members. The Communist Party was active in uniting students and workers in demonstrations against the continued British presence in Egypt, and it was a frequent target of Faruq's secret police.

The trends towards extremism in politics in the interwar period mirrored social trends. Just as bands of young men were joining fascistic or religious parties, they were also organizing neighborhood gangs. Bodybuilding, boxing, and wrestling all became popular sports, and impromptu as well as formal gyms became sites for the organization of *futuwwat* for neighborhood "protection" (Jacob 2005). *Futuwwat*, roughly translated as groups organizing around the concept of youthful masculinity, had existed in the medieval period. Historically, they were involved in heroic fights against crusaders and various types of popular protests as well as less-appreciated urban "protection" that one associates with gangsters.

In the liberal era, parties (or individual politicians) could recruit among new-fangled *futuwwat* who could canvass neighborhoods for strong-arm political support and carry out various dirty-work tasks against political enemies, including (attempted) assassination. On the one hand, the state did not have the power to control the illegal activities of such groups (extraction of protection money, prostitution, drug trafficking), and on the other, some groups representing the "state" used these

---

(AHMAD) NABIL AL-HILALI: SON OF A PASHA WITH A PASSION

Nabil al-Hilali (1928–2006) was born to a life of privilege as a son of a titled (Pasha) lawyer-politician (Ahmad) Neguib al-Hilali. Like his father he became a lawyer, but rather than joining the prestigious firm associated with the family name he and a colleague opened their own law office, which would eventually become famous for defending political prisoners of all varieties in Egypt. Hilali was an ardent Communist who practiced what he preached. He gave the land he inherited to the tenants who were farming it and virtually ignored other lucrative parts of his inheritance. He met the love of his life Fatma Zaki (d. 2004) during their student days of activism in the Communist movement. Both he and Zaki were imprisoned multiple times. He once remarked, "I have been imprisoned under the monarchy, under Nasser, and under Sadat." With his wry smile, he indicated that there was still time left for Mubarak to change his mind given his workload and activism. (to author and then fiancé (now husband), 1991)

FATMA ZAKI: LEADER AND CONTENDER

In eulogizing his beloved wife Fatma Zaki (1921–2004), Nabil al-Hilali, said "If you were fighting for Communism, thinking about Communism, and living Communism, then you were the happiest person in the twentieth century" (Hilali 2004). Born to an upper-middle-class family, one of eight children that survived to adulthood, Fatma learned from an early age that life was not necessarily fair. She worked hard to succeed in school, enrolling in the Faculty of Science at Fuad I University (Cairo University) at a time when few women pursued higher education, let alone science. She was also an athlete, instrumental in creating the National Women's Basketball team. During her university days she helped form a Committee of Workers and Students seeking social reform, and it was at this time that she met her husband. She spent her life teaching, both professionally through her chosen vocation (until she was banned) and informally through her passion for true Communism and democracy, which continued right up until the end of her life.

---

groups to further their political objectives. The nature of triangular politics meant that each of the players needed a special force: the British had their armed forces, the king his money and his secret police, and the politicians had their own money with which they could deploy *futuwwat* or more conventional forces, for example, the police. The losers were the Egyptian people who still lived under occupation in a system that looked like a parliamentary democracy but did not necessarily function like one.

HOLLOW SUBSTITUTES FOR DEMOCRACY, 1952–1976

The Revolution

The Free Officers who carried out the Egyptian Revolution on July 23, 1952 claimed that Egyptian political life was completely flawed, and the only way to correct the problem was to purge the political parties of the most corrupt elements. Meanwhile, in an extremely popular move, on July 26, 1952, they sent King Faruq to Italy on the *Mahrussa*, the royal yacht that had also sent his grandfather Ismail into exile. The politicians, unscathed by the warnings, made claims based on the 1923 constitution, while the Muslim Brotherhood demanded the recreation of the state along Islamic lines. Nasser weakened his potential opposition in a number of ways. Materially, he confiscated the land base that supported the monarchy, and he limited land ownership to 200 *feddans* (a *feddan* is slightly more than 1 acre). Furthermore, he abolished the practice of family endowments (*waqfs*), which were a means of skirting inheritance and tax laws. These measures were detrimental financially to the large landowning class of political opponents. While the land redistribution took many years and its success was debatable, the move was immediately popular politically.

For a short time Egypt remained a constitutional monarchy with the infant Ahmad Fuad II as the monarch and the new regime promising to hold elections once the political cleansings had taken place. Instead, the Free Officers banned all political parties, suspended the 1923 constitution, and ended the monarchy in June 1953. The Islamic Socialist Party (Young Egypt) initially supported the revolution as did the Muslim Brotherhood; however, the Revolutionary Command Council (RCC) controlled by Nasser could not tolerate competing centers of power. The Communist Party and other keen political observers, for example, Doria Shafik watched along the sidelines with a more critical eye. The assassination attempt on Nasser in October 1954 was an opportunity for Nasser to lash out against the Muslim Brotherhood and to step out from behind Muhammad Neguib, the figurehead leader of the revolution. In essence he would be creating a presidential republic in which the legislative function would be dominated by the executive branch and shared with a weak legislative branch.

The Liberation Rally, National Union, and Arab Socialist Union

In the absence of real political parties, new structures or entities had to be created to fill the vacuum. Nasser's first two attempts at containing the socio-political passions of his citizenry through mass structures were also aimed at his desire to control labor unions and syndicates. In other words, Nasser was attempting mass mobilization of society and containing all possible sources of discontent. Nevertheless, since eventually everyone was (or at least could be) a member of these groups, there was no benefit associated with joining or supporting either one. The first organization, the Liberation Rally (LR), lasted from 1953 to 1958. Nasser's ability to get segments

---

DORIA SHAFIK ON THE REVOLUTION (AUGUST 1952 IN *DAUGHTER OF THE NILE*)

Before today people have not witnessed such complete support for a movement as the people of Egypt. . . . they support the blessed renaissance, undertaken by the intrepid Egyptian army and its leader rescuer of the constitution and defender of sacred individual rights . . . [this] earnest renaissance purged and reformed (society), removing causes of corruption and uprooting them . . . all of which advanced the blessed renaissance in its decreed path, increasing the happiness of the people. . . .They are delighted in the complete renaissance which reflects the people, their rights, and their authority. . .

The Egyptian woman. . . announces her readiness and her suitability to take her proper place in the nation's lines behind the army to bring forth the nation's glory, its freedom, and the happiness of its citizens, men and women together.

God bless the rebirth of a new Egypt and protect the guardianship of the constitution and the rights of the people so that they will be uplifted [and] brought closer to success.

ASSASSINATION ATTEMPT ON NASSER: THE IMPLICATIONS

On October 26, 1954, while giving a speech in Alexandria, Nasser was shot eight times at close range by Mahmoud Abd al-Latif of the Muslim Brotherhood. Amazingly enough, none of the shots hit Nasser, and more amazing, Nasser continued apace in his speech, incorporating the event: "Let them kill Nasser! What is Nasser but one among many? Even if I die, all of you are Gamal Abd al-Nasser." Afterwards, even more fortuitously, Nasser was able to do two things. First, he was able to brutally repress the Muslim Brotherhood, which was a potential threat to his power. Secondly, he moved against Gen. Neguib the figurehead leader, who stood behind elements of the Revolution that supported the notion of pluralism. With the Muslim Brotherhood and Neguib pushed aside, he could easily maneuver politically, leading to conspiracy theories that Nasser himself was behind the assassination attempt. Such theorists support the notion with both the outcome and the slow response to the shooting by Nasser's bodyguards.

Doria Shafik, fourth from left, Egypt's suffragette leader, is shown with other women taking part in a hunger strike in demand for the inclusion of women in Egypt's forthcoming constituent assembly, March 13, 1954. (AP Photo)

of the labor movement in the LR, for example, the Cairo Transport Workers, was critical in his bid to bring down Neguib. While the LR in and of itself was not that significant, the fact that Nasser succeeded in his power bid, brought forth a new constitution in 1956, dissolved the RCC, and reached new heights of international popularity during the Suez Crisis, were significant.

Gamal Abdel Nasser (1918–1970) was the force behind the Egyptian Revolution of 1952. He took power from figure-head president Neguib in 1954 and remained active in regional politics until his death in 1970. (AP Photo)

The 1956 constitution provided for the eventual dissolution of the LR to be replaced by a new organ, the National Union (NU) (1958–1961), in which all adult Egyptians would be members. The slogan for the LR had been "Unity, Liberty, and Work" that made the transition for the NU easy when the union with Syria took place. The Syrian Ba'th party slogan was "Unity, Freedom, and Socialism." The NU reflected the new posture in its slogan which also demonstrated its desire to control: "Socialism, Cooperativism, Democracy." The new UAR would have a 600-member parliament, 400 from Egypt and 200 from Syria (Waterbury 1983). It was only in July 1957 that the first parliament (People's Assembly) since the revolution had been convened based on the 1956 constitution. While "socialism" may have been part of the platform, Nasser brutally cracked down on Socialists and Communists in Egypt and Syria in an infamous New Year's Day round up in 1959.

After Syria withdrew from the UAR in 1961, Nasser feared negative consequences and he created yet another mobilizing institution and reorganization of society, the Arab Socialist Union (ASU). He planned to retool society along his own Arab socialist lines, while the "real" leftists were still perishing in his prisons and labor camps. The ASU would bear some similarities with its predecessors, in that all adults could be members. Following along the lines of Communist or other radical parties, there would be different levels of membership, and furthermore, one had to apply to be a member. Membership in other professional unions or syndicates, and therefore leadership positions therein (e.g., teacher's union), might also be contingent on membership in the ASU. Peasants and the urban poor did not need to become card-carrying ASU members, but urban professionals who wanted to advance in their careers did.

A series of laws, nationalizations, and sequestrations of property aimed at enabling the principles of the ASU, which included such lofty goals as the elimination of class differences and mobilization against the enemies of the revolution, occurred between 1960 and 1962, culminating in a new National Charter. André Aciman's *Out of Egypt* and Samia Serageldin's *Cairo House* (see Chapter 6) vividly depict this era for the Jewish community and the Egyptian elite, respectively. Land ownership was now limited to 100 *feddans*. While the "enemies of the people" had their properties taken, peasants and workers were assured of 50 percent of all elected seats at any position—industry, government (all levels), unions, or cooperatives (Waterbury 1983). Issues of definition always plagued this law as did the notion of which seats were supposed to be elected.

During their incarceration, Egypt's leftists welcomed the idea of Arab socialism; however, they combed through the charter and debated its meaning. Nikita Khrushchev's 1964 visit to commemorate the completion of the first stage of the Aswan High Dam compelled Nasser to release Egypt's Communists. Nasser felt that perhaps the ideological bent and frustrations of his former enemies could be put to better use in the ASU. Between 1965 and Egypt's defeat in the June War of 1967, Nasser allowed the ASU greater leeway for truly restructuring society along socialist lines; however, he and his left-leaning cronies sometimes found it difficult to contain the socialist beast, imprisoning a number of leftists in October 1966 and expelling some Marxists from organizations that had previously been given prestige, for example, the Institute of Socialist Studies and the Socialist Youth Organization.

The Muslim Brotherhood also had a reprieve in 1964 and its members were released from prison. Nevertheless, after less than a year, the organization's ideologue Sayyid Qutb was imprisoned along with a number of other brothers. Qutb was highly critical of the regime and its secular Arab Socialist philosophy, which he believed was in the midst of a new age of ignorance, similar to the one that had prevailed before the rise of Islam. The regime held a spectacular trial after which the defendants were found guilty of treason and hanged. There was some evidence that the group was in conspiracy with Saudi Arabia's King Feisal to bring down the government. The two states were at war supporting opposing sides in Yemen.

The Harsh Reality of Nasserist Authoritarianism and the June War

Even during Nasser's short-lived experiment with greater participation in social restructuring, Egypt was a police state in which the president was elected by referendum, there were no political parties, and parliament exercised little authority. The instruments of Nasser's police state could be tools for abuse wielded by the managerial class of technocrats against the old elites. By 1959 all newspapers came under the purview of government and the turn-of-the-20th-century haven for Middle Eastern journalists became a hollow shell of its former self. After the creation of the ASU all journalists had to be members. Nasser depended on the army, his police force (especially the secret police), and the ASU to maintain order, all of which functioned effectively in the 1950s and early 1960s. Nevertheless, Egypt's defeat in the June War of 1967 presented a huge challenge, effectively diminishing the status of the army

---

SAYYID QUTB

Sayyid Qutb (1906–1966) has probably had more influence on modern radical Islamic thought than any other 20th-century writer. Like Hasan al-Banna, the founder of the Muslim Brotherhood, Qutb's background was as an educator. Born in a small village outside of Assiut (upper Egypt), he moved to Cairo to pursue his education. His early career entailed working for the Ministry of Education, which eventually sent him to the United States, first to Colorado and then to Stanford, to study educational administration. Qutb endured severe racism, due to his coloring, and he was disgusted by what he considered to be an acute lack of morals in the United States. He returned to Egypt, and joined the Muslim Brotherhood where he became its chief writer. His most famous work is *Milestones,* and his most infamous posthumous followers are Ayman al-Zawahiri and Osama bin Laden. They became acquainted with him through Muhammad Qutb, a professor of Islamic studies, and editor of his late brother's work.

---

and calling into question the unwavering support of the ASU and large segments of the population.

Nasser first tried unsuccessfully to resign, which would have relieved himself of numerous problems. The people of Egypt would not allow it—demonstrating in the streets—not so much as a show of popular support, but as a sign that he got them into this mess and would now have to get them out of it. The armed forces would have to bear the burden for this disgrace, and the weight fell on the shoulders of Abdul Hakim Amir head of the armed forces. Amir and a number of other high military and intelligence officials who had stepped down in the wake of the debacle on June 10, 1967, had begun speaking in terms of a platform involving democratization, civil rights, free press, overhauling the ASU, creating a multiparty system, and reorienting foreign policy, all perhaps in a bid to save their careers. Unfortunately, Amir died in what the regime referred to as a suicide on September 15, 1967 while he was in detention. With respect to Amir's platform, even those close to Nasser, for example, *al-Ahram's* Muhammad Hassanein Heikal, began to speak out about some of the very same things. Nasser slowly began to work toward mending some of the abuses of the system, such as returning sequestered property and promising reform.

The ASU, students, and workers represented potential sources of unrest for the government. Following the trials of air force officers in February 1968, who received relatively lenient sentences, riots broke out across the country. The demonstrations represent an interesting historical moment, since in all fairness to both the High Military Court who tried the officers, and the men themselves, what could either of them have done? As for the officers, most of their entire fleet had been destroyed; the court had no choice but to offer some type of sentence to meet public demand. Anger, frustration, resentment over the humiliating loss, lack of democracy, and a failing economic system fueled the demonstrations. What started with workers at the

---

ABDUL HAKIM AMIR: SUICIDE OR LIQUIDATION

Abdul Hakim Amir was one of the Free Officers that comprised the Revolutionary Command Council, and was probably Nasser's best friend. They lived next door to one another, vacationed together, and had connections through familial marriage. In addition to being Nasser's Chief of Staff, Amir was also head of the Egyptian Soccer Federation, two positions that allowed him to accumulate wealth. Nasser was an intensely paranoid individual, and clearly Amir posed the biggest threat to his power. Some historians have argued that Amir believed that an Egyptian victory in 1967 was in his grasp and that this victory would facilitate his power bid over Nasser, which led Amir to make a number of careless moves leading to the Israeli preemptive strike. Whether his death was a suicide or a targeted killing is open to debate. While suicide is fairly uncommon in Islamic society, others have argued that Amir's act represents his ultimate act of desperation.

Helwan munitions plant outside of Cairo spread to students, who were coincidentally commemorating demonstrations against the monarchy in 1946, in what is known as Students' Day. Nasser countered with promises of reorganizing the ASU and greater democratization generally. Nasser hoped to contain the student threat by recruiting student activists into a special arm of the ASU, the Socialist Vanguard.

The ASU elections of May 1968 have been widely contested by those inside Egypt; however, some outsiders dispute vote rigging. What is clear is that the elections did allow a number of previously disenfranchised people to participate in the ASU elections, namely Communists. Egypt's Communist Party had been voluntarily disbanded since 1965, and thus a number of new thinkers were brought into the ASU, even if as some have alleged, the gate of entry was somewhat restricted.

The ASU did not remain at center stage. The Arab–Israeli conflict loomed at the forefront. An Israeli helicopter raid in Nag Hammadi in Upper Egypt spurred a new round of demonstrations in November 1968, which also overlapped with a highly unpopular Education Act, which would restrict the number of times a secondary student could stand for exams. Nasser's approach was multipronged. Against the Israelis he launched the War of Attrition, and to quell internal dissent, the former would be popular, but he also arrested and dismissed the head of the ASU. Although later released and still a member of its Supreme Executive, Ali Sabri lost his place of preeminence, as did the organization. The War of Attrition against Israel would effectively unite workers and students against an external enemy instead of an internal one. The Arab–Israeli conflict and its discontents remained more significant right up until Nasser's death in September 1970, which occurred just after convening a conference of Arab heads of state in the wake of Black September in Jordan, the event that forced the PLO out of Jordan. As would be typical of Middle Eastern politics for years to come, focusing on the conflict and other external enemies would be far more satisfying than overcoming domestic struggles.

THE WAR OF ATTRITION (1967–1970)

The humiliating loss for its client encouraged the Soviets to resupply the Egyptians with weapons, but Egypt was in no position to fight a full-scale war. The Soviets continuously resupplied Egypt with their latest equipment, often training and flying missions with their clients. Israel occupied the Sinai Peninsula all the way up to the eastern bank of the Suez Canal, which remained closed. Nasser's hope was that the War of Attrition would be a limited war that would enable him to regain the Sinai and reopen the Canal. The Israelis viewed the conflict as a test of their willingness to hold on to territorial gains made in the 1967 war. Syria, Jordan, and the PLO would also participate in this test that ended in a ceasefire in August of 1970.

Sadat: The Early Years, Consolidating Power

Sadat did not have nearly the internal power base that a number of other people in either the army or intelligence had, which is why no one opposed him initially. He was Nasser's last vice president, but many scholars question whether Nasser himself intended for Sadat to be his successor. People referred to him variously as either Nasser's lap dog or *Bikbashi Sah-Sah* (Colonel Yes-Yes). Less than a year after taking office (May 1971), he instituted a "Corrective Revolution" in which he replaced a large number of government and ASU officials. Sadat created a new constitution in 1971 that tilted the powers of government inordinately toward the executive.

1971 CONSTITUTION

The chief executive (president) has the power to appoint and dismiss the prime minister and cabinet ministers, start impeachment proceedings, issue decrees and referenda bypassing parliament, convene emergency sessions of parliament, proclaim a state of emergency, and appoint 10 members of parliament. At the local level, a governor presides over each of the 27 governorates, each of which has a local council. Theoretically, the overwhelming executive powers are checked by guarantees of civil rights and freedoms, similar to the ones in the American Bill of Rights. There are also prohibitions against torture and mistreatment of prisoners. All "rights" are determined by law and can be interpreted or abridged by the government. Article 62 compels Egyptians to participate in public life. Previously, there had been presidential term limits in the constitution; however, Sadat amended the constitution before his death to allow for an unlimited number. Finally, the Judiciary is an independent branch of government and it regulates the practice and function of the other two branches. (CIA *The World Factbook*)

Shortly thereafter, he began to publicly tear apart huge portions of Nasser's highly unpopular security apparatus, after which he announced that he would reform the ASU. The reformation that ensued ultimately entailed its dissolution. Another wave of student demonstrations pounded Sadat's early presidency (1972–1973) in which protestors demanded action on the Arab–Israeli conflict, democratization, and economic reform.

Much of what Sadat ended up doing was outlined in Abdul Hakim Amir's platform just after the 1967 war; however, Sadat faced many obstacles including a looming state socialist bureaucracy, a lingering unresolved conflict with Israel that left the Suez Canal closed, a veritable army of Soviet military advisors, and numerous opponents, particularly on the left. As early as 1971 he changed Egypt's investment code, he dismissed the Soviet military advisors in 1972, and indicated a desire to return Egypt to the Western fold, a position it held at the time of the revolution in 1952. Nevertheless, the United States still mired in Vietnam ignored Sadat's gestures. As odd as it sounds, he took the calculated risk of starting war with Israel in 1973 to reignite the peace process. Coordinated with Syria, the October War of 1973, also known as the War of the Crossing, due to the successful Egyptian crossing of the Bar-Lev line, defeated the myth of Israeli invincibility. This political gamble, along with the deployment of the oil weapon by Arab oil producers, catapulted Sadat to international fame. It set him on a course that could enable him to reopen the canal and regain the Sinai (see Chapter 2).

INFITAH POLITICS, MID-1970s TO 2000s

Controlled Democracy under Sadat

Sadat had been highly underestimated by his competition both domestically and internationally. He had come from humble origins, born in the small Delta village of Mit Abu al-Kum in the governorate of Minufiyah. As a youth he had tasted a variety of political flavors from among the radical groups that existed in the 1930s and 1940s, including affiliations with Germans (during World War II) and the Muslim Brotherhood. His generally right-wing inclinations, along with the reality of his opposition, led him to stave off the Nasserists and leftists with the assistance of Islamic organizations, which were allowed greater freedom in the country. Once again the Muslim Brotherhood was allowed to legally publish, and its two papers became immediate successes. Another area where Muslim groups spread rapidly was in student organizations where they began to counter the Marxist and Nasserist groups that had been staples of the previous era.

With respect to the dismantling of the ASU, Sadat began in 1976 with the creation of *manabir* (platforms) within the union to contest parliamentary elections, which would later evolve into functioning parties as the ASU dissolved entirely. By 1978 the ASU no longer existed. Many groups and individuals expressed an interest in participating in this process, including groups as far-reaching as a so-called Akhneton platform. Nevertheless, Sadat controlled the process entirely, naming and creating the platforms and leaders from within the executive committee of the ASU, a move that drew heavy criticism from Fuad Serageldin, the fiery, cigar-smoking Wafdist politician who reemerged after a quarter century of political nonexistence to give critical speeches, not only of issues related to election reform, but also of the revolution in general.

The platforms included a centrist one, representing the interests of the regime, known as the Socialist Democrats (later Egypt Party) and led by Mahmud Abu Wafia, the president's brother-in-law; the "right" platform represented the interests of infitah (or opening of the economy), known as the Socialist Liberals and led by Mustapha Kamal Murad, Free Officer, MP, and President of Cotton Exporter's Association; the Left, known as Progressive Nationalists, led by Khalid Muhi al-Din, Free Officer (member of RCC); and Nasserists (distinguished from the Leftists by their non-subordination to Moscow), led by Kamal Ahmad Muhammad. The Leftists and the Nasserists ended up as single alignment in the first elections of 1977, but since they represented Sadat's version of the left, they were not particularly radical. Sadat appointed a number of MPs, including eight Copts and two women (Waterbury 1983; Hinnebush in Oweiss 1990).

As Sadat faced the challenges of the opening of his economy, the pressures of the IMF, and bread riots (see Chapter 2), along with the reorganization of the New Wafd party in 1977, he created a series of laws in May to put the brakes on party formation requiring that other parties be distinct from the three in existence: that they conform to basic government documents; for example, the constitution and the charter; that they not be based on sectarian, class, regional, or gender interests; that party members cannot come from other privileged groups, for example, judiciary, officer corps, or police; that parties not accept foreign funding; that parties must have at least 20 MPs to found a party; and finally that a special committee of the (nearly defunct) ASU would oversee the process.

The New Wafd found support among independent MPs, and Sadat was forced to find creative ways of containing his arch enemies. His ruling party had a majority in parliament through which he could push through referendums, for example, one denying rights to those who had been convicted of crimes against the state in the early days of the revolution, a bill that would nicely suit the threat of Serageldin and any other formerly powerful pasha who might wield his ugly head. Ever the crafty politician, Serageldin dissolved his party rather than to bow down to the pressures of Sadat's window-dressing democratization. His public speech condemning Sadat came on the heels of the latter's visit to Israel, and not surprisingly Serageldin, by then a septuagenarian, was one of Sadat's 1981 roundup of political prisoners.

Even without the Wafd, Sadat's efforts continued apace. In 1978 he renamed the government party the National Democratic Party (NDP) to reflect to new orientation of the country. Where just two years earlier "socialist" had permeated nearly all the parties' names and the umbrella organization, now there would be a new catch phrase associated with the ruling party to reflect its image and relationship with the West (eventually all of the original parties would drop the word socialist). Nevertheless, Sadat had to also please his Islamic constituency. He was building a state based on "science and faith" that affirmed the core values of the country, one in which the shari'a would be the principal source of law, or so he would claim in the constitution.

At the same time he could not forget his Coptic citizens, and he promised national unity and the reconciliation of individual and collective interests. Finally, despite the fact that his trip to Jerusalem alienated his Arab neighbors, he never gave up hope of replacing Nasser as the great Arab leader; he would strive for Arab unity.

The other party that emerged at the same time with the NDP was the Socialist Party, which would eventually become known as the Socialist Labor Party (SLP), led by Ibrahim Shukri. This party has been known for its broadly socialist and Islamic principles. By 1979 Sadat's NDP won 330 of the 392 seats, the SLP won 29, and Murad's Socialist Liberals (still using the outdated name, would eventually be known simply as the Liberal Party) won only three seats. Khalid Muhi al-Din's Unionist Progressive party (NPUP), the coalition of watered-down leftists and Nasserists, were eliminated in this election, while more powerful versions of the same were not allowed to participate. The Muslim Brotherhood, since it was an organization based on religious interests was not allowed to participate. Sadat appointed 30 women and 10 Copts to insure representation of these groups (Waterbury 1983). An additional party that formed in this early period but that did not fare as well electorally was the Arab Socialist Party of Egypt, another socialist party with Islamic overtones.

Even with the NDP's incredible majority, Sadat found ever more creative ways for dealing with his opponents. In 1980 he created an upper house for the parliament, a consultative council over which the president would control one-third of the appointments of the members who would serve six-year terms. Ultimately, the council would not be as powerful as the People's Assembly, whose 454 members were nearly all elected, and according to the constitution had to represent workers and peasants by at least 50 percent (CIA *The World Factbook*). Sadat was still troubled by his less than

Anwar Sadat, president of Egypt from 1970 until his assassination in 1981. Sadat is remembered for his part in concluding the 1979 Camp David Peace Treaty between Egypt and Israel. (U.S. Department of Defense)

THE LEFT, SOCIALISM, COMMUNISM, AND ISLAM

Most Americans see a vast difference between Socialism and Communism when most states to which we refer as "Communist" are state socialist because the state controls the means of production, land ownership, and distribution of resources. Leftist parties desire an equitable distribution of resources and see an active role for the state and its citizens in this process. Westerners see Communism as atheistic because Marx, its most prominent ideologue, referred to religion as "the opiate of the masses." Nevertheless, Muslims interpret Marx differently. The attraction of Marx to Arab Muslims was as a philosophy of social justice in keeping with their religion, but it was not exclusively Muslim—it could be shared with minority communities. After the 1967 defeat, many leftists were attracted to the local ideology of Islam, but politically they still adhered to some socialist principles. Thus, one finds that some abandoned socialism or communism altogether for Islamism, whereas others joined one of the many socialist parties that adopted Islamic principles.

---

loyal opposition, leading him to pass the Law of Shame in May 1980. The charges for violations of this law were so ambiguous that anyone could fall victim to what amounted to government witch hunts tried before a special Ethics court. The Law of Shame basically meant that if a person or news agency insulted the government, the president, or anyone in his family, then he, she or it would lose political rights, fall under house arrest, be banned from travel, or suspended from economic activity.

The Law of Shame made left of Center press activity difficult. On the one hand, now journalists were no longer constrained by membership in the ASU, and with the creation of platforms Sadat reinvigorated a number of the major papers. Nevertheless, he feared anything left of center, and these papers were monitored so heavily that a number of them struggled to survive after numerous shutdowns, for example, *al-Ahali* of the NPUP, while independent *Ruz al-Youssef* and the SLP's *al-Sha'b* carefully monitored their words.

Sectarian conflict marked Sadat's presidency, which helped to highlight the Islamic militancy that tragically marked his end. Because Sadat had played Islamists against Nasserists and Leftists, by passing legislation to suit the former's interests he alienated his Coptic citizenry. His constitutional amendments first making the *shari'a* "*a* principle source of legislation" in 1971, and changing it in 1980 to "*the* principle source of legislation," greatly annoyed the new Coptic patriarch Baba Shenouda (1923–2012), who assumed his office in 1971. As Muslim groups grew in power and authority, the firebrand patriarch vigorously defended the rights of his community, going into retreat, fasting, and taking other desperate measures in the face of legislation including a draft law suggesting death for apostasy. Historically, Copts have married Muslims and returned to their original faith after the termination of the marriage, either through divorce or death of a spouse. Ultimately, Sadat also protected the Copts, not allowing the apostasy law to pass, protecting the Copts' rights to

---

CONSTITUTION AND THE *SHARI'A*

Sadat's moves in 1971 and 1980 were bold and calculated to pacify Islamists; however, if one looks at the legal history of Egypt, most laws were already in conformity with the shari'a, particularly those governing contractual and legal obligations. As for Personal Status laws (marriage, inheritance, divorce), again most were based on the shari'a, generally favoring the liberal Maliki school of law. Thus, the entire corpus of existing law was not out of conformity. The problem has been that extremists want the application of Quranic punishments (without necessarily the prescribed witnesses or procedures) for crimes, for example, adultery and theft, as well as a thorough examination of all legislation for its harmony with the faith. Mubarak waffled on how to deal with the potentially thorny issue, neither wanting to become embedded in legal reorganization nor a "return" to the Quran as constitution.

---

build churches, and giving Copts of his choosing representation in parliament. Meanwhile, a radical group *takfir wal-hijra* (repentence and holy emigration) carried out a high-profile kidnapping and assassination of a government official in 1977 in its bid to recreate the state. As Islamic groups grew more militant in the wake of the success of the Iranian revolution of 1979, more clashes between Muslims and Copts took place in those areas where high concentrations of Copts live (see Chapter 5). In June 1981 there were violent sectarian clashes in Zawiya al-Hamra, outside of Cairo, where a Coptic Church was supposed to be built. As Sadat collected evidence from a number of these incidents, he found that one of the groups involved, Egyptian Islamic Jihad, was also conspiring against the state.

It was on September 5, 1981, that Sadat rounded up his opposition that included a variety of young radical Islamists, most of whom were well educated and from the middle class; however, he overlooked a few cells including one in the military. Sadat arrested figures from all shades of the political spectrum that included 1,500 people, among whom even Pope Shenouda was forced into seclusion. The vast majority of these individuals had nothing to do with any plot against the state; they were merely free thinkers and vocal advocates of policies contrary to those of Sadat. Ever the "democratizer" Sadat put the issue as a referendum before parliament where it passed with more than 99 percent of the votes (Waterbury 1983).

Just over a month later (October 6), as he reviewed a military parade celebrating Egypt's successful crossing in 1973, Sadat was gunned down by Lt. Khalid Islambouli, assisted by three other Islamic militants who jumped out of one of the trucks as horrified dignitaries, journalists, and foreign observers watched. State-controlled Egyptian broadcast immediately shut down. Sadat and seven others lost their lives, although the government waited sometime before announcing the president's death. In an unprecedented display of support, three former U.S. presidents, Nixon, Ford, and Carter, attended the funeral along with France's Mitterand, the United Kingdom's Prince Charles, and Israel's Begin. Aside from Sudan, Oman, and

Somalia, the Arab League lacked representation, thus demonstrating Egypt's weakened position in the Arab world. More importantly, unlike the funerals for his predecessor Nasser, or public icons, for example, Umm Kulthum and Abdel Halim Hafez (see Chapter 6), the streets were not filled with grief-stricken Egyptians. Where people were in the streets, it was generally because of sectarian strife. Nevertheless, Sadat, ignominiously murdered after Islambouli shouted the words, "Death to the Pharaoh!," Sadat was buried in a pyramid-like structure along with a monument to unknown soldiers.

Mubarak: A Path Clearly Beaten or a Clearly Beaten Path, the First Decade

In 1981 Egypt's vice president Hosni Mubarak succeeded Sadat according to the terms of the constitution, whereby the People's Assembly ratified the choice and a national referendum endorsed this selection. Since that time he has been reelected by the same process three more times (1987, 1993, and 1999) and in his fifth election in 2005 Mubarak allowed for a constitutional amendment in which the presidential election would not merely be a referendum, but would allow for an opposition candidate (el-Amrani 2005).

Much like Sadat in his early years, Mubarak was highly underestimated. Referred to as the "laughing cow" (a satirical dig at his simplicity and resemblance to the figure on the cheese package), Mubarak endured a significant test of time and perhaps a new image will replace sources of political humor. Writing less than 10 years after Mubarak took power, Afaf Marsot argued that jokes about Nasser focus on him as a hero because of his "larger than life" image, whereas Sadat although underestimated in his early years, by the time of his death was joked about as a crafty, conniving figure. Meanwhile, she maintained that Mubarak jokes center on him as the simple, well-meaning average guy (Marsot in Oweiss 1990). At least part of Mubarak's success can be attributed to Sadat, who paved the way for him with his corrective revolution, effectively removing many potential sources of opposition. At the same time, many of the stalwart figures of the revolution had previously been removed from positions of power (e.g., Amir), retired, or faded into obscurity. Mubarak (b. 1928) himself represents a slightly different generation than Nasser and Sadat, having risen quickly to high positions of authority after the October War. Sadat's assassination gave Mubarak an additional opportunity for creating an Emergency Law that gives the president wide-ranging authorities against a vast array of potential opposition with additional powers for censorship, arrest and detention, and so on. More than a quarter century after Sadat's assassination the law was still in existence, with human rights groups estimating that up to 15,000 people were under detention in the mid-2000s. Before his removal, the law would undergo periodic renewal in parliament where it faced opposition from about one quarter of the MPs (Moustafa 2004; Shehata and Stacher 2007).

Shortly after taking power, Mubarak did allow many of Sadat's political prisoners to be freed, and he allowed the Wafd to reform as a political party; however, he too reformed election laws not allowing opposition parties to enter parliament unless they could attain 8 percent of the vote. While not actually permitted to form as

(Muhammad) Hosni Mubarak (b. 1928) succeeded Anwar Sadat in the presidency of Egypt. Mubarak was brought down by the Revolution of 2011. (U.S. Department of Defense)

a political party, the Muslim Brotherhood entered mainstream politics as a partner with other legal parties. In 1984 a New Wafd and Brotherhood coalition garnered just over 15 percent of the vote, whereas none of the other opposition parties could muster up the 8 percent minimum. By 1987, the Brotherhood switched partners, moving to the Liberal Party where its candidates received just over 17 percent of the vote, whereas the New Wafd's numbers dropped down to just under 11 percent and the NPUP less than 3 percent (Wickham 2002). Other parties struggled to enter the political scene through court battles. In 1983 the *Umma* party with its quirky leader the *hajj* Sabahi stood in distinction to other vaguely Islamo-socialist parties, in that it looked favorably on the Israeli peace process. Nevertheless, Sabahi, a renowned fortuneteller, would often refuse to disclose party platforms before elections on the basis that others might steal them. Thus, it made it hard for the party to earn much respect or support. Despite the fact that the political process was seemingly expanding, the dominance of the ruling NDP was evident in the fact that it continued to win 87 percent of the seats in 1984, 69 percent in 1987, 58 percent in 1990, and 71.4 percent in 1995. These figures do not include NDP independents or those who joined the NDP after winning an election, which would increase those figures to 79 percent in 1987, 86 percent in 1990, and 94 percent in 1995 (Wickham 2002).

On what principles did the NDP win these victories? Preserving the interests of the state and the bureaucracy have been the party's main functions; however,

ISLAMIC TRENDS

The success of the Muslim Brotherhood coalitions obviously mirrored what was taking place at other levels of society. Political scientist Carrie Rosefsky Wickham has used the term parallel Islamic sector to refer to the way in which Islamic voluntary associations, some of which are funded from abroad and some of which survive on funding from *zakat* (religious donations), to fund various ventures ranging from the charitable, namely, schools, clinics, and daycare, to the profitable, like Islamic banks, construction, and manufacturing interests (Wickham 2002). These groups have their own publications and indeed have their own presses. Mubarak allowed many of these institutions to continue their work because they provided services that the state was unable or unwilling to offer its citizens. Many of the people involved in these trends had been student activists of the 1970s, and by the 1980s and 1990s, some found membership in the Muslim Brotherhood as an organized means for channeling Islamic activism.

its platform continued to include rather lofty goals regarding equality of citizens, the role of the state in achieving development, and the significance of Egyptian national identity. The party also promoted the private sector, the development of civil society, and women's rights. How has the party managed to achieve either its success or its goals? The NDP maintained a unique system of clientage, rewards, and favors; and it depended on uneven voter turnout to maintain its strength. For example, if a village wanted a new school, the NDP would work to nearly finish the project BEFORE the election, but would not complete it until AFTER the NDP guy or gal got elected. Opposition party candidates learned these tricks as well, and many large merchants, bankers, and investors have become politicians in recent years, usually aligned with the New Wafd or Liberal parties.

Historically, between the 1952 and 2011 revolutions, voter turnout has been alarmingly low in Egypt, and this apathy worked in favor of the NDP. Although the old regime frequently made claims, for example, 40–50 percent voter turnout, these figures were based on adult citizens registered to vote. Political scientists estimate that at that time perhaps only half of Egypt's adult citizens were registered to vote. Furthermore, by examining voter participation, it is clear that it was higher in the countryside. In fact, voter apathy has been poor in areas where the citizenry is most educated, with turnouts as low as 1 in 12 or 13 adults.

Elections of the 1990s and the Early 2000s

Despite the fact that clear patterns in Egyptian electoral process reflected little hope for opposition parties, new ones continued to emerge. In 1989 Young Egypt returned as yet another Islamo-socialist party. While parties are not supposed to accept outside monies, Young Egypt had acknowledged its connection to the former Libyan regime and its connections to the notion of pan-Arabism. The following year, the Democratic Unionist party formed, with a generally a "liberal" platform, but it distinguished itself from either the Liberal Party or the Wafd party with its emphasis on separating religion and politics. The Democratic Unionist party emphasized the importance of rejoining Egypt with Sudan. While some have chastised the Democratic Unionist party for this aspect of its platform, Egypt's integration with Sudan exists as part of the New Wafd's platform, as well as some other small party platforms. Quite literally a fresh new breath of air on the political scene in 1990 was the Green Party, which aside from its emphasis on the environment bears some resemblance to a number of the Islamo-Socialist parties in terms of social programs, and the Liberal or New Wafd party in terms of economics. The party was also concerned with issues related to Egypt's historic sites and the environmental issues connected therein, as well as health issues. The Green Party has been extremely small and publishes a paper, *al-Watan*, not to be confused with the newspaper of the same name published in Qatar or Oman. Few of the opposition newspapers have much of a following. Only the Wafd's *al-Wafd* is a daily paper, with an estimated circulation of 150,000–180,000 in 1991 (Wickham 2002). In order to maintain its circulation, *al-Wafd* tends to be both highly critical of the government and of Israel. The SLP's *al-Sha'b* claimed much lower circulation rates during the same year; however, it boasted higher reading rates due to shared reading particularly during the Gulf War. At one time NPUP's weekly *al-Ahali* boasted circulation rates of approximately 150,000; however, that was in the mid-1980s (Wickham 2002).

The 1990s also saw the creation of some small parties some of which did not last much beyond the 2000 elections, nor did they differ vastly from those already on the political scene. The People's Democratic Party formed in 1992, with its newspaper *Sha'b Maṣr*, garnered less than 300 supporters, and while it was still registered with the State Information Service before the 2011 revolution, it did not appear active. Founded in the same year, the Arab Democratic Nasserist party distinguishes itself from the NPUP and the SLP as being the "true heir to Nasserism," the party which claims it really cares about workers, peasants, the people, and the public sector in the face of rampant privatization and economic crisis (Wickham 2002; State Information Service; *al-Ahram* 1995). In 2003, its weekly newspaper, *al-'Arabi*, while avoiding direct confrontation with the regime by insulting Mubarak, resorted to critiques of his son Gamal after he became head of the NDP's steering committee (2002), raising the specter of the inherited presidency.

There was still room for more Islamically oriented parties in the early–mid-1990s. In 1993 the Social Justice party was founded as another party seeking to maintain a more equitable society based on the principles of the *shari'a*. One notable feature about its platform is a desire for greater cooperation and respect between ruling and opposition parties. Dr. Osama Shaltout founded the Mutual Support Party in 1995, which enabled him to create what is essentially a flat-tax religious party. His desire was or is to rid the country of its current tax structure replacing it with a 1 percent tax on the wealthy that would be returned to the people who need it along with free (quality) medical care. Furthermore, he advocates a spiritual uniting of Sunni and

Shiite Muslims, a rather controversial issue in a country where the most radical of Muslims do not accept the philosophy of their Shiite counterparts. His slogan is "Determination and knowledge against money and profit" (*al-Ahram* 1995).

The 2000 election revealed the multiplicity of problems and inconsistencies in the electoral process. The New Wafd and the Liberals, who had ridden on the coat tails of the Muslim Brotherhood in the previous elections, respectively had alienated their base by going against their secular, liberal principles. Indeed, the Wafd party had been founded even before the (independent, modern) Egyptian state by wealthy Muslims, Copts, and Jews. The New Wafd's stand on censorship of a controversial novel and amendment of personal status laws for women contravened its image as the secular party of Western-style liberalism. Meanwhile, as the Muslim Brotherhood moved away from allying with traditional parties and running more candidates as independents, the traditional opposition liberal parties were left with neither the numbers generated by an alliance with the Brotherhood nor their reputations. They had alienated some of their base constituency through the alliance with the Muslim Brotherhood, including Copts and some women's groups. The Brotherhood's dramatically growing numbers and electoral presence through nonviolent confrontation began to threaten the government even more than extremist Islamic groups' traditional techniques of attempting to overturn the government by more radical means.

Egyptian voters flee from tear gas fired by riot police after supporters of independent candidate Mohammed Oda (shown on poster) were denied entry to polling stations by police in Cairo on November 8, 2000. (AP Photo)

SAAD EDDIN IBRAHIM AND THE REGIME

The politics of patronage can be a difficult balance. One cannot succeed in Egypt without connections. Dr. Saad Eddin Ibrahim (b. 1938) is an intelligent, well-published sociologist, passionate about advancing the cause of civil society in Egypt. As a youngster he was attracted to various revolutionary philosophies, and he came to the United States to pursue higher education in the midst of the anti-war and the civil rights movements, which influenced his activism. Married to Barbara Lethem Ibrahim and holding dual American–Egyptian citizenship Dr. Ibrahim taught for many years at the American University in Cairo, where among other things, he served as a thesis advisor to Suzanne Mubarak and taught Gamal Mubarak. It is most likely his association with the first family and support of the peace process that facilitated the creation of the Khaldun Center in 1988. Ibrahim has also been a representative of the "Egyptian" voice abroad, as well as being a voice for normalization of relations between Muslims and Copts in Egypt.

Through the course of the electoral process on the campaign trail and in polling places, the Brotherhood candidates (including one woman) and their supporters all began to suffer the same consequences that radical groups suffered—arrest, detention, and even beatings. The Emergency Law could flexibly be applied at any time both to political candidates and to ordinary citizens. Saad Eddin Ibrahim (b. 1938) Egyptian American democracy activist and founder of the Ibn Khaldun Center for Development Studies, who had monitored the 1995 elections, was arrested in June 2000, just months before the election. At this point Ibrahim suffered only 45 days of incarceration; however, the indictments would tie him up for years thus allowing the elections to proceed without his scrutiny. Dr. Ibrahim was accused of embezzling funds from the European Union—grants received for his center's work. Ibrahim underwent a series of trials and convictions by state security courts in 2001 and 2002 after which he and a number of his coworkers received sentences ranging from prison terms to hard labor. After his third trial in 2003, he was released only to be sentenced again in 2008 after his support of Ayman Nour (see subsequently). Ironically, Egyptians did not come out in large numbers to support Ibrahim because of his association with the U.S. government through his citizenship and because of his support of the Israeli peace process.

DYNAMISM AND STAGNATION IN RECENT POLITICS, 2000 TO PRESENT

The second Palestinian *intifaḍa* (September 2000), the return of Ariel Sharon to Israeli politics (September 2000), the death of Hafez al-Assad of Syria and the succession of his son Bashar (June 2000), the election of George W. Bush and the policies pursued by his foreign policy team (January 2001 to January 2009), and the repercussions of September 11, 2001 worldwide, all reinvigorated the opposition political party scene in Egypt with the creation of new parties and new demands for electoral reform. Founded just months after the start of the second *intifada* and rising criticism in the Egyptian press about Egypt's peace with Israel, the National Conciliation Party formed as a group seeking a just solution for the Palestinian issue through regional cooperation. This small party used the old language of pan-Arabism to seek European Union-style economic cooperation, while simultaneously taking a strong stand against imperialism. Founded the following year, the Egypt 2000 party was essentially an anti-Western and anti-globalizing party that takes a strong stand regarding Egyptian identity, the Arabic language, and promoting greater freedom through media and party pluralism. Egyptian identity plays a powerful role in the Democratic (Young) Generation party's platform as well (2002), where the focus is on the country's strength as an agricultural producer and the need to develop better education programs for youth, who represent a large proportion of the population. The Free Constitutional party founded in 2004 also sought sweeping reforms, not only of education, but also of the constitution, health care, the budget, and the bureaucracy.

The most important party formed during the era before the 2005 elections has been the Tomorrow Party. The party was created by unhappy Wafdists who felt that the political spectrum needed a new centrist liberal party that could speak in the idiom of the people. Its charismatic leader, Ayman Nour, is a dynamic orator able to rally masses with his party's message of limiting presidential powers, expanding human rights, and constitutional reform. He would play an important role as Mubarak buckled under and amended Egypt's constitution to no longer simply hold a yes or no referendum on the candidate chosen by his NDP-dominated People's Assembly (PA). The previously discussed exigencies of voter turnout and the NDP control do not even address the Ministry of the Interior's control of the vote count and electoral process. In the spring of 2005, the PA amended the constitution such that legal opposition parties could run candidates against Mubarak in the November election. Nevertheless, this would make it impossible for the independent Muslim Brotherhood MPs to stand as candidates. To register their unhappiness, a few parties boycotted the process by refusing to run candidates, for example, NPUP and the Arab Democratic Nasserist party, while others ran candidates without hope. The only high-profile opposition candidates were the New Wafd's Numan Goma and the Tomorrow party's Ayman Nour. In fact, some have even suggested that Goma's candidacy was a behind-the-scenes deal between the Wafd and the NDP to reduce the number of votes for the rising-star candidate, that is, an effort to split the opposition vote.

In the months leading up to the 2005 election Mubarak worked on his image. In television ad campaigns of which the NDP seemed to have an inordinate share, he appeared younger than 77 years and often in more casual clothing (shirt and tie instead of the heavy dark suit). Since the Muslim Brotherhood could not run its own candidate, its support would be crucial in the election, and interestingly enough, over the course of the summer before the November election masses of Brotherhood detainees were released. In fact, by the time of the election it was the first time in a decade that no Brothers were incarcerated.

KEFAYA: ENOUGH!

The presidency of Bashar al-Assad in Syria started rumblings in Egypt that the same could take place—inherited presidency. As Gamal Mubarak moved into the third highest position in the NDP in 2002 on the steering committee and by 2004 his cabinet was in place in government, many were shouting "enough" or "*kefaya.*" By 2005 a coalition of Egyptians, who rarely agree on anything, running the entire range of the political spectrum, opposed the presidency, generally, along with the idea that Gamal might succeed his father, and the Emergency Law of 1981, in particular. Many of these groups had been engaging in protests against Israel, the Iraq War, and Egypt's relationship with the United States. Although Mubarak changed the election law to allow opposition, most within the movement saw this as a hollow gesture aimed at satisfying international criticism. Kefaya ran no candidate and boycotted the 2005 elections after a number of distressing confrontations with the regime at what were meant to be nonviolent protests.

Not surprisingly, Mubarak won the election, in which there were widespread accusations of fraud despite a huge foreign media presence, which did reduce (but not eliminate) the violence that characterized many of the previous elections. Voting irregularities existed even in the referendum for the amendment to the constitution (which also entailed regulations about who could run). There were districts that reported 100 percent turnout, leading the judge filing the report to question why no one was sick, working, or lazy, therefore unable to make it to the polls (el-Amrani 2005).

Perhaps the biggest irregularity related to the 2005 election was the arrest and detention of the most successful opposition candidate Ayman Nour who received approximately 12 percent of the vote. Numan Goma won approximately 5–7 percent of the vote, and Mubarak claimed the majority of the remainder, something of the order of 78 percent (el-Amrani 2005). The government claimed that Nour falsified documents that he submitted in his presidential bid; however, after then U.S. Secretary of State Condoleezza Rice cancelled a visit and chastised Egypt for its actions Nour was briefly released and allowed to stand for the elections. Nevertheless, Nour's release was merely a delay of his trial, which ended in 2006. He remained imprisoned until February 2009, shortly after the inauguration of Barack Obama, when he was mysteriously released nearly two years short of his five-year sentence. In June 2009 Obama chose Cairo over other locations to make his historic speech to the Islamic world. Several days before Mr. Obama's visit, his face visibly singed from a recent attack, his personal life marred by rumors of divorce from his lifetime partner in love and politics Gamila Ismail, Nour announced that he wished he was back in jail. He insisted that the government was maximizing its benefit from his release, while he was unable to return to political life. Meanwhile, his supporter, Saad Eddin Ibrahim remained in "self-exile" in the United States even after the Egyptian government overturned charges of defamation because he still faced charges of treason.

SAAD EDDIN IBRAHIM: LETTER TO THE *WASHINGTON POST*

In a brutally honest August 2007 piece in the *Washington Post*, Dr. Ibrahim highlighted the plight of imprisoned political leader Ayman Nour, his torture and mistreatment in government prisons, and the general conditions in Mubarak's police state. Ibrahim suggested that the United States tolerated the situation in Egypt not just because of the war on terror or Egypt's role in the peace process, but because of the Egyptian regime's stance as a moderate in a sea of Islamic radicals. He dismissed the Egyptian government's claim that he was responsible for connecting aid to specific changes in governmental behavior; however, the phrasing and tone of his statements made clear that the United States could go much further than the one small instance cited. He closed the article with the revelation of his fear of returning home to face charges in a state that has "strayed so far from the rule of law."

As for the legislative elections, despite voter intimidation and ballot-stuffing, the independent Muslim Brotherhood candidates won a landmark 88 seats in parliament (Shehata and Stacher 2007). The brief respite that the organization received prior to the election to get support for Mubarak's candidacy was short-lived as members were rounded up to keep the new parliamentary voting bloc in line. The group has demonstrated remarkable solidarity by carrying out brazen acts, for example, wearing matching "No to Emergency" sashes in 2006 when the Emergency Law, in place since Sadat's death, was up for renewal. They also supported the government by literally eating chicken and drinking water on the steps of parliament when Avian flu struck in 2006, in addition to visiting poultry-producing regions of the country and providing factual information about the disease when the country was in a state of panic.

No other opposition group or party or even all other independents collectively were as successful as the Muslim Brotherhood independents. The ruling NDP managed to elect 311 MPs, as well as the president's 10 appointments, but the showing of all other opposition parties was poor. The New Wafd received only 6 seats, the Tomorrow Party despite its presidential success elected only 1 MP, and other independents received 24 seats. The Muslim Brotherhood's tactic of moderate reform within the system had been successful (el-Amrani 2005).

The other recent challenge to the electoral process has been from women. The first change had come in 1979 to give 30 seats to women; however, it was challenged on constitutional grounds in 1988. In 2009 the number of seats in the PA was increased to 518, allocating 64 for women, which would have impacted the 2010 elections and 2015 elections only (author interview with Farkhonda Hassan 2009). The initiative received a great deal of support from a number of women's groups including the National Council for Women (NCW), headed by Suzanne Mubarak, but run on a more practical basis by its secretary general, long-time MP Dr. Farkhonda Hassan (see Chapter 5). Male and female activists in the NCW had been keen on recruiting women into the political process at the provincial level, helping them to overcome obstacles, for example, education, funding, and lack of family support. Other women's groups have stressed the need to press parties to have a proportional system on the party slate guaranteeing a number of positions on party lists. After the 2011 revolution, there are no seats guaranteed for women; however, party lists must contain at least one woman's name for the PA.

EGYPT'S COURT SYSTEM

Lawyers and the system of justice in Egypt have long been checks on an authoritarian system. Westerners have many misconceptions about the *shari'a* and how it was applied through the course of Islamic history. In fact, much of what we now refer to as international trade law has roots in the interactions between Europeans and Muslims during the crusades as the former learned the fair-trade practices of the latter. Evidence of the intercultural exchange is in English words with Arabic origin, for example, check from *ṣaqq* meaning contract for later payment. One problem is that Westerners tend to focus on certain aspects of the *shari'a*, namely the *ḥadd* punishments, which are retaliatory in nature, for example, amputation for theft. Second, even with respect to the *ḥadd* punishments, the Quran prescribes specific circumstances for the implementation of the punishment, for example, for adultery there must be four witnesses to the actual act. Third, the *shari'a* is meant for Muslims only. Thus, in early Islamic history customary law played an important role with respect to administering justice in Egypt and worked its way into the corpus of *fiqh*, the body of jurisprudence. Historically, the courts were a place where one's property rights were protected and one could expect to redress grievances. During the Ottoman period, for which we have records, it is clear that *ḥadd* punishments had no place in the system. The Ottoman state preferred to fine subjects for sexual and other indiscretions rather than to carry out these extreme punishments. This practice did not appear to be a departure from the eras that preceded it.

SHARI'A

Technically, the *shari'a* is God's law, which is divine law; it is unchanging and immutable. Allah expressed certain wishes or mandates through the Quran, but man is the one who interprets them. The shari'a as it is applied in a corpus of law, that is Islamic jurisprudence, is known as *fiqh*. Historically, these were two distinct terms; however, over time they have come to be used interchangeably. A legal opinion is known as a *fatwa*, and it can be rendered by any recognized scholar. According to Islamic law, anything which is not expressly forbidden is allowed, and among allowable behaviors there are categories: obligatory, for example, prayer; commendable, for example, charity beyond that which is required; permitted, for example, four wives; reprehensible, for example, divorce.

The modern court system has its roots in the age of Muhammad Ali and the need to regulate the vast governmental changes along with the large numbers of foreign merchants. Therefore, he created a *Majlis al-Aḥkam* (Council of Justice) and a Merchant's Court. It was not until after the *Tanzimat* reforms (1839–1876) and the arrival of large numbers of foreigners during the reign of Said (see Chapter 2) that the justice system truly necessitated an overhaul. The *shari'a* courts would gradually be stripped of their functions and bypassed for what would become the newly created national courts.

During the reign of Ismail matters came to a head as the Khedive was collecting taxes in advance to pay the current debt, and the large foreign community in Egypt was exerting its will in new ways lending money to Egyptians, from peasants to large landholders, at exorbitant rates. The rising number of conflicts led to the creation of a new court system in 1876: the Mixed Courts to adjudicate civil and commercial cases between Egyptians and foreigners. Ordinary criminal cases against foreigners were tried in special consular courts. The language of the Mixed Courts was French, and the judges consisted of two-third foreigners, including Europeans and eventually Americans, and one-third Egyptians (or at least lawyers having passed the Egyptian bar that might include Levantines, Greeks, and Italians who had made Egypt their home). An American who wrote one of the landmark studies of the courts remarked decades later that he found his colleagues to be the keenest legal minds on any court in the world, surpassing even the U.S. Supreme Court (Tracy 1970). The Mixed Courts had branches in Cairo, Alexandria, and Mansura, with an Appeals court in Alexandria. Although the Mixed Courts were theoretically based on French law, since most of the laws dealt with trading and contractual obligations, Egyptians who were on the commission were careful to draft the laws with the *shari'a* in mind. Furthermore, the courts allowed for following the principles of "natural law and equity" where the law was lacking or obscure. This phrase gave the judges greater leeway in applying local principles. Nevertheless, Egyptians associated the Mixed Courts with the protection of foreigners and foreign interests.

The development of the Mixed Courts had a formative influence over the creation of Egypt's National Courts in 1883. The Egyptian lawyers who compiled the code looked to the example of the Mixed Courts for setting up their system. The new system came at the beginning of the British occupation, and much to the consternation of the occupiers Egypt's lawyers and judges played a decisive role in shaping the system. This theme, the independent (and even maverick) judiciary, would continue to be a theme in Egypt's modern history. The occupiers would, however, make sure that Egypt had a firm, new criminal code in place at the turn of the century. As these changes took place the *shari'a* courts became marginalized dealing more or less with personal status issues: marriage, inheritance, and divorce. The minority communities would continue to use their own courts for these matters.

The Mixed Courts, the continued British presence, and the existence of unequal trading agreements thwarted the Egypt's development generally and its legal system specifically. The negotiations for the Anglo-Egyptian Treaty of 1936 helped to spur dialogue on these issues, which were concluded in the Convention of Montreux the same year. This agreement ended the Capitulations (the unequal trade agreements), and it phased out the Mixed Courts over a 12-year period ending in 1949. In the meantime, a separate Court of Cassation had been set up in 1931, and in 1946 the Judiciary Advisory Council began adjudication, creating the *Majlis al-Dawla*. A High Administrative Court was added in 1949 as well as a High Court in 1969 to handle interjurisdictional conflicts. The latter was replaced in 1979 by the Supreme Constitutional Court, which has played a pivotal role in Egypt's elections. It should be noted that in no Egyptian court does a jury play a role. All legal decisions come directly from judges, who are part of an independent judiciary.

Throughout the 1930s and 1940s both civil and criminal law codes began long processes of revision. The Egyptian Civil Code of 1949 stands as an example throughout the Middle East as an amalgam of Islamic and Western law. Although scholars debate the relative amount of each element on the final product, both influences are there. Its author, Abd al-Razzaq al-Sanhuri, with the assistance of Edouard Lambert (a French law professor), drafted the document. The code calls for the judge to use the following in making any decision (in order) (1) the applicable law, (2) custom, (3) the *shari'a*, and (4) natural law or equity. As for the criminal code, its revisions were completed in 1950. Some revisions to Personal Status laws took place at the behest of women's groups (see Chapter 5) in the 1920s, and these were in accordance with the more liberal Maliki school of Islamic law.

Nasser brought some change to the judicial system. Although at first he worked with the legendary Sanhuri, architect of Egypt's civil code, to draft some of the early legislation of the revolution, by 1954 the two were at odds and Sanhuri, by then chief justice of the *Majlis al-Dawla*, retired from public life. In 1955, Nasser integrated the *shari'a* courts into the mainstream court system along with the other religious community courts. He created various "special" courts with which he could try enemies of the state. In this manner he could bypass the independent legal establishment that managed to seep through his shackles of control. When this was not enough, Nasser

---

COURTS TODAY

At the base of Egypt's court system are its district tribunals, over which single judges hear civil cases involving less than 5,000 Egyptian pounds and criminal cases involving misdemeanors. In each governorate there is a Court of First Degree that hears cases on appeal from the tribunals, as well as civil cases involving more than 5,000 Egyptian pounds. These courts have a presiding judge and two sitting judges. A higher Court of Appeals exists in seven major cities. It hears civil, commercial, and criminal cases on appeal from the Courts of the First Degree. The Court of Cassation in Cairo hears cases on appeal based on violations of due process or faulty application of the law. There are various special courts, for example, labor tribunals, which fall under the jurisdiction of the Supreme State Security Court. Finally, the Supreme Constitutional Court consists of nine justices and a Chief Justice. This court settles disputes between courts and renders decisions about the constitutionality of laws.

carried out a "massacre of the judges" in 1969, to force them under the control of the ASU. After the General Association of the Magistrates had collectively voted against joining, those who voted "yes" to remaining independent were purged and replaced by appointments from the Ministry of Justice. Nasser found this maneuver necessary because Egyptian judges are appointed for life, and thus he felt powerless in the face of this large group that would not toe his line. Egypt's independent judiciary would not tolerate such an action again, and by 1984 the *Majlis al-Dawla* assured internal appointment for judicial openings. The Lawyer's Syndicate represented another challenge for Nasser, and in order to get the proper number of loyalist ASU members in this recalcitrant syndicate, he required that the syndicate admit all graduates of law faculties working in public-sector companies.

As a general rule Sadat respected the judiciary more than Nasser and did not find it necessary to purge judges. Like Nasser he would occasionally create the special tribunal to deal with his enemies in order to bypass the independent judiciary. These were especially important after he created his Law of Shame in 1980. The most important change to the judiciary that took place under Sadat was the creation of the SCC in 1979. It has taken an activist role in challenging laws and the electoral process.

Among the more infamous of the court's early rulings was its 1985 decision to throw out "Jehan's Law," notoriously named after President Sadat's wife who took an activist role in promoting this 1979 law that enabled women to have easier access to divorce, along with a number of other rights (see Chapter 5). Ironically, most commentators at the time were surprised that the court dismissed the law on procedural grounds making the assumption that the law was not in accordance with the *shari'a*. Interestingly enough, the judges must have understood the finer points of the *shari'a* since the changes in personal status legislation in 2000 utilized Islam as the basis for its passage.

LAWYERS AND THE LAWYER'S SYNDICATE

Although some scholars have questioned the radicalism of the Lawyer's Syndicate, the group's support of the independence of the judiciary has been unwavering. Those that see the lawyers as more radical take a longer view of the association's history (1912), demonstrating it as a location of antigovernment activity since before the creation of the Egyptian state. Some of the key opposition figures highlighted in this chapter are all lawyers, including Nabil al-Hilali, the Communist who spent the greater part of his career defending prisoners of conscious of all varieties; Fuad Serageldin, the founder of the New Wafd; and Ayman Nour, presidential candidate in 2005. Nasser tried to use the ASU to control or pack the syndicate, and Sadat tried to assure loyalty with proper leadership; but under Mubarak the syndicate returned to greater member control. Recently, the issue has been controlled by the Muslim Brotherhood, which handily won the election in 2009 over the NDP candidate.

The SCC has spent much more time dealing with electoral matters. When Mubarak tried to restrict the means by which parties could organize and thwart small parties from entering the political arena, the court has intervened repeatedly to allow plurality in the political scene, even for small obscure parties with vague platforms. Nevertheless, despite the fact that the judiciary is supposed to have control over the electoral process, the former government ignored this role, thus the SCC declared the then current PA invalid in 2000 based on the 1995 elections. Thereafter, Mubarak allowed the judiciary greater oversight in elections. Previously, the Ministry of Interior reigned supreme in the oversight of the electoral process, but due to the court's decision 8,000 judges would supervise not just main voting stations, but auxiliary ones as well by extending the voting process over several weeks. Nevertheless, one of the huge sticking points in this ruling has been the meaning of the term "judicial body," which oversees the process. The government has frequently seen fit to send its own legal officers to polling sites in contentious elections that followed; however, overall elections have been cleaner resulting in more victories for opposition candidates, generally, and more Muslim Brotherhood candidates, in particular. Judges have also been critical of the government's handling of the process, which led to disciplinary action against two Court of Cassation judges who spoke out against the 2005 election, where one was found guilty of disparaging the Supreme Judicial Council and discussing political affairs with the press (el-Ghobashy 2006).

As Islamic trends have become more widespread in Egypt, there has been a rise in the number of cases involving Article two of the constitution, that is, regarding Islam as the religion of the state and the *shari'a* as the source for legislation. Furthermore, a *hisba* suit can be activated if God has been insulted, particularly by a person's words or actions. Activist Islamist lawyers, in particular, have targeted intellectuals, for example, Nasr Abu Zayd and Nawal el-Saadawi (see Chapter 5) as apostates. The

---

THE CASE OF NASR ABU ZAYD

In the United States, Dr. Abu Zayd would be another obscure academic whose work on the linguistics of the Quran would probably not receive much attention. When he first came up for promotion to full professor at Cairo University in 1992, his discussion of the Quran as an interpreted text with internal inconsistencies, was offensive to some members of the committee resulting in a close but negative promotion decision in 1993. In 1995 he received the promotion; however, his case had raised the ire of Islamist lawyers who successfully filed for divorce on behalf of his unwilling wife, Dr. Ibtihal Younis, on the grounds of apostasy. By 1995 the case had gone to appeal, and it reached the Court of Cassation in 1996, which upheld the ruling of the lower courts. Abu Zayd and his wife lived in exile in the Netherlands until shortly before his death in July 2010. The Supreme Constitutional Court in 2000 also rejected his appeal submitted from abroad.

goal of making the individual's life miserable by forcing the state to grant a divorce to his or her spouse (on the basis of apostasy) would then highlight the infamy of the intellectual's work, perhaps leading to some or all of them being banned in Egypt or beyond. While the Islamists were at least partially successful in the case of Abu Zayd, they were not successful in the el-Saadawi court case. All the cases begin in personal status court and some work their way up to the SCC. The SCC has been charged with the issue of Christian "apostates," that is, those who return to their religion after being married to Muslims. In a 2009 case the SCC upheld the 2008 position of the Supreme Administrative Court in allowing these individuals to have their Christian identity documented in public records and identification cards. Rather than substantively discussing the issue, the SCC simply deferred jurisdictional status.

Most significantly for the 2011 revolution, in June 2012 the SCC ruled that the democratically elected parliament was illegitimate based on procedural grounds. According to the SCC, the new parliament, dominated by Islamist parties, was illegitimate due to an aspect of the parliamentary election law that allowed party members to contest one-third of the seats that are reserved for independents. According to the court, this violates the principle of equality. In a separate hearing, the court agreed to allow Ahmed Shafiq, former prime minister, to run for president (see Chapter 7). Many Egyptians wanted to prohibit elements of the old regime (known in Arabic as *felool* or remnants) from participation in the new government; however, the SCC ruled that this too violated the principle of equality.

CONCLUSION

Although various laws have been used in some legal cases that in the West would be classified as religious persecution, the courts were applying and upholding Egypt's laws. Generally, Egypt's court system has been an important balance to a system that has not represented its citizens adequately. In the colonial period, the modern court system was created as a restraint to European power over its citizens, even if the Mixed Courts were viewed at times as representing those interests. In the liberal era, while the structure of parliamentary democracy existed, the foreign monarchy wielded an extraordinary power as did the British who retained four points of control up until 1936 and remained in the canal zone until 1956. Furthermore, the political parties represented large landowners with strong economic ties to the British. The revolution of 1952 brought Egyptian leadership to power, but the executive has retained an inordinate amount of control. The changes wrought by the 2011 revolution are yet to be seen.

REFERENCES

Abdullah, Ahmad. *The Student Movement and National Politics in Egypt, 1923–1973.* London: al-Saqi, 1985.

Abou el-Magd, Nadia. "Presidential Trip Gets Credit for Good News and the Not So Good News." *The National*, June 1, 2009. http://www.thenational.ae/article/20090601/FOREIGN/705319847/1011/rss.

el-Amrani, Issandr. "Controlled Reform in Egypt, Neither Reformist nor Controlled." *Middle East Report*, December 2005. http://www.merip.org/mero/mero121505.html.

Brown, Nathan. *The Rule of Law in the Arab World: Courts in Egypt and the Gulf.* Cambridge: Cambridge University Press, 1997.

Carr, Sarah. "Supreme Constitutional Court Rules in Christian Reconverts Case." *Daily News Egypt*, June 9, 2009. http://www.thedailynewsegypt.com/article.aspx?ArticleID=22302.

CIA, *The World Factbook.* "*Egypt.*" https://www.cia.gov/library/publications/the-world-factbook/geos/eg.html.

el-Ghobashy, Mona. "Egypt's Paradoxical Elections." *Middle East Report*, Spring 2006. http://www.merip.org/mer/mer238/elghobashy.html.

Goldschmidt, Arthur, Amy Johnson, and Barak Salmoni, eds. *Re-Envisioning Egypt, 1919–1952.* Cairo: AUC Press, 2005.

al-Hilali, Ahmad Nabil, et al. *Fatma Zaki: Leader and Contender, 1921–2004.* Cairo, by author, 2004 (in Arabic).

Ibrahim, Saad Eddin. "Egypt's Unchecked Repression." *Washington Post*, August 21, 2007.

Jacob, Wilson Chacko. "Working Out Egypt: Masculinity and Subject Formation between Colonial Modernity and Nationalism, 1870–1940." Ph.D. Dissertation, New York University, 2005.

Marsot, Afaf Lutfi al-Sayyid. *Egypt's Liberal Experiment, 1922–1936.* Berkeley, CA: University of California Press, 1977.

Moustafa, Tamir. "Protests Hint at New Chapter in Egyptian Politics." *Middle East Report*, April 9, 2004. http://www.merip.org/mero/mero040904.html.

National Council for Women. *The National Council for Women.* Cairo: YAT, 2009. (Also interview with Farkhonda Hassan and tour of the facilities by officials in June 2009.)

Oweiss, Ibrahim, ed. *The Political Economy of Contemporary Egypt.* Washington, DC: CCAS, 1990.

Serageldin, Samia. *Cairo House.* Syracuse, NY: Syracuse University Press, 2000.

Note this is a work of fiction; however, it is based on the author's life and in particular for this chapter, events surrounding her uncle Fuad Serageldin.

Shehata, Samer, and Joshua Stacher. "Boxing in the Brothers." *Middle East Report*, August 2007. http://www.merip.org/mero/mero080807.html.

"Small Fry by the Half Dozen." *Al-Ahram Weekly,* November 23–29, 1995. http://weekly.ahram.org.eg/archives/parties/smallp.htm.

State Information Service. http://www.sis.gov.eg/En/Politics/.

Tadros, Mariz. "Egypt's Election All About Image, Almost." *Middle East Report*, September 2005. http://www.merip.org/mero/mero090605.html.

Tracy, William. "Jasper Yeates Brinton: An American Judge in Egypt." *Saudi Aramco World* (September/October 1970): 18–21.

Waterbury, John. *The Egypt of Nasser and Sadat: The Political Economy of Two Regimes.* Princeton, NJ: Princeton University Press, 1983.

Wickham, Carrie Rosefsky. *Mobilizing Islam: Religion, Activism, and Political Change in Egypt.* New York: Columbia University Press, 2002.

CHAPTER 4

Economy

Ramsey M. Awwad, Patrick F. Herman,
Aly Mansour, and Mona Russell

OVERVIEW

The Egyptian Economy Today

At the start of 2011, Egypt's economy was the 26th largest in the world. After the chaotic revolt against President Hosni Mubarak in January of that year, the economy has faced economic and political uncertainty resulting in a loss of productivity worth US$40 billion in 2011 (Euromonitor, "Egypt Country Profile," 2012) and a 12 percent decrease in output for the country's primary industries (Datamonitor 2012), with industrial output in the country's major industries falling approximately 12 percent by the third quarter (Datamonitor 2012). The turmoil that spilled onto the streets of Cairo, marking the final chapter of Mubarak's nearly 30-year rule, put an abrupt end to an average real GDP growth of 6.2 percent per year from 2006 until 2010. Egypt's GDP growth fell to a mere 1.6 percent ($1.23 billion) in 2011 (World Bank 2012), with total GDP listed at $214.18 billion. Following the unrest, the interim military-council government then led by Prime Minister Kamal Ganzouri requested aid to finance the new national budget and repair the damage wrought on the capital by weeks of violent protests. The United States responded by relieving $2 billion of Egyptian debt, and the World Bank offered $4 billion to assist in the creation of a new government. The International Monetary Fund (IMF) also offered $3 billion, but this fell short of the interim government's estimated need of $10 billion. The offer was therefore rejected with the hope that neighboring countries would pledge more money to Egypt's cause. Egypt has been in negotiations with Saudi Arabia and the United Arab Emirates (Euromonitor International, "Passport GMID," 2012), but the social unrest throughout the region has made it difficult to obtain the cooperation of other Arab neighbors. Egypt's upheaval was predated by Tunisian protests that overthrew President Zine El Abidine Ben Ali, and within months there were signs of unrest or instability in Libya, Bahrain, Syria, Yemen, and to some extent in Oman and Jordan as well.

While Egypt's new leaders were seeking to rebuild their nation, the outbreak of civil war in neighboring Libya intensified Egypt's economic hardship. Among other issues, the country has faced a sharp increase in unemployment as more than 150,000 Egyptians fled Libya to avoid the ensuing violence. As social and political unrest continued to wreak havoc throughout the Middle East and North Africa (MENA) region in what would become known as the "Arab Spring," investments in Egypt remained stagnant as inflation, unemployment, and regional instability continued to threaten local businesses, the industrial sector, and financial markets. Egypt's credit rating stands at near-junk status in 2012 as public debt equates to approximately 76 percent of the country's GDP and is expected to grow as the country invests in a range of new public projects: the government is working to enhance productivity in its industrial sectors and develop infrastructure to facilitate efforts by farmers to sell their agricultural products in Egypt's rural communities (Business Monitor, *Egypt Agribusiness Report*, 2011). In spite of these economic complications, the country did survive the crisis and has ultimately recovered from the 2008 recession nicely, despite major drops in foreign direct investments (FDIs) and widespread corruption (in 2011 Egypt was ranked 111th out of 180 countries listed in the Corruption Perception Index) (Datamonitor 2012).

Although the Arab Spring came with costly ramifications at social, political, and economic levels for the entire MENA region, the overthrow of autocratic regimes has opened up financial markets for new foreign and domestic investments. The economic control favored by Hosni Mubarak ensured that Egyptian financial markets remained generally isolated from the rest of the world and out of touch with the needs of local residents. Since his overthrow, the financial industry has liberalized, and its continued privatization has permitted expansion of the much-needed private sector. To date, most of Egypt's manufacturing output has been in the production of metals and fabrics, but the metals industry has stagnated in recent years despite persistent GDP growth. Domestic economic policy has taken a noticeable step toward reform since the interim government has taken control, but measures have yet to reduce unemployment, poverty, or narrow the income distribution gap. Despite a sharp rise in unemployment and an oversupply of labor, Egypt has implemented a 20 percent wage increase for the public sector as public works projects are expected to increase from 2012 onward (Euromontior International, *Passport GMID*, 2012). The new government is expected to enact laws that would make foreign investment and local business startups more attractive including bankruptcy laws, public–private partnership laws (that would greatly enhance public works projects), and a new tax collection policy. These reforms could create a promising economic future for Egypt, but current political uncertainty ensures that the short-term outlook remains pessimistic.

With businesses and investments threatened by continuous political tension and social unrest, unemployment in Egypt rose from 8.9 percent in 2010 to almost 12 percent in 2011. One of the main causes for this jump was the return of hundreds of thousands of Egyptian workers fleeing from unrest in Libya and Syria. A decrease in steel production in 2011 has also taken a toll on industrial workers, who account for roughly 15 percent of the labor force. With foreign investors wary of Egypt's stability, the country faces a difficult task in developing a sustainable economy that will both employ the Egyptian workforce and ease poverty to decrease government spending on welfare. As of 2011, welfare and social security expenditures accounted for almost half of the overall government budget. Additionally, Egypt's trade imbalance has been growing as annual imports have persistently exceeded exports by an average of almost 50 percent since 2006, indicating a severe need for local production that can withstand competition with Asian Pacific nations. Whereas the country had been a suitable and cheap export platform for foreign investors, revenues from foreign investors in the export sector have dropped as the political situation destabilized.

Egyptian anti-government activists clash with riot police in Cairo, Egypt on January 28, 2011. (AP Photo/Ben Curtis, File)

Egypt's Economic Structure

In comparison with most of the region, Egypt's economy is relatively well diversified, specializing in the manufacturing of metals, textiles and fabrics, oil and petrochemicals, and agricultural products. Its revenue from the Suez Canal, exports, and tourism is also higher than most regional competitors. Though much of the population is impoverished, the Egyptian economy invests in a range of industries that give it a comparative advantage over other MENA member states. Egypt's investments in agricultural products such as cotton, fruit, and livestock ensure that it is not dependent on any one source of income in the way some oil-exporting Gulf States have been for decades. Despite this diversification, Egypt's economy has been on a continuous path to hardship. The country's currency is the Egyptian pound (LE), which has remained unpegged since 2003 and has inflated at an annual average rate of 10 percent ever since (World Bank 2012). In the face of being the most populated country in the Arab world with approximately 84.2 million residents as of 2011, it unfortunately has one of the highest poverty rates in the region and one of the highest unemployment especially among youth (the bulk of the unemployed population is between 20 and 24 years old). Nevertheless, Egypt ranks among the top in the MENA region in terms of equality of wealth. This score is based on its Gini index ranking of 36.3 percent (100 represents the lowest extreme of income distribution and 0 represents the highest extreme of income distribution).

The agricultural sector remains the country's leading industry. This sector employs 32.9 percent of Egypt's labor force, and it was left almost intact in 2011 as productivity rose by just over 4 percent. Despite Egypt's desire to develop and modernize its urban communities, government officials plan to expand the agricultural sector even further to become almost entirely self-sufficient for wheat by 2022. Near the Nile River delta, cotton continues to be heavily cultivated and remains Egypt's most cherished cash crop; exports of cotton and related fabric grew by $200 million per year from 2007 to 2011. Famous for its quality, Egyptian cotton is among the most in-demand and exported cotton fabric in the world. The sugar, wheat, corn, milk, and cheese industries have maintained a steady growth rate for several years averaging hundreds of tons annually.

Irrespective of sustained economic growth, Egypt's large unemployed labor force is an ominous indication of the lack of skilled laborers in the general population. While there is no shortage of workers, many public sector businesses have trouble finding skilled and competent workers. Productivity has been on the rise though, nearly doubling from $4,902.0 per worker in 2006 to $9,224.7 in 2011. While gender inequality in the workforce is generally seen as less extensive in Egypt than the rest of the region, 30.8 percent of employable Egyptian women are unemployed—a stark contrast to the 6.0 percent of unemployment rate for men. Other major employers in Egypt's economy are educational, social, health, community, and personal services sectors that combine to employ just over 20 percent of the workforce. Employment in construction has grown to 11.0 percent of the workforce in 2011 with high demand for housing in an improving real-estate sector. Labor issues remain at the forefront of Egyptian economic problems, which will be treated at greater length later in this chapter.

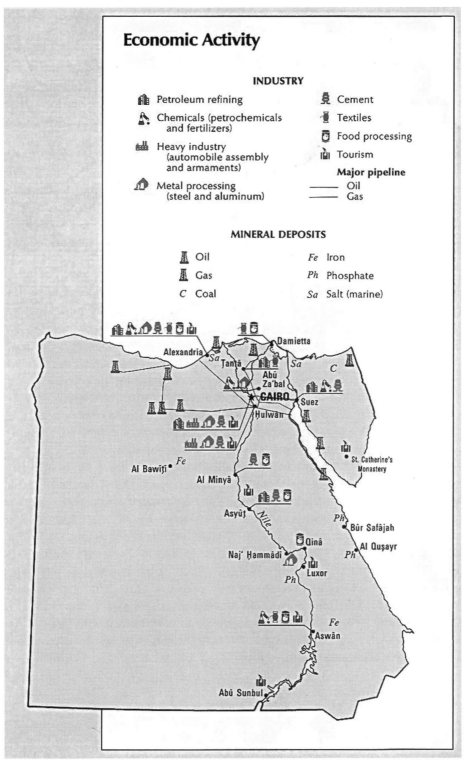

Economic activity map of Egypt, 1993. (Perry-Castaneda Library/University of Texas at Austin)

EGYPT'S INDUSTRY

Egypt's Industrial Revolutions

The first industrial revolution in Egypt occurred in the 19th century during the rule of Muhammad Ali (1805–1848). As discussed in Chapter 2, Muhammad Ali has also been known as the founder of modern Egypt. His renaissance began by building shipyards on the Nile and in Alexandria, building factories to produce for mass domestic consumption, building small dams and water gates to regulate and maximize the use of the Nile water, renovating and introducing mechanization to agriculture, and building military factories. In general, there were a number of industrial projects designed to benefit Egyptian society and stimulate economic growth. He continued the revolution in the agricultural sector and expanded the cultivated land in Egypt from 1 million acres before his reign to almost 5 million acres by the end of Ismail's in 1879. By 1952, it had grown to 6 million acres. Ismail continued to aggressively rebuild the cities of Cairo and Alexandria until Cairo was sometimes known as the "Paris of the East" or "the new Paris" (see Chapters 2, 5, and 6).

In the mid-19th century, Great Britain succeeded in freezing or shutting down most of the industries built by Muhammad Ali and his sons. International geo-strategic interest grew in the region after the opening of the Suez Canal in 1869 (see Chapters 1 and 2), particularly for the French who sponsored the multi-national company that built the canal and the British who bought Egypt's shares in the canal in 1875. Egypt was forced to sell its shares due to bankruptcy, and this moment of economic vulnerability came after cotton prices had spiked in Egypt during the American Civil War (1861–1865) and then declined or stagnated thereafter. This vulnerability, which was followed by loans and indebtedness, would be one of the major contributing factors to the British occupation in 1882.

After World War I, an uprising of intellectuals tried to fight the British occupation by rebuilding the Egyptian national economy. The most successful project was the Banque-Misr group founded in 1920. It was founded as an agricultural bank and was also the first private national bank in Egypt. By 1925, Banque-Misr had started to become an industrial bank, and since then has been responsible for most of the industries that exist in Egypt to this day. It is the only private bank that has survived for more than 91 years without ever filing for bankruptcy, despite numerous attacks and instances of government interference since its founding. The establishment and success of Banque-Misr can be considered as Egypt's second industrial revolution. Banque-Misr succeeded in building and promoting companies in almost every sector. A far more detailed account of how the bank was able to help build and shape the Egyptian economy can be found later in this chapter.

Corruption and Revolution

After the 1952 military coup d'état, Egyptian policy shifted to focus on ventures in heavy industry. This plan was supported by eastern-bloc countries and coincided with the government's interest in adopting, or rather imposing, a socialist system.

Most of the heavy industries built during the 1960s failed after heavily indebting the government, and Banque-Misr companies worked for more than two decades to pay off these debts and projects. By the mid-1970s, President Anwar Sadat adopted an economic open-door policy (infitah) in order to encourage new investors and end the socialist system that had hurt the national economy for more than a decade. The policy seemed necessary, but being loosely applied, it allowed for numerous problems (which will be discussed in greater detail later in this chapter) that counteracted the benefits it might have brought to the Egyptian economy. The 1980s were a time of economic fluctuations, but by the mid-1990s corruption started growing exponentially and has been a huge feature of the Egyptian economy until present day.

Between 1990 and 2011, the economy and industrial sector could best be described as chaotic. Corruption appears to have become an institutionalized norm of Egyptian life. As records are made public, it appears that state property was frequently gifted or sold at nominal values to friends and associates close to the ruling family and party, and many new companies were founded with little potential benefit to Egyptian society. While the older Banque-Misr companies had been directly concerned with building companies that would promote Egyptian society, the new corporations concerned themselves entirely with their own profit and revenues without any focus on societal improvement. The success of these companies was often based on their affiliation with a corrupt regime that granted them illegal privileges and opportunities that were not offered to other corporations.

As of 2011, the industrial situation in Egypt has radically changed. Inspired by a successful Tunisian revolution a little over a month before, thousands to millions of protestors converged on Tahrir Square in the heart of downtown Cairo in January 2011. Despite government efforts to cut off mobile telecommunication facilities (violating codes of the telecommunication industry), demonstrators were able to communicate via landlines, Facebook, Twitter, and other social networks. Demonstrations led by youth groups, human rights activists, and employees and workers in various government and public sector industries soon spread to almost all Egyptian cities. Hundreds of young men and women were shot dead or beaten by riot central security police and government security snipers in a failed attempt to end the revolution. In the major cities, demonstrators spanning the economic spectrum expressed their anger at the dictatorship and police state that lasted for almost 30 years under the presidency of Hosni Mubarak. In smaller cities and towns, demonstrators from various industries (especially state-owned industries) demonstrated against poverty, corruption, unemployment, and the autocratic governance. The activists took their anger to the streets determined to make a change, and after 18 days of protests, bloodshed, and sacrifice, most of government officials, including Mubarak, were either ousted or fled the country with unknown sums of money stolen from Egypt via government-owned banks. The revolution resulted in a fear of economic collapse stemming from expected strikes by employees from several public sectors as chaos devastated the country's commerce. The demonstrators during the January revolution complained that the ousted regime's pessimistic portrayal of the country's recovery prior to the revolution spread a gloomy picture among the public, and in some ways kept Egypt in a continuous state of unrest. The demonstrators have also voiced that the post-revolution media has further harmed the economy, and some have speculated that it is pushing for a return to the ousted regime in order to save Egyptian society. While the economic concerns of the revolutionaries have been varied, the standard of living continues to be a clear, widespread complaint; the World Bank estimates that as many as 40 percent of Egyptians were living under the poverty level in 2010 prior to the revolution. Other local sources put the estimate for the overall poverty rate at almost 70 percent prior to the events in Tahrir Square.

Egypt's Industries after the Revolution

Prior to the 1970s, agricultural products made up 87 percent of all exports from Egypt, but this changed in that decade as agriculture lost its position as the country's leading economic sector. Agricultural exports dropped from being 87 percent of the total Egyptian exports in 1960 to 35 percent in 1974, and by the year 2001 they had fallen to only 11 percent. In the year 2000 the agricultural sector accounted for only 17 percent of the gross domestic product (GDP) and employed 34 percent of the total workforce. In 1999, the largest agricultural outputs included corn (9.35 million tons), wheat (6.347 million tons), rice (5.816 million tons), potatoes (1.9 million tons), and oranges (1.525 million tons). Egypt is also a substantial producer of sugarcane, fruits and vegetables, and animal fodder. Citrus, dates, and grapes are the main fruits by acreage. The government has historically exercised a strong degree of control over agriculture to both ensure the best use of irrigation water and curtail the planting of cotton in favor of food grains. As of the late 1960s substantial quantities of wheat were imported, especially from the United States and Russia, but wheat yields have increased significantly since 1970, and as mentioned earlier in this chapter Egypt has a goal of being self-sufficient in wheat production by 2022. Rice production has also been high enough since the mid-1970s that significant quantities have been exported.

The revolution has certainly impacted the agricultural sector in Egypt, and by the end of 2011, Business Monitor International (BMI) summarized their view of the situation as follows: "Because the political situation has not yet been completely settled, the Egyptian government is still cautious about food price inflation. In fact, the interim government has taken several measures to boost the country's main crop production in order to increase supply on the domestic market. For example, for grains the government introduced new seed varieties, boosting yields and thus output. For rice the government was reluctant to impose the normal area restrictions on water preservation and extended a ban on rice exports to ensure that the local market is well supplied" (Business Monitor International 2012). In line with interim government's agricultural measures to boost main crop production, it is expected that the livestock industry would recover on a cheaper and more available feed stock.

The outlook for the agricultural sector is generally quite positive. Egypt's fertile area today totals about 8 million acres (3.3 million hectares), about one quarter of which is land reclaimed from the desert over the past 60 years. The reclaimed lands add only 7 percent to the total value of agricultural production. Even though only 3 percent of Egypt's land is arable, it is extremely productive and can be cropped two or even three times annually. Most arable land is cropped at least twice a year, but agricultural productivity is limited by salinity, which afflicts an estimated 35 percent of cultivated land. In a 2011 report released by BMI, forecasts expect wheat production growth of 19.7 percent (9.4 million tons) by 2016. This growth is expected in part thanks to government support and the liberalization of state-owned arable lands. Sugar consumption is forecasted to grow 10.9 percent (3 million tons) by 2016 as a result of growth in the confectionary and soft drink sectors with an increasing population and rising disposable incomes stimulating demand (Business Monitor International 2012). Increasing domestic demand should have a positive impact on the sugarcane industry. In October 2011, the interim government, then headed by Dr. Essam Sharaf, announced that it would extend the ban on exporting rice until further notice. The decision was taken to avoid any shortage in basic food supplies or price increase. The ban started in 2008 and will probably continue at least through the end of the interim government in June 2012. Interim government officials carefully considered decisions increasing the price of basic commodities and further hurt consumers after the revolution (Business Monitor International 2012). This government was the first to candidly speak of ending subsidies, and its approach was cautious and gradual. Its recall by the SCC, interim replacement by SCAF, and uncertain parliamentary future make the future of subsidies and their abatement open to question.

Egyptian cotton has long been a staple of Egyptian economy, but exports have decreased in 2011 thanks to the controversy between farmers and traders over the price at which the country's 2011–2012 cotton crops should be sold. The price of cotton has dropped sharply following the global recession in the first decade of the 21st century, and the price controversy has reduced the 2011 cotton export from August until the end of October to only 6,854 tons of cotton, compared to 110,000 tons over the same period in the previous year. The primary reason for the reduction is believed to be promises and poor forecasts made by the Mubarak ministry of agriculture encouraging farmers to increase cotton plantings considerably for the 2011–2012 season. Cotton production is forecasted to grow 15.7 percent (694,600 tons) by 2016. This increase will come as a result of higher prices that have encouraged farmers to increase planted area and yields, and is expected to continue for at least few more years (Business Monitor International 2012). The ministry promised high export prices, but local cotton wholesalers have significantly reduced their buying price as a result of lowered global prices (Business Monitor International 2012).

In 2012, al-Azhar University hosted a conference attended by almost the entire political spectrum of post-revolution Egypt. It was announced at this conference that Egypt did not receive a penny from any Western or non-Western entity during

Workers handle raw cotton at a mill in Tanta, Egypt, November 8, 2001. It is Egypt's second-largest export earner after oil, roughly $500 million a year, including textiles. (AP Photo/ Philip Mark)

or following the January 2011 revolution. This statement does not reflect debt relief discussed earlier in this section, nor does it take into account Egypt's relationship with the United States since 1979. Nevertheless, the U.S. Congress put new restrictions into play to make sure that Egypt remained in conformity with free and fair elections, and the Obama administration while able to maneuver around restrictions bristled at the treatment of pro-democracy NGOs even after the elections in late 2011.

The fact that Egypt has been able to survive without significant external help (especially considering its heavy payments of past debts totaling almost $3.2 billion) shows that Egypt probably has one of, if not, the strongest economies in the region. Despite the turmoil of revolution, the economy has proven resilient, and the interim governments have been able to keep prices from rising to any great extent. In January 2012, *Daily News Egypt* reported that the World Economic Forum emphasized that Egypt's economic recovery and future growth in the industrial sector should be based on long-term private-sector small business enterprises. The forum focused on a long-term vision for Egypt's economic well-being rather than the short-term solutions designed to achieve immediate social justice. The forum advised the interim government not to push the economy too hard and to minimize government interference and avoid any quick fixes. They suggested focusing on domestic and regional markets by supporting small businesses in an effort to promote sustainable long-term economic growth. Once production resumes, cotton prices rise again, and corruption is under control, the GDP is expected to witness a growth rate equal to or higher than 2010. The revolution's main objective was to restore human rights and increase the national standard of living; the active public and youth groups involved in the revolution mainly concerned themselves with the problems of social injustice, the disconnectedness of the ruling regime, the high rates of unemployment, and the lack of adequate health and educational services. Nevertheless, the World Economic Forum's suggestions clearly emphasized that social gains from the revolution should not come at the cost of Egypt's future economy.

At the end of 2010, Egypt's foreign reserves were at $36 billion. By the end of 2011, the foreign reserves had dropped to approximately $18 billion (Abdellatif 2012). It would seem that this sharp drop could jeopardize Egypt's ability to cover the cost of imported goods in the near future, but the reduction in foreign aid or loans coupled with factors like the drop in cotton prices and lower tourism rates means that the risk of depletion is almost negligible. There is also some speculation that the ousted regime (or its emergence in some new form) has been exerting restless energy to cause as much damage to the Egyptian economy as possible in an attempt to prove the failure of the January revolution and to escape any trials that might deprive it of ill-gotten wealth from the past 30 years. In January 2012, Reuters reported that FDI in Egypt dropped from $1.6 billion to $0.44 billion; in essence, 75 percent of FDI projects were terminated, suspended, or liquidated (Abdellatif 2012). Although this phenomenon at first appears entirely negative, there are some upsides to these numbers. Long-term economists and entrepreneurs view this amount of drop as a positive indicator of a strong economy that was only marginally affected by tremendous weakening factors. To this point the Egyptian economy has proven itself strong and stable, and also capable of withstanding expected and unexpected shocks. Hoda Selim, an economist at the Economic Research Forum, blamed the interim governments for not implementing measures to improve employability rates (especially for youth) by offering incentives for employers to hire in 2011. She suggested that incentives could include a taxation grace period for young or initial entrepreneurs, and on-the-job training subsidies to boost new projects and decrease the unemployment rate (Abdellatif 2012).

Alaa Ezz, secretary general of the Federation of Egyptian Industries, has indicated that the infrastructure projects being initiated at the time of writing are largely being subcontracted in order to create jobs and lower the unemployment rate. He added that the Federation of Industries is planning to design mega-infrastructure projects in order to enhance investments (mainly local investments) and offer new job opportunities for youth and the unemployed. Ezz also announced that in September 2011, Deauville, a French investment company, offered a loan of $73 billion to some Arab Spring states: Morocco, Tunisia, Egypt, and Jordan. Almost $38 billion will be funded by the G8 (a panel of the eight world's largest economies), and $35 billion will be funded by the IMF for infrastructure projects planned to take place in the region. Ezz suggested that an effort should be made to solicit local engineers and consultants to propose feasible projects that would generate interest from local and foreign investors. Ezz imagined large-scale infrastructure improvement projects such as new airports, water plants, and highways that would create jobs for contractors and subcontractors. The necessary industrial products such as building materials and construction equipment would also create new industries and add liquidity to the market (Abdellatif 2012).

Minoush Abdelmeguid, managing director of Union Capital, has observed that Egyptian banks often ignore smaller businesses in favor of supporting mostly bigger corporations. She points out that similar penalties and policies are applicable to smaller businesses as to larger corporations, a practice that has forced hundreds of young entrepreneurs to go out of business or declare bankruptcy. She also notes that banks have not been willing to compromise or offer grace periods for young entrepreneurs, as was the policy of Banque-Misr prior to 1960 (Mansour and Khalifa 2011).

Magda Kandil, head of the Egyptian Center for Economic Studies, summed up the economic goals of post-revolution Egypt nicely for the *Daily News of Egypt* saying that democracy cannot be fostered without a basis of economic prosperity. She added that the economic crunch remains the primary threat to the ongoing January 2011 revolution and warned that economic pressures are an obstacle to social stability (Abdellatif 2012). She felt that the Supreme Council of the Armed Forces (SCAF), the interim ruling government after the January revolution blamed the economic decline on strikers and protesters, but lacked an in-depth economic vision. Since its inception, the interim government has increased pensions, salaries, and subsidies instead of focusing on stimulating the economy, and Kandil questioned the logic of appealing to the masses with a social agenda without stimulating the production necessary to support it. She also mentions that the interim governments did not support small businesses when they could have done so by facilitating credit offerings that could lead to thousands of jobs and result in a sustainable economic boost. The policy presented by SCAF and implemented by the interim governments led to worse results for both democracy and the economy. Thanks to low production in some sectors the economy has been slow since the revolution, and inflation rose by more than 1 percent in 2011. Kandil refused to accept government claims that it would provide jobs; she maintained that jobs are provided by the private sector and the role of government is to offer credit opportunities so that the private sector, especially small enterprises, can start producing to benefit society through a strong economy (Abdellatif 2012). So while Egypt's economy works to rebound from the chaos of the revolution, the exact ways in which the government should support industry remain controversial and unclear.

LABOR

Labor Market Conditions in 2012

Among the many complications facing Egypt in terms of its economic progress and development is the major inefficiency of the nation's labor market. This problem is a contributing factor to the high unemployment that has plagued Egypt's economy for decades and causes stagnation in overall productivity. There has been improvement as the country continues to make significant strides toward privatization, but the general business environment still suffers from a significant lack of skilled workers and frequent mismatching of workers to their talents. Unfeasible labor codes and a lack of adherence to contracts make human resourcing a challenging aspect of day-to-day business in the country. The continuity of the population's "brain drain" continues to deprive much of the labor pool of its supply of educated or skilled workers, with many Egyptians expatriating to find work in other countries, typically in emerging markets such as the Gulf Cooperation Council (GCC) states, which possess greater economic prospects and opportunities.

There are many factors influencing Egyptians' preferences for expatriating such as offerings of relatively higher salaries from foreign entities, flexibility of wage determination, the relative ease of starting a business or finding work, opportunities for continuing education, and better working and living conditions. In 2010, out of 183 listed countries, the World Bank ranked Egypt 106 for "Ease of Doing Business," 156 for "Dealing with Construction Permits," 148 for "Enforcing Contracts," and 132 for "Closing a Business" (World Bank 2012). Egypt's rankings suffered even more as a result of the uprisings in 2011, dropping to an overall ranking of 108 for "Ease of Doing Business" that year, followed by another drop in 2012 to 110. Prior to the 2011 uprising, however, the easing of restrictions on foreign investment and laws protecting the interests of foreign investors, such as Investment Law No. 8 of 1997, contributed to high inflows of FDI in the years leading to the uprising. The law states that "companies may not be confiscated or nationalized. . . . may be entirely owned by foreigners. . . . [and] foreign experts' salaries are exempted from income tax if their stay in Egypt is less than one year" ("Laws Library" 2012, Investment Law No. 8 of 1997, 2009).

Dependency ratio is the ratio of anyone aged 0–14 years and 65+ years to anyone aged between 15 and 64 years to account for Egyptians who do not depend on their own source of income. Despite a growing population, the level of dependency among Egyptians remains at healthy levels. The dependency ratio has gradually dropped since its 25-year high of 78 percent in 1986 to just below 57 percent in 2011. Thus, for every person in the population that is between 15 and 65 years of age, there are approximately 0.57 persons who are either younger than 15 or older than 65. One major cause for the drop is improved family planning. Birth rates have declined by 25 percent over the past 35 years while fertility rates have decreased by half. Still, the average number of births per family stands at more than two children; since the vast majority of Egyptians who are emigrating from their land to seek opportunity abroad are only expatriated temporarily, the population of Egypt is expected to continue its growth to 105 million inhabitants by the year 2030. Drops in infant mortality rates will also contribute to the growth.

Another current detriment to domestic economic efficiency in Egypt is the lack of accessibility to loans and external financing. Interest rates have remained above 10 percent since 1978, reaching as high as 20 percent in 1992, and finally lowering to 11 percent after a gradual 20-year decline. Such high rates can be attributed to long-term regional political and economic issues that were worsened by unreasonable collective bargaining practices used in NDP reform negotiations by Egypt's influential trade union. Efforts to privatize the economy were stunted by such practices on several occasions. Despite the fact that Egypt's former president, Hosni Mubarak, is facing a life sentence for failing to stop the killing of protestors in Tahrir Square, he managed to escape corruption charges alleging that he looted billions of dollars from the country's foreign aid receipts and public businesses. Currently, his sons await trial on separate charges of corruption.

Regional conflicts have had a tremendous impact on economic policy in the country. In 1992, the economic effect of the Gulf War was still felt throughout the region, as many Egyptians who were working in Kuwait returned unemployed. Additionally, Suez Canal revenues suffered losses as a result of the conflict. The beginning of Egypt's privatization plan and its collaboration with the IMF and World Bank on the Economic Reform and Structural Adjustment Program were in the negotiating stages in 1991. The proposed plan and proceeding talks prompted uncertainty for global investors for over a year as fragile and unprecedented discussions that would perhaps reshape Egypt's economy were, with regard to their ultimate outcomes, unclear. Cairo's cooperation with the West in the midst of the conflict with Iraq provided favorable grounds for the Egyptians over the course of the negotiations, in which the United States Agency for International Development (USAID) and the European Union (EU) among other international organizations participated. At the same time, internal pressure from unemployed Egyptians was mounting on the government to resolve the unemployment issue.

A boat coasts through a section of the Suez Canal in Egypt. This waterway is vital to Egypt's economy. (Corel)

Labor Laws and Unemployment

Although the country experienced a healthy rate of GDP growth between 1993 and 2011, economists assert that "only a small proportion of Egyptians actually benefited from this economic growth" (Euromonitor International, Economic Briefing, 2012), citing the use of "political connections" as a typical business practice that carries major economic advantages for those who are well connected professionally. Advantages in job security, level of salary, and retirement packages were commonly associated with a worker's business contacts and reputation. Such practices can be rightfully attributed to the mismatching of workers to their appropriate positions, either undermining or exaggerating their talents or level of expertise. With an estimated total labor force of 27.1 million participants, Egyptian unemployment reached a new high of 11.7 percent by 2012, representing 23 percent of the total unemployed population for the entire MENA region. For a country with the highest population in the Middle East, accommodating more than an estimated 82 million residents, such statistics bear a heavy burden on regional economic performance. While labor in the region is cheap, the inefficient employment of such a populous labor market—comprising more than 20 percent of the entire region's workforce—carries major economic consequences, such as, the impact on regional consumer expenditure or international trade.

TRADE, FINANCE, AND BANQUE-MISR

The Egyptian Financial System

In the early 1920s, the Egyptian financial system developed with the founding of the Banque-Misr. The bank was founded by Talaat Harb, an Egyptian entrepreneur who obtained his law degree from Fuad I University (now Cairo University) and who later visited several European countries after World War I to study banking and financial systems. During the war, Harb was charged with organizing estates of large landowners, and he was able to win their confidence as well as that of other merchants affiliated with large land companies such as Société Foncière d'Egypte (Radwan 1970).

Banque-Misr was founded in 1920 as an agricultural bank by a conglomeration of landowners, land companies, merchants, factory owners, high ranking officials, and the president of the General Agricultural Syndicate. The bank had a startup capital of LE80,000. In its first decade, the bank went through a series of expansions as the General Agricultural Syndicate pushed the founders to form joint-stock companies in order to minimize or prevent speculation, decrease the middlemen between cultivators and consumers, supervise the trade of crops, and establish agricultural cooperatives (Deeb 1976). The addition of new shareholders increased the available capital to LE400,000, and soon after the bank was able to found several new national companies between 1924 and 1927 including Misr Paper Manufacturing Company, Misr Trading and Ginning Company,

Misr Silk Weaving Company, Misr Fisheries, and Misr Cotton Weaving and Spinning Company (Deeb 1976).

Recruiting Diverse Investors for Banque-Misr (Deeb 1976)

Egypt's post–World War I economy was extremely unstable, and 81 labor strikes shook the country from 1919 to 1921. The national companies founded by the Banque-Misr eventually solved most of the economic problems in the aftermath of World War I, but the sole dependence on shareholders from one economic sector constituted a weakness and a threat to Banque-Misr operations. The generous investment of landowners recruited by Talaat Harb had allowed the Banque-Misr to start its first bank-owned or shared national companies, but diversification of products and investments was not enough to guarantee the bank during the great economic depression. Banque-Misr had to lower its dependence on landowners and work toward strengthening its ties with local merchants.

Talaat Harb and other founding members of Banque-Misr were prominent members of the first Egyptian chamber of commerce established in November 1913, and in 1919 Harb used the Cairo Chamber of Commerce to call on all Egyptians to buy shares of Banque-Misr. Although Cairo had the sole chamber of commerce in 1919, after the revolution of that year the Cairo branch helped establish five further chambers of commerce in Daqahlia, Gharbiya, Alexandria, Mit-Ghamr, and Zifta over the following three years.

Talaat Harb played a vital role in forming and restructuring new and existing chambers of commerce in the mid-1920s and helped them focus on strengthening the ties between merchants and industrialists while improving and encouraging national industries. After the cotton crisis in 1926, the cotton prices dropped significantly causing a critical loss for cultivators as well as merchants. The chambers of commerce were well situated to address this issue by emphasizing cotton ginning, weaving, and textile industries to consume the national cotton crop while promoting diversification of crops. They also favored increasing railway freight rates and customs duties on similar imported products to help protect domestic industry.

Joint-Stock Companies Established by Banque-Misr 1929–1939 (Banque-Misr 2012)

In 1929, a Banque-Misr report emphasized the dire need to establish a national industrial bank to finance new industries as a continuation of the economic independence policy following the instability after World War I. The Egyptian government agreed with Banque-Misr on creating protective tariffs, giving preference to local products even when they exceeded the cost of foreign duplicates by as much as 10 percent and giving preferential railway freight rates to local industries, but did not establish an industrial bank. The national government's failure to do so left the ambitions of the new national petty bourgeoisie unrealized, and so the Federation of Industries (an industrial chamber of commerce) started inviting Egyptian industrialists to join in order to expand its activities and capital. The federation had once been almost entirely dominated by non-Egyptians, but as can be seen in Figure 4.1, Egyptian industrialists began joining in large numbers. In less than 15 years (between 1925 and 1939), the number of Egyptians in the federation increased from 16 to 67, or from roughly 12 percent of the organization to more than 50 percent.

At least part of this movement was based on Egyptian desire to be involved in rebuilding the country. Taylor described it as a petty bourgeois movement hallmarked by a need for participation, a desire to contribute to decision making, and an aspiration toward identity, sense-of-belonging, and self-confidence. By joining the Federation of Industries the petty bourgeoisie gained access to capital to start new ventures through Banque-Misr or via the joint-stock companies that it started. Also, the investors realized the benefits of new industrial projects as a means to lower unemployment rates and offer better social, health, education, and infrastructural services to the society at large (Banque-Misr 2012).

During the 1930s, Banque-Misr took over the mission of establishing needed industries by inviting local and foreign investors to establish 28 new industrial and business projects employing some 250,000 workers with a combined startup capital of approximately LE120 million. Examples of these industries can be found in Table 4.1.

As is evident in Table 4.1, there was great diversity in the projects funded by the bank. This was necessary to reduce the market risk of loss and to optimize on revenues and profits. To this end most companies simply did not establish their headquarters in either Cairo or Alexandria, the two largest cities in Egypt, and the

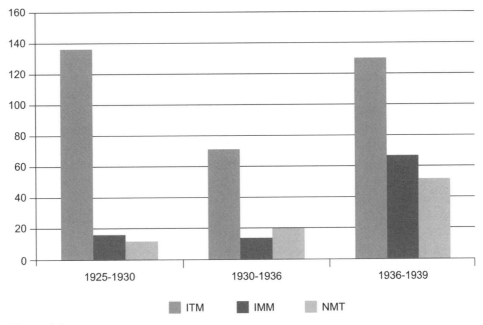

Figure 4.1

TABLE **4.1**

Company	Egyptian	Location	Partnership	Year	Capita
Misr-Air	60%	Cairo, Alexandria, Luxor	British (40%)	1932	LE20k
Misr Insurance	43%	Cairo, provinces	Bowring/ Assicurazioni	1934	LE200k
Misr Maritime	85%	Alexandria, provinces	Cox & Kings	1934	LE40k
Misr Tourism	51%	Cairo, Alexandri, Luxor, Red-Sea	Non-Egyptian shares (49%)	1934	LE7k
Misr Beida Dyers	51%	Simuha, Alexandria	Non- (Egyptian) shares (49%)	1938	LE52k
Misr Spinning & Dying of Fine Cotton	51%	Kafr-al-Dawar	Non- (Egyptian) shares (49%)	1938	LE500k
Misr des Tabacs et Cigarettes	100%	Giza	n/a	1938	LE40k
Misr pour l'Industrie d'Huiles	100%	Kafr-al-Zayat	n/a	1938	LE30k
Misr des Mines et Carrieres	100%	Red-Sea	n/a	1939	LE40k

Source: Radwan (1970).

few companies that were based out of Cairo and Alexandria also had branches in other provinces. Egyptian ownership of these companies ranged from 43 to 100 percent as foreign involvement was often encouraged to promote investment, and sometimes necessary for either funding or for expertise that could not be found in Egypt.

As is evident in Table 4.2 and Figure 4.2, the initial capital of Banque-Misr from 1920 to 1940 was almost LE1 million, but jumped to more than 2.7 million Egyptian pounds by 1945. By 1960, the available capital of Banque-Misr jumped again to 9.2 million Egyptian pounds. In essence, Banque-Misr capital increased more than nine times from 1920 to 1960.

Religious Guidelines for Banking

While creating new companies, Banque-Misr always needed to be conscious of societal religious expectations. According to the Torah, the Bible, and the Quran,

TABLE 4.2

Company	Year	Egyptian %	Capital-Initial (LE in 1000)	Capital 1945 (LE in 1000)	Capital 1959–60 (LE in 1000)	Bank Misr share (LE in 1000)
Misr Printing & Publishing	1922	65%	5	50	50	36
Misr Cotton Ginning	1924	23%	30	250	250	58
Misr Shipping	1925	85%	40	150	150	127
Misr-Studios	1925	81%	15	75	100	81
Misr Silk Weaving	1927	74%	10	250	1000	741
Misr Fisheries	1927	95%	20	75	75	71
Misr Cotton Exporting	1927	61%	120	160	400	245
Misr Industrial-Mart	1932	28%	5	80	500	138
Misr-Air	1932	60%	20	80	1350	810
Misr Insurance*	1934	43%	200	200	500	215
Misr Maritime	1934	50%	100	200	750	375
Misr Tourism*	1934	48%	7	7	50	24
Misr Baida Dyers*	1938	36%	52	52	2000	720
Misr Concrete*	1938	5.60%	6	6	300	17
Misr pour l'Industrie d'Huiles*	1938	78%	30	30	75	58
Misr Spinning & Weaving, Mahala	1938	26%	300	1000	4000	1040

(Continued)

TABLE 4.2 (*Continued*)

Company	Year	Egyptian %	Capital-Initial (LE in 1000)	Capital 1945 (LE in 1000)	Capital 1959–60 (LE in 1000)	Bank Misr share (LE in 1000)
Misr des Mines et Carrieres	1939	88%	40	40	40	30
Misr Pharmaceuticals*	1940	10%	10	10	300	30
Misr Polyester	1946	8.60%	2000	—	3000	257
Misr Hotelier	1955	5%	1750	—	100	2000
Misr Dairy and Food	1956	19%	400	—	750	143
Misr Chemicals	1956	25%	2000	—	2000	500
Misr Spinning & Weaving, Shebeen-el-Kom	1959	25%	2000	—	2000	500
Total	1945		1010	2715		
Total	1960				19740	8216

Joint-stock companies established by Banque-Misr 1920–1960 (Radwan, F; Kamel, R; Banque-Misr Web site)
Source: Kamel (1993).

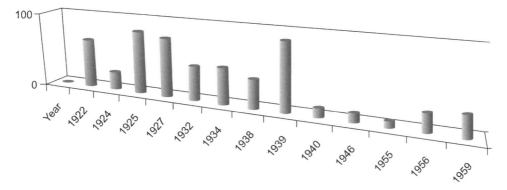

Figure 4.2:

charging interest of any kind is forbidden and considered a major sin (Feiglin 2010). Banque-Misr and its projects needed to abide by this teaching. Bank-owned projects are considered interest-free operations since all investors share the net revenue after deducting all administrative and other bank expenses. Islamic banking also offers a variety of interest-free programs that follow religious guidelines. Several of these programs are listed as follows:

- *Murabaḥa*: Selling needed commodities to customers for a price higher than wholesalers, but within the range of most retailers and therefore at market value. Installments on a loan are paid without interest and several grace periods may be granted. If the customer defaults completely on paying back the loan, the bank has the right to repossess the item after settling a fair arrangement with the customer where the customer may regain some of what he or she has already paid.
- *Ijara*: Leasing a property with the option to apply all payments toward buying the property at its regular value with a marginal increase for repairs. All repairs are borne by the bank except for regular maintenance, for example, oil changes. No interest is charged for faulty payments as there are grace periods built into such contracts.
- *Musharaka*: Joint projects shared between the bank and other companies, entrepreneurs, manufacturers, or contractors. Losses and gains may be split between both parties (bank and business partner) according to shares or mutual agreements specified in the contract.
- *Mudaraba*: Either 100 percent bank-owned projects or money borrowed by a credible contractor or entrepreneur who shares profits according to contract. Losses are totally borne by the bank, and for bank-owned projects revenues and profits are distributed among all shareholders according to their shares after deducting all expenses and a percentage for reinvestment in existing or new projects. The bank has no right to earn any profit for itself.

- *Takaful*: An insurance pool by a holding company that invests part or all its assets in any Islamic banking activities. The investment has to be within the region where the insurance policyholders live, and revenues are distributed to policyholders on a periodic basis. These are usually smaller than banking deposits as a bigger share of the revenue is kept to meet insurance needs within the society.

After centuries of almost complete negligence, the Islamic banking system restarted in Cairo in 1975, when it became an option to the general public. It soon spread to the Arab World, the near-east, Asia, and even in Europe and the American continents. The success of Islamic banks and Islamic banking systems have attracted huge masses from the general public due to their low risk and steady revenue for their customers. In addition to pure Islamic banks, most banks in European countries have started to have at least Islamic windows. In 2009 the Vatican endorsed Islamic banking systems as a way to solve the economic and financial crises in Europe and the West, but it would seem that Islamic banking was spreading well before any such endorsement (Segre 2009).

Although Islamic banking and financial systems contributed positively to individuals and helped a great deal in the economic development, some of the newer Islamic banks forgot one of the most important parameters and missions of any bank; a bank must improve and boost economic growth within any society.

Banque-Misr Achievements, 1920–1960

The primary focuses and achievements of Banque-Misr between 1920 and 1960 can be summarized as follows:

- Projects were undertaken both solely by Banque-Misr, and in partnership with any number of national, regional, or international partners.
- Bank-owned projects proved that patriotism and nationalism did not mean secluding Egyptian society from interacting and partnering with other regional and international entities—so long as it did not harm society.
- Bank-owned projects were based on studies demonstrating economic need for specific commodities, raw materials, semi-finished or finished products at affordable prices for merchants, industrialists, farmers, and the general public.
- Bank-owned projects aimed at and contributed to the economic growth of Egyptian society.
- Banque-Misr projects were mostly built and operated in rural areas or urban outskirts to improve economic growth for the rural and poorer segments of Egyptian society.
- Bank-owned projects guaranteed the sustainability and the profitability of the institution without the need to collect any revenues from loans and mortgages to private households with unreasonable interest rates (Feiglin 2010).

- Banque-Misr constantly diversified its projects in order to lower market risk and guarantee the sustainability of its operations.

- Bank-owned projects increased the efficiency of dealing with regular banking customers by attracting more customers through projects.

- Banque-Misr recruited some 250,000 additional customers by 1939 by hiring them to work on bank-owned projects and giving them shares. Share amounts varied according to how much workers could afford, but they involved employees while adding to the bank's capital.

- Bank-owned projects helped develop rural towns, decrease the unemployment rate, build schools and hospitals for its workforce, which would also serve the general rural population, and build rural infrastructure.

- Banque-Misr projects proved to be highly stable and showed exponential growth in capital and revenues.

- Bank-owned projects helped protect the environment by saving on importing goods from overseas by promoting domestic production.

- Bank-owned projects contributed significantly in reducing the crime rates in rural and urban areas where they exist.

Trade and Finance, 1960–2011

It is not fair to consider 1960–2011 as one financial period, especially considering the severe global financial and economic crises during the first decade of the 21st century. Yet, after 1960, the financial system moved toward privatization of industries that swung the national attitude from extreme socialist to extreme capitalist. The sharp swing to extreme capitalism was accompanied by problems associated with corporate corruption and the consequent potential to cause societal harm.

In the 1960s, the Egyptian government opted to adhere to socialist financial and economic systems. Although most banks and financial entities had to track global financial systems, trade was almost entirely limited to eastern-bloc socialist countries. Heavy industry was especially supported technically and financially by the Soviet Union and other eastern European countries. The Aswan High Dam (1960–1970) is an example of a major Egyptian project that was built only with Soviet monetary aid. Most of the country's import–export trade was limited to eastern European countries, especially the Soviet Union. After the 1967 war, military armaments were exclusively supplied by the Soviets as well. Soviet consultants were active in every field of production trying to ensure Egypt's total dependence on them.

In 1972, President Anwar Sadat ousted all Soviet military consultants and trainers (see Chapters 2 and 3). The reasons for this expulsion are not well documented, but it was rumored that the consultants' lack of support for plans to regain the Sinai Peninsula (which was claimed by Israeli forces in the six-day war) ensured their unpopularity with the president. After the October War, the post-war government adopted an open-door economic policy (see Chapters 2 and 3). This policy largely opened the door for corruption among both investors and government officials.

From the mid-1970s until the January 2011 revolution, the Egyptian economy faced a host of problems brought by the open-door policy. Economic growth deteriorated, national resources were wasted, and public officials up to the highest levels were often surrounded by elite citizens hoping to profit by exploiting national properties. Despite the increase in the country's GNP, the overall quality of health services, housing, education, transportation, infrastructure, and other services were declining at a steady rate. Unemployment rates grew and became one of Egypt's largest problems in the recent decades as has been discussed elsewhere in this chapter.

By the end of the 1970s and throughout the 1980s, there was great potential for a strong economy. Some private investing companies such as Al-Rayan and Al-Saad groups appeared to follow the original Banque-Misr model, but soon ventured into fast revenue investments both locally and overseas. They were able to engage in diversified range of industries including land reclamation, poultry, livestock, plastics, soft drinks, textiles, gas stations, real estate, publishing companies, jewelry, and many more, but their focus on quick returns over societal interests ensured that they violated the Central Bank limits on investing overseas. Charges were brought against the companies so that the government could confiscate all their assets. The government's main concern was that during the 1980s private investment companies had been able to convince the populace to withdraw their deposits from national and private banks to invest with other companies. The situation had become dire when the Central Bank had to borrow from such companies due to low cash liquidity.

After the government confiscated the assets of Al-Rayan, Al-Saad, and some other similar private investment companies, hundreds of thousands became unemployed, several related health and educational services were closed, and millions of investors lost most of their deposits. Some economists justified the government action as necessary citing that the revenue paid to depositors in those private investment companies in the 1980s exceeded 16 percent, whereas the national banks were striving to reach a revenue of 8 or 9 percent.

By the early 1990s, a new elite class of entrepreneurs had appeared in Egyptian society. They tended to be affiliated with influential Egyptian figures such as the president's family, prime ministers, ministers, and various subordinates. Corruption began to spread in both public and private sectors while common Egyptians were increasingly marginalized as services were constantly deteriorating. Divisions between rich and poor grew increasingly apparent as younger Egyptians had problems securing jobs or getting married while elites were building new compounds and lavish resorts with high walls to separate themselves from the rest of society. Public alienation grew increasingly common especially among the country's youth as poverty rates increased side by side with the number of corrupted elites.

Corruption was not limited to the economic sector, but was also rife in the political arena. In order to protect elite status and socioeconomic crimes committed by elites, elections were often of questionable legality and hundreds of honest citizens were detained, tortured, and harmed financially and physically for their opposition to the government. Corruption was effectively instituted as a system and any objectors were harshly punished and prosecuted.

During the 1990s, some opposition youth groups were so frustrated by the deteriorating human rights that they decided to start suicidal attacks against government establishments and corrupted powerful individuals. Unfortunately, tens of innocent citizens were injured or killed due to attacks launched by desperate youth against government officials. By the end of the 1990s, security measures surrounding government officials and potential targets ensured that the majority of victims were innocent citizens. Upon realizing this, the militant youth groups announced that they would stop their attacks.

The confrontation between youth groups and the government during the 1990s affected the economy, and the tourism industry was especially hard hit given the lack of public safety. Although the militant youth groups abandoned their patriotic operations when they realized that their acts were hurting Egypt more than helping, the government went on building a central security force of almost 1.5 million troops. The Central Security Forces were primarily used to protect elite property and combat any riots or rebellious activities from the society that had been exploited and abused to attain such property.

Trade and finance was further affected by the turn of the 21st century, especially after the events of September 2001. The Egyptian government and political regime seized that opportunity to violate all constitutional rights with the excuse of fighting terrorism and ensuring internal security. This security was also meant to ensure the safety and position of corrupted elites within society. Trade and finance were kept as private activities and a privilege only for the elite. Not only did this group claim the wealth of the country without contributing to economic growth or needed social services, but they also went as far as fighting any effort to supply the society with any necessary health or educational service not approved by them. Approval for a new hospital, school, or even a charitable organization required a license that could only be obtained with huge bribes for officials.

Throughout the past two decades, economic and political instability have been defining characteristics of Egypt. The economic instability affected all economic sectors including finance, foreign trade, and small or independent business. The widespread problems stagnated the economy and made any attempt at honest business very difficult given the institutionalized system of corruption.

January 2011 and Its Impact on the Financial Situation

Following the January 2011 revolution, the financial situation in Egypt looked very negative. The antirevolutionary coalitions were able to start a series of strikes among several production sites that affected production, trade, finance, and both internal and external investments. The security conditions were deteriorating in both rural and urban areas.

In reality, the revolutionary youth have proceeded to initiate and revive tens of projects in almost every province in order to increase production, improve health services, raise educational standards, decrease unemployment levels, lessen traffic

Egypt's Prime Minister designate Essam Sharaf, surrounded by supporters in Tahrir Square, Cairo, Egypt, Friday March 4, 2011. He vowed before thousands of mostly young demonstrators to do everything he could to meet their demands and pleaded for them to turn their attention to rebuilding their country. SCAF picked Sharaf to replace Ahmed Shafiq as prime minister. (AP Photo/Khalil Hamra)

problems, clean up urban areas, and promote environmentalism. In short, they have started projects badly needed to raise the standards of living, and above all to rebuild the sense of belonging and identity within Egyptian society.

Dr. Essam Sharaf, the first prime minister after the 2011 revolution, was optimistic about the potential for increases in trade backed by a strong financial system within two to three years. His statements were based on the fact that with a new freely elected parliament, antirevolutionary coalitions would fade away leaving the new parliament, new government, and the revolutionary youth to be fully dedicated to production to enhance and revive high standards of local and foreign trade and investment. Every day youth groups have started productive projects around the country, and Sharaf's outlook is increasingly realistic with the grassroots movements for positive change sweeping through the country.

REFERENCES

Abdellatif, Reem. "Egypt 2012: Time for a New Economic Vision." *Daily News Egypt*, January 25, 2012. http://www.thedailynewsegypt.com/egypt-2012-time-to-for-a-new-economic-vision.html.

Banque-Misr official site: www.banquemisr.com/sites/EngBM/pages/TalaatHarb.aspx.

Business Monitor International—Country Risk, Industry, Company Intelligence. "Economy Recovering, but Not Meeting Expectations." *Middle East and Africa Monitor*, February 2012. http://www.meamonitor.com/file/109646/economy-recovering-but-not-meeting-expectations.html.

Business Monitor International—Country Risk, Industry, Company Intelligence. *Egypt Agribusiness Report Q2 2011*. Business Monitor International, n.d. Web. February 1, 2012. http://www.businessmonitor.com.

Datamonitor "Country Analysis Report: Egypt 2012." http://www.datamonitor.com.

Deeb, Maurius. "Bank Misr and the Emergence of the Local Bourgeoisie in Egypt." *Middle Eastern Studies* 12 (3) (1976): 69–86. http://www.jstor.org/stable/4282607.

Euromonitor International. "Egypt Country Profile." http://www.euromonitor.com/egypt.

Euromonitor International. "Egypt in 2030: The Future Demographic." http://www.euromonitor.com/egypt.

Euromonitor International. "Passport GMID." www.euromonitor.com/passport-gmid.

Feiglin, Moshe. Jewish Banking. August 29, 2010. http://jewishisrael.org/eng_contents/articles/70/article7064.html.

Kamal, Rashad. *Talaat Harb: Conscience of a Nation* [in Arabic]. Cairo: Susana, 1993.

"Laws Library." *Gafi.* Web. February 1, 2012. www.gafinet.org/LawsLibrary/Forms/AllItems.aspx?SortField=LinkFilename&SortDir=Asc&View=%7bB9C5A7DE%2dC673%2d4CCC%2dA939%2d691C7F11841D%7d.

Mansour, A., and Khalifa, S. "Impact of bank-owned projects on urban and rural economic growth: Bank-Misr model, 1930–1960." Paper Presented at the MCRSA Conference, Detroit, MI, June 2–4, 2011.

Radwan, Fathi. *Talaat Harb: In Search of Greatness*. Cairo: Dar El Maaref, 1970.

Segre, Claudia. "Vatican Offers Islamic Finance System to Western Banks." L'Osservatore Romano, March 6, 2009. www.worldbulletin.net/index.php?aType=haberArchive&ArticleID=37814.

World Bank. "Economy Profile: Egypt 2012." Doing Business-Measuring Business Regulations-World Bank Group. http://doingbusiness.org.

CHAPTER 5

Society

RELIGION AND THOUGHT

Islam: A Way of Life

Egypt is about 90 percent Sunni Muslim. A young engineer explained Egyptian sentiments nicely, comparing himself to Christians and Jews. He said "the other religions have rules, but there is room for error . . . Islam is a way of life." In other words, it is not something to be taken lightly, done over, or taken back at a confession. Life is a straight path for which one must work ceaselessly to maintain one's course. It is not a lonely road, nor one without guidance. If family, friends, or even well-meaning strangers see someone veering too far off the path, an intervention is likely to remind the errant Muslim of the consequences of his or her behavior. Where many in the United States would see this action as a form of "interference," in Egypt it would be considered care for one's brother or sister in the Muslim community (*umma*). These statements do not mean that all Egyptian Muslims conform perfectly to some idealized conception of their religion, and those who do not are immediately corrected. In its interpretation, just as any other religion, Islam has been influenced by a larger constellation of social, economic, and political factors. Furthermore, there are a number of things attributed to Islam, but may have absolutely nothing to do with the religion whatsoever. The most notable issue in this category would be the genital mutilation of women, which predates Islam (see Chapter 7).

Islam: The Basics

Understanding Islam as it is practiced in Egypt means understanding the basic pillars of the religion. In order to be a Muslim, one is either born to a Muslim father or one must bear witness to the first pillar of Islam, the *shahada*, the testimony of faith in front of two witnesses: *"la ilaha ila-lah wa Muhammadan rasul Allah."* In doing so, he or she is stating that "there is no God, but God (Allah), and Muhammad is his Prophet." Of the five pillars of Islam, the first pillar of Islam is the only pillar that deals with belief, all the other pillars deal with practice. It deals with the meaning of Islam, coming from the Arabic root s-l-m that connotes peace, which in its fourth form, Islam, means to make peace with (submit to) Allah.

Any visitor to Egypt is quickly going to understand the second pillar of Islam: prayer (*salat*). Daily life for the Muslim is punctuated by five pauses to remember Allah in prayer: dawn, noon, mid-afternoon, sunset, and evening with a call from the minaret of each and every mosque. Historically, prayer callers were chosen by their melodious voices and ability to be heard from the minaret. Technology, recordings, and amplification have allowed many who are less than qualified, not to mention multiple and competing calls, to create a veritable cacophony at prayer time. The Muslim does not have to pray immediately at the call to prayer, but should finish the prayer sometime preceding the next call to prayer.

Before beginning, the Muslim has to complete a series of ritualized ablutions, which begin by stating one's intention to cleanse and saying *"bismi-llah ar-rahman ar-raheem"* (in the name of Allah, Most Gracious, Most Merciful), then the actual washing starts with the hands, moves to the mouth, nose, face, arm to elbow, hair and ears, and finally feet. Actions are performed right side first and repeated three times. This *wudu'* is the ordinary ablution. If one performs an act of sexual inter-course, is ending one's menstrual cycle, discharges any type of sexual fluid with or without contact, or even has any type of physical contact with the opposite sex, a more thorough type of ablution is necessary. Basically, it involves cleansing the private parts before a *wudu*-type cleansing and a shower-type cleaning afterward. Defecation requires special cleansing as well. Anyone who has visited Egypt and wondered why toilet paper seems to be such a scarce commodity in many places, but all bathrooms are equipped with either bidets or in-toilet spigots, can now understand that simply "wiping" would not do the job required to be "clean" for prayer.

The dawn prayer is the shortest with only two *rakahs* (or sections) of prayer. After ablutions, the Muslim places a prayer carpet facing Mecca, and covers his or her body appropriately. A woman needs to have everything covered aside from her face, her hands, and her feet. A man should not wear anything that discloses his body from midriff to knees. The Muslim then states his or her intent to give the two *rakahs* in prayer and assumes the first position of prayer with his or her hands by his or her ears, hands open palms facing Mecca, and states *"Allahu akbar"* or God is the greatest. The volume of the prayers should be just loud enough for one to hear it himself or herself. The second position of prayer is standing with the right hand over the left at the chest. Next, it is recommended that the Muslim asks for Al-lah's assistance and protection from the devil. The Muslim then recites the opening chapter of the Quran, *al-Fatiha*, which is said to contain the essence of the Quran (and it must be in Arabic):

In the name of Allah most Gracious, most Merciful,
Praise be to Allah The Cherisher and Sustainer of the Worlds:
Most Gracious, Most Merciful;
Master of the Day of Judgment.
Thee do we worship, and Thine aid we seek.
Show us the straight way,
The way of those on whom
Thou has bestowed Thy Grace,
those whose [portion] is not wrath,
and who go not astray. (Trans. Abdullah Yusuf Ali 2004)

He or she should then recite another short chapter or a set of verses from a longer chapter. When this is completed the person moves into a bowing posture such that the hands rest on the knees and the torso is perpendicular to the legs. In this position the Muslim says "*subḥana rabbi al-azeem*" (praise be to my lord, the great one) three times. One then straightens completely and there are various formulaic things one can say to assure that he or she stays standing straight for the appropriate amount of time; these are not obligatory, only recommended. It is recommended to raise hands again, and say "*Allahu akbar.*" Afterwards, one goes down to the prostrate position, forehead on floor, palms on floor by ears, knees on floor, toe tips on floor, and heels in air. In this position, one says, "*subḥana rabbi al-'alaa*" (praise my Lord, the most lofty one) three times. Finally, one moves into sitting position with feet under buttocks and hands on quadriceps and says "*Allahu akbar*" again. Rising to a standing position the Muslim says "*Allahu akbar*" and this completes one *rakah.* Everything is repeated from the saying of the *Fatiḥa* onward. The conclusion of the session is achieved in the seated position by turning one's head to the right and saying "*as-salaam 'alaykum* (*wa raḥmatu-llahi* optional)" (peace be upon you (and the blessings of God)), and then the same is repeated on the left side. To a non-Muslim this probably seems like an extraordinary amount of work, and it is the shortest prayer, consisting of only two *rakahs.* There are three at sunset and four at other times. Prayers take no more than a few minutes for a Muslim to complete. People are so accustomed to the movements and repeat verses with grace and ease. When unable due to health or circumstance to complete a standing prayer, one might see people going through modified prayers in a seated position. This is generally reserved for the elderly, although in recent years more middle-aged believers resort to the chair (at least in Cairo). Changes in diet, sedentary lifestyle, the extreme pollution in Cairo, and other markers of modernity have taken their toll on individual lifestyles and customs. Regardless of standing or sitting positions, one cannot disturb the *qibla*, or orientation toward Mecca. One should not cross in front of someone who is praying. Disturbing the *qibla* will negate the prayer. Given the extreme population density of Cairo, in particular, and the ease with which one can disturb an *qibla*, measures can be taken to protect it. Placing some sort of object in front of the individual praying will protect one from this occurrence, for example, a pair of sandals or a small table.

People can pray anywhere—at home, at work, stopped on the side of the road, or in a mosque. The Friday noon prayer is the only prayer for which people generally attend a public service; and this is usually for men, although mosques typically have areas set aside for their sisters. Given the nature and posture of prayer, having women's posteriors rising and falling before male observers would be considered a distraction. Most men attend their neighborhood mosque; however, popular *imams* can receive quite a following and their mosques on Friday literally spill out into the surrounding sidewalks and streets. By the late 1970s, popular Friday *khuṭbas* were recorded and disseminated on cassette tapes. Now the most popular clerics have TV audiences, can post video clips online, and provide interviews to much larger audiences. One cleric taking to the airwaves to spread his word beyond his flock is Safwat Higa, recently airing his anti-Starbucks sermon in which he hypothesizes that the female figure in the logo is Queen Esther of the (ancient Persian) Jews and that the multinational giant should be shutdown in the Islamic world, particularly in the holy cities of Mecca and Medina.

The third pillar of Islam is *zakat*, or mandatory alms-giving. This practice dates back to a difficult time in Islam when the early community was fighting a number of different enemies and there were many orphans, widows, and other problems as a result of these wars. Creating a fund to take care of the needy by having everyone give a small amount of his or her personal fortune solved many problems. Muslims are supposed to give about two and a half percent of their annual income for this mandatory charity. *Zakat* is distinct from other forms of charity and volunteerism that are encouraged but are not mandatory. Egypt is an extremely poor country, and even that which is "mandatory" is not expected from everyone. Only those who have 85 grams in gold or about 14,159 Egyptian pounds are required to give; however, there are even discrepancies about how this figure is calculated, that is, whether this is one's total income or net worth, or whether one has this amount available after expenses are met. Less than half of the people in Egypt paid this obligation in the early 2000s (when it was worth about 6,800 Egyptian pounds), and even fewer are likely to be able to do so given recent inflation and economic hardship. The easier *zakat* requirement to fulfill is the *zakat al-fiṭr*, which about 85 percent meet because it only requires a few extra pounds or food staples (*zakat*). This requirement was also established in the lifetime of the Prophet Muhammad, who did not want anyone going hungry during the time of the feast following the month of Ramadan. Therefore, before prayers on the first day of the feast, each family with enough money for extra food should set aside extra provisions for the needy. Sometimes this process involves creating actual meals, many people dispense aid directly to their favorite panhandlers or go where they know they will find beggars, others choose to utilize some type of agency. The idea behind all *zakat* is that it is supposed to be local and benefit the "deserving poor" of one's community.

The fourth pillar of Islam is *ṣawm*, or fasting during the month of Ramadan. Muslims are not supposed to eat from about one hour and 25 minutes before dawn, according to the traditions of the Prophet Muhammad, until the sunset call to prayer. Unlike Christian fasts, which allow clear liquids, Muslim fasts are extremely strict with absolutely NO food or drink, including water. The fast also includes abstinence from sexual intercourse, foul language, and cigarettes. Since Islam follows a lunar calendar, the holiday rotates, and it can be quite challenging when it falls during the long, hot days of summer. This type of challenge is precisely the purpose of the practice, which is meant to help bring the Muslim closer to Allah as he or she gets through the day in thoughtful contemplation. Many Muslims work their way methodically through the entire Quran over the course of the entire month. While the holiday is supposed to be spent more in religious pursuits, evenings are spent with family and friends eating breakfast and *suhur* (see Chapter 6), and often time is spent watching television. Frequently dramatic miniseries are created specifically for the time during Ramadan. TV producers know people will be at home with the premier time slot being about one hour after breakfast, and Ramadan commercials are somewhat like Super Bowl commercials because they sell for the high-demand time slots. While marketing is not as sophisticated as in the United States, nor packaged in the same manner, after the rise of infitah economics, much has changed, particularly in the past 15 years.

The origin of this holiday goes back to the earliest community of Muslims, who used to fast with the Jews of Medina on their Day of Atonement. When the Jews of Medina split with the Muslims and no longer upheld the Constitution of Medina (an agreement that bound the citizens of Medina to an intertribal alliance), distinctions

A page from the Quran. (© Yamo/ Dreamstime.com)

had to be made between the two communities (see following text). Ramadan was a significant month because it was the month when Muslims believe the Quran was first revealed to Muhammad, and it was also the month during which the pivotal Battle of Badr was waged. Not all Muslims must fast during Ramadan. Children are not expected to fast. As they approach adolescence, they begin to develop a tolerance for fasting more days each Ramadan, so that when they reach maturity they can fast the full month. Women who are pregnant, menstruating, or breastfeeding are additionally not required to fast, although many still fast. Those who are traveling, ill, convalescing, or have certain chronic conditions are exempt; however, those who have "temporary" issues are supposed to make up the days at a later time. During the month of Ramadan the pace of life in Egypt slows down significantly. Many public offices restrict hours and expectations decrease. With the rise of infitah economics and the creation of the private sector, this slowdown has changed somewhat since companies competing in a global economy cannot simply grind to a halt for a month. When the sunset call to prayer takes place, the streets are nearly emptied. Nevertheless, one can witness acts of generosity, such as a coffee-shop owner standing in the street with a tray of date and fruit compote cups so that people like cab drivers and other busy workers can quickly stop to break their fast. Egyptians have tremendous hearts.

The final pillar of Islam is the *ḥajj*, the obligation of all Muslims to make a pilgrimage to Mecca as long as they are physically and financially able to do so. The official period of pilgrimage is during the 7th to 10th days of *dhul al-ḥijja.* If it is made at another time of the year, it is referred to as an *ʿumra*. There are a basic series of rituals established during the lifetime of Muhammad that adherents must follow, including circumambulating the ka'aba a certain number of times fast and slow in a counterclockwise direction, touching or kissing the black stone of the ka'aba (rather difficult given the crowds), visiting the well of Zamzam, cursing and stoning the devil (has been modified to deal with the crowds), and finally the festivities culminate at Mount Arafat where the feast of the sacrifice is ritually reenacted (see Chapter 6). To accommodate the large number of pilgrims from Egypt, there are routes by air, land, and sea. Travel agencies can provide women with proper guides, since women are supposed to travel with husbands, fathers, (adult) sons, or brothers. Male pilgrims wear a simple garment composed of two pieces of unhemmed white cloth, one over the torso and one around the waist held together by a rope or sash, with only simple sandals. Women are to wear unadorned white or neutrally colored garments with their heads covered, but face and hands showing.

The Saudi government issues each country a specific number of visas annually to participate in the *ḥajj* festivities. In a country such as Egypt, demand outstrips the supply. There are people with resources to make the *ḥajj* annually or even biannually (*ʿumra*) (during the *ʿEid al-Fiṭr* as well). In the past, this problem has been resolved by obtaining visas from countries where demand is lower, for example, Europe, and reissuing them to Egyptians desiring to make the *ḥajj*. In the past few years, problems of forgery, fraud, and overcrowding have caused the Saudi government to crack down on these practices leaving many Egyptians denied entry, sometimes from their own airport and sometimes actually in Saudi territory after paying thousands

Stereograph showing a crowd watching a Muslim procession with banners, starting for the Hajj pilgrimage to Mecca. (Library of Congress)

of pounds for tickets and visas. Theoretically, as the benevolent and oil-rich keeper of the holy cities, the Saudis donate a certain number of visas to Egyptians annually, so that earnest Muslims can make the trip, and also do so spiritually for loved ones who were not able to do so in their own lifetime. The government used to give 50,000 visas earlier and now offers 70,000, and while this is a significant cost (20,000 Egyptian pounds per visa), it still does not represent the cost of transportation, housing, food, or the special clothing requirements (while simple). It still represents an outlay of expenses. Tour operators tend to receive these "free" visas for which they charge Egyptians, and the typical pilgrimage costs somewhere between 40,000 and 80,000 Egyptian pounds depending on the level of accommodations (Shihane 2002; Emam 2008).

Islam: A Religion of Social Justice, the Origins

To fully understand Islam's contemporary appeal or how it spread as a form of government and as a religion in the Middle Ages, it is important to understand how it began in the Arabian Peninsula in the seventh century. The Arabian Peninsula was and is a land of extremes: harsh climate, topography, and difficult access to water.

The only agriculture available is at the southern end of the peninsula (Yemen) and around scattered oases. In the early seventh century, most people lived by herding animals that could withstand these conditions, for example, camels, and moving from place to place in search of water. Nevertheless, there were trade routes that connected the agricultural south, with its highly valued commodity of frankincense, and the markets of Syria to the North. Mecca was a convenient watering point in between where people came to rest and to visit a shrine with appeal to many: the ka'aba, which Jews believed that Abraham built, which had connections to Allah, lord of creation and divinity (the same word that Arabic-speaking Christians used for their one God), and which housed many pagan entities worshiped by pre-Islamic Arabs. The Quraysh tribe had settled and was no longer nomadic, having found its niche in protecting the ka'aba and fulfilling the needs of the service economy that had been generated by the market city.

Muslims believe that Muhammad is the messenger of God, the "seal" in the series of messengers that begins with Abraham in the Old Testament and its prophets and continues with the message brought by Jesus, who is also considered a prophet, but not divine. Muhammad was troubled by conditions in early seventh-century Mecca. Tribal values, like generosity, equality, and concern for the community, had given way to individualism, materialism, and greed. The clans that were closer to town and therefore the well and the ka'aba had grown much richer than those further away and these disparities had given rise to new values. It was after meditating about these issues in a cave on Mount Hira that Muslims believe that Muhammad received his first revelation in 610, verses 1–5 of Sura 96. At first Muhammad kept the message of Allah within his household, but eventually the message came that he needed to spread the word, which brought him in conflict with the powerful members of his community. Their economy depended on belief in many gods, and belief in just one was not only a threat to tradition, but it was also a threat to the economy and to the prevailing social order.

Muhammad's religion attracted not only slaves, the weak, the poor, and women with its message of equality, but it also attracted members of the younger generation from some of the more powerful clans of his tribe. As well, those who were open-minded and perhaps those who had come into contact with other monotheists through trade had a greater inclination toward Islam. Nevertheless, the powerful and wealthy among the Quraysh fought hard against Muhammad, even forcing him to flee for his life. In this process, he emigrated to Medina in 622, where he created the first community of believers. Whereas in Mecca he simply had a group of followers, the Medinans accepted him as a leader, including the Jewish clans (Constitution of Medina). Muhammad had arbitrated a number of longstanding feuds among the tribes and clans of Medina that allowed him to enter the city as a statesman and a leader. So significant is this emigration and the creation of this community that Muslims mark this moment as the beginning of the Muslim calendar.

His uprooted Qurayshi Muslims had no way to make a living in Medina, and after doing the basic work of building his new home and meeting place (the first mosque), there was little to do but raid (pagan) Qurayshi caravans making their way to and from Syria, which was at least partially fair given the economic boycott that had been placed on Muslims prior to their emigration by their Meccan opposition and the looting of their households afterward. The caravan-raiding necessarily led to blood-vengeance. By the mid-620s some Jewish tribes grew tired of the intertribal alliance that had been created in the Constitution of Medina, and they began fighting the Muslims. In essence the Muslims were then fighting a two-front war: the Jews of Medina and the Quraysh of Mecca. The oft-cited Quranic verses (usually by conservative Western commentators or by radical Islamists) that have an anti-Semitic tone are revelations specific to this time period when some of the Jews of Medina abrogated the constitution because they felt nothing could be gained by the protracted state of war. Indeed, revelations were quite often context-specific. Ultimately, the Muslims expelled some of the Jews from Medina.

Muhammad due to his skill as a diplomat and a warrior was able to return to Mecca as a conqueror and to convert the entire Arabian Peninsula by what might be termed an intertribal alliance before his death in 632. Great gains do not come without some cost. Muhammad married the daughter of his bitterest enemy Abu Sufyan, his son Muawiya became Muhammad's secretary, and after Muhammad's death the Muawiya would become governor of Syria, eventually founding the Umayyad caliphate in 661. In Muslim historiography the story is the victory of good over evil, whereas in most things in life it was a complicated negotiation of competing sources of power.

Although the entire peninsula had "converted," this change did not necessarily translate into religious observance. It simply meant that the tribes accepted Muhammad as a leader and paid *zakat* (mandatory alms) to the central treasury. In reality, other tribal leaders admired his skill as an Arab. He possessed outstanding qualities in leadership for Arabs: bravery, strength, generosity, eloquence, and concern for his community. His gift was his ability to take the tribal structure and values and impose it on a structure that transcended the tribe. Nevertheless, after his death, there would be no assurance that the disparate groups of followers on the peninsula ranging from his earliest followers in Mecca, to the Medinans who created his first community, to other tribes that became early followers, to the Quraysh that were his bitterest enemies yet still rose to high positions due to skillful negotiations and powerful manipulations, to ordinary tribes who joined for the ride, would remain Muslims and abide by the rule of his caliph, or successor Abu Bakr (r. 632–634) (see Chapter 2). Furthermore, the Quran contained only 114 chapters, some containing only a few verses, which were meant to guide people in this holistic way of life. Therefore, in the coming centuries interpretation and techniques for interpretation would be developed among early Muslims.

Islam: The Misunderstood Aspects

In a roomful of adherents, if one asks what the "true" meaning of Christianity, Judaism, or any other religion is, there would probably be as many different answers as there were people in the room. While many Egyptian Muslims can agree on certain points of religion, there is heated debate about other points. In the West, perhaps the most confusion about Islam arises over issues pertaining to the concept of jihad and issues relating to women.

Westerners have a number of misperceptions regarding women and Islam, and all (Muslim) Egyptians are defensive about these misperceptions, but none more so than women. A typical Egyptian woman will proudly inform any listener of the liberating aspects of her religion. She would likely begin in pre-Islamic times and tell her Western listener about the days when female infanticide, prostitution, and unregulated slavery ran amuck on the Arabian Peninsula in the days of ignorance (*jahiliyya*). Islam guaranteed women rights in marriage, property, and divorce, which could be upheld in a court of law when Western women could not even hold property in their own name. She is most likely to quote from Sura 33 verse 35, which demands equal adherence to the faith from both women and men. This chapter is entitled *al-aḥzab*, or the factions (parties); and it is a Medinan sura dating back to the time when Muhammad was dealing with the unruly Jewish factions in Medina as well as protecting and safeguarding the religion for 50 percent of its adherents.

Despite Islam's call for equality, the Western listener might ask the Egyptian woman her opinion of Sura 4:34, an even later Medinan sura, which states that "men are protectors of women" and must maintain them because Allah has given "one more than the other." Our imaginary Egyptian woman would most likely be laughing at our Western listener and say that Westerners have such silly notions of equality. Muslim women do not want to be like men. In other words, she does not view equality as the same rights, but different ones suited to her needs. Of course, she wants her husband to protect and maintain her because his money provides for the household, and her money is her money. The reality may not be the case, but this is her most likely response. If she wears a headscarf (80 percent or more of adult women do), then she will insist that the religion demands this of her and that only her face and hands should be exposed in public; however, women who choose not to veil are quick to point out that the Quran demands only modesty and that veiling was meant only for the wives of the Prophet. The Quran 24:30–31 takes up the subject of both male and female modesty, and adherents of both sexes are instructed to lower their gaze and attend to their modesty, with women being told not to display their ornaments and to draw their cloaks (sometimes translated as veils) around their bosoms. With respect to advice for the Prophet's family, this instruction comes in Sura 33, when there was great concern for the well-being of the women of the community. Verse 59 warns the Prophet to tell his wives, daughters, and believing women to wear the *jilbab*, a long cloak covering the entire body and neck, when they go out so as not to be molested. Commentary as to the meaning and application of this particular verse is profuse.

With respect to the concept of jihad, the word originates from the Arabic root dealing with struggle, effort, initiative, and in its third form from which jihad comes it deals with battle or even holy war. In some cases in the Quran, it is clear that this jihad is internal and it is a struggle to maintain one's course on the right path, for example, in 22:78, where the parallel with Abraham is drawn. In other cases, where actually "killing in the way of God" is prescribed, the word jihad is not used, but the command *"qatilu fi sabil Allah"* (2:190). This command is followed by instructions only to do so against those who have attacked first and by a warning not to transgress limitations. The only other mention of jihad is in a more or less ambiguous context between the two extremes. In 25:52 believers are warned that the weapon they should use, according to most commentators, is their own faith. (Contemporary discourse on jihad will be addressed in Chapter 7.)

Islam, like all monotheistic traditions, has two basic tendencies, one toward intolerance or even holy war and one toward erasing all differences. Believers in one God have a universal tradition that cuts across class, ethnicity, gender, and national boundaries. Nevertheless, others believe that if everyone worships one God this implies that belief should be uniform. Historically, more tolerant trends have prevailed, but a quick read through Chapter 2, as well as the previous discussion, highlights some blatantly obvious examples of the second tendency. During times of social and economic stress, subjects (or citizens) often look toward religious or other minorities as scapegoats. In the 19th and 20th centuries as Egypt defined itself as a nation-state, determining what role religion would play and how Egypt's minority communities, particularly the Copts, would fit into that picture have been particularly difficult. The Copts represented the link to pharaonaic Egypt, a time when Egyptians were powerful, yet they also represented a link to the European occupiers with their Christian religion.

Islam itself represented another great time in history and nationalist debates ranged from pan-Islamic, to pan-Ottoman, to territorial Egyptian, and to various combinations thereof. Copts themselves developed a form of nationalism in response to these debates as "the true Egyptians." As political and economic events waxed and waned for the Copts, their condition within the country rose and fell.

The Copts in Egypt

The history of the Copts in Egypt has been one of harsh persecution interspersed with long periods of relative calm. Between the death of St. Mark in 68 CE, who founded the first church in Alexandria and the early fourth century when Christianity became the official religion of the Byzantine empire (Eastern successor to the Roman empire), the majority of Egypt's inhabitants abandoned paganism. According to legend, St. Mark had returned from travel abroad and was celebrating Easter (Pascha), which coincided with the old pagan celebration of Serapis, and the influential individuals who felt threatened by his powers of persuasion killed him and dragged his body through the streets. This account still does not answer the question of what specifically he was doing to attract negative attention and how many observant followers he had to garner such a punishment.

According to anthropologist Clifford Geertz, religion makes sense only when it can provide a system of order that corresponds to people's everyday lives, one that creates a system of symbols that motivates mankind to believe (have faith) in that which is not necessarily humanly possible (e.g. immaculate conception, resurrection, etc). Scholars often point to parallels between Egyptian mythology—stories of Horus, Isis, Set, and Osirus—with Horus or Osirus representing various incarnations of Christ and the Holy Spirit; Isis, the Virgin Mary; and Set, Satan. While the most

---

SERAPIS

Serapis represented an amalgam of Greek and Egyptian gods, the most significant of which are represented in his name. Osiris the god of the underworld had many forms, and in his element as a bull he was known as Apis. The Ptolemies, who first encouraged his worship in the fourth century BCE, wanted support from both the Egyptians and the Greeks so Serapis included elements from Zeus, Hades, Dionysus, and Asclepius. Since the Greeks did not particularly enjoy animal worship, he took a human form. The cult of Serapis spread beyond his huge temple, the Serapeum, in Alexandria. By the first century CE even Rome had followers. Scholars of early Christianity maintain that there was a great deal of overlap and/or confusion between followers of Jesus and those of Serapis in the early years of the religion. At the end of the fourth century, supported by imperial policy from Byzantine Emperor Theodosius, violent confrontations between Christians and pagans ended in the destruction of the Serapeum

---

radical claim that Christianity (and Judaism) plagiarized from existing religions in the region, the more satisfying answer for the faithful is that all the messages come from the same source (God) and were therefore tailored to meet the needs of each community in its time. An answer in between the two is that new religions accommodated symbols to fit within the accepted realms, for example, celebrating holidays at traditional times and incorporating recognizable motifs and even music (see Chapter 6). Thus, the birth of Christ overlaps with the Roman celebration of Saturnalia (which it adopted from Babylon), which coincided with the winter solstice, a time that would be significant for a developed agricultural society, such as Egypt.

Egypt was an important center for the development of early Christianity, and Alexandria became a great center for Christian learning. Religion and politics in Egypt always seemed to be intertwined, and the heresy regarding the nature and substance of Christ offers a case in point. The argument began as to whether or not Jesus was literally or simply metaphorically the son of God. These two viewpoints represented political or ethnic viewpoints as well since the Greek population clustered around Arius, who supported the latter view, and the Egyptians, Athanasius, who supported the former. What began as a simple scholarly debate in Egypt was settled formally at the Council of Nicaea in 325 to favor the Egyptian viewpoint. Nevertheless, the Monophysite controversy over the nature of Christ grew out of the old debate. The Egyptian (Monophysite) position was that Christ had a single (divine) nature formed by a fusion of its human and divine aspects. This position was overruled at the Council of Chalcedon in 451 leading to formation of a separate Coptic Church. The stand was political since it opposed the ruling Byzantine position.

At the time of the Arab conquest, Egyptians viewed the Muslims as far superior administrators to the Byzantines in terms of both taxation and freedom of worship. One of the Prophet Muhammad's companions, Maria, was a Copt and based on her very existence even Copts accept the notion of *hadith* in which Muhammad preaches kindness to Copts. As discussed in Chapter 2, the process of Arabization and Islamization was a slow one, helped along by the Hilalian migrations and the Crusades. Nevertheless, a significant proportion of the population retained its Christian identity.

Coptic Christians emphasize their religion's physical and metaphorical proximity to the early teachings of Christ. They uphold the sacraments of Baptism, Confirmation, Eucharist, Confession, Orders, Matrimony, and Unction. The general tone of the religion is much more ascetic than most Catholic or Protestant churches in the West. Nearly 60 percent of the year is spent in modified forms of fasting that basically amount to a vegan diet. The Coptic Church is headed by the Patriarch of Alexandria. Up until March 2012 this post was held by Shenouda III, known to his followers as "Pope" or "Baba." Since 1971 he represented the Copts of Egypt as a fiery advocate of their rights, although in recent years his message was to preach both Christian unity and spiritual unity with his co-citizens. In the wake of the January 25 movement, the Pope praised the demonstrators for the peaceful resolve with which they led the nation.

In places where Copts remain, their numbers have been statistically significant. In Upper Egypt and in certain neighborhoods in Cairo, for example, Imbaba, Copts represent as much as 30 percent or more of the population. It is in these pockets of higher density that sectarian conflict and violence have occurred recently. The role that the Copts played historically, for example, their greater literacy and therefore their positioning for government service during the British occupation, created resentment among the Muslim population. The post-1967 era opened a new chapter in sectarian relations with the rise of Islamist trends, and in particular the deepening of the economic crisis in the region in the past two decades has made the minority community vulnerable. The outbreak of the swine flu in 2009 and the culling of a quarter of a million pigs and the sectarian violence that followed is evidence of the continuing tension between the communities.

The Egyptian state has been slow to respond to individual or mass lashings at Copts because this outlet represents a vent for pent-up frustration that has not been directed toward the government. One of the major issues of contention has been church-building and renovation. Just as Egypt's Muslim population has grown, so too has its Coptic population, and hence the need to build more churches and add on to those that exist, but with space at a premium these processes have been slow, difficult, and fraught with violence directed against the Copts. The laws regulating such measures date back to the Ottoman era.

While Westerners are accustomed to the separation of religion and state, the trend in the post-1967 era has been toward an increasing penetration, which has only added to the discomfort of Egypt's minority community. Sadat added constitutional amendments to make Islamic law the source of all law, and after his death the Muslim Brotherhood, while officially a nonentity has slowly received growing popularity in the parliamentary realm (see Chapters 3 and 7). Thus, by Mubarak's 2005 reelection Egypt's Coptic community was uncertain about which direction it would turn. It was also the year of intercommunal crises, including church burnings and sectarian riots. At the tail end of 2004, Wafa Konstantin, the wife of a disabled Coptic priest had taken refuge in a Cairo police station, declaring her conversion to Islam. In all likelihood the conversion was a means to escape her marriage, since the Coptic Church generally does not allow divorce, and seeking an annulment or a divorce from a priest would be near impossible. Copts insisted that the conversion was forced by Muslims. The stand taken by Mrs. Konstantin generated interest by none other than Pope Shenouda himself, who went into retreat and implied he would not even be presiding over Coptic mass on January 7 (Coptic Christmas), if the issue were not resolved. Mrs. Konstantin was turned over to a monastery much to the dismay of human rights organizations. Indeed, Konstantin's case is not the only one in which the state has sided with the church against the citizen over his or her individual rights, fearing the larger issue of sectarian violence. On the other hand, there have been allegations of young Coptic women going missing, allegedly having been taken as sex slaves by Muslims. Thus, the government has tried to pursue the safest course between the two extremes.

The two communities take great pleasure in highlighting the shortcomings of "the other." Notable in this category is the 2001 scandal erupting from the publication of lurid photographs involving a (former) Coptic priest and female parishioners at one of the holiest sites in Christianity, the Deir al-Muharriq Church near Assiut. The newspaper *al-Nabaa* published the graphic photographs along with a story that described the church as something along the lines of a brothel. At the commemoration of the events surrounding the Church's fame, the Virgin Mary's release of Christian converts, it was apparent that the Copts of Egypt would not soon forget the humiliation, despite the prosecution of the newspaper and its editor. The veracity of the pictures has been called into question, and the publication of such pictures is a criminal offense in Egypt.

Similarly, a DVD entitled *I Was Blind, but Now I Can See* involving a Copt who becomes a Muslim due to the machinations of fundamentalists but ultimately "sees the light" and returns to his faith was created and distributed to embarrass Muslims. The Coptic Church officially banned the play turned DVD, but it resurfaced in a voting district where a Copt beat several Muslims to become the then ruling party (NDP) candidate.

Another Coptic member of the NDP became Egypt's first female mayor in late 2008, presiding over Komboha in Middle Egypt. She demonstrates that in her town such sectarian bickering is not necessary and that relative peace exists between the inhabitants. Eva Habil Kyrolos replaced her father a short time after his death. The Ministry of the Interior appointed her since she had in effect been gradually taking over the functions of her father during his illness, and she had the twin credentials of being a party member and a lawyer. The role of the mayor is often one that is inherited. In the 19th century, the state granted her great-great grandfather permission to establish the town, build a church, and create a community oven. Her family's story is telling of how major Coptic families established themselves.

Forgotten Citizens: Jews of Egypt

Although those who know their Biblical history are aware that Pharaoh cast the Jews of Egypt out, in later eras (see Chapter 2) Egypt became a place where Jews could thrive and prosper in comparison to other parts of the world. Although some Jewish scholars claim that Jews were "second-class citizens" in Islamic Empires, nowhere prior to the American and French revolutions did modern notions of citizenry exist, and even in those countries it did not apply to all citizens until much later. Therefore, the idea that Jews were treated as "second-class" citizens in various Muslim empires—Umayyad, Abbasid, and Ottoman—is not particularly fair since "equal" notions of citizenship spelled out in constitutions did not exist anywhere until quite recently.

Estimates vary as to how many Jews lived in prerevolutionary Egypt—some as high as 150,000 in the capital alone; however, only some had Egyptian citizenship. Many had migrated from other parts of the Ottoman Empire. Only 65,000 Jews were listed in the 1948 census, but most consider this figure to be severely under-enumerated (Beinin 1998). Many Westerners erroneously believe that most Egyptian Jews left after the 1948 Arab–Israeli War. In reality, most Jews left in the era of nationalizations and sequestrations of property after the Suez Crisis of 1956. Even after that period of time a small community remained, but the 1967 and 1973 wars had devastating repercussions for the minority community and called their national identity and citizenship into question. Jews had been important figures in the creation of the Egyptian nation-state, and the original flag of Egypt was Nile green with a crescent and three stars to represent its three religious communities. The flag, adopted by 1952 Free Officers, adopted new colors to symbolize revolutionary meanings and the eagle on the crest initially contained the crescent (an Islamic symbol) and three stars; however, in the wake of the Suez Crisis and the creation of the United Arab Republic (UAR), a new flag with simply two stars for the two states replaced it. After the dissolution of the UAR, the hawk of the Quraysh (1972–1984) and the Eagle of Saladin (without symbols to include Egypt's minority communities) appeared on the flag—statements about the (non)recognition of minorities in the national family.

Now it is estimated that less than 200 Jews remain in Egypt. There are not enough men to form a quorum (10) for a prayer at the few synagogues that remain open. Writing 10 years ago, Cairo historian Samir Raafat lamented the death of Robert Nahman stating that the loss meant 25 percent of the community's male population. While one cannot be sure whether Raafat is simply basing this figure on synagogue attendance, registration, or something else, anecdotal evidence from other researchers on the Jewish community indicates that the population in both Cairo and Alexandria is almost entirely elderly and female.

The Jews of Egypt are Arabic-speaking Rabbinites and Karaites, some of whom can trace ancestors to pre-Islamic times. In other words, they are every bit as "Egyptian" as their Muslim compatriots. The Karaites are a small breakaway sect of Judaism that began in Mesopotamia in the eighth century, but was well established in Fustat (just outside Cairo, or Old Cairo) by the ninth century. They are distinct from other Jews in their rejection of the Talmud as a source of law. While a small, minor community worldwide, they represented a significant force in medieval Egyptian Jewry. During the Ottoman period the Karaite population declined, and by 1948 they numbered only 5,000 in Egypt.

Rabbinite Jews include both Sephardic and Ashkenazi Jews. The former include Spanish Jews seeking shelter from the Almohads and intolerant Christians of the Iberian Peninsula. Some came directly in the 12th century, others came directly to

Church of St. George in Old Cairo. (Courtesy of Mona Russell)

Egypt after that time, and still others settled in various cities of the "would-be" Ottoman Empire and made their way to Egypt subsequently, particularly after business opportunities became available in the 19th century. Business as well as relative religious freedom brought Ashkenazi Jews from Europe in 19th century. Marriage between the various sects of Jews was not uncommon; however, marriage across class lines was less common. There were larger numbers of middle to lower class Arabic-speaking Jews than Ashkenazi Jews, but there were elite among all sects.

We Cannot Be Citizens Because There Is No Field

As the world has become a globalized, digitalized entity, Egypt too has entered this age with national identification documents that require one to record this information with qualifying documents, for example, birth certificates, marriage certificates, and so on. Baha'i Egyptians fought an eight-year battle to receive recognition and citizenship rights. The Baha'i faith is an offshoot of Shia Islam, although not viewed as "legitimate" by mainstream Sunni Muslims. Embracing one concept of Islam to the extreme, *tawḥid* (unity), this faith embraces unity of God, religion, and man, viewing history as a cycle of continuing and expanding revelations. While tolerant to the extreme of all faiths and demanding of equality among all people regardless of class, gender, or ethnicity, Baha'is worldwide have endured extreme discrimination.

One would hardly even know that there are Baha'is in Egypt had the controversy over identification documents not arisen. Baha'is who tried to register through the new system found only three fields (Islam, Christianity, and Judaism) in which they could enter a religion, and they utilized Egypt's courts to ask why it is even necessary to register a religion for citizenship papers. By 2004 the Ministry of the Interior insisted that Baha'is fill in one of the three acceptable fields or surrender their supporting documents. This action meant that they would not be able to collect pension checks, immunize their children, obtain visas, open bank accounts, and so on because they would not have the acceptable government identification documents. It was only in 2008 that the Supreme Administrative Court upheld the right of Baha'is to receive such documents without declaring their faith. It is estimated that Baha'is number about 2,000 in a country of about 83 million. The story of Baha'is and their struggle in Egypt is significant because it is telling of the struggle of any religious minority or dissident in Egypt. There are also small numbers of Shiites, agnostics, and atheists, but due to persecution (particularly of the latter two) it is difficult to assess their numbers. Because religion is intimately connected with all realms of life, and "wrong" answers yield obstacles in life, minorities are difficult to enumerate.

Popular Religion: Sufism and Other Trends

As Islam developed as a religion and became codified with an official version of the Quran (after Muhammad's death), the creation of a corpus of Islamic law, and the development of a science to study the life and customs (*hadith*) of the Prophet, another tradition arose in rejection to these written and mostly interpretive means of understanding religion. Scholars disagree about when or how it arose; there are even religious scholars who see pre-Islamic mystical trends in Egypt as breaking the ground for Sufism. Sufism probably helped Islam spread not only among Egyptian Copts with their ascetic traditions, but also in the further East with its syncretic ability to blend with other forms of spiritualism. With respect to mainstream Islam, most scholars believe that Sufism was rejection of the intellectual or interpretive or legalistic and written trends that took believers away from the spiritual and oral origins of the early community. The name Sufi comes from *sawf* or wool, from the simple garments worn by Sufi ascetics.

In Egypt organized guilds or brotherhoods, *tariqa* Sufism, began around the 12th century and merged with trends of saint veneration that had been established in the time of the heterodox Shiite Fatimids (r. 969–1171). Thus, contemporary Sufism incorporates four different and at times contradictory elements: desire for a spiritual path to Islam, asceticism, the veneration of saints or spiritual guides, and organization into guilds. The goal of Sufism is to achieve a spiritual unity with Allah, and various brotherhoods or orders utilize different means. Perhaps one of the most famous, still in operation in Egypt is the *mawlawi* order (*mevlevi*), better known in the West as whirling dervishes, who achieve this state by drawing energy from one hand directed toward the earth and one hand to the heavens as they spin. The leader of a brotherhood, the *shaykh*, establishes the rites for his group along a path of spiritual stations meant to elevate the individual's spirit to a greater love, devotion, and/or affinity for Allah. Explaining this experience to the lay person or the uninitiated is a bit difficult or even historically dangerous since the relationship between orthodox religious elements, the state, and *tariqa* Sufism has been controlling tolerant at best. Currently, the state oversees (read dominates) such groups with a Supreme Council of Sufi Orders under the purview of the Ministry of the Interior.

The epicenter in Cairo for such worship is the area between the Sayyida Zeinab mosque, built over the shrine for the Prophet Muhammad's granddaughter, and the Mosque of Hussein (Prophet's grandson), believed to contain the namesake's head, after his defeat at the battle of Karbala. In the annual event commemorating the Prophet's birth, a march of the 77 registered orders between the two sites draws about half a million Sufis. Scattered throughout the delta are other shrines, such as those for Ahmad Badawi (d. 1276) in Mansura or that of Shaykh Khalil (1872–1956) in Mansura where people gather, many of which date back to the medieval period, but some like the latter are relatively recent. The spiritual leaders or guides are thought to have significant enlightenment or power, and people seek their assistance for everything from marriage counseling to general healing to treatment for infertility.

The central aspect of Sufism is the *dhikr* or ceremony of remembrance. Breathing, meditation, recitation of the 99 names of Allah, counting beads, dancing, and chanting, are just a few of the pathways of achieving spiritual unity with Allah at a *dhikr*. Although Sufism is usually associated with men, women historically have attended *dhikrs* and have even been spiritual guides themselves. The presence of women at such functions has of course given more ammunition to mainstream religious elements to condemn them.

Furthermore, women have participated in their own popular religious practices, for example, the *zar,* which is usually described as an exorcism; but this term is not really accurate. One could potentially think of the *zar* as achieving a level of religious ecstasy in which evil spirits are placated and heightened awareness achieved through ritual actions. In other words, when men are engaging in this practice it is described as a form of mysticism, but when a group of women get together and engage in the practice it is described as superstition and hysteria. Like many of the practices of current religions, there are antecedents that predate Islam with connections to a time in Egypt when female priestesses healed other women. The religious establishment has come down hard on women, both contemporarily and historically for the *zar* as well as practices, like the veneration of saints and visiting shrines.

A practice that cuts across both the Muslim and Christian communities in the category of popular is the *subu',* a ritual held seven days after a baby's birth. The practice dates back to pre-Islamic and pre-Christian times, and the kinds of rituals hearken to ancient Egyptian or African traditions. The baby is carefully washed and dressed in new clothes, while an animal (usually a sheep) is ritually slaughtered, with salt scattered about the home to protect the newborn from the evil eye (see Chapter 6). The child carried in a decorated (large flat) sieve tours his or her new home accompanied by candles. The mother steps over the child seven times as older women chant and make noise with a copper mortar and pestle. Various types of gender-based admonitions are heaped on the child from the elders, mostly warning him or her to listen to his or her parents (especially the father). Symbolic gifts are exchanged between the host and visitors, who receive boxes of candy, nuts, and roasted chickpeas. The hosts receive variations on a clay jug, the shape of which depends on whether the child is a boy or a girl. The occasion is generally more festive for the birth of a boy where traditionally he was circumcised and named. Girls would traditionally get their ears pierced. Now only the symbolic gestures remain. In a country bitterly divided by sectarian conflict it is often these small but significant reminders of the ties that bind Egyptians.

REFERENCES

Abu Khalil. "Spiritual Training." Translated by the Domestic and Charitable Association of the Mosque of Abo Khalil and approved by Mosleh Ibrahim Mohammed Khalil. http://www.abokhalil.com/english.htm.

Ali, Abdullah Yusuf, Trans. *The Meaning of the Glorious Quran* (11th edition). Beltsville: Amana, 2004.

el-Amrani, Issandr. "The Emergence of the 'Coptic Question' in Egypt." *Middle East Report,* April 28, 2006. http://www.merip.org/mero/mero042806.html.

Armbrust, Walter. "The Riddle of Ramadan: Media Culture, and the 'Christmasization' of a Muslim Holiday." In *Everyday Life in the Muslim Middle East,* 335–48. Donna Bowen and Evelyn Early, eds. Bloomington: Indiana University Press, 1993.

Beinin, Joel. *The Dispersion of Egyptian Jewry: Culture, Politics, and the Formation of a Modern Diaspora.* Berkeley, CA: University of California Press, 1998.

"Egypt's ID Cards and the Baha'i Struggle for Privacy." *The Review of Faith and International Affairs,* December 11, 2009. http://www.rfiaonline.org/extras/articles/587-egypt-bahai-id-cards.

Emam, Amr. " Egypt's Hajj Business." http://www.islamonline.net/servlet/Satellite?c=Article C&cid=1227019238932&pagename=Zone-English-News%2FNWELayout.

Entry for Zakat, Philanthropy for Development. http://www.neareast.org/phil/en/page.asp?pn=27.

Geertz, Clifford. "Religion as a Cultural System." In *The Interpretation of Culture: Selected Essays.* New York: Basic Books, 1973.

Luisard, Pierre-Jean. "Le sufisme égyptien contemporain" (Contemporary Egyptian Sufism). *Égypte Monde Arabe* I (2) (1990). http://ema.revues.org/index218.html.

Minkin, Shane. "The Graveyards of Imperialism: Cemeteries in Alexandria, 1917–1972." Presentation at Middle East Studies Association (MESA), 2007.

Raafat, Samir. "Robert Nahman, the End of His Era." *Cairo Times,* November 10, 1999. http://www.egy.com/judaica/99-11-10.shtml.

Shihane, Gihan. "No Way Round the Hajj Quota." *al-Ahram Weekly,* February 21–27, 2002. http://weekly.ahram.org.eg/2002/574/eg5.htm.

Sonbol, Amira. "Society, Politics, and Sectarian Strife." In *The Political Economy of Contemporary Egypt.* Ibrahim Oweiss, ed. Washington, DC: CCAS, 1990.

St. Takla Coptic Church Alexandria. http://st-takla.org/.

SOCIAL CLASSES AND ETHNICITY

Ancient Egyptian Society: Setting the Stage

The highly centralized nature of Egyptian government necessitated by the Nile River made for a highly stratified society from ancient times. At the top of the social pyramid was the Pharaoh, followed by the high-level priestly class, the nobility, the ordinary priestly class, and finally the scribes and worthy professions (e.g., engineers and doctors). All of the preceding groups would be considered of a higher social order. Most Egyptians or ordinary Egyptians were working-class folks who were urban craftsmen, peasants, ordinary soldiers, or even tomb builders. There was not much slavery in ancient Egypt, although it did exist and there were also social outcasts, beggars, outlaws, and misfits who formed a small group below the working class. It should be noted that the military and the priestly class recruited from all walks of life, and with respect to the former, many different ethnicities (in addition to Egyptians) participated (e.g., Jews, Nubians, Armenians, etc.) at different points in history. The existence of a vast surplus and the needs of a highly organized bureaucratic state led naturally to a wide gulf between the social classes. As different occupiers came to control the surplus (Persians, Greeks, Romans, Arabs, Turks, etc.), they would move into the position of power and ordinary Egyptians would remain in their stations (see subsequently).

The Riddle of Modern Egyptian Identity

In a famous book outlining the principles of the Egyptian Revolution (1954), Nasser (d. 1970) states that modern Egypt falls into three circles: Arab, African, and Muslim. His purpose was to examine Egypt's intended place in world affairs. He envisioned the country taking a leadership role at the helm of these three overlapping circles. In doing so, he was defining Egypt's identity and evaluating its history. While he acknowledged the unique role of ancient Egyptian history and the contributions of Greco-Roman knowledge to that civilization, his concern was for the present state of Egyptian identity and its various components. The most important circle for Nasser was the Arab circle, comprising the "Arab Nation" from the Atlantic Ocean to the Arabian (Persian) gulf, the countries united by common language and scarred by imperialism. Great potential existed for this group that could be rallied under his leadership. Certainly all Egyptians could counter the force of imperialism, which also united the circles of Africa and Islam. While the Arab circle was the most important circle for Nasser, it presented some questions since potentially some of his population was not really Arab, although few would question the Arab identity of the Copts. Prior to the rise of Islam, Egypt was not an Arab state, and while the Coptic population had become culturally Arabized (see Chapter 2 and the section "A History" in Chapter 6), due to strict measures regarding non-marriage outside the faith, they are not necessarily blood "Arabs" particularly in Upper Egypt.

Nasser connected Egypt to two other circles that would help to keep his country united spiritually with millions of other Muslims as well as millions of other Africans seeking to cast off the yoke of imperialism. As for the latter, while Nasser made the statement that he stood by other Africans and recognized Egypt's existence in the continent, he did not acknowledge its Nubian population or its role in African imperialism in the Sudan, which happily seceded from its (imposed) union with Egypt in 1956. The final circle, or the Muslim circle, unites Egypt with Muslims beyond the Middle East, perhaps alienating the non-Muslim population (approximately 10 percent). This portion of the *Philosophy of the Revolution* that was meant to define Egypt's identity is telling of the problems in determining ethnicity in Egypt.

According to the current CIA *World Factbook,* Egypt is 98 percent "Egyptian" (which includes Muslims and Copts); however, the question of whether "Egyptian" comprises a separate ethnic identity is a difficult one. Egyptians do not form a separate race, but race and ethnicity are not necessarily the same thing. So contentious is the issue of whether Egyptians are Arab, African, or a composite race due to their position in North Africa that even the CIA decided to settle the issue by utilizing the cultural definition of ethnicity to embrace the majority of the citizenry; yet it distinguished a number of other minorities. Another 1 percent is divided among Berbers (mainly around Siwa oasis who speak Arabic rather than Berber), Nubians (many of whom have mixed with Arabs), Bedouin (Arabs who still herd and graze animals), and the Beja (distinguished by Beja language and found mostly in southeastern Egypt). The final 1 percent is divided among non-Coptic Christians, such as Armenians, Greeks, and other Europeans. If the CIA had used Arab blood as a determinant, then some of the Copts, the group with the continuous link to Egypt's past, might not appear as the "real" Egyptians. If the reverse were portrayed, then the Muslim majority would shout Christian favoritism.

Race, Religion, and Class

The issues of race, religion, and social class have been intertwined in Egypt since at least the days of the Greeks (331–30 BCE, which makes the subject extremely sensitive and thus the need to create new categories or to subvert old ones. The Greeks gave privileges to the ethnically Greek, Greek-speaking elite; however, it is clear that these boundaries were often porous and Egyptians utilized various means to advance themselves socially and financially. Greek remained the language of rule after the arrival of the Romans (30 BCE) and for several decades of Arab rule (639–706). With the emergence of Christianity in the region, another facet to the multidimensional nature of social status arrived. At first the Romans did not accept the new religion and persecuted Christians, but after the Romans (Byzantines) converted, the manner of worship became badge of Egyptian character intertwined with a rebellion against the foreign ruling authority, leading to the creation of a separate Coptic Church in 451.

After the arrival of Islam, a new social order came into place whereby an Arab, Muslim military elite ruled over a non-Arab, non-Muslim (Christian and Jewish) population (*dhimmis*) that supported the state by paying taxes, including an extra poll tax in return for not having to serve in the military. The *dhimmis* had complete autonomy over personal status matters to which they turned to their patriarch or rabbi to consult on personal status issues. As more people converted to Islam adjustments were made to the system so that Arabs could settle and mix with the population and the indigenous people could convert. Over time rather than Arab Muslims serving in the army, Islamic empires imported slaves from the territory between Europe and Asia just beyond the Black Sea, *mamluks* (see Chapter 2), to serve as an elite military force. These individuals fought some of the worst enemies of Islam in the Middle Ages, including crusading Christians who invaded Egypt and rampaging Mongols who threatened to do so. This military elite, distinguished by Turkish language, superior fighting skills, and the distinction of riding on horseback, was generally much fairer in complexion than the rest of the population, given their origins in Caucasus, Georgia, the Urals, and so on. They imported women from similar backgrounds for their harems. Thus, the military elite was associated with both power and whiteness, despite the fact that as individuals they began life as slaves. There were also African slaves, but they were generally used for the household and other sorts of menial positions (both male and female), although the children of any slave woman (regardless of color) inherited from the master as any other child. Therefore, families could potentially be multiracial.

Historically, another powerful group was long-distance traders (*tujjar*) who often intermarried with the blood children of mamluks, since mamluks often did not consider their own children strong enough to enter the military system. Remember, the mamluk system did create fictive bonds of kinship that tied slave children (mamluks) to their household even after their manumission (see Chapter 2). Eventually, these mamluks might be strong enough to marry their sons into the ranks of the *tujjar,* if they were not killed fighting external enemies in internecine battles against other mamluks, or in recurring bouts of the plague.

The only other significant force in medieval times was the religious establishment, the *'ulama,* who served as a bridge between the rulers and the ruled. They also had independent sources of wealth from administering religious endowments and various other types of duties that enabled them to function autonomously from the state up until the 19th century. High-ranking members of the *'ulama* often invested in trade and married into important commercial families. They provided rulers with legitimacy, and in times of hardship the people could call on them to petition the rulers with grievances. Together the high-ranking *'ulama,* the long-distance traders, and the military elite formed a class known as the *khaṣṣa,* or the elite, as opposed to the *'amma,* or everybody else, the masses. The *khaṣṣa* worked selfishly to defend its political, economic, and social self-interest, while the *'amma* clung to the only thing that it maintained: its authenticity, its roots, and its local knowledge as various groups representing the military or political branch of the *khaṣṣa* came and went (see Chapter 2). Egyptian agriculture and surplus depended on this knowledge.

The large body of peasants, who made up the majority of the population, for most of Egypt's history formed the backbone of the *'amma,* whether they were Muslim or Christian (most Jews were urban). At different points in time during the medieval period and during the Ottoman period there were people in urban areas who defied categorization in either the *khaṣṣa* or the *'amma,* people in what we might term a middle class. These were often people involved in urban professions, for example, artisans and craftsmen who perhaps had some modicum of education, but lacked the financial means, the social status, or the completion of the education to be considered among the *khaṣṣa*. Historian Nelly Hanna has studied probate records and argued that compared to Europe where a middle class slowly emerged, in Egypt, or at least Cairo, the middle class waxed and waned according to the city's economic fortunes (2003).

Nineteenth-Century Change

The reforms of Muhammad Ali and his successors in the 19th century changed class structure in Egypt. First, he defeated the most powerful mamluks and his successors phased out their personal use of slave retainers; however, manumitted mamluks and their descendents remained powerful. Even by the mid-late 19th century, manumitted mamluks still formed a key component of men in government service. Second, Muhammad Ali took away the independence of the religious establishment. Instead of having their own sources of wealth and means to make their own decisions, he made them salaried officials of the state. Third, he created private property and rewarded

Muhammad Ali, a professional soldier of the Ottoman Empire who seized control of Egypt in 1805 and ruled the country for more than four decades. (Library of Congress)

loyal citizens with large tracts of land. These benefits went to village noblemen who sent their sons to his new schools, as well as family members and hard-working bureaucrats. Fourth, with the expansion of the government, the bureaucracy, and the educational system to support it there was a subsequent and sustained growth of the middle class. Finally, Egyptians would be allowed to serve in the military (whether they desired it or not). This change restructured society such that anyone, regardless of religion or class could enter into the military, where previously it had been restricted to the *khaṣṣa*. The Ottoman Empire's *tanẓimat* reforms echoed many of Muhammad Ali's changes with the creation of an Ottoman Land code of 1858 and two proclamations that made all citizens equal before the law regardless of race or religion with equal access to government jobs including the military (1839 and 1856). Muhammad Ali's successors Said and Ismail worked toward the abolition of the slave trade, which for white mamluks had already ended, but continued for African and female slaves of all colors.

Nineteenth-century changes brought shifts to the nature and composition of the *khaṣṣa* and *'amma*. The religious establishment, aside from members who had commercial wealth and one or two high-ranking members, moved down into the ranks of the middle class or even the *'amma*. The Ottoman Egyptian elite included the manumitted mamluks and their descendents, the extended royal family, and the commercial bourgeoisie, who now sought marriage alliances with the newer members of the elite, that is, the large rural landowners. Together this group formed the new *khaṣṣa*. Particularly, after the end of female concubinage and the rise of bourgeois companionate marriage by the late 19th century, the *khaṣṣa* reinvented itself to maintain its position in the face of a growing European presence. Nevertheless, even some of the members of the *khaṣṣa* came from Southern Europe (mainly Greece and Italy). These were people who came to take advantage of the economic benefits that began during the reigns of Said and Ismail; and many adopted Egypt as their home—the so-called "*mutamiṣrun*"—"those who have become Egyptian." They are distinct from "foreigners," agents of large, foreign business interests without concern for the country.

With respect to marital practices, whether one was choosing a bride or a groom, fairness of skin color was a desired objective because it connected an individual to the old elite or simply to a background of nonmanual labor. Those individuals who made their living by long-distance trade would not have the same color as someone (even of the same skin tone) who toiled in the fields day after day. Wealthy women would have the leisure to stay indoors. Nevertheless, large tracts of land might make up for a darker skin tone in the politics of elitism, whether in the hands of a rural land-holding man or as part of a diminished dowry owed to a bride to be. By the turn of the century, skin whiteners advertised in newspapers and magazines seeking a non-gender-specific market.

Because the *khaṣṣa* was limited and the perks unevenly divided, by the last quarter of the 19th century, there was a movement for change. The nature of the *khaṣṣa* is to selfishly defend its interests, and it may even be divided over the best way to achieve these ends, particularly at a time when foreign interference was high, for example, before, during, and after the deposition of the Khedive Ismail (r. 1863–1879). One of the major problems was that extremely few ethnic Egyptians could rise up through the ranks to become officers in the army. They would be passed over for promotions or pensioned off before they could achieve this rank. By 1880 only a handful had made it. The *khaṣṣa* was not united on this issue since there were elements of the old *khaṣṣa* who wanted to maintain the privilege; however, with the rise of a new, mixed elite there was greater openness to the idea of allowing Egyptian promotion and support from the growing middle class. A second problem was that there was no constitution guaranteeing the rights of citizens or setting limitations on the authority of the Khedive, both the *khaṣṣa* and the nascent middle class could agree on this problem. After the deposition of Ismail and the rise of Tawfiq, the large number of financial cutbacks in government and the educational system brought criticism from all classes. Finally, the presence of foreigners and foreign interests cut across class boundaries leading to the cry of "Egypt for the Egyptians." This foundation helped spark the Urabi Revolt (see Chapter 2) that ultimately led to the British occupation. Naturally, the army would no longer be able to serve as a powerful arbiter of disputes in society. The British greatly reduced its numbers. The religious establishment, the historical bridge between the *khaṣṣa* and the *'amma,* was no longer in a position to intervene either.

From the 1919 Revolution to the 1952 Revolution

The 1919 Revolution was another attempt by the *khaṣṣa* to renegotiate its position for greater gain vis-à-vis the occupation (see Chapter 2). Egypt's nationalists, the politicians of the succeeding liberal era, were its large landowners who benefited from an economic relationship with the British occupiers. The British had greatly reduced the size, power, and ability of the military to act, and with four points of control and power shared between a powerful monarch and parliament, it would be highly difficult for Egypt to attain true independence. Where the nationalists had been highly critical of the British with respect to a wide range of health, education, welfare, and social programs, once they were in control of the purse strings they continued to pursue policies that advanced the export of cotton to the former occupiers. There were some modest gains, but they did not change the nature of the system. There were the beginnings of industrialization, but everything moved slowly with little protection for the peasant and the worker. Both struggled to exist as the gap between the rich and the poor expanded.

Meanwhile, by 1936 the ranks of the middle class had also widened and both the middle class and the *'amma* had grown fed up with the presence of the British on Egyptian soil. It was at this moment that the greedy *khaṣṣa* overplayed its hand in its negotiations, setting forth in motion the events that would ultimately lead to its demise as a force in governing Egypt. One of the pieces of fine print in the Anglo-Egyptian Treaty of 1936 was a clause that enabled Egypt to control and expand its armed forces, as well as allowing men of more humble origins to enter the new staff college. Most of the inner circle of the Free Officers entered between 1937 and 1939, the key figures enrolling the very first year.

Scholars are divided over what degree Egyptians considered themselves "Arab" in the period between the two revolutions (1919–1952). Reading elite memoirs would suggest less self-consciousness of Arab identity and more of a cosmopolitan Egyptian-ism, whereas reading the journal of the Muslim Brotherhood or even women's journals geared to the middle class indicate a higher level of concern for regional issues than writings emanating from the *khaṣṣa*. In other words, the *khaṣṣa* while demonstrating a wider notion of what it meant to be an Egyptian (inclusive of the Coptic and Jewish minorities) had a much more narrow vision of class and Egypto-centric interests; while the middle ranks of the middle class into the *'amma* were more concerned about regional issues such as the mounting crisis in Palestine. Advertising in journals represents the hopes and fears of these classes. Again, the skin-whitening advertisements serve as a barometer of change. The focus of the advertisements became more geared toward women; however, there were still advertisements that targeted men. The advertise-ments played on people's doubts regarding appearance, depression, and even divorce.

In 1952 the Free Officers movement within the army began a process to completely restructure society. Nasser wanted to break the monopoly of the 16 most powerful families that controlled political, economic, and social interests of the country. The *'amma* was willing to put its faith and support behind someone representing native Egyptian authenticity (Nasser), not a foreign entity—as the old *khaṣṣa* in its various iterations had been (British, the Muhammad Ali dynasty, the landowning politicians with foreign economic interests, the Ottomans, the mamluks, etc.). The measures that the new regime took to restructure society and the economy benefited the state and its powerful managerial class (especially of officers) rather than individual en-trepreneurs. It was this new group of technical and managerial *apparatchiks* who be-came the elite of the *khaṣṣa*, supported by the military. Arab socialism pushed down the upper middle class and elevated the impoverished, creating a new, improved *'amma.* The *'amma* paid a high price for its gains as Nasser dismantled the tools for democracy, for example, political parties, the 1923 constitution, and other indepen-dent means of citizen organization; he replaced them with hollow substitutions. Even in the liberal era (1922–1952) the tools for democracy had mainly served the interests of the large landowning class (*khaṣṣa*), but the potential for change existed.

Social Class in the Era of Infitah

The era of the 1970s presented a moment for *khaṣṣa/'amma* realignment once again. Egypt's defeat in the June 1967 War and the failure of Arab Socialism led Sadat to experiment in the realms of both foreign and domestic policies (see Chapters 2 and 3). With respect to the economy, Sadat opened the door for private investment in Egypt, which rapidly led to the rise of a new wealthy class. Although there were rapid rates of economic growth, its benefits were not widely felt in the country. Investment centered on construction of hotels, tourism, banking, and import or export ventures. The "new" *khaṣṣa* was not entirely new as a significant component of it was composed of the old elite families, many of whom had married into the revolution either literally or figuratively. Nasser's officers did not necessarily have the know-how or where-withal to run the private-sector companies that had been nationalized, while others connected their children to the children of key revolutionary figures (Abaza 2006).

These trends that started before Sadat's death escalated under Mubarak especially after the economic restructurings in the wake of the Gulf War with the debt relief and the monetary assistance that followed. Some of the aforementioned old families bided their time in the Gulf or Libya, earning investment money and making contacts that would facilitate their reemergence as joint investment groups rather than simply the blacklisted family name. Once again an extremely small, powerful *khaṣṣa* with strong external protection, like Gulf princes, seeking to maintain its significant holdings reemerged as a player on the Egyptian scene. Although the number has gone up to about two dozen, this handful of families with intricate ties to large holding companies and connections to the Mubaraks is eerily reminiscent of an earlier age. Bahgat, Orascom, and Osman are all examples of these groups with multiple and monopoly interests. For example, the Sawaris family controls a substantial interests in Orascom, a holding company for various subsidiaries including a large construction company, a cement company, a natural gas company, the largest tourism company, rights to the largest (and the first and for many years only) cellular and internet provider, Microsoft, and McDonalds (Abaza 2006). In the wake of the January 25 movement, some of these families have emerged as the biggest critics of the Mubarak regime. Some scholars claim that in recent years, the Mubaraks, in general, and Alaa and Gamal, in particular, have marginalized or outmaneuvered some of the most powerful men and families in Egypt.

When traveling in Cairo one would think that it is a wealthy place with the sight of Harley–Davidson dealerships, Hummers, and other luxury stores, along with Western restaurants such as Chili's, Fuddruckers, and fast-food chains such as McDonalds, Kentucky Fried Chicken, and Pizza Hut that deliver to homes and hotels. In fact, when Cairo reorganized phone numbering system in order to create more available numbers, all delivery numbers received special codes to indicate service. Nevertheless, the prices at these restaurants are beyond the reach of the average civil servant. For example, a Big Mac value meal costs 23 Egyptian pounds or about $4, potentially one to two days' salary of a civil servant. The disparities between the poor and the rich are incredible, with nearly half the population living below, at, or near the poverty line in the mid-1990s. The situation of unemployment and inflation has only worsened, and the World Bank has not yet released the statistics for this decade. In particular, with the inflation and increase in food prices in 2008, the levels of misery have increased astronomically in Egypt. The luxury goods market is meant to satisfy the needs of 5–10 percent of the population. The wealth is so

TABLE 5.1 Weekly Wages **with LE** for Public and Private Sector Employees

	1999	2000	2001	2002	2003	2004	2005	2006	2007	2008
Public	158	165	171	182	195	232	257	303	308	406
Private	120	137	138	141	149	175	168	172	214	275
Total	143	162	154	163	174	190	207	229	252	329

(*Source*: CAPMAS): http://www.capmas.gov.eg/eng_ver/sdds/SDDS2.htm, http://www.capmas.gov.eg/pages_ar.aspx?pageid=922.

TABLE **5.2** Inflation Rate Represented by Consumer Prices

Year	Inflation Rate
2003	4.3%
2004	4.3%
2005	9.5%
2006	4.9%
2007	6.5%
2008	9.5%*

*Other sources have indicated higher rates of inflation. (*Source:* CIA *The World Factbook*) https://www.cia.gov/library/publications/the-world-factbook/geos/EG.htm

heavily concentrated that the market focuses on selling extremely high-end items to the *khaṣṣa* because its members have so much disposable income that it makes more fiscal sense than selling cheaper (low-profit) items in volume to the masses.

Official statistics on the economy are nearly meaningless since the unofficial economy in Egypt exceeds the real one. A public-sector teacher might have an imported cigarette habit that far exceeds his monthly salary, but lives in a rent-protected apartment that costs only $1 per month; however, since he drives his brother's cab at night he earns extra money to send his kids to private school, make ends meet, and feed his Marlboro addiction. This is why *khaṣṣa/'amma* works better than the traditional classification because our teacher defies classification. His salary might be less than $5 a day and he probably has no money for savings or investment, although his children's education is potentially a form of investment and his own education is somewhat of a class marker. However, with the massification of education it became less of one, particularly since he did not do well enough on the General Secondary Exam (GSE) to achieve a status position.

As the gap between the rich and the poor widens, so too does the criticism, and not just from the poor. A middle-class supervisor of a public-sector textiles firm with two grown up (but unmarried) children and one teenaged child still in her home, married to a retired naval officer now working in the public sector as an engineer, remarked with disgust at the elite 5–10 percent of her compatriots, "they have the money to put their dogs in hotels and buy them fancy foods while the sons of the country go hungry. Are we Muslims?!" Even middle-class Egyptians were feeling an economic pinch in the summer of 2008, and someone, for example, the textiles supervisor living on her public-sector salary, her husband's military pension, and his salary from his private sector job, still had to think about the unmarried children at home and their futures.

The *khaṣṣa* is well aware of this resentment that the underbelly of the *'amma* feels even more keenly. They isolate themselves by creating new gated communities with fanciful names such as Dreamland and Beverly Hills, where they can parade in their new designer clothes and safely hide in their mansions, pools, cars, and golf courses.

Some have even taken to hiring Indonesians, Filipinos, and other Asians who are seen as more tractable than Egyptian domestics and do not demand returning home to their families. As Egyptian domestics face loss of work at home, they have turned to working in the Gulf, a mark of shame for the rapidly diminishing *'ammafied* middle class that once proudly sent doctors, lawyers, teachers, and other professionals to fill positions that the once uneducated oil-wealthy *khaligis* (Gulf Arabs) could not fill. They are now faced with sending their most vulnerable male and female citizens to work as domestics where they face verbal, physical, and sexual abuse.

Despite the many changes in the economy and fluctuations in the composition of the *khaṣṣa*, its general nature has remained the same: self-interested. Meanwhile, the *'amma* has remained remarkably steady throughout Egypt's history. The peasant was the central element; however, after the opening of the economy there was a shift. Service industries, which are broadly defined to include vocations from teacher to tour guide to barista, now account for more than half of the workforce population (51 percent). Nevertheless, agriculture (including fisheries) still accounts for 32 percent of labor force. Only 17 percent of the workforce is in industry. The *'amma* stands as a reminder to the *khaṣṣa* of what it means to be Egyptian, even as the *khaṣṣa* seeks shelter in its gated communities. Historian Amira Sonbol views the Islamist trends of the post-1967 era as the *'amma* seeking to restore a lost authenticity, one to which it has not had full access since the reforms of the 19th century (2000).

As for social mobility, historically there have been a number of keys to success: education, language, connections, and strategic marriage. These factors have often been interconnected. A poor peasant who does not have the means or ability to attend school will not likely learn the language(s) necessary to advance in Egypt at any particular historical moment (see Chapter 6). In the Ottoman era a peasant who chose to give up the labor of one of his children and sent him to al-Azhar for education meant that he would have one child who could break the barrier and reach the *khaṣṣa*, just as a maid knows today that working extra shifts and/or working for foreigners who pay more money will give her the opportunity to give her intelligent daughter private lessons so that she can succeed on the GSE and achieve a score to go into medicine or engineering. Frequently, it is in school that connections for work and advancement later in life are made. Nevertheless, the "free" educational process is one that is fraught with difficulty and expenses, but it is an investment that can produce long-term benefits. Given the nature of marriage and courtship rituals, it is not uncommon for an enterprising young man to marry his superior's daughter. Fairness is still a desired trait and a sign of beauty. Advertisements for skin whiteners still link the product with notions of status, but also with youth, happiness, and marital success. Currently, in Egypt these products target the female audience (Ghannam 2008).

REFERENCES

Abaza, Mona. *Changing Consumer Cultures of Modern Egypt: Cairo's Urban Reshaping.* Leiden: Brill, 2006.

Baron, Beth. *Egypt as a Woman, Nationalism, Gender, & Politics.* Berkeley, CA: University of California Press, 2005.

CIA *The World Factbook. Egypt.* https://www.cia.gov/library/publications/the-world-factbook/geos/eg.html.

Ghannam, Farha. "Beauty, Whiteness, and Desire: Media, Consumption, and Embodiment in Egypt." *International Journal of Middle East Studies* 40 (2008): 544–46.

Hanna, Nelly. *In Praise of Books: A Cultural History of Cairo's Middle Class, Sixteenth to the Eighteenth Centuries.* Syracuse, NY: Syracuse University Press, 2003.

McCloskey, Denise. "Race before 'Whiteness': Studying Identity in Ptolemaic Egypt." *Critical Sociology,* 28 (1–2) (2002): 13–39.

Mitchell, Timothy. "Dreamland: The Neoliberalism of Your Desires." *MERIP,* August 9, 1999. http://www.merip.org/mer/mer210/mitchell.html.

Nasser, Gamal Abd al-. *Philosophy of the Revolution.* Buffalo, NY: Smith, Keynes, and Marshall, 1959.

Russell, Mona. *Creating the New Egyptian Woman: Consumerism, Education and National Identity, 1663–1922.* New York: Palgrave, 2004.

Sonbol, Amira. *The New Mamluks: Egyptian Society & Modern Feudalism.* Syracuse, NY: Syracuse University Press, 2000.

WOMEN

Introduction

Feminist Nawal el-Saadawi (discussed later in this section) argues that contemporary Egyptian women's lives are not filled with as much prestige, privilege, or equality as their ancient Egyptian sisters whose career paths were as diverse as priestesses, healers, and brewers. Then, as through most of Egypt's history, most women stayed at home to pursue roles of wives and mothers. Women in ancient Egypt, like women after the rise of Islam, could own and inherit property. A major difference with their Muslim counterparts (until quite recently) was that they could seek and obtain divorces. Understanding women's lives today means understanding how agricultural life has been dominated by the Nile River (see Chapters 1 and 2); the coming of monotheism, first Christianity and then Islam (see Islam: A Way of Life); and examining the impact of modernization on women's lives from 1800 to the present day.

1800–1848

Although the 19th century was an extraordinary period of change for women and men, the life of the typical woman in 1800 was very much like the typical woman's life in 1600s or 1700s. Most women were peasants who worked alongside their husbands in the production of wheat or sugar. Some women were involved in family-based urban or rural craft production, the most common being textiles. In cities there were women who practiced professions such as traders, bathhouse keepers, musicians, vendors, or dancers. Working, even as a dancer or a musician did not necessarily stigmatize a woman, but practicing a profession in front of men or even women of a lower class would.

Slavery was a component of upper-class life in Egypt before 1900. Elite households would purchase Circassian or Georgian female slaves to serve as companions or entertainers in their homes. Female slaves of African origins generally held lower positions in the household; however, these divisions were not impermeable. Any slave, white or black, who produced a child for her owner would achieve the status of *umm walad* (mother of child) and could not be sold, and her child would inherit as much as any other heir. Many of these women, some of whom married their owners and/or inherited property, became quite wealthy. Like other elite women, some of them became businesswomen by investing their wealth. They also extended their influence by donating to charitable causes such as mosques, schools, asylums, fountains, and soup kitchens. Although all elite women, freeborn or slave, followed Islamic norms with respect to gendered segregation, this restriction did not mean that they led boring lives. Modesty garments and architectural styles, both of which physically separated women from men, allowed the former freedom of movement to visit one another, attend religious and secular festivals, and go to the cemeteries or for regular trips to the bathhouses. Women's participation in some of these activities caused great tension and fear among some segments of the religious establishment, who continued to write and warn about the dangers of women in public spaces. The existence of these writings would seem to indicate that women did these things on a regular basis despite such denunciations.

Muhammad Ali's (r. 1805–1848) reforms had far-reaching implications on the lives of ordinary and elite women (see Chapter 2, section on age of Muhammad Ali). He set out on an aggressive program of economic and military expansion aimed at making Egypt more autonomous from its Ottoman overlord. A new army, bureaucracy, educational system, and economic infrastructure were required to sustain his development plans. Muhammad Ali turned Egypt into a monopoly whereby he was the single buyer and seller of all goods. He dismantled the tax-farming system, created private property, and introduced long-staple cotton to the country. He played to Egypt's strengths by creating factories to produce textiles, broke tradition by employing women in those factories but maintained cultural mores by keeping female employees segregated.

Muhammad Ali founded the first national army in Egypt, which involved conscription; he utilized large numbers of men in public works projects. Early in his reign campaigns and projects tended to be shorter and closer to home. Women and children might even follow trying to maintain production of the family unit; however, as the campaigns and the projects became longer and more complex, women and children were left behind to fend for family plots of land. Women were often abandoned or widowed without confirmation, and given the nature of Islamic law there was often little hope of remarriage. Although schools of law differ on the issue, most require that a woman wait a period longer than a typical lifetime for her husband to return before she could entertain the (im)possibility of remarriage. Such a woman might also face the prospect of fighting her husband's family in court for her share of the property. With respect to public works projects, rather than being an innovation, recent research indicates that the Ottomans as well carried out increasingly complex projects in the previous century, with similar implications for women. Given the demands of conscription, the continued public works projects created more difficulties for the women left behind.

Although Muhammad Ali created factories, the bulk of production still remained home-based. The state-created monopolies meant that families had to buy and sell materials at state-set prices. Although the textile industry suffered from severe foreign competition, other women's crafts flourished, for example, embroidery and rug-making. The existence of the factory system tended to institutionalize gendered division of labor.

The state's desire for increased production led to an increased awareness regarding public health. Muhammad Ali needed a healthy populace to produce his goods and to conscript his army. Furthermore, he needed 100 percent of his population to be healthy, not just 50 percent. His medical advisor Antoine Clot suggested training women as midwives when there was an outbreak of venereal disease in the army because women refused treatment from male doctors (and/or their families refused them this treatment). Similar restrictions prevented Egyptian women from studying with male instructors. Clot solved the problem by buying the first few students (African slaves) and a couple of eunuchs to monitor the school. While the first teachers were men, the school eventually produced its own instructors. As time passed orphans and others severely affected by state policies found their way to the School of Midwifery, which opened in 1832. It provided housing, clothing, food, tuition, and even pocket money for students. Recruitment remained a problem, and despite the fact that graduates received the same rank as men from the School of Medicine, it was not a desired career track at any time in the 19th century. Some scholars have disputed the role of female doctors arguing that they were simply tools that the state utilized to extend its authority over women's bodies, while others emphasize their importance in extending healthcare to other women. Regardless, when the British arrived in 1882, they revised the curriculum, reduced the number of students, and created a program geared toward producing nurses rather than doctors. As early as 1836, the Committee of Public Instruction acknowledged the importance of education for all members of society; however, it did nothing to sponsor other schools for girls.

Despite their prestigious position in society, elite women suffered from the reforms of Muhammad Ali. Previously, the old mamluk system kept men away for long periods of time, and women ran large households. Even to call a mamluk household a household is somewhat of a misnomer, since it was more like a compound or a campus with multiple buildings. In the case of a truly powerful mamluk grandee it housed something on the order of 200 inhabitants, including male retainers and female concubines and servants. When Muhammad Ali created a national army and killed most of his mamluk enemies, he eliminated this system. Therefore, only female slavery existed in large measure. Elite women now lived in homes with a full-time, resident patriarch. The state had taken many of their lucrative sources of wealth. Muhammad Ali distributed private property to loyal, male servants of the state, as well as to members of his own family. Although women could inherit land and royal women held significant tracts of land, land ownership in the new state was male dominant. While elite Muslim women had always lived by a system in which men could marry up to four wives and take unlimited concubines, the stakes seemed to have changed with the new household and the new state.

1848 to World War I

Over the course of the second half of the 19th century, great changes occurred in the lives of Egyptian women as the country was drawn further into the world economy and came largely to function as a supplier of raw cotton to the United Kingdom. Most women were still peasants, but the nature of agriculture changed with the introduction of cotton and private property, further codified by the Ottoman Land Code of 1858. Peasant lands eroded with the creation of large, landed estates. More and more men went to work for salaries on these estates, whereas women tried to eke out an existence on the family's subsistence plot back at home. By the turn of the 20th century, subsistence was nearly impossible, and the value of women's labor had become marginalized with the rise of wage labor for men.

As a result of land dispossession and dreams of a better life in the city, many peasants (with or without their families) fled to Cairo, Alexandria, Port Said, and some of the larger cities of the delta. Conditions in the cities for newly arrived peasants were not better than the ones that they left, and for the women who remained, it was a similar story of struggling to hold on to any property (moveable or otherwise) or being forced into domestic service.

The influx of foreigners, Egypt's integration into the world economy, and the urbanization that took place was not entirely negative. For women of the growing middle and upper classes more positive changes were taking place. Daughters of officers and bureaucrats would have greater opportunities by the turn of the century with the spread of education. Ismail (r. 1863–1879) opened the Siyufia (Sania) School, the first primary school for girls, in Cairo in 1873. Like the School for Midwifery there was an immediate difficulty finding students. The poor did not want to send their daughters to school because they needed their labor, the elite could afford to educate their daughters at home, and those in between the two extremes were few in number. Once again the first students were slaves from the royal family as well as some from prominent Cairene families.

Ismail told the U.S. consul-general that he viewed female education with an eye toward the end of the slave trade (1877), hoping to substitute educated Egyptian peasant girls. The linkage between slavery, domestic service, and education meant that few girls with options chose to go to the Siyufia (Sania) school. Other options included schools run by missionaries and minority communities, private schools, tutors, European governesses, and schools attached to mosques (*kuttabs*). Thus, education for girls in the latter half of the 19th century ran the gamut from entirely free including room, board, and pocket money in government schools to free at some of the missionary schools to nominal and sliding charges in some mission schools to hefty fees at some of the exclusive private schools. Curriculum in the Sania and Abbas (opened 1895) government schools pushed a domestic curriculum (cooking, laundry, childcare, sewing, and embroidery) in addition to the basics of Arabic reading and writing, religion/morals, French, and history. Private and missionary schools offered a wide range of subjects, some teachers focusing solely on literacy via the Bible to sophisticated programs of study involving multiple European languages, art, and music. The more exclusive the school, the less likely the curriculum was to include practical home economics. Great debates took place in the mainstream and burgeoning women's press about what this curriculum should include; it was often divided along class and gender lines.

In the period between 1892 and 1914 there were 20 journals founded, by and/or for women. The contributors and readers included a number of foreign and minority communities including Syrian Christians, Jews, Armenians, and Greeks, many with longstanding ties with Egypt (Baron 1994). With increasing numbers of schools more Egyptian women could read. Although overall female literacy rates remained at about six percent, rates in the large cities of the delta were double or triple the national average, with rates for unmarried women surpassing those levels. Arabic's oral tradition allowed younger, literate women to share print culture with others. The household became the key to reform, and without an educated woman at its helm, there would be no redemption for a new Egypt.

The nature of the elite household had greatly changed with the suppression of the slave trade. Architecture reflected the changes in the new home with Western styles replacing Islamic ones. The Turkish-speaking elite began to intermarry with the Egyptian elite, and bourgeois monogamy formed the marital ideal. Servants, governesses, and other unprotected female workers now became the targets of male attention, which had formerly been the domain of concubines. Commentaries in the women's press vigorously opposed marriages and relationships that crossed boundaries of class, culture, or ethnicity. Within another few decades one of the most common motifs in cartoons would be of the innocent child revealing the kiss he or she witnessed between his or her father and the maid.

The household and household politics were topics of both the mainstream and the women's presses. While elite and upper-middle-class women deemed practical home economics beneath them, the "science" of home management was an honor worthy of national attention. Male nationalists used the trope of the family and the household to criticize the monarchy and the occupation, as well as a call for reform from within (Pollard 2005).

World War I, 1919 Revolution, and Egypt's Liberal Era

As discussed in Chapter 2, World War I came to a close and the British occupation continued. It provided new fuel for the women's press and an organizational structure for a women's movement. A delegation (*wafd*) of Egyptians led by Saad Zaghlul went to the residence of the British High Commissioner to ask permission to attend to the Versailles Peace Conference (January 1919) to call for Egyptian independence. The British rejected Egypt's request, and by March 1919 wide-scale rioting in Egypt occurred among all classes. Upper-class men and women of the "Wafd" party organized controlled protests, signed petitions, and waged a campaign against the British in the press. Demonstrations, arrest and deportation of leaders, and celebrations marking the return of such leaders characterized the period between 1919 and 1922, when Egypt gained its partial independence. Women were crucial players during this time period since many of their husbands, fathers, and brothers were arrested, and they were thrust into leadership roles. Some scholars have questioned why male nationalists, who utilized women so effectively in the 1919 Revolution, then turned their backs on women's rights and issues in the writing of the 1923 constitution and other legislation that followed in the so-called "liberal" era (Badran 1995). More recently, scholarship has focused on how women's participation in demonstrations did not have a feminist agenda in its early years and that historical memory has clouded the events by using pictures of women protesting and infusing that memory with a feminist consciousness or that male nationalists were never actually focused on women, but using the home and family as a metaphor for the nation and their own selfish interests (Baron 2005).

The key players in the early mainstream secular women's movement include Huda Shaarawi (d. 1947), who headed the Wafdist Women's Central Committee (WWCC) and later founded the Egyptian Feminist Union (EFU); Safiyya Zaghlul (d. 1946), wife of the exiled political leader; Princess Chevikiar (d. 1947), the first wife of King Fuad and leader of the New Woman Society; Esther Fahmi Wisa (d. 1990), a Copt-turned-Protestant social activist who took leadership of the women's Wafd after Shaarawi; Munira Thabit (d. 1967), activist and journalist; Fatima (Rose) al-Youssef (d. 1958), Syrian-born actress and journalist; and Doria Shafik (d. 1975), French-educated activist and journalist.

Women worked actively together during the 1919 Revolution because their goals were united. As the women continued to meet, organize, and discuss other objectives, it became clear that there would be breaks in the movement related to personalities, politics, and visions of the role of the monarchy. Shaarawi founded the EFU even before her break with the Wafd party. Those following Huda Shaarawi followed the path of Western feminism and joined international women's conferences; however, by the 1930s and 1940s it was difficult for Egyptian and Arab participants to make Europeans understand their feelings regarding Zionism. Within Egypt, it was difficult to make inroads with male politicians with respect to women's suffrage. Modest gains were made with respect to expanded education (compulsory primary education 1923), raising the legal age of marriage to 16, and just prior to the revolution (1951) ending state sanctioning of prostitution (a vestige of the colonial state). The personal experience in households with multiple wives and/or concubines marked these women's activism; yet at the same time, very few of their compatriots lived in such households.

While Shaarawi represented the rising hopes and dreams of what would become the new class of politicians, Princess Chevikiar represented an opposing pole of feminism, nationalism, and philanthropy embodied in the monarchy. Although divorced from her cousin King Fuad (r. 1917–1936), she still represented the family since Fuad kept his wife Nazli secluded. Her New Woman Society and magazine competed with Shaarawi's EFU and its *L'Egytienne*. Doria Shafik had ties with both Shaarawi and Princess Chevikiar. Shaarawi had sponsored her studies abroad at the Sorbonne where she received a *Doctorate d'Etat,* but when she returned she worked for the Princess's magazine. Shafik believed she could help the maximum number of women by utilizing any resources available to mobilize middle-class women. She tapped into Chevikiar's resources to start her own magazine, *Bint al-nil* (daughter of the Nile), and after the death of both of her benefactors, she began a political organization with the same name.

Rose al-Youssef played an important role in making Egyptian women aware of the events of the day with the founding of a publication bearing her name in 1925. The magazine originally conceived as cultural journal, owing to the editor's background as an actress, quickly demonstrated its political flavor with its famous covers and political cartoons, as well as stories and articles incisively critiquing Egyptian politics. Other women, for example, Latifa Zayyat (d. 1996), Inji Aflatun (d. 1989), and Fatma Zaki (d. 2004), chose to oppose the political system by joining radical groups, namely various incarnations of the Communist party. Egyptian Communism had its roots amongst intellectuals, and it spread through student groups in the 1940s. These women opposed both gender and class oppression.

Some women who had previously been active in the original feminist movement began to splinter when they disagreed with the goals of Western feminism. They sought an indigenous model of feminism, and looked for a more inclusive model of organization. Labiba Ahmad (d. 1951) utilized her journal *Female Renaissance* to seek not only political, but also economic, cultural, and moral independence from the British. Zainab al-Ghazali (d. 2005), a one-time supporter of the EFU, broke ranks and formed her own Muslim Women's Association in 1936; and by 1948, she joined the Muslim Brotherhood, which helped newly relocated peasants in the city with soup kitchens, workshops, and job-placement programs.

1952 to Present

Male politicians of the liberal era had done little to deal with the major problems affecting women's lives in the 20th century: illiteracy, poverty (related to landlessness), and inequality in the political and judicial systems. Even where legislation existed, for example, compulsory education, it had not been implemented. A group of young army officers headed by Gamal Abd al-Nasser spearheaded a revolution in July 1952 that would have far-reaching implications on the lives of women at many levels, yet continuity on others.

Although many credit the Nasserist regime for its track record on education, much can be attributed to the sheer need after the expulsion of foreign technicians as a result of the Suez Crisis (1956) and the migration of many educated foreigners in wake of the nationalizations that followed. By the early 1960s, the regime had made the educational system free at all levels, promised jobs to all graduates, and granted maternity leave. The numbers of children in elementary school more than quadrupled between 1952 and 1965, and nearly half of those children were girls. The growth rate for women attending higher education was astounding, increasing sixfold between 1960 and 1976, with more than half of those women entering the sciences by the end of that period. While not entirely gender-blind, the state education and civil service system facilitated the hiring and promotion of women. The "massification" of the educational system under Nasser and his successors, nevertheless, meant a severe decline in its quality.

Although the Mubarak government boasted of high enrollments, the latter did not translate into high rates of attendance nor equate with literacy. The reality is that Egypt today remains on UNESCO's list of E-9 countries with high populations and high rates of illiteracy. Mothers continue to struggle in the role defined at the turn of the previous century as the individuals responsible for their children's educational development. These struggles take place in a variety of class settings whether it is a maid working from dawn to dusk to send her child to a private school, or a working mother rushing home from her job to shuttle her children to their various private tutors so that they can succeed on the GSE that determines where and what they can study at the university level.

With respect to land, on the eve of the revolution the wealthiest 2 percent of the population owned 50 percent of the land. Nasser limited land ownership to 200 *feddans* (approximately 208 acres) and later reduced it again to 100 *feddans* by re-distributing land to peasants. These measures improved the overall quality of life, but without other alternatives, there have not been remarkable improvements over the course of the last half century. It was only in the later years of Sadat and under Mubarak that peasants were allowed to leave the country and work in the Gulf, sending remittances back to Egypt. While this served to raise the wages of those

The new campus of AUC in New Cairo. Since its founding in 1919, the university has been closely identified with Egypt's elite. (AP Photo/Maya Alleruzzo)

who remained home, namely women and children, it once again placed those women left behind in a precarious position as their husbands were often subject to conditions beyond their control: foreign immigration, dual households, and conscription (Iran–Iraq war). Many middle-class women participated in labor migration to the Gulf with their husbands, but this luxury was not afforded to peasant women or the urban poor. Egyptian women cannot travel without the permission of their husbands, and while not always enforced, a poor woman would find it as difficult to leave as a political dissident.

With respect to political participation, initially the Nasser regime was no more committed to women than the politicians of the liberal age. Activist Doria Shafik had challenged the old regime to offer the same political and civil liberties to women as men, and her *Daughter of the Nile Union* and other women's groups, managed to gain female suffrage from the new administration in 1956. Nevertheless, such a right was growing meaningless with Nasser's increasing authoritarianism. The government had already liquidated political parties and was moving toward the absorption of women's organizations by the early 1960s under the Ministry of Social Affairs headed by Hikmat Abu Zayd. The Ministry and the Arab Socialist Union (ASU) now took over many functions previously dictated by elite women's groups, and it ventured into new areas such as family planning.

There were some elites who survived the revolution by creating business, personal, and marriage alliances with the new officer class. These connections were celebrated by conspicuous consumption in marriages and vacations in the 1960s that would open the path for Sadat's open door economic policies of the 1970s and the new consumption of the Mubarak years. While women had some new paths open with the freer economic and political systems, Egypt was still constrained with its old socialist promises and system.

Female politicians, academics, and lawyers have been key in bringing about change for other women by working against the system, within the system, and with other women around the world. Notable in the latter two categories is Dr. Farkhonda Hassan (b. 1930), a scientist, a women's activist, and a parliamentarian. Trained as a geologist, Dr. Hassan's interests naturally extend to a concern for the environment; she is a member of the international organization Scientists without Borders. Until the 2011 revolution, this professor emeritus at the American University in Cairo served parliament continuously since first elected in 1979. She resigned her post as women's secretary-general for the ruling NDP so that she could be the secretary-general for the National Council on Women (NCW). Her role in UN institutions and NGOs are too numerous to list as she demonstrates what one woman can do for her country. Since the NCW was so intimately tied to the ruling party it is unlikely this institution will outlive the 2011 revolution since its titular head was Madame Mubarak, thus tainting the work of the group in the eyes of many women's groups.

Infamous for her outspoken views on sexuality, patriarchy, government, and world politics, Dr. Nawal el-Saadawi (b. 1931) has a larger following among foreign feminists than among Egyptian women; her Arab Women's Solidarity Association has been shut down by the government a number of times. Her conflicts with Islamic militants actually earned her house arrest by the government in the early 1990s (which feared blame if she were assassinated), and militants unsuccessfully tried to divorce her from her husband on the basis of apostasy in 2001. She has published more than two dozen works (fiction and nonfiction), which have been published in 30 languages.

In 2000 lawyer and activist Mona Zulfikar was part of a team that successfully utilized rights guaranteed to women by Islam to make divorce more accessible to women. In 1979 women's organizations had utilized the executive branch via Jehan Sadat to make these changes, but they had been overturned on constitutional grounds.

Women were prominent members of the January 25 movement to overthrow the regime of Hosni Mubarak, just like the 1919 Revolution. The role played by social networks, telephones, and instant messaging in the early period was particularly important. One video that went viral on YouTube of Asma Mahfouz, represents the spirit of Egyptian womanhood, in which she encourages all Egyptians to take to the streets on January 25 and demonstrate like herself a single, young woman. Using gendered language she shamed the men of Egypt into joining her. After the movement's success in forcing Mubarak to step down on February 11, the Committee selected by the Supreme Council of the Armed Forces (SCAF) to amend the constitution contained no women.

Doctor and author Nawal El Saadawi of Egypt receives the Doctor Honoris Causa decoration from the French-speaking and Flemish Brussels Free University, November 28, 2007, in Brussels. (BENOIT DOPPAGNE/AFP/ Getty Images.)

Culture, Religion, and Marriage

Egypt's loss to Israel in the 1967 war combined with economic and political strains breathed new strength into fundamentalist currents that were already in existence, among both Muslim and Coptic women. The return of the *ḥijab* (headscarf) in the last two decades of the 20th century has been greatly debated by many scholars. There may have been a class (lower-middle) and age factor (20s) in the 1980s, due to a complex set of factors including Egypt's loss in the 1967 war and the overall failure of secular Arab socialism, the circumstances generated by urbanization, and the "massification" of the education system (see The Copts in Egypt). Nevertheless, by the late 1990s the overwhelming majority of adult Muslim women had adopted some form of the headscarf, although relatively few opted for the complete facial and head covering. The adoption of Islamic dress has heightened distinctions between Muslim and Coptic women, evidence of the growing tension between the communities since the 1970s.

While religion and the return of the *ḥijab,* for many women, is a critique of Western politics and consumption, ironically, it can be associated with new forms of consumption and sexuality. Large numbers of stores cater to the Islamic chic fashion, which can also be purchased online. Many, from anthropologists to casual observers, have noticed the liberating and concealing effect of the *ḥijab* on young lovers in a society that monitors premarital behavior quite rigidly. Egypt remains a society where nearly all women marry, engagement generally precedes courtship, and premarital sex is taboo. Although the internet and new venues for consumption (malls, new cafés, and bowling alleys) provide new means for meeting prospective mates, these means are limited to those members of the elite who can afford them. Family (broadly defined) remains the single most important facilitator for relationships, whether as a means of introduction or through cousin marriages. Estimates vary significantly; consanguine marriage rate is about 11 percent nationally; however, rates in Upper Egypt are easily triple of the national average.

Dating as Westerners know it does not exist in Egypt. The official courtship or dating process begins after one gets engaged, that is, after intentions are declared. At this time the couple may go to appropriate venues for specific amounts of time, perhaps even accompanied by a relative, depending on the conservatism of the family. Engagements are not taken lightly, but they can usually be dissolved without problem because this period is seen as the time when the couple decides if they are compatible.

One of the major crises of marriage in the late 20th century has been acquiring "key money" for an apartment. Given Nasserist rent controls and a new dual system of "rental" apartments for rent or sale to foreigners or the elite (to which the old rules do not apply), there is a major housing shortage in Egypt, generally, and Cairo, specifically, which is partially real and partially created. Families sit on old rent-controlled apartments whether in use or not (to which they have squatter's rights), and landlords have no reason to improve the buildings that take up prime real-estate space in Cairo. Meanwhile, new apartments are expensive, and it can take years for young couples to save the money to get married, often after the prospective groom spends years working in the Gulf.

The cost of weddings in Egypt has sky-rocketed, and on average Egyptian grooms and their fathers spend about 43 months' salary on a typical wedding. These costs include not only the food and entertainment, but also the *shabka* (jewelry gift) that a husband gives to his prospective bride, the *mahr* (the bride's price), provisions for the new home, which according to some interpretations includes the home itself, but can simply mean appliances or house wares by other interpretations. Those of a more conservative ilk opt for less jewelry and perhaps no dancer or even music, whereas the wealthy, particularly the nouveau riche, see the wedding as a symbol of their status. Thus, the *shabka* must be ornate and of precious stones, the *mahr* high, the food plentiful and of the highest quality, and the wedding in a five-star hotel. For the truly wealthy, however, the *mahr* can simply be a token price, for example, a few cents, meaning that the woman cannot be purchased. Even in smaller towns girls are opting to get their hair styled in a salon, wear a Western-style wedding gown, and even get professionally applied makeup. In Cairo one can find sharp-minded businesswomen who provide all services for the wedding from planning the clothing of the wedding party to styling the hair, makeup, and nails of the bride on her big day.

To escape the trap of consumerist, Western-style weddings with all the associated costs, many couples in the past decade or so have resorted to *'urfi* (common-law) marriage. All that is required for such a marriage is someone to marry the couple in front of two witnesses. *'Urfi* marriages provide couples greater leeway to have guilt-free sex, ease of marriage before "key money," and/or the ability to marry without expense; however, since the marriage is not documented like a regular marriage (by binding contract), there are a number of negative consequences for women. Up until the changes in divorce law in 2000, the government did not even recognize such marriages. Women can use the new law to leave a marriage, but they cannot seek alimony or child support; they can only do so if they have documentation—the "contract" signed by the two witnesses to the marriage.

Finally, acknowledging the practice, the government has had some doubts. First, the practice of selling *'urfi* contracts has become a cottage industry in Egypt, and the abuses of the practice widely known after the recent high-profile paternity case involving actor Ahmed el-Fishawi and stylist Hind el-Hinnawi. Furthermore, wealthy men from the Gulf come to vacation in Egypt "marry" *'urfi* brides only to abandon them at the end of the visit. In other words, the line between sexual freedom, free choice, and prostitution often blur with *'urfi* marriage. A girl might defy her parents' wishes and marry a young man through *'urfi* contract only to find herself abandoned on the streets, and soon she is seeking a new *'urfi* marriage just to get off the streets. New charitable organizations and hotlines are emerging to assist women dealing with such crises.

Although most men marry, some men carry on a double lifestyle. While many Americans might identify those men as gay or homosexual, aside from a small group of Westernized elites, most identify themselves by their active or passive role and do not construct such an identity. The 2001 raid of the Queen Boat discotheque, the arrest of 52 men and the trials that followed, highlighted the lack of human rights, generally, and gay rights, specifically, in Egypt. The rise of the internet and the ability of the government to monitor and entrap enemies of the state involved in "perversion" has been a concern since the time of the Queen Boat trials. Critics of the Mubarak government policy argue that it utilized persecution of gay men to shore up its Islamic credentials and as an outlet for the population's pent-up frustrations for a variety of problems.

Lesbians do not yet appear to be victims of any type of persecution. First, there is still the culture of denial that homosexuality exists and that women are involved. Furthermore, with respect to past government witch hunts, to accuse women would give them agency; such accusations are usually accompanied by conspiracy with foreign governments and other sorts of threats. Second, while parents might disapprove of this outlet for a daughter's sexual frustrations, they might also deem it safer than encounters that would end in pregnancy. Third, some have argued that as long as the lesbian is discrete, then parents sometimes seem willing to overlook what does not otherwise affect the family or its perceived honor. Fourth, those writing about the "lesbian scene" such as it exists seem to write from the perspective of young women as though older women are so deeply lost in the closet or entrenched in marital and household duties that seem to fall on women regardless of their sexual preferences.

The movement for civil and democratic rights that began in early January 2011 has sparked hope among gays and lesbians that it will include their rights too. Nevertheless, speaking from his chosen place in exile, Hassan el-Menyawi expressed his doubt about whether or not the short window of time to amend the same faulty constitution, which stripped him of his rights, would allow ample time to change the fundamentally flawed document.

REFERENCES

Abaza, Mona. *Changing Consumer Cultures of Modern Egypt: Cairo's Urban Reshaping.* Leiden: Brill, 2006.

Badran, Margot. *Feminists, Islam, & Nation: Gender and the Making of Modern Egypt.* Princeton, NJ: Princeton University Press, 1995.

Badran, Margot, and Miriam Cooke, eds. *Opening the Gates: A Century of Arab Feminist Writing.* Bloomington, IN: Indiana University Press, 1990.

Baron, Beth. *The Women's Awakening in Egypt, Culture, Society, & the Press.* New Haven, CT: Yale University Press, 1994.

Baron, Beth. *Egypt as a Woman, Nationalism, Gender, & Politics.* Berkeley, CA: University of California Press, 2005.

Huda Shaarawi. *Harem Years: The Memoirs of an Egyptian Feminist. Introduced, edited, and translated by Margot Badran.* Cairo: AUC Press, 1998 (1986).

Kholoussy, Hanan. *For Better or Worse: The Marriage Crisis that Made Modern Egypt.* Stanford, CA: Stanford University Press, 2010.

Marsot, Afaf Lutfi al-Sayyid. "Revolutionary Gentlewomen in Egypt." In *Women in the Muslim World,* 261–76. Lois Beck and Nikki Keddie, eds. Cambridge, MA: Harvard University Press, 1978.

el-Menyawi, Hassan. "Opinion: Will Egypt's Revolution Be in Vain," February 24, 2011. http://www.aolnews.com/2011/02/24/opinion-will-egypts-revolution-be-in-vain/.

Mikhail, Alan. "The Nature of Ottoman Egypt: Irrigation, Environment, and Bureaucracy in the Long Eighteenth Century." Ph.D. Dissertation, Berkeley, 2008.

Nelson, Cynthia. *Doria Shafik: Egyptian Feminist, a Woman Apart.* Gainsville, FL: University of Florida Press, 1996.

Pollard, Lisa. *Nurturing the Nation: The Family Politics of Modernizing, Colonizing, and Liberating Egypt 1805–1922.* Berkeley, CA: University of California, 2005.

Russell, Mona. *Creating the New Egyptian Woman: Consumerism, Education and National Identity, 1663–1922.* New York: Palgrave, 2004.

Tucker, Judith. *Women in Nineteenth-Century Egypt.* Cambridge: Cambridge University Press, 1985.

Whitaker, Brian. *Unspeakable Love Gay and Lesbian Life in Middle East.* Berkeley, CA: University of California Press, 2006.

Zayyat, Latifa. *The Open Door.* Translated by Marilyn Booth. Cairo, New York: AUC Press, 2000.

EDUCATION

Islamic, Coptic, and Jewish Traditional Education

Before the 19th century an education in Egypt was a religious education or an occupational apprenticeship. Learning to read was usually done in the context of learning to understand a holy book. The basic foundational unit of learning for Muslims was the *kuttab,* a small school usually attached to a mosque where students first learned to memorize the Quran. In Western tradition we generally think about the physical locality of the school being the most important feature of learning, but according to Islamic tradition it was the person from whom one was learning. This individual created a circle or *ḥalaqa* of study that created the appropriate learning environment, whether it was in a mosque, by a fountain, a home, or any other suitable space. At the elementary level this was less significant than higher levels of education, but good teachers attracted good students in a synergistic process, and even within the same school there could be diversity of teachers and curriculum.

CURRICULUM: LEARNING QURAN

The Quran is divided into 114 chapters, which aside from the opening chapter (*al-fatiḥa*) are arranged roughly from longest to shortest. A child learns the shorter chapters at the end of the Quran, which are actually the earliest Meccan suras. These are the simplest to understand, and they deal with the power and authority of Allah. In the time of the Prophet Muhammad, they were meant to catch the ear of potential believers. The later verses that were revealed in Medina deal with the specifics of life in the community, for example, marriage, inheritance, and divorce. They were revealed to a community that was already fixed in its beliefs, and thus they are more complicated.

Students engaged in a ḥalaqa or circle of learning at a Quranic school. Education is an important and valued pursuit in Islamic society. (Library of Congress)

At the basic level the *kuttab* simply included memorization of the Quran and a dose of *hadith* literature, but at the more diverse ones the course of study might also include poetry, mathematics, and Arabic. Theoretically, girls were allowed to attend *kuttabs* alongside boys, but in reality this did not occur frequently. Many scholars thought that subjects, for example, poetry and writing were not suitable for women. In point of fact, not many boys learned how to write either unless they were destined for careers that necessitated writing. Some women learned to read and write at home from tutors or male relatives, and they learned needlework and embroidery from female relatives or a special (female) teacher. Wealthy merchants housed small schools in their homes for their children and their dependents.

Coptic children attended the Coptic equivalent of the *kuttab,* and girls could attend school as long as they had their mothers' permission, which was common up to age eight or nine in Upper Egypt. In Cairo girls did not generally attend; however, home schooling was still an alternative. For Jews, it is a great irony that their secondary status with respect to the Muslim majority pushed them toward urban areas and occupations, which later resulted in their emergence in the fields of long-distance trade and banking. These occupations by their very nature necessitated literacy, and Jewish men and women had significantly higher literacy rates than both Muslims and Copts.

Higher learning existed among men of all three religions. The *madrasa* network led to the premier school of higher learning in Egypt, al-Azhar, the second oldest

CURRICULUM: *ḤADITH*

Ḥadith literature refers to a collection of traditions about the Prophet Muhammad. These can be things that he said, things that he did, or simply things that he observed. In the years after the Prophet Muhammad's death many people found it useful to put their own words into the Prophet's mouth for their own gain, hence the "science" of collecting *hadith* to verify its authenticity according to who told what story to whom. Certain collections of *hadith*, for example, those collected by medieval scholar al-Bukhari (d. 872) are considered to be the most valid and studied by Islamic scholars; however, Western scholars might doubt the authenticity of some parts of the collection. *Ḥadith* literature fills the void of many unanswered questions in the Quran. Young children learn *hadith* for its basic moral lessons and instructions, whereas more advanced students can compare *hadith*, and discuss the science regarding the authenticity of its *isnad*, or chain of authority, as well as the commentary made by revered scholars.

continuously operating university in the world. Paradoxically, this institution that is synonymous with mainstream Sunni orthodoxy opened in the late-10th century under the heterodox Shiite Fatimids (see Chapter 2). In the 12th century, Salah al-Din (Saladin) changed it to a center of Sunni learning, and he improved the *madrasa* system of higher learning that had first been created in the 11th century by a Seljuq vizier to restore order after a Shiite dynasty throughout Abbasid lands in the lands over which Egypt had control. *Madrasas* issued *ijazas* or licenses documenting what subjects a scholar learned in the circle of another and was then capable of transmitting on his own., During times when the economy was flourishing, education thrived and curriculums tended to be expanded, while in times of crisis, education suffered and they narrowed. As for Coptic education, Christian monastic tradition grew out of customs established in Egypt in the fourth century based on learning, discipline, humility, and submission to authority. Jewish education also had a long, venerable tradition. The Geniza collection, an enormous cache of documents, in combinations of both Arabic and Hebrew, reflects the social, economic, and judicial world of the Jewish community of medieval Cairo. About 10 percent of the 35,000 people in the documents are "prominent" individuals, and describe people actively involved in urban professions including commerce, banking, medicine, and faith. In other words, these are the people who would require an advanced education to practice their trade.

The Birth of the Modern Educational System

The modern educational system has its roots in the reforms of Muhammad Ali, whose development plans created new job opportunities to integrate Egyptian citizens into the workforce in new ways. Nevertheless, without training or education these opportunities could not come to fruition. Historians debate the nature and results of Muhammad Ali's reforms and whether or not to grant him the status as the founder of modern Egypt for his role in creating the modern army, bureaucracy, and educational system. The opposing camp points to Muhammad Ali's obviously non-Egyptian origins, his lack of intent on creating an "Egyptian" system, the dismantling of much of the system that he created by the end of his reign, and the overglorification of aspects of his system even during times of its operation. To this list one might add the fact that he built his system from the top-down with specialized schools for officers, engineers, and doctors, rather than from the bottom-up (primary schools), the way that the Japanese built their system.

Muhammad Ali's supporters would argue that in a relatively short period of time he built a parallel system of education that would not threaten or alienate the existing system of education. In fact, without building a huge network of primary schools, he had to utilize the existing schools as a recruiting base. By sending students abroad and creating massive translation projects he was able to utilize the native language of instruction quickly and take advantage of modern technology. Although he focused on higher education, he simultaneously tried to develop lower levels of education. One fascinating side note: Muhammad Ali himself did not learn to read or write until he was 40, and he placed an extraordinary emphasis on learning in his own household, among children of both sexes.

To feed his army and bureaucracy a battalion of students infiltrated his new school system, some 11,000 between 1809 and 1849. One of the first big changes with the new program was to make the physical location of the school and the system more important than the charisma of the individual teacher. Uniformity of curriculum and materials was essential, and the Pasha sent missions to the United Kingdom and France in order to learn methods of discipline and order that could be established in Egyptian schools—not just for soldiers, but for ordinary boys too. An undated report on the school system described punishment at the elementary level, sounding absolutely draconian: public humiliation, suspension, a "bread and water prison," the whip, and expulsion. At the preparatory level some students would be selected to monitor the behavior of their peers, and all schools had "prisons" to detain ne'er do wells and incompetents. The curriculum at preparatory level included Arabic, Turkish, Persian, mathematics, algebra, geometry, history, geography, calligraphy, and art. These schools fed into the specialized schools to train bureaucrats and officers, including a technical school of surveyors, a staff college, a medical school, a school of midwifery, a school of veterinary medicine, a school of pharmacy, a school of agriculture, a school of engineering, and an all important school of languages to translate for the other schools. The government press at Bulaq cranked out books at a healthy pace to meet the demands of the growing system. The military was so important that it had a number of specialized schools including one for artillery, cavalry, infantry, and the navy.

Shaykh Rifaat Tahtawi (1801–1873) had been sent by Muhammad Ali as the *imam* in charge of the spiritual guidance of an early mission to France in 1826. A keen observer and a quick learner Tahtawi would return to open the School of Languages, translate for the government, and become an architect of the modern educational system. He was an important link since many of Muhammad Ali's schools closed in the wake of the Treaty of Balta Liman, (1838). Abbas (r. 1848–1854) shut down more schools and sent Tahtawi for an extended tour of Khartoum. Said (r. 1854–1863) while more open-minded in some ways was still somewhat apathetic toward Egyptian education, and is remembered for saying "why open the eyes of the people, they will only be more difficult to rule."

Muhammad Ali's grandson Ismail (r. 1863–1879) restored education to its place of primacy. Having men like Tahtawi in the system who had worked their way through it, and who had traveled abroad facilitated the process of renewal. Tahtawi believed in the notion of education for promoting the ideals of citizenship, something that needed to be fostered in boys and girls (see Islam: A Religion of Social Justice; the Origins). Ismail believed that there was a connection between reform of the public body and reform of the schools, and he knew that new methods of funding and organization were needed. Thus, he combined the Ministry of Public Works and Ministry of Education and put the two in the capable hands of another talented Parisian traveler, Ali Mubarak. Tahtawi and Mubarak were both Egyptians who had worked their way through the school system to establish themselves in government positions, which represented another hallmark of Ismail's achievements in government and education: it is during his reign that Arabic became consolidated as the language of government. Ismail also hired many foreign advisors, but even here, ironically, his energetic Swiss school inspector Dor Bey saw a link between the teaching of history, education, and the development of national character; he encouraged Ismail to foster those links.

In addition to the large numbers of schools built during the reign of Ismail, including the first primary schools for girls, major curricular and organization changes were implemented: basic standards, establishing age limits for students, recruiting teachers, designating salaries and finding means for funding them, creating curricula and the means for assessment, and setting a sliding scale for school fees according to ability to pay.

Competing with government schools were large numbers of missionary schools as well as schools operated by foreign and minority communities in Egypt. While the goal of mission schools was to spread Christianity and Western education, the goal of the minority schools was to preserve language, heritage, and culture. Both types of schools affected and were affected by government trends in education. Muhammad Ali had laid the groundwork for the flourishing of missionary education in Egypt; they would provide a base for his specialized schools at no extra cost. He gave them free land and buildings and granted them (and their belongings) free travel by train within the country. Many mission groups were self interested as well. For example, about one-third of the Church Missionary Society's commissioners were bankers, brokers, or merchants. These groups varied as to whether they targeted Christians (both native Copts and Syrian Christians), Jews, or Muslims, or whether the work was nondenominational. Even individuals, for example, Mary Whately, the daughter of the Archbishop of Ireland, single-handedly undertook fieldwork in a popular neighborhood in Cairo and wrote a number of books about her experiences.

One of the longstanding and most influential in terms of numbers was the American (Presbyterian) Mission, which arrived in Egypt in 1854, taking over vacated buildings from departing British and Scottish missions in Cairo and Alexandria. By the turn of the century, there were 119 schools serving 8,000 students, and by the early 1920s there were 2,000 students in Cairo alone with schools established in 175 villages. Although Copts formed the majority of the student population, there was always a significant Muslim minority. The rapid spread of the American mission created a huge response, both among other Christian groups as well as among the Muslim majority. Catholic orders had been content servicing the needs of the Catholic community, and now they worked harder to reach Egyptian Copts. They also moved beyond the major cities of the Delta into Upper Egypt. The Coptic community, which had always been the bread and butter of American Mission schools, now felt uneasy. Some members of the Church hierarchy found the situation unacceptable. The American Mission worked with the Coptic community to establish new schools of their own, but the problem of raiding one another's schools for teachers existed. Jewish, Greek, Italian, Armenian, and other communities also rallied to improve and expand their schools. Muslims created new charitable associations to build schools for their children, particularly, when they felt the government was not responsive enough to the growing demand.

The Egyptian Mind Occupied

Ismail had rapidly expanded the school system, and as he did everything, he spared no expense. In the wake of Ismail's deposition in 1879, the rise of his son Tawfiq, and the British occupation shortly thereafter, new problems arose. The British revamped the educational system in Egypt by limiting access to education, increasing fees and the number of people paying them, changing the composition of the student body, and changing the curriculum within the schools. Previously, anyone could climb the ladder through education provided that his or her parent would give up his or her labor to allow him or her to attend school. The imposition of fees drastically changed the system, and a new two-tiered system was put in place whereby basic literacy and math would be taught at the base level and only a handful of individuals would have access to the quality level of education that would provide them with a ticket to government service or the ability to practice an urban profession. The British High Commissioner Lord Cromer chose his tennis partner, an irascible Scot and former missionary, Douglas Dunlop, to implement his educational reforms. This individual was a man who prided himself on knowing no Arabic after 30 years of residence in Egypt. Thus, education became a keystone issue for nationalists in the decades leading up to independence.

In addition to the problems of fees, access, and stratification, there was a perennial lack of teachers. For men, teaching was not a profession that garnered status, and for women the problem was two-pronged. First, there were not enough educated women, and second, once women were married they could no longer work as teachers. Even where fees were introduced elsewhere in the system, incentives remained to attract people to teaching through various types of scholarship.

The British had altered curriculum to suit the needs of the empire. In 1910 two of the biggest complaints of nationalists at a Congress in Brussels were that the British had forced their language and history in Egyptian schools, and to that list one might also add geography was taught from the perspective of the metropole. Archival materials reflect a shift from the Egypto-centric focus during the age of Ismail to an Anglocentric view of the world. Confronting the British occupation on the basis of education allowed the nationalists to have their cake and eat it too. Nationalists were large landowners whose major interests lay in selling cotton to the British, and what they were negotiating was not a major change in the basic system from which they were benefiting, but a larger piece of the dessert. Indeed, they shared many of the class-based assumptions of the British, which would become evident in the period after independence in 1922.

In one of the great successes for the nationalists, future prime minister and founding father of Egypt Saad Zaghlul became Minister of Education in late 1906 right in the midst of the Taba affair and on the eve of the Dinshaway incident (see Chapter 2). This change overlapped with the departure of Lord Cromer and the arrival of Sir Eldon Gorst, a much more sympathetic figure to both Egypt and education. Zaghlul implemented major changes including making sure that students of exceptional abilities and insufficient means could attend school without fees, created differential fees for Egypt's poorer governates, forming provincial councils to oversee and improve the lower-tier schools, teaching more subjects in Arabic, and allowing students to be able to respond to secondary-school exam questions in Arabic as long as the subject had been taught in Arabic.

Another great success story of the nationalist era was the creation of the Egyptian University (later renamed Fuad I, and Cairo University). First opened in 1908 it was the combination of a collection of higher schools and institutes that were already in existence. Nationalists ran short of resources and could not even pay the rent, so members of the royal family and other elite patrons came to the rescue by providing funds, a location, a palace, and even the library. The first rector of the university, a

---

THE HIGH COMMISSIONERS AND EDUCATION

Sir Evelyn Baring, Lord Cromer, was Egypt's first High Commissioner. Prior to his work in Egypt he had served in India under his cousin Lord Northbrook, and he was highly influenced with the ideas of Lord Macaulay, the architect of the Indian educational system; however, he did not want to make the same "mistakes" that were made in India where too many people were educated and hence a highly critical elite had emerged. Therefore, he developed the two-tiered educational system. Eldon Gorst, on the other hand, was the son of the Minister of Public Instruction in Britain, a man who enjoyed traveling to Egypt "during the season." Prior to his tenure as High Commissioner Gorst held other government offices that allowed him travel to Egypt. He came with a different perspective on Egypt and a different perspective on education. Furthermore, he had been in Egypt during the Dinshaway incident and felt that amends needed to be made to the Egyptians.

A UNIVERSITY FIT FOR A PRINCESS

The first location for the Egyptian University was a provisional one, where the old campus of the American University in Cairo is today in downtown Cairo. Classes were held here for two years until the administrators could no longer fund the rent, which was 400 Egyptian pounds, a significant amount in 1910. Princess Fatimah Ismail, one of the Khedive Ismail daughters, a sister of future Sultan Husayn Kamil and future King Fuad, heard from her personal physician, Dr. Muhammad Pasha Alwi, who was also one of the University's founders, about the crisis. Princess Fatimah allocated 40 percent of the revenue from nearly 700 acres of prime Delta land to support the University in perpetuity. She then donated another block of land and a palace in Giza that would serve as the nucleus for the campus. When funds were still lacking, Princess Fatimah gave a stash of jewels to Alwi Pasha to auction off in Europe.

candidate acceptable to both nationalists and British, was Prince (later King) Fuad, who actually taught marksmanship and equestrian skills. The university symbolized nationalist hopes and dreams by demonstrating that Egypt could provide advanced learning to its citizens; however, it was a dream attained by few.

Liberal Era

Once Egyptian independence was achieved, the class-based interests of the politicians kicked in and the programs of reform remained modest. The 1923 constitution demanded that education be both free and compulsory; however, it did not change the two-track educational system nor did the government necessarily have the will or

CREATION OF WOMEN'S SECTION

What began as a special lecture series at the Egyptian University when French feminist Marguerite Clement came to visit became a regular staple for women on Fridays, during the time the university was ordinarily closed. Egyptian feminist Huda Shaarawi organized the program, and Malak Hifni Nasif a female Egyptian writer was recruited to lecture. Famous European men lectured on topics pertaining to health, education, and hygiene. By late 1909, a French educator, Mlle. Couvreur, had been recruited to create a more formal program of study for the women, which was well attended by members of the royal family and Cairo's elite. The women covered a range of authors including Herbert Spencer, Gustav Le Bon, and Friedrich Nietzche. Labiba Hashim, a Syrian Christian with her own journal lectured in Arabic on the topic of family life and raising children.

EXPANSION AND DISSOLUTION OF WOMEN'S SECTION

By 1911, the Women's Section was so popular that greater facilities were provided to the women in Arabic. The university hired Nabawiya Musa, the first woman to receive a secondary school certificate to lecture on the history of Egypt, including ancient and Islamic history, women's history, and the French invasion. Rahma Sarruf, a prominent Syrian Christian, would teach home economics, which was more a theoretical class given the highbrow level of the participants. The women also had the option of attending special sections of courses taught by European faculty in ancient history and Semitic languages. Apparently, despite the fact that women's sections were held on Fridays, mornings, and during other off times, they garnered opposition from male students who violently opposed their existence. The women's section was cancelled for the 1912–1913 academic year. Women were not formally admitted to the university until 1928, although there were provisions for some women to attend before that time.

the means to implement the law that it had promulgated. First and foremost, there would be no means of enforcement. Girls whose parents did not wish them to go to school did not attend, and boys whose labor was needed, year-round or simply during harvest were not required to go to "compulsory" school. Less than half of students of eligible age actually enrolled at government schools, and girls attended in proportionately lower numbers than boys. The government really did not want everyone in school because of the second problem: lack of facilities and teachers. One way in which the government had been expanding the lower track of education prior to 1923, was taking over existing *kuttabs,* and putting them under government inspection. Now this process was greatly expanded to increase the number of elementary and compulsory schools, as the lower-track schools were known, to differentiate them from the primary schools. Only graduates of primary schools, or private schools, could take the primary certificate exam, which enabled successful candidates to go on to complete secondary school, receive a secondary certificate, and go to government service or higher education and/or urban professions. Meanwhile, the lower-track schools fed into al-Azhar, the School for Sharia Court judges, and Dar al-Ulum, the school that produced teachers for the lower track. The lack of facilities in both tracks made it desirable for students to opt out of the system or at the minimum for the government not to punish truancy.

The government could keep its two-track system by charging fees at the high level, which kept the numbers down; however, it put the lion's share of resources into the upper track of the school system. These policies generated a great deal of debate about democracy and access to education. Ultimately, the Wafdist government under maverick Minister of Education Neguib al-Hilali abolished primary school fees in 1943; however, his class-based views were no different than Lord Cromer's had been: that the lower track of education was meant to suit the individual for his station in life, that is, to keep him there not uplift him. While he wanted to improve and extend that education, he wanted to maintain the basic distinction between the two tracks. The government even backtracked on these measures by charging fees for lunches and books to all but a handful of gifted but needy students due to over-crowding by 1945.

The debate about education had begun, and by 1949 people were no longer questioning just the fees in the upper educational track but the entire bifurcated system itself. Nevertheless, some people questioned the problems associated with the "massification" of the system. Taha Hussein, the great writer and eventually a minister of education represented the interests of those who wanted to expand the system, while Ismail Qabbani, a Ministry of Education official, worried about the quality of a rapidly expanding system represented the opposing side. The Primary Education Law of 1949 would slowly bring the level of elementary schools up to that of the primary schools, set six years as the minimum period of study from the age of six years, and worked toward a unified curriculum (aside from foreign language). By 1951 a Wafd government passed a law that would eradicate the differences between the two tracks, but this would take time. The revolution took place before liberal politicians had the opportunity to carry out this process; however, they laid the groundwork of the Free Officers. Prior to the revolution secondary fees were also revoked (Ikeda 2005).

Compared to the British record, the elite politicians did quite well. The British spent only 1 percent of the budget on education in the early years of the occupation, increasing to about 3.5 percent once Egypt was financially solvent, while the liberal politicians spent 6.4 percent in the early years of independence, increasing it to 10 percent by 1935 and settling at about 13 percent for the remainder of the prerevolutionary period. Although the criticism has been raised that the proportion of money spent on the upper track of the educational system was extremely disproportionate to the numbers of students, the politicians did increase the numbers of students attending schools at a time when Egypt's population was increasing. Between World War I and 1951 the numbers of students attending government schools had grown from 324,000 to 1,900,000. Expressed differently, 27 out of every 1,000 Egyptians (of all ages) went to a government school in 1914, but by 1951 that number soared to 91, despite a population increase of 65 percent (Ikeda 2005).

Education after the Revolution

Thus, while it appears that the Egyptian Revolution was a radical departure, with respect to education, many of the changes were already under way. It was up to the new regime to implement the course of action taken at the tail end of the old regime—unify the educational system and make it truly free at all levels, including the university, at which the new government did succeed by 1962. The system expanded rapidly at all levels in the first 25 years. Enrollments in primary school nearly quadrupled from 1.5 million in 1952 on the eve of the revolution to 4.2 million 25 years later. Similarly, enrollments in preparatory school that were just under 350,000 would also more than quadruple, as would growth in secondary schools, which was just under

200,000. Since the government integrated a number of technical and higher institutes into the university system, some of those numbers dropped, but the figures for higher education generally increased ninefold to more than 450,000. In fact, in the early 1960s, more Egyptians as a ratio per 1,000 of the population attended higher education than Britons, the former occupiers.

The educational system created by the Free Officers still exists. Students follow a six-year course of primary school, followed by two years of preparatory school, and four years of high school. Students who want to continue to higher education must take the GSE. An individual's score on the GSE determines where he or she can study and what he or she can study. The prestige faculties continue to be medicine and engineering, and the faculty that requires the least success on the test is teaching. Most Americans would be appalled by how little free choice a student has in the decision-making process. Many factors come into play, for example, parental occupation and ambition, marital prospects, and so on; student interest often plays a small role in determining course of study. Since the reopening of the economy there has been a resurgence in degrees in law and commerce, which had little value in the public sector.

By 1952 there were three more universities—Alexandria, Ain Shams, and Assiut—to be followed in the years to come by more regional and satellite campuses. Cairo University has a great deal of prestige; however, other universities in the capital and Alexandria also have fine reputations; going to a regional campus or one in Upper Egypt is less prestigious. Since so much of one's future is determined by the GSE, a whole cottage industry exists in tutoring and study materials for the test, thus obliterating the theoretically equalizing nature of free education. In the two years preceding the GSE, as much as 25 percent of household income can be allocated toward private lessons. In 2008, a huge scandal broke out which involved the leaking and selling of an upcoming GSE, for which sentences ranged from 3 to 15 years.

In 1964 the government obligated itself to hire all graduates of universities, as well as various types of vocational, higher institutes, and secondary schools. In the wake of the nationalizations that took place the post-Suez era there was some need for educated specialists, but this kind of commitment was ultimately more than the public sector could handle. In many respects, however, this policy was a continuation of British policy because the old government certificate process attached to the upper track of the educational system was a gateway to government service. In times past, that gateway had been very narrowly restricted, but in the mid-1960s it was thrust wide open with the same level of expectation. By the 1970s and 1980s, the ranks of the public sector swelled enormously. The casual observer in Egypt will notice that what can be accomplished in one step in the United States takes five or six in Egypt simply because it creates jobs. When the price of oil dropped in the early 1980s and the regional economy slumped, the government began stretching out the period that applicants must wait before applying. University graduates are supposed to wait two years to apply in order to allow males to do their military service and secondary graduates to do an extra year of service. Now, after application, the wait for a government job can be anywhere from 8 to 13 years. The growth of the private sector has meant that many people have opted out of the system altogether. Nevertheless, government jobs remain popular because of the perceived security and benefits. The time commitment involved in a public-sector job usually allows an enterprising individual to pursue a second job in the private sector. Women have found employment at much higher rates in the public sector.

The revolutionary government realized that it could use its curriculum as a social tool. The old regime had utilized history as a melting pot for the three religious communities. It found Egypt's ancient history and the age of Muhammad Ali as the two periods worth emphasizing, avoiding Roman, Islamic, and Ottoman histories, while the revolutionary regime would emphasize Arab or Islamic history as the most significant period. New classes emerged, for example, Arab Socialism with textbooks in which the old feudal elite would become the target of societal criticism. The large landowners represented a cruel and vicious class, whereas the hard-working peasant received special emphasis. The nobility of the peasant had existed in turn-of-the-century textbooks, but the older depictions were foundational and unappreciated much like the legs of a table, without which it might topple, whereas now the peasant was like the meal, more central and appealing, truly at the heart of the story.

Although the Nasser regime has been portrayed as "secular" when compared to Sadat who courted Islamists or to Jihadists of a later period, one should remember that Nasser mobilized religion in particular ways. He gave important speeches from the minbar at al-Azhar, and he utilized the curriculum in religion to mobilize the population. Previously, the religion curriculum in the upper track of the educational system did not play that large a role and was not even taught the first two years in primary school. Nasser utilized religious instruction to inculcate young citizens with the notions of devotion to God and country and against external enemies, such as Zionism and imperialism. These methods of social control previously had been utilized heavily in the lower track of the educational system, but were now advanced throughout a uniform curriculum. Holidays—some with little connection to faith—would be celebrated in religion class, including the Prophet's birthday, Unity Day (no longer celebrated), and Mother's Day.

Another way in which uniformity of curriculum with respect to religion was needed was at al-Azhar. This bastion of Islamic learning was in need of a makeover in the eyes of the revolutionary establishment. During the days of the liberal politicians, al-Azhar had generally sided with the king against the Wafd and presented a strong face of conservatism in the modern era. Even though Muhammad Ali and his successors had been successful in divesting the religious establishment of its independent authority (see Chapter 2), they could not change the basic overall fact that the religious establishment since medieval times legitimated Islamic rule, and with or without independent authority, al-Azhar had the hearts and souls of true believers. In 1961 al-Azhar underwent a modernization process to offer a wider range of subjects, including various scientific and humanistic disciplines as well as a women's faculty. It also gave the government control over the curriculum that, to a degree, had been independent for nearly 1,000 years.

During the Sadat years religion took on an even greater importance. Sadat was walking a difficult tightrope while trying to turn away from the Soviets and toward the United States in terms of his foreign policy, and simultaneously fighting the Nasserist or Communist opposition internally. Thus, he turned to a "science and faith"

al-Azhar mosque and university in Cairo is one of the oldest degree-granting institutions of higher learning in the world. (Paul Cowan)

curriculum that actually reduced the number of hours of religion in primary schools, but extended the number of years of religious study. More importantly, he utilized Islamic student organizations at the university level to counter the leftist or Nasserist opposition, funding them heavily on campuses throughout Egypt. These student organizations mobilized and utilized the funds to deal with the major problems on college campuses including overcrowded transportation and classrooms, traveling and negligent professors, and general lack of facilities; they provided services to students that adhered to Islamic codes of behavior and dress.

By the 1970s the numbers of students at university level had grown dramatically, an 81 percent growth between 1969 and 1977 alone. Classrooms were crowded, dorms could not meet demand, and transportation taking students to campus were packed beyond capacity. For women going to the university, every day involved humiliating situations on buses and in classrooms as men were literally jammed up against them. The pay for faculty was less than a living wage, so professors often worked on several campuses to make ends meet and sold the lecture notes on which examinations would be based. The fears Ismail Qabbani voiced in the interwar years had certainly come to fruition. The revolution had paid a price for the rapid expansion of education.

Islamists devised unique solutions to these problems. They created their own system of minibuses with special seating for women and special areas in the classroom for women—provided they wore Islamic dress. These groups also purchased study notes and mimeograph machines to inexpensively reproduce lecture note packets. They organized study groups for students for prayer and recitation of notes in what can only be described as a *ḥalaqa.* They organized summer camps along the same lines as ones organized by the Muslim Brotherhood in the years before 1954, that is, before Nasser disbanded the group, creating disciplined activists promoting an Islamic agenda. While it appeared that they buttressed Sadat's rule, they filled gaps with which the state could not cope, and it was one of these groups that assassinated Sadat in 1981.

With the opening of the economy under Sadat and the continued strain on state education, a parallel system of education has grown alongside that of the state system: private school education. Certain aspects of private school curriculum are standardized and inspected by the government, along with standardized testing—culminating in the GSE or foreign equivalents for those not interested in working in the public sector. Roughly 3,000 of Egypt's 36,000 K–12 schools are private, which still puts an enormous strain on the government that must maintain standards at all of these schools. Private schools vary between those that give instruction in Arabic and teach English as a foreign language, and the foreign language schools: English, French, and German, which utilize the foreign language as the primary means of instruction. The language schools are perceived as the means for advancing in the global economy. One mother expressed it well when she explained that she sent her child to the German school because she knew he would learn all the languages there (German, French, and English) and he already knew Arabic anyway. There are a small number of schools that follow a narrow interpretation of Islam with an anti-Semitic, anti-Christian curriculum that cast a negative light over all the schools.

Under Mubarak Egypt's literacy rate only achieved 71 percent overall; and female literacy lags far behind, just under 60 percent (male rate 83 percent). Overcrowding of classrooms and lack of facilities means rotating shifts in crumbling government schools where teachers receive the lowest scores on the GSE. On the 50th anniversary of the revolution Egypt was spending some 20.4 billion Egyptian pounds on education; however, how much of that money was making it to Egypt's 15 million students and not wasted, skimmed, or misused is another question. Despite 200 years of modernization, education is still geared toward rote memorization in preparation for taking the GSE and reproducing the lecture notes of professors verbatim. In the last years of his rule, Mubarak and his wife announced several educational initiatives aimed at solving a number of Egypt's educational deficiencies. There were strategies for training more students in science, offering better technical and vocational training, utilizing information technology as a means of teaching critical thinking skills, narrowing the gender divide in learning, improving teacher–student ratios, utilizing the television as a teaching resource, eliminating illiteracy, and creating partnerships with private industries as well as other countries for mutually beneficial ventures in education and/or globalization.

While the education system itself was not a direct target of the January 25 movement, its (in)ability to prepare young adults for the job market has been an issue along with the lack of jobs upon graduation. Furthermore, government and NDP control of university elections has been a major bone of contention, just as it has been across the country.

REFERENCES

Abd al-Karim, and Ahmad Izzat. *The History of Education in the Age of Muhammad Ali* (in Arabic). Cairo: Maktabat al-Nahda al-Misriyya, 1938.

Abd al-Karim, and Ahmad Izzat. *The History of Education in Egypt from the End of the Rule of Muhammad Ali until the Beginning of the Rule of Tawfiq* (in Arabic). Cairo: Matba'at al-Nasr, 1945.

Égypte, Ministre de l'Instruction Publique. *Régulations approuvées par le Ministre l'Instruction Publique pour l'organisation des écoles sous Muhammad Ali* (*Regulations Approved by the Minister of Public Instruction on the Organization of Schools under Muhammad Ali*). Paris, n/d.

Goitein, S. D. *A Mediterranean Society: The Jewish Communities of the Arab World as Portrayed in the Cairo Geniza Documents.* Berkeley, CA: University of California Press, 1988.

Heyworth-Dunne, James. *An Introduction to the History of Education in Egypt.* London: Cass, 1968.

Ikeda, Misako. "Toward the Democratization of Public Education in Egypt: The Debate in Late Parliamentary Egypt, 1943–1952." In *Re-Envisioning Egypt, 1919–1952,* 218–48. Arthur Goldschmidt, et al., ed. Cairo: AUC Press, 2005.

Russell, Mona. "The Female Brain Drain, the State, and Development in Egypt." In *Women and Development in the Middle East and North Africa,* 122–43. Joseph Jabra, ed. Leiden (Netherlands): Brill, 1992.

Russell, Mona. *Creating the New Egyptian Woman: Consumerism, Education, & National Identity.* New York: Palgrave, 2004.

Starett, Gregory. *Putting Islam to Work: Education, Politics, and Religious Transformation.* Berkeley, CA: University of California Press, 1998.

CHAPTER 6

Culture

LANGUAGE

A History

The linguistic history of Egypt parallels the political history of Egypt. The current language of Egypt is a localized dialect of the Arabic brought by the Arab conquerors in the seventh century (see Chapter 2). Nevertheless, Arabic and the language of the Ancient Egyptians are cousin languages, that is, they come from the same language tree. They are part of a family called Hamito-Semitic (Afro-Asiatic) that includes ancient Egyptian, Coptic, and Berber.

The ancient Egyptian language that appears on tombs, papyri, and the like continued to appear all the way through the Ptolemaic and Byzantine periods. Writing was extremely important to the development of ancient Egyptian civilization. Centralized bureaucracies required writing to keep records for taxation, census records for counting workers and allocating resources, and in the case of Egypt to record the activity and significance of the Nile's annual flood. The ancient Egyptians believed that the God Thoth had given mankind this special gift. It is uncertain exactly when hieroglyphs emerged, since they grew out of predynastic art forms; however, evidence of hieroglyphs dates back at least as far as 3200 BCE. Hieroglyphs translate as "priestly writing" named after the elite class of scribes responsible for record keeping. Estimates vary, but potentially as little as one to two percent of the population had this valued skill. Most people think of hieroglyphs as picture writing, with each letter representing an idea or a symbol. While some hieroglyphs serve this function, the vast majority are phonetic, and a third category helps sort out meanings between the phonetic and ideographic varieties. The existence of the papyrus plant, the stem of which can be used to make a form of paper that holds up well in dry climates also facilitated the development of writing. This paper-making technology existed in Egypt as far back as the third millennium BCE. Eventually, simpler scripts were developed for ease of use; however, hieroglyphs did not vanish. The famous Rosetta Stone, which came from the Ptolemaic period (196 BCE), was written in hierogylphs, Greek, and Demotic, thus even at this later date it was still used as a sacred language. Its lingering existence on this decree allowed 19th-century scholars to decipher what had previously been an unknown language. Even by this time period the ancient Egyptian language was in flux with Demotic representing a transitional state between what the people were actually speaking and the traditional language, with Greek being the language of the elites.

Eventually, by the late Byzantine period, the ancient Egyptian language had gradually been supplanted by Coptic. Coptic is quite similar to the previously mentioned Demotic language; however, unlike Demotic, which appears almost like a cursive hieroglyphic system, Coptic is written in Greek script. Greek was the language of the rulers, and although both Greek and Coptic appeared on official documents, they were meant to be understood by both the rulers and the ruled. Those who wanted to advance in society needed to learn the Greek language (see Chapter 5, section on social classes and ethnicity). When the Arabs arrived, they utilized the administrators and scribes of the Byzantines. It was not until 706 that Arabic became the language of administration in Egypt. At that point, a slow linguistic decline began that meant ancient Egyptian would become a lost language, and Coptic nearly so due to the linkage between the two languages. Coptic would remain a liturgical language for the Coptic clergy known only to a small handful of people after the 15th or 16th centuries. The Coptic language remained nearly extinct until a "revival" in the 19th century as a part of the age of nationalism.

Arabic has a special connection to Muslims since it is the language of the Quran, and one must master the language in order to fully understand and appreciate the religion. In fact, translations of the Quran cannot actually be called the Quran, but will usually be called something like *The Meaning of the Glorious Quran* because of the strong connection between the language and belief. As the process of Arabization and Islamization took place in Egypt, so did the linguistic process of replacing the Coptic language with that of Arabic. Since the two languages are from the same language family, it was not too difficult a task.

As discussed in Chapters 2 and 5, Egypt was at the center of many empires and the treasured province of many others. Therefore, its agricultural surplus helped to sponsor Islamic learning in the medieval period, and the Arabic language played a key role in this. After the Abbasid Revolution, Persian (written in Arabic script) became an unofficial language in the Abbasid court and men of letters mastered it; however, it was less common in lands as far west as Egypt. When the mamluks took power in Egypt, Turkish became a language of the elite; however, Arabic remained the language of administration. After the arrival of the Ottoman Turks in the 16th century, Ottoman Turkish (written in Arabic script) became an official language of administration, but the provinces utilized their own languages in their courts and offices. Therefore, Arabic remained a language of learning and administration as well as the language of the people during Ottoman times. After the rise of Muhammad Ali, the use of Turkish in government administration became reinvigorated once again; however, it was already largely in usage among the elite due to the reemergence of the mamluks in the previous century.

Language and Education

When Egypt's educational system became modernized in the 19th century, the Arabic language still played a major role in its curriculum. The government press at Bulaq and the School for Languages enabled Muhammad Ali and his successors to facilitate modern education in the native tongue; however, foreign advisors, especially those from France were a key part of the new educational system and the government. French had actually been a language of interest since the time of the French invasion when the occupiers (1798–1801) tried to demonstrate the efficacy of Western science to the religious establishment. Although the occupation was unsuccessful, a number of mercenaries, technocrats, and advisors stayed on to assist Muhammad Ali. Thus, French became the second, third, or fourth language for many. By the reign of Ismail (r. 1863–1879), Arabic had largely supplanted Turkish in government administration.

After Ismail's deposition and the beginning of the British occupation in 1882, English began to replace French as the foreign language in higher track of the government schools and many private schools (see Chapter 5), which was a source of vast discussion in the British *Annual Reports to Her/His Majesty* each year as the struggle continued. Nevertheless, law schools continued to consider French as an essential core of the curriculum. Many famous nationalists and politicians were lawyers, whether they graduated from Egyptian law schools, studied in France, served as apprentices to lawyers, or some combination thereof. There was a major gender divide in the study of languages and the usage of government versus private schools. For boys, government schools were a ticket to government service and opportunity. Thus, when the government schools placed their primary emphasis on English as a foreign language, more boys began to study English than girls. Meanwhile, government schools for girls likewise were meant as a ticket to government service in teaching or medicine, but rather than being considered an opportunity, this was considered a stigma. Women of the upper classes at the turn of the century preferred not to work. They studied in private, missionary, and minority community schools where the curriculum focused heavily on foreign language (usually French, but also Italian, Greek, Armenian, or German) as well as music and art. Newspaper articles in the early 1900s lamented the poor state of young girls' Arabic due to this situation and the need to remedy it. By this point, as well, students in neither girls' nor boys' schools were studying Turkish since Egyptian national sentiment demanded study in Arabic.

The trends that were underway at the turn of century continued in Egypt's liberal era (1922–1952). Education expanded generally, and those who attended public schools learned English as a second language and French as a third language if they were in the upper track of the educational system (see Chapter 5). Knowing a number of languages was a sign of culture or refinement, and it qualified a person for employment in a range of fields from urban professionals to simple shopkeeping. The most demanding department store managers would not hire a person who did not speak at least French and one other language (in addition to Arabic), for example, Italian, Greek, or German.

Most of the officers who carried out the Egyptian Revolution came to the Staff College as a result of the liberalization of requirements after the Anglo-Egyptian Treaty in 1936. The officers' foreign language was English, not French, like the lawyer-politicians who ran the government before them. They deplored the state of Arabic language study in both the public and private schools and demanded greater uniformity of language curriculum. All citizens of the new Egypt would be conversant in spoken and written Arabic before graduating from high school.

Arabic in Egypt Today

The Arabic that students learn in school is Modern Standard Arabic (MSA). It is an updated form of the classical Arabic that appears in the Quran and the Arabic that was spoken by the seventh-century conquerors. Arabic, like most Semitic languages, reads from right to left and is based on three-letter roots that signify meaning. Put differently, the words for school, teacher, study, teach, and so on, all come from the same three-letter root (d-r-s). This three-letter root can potentially take 10 different forms and have various prefixes and suffixes to signify meaning, for example, possession or place. Understanding the system of roots, prefixes, suffixes, and forms helps the student of Arabic understand the language, which is beautifully systematic.

MSA is the same Arabic that appears in newspapers, in media broadcasts, and in official speeches. Nevertheless, people do not speak in MSA, but rather in Egyptian dialect, which differs from formal Arabic in a number of significant ways. There are two letters, the tha and the dhal, that are pronounced like the ta and zayn, respectively. The jim, which sounds like the letter "j" in classical Arabic is pronounced like a "g" in colloquial Egyptian. The letter qaf, which sounds like the "k" hawk in classical Arabic is a glottal stop in most words. For example, the word heart, *qalb*, would be pronounced *alb.* There are plenty of exceptions to the rule, including the word for law, *al-qanun.* The combination of vowels that form ay, and aw become ee or oo, for example, the word for house, *bayt* in classical sounds more like *beet.* The other types of differences are ones in which one would have to study the grammar of the language to completely understand that nature of the changes, compared to the above differences that are mostly in pronunciation.

Classical Arabic, even in its MSA version, is a language that carries case endings for nouns and adjectives, as well as mood ending for verbs. Nouns and adjectives also must agree according to gender. Egyptian colloquial is a bit simpler since it eliminates case endings for nouns and adjectives and masculine plurals generally take the same endings. Egyptian dialect has some different pronouns:

S = singular   Pl = plural   M = male/masculine   F = female/feminine

In a nutshell, Egyptian dialect is less complicated and less stilted than MSA. It is widely understood around the Middle East due to the popularity of Egyptian movies and television series. Contemporary authors are moving toward writing in the language of the people rather than in the MSA that many find difficult to read and understand.

GLOSSARY FOR TRAVELERS, STUDENTS, AND BUSINESSPERSONS

Everyday Phrases for Understanding the Culture

salaam 'alaykum: "May peace be upon you," the standard greeting, usually from one Muslim to another, but typically how one says hello or good bye. Copts would simply say *salaam.*

wa 'alaykum as-salaam: "And peace be upon you." The response said to the person above when saying hello.

m'a as-salama: "With Peace." It is the response to *salaam 'alaykum* when someone is leaving.

al-ḥamdu-li-lah: "Praise be to God." Muslims thank God for everything. Thus, whether it is something that occurs due to the sweat of one's brow, because intelligence and perseverance are traits for which one can thank God, or if it is something fortuitously lucky, it deserves this phrase. A poor turn of events can merit the phrase, with the proper intonation, for one can always be thankful to be alive, for example, after a car accident, a robbery, and so on.

in sha-allah: "If God wills it." This is another catch phrase for everything for the Muslim population of Egypt. Nothing happens, except by the grace of God, for example, an engine starting, a bus leaving on time, or the maid coming to clean on her appointed day. One uses it to refer to things that one hopes will happen as opposed to the previous phrase that refers to that which has already happened. A similar phrase is *bi-izni-lah*—by the permission of God.

fee mesh mesh (literally "in apricots"), or *bokra fee mesh mesh* ("tomorrow in apricots"): This means there is doubt that something will happen, the English equivalent might be "when hell freezes over" or more politely "when pigs fly" or "that'll never happen!," depending on intonation. Egyptians are infamous for saying that things will happen tomorrow—*bokra*—and to that add it will be during the extremely short but sweet apricot season. Thus, the intent is that it is unlikely that it will ever happen.

kifiya or *kifiya 'alayya:* "Enough" or "enough for me" (I am satisfied).

bil hana' wa shifa "To [your] health and well-being." Sometimes this can be said before a meal in praise of a delicious spread of food, or conversely, after the host or hostess has served guests beyond capacity one can signal his or her inability to eat more by praising the host or hostess with a toast to his, her or their health.

mabruk: "Congratulations."

Allah yubarak fik (to m) *Allah yubarak fiki* (to f) Response to congratulations. "May God bless you."

ubalak (to m) *ubalik* (to f): "You next." Often said in response to congratulations if it is appropriate, for example, after a young woman gets engaged, she might say "you next" to a girlfriend who is unmarried and has congratulated her.

istaghfiru-llah al-'azim: "God forbid!"

ya salam! Response to something unbelievable—"really!"

Rabbina yisahhal: "Our lord [Allah] will make [it] easier." Usually said after some difficult event or concern about the future.

la ilaha ila Allah: "There is no god, but God." This is half of the formulaic statement that Muslims make in order to be Muslims, the other half being that Muhammad is his Prophet, but this half is often said alone upon hearing that someone died.

al-ba'iyya fi ḥayatak (to m) *al-ba'iyya fi ḥayatik* (to f): This is said to express condolences—literally "the remainder in your lifetime."

Basic Pleasantries

ismak ay? (to m) *ismik ay?* (to f): "What is your name?"

ismee . . . : "My name is . . ."

shukran: "Thank you."

'afwan: "You're welcome."

feen?: "Where?"

feen al-ḥammam?: "Where is the bathroom?"

aywa: "Yes."

la: "No."

giddan: "Very."

fee . . .: "There is or there are . . ."

mafeesh . . .: "There is no or there are no . . ."

mumkin?: "Is it possible?"

mish mumkin: "It is impossible."

ma'alish: This is another all-purpose word that means "I am sorry," "get over it," or it "doesn't matter" depending on how it is used.

tasharrafna: Pleased to meet you (formal)—literally "we [royal we] are honored to make your acquaintance."

nuwwartina (followed by home/city): Literally means "you have brightened us with your presence"; it is a greeting meant to welcome visitors to a new place or to someone's home.

munawwara bi-ahlaha: response to above—"its people are the enlightened ones."

ḥamdillah 'ala as-salaama: "Thank God upon the peace [and your safe arrival]"—another way of saying welcome.

Allah yislamak (m) Allah yislamik (f): Response to above or to m'a as-salaama (goodbye); it means "God keep you safe."

izzayak? (to m) *izzayik?* (to f): "How are you?"

kweyis (m) *kweyyissa* (f): "Fine." (optionally add *al-ḥamdu-li-lah*). Try to always answer fine in English or Arabic.

min faḍlak (to m) *min faḍlik* (to f): please, literally "from your favor."

law samaḥt (to m) *law samaḥti* (to a f): "Excuse me" or "pardon me" (to get someone's attention).

'an iznak (to m) *'an iznik* (to f) *'an iznukoo* (to pl): "Pardon me" or "Excuse me" (to get past someone or inconvenience someone).

effendim: Pardon me, or I did not hear you (repeat what you just said).

assif (m) *asfa* (f): "I'm sorry."

Ṣabaḥ al-kheer: "Good morning." Variations include "*Ṣabaḥ al-ishṭa, Ṣabaḥal-ful*, and *Ṣabaḥal-'asl*." These literally mean "morning of cream," "morning of jasmine," and "morning of honey."

Ṣabaḥ an-noor: response to good morning. This literally means "morning of light."

masa' al-kheer: "Good evening."

masa' an-noor: response to good evening. This literally means "evening of light."

ahlan wa sahlan: Welcome.

ahlan bik (to m) *ahlan biki* (to f) *ahlan bikoo* (to pl) response to the above.

furṣa sa'eeda: Nice to meet you. This literally means "happy occasion."

Ana as'ad: I am happier—meaning it is even nicer to see or meet you.

tisbaḥ 'ala kheer (to m) *tisbaḥi 'ala kheer* (to f) *tisbaḥoo 'ala kheer* (to pl) : "May good come to you"; in other words, good night.

wa inta min ahlu al-kheer (to m) *wa inti min ahlu al-kheer* (to f) *wa intu min ahl al-kheer* (to pl.): response to above—"you are sweeter than the good." Variation is simply wa inta min ahlu, meaning you are sweeter than it.

wahashtny (to m) *wahashteeny* (to f) *wahashtoony* (to pl.) : I missed you. This literally means "you have been absent in me."

Na'eeman: heavenly—usually said after someone has just showered, bathed, or gotten a haircut.

inta bititkalim ingleezee? (to m) inti bititkalimee ingleezee? (to f) intu bititkalimoo ingleezee? (to pl): "Do you speak English?"

ana mish batkalim 'araby: "I do not speak Arabic."

wa ana kaman: "And neither do I."

ana mish fahim (m) *ana mish fahma* (f) *ihna mish fahmeen* (pl): "I/we do not understand."

Transactions, Real Estate

bi kam?: "How much?" Usually one would use it in a complete sentence, but simply pointing to the object in question and asking will bring the needed response.

da ghali khalis: "That's too much."

rakhees: Cheap, inexpensive.

feloos: "Money."

ba'sheesh: Tip. People expect tips for just about everything. Travelers and business-people should be firm about not accepting services that they do not desire—for example, bag carrying—and should have small notes in a pocket ready for tipping so that they do not have to pull out their wallet for every tip. When changing money ask for small bills for this purpose (fakka).

da akhir kalam: "That is the final word." Deploying this phrase is the equivalent of saying I will not pay any more than my last offer.

imshi: "Get away." This is useful when pesky salespeople continue to follow tourists, particularly kids. A simple, la shukran, usually works in most business situations when the intention is no, thank you.

bawwab: doorman.

simsar: real-estate broker, apartment locater, or middleman.

wahid: One.

itneen: Two.

talata: Three.

arba'a: Four.

khamsa: Five.

sitta: Six.

seba': Seven.

tamaniya: Eight.

tis'a: Nine.

'ashra: Ten.

Forms of Address

Although titles and ranks went out with the Egyptian revolution, remnants of the old system still exist in colloquial dialect. Egyptians are extremely class conscious and address people accordingly.

Basha: From the old Turkish Pasha; this title is often used to address people who are senior in rank, most commonly among army officers and personnel. It can also be used teasingly or sarcastically, and even flirtatiously with a member of the opposite sex.

Bey: Another remnant of the old Turkish system, travelers might even hear this or the above applied to themselves by obsequious hotel employees or anyone trying to receive a large tip. It is applied to people of a higher class as a form of respect.

Hanim or *Sitt Hanim:* This is applied as a term of respect to women. Generally, this type of respect is not accorded to females who are not married.

Ya Seedy (to m) *Ya Sitty* (to f) *Ya Ibny* (to m): Used between two people of equal rank often when disagreeing. The word "ya" is the vocative particle that is used in Arabic prior to addressing someone. Thus, these correspond to "my man," "my woman," and "my son" in their literal meanings; however, conversationally they might be something more along the lines of "dude!" or "girlfriend!".

Ya 'Amm: When dealing with service people who are of a lower class, one would use this term, for example, with the older sandwich vendor, the doorman, or the garbage collector. Friends might also use the term jokingly with one another. 'Amm is the same word that people use for a paternal uncle, however, if they were related to a person they would use a suffix indicating that relationship.

Shaykh (m) *Shaykha* (f): This is a title given to men of religion, for example, imams. It is also used in a teasing fashion with children or friends when disagreeing.

Ḥagg (m) *Ḥagga* (f): Most often it is used for people who have literally made the pilgrimage (*hajj*) to Mecca, but it can also be used simply as a term of respect for elderly individuals. It is like the term sir or ma'am, but reserved only for the elderly.

Bashmuhandis: This is a title of respect given to educated individuals as a form of flattery, but it can also be applied to any skilled worker, for example, drivers, craftsmen, plumbers, electricians, and so on (Tonsi 1986).

Any attempt to be friendly and speak some Arabic, particularly greetings will be seen as a kind gesture—and may even save money. Most travelers to Egypt are surprised to find how many Egyptians speak passable English, and after practicing numerous Arabic phrases and terms, they find little opportunity to use them. From major five-star chains to two-star student pensions, the staffs at most hotels speak fluent English and can direct the traveler to anything he or she needs. This section does not contain any medical terminology or terms from the pharmacy because doctors and pharmacists rank among the highest on the GSE in Egypt and are generally fluent in English. If a traveler encounters someone in a pharmacy not fluent in English, then most likely it is not the pharmacist himself or herself but one of his or her relatives manning the desk—ask for the pharmacist, or simply go to another one—there is literally one on every corner in Cairo.

REFERENCES

al-Tonsi, Abbas, and Laila al-Sawi. *An Intensive Course in Egyptian Colloquial Arabic, Part I.* Cairo: American University in Cairo, 1986.

al-Tonsi, Abbas, Laila al-Sawi, and Suzanne Massoud. *An Intensive Course in Egyptian Colloquial Arabic Part II.* Cairo: American University in Cairo, 1987.

ETIQUETTE

Overview

Egyptian etiquette is a complex combination of rituals that predate the Islamic conquest and have been accommodated to Arab culture. First and foremost, where etiquette is concerned, Arab culture centers around notions of hospitality and generosity. When a guest arrives at someone's home, the first few minutes are spent exchanging a series of ritualized and formulaic greetings of welcome in which the guest is meant to feel at home and the host is meant to feel special for having invited the guest. Male guests shake hands with male guests, but it is not a macho gripping contest, so some Westerners may find the shake less firm than the one they are accustomed. If a woman extends her hand to a male visitor, then she has no objection in doing so, but some women will not want to shake hands with men outside their family, so check if it is extended. Female guests will kiss each other on both cheeks (if they know one another well); otherwise a simple handshake will suffice. Women, who wear the *hijab* or headscarf, will cover their heads in front of all men, except for their brothers, sons, husband, and father-in-law. The basic rule of thumb is that they are covered in front of all adult men whom they can or could marry (apart from their husband). Thus, when the doorbell rings, one often hears a scurrying as women who prepare the meal rush to cover. They do not consider it an imposition to re-cover as it is a natural part of their life. Most women keep an all-purpose covering near the door in case they are alone. One finds that children or men often answer the door if guests are arriving as women are often involved in food preparation or its supervision. If invited to someone's home, it is not necessary to bring the host or hostess a gift, but getting a box of gateaux, petit fours, local sweets, or simply chocolates will be a nice gesture. Bear in mind that there may be an overwhelming amount of food and getting something that might spoil will not be a good idea if it is a formal affair, but something that can be kept for the host or hostess might be better. Flowers or a plant is another good choice. Since the overwhelming majority of the country is Muslim, getting alcohol will not be a good option even if the hosts drink as other guests may not, which might embarrass the host. Getting a bottle of wine is not a problem for a Coptic family, but again, if it is a mixed gathering then it is better to go with a different gift.

Once inside, the guest will find that young and old are equally responsible for hospitality. Whether expected or unexpected, the guest will be offered something either hot or cold depending upon the season—or both if he or she stays long enough—which the host will usually insist upon. It is not in good form to reject something that has been offered particularly if it is something that has required a good deal of preparation. Thus, the strict vegetarian traveling to Egypt needs to be extremely careful while accepting offers (as is anyone with strict dietary restrictions). "Vegetables" are usually cooked with meat (especially if company is coming) and it will be difficult to explain nonconsumption. Even if a dish is supposed to have been vegetarian (or substitute any special dietary request) the maid or cook may have decided that it would be "better" to add a bit of meat (or something else). If the lady of the house did not prepare the food herself, she would have firmly and steadfastly supervised its proper preparation and will be extremely insulted if it is not consumed by the guest. It will be seen as a sign of not pleasing the guest and is therefore problematic as is not eating enough. The Western visitor most likely will not be able to eat enough to please the Egyptian host, who will continue to pile food on his or her plate. This is when the guest must say he or she has had enough or simply toast the host and the great bounty of food as a sign that enough is enough. The only thing worse than non-eating by a guest is running out of food by the host. Most hosts put out a spread of food that is quite shocking in terms of quantity and variety. Gazing at family photo albums will reveal numerous pictures of such feasts for relatively ordinary occasions.

There are a few basic rules of thumb when in someone's home. First, be gracious and honor the host. Second, when asked "how are you?," one should always reply as positively as possible. Simply saying fine and thanking God is the most culturally correct thing to do (see Language). If it is clear that one is not feeling so well, then simply praise God, or say "I am feeling a little tired," but never say "I am not feeling well." Indeed, one will find that Egyptians do not speak frankly about health issues at all. One is not likely to hear the words "death," "cancer," "tumor," and so on. Instead, various euphemisms for all serious health ailments exist. Do not expect people to speak candidly about the illness of a loved one. Another faux pas: do not extend the feet so that the soles are facing the host (or anybody else for that matter). Also, if something can be done with the right hand or side first, do it with the right hand or side first, for example, putting on one's shoes or socks.

Here are a couple of things that a visitor to Egypt may find different than the United States at meal time; these vary according to class and region. In upper class households, the meal is much more formal than most meals in typical American homes, particularly if they have invited guests. There might be servants dressed in livery, silver cutlery, cloth napkins, and a multiplicity of dishes. The ordinary upper class meal (not a formal affair) will mostly resemble an American meal, except perhaps the presence of servant(s). In a family of more humble origins people might prefer to simply eat with spoons; however, knowing that a Western guest is in the home they may offer a fork (even though a spoon might be a better option for some of the foods offered). If one is eating truly *baladi*-style, there may be no silverware, the bread will be the vehicle for moving the food to the mouth (but one is likely to see this only in the countryside or poor urban areas). There may or may not be napkins as people would wash up hands before and after the meal. There may be no water offered with the meal. Many prefer to drink water after the meal is completed. Unless the family drinks bottled water or purified water, one should abstain from drinking tap water. Do not eat and run. In fact, one should wait for awhile after the hot beverage after the meal has been served to even contemplate leaving.

When offered anything, for example, coffee, tea, or even orange juice, the traveler to Egypt will find that the beverage is sugared beyond the limit to which he or she is accustomed. For those who do not care for much sugar, it is best to order anything sugarless (*min gheer sukar*) because there is no confusing this order, as "one spoon" can mean different things to different people. One man's "spoonful" is another's shovel. The idea behind the sugar is that the host wants everything to be literally as "sweet" as possible for the guest. In other words, he or she would not want the guest to leave with a bitter taste in his or her mouth. Unless in an upper-class home, tea is usually served in a plain glass with the leaves at the bottom, so let the tea rest a few minutes, gingerly hold it from the rim to drink, and leave the leaves and the last bit of liquid at the bottom. (See Food for the wide variety of teas and beverages).

Aside from the elite, who often mimic Western trends, children's birthday parties are quite different from those in the United States. The child is still the center of attention and has a huge party with an enormous spread of food, but the participants are the extended family: grandparents, aunts, uncles, and cousins. The family gathers to eat, tell stories, listen to music, and dance (unless their religious views prohibit them from doing the latter two).

A brief anecdote about a middle-class student and his family studying in the United States and the culture shocks that his family experienced tells about the differences in hospitality and etiquette. This man, his wife, and young child came to the United States so that he could pursue a Ph.D. at a U.S. university. The university had a program to "adopt" international students and make them feel more at home. The American family, in true American tradition invited the Egyptian family to a cookout one weekend early in the semester. In making the arrangements, one of the first things the Egyptian wife did was to call the American wife and inquire about the family religion. Being particularly religious (of the fundamentalist variety), she followed *hadith*—traditions of the Prophet that forbade her from eating with people who were not monotheists. Having obtained a satisfactory answer, the family went to the cookout. They thought the food was a bit slim but knowing about American culture they understood that lunch was not the biggest meal of the day—unlike Egypt. They enjoyed their small, simple meal, but being Egyptian, they felt they still had to reciprocate. They invited the host family for an Egyptian feast, and to fit into American culture it was a dinner. The entire table was covered from end to end in delicacies that probably cost the student's entire monthly grocery budget to please his American guests. The American host family must have felt the need to reciprocate the Arab generosity because the Egyptian family was also invited to dinner. The Egyptians were literally eager to see what the Americans would cook up. They were hoping to learn more about U.S. culture through the process of reciprocation and eating more new American foods. The Americans were quite typically American: spaghetti, salad, bread. The Egyptians had come ready to eat—and there was not even enough! In fact, the American wife seeing the heartiness of the Egyptian appetites, squirreled away some of the food for her child who was coming home late from sports practice. The Egyptians could not possibly have been more offended. Spaghetti is an appetizer in Egypt and not really a main course. Then, there was not enough of it. Finally, the host took away some of the food from the guests. Most Americans would not think twice about offering this meal to company; after all, everybody likes pasta, but it created an intercultural conflict. The Americans had probably also done research on what foods not to feed Muslims (i.e., no pork and no alcohol), but these basic misunderstandings still remained. Nevertheless, they violated the most essential rule of etiquette—generosity—never run out of food and never take food away from a guest.

The incident is useful for discussing other social differences and basic etiquette that one finds in Egypt. Religion is extremely important. When the wife asked about the religion, it is quite typical; however, her desire to eat only with a mono-theist is common to more those of a more fundamentalist ilk who have studied *hadith*. Both Muslims and Copts will ask a traveler about his or her religion in one of the first two to three questions asked, perhaps after where one is from. While dishonesty is rarely advised, a person would find himself or herself quite uncomfortable if he or she were to say that he or she had no religion or was an agnostic. This concept is alien and alienating to most Egyptians. While Egyptians may not like the state of Israel, they are quite accustomed to Jews. They may not agree with Zionism, but Judaism is respected as a religion, except among a small fringe of extremists.

Most Westerners would find the level of questioning of taxi drivers and other folks whom one meets disconcerting. Egyptians are extremely friendly. Since the Iraq War (2003), there has been a general level of cooling to Westerners, but many still engage in conversation and certainly in business or other situations, people permeate boundaries much sooner than levels to which some Westerners are accustomed. The next question on the list is whether or not one is married, and if so whether or not one has children. In Egypt, children live with their parents until they have the money to establish their own households, and thus most do not have that period of transitional independence in college where they learn to manage money, live on their own, get an apartment, and so on. Until one is married one is considered in a "child-like" state, and his or her affairs are managed by a parent or an older brother. Even elderly spinsters often have their medical, legal, and financial matters handled by a sibling or a nephew. Marriage connotes a level of maturity and independence. In addition, the society frowns upon premarital sexual relationships (see Chapter 5). A married woman carries with her experience and knowledge that an unmarried woman simply could not or should not have. Once a woman is married she can participate in a whole new level of humor and bawdiness (which varies according to class and personality) that might make a sailor blush. Egyptian women keep their maiden names and what changes is one's title.

Muslims and Copts in Egypt follow Arab naming practices. First a newborn is given a name, an *ism*. Then he or she is located by his or her heritage, usually up to the level of his or her father and grandfather, known as a *nasab*. A boy named Muhammad with a father named Sayyid and a grandfather named Muhammad would be Muhammad Sayyid Muhammad, or Muhammad ibn Sayyid ibn Muhammad. Usually the *ibn* (son of) or *bint* (daughter of) has been removed from the name. After someone has given birth, usually to a boy, they are known as *Umm* followed by the name of the child (mother of . . .) or *Abu* (father of . . .). This is known as a *kunya* or honorific name. One's *kunya* would be used in the neighborhood, or by one's close friends, but not in a professional environment. A *laqab* is an epithet or superlative title, for example, if someone were extremely honest, then they might be known as al-Ṣadiq or simply Ṣadiq (truthful one). The *laqab* might even come to replace the *nasab*. Finally, names can describe occupations, original hometowns, or tribes of origin; these are known as *nisbas*, for example, Karim al-Ahwaggi (Karim the Coffeeshop owner) or Abdullah Minyawi (Abdullah from Minya). People do not go by their "last" names, but rather by their first name and a title, for example, "the engineer Fawzi," "professor Laila," or simply Miss Nabila or Mr. Hamdi. Women never "lose" their identity, whether by genealogy, occupation, or location; however, if they choose not to marry it is difficult to achieve full societal status. Women retain their names apart from the first lady. For example, Mubarak's wife was known as "Mrs. Mubarak" or *haram al-ra'is* (wife of the president)—*haram* from the same root meaning sacred possession (all Arabic words are derived from three letter roots that connote meaning).

Some unmarried women visiting Egypt for longer or shorter periods of time have created fictitious husbands for themselves just to achieve the appropriate status and to avoid the hassle of unwanted sexual advances—complete with ring. Obviously, this lifestyle has its pitfalls as one scholar found when she could not remember whether her "husband" was an architect or a lawyer because she had not given her fictitious husband a uniform personality and ran across the same people again. Many men wanting to come to the United States on a green card will seek out an American bride as a means to an end, and some comb hotels and tourist spots for this purpose, whereas others simply look for opportunity when it knocks. While lunching at what was then a Club Med in Manyal Palace in the early 1990s, an embassy official shared the story of a wealthy woman who married a man from one of the shops surrounding her hotel and came to the American embassy saying "I think it was a mistake." She probably was not the first or the last. Foreign couples who are not married will also find it difficult to explain being unmarried and may find it easier to be temporarily "married" for their duration in Egypt. Again, dishonesty always has its downfalls since people often establish friendships in Egypt that last a lifetime.

The anticipated outcome of marriage is children, and Egyptians love children. Many Egyptian families will continue having children until they have a boy and find Western households with one child or children of only one gender strange. Even if there is the treasured boy, just as often will a mother also want a girl. Men and women value male children—men especially—a taxi driver from the airport on a recent trip had two wives (Islamic law allows four contingent upon their equal treatment—although polygamy is fairly rare) clearly in the hope that the second would give him a son. Instead, he had seven daughters and two wives to support. (Or perhaps the whole story was crafted in order to garner a larger tip, but it is entirely plausible!) Older children spend a lot of time playing with younger children and entertaining them. Where American adolescents and teenagers would groan and complain about caring for their siblings and cousins, Egyptians relish the opportunity to watch them thrive and grow.

Do not fuss over the beauty of an Egyptian baby the way one would for an American baby. Simply saying *"ma sha Allah,"* "whatever God intended," several times with appropriate happiness and glee will suffice. It is the same thing said after getting back exam results as it is a congratulatory compliment to the person who produced the result, but giving God the ultimate credit. Another common compliment is to say that the baby's face looks like the moon, *"zay al-amr."* Egyptians of the middle and upper classes will steadfastly deny it—perhaps because they are somewhat removed

HORUS, THE ORIGINS OF THE EVIL EYE, AND ISLAM

The evil eye is one of the beliefs in Egypt that predates Islam, but has been adapted to take on an Islamic guise. Nevertheless, some Islamic scholars would bristle at the thought of condoning the notion of the evil eye, particularly with practices that resemble idolatry. In ancient times, the eye of Horus was used to ward off the evil eye. Horus, represented as a falcon head with a human body, was known for his battles against his evil Uncle Seth. At one time he lost his eyes, but in a process of renewal, regained his sight, and the eye of the falcon with the teardrop cleanses the potential evil. After the arrival of Islam, this belief could find scriptural support since envy is not a characteristic condoned by monotheistic tradition (113:5). Authoritative collections of *hadith* definitively state that the evil eye is a reality and ritualized washing a remedy.

from it—but the reasoning behind the lack of complimenting is old folk superstitions regarding the safety of the baby and the evil eye. Even if 8 out of 10 people in an extended family do not believe in the evil eye, the two who do can make life difficult. The evil eye is a form of jealousy, so if a person is too complimentary then this attachment will be seen as a form of bewitchment that might bring harm to the baby unless certain precautions are taken, for example, reciting specific verses of the Quran. Some still use amulets, an updated derivative from the eye of Horus, which have become Islamized; many now use the hand of Fatima or various types of beads. Travelers will find the whole range of amulets, beads, and eyes of Horus when visiting Egypt, both as decorations and jewelry. With the age of modern marketing, New Agers can purchase them via the internet. The person who creates the problem of the

EVIL EYE: HAMSA AND OTHER CURES

Although Islam does not condone idolatry, various amulets continued to be used for the evil eye. The *hamsa*, similar to the word for five "khamsa"—perhaps for the five fingers—also known as the hand of Fatima (the Prophet's daughter) is the most popular. The hand of Fatima bears striking similarity to the hand of Miriam in Jewish tradition. Sometimes the hand of Fatima contains the eye of Horus (or simply an eye) in its palm. Prayer beads made with "eyes" as beads or dangling at the bottom represent the syncretic blending of Islamic and pre-Islamic culture. Those familiar with other cultures that follow "evil eye" belief systems will be aware of other cures—not usually deployed in urban or upper class settings—spitting. If these measures are not carried out, then there is a belief that the person who is the recipient of the evil eye will receive illness, bad luck, or misfortune of some kind.

"evil eye" is not seen as guilty, but rather he or she is an innocent victim of the beauty of the child. Modesty is another virtue in Egyptian society. As one looks at Egyptian babies, one should not assume gender based on the color of the clothes. Egyptian mothers dress their babies according to how they feel. This has changed somewhat in the past few years, but it is not uncommon to see a boy in pink.

Walking about the streets in Egypt the Westerner will see many things that are unfamiliar or uncommon at home. Egyptian men are less likely to engage in individual displays of strength. They would rather work cooperatively. Thus, at the airport where one would see two American relatives bickering over who was the strongest to carry the "big" suitcase, in Egypt each man would take one handle and the two would carry the suitcase together. Westerners, generally, and Americans in particular, have relatively large requirements for personal space, and thus they often find Egypt, in general, and Cairo, specifically, overwhelming. Egypt is densely populated in the areas where people live, with vast expanses of desert surrounding the Nile Valley. More than 18 million people live in Cairo, and even more commute in and out to work there on a daily basis. In order to speak to one another on the street and to be heard above the honking horns, screaming children, and blasting music, people walk closely together arm in arm. Culturally, even without the noise, men have no difficulty displaying this sort of bond with one another. Two male friends or female friends will link arms or hold hands affectionately, but nonsexually, and

Statue of Horus at the Temple of Horus in present-day Edfu, Egypt. The temple was built between 237 B.C. and 57 B.C. (Corel)

go about their errands downtown. At the same time, however, men and women do not engage in public displays of affection. Women do not generally smoke on the street and some not even in public at all. Modesty is important for men and women and even Egyptian men do not wear shorts in Cairo on the hottest days of the year. Female travelers will find it easier to get around in loose-fitting, capri-length pants and short-sleeved shirts (not shorts and tanks), and male travelers will similarly find it easier in very long shorts and t-shirts. Clothing marketed under the title of "safari" collections are good choices. This does not mean dressing like Indiana Jones, but in loose-fitting cotton clothing that covers large portions of the body often with air vents or other means for keeping cool. Unless one is in a closed resort, cruise ship, or hotel, revealing fashions are not a good idea. Nevertheless, it may surprise the traveler to find "covered" women in tight or otherwise revealing clothing; however, the best suggestion to visitors is to avoid hassles. Many women who dress in this manner drive themselves or have a car and a driver, whereas travelers need the assistance of others. If nightclubbing, wearing "revealing" fashions is OK, but women should wear an appropriate wrap and pay the extra cab fare to get door-to-door service. Inside the club, one is likely to see many women from around the world in revealing designer fashions. In fact, Saudi women (and men) come to Egypt to engage in meeting and courtship rituals that are impossible in their own country. In the cooler months of the year, October to April, getting around in jeans is comfortable. Again, despite what the traveler might see others doing, it is a good idea not to have the female form revealed—an untucked or long shirt usually does the trick. For women who prefer dresses or skirts, below the knee level is recommended unless heading directly to a nightclub.

Nothing happens quickly in Egypt. Even a phone call with one simple task at hand requires formulaic greetings, multiple inquiries into the health and well-being of whoever answered the phone and to all of his or her kinfolk, achieving the business of the call, and speaking to anyone else who might want to chat. Similarly, buying from stores requires patience. In the old nationalized department stores, one person will help a customer locate an item, someone else will take the item somewhere else to be wrapped by a third person, a fourth person will serve as a cashier, and pickup will take place after proof of purchase has been established. A trip to the bank may require a long wait in the queue only to find that the call to prayer has summoned the person at the teller window to his or her duty. Asking for directions may lead to long-winded explanations that have little to do with the intended route, simply because the well-meaning Egyptian does not want to let you down by telling you he or she does not know where you are going either. There is a saying that God is with those who are patient, and the faithful need to remember it daily in Egypt.

These kinds of challenges require Egyptians to value sense of humor, and they will spend hours telling jokes. If someone has a good sense of humor or is lighthearted, they refer to him as light blooded (*dammu khafif*), and conversely if he has no sense of humor, then his blood is heavy (*dammu ta'eel*). One favorite subject of humor is *sa'idi* jokes, which are jokes about people who live in Upper Egypt. The cosmopolitan Cairenes and Alexandrians make them a butt of humor in the same way that certain ethnic groups were once a target in the United States. While many in the West might find these jokes offensive, Egyptians themselves, including transplanted *sa'idis*, relish telling them. See a few examples:

Joke #1

Sa'idi:	Sir, I want to buy this television.
Salesman:	Sorry, we don't sell to Sa'idis.
	(Sa'idi goes home, grows a beard and goes back to the same store after a few days and finds a different salesman.)
Sa'idi:	Sir, I want to buy this television.
Salesman:	Sorry, we don't sell to Sa'idis.
	(Sa'idi goes home, shaves the beard, puts on his wife's clothing, a wig, and makeup, then returns to the store and finds a third salesman.)
Sa'idi:	Sir, I want to buy this television.
Salesman:	Sorry, we don't sell to Sa'idis.
Sa'idi:	I don't understand. How on earth did you know I was a Sa'idi—I changed my disguise, and I went to three different salespeople?
Salesman:	That's easy—this is a microwave, not a television!

Joke #2

A Sa'idi built mosque for his village, but when he saw the crowds of people coming, he turned it into a restaurant.

Joke #3

A Sa'idi was fasting during Ramadan and listening to his favorite call-in radio show. He decided to call in a request, and when asked what he wanted to hear, he said, "the *maghrib* call to prayer." (The prayer that comes at sunset to break the fast.)

Proverbs

Proverbs are a useful way for understanding the traits and relationships that Egyptians value. As a general rule, it is mothers and grandmothers who pass the wisdom of proverbs to their children on a regular basis. These values include cleverness, resourcefulness, respect, friendship, generosity, humor, and love, but also caution, patience, endurance, and the ability to put up with hardship and enemies. For each proverb, the literal translation, an easier meaning or similar English proverb, and a usage guide is provided.

P = Proverb   M = Meaning or Equivalent proverb   U = usage

P: The ability of the daughter's mouth equals that of her mother's.
M: Like mother, like daughter. The apple doesn't fall far from the tree.
U: Used when daughter engaging in a behavior, usually negative like mother.

P: The cub is from that lion.
M: He is a chip off the old block. Like father, like son.
U: Son behaving positively or negatively like father.

P: Stab him in the back so that you can go to his funeral.
M: To rid yourself of an enemy, outlive him. It is a backwards way of saying "watch your back" because your enemy is not watching his.
U: When someone is being naïve about a situation and needs to outmaneuver his or her opposition.

P: Seek to hunt and you will be hunted.
M: Obviously this proverb seemingly negates the previous proverb—folk wisdom can be contradictory and must be dispensed according to the situation. Another similar one in English—Don't make a mountain out of a molehill.
U: This is used to warn someone not to make an already dicey situation worse.

P: The person who burns his tongue on soup, blows on yogurt.
M: Once bitten, twice shy.
U: Warning to tread lightly with a person who has been betrayed or to a person who is overly cautious having been betrayed, not to worry so much.

P: Those who are afraid of snakes are afraid of [a piece of] rope.
M: This is a combination of the previous proverb and you can't judge a book by its cover.
U: Warning not to generalize, stereotype, or to be irrationally overcautious.

P: Dress up a stick, and it will become a bride. *Variation (similar proverb): Bathe her and then look at her.*
M: You can't judge a book by its cover. Appearances can be deceptive.
U: Advice dispensed to a man interested in a woman who is all glamour and no substance.

P: Marry a monkey for its money and it will still be the same [a monkey].

M: Love and marriage are enduring, but money is fleeting (especially if you are married to a monkey).

U: Islamic concepts of marriage involve equality on many different levels, and this proverb is a reminder of the violation of two, that the man is somehow "beastly," but rich and the woman of more humble origins has greater humanity.

P: The beating of a loved one (male) is like the eating of a raisin.

M: Women should endure the literal or metaphorical hardship of relationships.

U: When a woman complains about how her husband is treating her, she might hear this piece of "wisdom." *Note most proverb collections in English will not include this one, but it is still frequently used. People often use it laughingly to say that people stick together through the good and the bad, and even the bad is sweet.*

P: When the cat is away, the mice will play.

M: When the cat is away, the mice will play.

U: Warning not to take advantage of a seemingly easy situation, for example, when parents or spouse are away.

P: If you are going to be passionate, then be passionate with someone as beautiful as the moon, and if you are going to pilfer, then steal whole thing.

M: Any job worth doing is worth doing the right way.

U: Encouragement to never do things halfway—always put one's full effort in all endeavors, whether related to work or to love.

P: That which has passed is dead.

M: What's done is done. [Original quotation is what is done cannot be undone.]

U: Warning to not let past problems or conflict endanger future relationships. Think before you act.

P: If the boss likes you, then your hand will be free to sail.

M: A little brown nosing goes a long ways. If the boss likes you, then you can do what you want.

U: Advice dispensed to free-willed young men (or women) to buckle under and accept the authority of superiors.

P: The clever one (female) can spin with the leg of a donkey.

M: Make due with what you've got.

U: When someone blames the tools or lack thereof on the poor job, or conversely after someone has put his or her best foot forward with scarce resources. For example, one would say it after a woman fixed a creative dinner casserole with nothing but odds and ends in the cabinet and left-overs in the fridge.

P: A person with a wound on his head feels it the most. (He can't stop picking at the wound.)

M: A person sees his own faults the most. Actions speak louder than words.

U: Often unwittingly a person will display the vice or trait he or she so desires to cover, but he or she cannot help himself or herself.

P: They couldn't beat the donkey, so they beat the saddle.

M: Be fair and just in your dealings.

U: When people blame something other than the real source of the problem.

P: If the person you care about is like honey, then do not lick it all.

M: Do not wear out your welcome.

U: Although Egyptian culture values generosity, a person should never abuse another's generosity. A third party might intervene and remind the abuser or the person who has let himself or herself be abused.

P: Stretch your legs as far as your quilt goes.

M: Live within your means.

U: Reminder not to live extravagantly—not to push beyond reasonable limits or boundaries. Thus, if a son who was about to get married picked out an apartment that was unaffordable, his parents (who might be footing part of the bill) would remind him.

P: When angels arrive, devils leave.

M: Good prevails over evil.

U: Usually jokingly said after one group leaves a function when another one arrives.

Many of these proverbs were collected in an Arabic class taken many years ago. As an assignment, students were supposed to go and ask Egyptians about proverbs and then we came back to the classroom and discussed our findings. As I collected proverbs for the assignment, I noticed a great gender divide. Men tended to remember only one or two proverbs that stuck with them, whereas women tended to know many more because they were the purveyors of the knowledge and needed to have the proverbs in readiness for deployment to their children. It was telling of the relationships in households. Men are perceived to be all powerful in the home, the one whose "beatings" are as sweet as raisins and contributors to the gene pool, yet still are powerless at providing the basic skills and knowledge that mold the individual in readiness for adulthood.

REFERENCES

Lane, Edward. *An Account of the Manners and the Customs of the Modern Egyptians Written During the Years 1833–1835.* Cairo: AUC Press, 2004.

Seton-Williams, Veronica, and Peter Stock. *Blue Guide to Egypt.* Third Edition. New York: W. W. Norton, 1993.

LITERATURE

By Pamela Allegretto-Diiulio

On Cairo's horn-honking streets, a new intellectual spirit offers a reprieve from over-whelming exhaust fumes and incessant noise. A breath of fresh new writers is giving life to the literary world in Cairo at the dawn of a new century. Their audience? Young intellectuals in their early 20s who might be skipping conventional university classes, but instead find their way to lectures, salon conversations, and local book stores for a taste of the magical realist movement penetrating the Egyptian culture today. Seasoned professionals, familiar with the works of classic and traditional Egyptian literature, attend readings, lectures, and discussions by emerging writers, at regular forums in the cultural center of the Middle East: Egypt. Unlike many cultural cities in the world, Egypt is a cobweb of literary connections; one discovers that even taxi drivers are often familiar with the emerging writers that are adding a new hue to the already brilliant landscape of Egyptian life.

Egyptian literature grew out of several millennia of change: from biographical narratives in the Old Kingdom (2650–2134 BC) through classical tales in the Middle Kingdom (2040–1640 BC), for example, Tale of the Eloquent Peasant, The Ship-wrecked Sailor, The Tale of Sinuhe to an imaginary geography in the Late Period (1070–332 BC). Indeed, some scholars believe that Egyptian writings influenced world writers from the Greeks to modern-day novelists, for example, Robert Louis Stevenson and Alexander Dumas. Egyptian literature has impressed a global audience through a history of world-famous classics in both poetry and drama. Two other areas where ancient Egyptians excelled were "wisdom" or advice literature and what might be termed more generally critical literature. Perhaps ancient-Egyptian literature peaked with Demotic (see the section on language in this chapter) works critical of Egyptian rulers under the Persians and Ptolemies. Unfortunately, much of the literature from the fifth-century BCE until the early 19th century has been lost because of the influence of foreign nations that have conquered Egypt. Many of the written pieces were not translated properly so they remained unknown for centuries until J. F. Champollion broke the code of hieroglyphs on the Rosetta Stone in 1822.

It was the Arabic awakening or renaissance, called *al-nahḍa*, which began in the late 19th century and early 20th century in Egypt, which gave birth to an intellectual age of reform and modernization. In the *nahḍa*, there was an attitude for one to learn from the world, with its geographical center situated in Cairo. An Egyptian scholar, Rifa'a al-Tahtawi (1801–1873) was instrumental in helping the *nahḍa* grow, partly because of the time he spent accompanying an educational mission to Paris. Later, he returned to Egypt reforming the educational system, translating books, and writing his own including his views explained in *An Extraction of Gold in a Summary of Paris* published in 1834. The vibrant press of late 19th-century Egypt also offered writers from all over the Middle East a somewhat freer environment to spread their thoughts and ideas.

Poets such as Hafez Ibrahim (1872–1932), known as the "poet of the Nile," captured social and political strife in his famous poem, "Egypt talks about herself." Ahmed Rami (1892–1981), another poet, referred to as the "poet of youth," tapped into internal expressions and emotions in lyric writing for famous Egyptian singers such as Umm Kulthum and Mohammed Abdel Wahab. Rami's gift extended into translations of several Shakespearean plays and quatrains of the Persian author Omar Khayyam (1048–1122). These were only a few of the many Egyptians who illustrated their art through the poetic pen. It is because of poetry's preferred position in the Middle Eastern world that the development of the novel had a late start in the Egyptian literary scene. Only recently has the novel found its place on Egyptian bookshelves, blowing the dust off of untouched classics of the past. Authors such as Taha Hussain and Naguib Mahfouz (both listed subsequently) are credited for ushering in the modern Arabic novel, although Muhammad Hussein Heikal's (1888–1956) *Zeinab* is considered to be the first modern novel in Egypt.

Writers in Poetry and Fiction

These authors, poets, and dramatists are only a minute representation of the numerous classical and traditional writers of Egyptian culture and behavior. Since the merging of the 20th century into the 21st century, the reading audience of Egyptian literature has been introduced to an entirely new wave of writers and publishers who stake their claim from the pebbles of Egyptian landscapes. Although the 20th century stimulated the interest in social realism, which depicts social injustices and economic hardship through people's struggles, some began to experiment with more symbolic types of literature. Within a decade of the turn of the 21st century, the new-wave writers have begun to show their spirit and their bravado with subjects that are generally considered taboo in Egypt, such as political and revolutionary ideas. Perhaps it is this new generation of writers that helped to give spirit to the January 25 movement.

The previous dilemma of neutralizing the brain drain in order to keep Egyptians in the homeland seems to have found new life through the spirit of these new authors. They include the more contemporary cult authors, bloggers, off-beat poets, writers in exile, and those writers who find their catharsis in releasing their internal turmoil to the reading public. These new trends are in contrast to the most appreciated literary genre for centuries in the Arab world, which had been poetry. The touchstone classic of all Arabic literature remains the suras of the Quran, to which no poetry can compare. However, the young generation of the 21st century is awakening to a new day in Egyptian literature, giving writers the courage to speak up, to question restraints in their living conditions, to sometimes defy government censorship of literature, and to find avenues for the publication of their voices.

Respected Writers of the Past

One of the newest genres in Egyptian literature and one of the unique developments in Arabic culture since the mid-20th century is drama. Tawfiq al-Hakim (1898–1987) caused the adrenalin to flow with both his political contemporaries and the reading public to become a household name. Likewise, he was the most visible figure in Egyptian drama, and he found international fame as a result of his work; however, critics often disagreed in their assessment of Hakim's worth as both a dramatist and a writer. A number of his major works were translated into English by William Maynard Hutchins, a leading authority on the life and works of the Egyptian author. They include *Return of the Spirit, In the Tavern of Life and Other Stories,* and *Plays, Prefaces and Postscripts.*

Taha Hussain (1889–1973) has been recognized as a major literary figure in Egyptian literature; his novels breathe a sense of his intuitive nature and his sensitivity for justice and equality into the reader. Born in a lower middle-class family, and as a result of an ill-equipped doctor, he got an eye infection that caused blindness at the age of three. Greek thought influenced much of his literature, politics, and civilization. He fought for man to use reason and for enlightenment ideals including women's emancipation. As a result of his concern for the welfare of the human condition, in 1973, he received the United Nations Human Rights Award. Although Taha Hussain won the admiration of many Egyptians, it was Naguib Mahfouz who elevated the novel form in Arabic literature.

It was only natural for Naguib Mahfouz (1911–2006) to acquire the respect of his countrymen with his ability to depict Cairene culture caught in the upheaval of British occupation and political strife. Mahfouz is generally regarded as modern Egypt's leading literary figure and was the first and only Arabic-language author to date, who was awarded the Nobel Prize in literature (1988). Mahfouz's characters are often deprived, disillusioned, and victims of escape; in his major novels, there is an uncomfortable reality on the oppressive treatment of the female as a victim of society. *The Cairo Trilogy*, Mahfouz's noted masterpiece, is set in the areas of Cairo where Mahfouz had lived. The three novels in this trilogy, *Palace Walk*, *Palace of Desire*, and *Sugar Street* are the names of Cairo streets. The story centers on the dictatorial patriarch, al-Sayyid Ahmad Abd al-Jawad and his contradictory life as a stoic husband, father, and illicit playboy. The three generations of his family are juxtaposed with the events from World War I to the overthrow of King Faruq. Many of his novels, including the trilogy, up through the mid-20th century are representative of a genre noted as social realism. Another favorite, *Midaq Alley*, is a short novel depicting the characters' needs to escape their entrapped existence amidst the tension of British occupation.

Mahfouz's style changed as a reflection of the changes happening in 20th-century Arab reality. His work moved from heroic through realist to magical realist (magi-

Naguib Mahfouz is the author of more than 50 literary works that have chronicled the growth of modern Egypt. In 1988, he became the first Arab writer to be awarded the Nobel Prize for literature. (AP Photo)

cal elements or illogical scenarios happen in a normally realistic setting as is noted in his *Arabian Nights and Days*) or symbolist, showing evidence of more maturity in his work. This element is prominent with his introduction of *Children of Gebelawi*, in which he depicts the prophets of religion as ordinary men in their sinful natures in search of God. His use of symbolism in this novel was intended to convey that the search for Gebelawi was basically a journey into one's soul in search for an internal peace. Mahfouz had been honored with Egypt's National Prize for Letters in 1970, followed in 1972 with the Collar of the Republic, his nation's highest decoration. Mahfouz's distinction as a literary artist was realized in the many novels that have been made into films; thus, many of his characters have become household names. As one of Egypt's noted intellectuals, Mahfouz has often been compared to Balzac, Dickens, Tolstoy, and Galsworthy because of his diversity in characters while posing them in psychological and traumatic episodes. Mahfouz and a number of male and female authors spoke out against the abuses and oppression that served as weeds among the flora and the fauna. These voices are often recognized in the characters that inhabit the numerous pages of fiction in Egypt, which boasts a great diversity of writers who have found their works in English translation.

Somewhat younger than Mahfouz, Baha Tahir (b. 1935) is an Egyptian novelist writing in Arabic, who is the winner of the inaugural International Prize for Arabic Fiction in 2008, after previously winning the State Award of Merit in Literature in

1998, which is Egypt's highest literary award. Born in Cairo, he graduated from the University of Cairo, majoring in literature. Tahir left Egypt, traveling extensively in Africa and Asia, while working as a translator. His *Sunset Oasis* focuses on one man's journey that fragments the existential crisis of a man fully defeated. In his *Love in Exile*, an exiled journalist is living in Europe after his support of the Nasser regime turns sour. The narrator finds himself drawn back into the world of chaos when he hears about the massacres in Palestine. This novel, set in 1982, won the Egyptian State Prize.

Another writer who contributed to the emerging literature of the 20th century in Egypt is Ibrahim Aslan, who was born in Cairo in 1936. A leading Egyptian novelist and short-story author, he won the Sawiris Foundation Award for Egyptian Literature in 2008 for *Stories from Fadlallah Uthman* for the best collection of short stories. Two of Aslan's novels, *The Heron* and *Nile Sparrows* used the neighborhood of his youth for settings, which figured prominently in the story lines. An innovative writer with a genre all of his own, Ibrahim Aslan writes fiction mixed with autobiographical elements, teasing a style that knows no boundaries in the world of art. A master of language, with an expertise of a musician's ear, Aslan works his plots into the life of his readers by incorporating an artist's sense of texture to find the magic in normally dull aspects of life. Besides Aslan, other authors born at about the same time, have added great diversity to the literary landscape.

Close in age to Aslan is Sonallah Ibrahim (b. 1937), who has become a prominent voice in contemporary literature, featuring those areas of life that often awaken one's consciousness in the rife of civil war, revolution, and prison life. The private lives that are concocted by inmates in their world of fantasy to fill the void of isolation and sexual appetites are illustrated in his novels, *Tilk al-Ra'eha* (*The Smell of It*, 1966) and *Sharaf* (*Honor*, 1997). A number of his works have been translated into English, most recently *Stealth* by Hosam Aboul-Ela in 2010.

A well-known author, Gamal al-Ghitany, born in 1945 in Upper Egypt, has found exceptional success as a novelist, essayist, and writer. Just 14 when he penned his first short story, Ghitany has contributed literary works to Egyptian and Lebanese

---

GAMAL AL-GHITANY

Gamal al-Ghitany, upon receiving the Lettre Ulysses Award: "I reject unequivocal labels, like those who speak of an absolute Occident, or a fixed Orient. There is not just a single Occident, nor a single Orient; on the contrary, we learn to see that the sinking of the sun on the horizon is a process that continues throughout the year, which cannot be the possession of one region to the exclusion of the others. It arises from the spray of the dawn, as our ancestors, the ancient Egyptians, already saw millennia ago. There are sensible voices in the Occident, who know that the richness of humanity is to be found in the intermingling of its cultures and the complementariness of its elements, and not in building one sole culture and smashing the others."

newspapers, and as a result of his critical views toward President Nasser, he was held in a prison camp for six months. He was awarded the Egypt's State Prize for Novels—a Merit of Science and Arts—First Degree, and the Lettre Ulysses Award for the Art of Reportage. Many of his books have been published in various languages including German, French, Hebrew, and English. Some of his noted works include *The Cairo of Naguib Mahfouz* and *Zayni Barakat*, a postmodern historical novel, serving as an allegory of Nasser's police state.

The Woman's Role in Egyptian Life and Literature

There have been numerous Middle Eastern women who have written poetry dating back to the Abbasid period between the 8th and 13th centuries. Although most have never been recognized for their writing, researchers have counted 242 female poets, from al-Khansa' to Wallada Bint al-Mustakfi. The latter, it is claimed, had two lines of her poetry embroidered on her clothing in gold, giving way to the daring attempt of women to attract the public eye.

The landscape of Egyptian literature had inspired a new life rooted in the works of Rifa'a al-Tahtawi (1801–1873) and Qasim Amin (1863–1908). Rifa'a al-Tahtawi an Egyptian writer and reformer, teacher, and translator from Upper Egypt, was one of the first to write about Western cultures in order to bridge the divide between the Islamic and Western world and to address the woman's question in Egypt. These authors and feminists, through their belief in human rights, had started the discussions on women's rights. Qasim Amin in 1899 had published *The Emancipation of Women*, which met with much opposition from the Egyptian patriarchy including ministry and government officials. His understanding was that the "freedom of women and the status of the nation were entwined; education, then, would be the key that would," according to Amin, "emancipate women." Liberate women, it did. Although Amin was not the first to write on the topic of women's emancipation, his writings inspired debate.

Two women of the late 19th and early 20th centuries provided valuable insight to the plight of authorship in Egypt. 'A'isha Taymur, also known as al-Taymuriya (1840–1902) and Labiba Hashim (1880–1947) gave voice to a sense of the expected difference between writing by men and writing by women and expressed their reasons for the difference. This attitude is born from Taymur's anger as a child when she was restricted from unfeminine intellectual pursuits and forced to sew with her mother. Women's writings opened new avenues of expression and experience even if they experienced confrontation.

Some of the ongoing themes dealt with women's public presence, their comingling with the public, and the acceptance of women as intellectuals. The first generation of women in the Arab world to write, produce, and publish in any amount was evidenced in *al-Fatat*, a monthly journal appearing in 1892 and followed by many other journals; however, even before this time, *Tadbir al-Manzil* (household management) was a column that appeared in *al-Muqtataf*, a periodical from the 1870s that survived into the 20th century, which developed into a leading secular modernist voice of the Arab Renaissance. The first women writers participated to a great degree in literary debates, which broadened the discussion on women's roles in Egyptian society in the 19th and early 20th centuries. They responded to the challenge of the West and by the early 20th century, a great awakening was happening in Egypt with regard to women's writing. Among the genres that motivated women's writing in pre- and post-1919 Egypt were those biographies that focused on conduct literature. Ironically, Egyptian female writers often used Western women's biographies as the exemplar for Egyptian women's success.

Beth Baron's *The Women's Awakening in Egypt* documents women's contributions to Egyptian public discourse at the turn of the 20th century. The fact that some belonged to a new middle class was a feature of these writers' subject areas. As a result, their writings reveal the disparity between male and female intellectuals. Males traveled abroad to further their education, whereas women had fewer opportunities to take up professional careers. There were contradictions felt by women intellectuals. Often they used pseudonyms to hide their family ties—another irony, in that they veiled to keep their anonymity too. New topics were being born as women began to address a national identity under colonial rule.

One of the defining characteristics of the postrevolutionary era (1952) for women was the work of Latifa al-Zayyat, who published critical works in English and in Arabic. She wrote *Images of Women in the Arabic Novel* and *Lights: Critical Essays* along with many others while introducing the New Criticism movement and Marxist literary theories. Although she ended up in prison for her efforts against the normalization of relations with Israel, she discovered that the experience was rich, which enabled her to discover her inherent human potential. As a result of her prison experience, she produced her memoirs, a collection of short stories, followed by novellas and novels.

Many Egyptian women have paved new roads in the modern and contemporary literary arena, often evoking scrutiny from the conservative community, through their autobiographical works. Authors such as Jalila Rida (*The Weeping Melody*), Su'ad Zuhar (*Confessions of a Masculine Woman*), Asma Halim (*Ḥikayat 'Abduh 'Abd al-Raḥman*), and Iqbal Baraka (*Diaries of a Working Woman*) purposely used autobiographical elements in their novels. The memoir, like the autobiography, has contributed to boldness and bravery in Egyptian women's writing as evidenced in the writings of Nawal el-Saadawi (b. 1931). In her *Woman and Sex*, el-Saadawi reveals the horrors and abuses of female genital mutilation, an abuse still practiced in Egypt today (see Chapter 7). Numerous female writers such as Nabawiya Musa and Fatima Rushdi have contributed their voices through memoirs; the prison memories of Farida al-Aqqash, Zaynab al-Ghazali, Nawal el-Saadawi, and Safinaz Kazim make up much of the inventory women's writing.

Female Writers

Alifa Rifaat (1930–1996), a controversial author who originated from rural Egypt, shocked much of the reading public not only in Egypt, but also worldwide after her works were translated into English, Dutch, Swedish, and German. In *Distant View of a Minaret*, Rifaat explores the sexual and human needs of a woman, calling on husbands to understand the sexual appetites of their wives. Mainly a short-story writer, her traditional Muslim background posed Rifaat as being quite instrumental in the Egyptian literary scene where her voice had resonated through the dark halls of loneliness, finding its way to public awareness.

Radwa Ashour, an Egyptian Palestinian (b. 1946), has prospered as a literary critic, novelist, short-story writer, and university professor at Ain Shams. Her award-winning fiction includes the novel, *Granada* (1994), a trilogy that focuses on the Spanish Muslim community during the Inquisition. One of her readers claims that "you feel as if you are involved in a fairy tale; at the same time you feel it is the very real story of us Egyptians." Once, when asked why *Granada* was considered a subject for an Egyptian writer, Ashour relates that she was drawn to it because no one had written about how the lives of the people involved in the Andalusian civilization had been devastated by the defeat. She adds that she understood what it means to be defeated and to lose hope. Coauthor of *Arab Women Writers: a Critical Reference Guide* 1873–1999, Ashour has been instrumental in providing a historical context to both her scholarly work and her fiction, making her a valuable resource for Arabic literature in general. Her critical exploration of American society is realized in *The Journey: Memoirs of an Egyptian Student in America.* Ashour has found success in much of her writing: *Apparitions*, an autobiography; *Khadija and Sawsan*, by mother and daughter narrators; and *Siraj*, a novel set on an imaginary island, to name a few. Considered a radical by some, Radwa Ashour has offered not only the Egyptian world an important intellectual perspective of the life of Egypt, its society, its problems, its politics, and its landscape of individuals, but she has also provided the international community, a broader perspective of the modern literary movement in Egypt.

RADWA ASHOUR

Siraaj: An Arab Tale by Radwa Ashour (*from a review by Rana Harouny*) *Siraaj* is ultimately both timeless and topical. It has a mythic, fable-like quality that avoids heavy characterization and detailed description in favor of ambiguity and poetic simplicity. Yet it is also a political allegory of contemporary neocolonial realities, wherein the strategic and economic ambitions of the West often betray their consumer-friendly rhetoric of freedom and democracy. Whether or not popular rebellions such as Orabi's or Siraaj's could have produced sustainable formulas for change is an open question, just as much a mystery as the contents of the Sultan's locked vault. One does know, however, that Ashour's novella is not a cautionary tale—when Said is told that man is surrounded by evil, without the strength to overcome it, and that Orabi was wrong to fight the English, the boy replies: "But at least he tried, father" (p. 43). The novella may have opened the sea, but in the end, it closes the stars. —Rana Harouny

Somaya Ramadan (b. 1951), a translator and a short-story writer, earned her Ph.D. from Trinity College in Dublin. Her two collections of short stories, *Brass and Wood* (*Khashab wa Nuḥass*) and *Phases of the Moon*, preceded the 2001 publication of her pseudo-autobiographical novel, *The Narcissus Leaves*. Somaya Ramadan elevated her novel to a new type of aesthetic through the subject matter by using sophistication in language along with a new, more innovative form. She did this by nesting the ambivalent within the allegorical and using the informative within the imaginative.

Latest Trends and Writers

The chaotic traffic jams of Egyptian cities and villages have been a backdrop for avenues of recognition and diverse talent. The incessant competition to escape the tumultuous life of the smog, litter, and noise is, in part, accomplished through the new wave of authorship—adding new voices that sometimes cause the government to find innovative methods for silencing them. Some of these new authors find their venue in coffee shops and book shops, where they enjoy reading and reciting lines from their current publications. Suddenly, with no explanation, these authors often find themselves encouraged to discontinue their salon-style discussion groups, moving on to new locations, which are not heavily advertised to the general public. Ultimately, they continue to find creative means in which to recite and to sell their themes of clandestine antiestablishment rhetoric along with the ongoing internal turmoil that tugs constantly at their souls' desperation to find an appreciating audience.

Alaa al-Aswany (b. 1957) is proof that creativity is not restricted to literary scholars. As a dentist-turned-writer, he has exposed the exploitation of the weaker segments of society while addressing corruption in its most venomous lens: politics, religion, and corporate wealth. In *The Yacoubian Building*, readers and critics alike hail Aswany for writing one of the best-selling novels in Arabic. The building itself is the location of the author's first dental practice, although the characters are fictitious. Aswany has enjoyed writing novels, short stories, and political articles—some of which raise the hairs on the political structures in Egypt. In fact, the film version of *The Yacoubian Building* (2006), likely to reach a much larger audience, departed from the novel in a small number of key ways that would be less likely to offend the government and already-angered religiously sensitive groups.

Aswany, who welcomes diverse groups to his salon-type lectures throughout the literary arena in Cairo, asks of his audience: Why does the Egyptian go abroad to university and remain there for his life when Egypt calls its sons and daughters back? This rhetorical question provokes him to illustrate his yearning that "it is better for them and for us to stay in our country and try to make it better. If we do not, nobody will do it for us." Aswany backs those words with action. He has been at the forefront of the 2011 revolution, maintaining harsh criticism of policies not linked with true democratization.

Other writers besides Aswany use the local culture to illustrate their writing talents. Khaled al-Khamissi (b. 1962), a journalist, writer, film director and producer, and publisher, uses 58 conversations from some of Cairo's 80,000 cab drivers, and takes the reader on a memorable ride in *Taxi* in a city of unending noise. The 58 fictional dialogues with Cairene cabbies are extrapolated from the author's experience of chaotic maneuvering among rundown buildings decorated with falling debris, and ironically juxtaposed alongside the tales of struggle and survival. Khamissi asserts that some of the motivation for writing this story is due to the fact that taxi drivers belong to a very economically deprived stratum of the population. Their jobs are physically exhausting from sitting in dilapidated cars that wreck their spines. The ceaseless shouting that goes on in the streets of Egyptian cities destroys their nervous systems. There is a tremendous psychological factor in dealing with the endless traffic and incessant honking, while coping with constant arguing back and forth with passengers over fares since historically there has been no system for calculating them. (Recently meters have been reintroduced.) Add to this, police brutality mixed with a sense of irrelevance that overshadows cab drivers. Oddly, these taxi drivers gain a broad knowledge of society because in practice they live on the streets, encountering a cross section of Egyptian society every day. Through the conversations with such a diverse population, taxi drivers gain an amalgam of points of view that are most representative of the poor in Egyptian society.

Many Egyptian writers have come to their craft without familial influence or literary backgrounds; however, there are some notable exceptions. Essam Youssef, born in Cairo in 1965, originates from a family of literature lovers and perhaps was not fully prepared for the overwhelming interest that his social novel is receiving. Based on a true story, *The Quarter Gram* is a painfully honest insider's account on Egypt's drug life. Reactions from *The Quarter Gram* Facebook blog illustrate the fine reception that this 648-page novel has received: "What did *The Quarter Gram* do to a group of friends for ten years and more?" The novel examines the way heroin abuse affected the Egyptian landscape in the 1980s and highlights the effects that a quarter gram had on the lives of one group of friends. On the novel, one reader states, "I'm on page five hundred + and I stopped doing anything since I saw that book." Another reader raises even more curiosity with his letter: "Dear Essam, Just to let you know what a great writer you are in visualizing the characters and making us truly live that whole experience, while reading the novel. At the parts when I felt something bad was going to happen, I'd just close it and leave it for a few minutes in an attempt to get out of that consuming feeling you get when reading the novel. You feel so consumed by it as if Salah is telling only me these details!!! I think this is the best Arabic novel I've ever read. It sends a powerful message about the disease of drug addiction."

Many of Egypt's new authors originated in Cairo; however, the voices of nonconventional writers have been permeating the Egyptian bookstores. For instance, Hamdi Abu Golayyel (b. 1968), is one of Egypt's latest gifts to literature. A Bedouin, he finds his voice through a conglomerate of society's inhabitants. Like some authors before him, such as Naguib Mahfouz, who focused on a cross section of fragmented life in the alleys of Old Cairo, Golayyel exposes what he calls the "social disorder" of not only society in general, but also of the Bedouin families living in Egypt. Hamdi, himself, originates from one of the poorest branches of a huge Bedouin family, from which he finds the threads of alienation and disillusionment that he intricately sews into the pages of *Thieves in Retirement*. This novel, published in 2006, focuses on a similar society within the confines of a smothering Cairo apartment building, where inhabitants suffocate from a sense of displacement. It unfolds around a central theme in Egyptian literature, providing a sense of man as an individual lost in a world of faceless existence. One can easily find Hamdi Abu Golayyel in a smoke-filled, stuffy, paper infested room of the Merit Publishing Co. as he prepares for one of the Wednesday evening forums or discussions on one of the new local writers, where he eagerly greets other literary folk like himself.

An aspiring writer since his college days, Yasser Abdel Latif (b. 1969) from Nubia, which is located south of Egypt along the Nile and in northern Sudan, first published "A Devil of Light," a short story in 1989 in *Rose al-Youssef*. Six years later he published a collection of poems entitled *People and Stones* focusing on life during the 1990s in and around Cairo. A quiet man of moderate height, with somewhat cautious reservation, Yasser gives the impression that he is waiting for his next novel to move his pen. After his success with *The Laws of Inheritance*, Yasser proudly explains that this is a narrative of three generations of an immigrant family from Nubia. Yasser clarifies that "Laws" in the title mean "genetic" in Arabic; therefore, the novel illustrates three approaches of the three generations to be integrated into Cairo society. Admittedly, it is autobiographical in nature and the author explains that the first generation focuses on the early 1930s between the two wars, whereas the second generation, in the 1960s, develops through the Nasser years, followed by the third generation, during the 1990s and the Gulf War. Construction of the novel is one of its fascinating traits since it is not chronological. Instead, it uses a series of flash-backs, which help to explore four extended moments from the life of this family. This new rising star can be seen in Al-Kotab bookstore on Wednesday evenings conducting writing workshops for aspiring writers.

The newer authors of Egypt's brave new literary world find life through fragmented discourse. One of these authors, Ahmed Alaidy (b. 1974), found almost instant success with *Being Abbas El Abd*, which boasts a multitude of fragmented characters, none more revealing than the narrator's best friend, Abbas. The words of "An Introduction You Can Suck or Shove," greets the reader upon turning the first page, which guarantees that sucking up to this novella will end up shoving its multiple personalities into one's memory for quite some time. Alaidy has provided a spark in the potential for a true fictional renaissance, which has created an instantly rewarding read embraced by an extremely diverse range of literary figures. The opening dialogue of Alaidy's ambiguously humorous, yet angry novella, provokes anticipation from his audience with a series of questions such as, "Have you ever tried taking a cigarette from a pack in your sleeping father's pocket?" Alaidy is bound to remind his audience of their own past indiscretions with his brutal honesty.

Literary Journals and Magazines

Alif is the Journal of Comparative Poetics, a refereed multilingual journal appearing annually in the Spring. It presents articles in Arabic, English, and occasionally French. The editor, Ferial Ghazoul, is chair of the Comparative English Department at AUC, and author and critic of numerous articles and books on literary topics.

Banipal, an independent magazine of modern Arab literature, publishes contemporary Arab authors in English translation. *Banipal's* three issues a year present both established and emerging Arab writers for the first time through poems, short stories, or excerpts from novels, with regular columns for book reviews, photo-reports of literary events, and author interviews.

The New Literature: Literary Blogosphere and Online Presence

The annual Cairo International Bookfair held in January 2009 brought together global voices in a seminar titled "Bloggers' Literature: The Screams of Youth or Kleenex?" The seminar, organized by writer Youssef Al-Ka'eed focused on the simplicity of blogging, while highlighting it as an art form. Blogger Ghada Abdel Aal describes bloggers' literature as "express[ing] a human being's thoughts, feelings, and inhibitions." Furthermore, she quotes Tawfiq El-Hakim by stating that "the essence of real literature" is "the open air literature; the literary expression of freedom and passion; words that reach out from one heart to another exposing the depth of the human psyche in freedom, honesty, and sincerity." As a result of the current interest in the blogosphere, Dar al-Shorouk, publisher for over 30 years, has been building a reputation for the publication of popular Arab blogs. Without the latest online presence and the existence of social networks, the January 25 movement would not have taken place.

The contemporary genre and phenomenon of experimental writers is the favored blogosphere, which in some uncanny way, permits fresh air to enter through the electronic pages of public spaces. A new, interesting collection of narratives has been introduced by Rehab Bassam (b. 1977) in her *Rice Pudding for Two* in a language that allows the flavor of Egypt to seep through its colloquialism to represent the middle class as though she can feel the pulse of the country's psyche. The blog named *Hawadit* (tales), the forum for Bassam's refreshing yet unique voice for people clothed in diversity, is published in Arabic.

Amy Mowafi is editor of *Enigma*, an international English lifestyle magazine published in Egypt. The magazine was the source from which her book, *Fe-Mail: the Trials and Tribulations of Being a Good Egyptian Girl*, now in its 3rd edition, was taken. Many readers have become familiar with Amy's writing because of her online presence. Mowafi's audience for *Fe-Mail* has been evident in the reception of this compilation of stories on her Facebook page. A comment from *Alter Ego* magazine reveals that Amy "skillfully combines a sarcastic wit with a disarming self-deprecating honesty. This book will garner quite a following from both men and women alike." Likewise, the *Herald Tribune* acknowledges *Fe-Mail* by stating that it "will have you laughing all the way." Interestingly, as a result of *Fe-Mail*, her mother prematurely claimed that Amy would never find a nice Egyptian man who is willing to marry her.

Authors in Exile

Waguih Ghali (1930–1969), an Egyptian Copt, produced in his only novel *Beer in the Snooker Club*, a realistically devastating insight of the human and political conditions that existed in Egypt during the 1940s and 1950s. He accomplishes this in a well-written narrative of two friends, unhappy with the Nasser era, who go to London. Denys Johnson-Davies relates that these two friends "are both alienated by the air of unaccustomed sophistication that surrounds them." Upon "returning to Cairo the characters find it difficult to readjust themselves, particularly in their relations with the opposite sex." Although Ghali was raised in Cairo, he spent most of his adult life studying and working in the United Kingdom, Sweden, France, and Germany, committing suicide in 1968.

Women's voices have been prominent even in works written in exile. Ahdaf Soueif (b. 1950) is an Anglophone female Arab writer living in London, whose book, *The Map of Love*, had been shortlisted in 1999 for the Booker Prize for Fiction. Set in two time zones, it reconnects Anna Winterbourne of the past to Isabel Parkman, 100 years later. Soueif juxtaposes events and themes that merge the British ruling classes with the Egyptian landscape. In doing so, she captivates the reader with the coincidences that bring Anna together with Sharif, which ultimately bestow on them far more adventure than they had expected. Her *In the Eye of the Sun*, lays out the raw truth and uncompromising determination of a young Egyptian woman's life in Egypt and England. Her more current works include *Mezzaterra*, a book of nonfiction published in 2004 and a collection of short stories, *I Think of You*, in 2007.

Anglophone Egyptian writer Ahdaf Souief, June 2012. (David Levenson/ Getty Images)

Some writers in exile have made much progress in the field of literary criticism. Leila Ahmed (b. 1940) has contributed exceptional wisdom to the literature of Muslim women; her work has been respected and cited by numerous scholars worldwide. Ahmed's 1992 book, *Women and Gender in Islam* is responsible in part, for setting the foundation in understanding how women's roles in the Muslim world, and more specifically in the Middle East, have contributed to the history of what the reading audience knows about gender issues. Her other contributions include *A Border Passage: From Cairo to America—A Woman's Journey*, a memoir that focuses on Ahmed's education and her increasing awareness of her identity. Part of the conflict in her quest for answers lies in part with being Egyptian, but also trying to identify with her Arabness—all in her journey to the United States to establish herself as a scholar in Women's Studies.

Finally, one of the most accessible authors who has kept her homeland close to her heart is Samia Serageldin, born in the early 1950s and the author of *The Cairo House*. She chose to script her narrative as a novel because "Only in a novel would one have the license to conveniently conflate two aunts into 'Tant Zohra,' or to explore 'the path not taken,' at a crucial juncture in the story." *The Cairo House* is the meshing of two identities, two cultures, two time periods—one in Cairo and one in America. In her latest book, *The Naqib's Daughter* (2010), Samia claims that two characters, Nafisa and Zeinab represent reverse sides of the coin in Egyptian women's roles during the French occupation. While researching this novel, she was struck by the parallels between the French in Egypt in 1798 and the U.S. occupation in Iraq. The French also had their "Green Zone," the Tivoli. A collection of short stories titled *Love is Like Water* (2009), interestingly reads like a novel since it is set chronologically with a common narrator. The last three chapters address the post 9/11 experience of Arab Americans. Serageldin has lived for more than two decades in United States, having left Cairo after the assassination of Anwar Sadat and in the wake of fundamentalist trends.

New Wave Publishers and Bookshops to Whet the Reader's Appetite

Bookstores in Cairo, in general, are run-down and shabby. They are small, dusty, and are concentrated in the center of town which in the 1930s, 1940s, and 1950s was the apex of culture, architecture, and fashion, but has since fallen into decrepitude. Hind Wassef, coowner of *Diwan*, relates that with the 1952 socialist revolution, books were treated as staples that had to be provided by the state to its people at subsidized prices, which until today, has negatively impacted the economic viability of publishing. It is only natural to realize that few would have any interest in investing in book production or consumption when the market is overpopulated with cheap and poor quality editions. This process culminated in a trend toward the closure of bookstores in the 1970s. Fortunately, the appetite for books and reading, especially amongst the educated classes was not affected, but they were getting their annual supply when they travelled to Europe or the United States.

Diwan, is the first Western-style bookstore established in Egypt and they have a strong and active role in the local literary scene. Hind Wassef and his wife Nadia established the company in September 2001 and the first Diwan Bookstore opened its doors on March 8, 2002 in Zamalek, an upmarket, yet diverse and very pedestrian area of Cairo. Diwan sells books for children, teenagers, and adults in four languages (Arabic, English, French, and German), with a select film and music section, a stationery corner, and a café. They now have six branches with more on the way. Diwan has become a family outing, a refuge from Cairo's hustle and bustle, a meeting place for young people, friends, and intellectuals, and above all, a source of enrichment.

Diwan was the prototype for other bookshops that are finding popularity in and around Cairo. When the first-time visitor finds Al Kotob Khan for Publishing and Distribution, snuggled between other shops along El Lasilky Road in the upbeat Cairo suburb of New Maadi, the first impression will be the inviting coffee-shop atmosphere, filled with refreshing new Egyptian literary talent. According to Karam Youssef, the owner of Maadi's first serious bookshop, "since we have been in the Egyptian culture scene, we have made a huge difference. From the first day, there has been a book discussion each month where clients can meet the author, becoming engaged in interactive discussion with him or her. We hold creative writing workshops and have now accomplished the first workshop for beginners. As a result, we had the honor of publishing the first book with the title *Half Past Seven on Wednesday Evening.*" The workshop was moderated by author, Yasser Abdel Latif. Al Kotob Khan is working on their second creative writing workshop under the title *The First Novel*, from which they expect to produce two or three novellas.

At Al *Kotob Khan*, they also screen low-budget movies and documentaries made by independent film makers. Karam has been influential in gaining more readers to original Arabic titles. In part, she wins over newcomers through intrigue and the innovative activities mentioned above: a series of activities including Wednesday evening writing workshops, a literary criticism workshop headed by Dr. Sayed al-Bahrawy, a well-acclaimed Egyptian critic, book signings, and book-of-the-month promotions. Karam's diligence grabbed the attention of Manal el-Jesri who interviewed her for the May 2009 issue of *Egypt Today*. At that time the bookshop was celebrating its third anniversary, building its popularity on Egypt's newest and most unique talents in writing.

There are publishers springing up in the alleys and hallways of dilapidated buildings in Cairo. An example is *Merit Publishing*, which has distinguished itself as an independent publishing house over the past 10 years, as a result of author Mohammed Hashem's dream and vision for transforming the contemporary literary world in Egypt. Dar Merit was awarded the Jeri Laber International Freedom to Publish Award in 2006 by the Association of American Publishers' International Freed to Publish Committee in New York City. As a believer in fresh talent, Hashem supports, encourages, and publishes new writers, some of whom have been featured in *Banipal's* volumes 25 and 26. Hashem proudly states that the alternative literature that Merit publishes is different than the classics because it often goes against traditions and political structures, pushing people to reevaluate one's life values and lifestyle. On any Wednesday evening at about 7:00 P.M., one can experience new authors reading excerpts or parts of newly published novels in a reading forum. Hashem admits that he has been brave in allowing Merit to break the taboos of sex, politics, and religion.

REFERENCES

Abu-Haidar, Farida. "Tawfiq al-Hakim: A Reader's Guide." *Research in African Literatures Review*, 35 (1) (Spring, 2004), 198.

Allen, Roger. "Contemporary Egyptian Literature." *Middle East Journal,* 35 (1). *Egypt Today* (Winter 1981), 25–39.

Ashour, Radwa, Ferial Ghazoul, and Hasna Reda-Mekdashi, eds. *Arab Women Writers: A Critical Reference Guide, 1873–1999.* Cairo: AUC Press, 2004.

Baron, Beth. *The Women's Awakening in Egypt, Culture, Society, & the Press.* New Haven, CT: Yale University Press, 1994.

Davies, Denys-Johnson. "Travellers Tales." *Al-Ahram Daily.* August 10–16, 2000. http://weekly.ahram.org.eg/2000/494/books5.htm.

Egyptian Government. "Literature in Ancient Egypt: A Prominent Component of Civilization." Online. http://www.touregypt.net/featurestories/liter.htm.

Elsadda, Hoda. "Egypt." In *Arab Women Writers: A Critical Reference Guide. 1873–1999.* Cairo: AUC Press, 2004.

ART AND ARCHITECTURE

By Jelena Bogdanović

Overview

The world knows Egypt best for its rich artistic legacy. People identify Egypt through its great pyramids, ancient funerary art, and mysterious concepts of death, afterlife, and eternity. The original contexts of funerary objects and rituals show that Egyptian art is, however, primarily about life and the continuation of life in the hereafter. The artistic accomplishments of Egypt are made according to long-established pictorial and architectural conventions, which convey highly abstract concepts. The art of Egypt tangibly and subtly reveals various cultural and personal identities from the prehistoric times up to the present. Simultaneously, the ways in which people perceive Egyptian art disclose global attitudes toward Egypt.

Egyptian prehistoric art is generally understudied because it was made of perishable materials and because scholars are predominantly interested in Pharaonic Egypt. Yet, millennia before the powerful dynasties known for wealth-laden tombs, prehistoric societies in Egypt developed rapidly due to the good climatic conditions in the Nile valley (see Chapters 1 and 2). Neolithic sites (ca. 7000–3100 BCE) consisted mostly of oval-shaped mud-houses organized along the passageways and streets. The prehistoric Egyptians used pleasingly shaped and decorated artifacts in their permanent settlements along the Nile. The natural environment influenced not only the choice of themes for art objects, but also the artistic material.

Clay was often used for vessels and votive figurines. Characteristic pottery has a polished red surface contrasted with the black rim of the mouth, occasionally with geometric and stylized animal patterns. The clay head from Merimda, a Neolithic site 37 miles (60 kilometers) northwest of Cairo and dated to ca. 5000 BCE is the oldest known three-dimensional Egyptian work of art. This carefully sculpted terracotta resembles a male human head pierced to receive hair and a beard. Although its original function remains unverified, the Merimda head may have been initially mounted on a post and used as a ritual object.

In addition to ceramics, numerous stone objects existed. Vases, votive tables, and cosmetic slate pallets for grinding eye-paint were produced in a variety of shapes, wares, and surface treatments. Seldom were two objects identical reflecting the great creativity of prehistoric Egyptians. The techniques and experiments in prehistoric art became the basis of the recognizable ancient Egyptian art. Eventually even the repertoire of visual symbols expanded into pictographs and initiated the development of hieroglyphic script.

Shortly before 3000 BCE, many artistic traditions and styles framed the ancient Egyptian art for the next three millennia—codified art that employs hierarchical scale, canon of proportions, fractional representation of human figures, and combination of realistic and symbolic images. The Narmer Palette, carved on both sides in low relief, exemplifies these common stylistic features of ancient Egyptian art. On the front, the intertwined long necks of the two fantastic creatures form a round depression indicating the place for grinding eye-paint. The object looks like a cosmetic palette but its scale and significant weight suggest that the palette was meant for display and ceremonial purposes. The palette communicates a large amount of information within a limited space with a strong message.

The palette commemorates King Narmer. King Narmer, the largest figure represented on the palette, is usually identified with the legendary King Meni, who founded the capital city of Memphis and unified Upper and Lower Egypt. The palette itself does not offer any connection between Narmer and Meni, but the narrative reliefs show Narmer as a divine ruler of the two kingdoms. On the front of the palette King Narmer wears the red cobra crown of Lower Egypt, whereas on the back he wears the white crown of Upper Egypt. In the uppermost registers, the goddess Hathor protects the palace of King Narmer, identified by a phonetic hieroglyphic inscription of his name. The central images show victorious Narmer surveying decapitated enemies and receiving a captive from the Delta region ready to smite him with a mace. A bull's tail hangs from waist of the king and signifies his strength. Narmer is also represented as a bull, razing a fortified town.

The palette communicates the territorial claim and political message of unified, dynastic Egypt by using both the realistic images of a king as human and symbolic images of the bull representing the king and his power. The work reveals schematic

Detail showing Egyptian Pharaoh Narmer, founder of the First Dynasty, subjugating a priest with a mace. From a facsimile of the Palette of Narmer, Hierakonpolis, Egypt, ca. 3000 BCE. (The Art Archive/Corbis)

and conceptual manipulation of the two-dimensional representation of human figure to accommodate Egyptian ideals. State policy declared the king divine, and therefore he is the most important figure and is shown much larger than the other figures. Hierarchical representation is combined with the fractional representation, showing Narmer with his head and legs in profile and torso in frontal view.

Most of the surviving ancient Egyptian art is funerary and reflects beliefs in the afterlife tied with concepts of divine cosmological continuity and order—*ma'at*. Seemingly unending effort to impede time and death prompted ancient Egyptians to create structures that would preserve their remains for eternity. The royalty built tombs to glorify and perpetuate the memory of the ruler. The tomb provided a permanent resting place for a ruler's mummified body, his *ba*—the nonphysical aspect of an individual similar to the concept of personality in modern society—and his *ka*—life force, similar to the Western understanding of spirit. Egyptians linked the stability and continuity of Egypt with the east–west movement of the sun across the sky and the south–north flow of the Nile. Thus, architects set linearly organized burial complexes along the cardinal lines and within fixed patterns that corresponded to the size, mass, and solidity of the tombs.

Among the most impressive tombs from the Early Dynastic period are *mastabas*, royal and high official burials, found at Saqqara, Abydos, and Naqada. *Mastaba*, via descriptive Arabic word for "bench," is a mud-brick, flat-topped monumental tomb with slanted walls erected above an underground burial chamber. The tomb housed the mummy, the *ka* statue, and various goods the deceased would need in the hereafter. The burial chamber had access only through a vertical shaft on the *mastaba's* roof, which was sealed after the burial. *Mastabas* often had false doors to deceive tomb robbers. Located on the western bank of the Nile, groups of typically 30 feet (10 meters) high *mastabas*, laid out on a grid plan to resemble streets, literally formed the *necropoleis*, cities of the dead, as the ancient Greeks named these huge cemeteries. The earliest *mastabas* were relatively simple, but over time their physical appearance changed. The offering chapel was incorporated into the superstructure and during the Old Kingdom *mastabas* evolved into famed pyramids.

The step pyramid of King Djoser (r. 2630–2611 BCE) at Saqqara, built during the Third Dynasty just outside of modern Cairo, begun as a large *mastaba* and ended up as a group of six stacked *mastabas*, more than 200 feet (60 meters) high. Djoser's pyramid, the first of its kind, and at its time undoubtedly the tallest edifice in Egypt, was a marvel by its sheer size. While ancient Egyptians built vernacular buildings including royal palaces of perishable materials, primarily of mud-brick, architect Imhotep constructed this funerary complex of huge limestone blocks to last forever. Massively built, suggesting continuity and durability, the expressive content of Djoser's funerary complex shows the primacy of life after death in Egyptian society.

King Djoser was buried in accordance with *mastaba* convention, in a chamber at the bottom of a 92-feet (28-meter) deep shaft. The funerary complex enclosed by

The step pyramid, designed for King Djoser of the third dynasty by his architect and vizier Imhotep, is located in Saqqara, the main necropolis of Memphis. The structure, considered the first great monument built of stone, was started as a masataba and enlarged twice to its current six-step shape. (Corel)

IMHOTEP

The first artist known by name in recorded history is the architect Imhotep, whose name means "the one that comes in peace." Imhotep is one of the few nonroyal ancient Egyptians who became a legend. Originally trained as a priest and a scribe, and later revered as a god, Imhotep remains famous as the inventor of a stepped pyramid for King Djoser's mortuary complex in Saqqara (ca. 2650 BCE). Inscriptions on the base of a now lost statue of Djoser (Cairo JE 49889) celebrate Imhotep as a high-ranking government officer, first to the king. In the *Aegyptiaca* (ca. 300 BCE) the historian Menetho described Imhotep as the inventor of building with stone ashlar. Though archeological findings contradict this claim, Imhotep is still credited as the first architect who used limestone instead of mud-brick for the construction of monumental Egyptian tombs. The Greeks associated Imhotep with Asklepios, their god of wisdom and medicine, and organized cults for his worship at Philae and Memphis. Numerous bronze statuettes from the Late Antique period show Imhotep in a divinized pose, seated and holding a papyrus scroll in his lap.

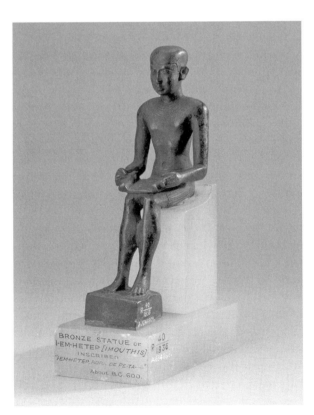

Imhotep, means "the one that comes in peace." (SSPL/Getty Images)

a high wall and built as the palace for the dead, contained large courts, various structures, and sham buildings. Many parts of the complex served either as a backdrop for the performance of the rituals or as the permanent setting for the dead king to reenact rituals of kingship, rituals that Egyptians believed ultimately maintained order among the living. The king's presence in the complex was assured by the installation of his life-sized statue in the *serdab*—a sealed room for the *ka* sculpture—to the east of the funerary complex. Two holes in the *serdab's* front wall enabled the king's *ka* residing in the statue to observe the rituals in his honor and draw sustenance from offerings of food and incense. The entire complex was oriented along a north–south axis. The king's statue looked toward the circumpolar stars in the northern sky. The ancient Egyptians believed that within the precinct dominated by the step pyramid, which assisted the ascension of the king towards the sun, the king's *ka* would remain eternally alive and vigilant.

During the Fourth Dynasty (ca. 2575–2465 BCE), marked by social cohesion, political stability, and increasing wealth of ruling families, funerary art changed dramatically. The most obvious shift was the modification of a step pyramid to a smooth-sided one. This formal change in the physical appearance of pyramids shows how Egyptians viewed the king as the supreme ruler of life on earth and beyond. The king and his tomb were tangibly associated and centered around the divine sun cult. Egyptians added the king a new attribute, which meant "son of Ra," the sun god. The smooth-sided pyramid emulated on a large scale the sacred *Benben* stone from Heliopolis, "Sun City," the center of the sun cult.

The first and the largest smooth-sided pyramid is that of Khufu, whom Herodotus called Cheops. Righteously named the Great Pyramid, it covers 13 acres at its base and, stripped of its limestone casing, now rises to about 450 feet (479 feet— 146 meters originally), which is the height of a 45-story (48-story originally) skyscraper. Built on the western bank of the Nile in a suburb of modern Cairo, the Great Pyramid is accompanied by those of dynastic successors Khafre (Chephren) and Menkaura (Mycerinus), surrounded by smaller queen and royal pyramids, *mastabas* of engineers, priests, governmental officials, and others, including the dwarfs who often held important posts in ancient Egypt. Each complex had funerary temples and additional structures. The pyramid complex of Khafre is guarded by the 65-feet (20 meters) high Sphinx, the composite creature with a lion's body and royal head, possibly of Khafre himself.

The Great Pyramids of Giza remain the most famous of all landmarks in Egypt. Each of the three great pyramids was enclosed by precinct walls like at Djoser's complex. In contrast to Djoser's complex laid out on a north–south axis, the complex at Giza was organized along an east–west axis. This change in orientation meant that the complex did not face the northern stars anymore, but instead the rising sun in the east, incorporating the ruler into the eternal cosmic cycle of rebirth, similar to the daily cycle of the sun. The Egyptians believed that when a pharaoh died he became a god and joined Ra in his daily passages through the heavens. The pyramid itself, called by Egyptians *m(e)r*, or "place to ascend" acquired the shape of the back-to-back stairs while angled sides may have represented slanting rays of sun, becoming a symbol for the ruler's divine ascension into the heavens.

THE DWARF SENEB AND HIS FAMILY

Dwarfs and other handicapped people were integrated in ancient Egyptian society. Wisdom literature advised people to accept those who were physically or mentally challenged. Ancient Egyptians even had two dwarf gods: Bes and Ptah. Images of dwarfism found on art from the Pre-dynastic and Old Kingdom periods confirm that dwarfs were accepted in ancient Egypt. They worked as personal attendants, overseers of linen, jewelers, dancers, and entertainers.

Impressive funerary sculpture of the dwarf Seneb is done in the typical Old Kingdom style. Seneb is on a bench cross-legged in a position of a scribe. His wife, Senetites, sits behind him with her arm around his shoulder, a gesture of affection. The sculptor has disguised Seneb's physical deformity, by placing their two children as a symbolic extension of Seneb's legs. The inscriptions reveal that Seneb was chief of all the dwarfs responsible for the royal wardrobe. He and his wife held priestly positions and possessed cattle, which indicates their wealth.

SPELLS FROM THE BOOK OF THE DEAD WHICH EXPLAIN THE PYRAMIDAL SHAPE OF MONUMENTAL TOMBS IN THE OLD KINGDOM PERIOD

Spell 267: A STAIRCASE TO HEAEVEN IS LAID [FOR PHARAOH] SO THAT HE MAY MOUNT UP TO HEAVEN

Spell 553: HEAVEN STRENGHTHEN FOR YOU THE RAYS OF THE SUN IN ORDER THAT YOU MAY LIFT YOURSELF TO HEAVEN AS THE EYE OF THE RA

The passages quoted in I. E. S. Edwards. *The Pyramids of Egypt* (Baltimore, 1961), 288–91 and taken from: Roth, Leland M. 2007. *Understanding Architecture, Its Elements, History, and Meaning.* (Boulder, CO: Westview Press), 201.

The precision, sophistication, and mathematical calculations used for the construction of the pyramids are impressive. Built of huge stones, some up to 15 tons in weight, the pyramids' measurements deviate from perfect geometric forms within inches (centimeters). Square in plan, their four sides with a 52-degree incline, shaped as equilateral triangles, taper up from the desert sand towards the sky. At any time of the day one side holds the sun's full glare, while another is cast in shadow. Each pyramid was dressed with polished slabs of white limestone, now preserved only on the pinnacle of the Khafre Pyramid. A capstone in the shape of a mini-pyramid with thin lustrous plating of electrum covered the very top of each pyramid.

The rulers of the successive dynasties continued to build pyramids, though smaller in size, while the attached places of worship became larger and more complex. After

Pyramids served as royal tombs for Egyptian pharaohs beginning in the era of the Old Kingdom. The pyramids of Giza demonstrate a highly sophisticated level of engineering, and the method of their construction is still debated today. (Corel)

numerous civil wars and intrusions of the Hyksos people from the east (see Chapter 2), Egypt was no longer an isolated and monumental polity. Having witnessed the loss of order when royal burials were robbed, the kings of the 18th Dynasty stopped building pyramids. Instead, they preferred concealed rock-cut tombs, like the famed mortuary temple of Hatshepsut In Deir El-Bahri. Cult temples built in honor of particular gods became important religious and administrative centers. Art was a way of communication and changes in artistic conventions reflected societal complexities.

HATSHEPSUT

Hatshepsut (r. 1479–1458 BCE), chief wife and half-sister of Thutmose II, became the regent for minor Thutmose III after her husband's death. She assumed the role of a pharaoh, male ruler. Her public images often show her in typically male postures and ceremonial dress. By transcending gender limitations within the power structure, Hatshepsut's "cross-dressing" exemplifies the authoritative political message of the Egyptian kingship communicated through visual perception imbued with symbolic meanings. Nevertheless, Hatshepsut's oval gentle face, with the hint of smile, high cheekbones, and large made-up eyes, remain feminine, perhaps intentionally emphasizing the personality of the queen.

Because one of the most important duties of a king was to build cult temples, later rulers frequently replaced earlier structures by new buildings. Hence, most of the surviving temples are from the New Kingdom period. Egyptians thought that the temple was the house of divinity. Thus, the cult temples architecturally resembled houses, but on a colossal scale. The complex of the Great Temple at Karnak covered about 60 acres or the area of a dozen football fields. A massive gateway, known as a pylon, and a pair of obelisks marked the entrance to the temple. Sloped walls of the pylon and faces of the obelisks were ornamented with reliefs detailing the king's military exploits, official regalia, and the king's communication with the gods.

During the so-called Amarna period (ca. the 1350 BCE), when King Amenhotep IV proclaimed himself Akhenaton, son and prophet of Aton, god of the sun, art reflected changes in Egyptian religion (see Chapter 2). Gigantic statues of Akhenaton found in Karnak and various other images of the pharaoh show remarkable individual characteristics of a ruler with an emaciated face, slit eyes, protruding full lips, delicate bust, and feminine hips with swollen thighs. It is difficult to discuss the extent of realism of Akhenaton's statues. Yet, the innovative representation of the male human body, different from the traditional Egyptian canon, marks the break in traditional art. This novel vision of divine sovereignty, where feminized appearance captured the androgynous fertile character of the king as the life-giver is expanded to affectionate and intimate royal family portraits with his chief wife Nefertiti and occasionally with their daughters, emphasized the regenerative, life-giving, supreme force of Aton. Unlike traditional deities, Aton could not be depicted. The sun disc with rays, prominent in Amarna art, is an expanded version of the hieroglyph for "light." Changes also occurred in architecture. A sanctuary open to the sky and an altar facing the eastern horizon replaced the mysterious darkness of the inner sanctum, while rock-cut tombs displayed joyful scenes of everyday life and royal family intimacy, worshiping Aton.

OBELISKS

Obelisks, nail-like monuments topped by a small pyramid (*pyramidion*), are prominent features of Egyptian architecture. Usually set in pairs, the obelisks marked the entrances into ancient temples. Inscribed with names and accomplishments of kings and queens who built temples, the obelisks functioned as modern billboards. The *pyramidion* they called *ben* or *benbenet*, making references to the verb *ben*, which means "to shine, radiate," and *Benben* stone, a cult object of the sun temple at Heliopolis, associated with the place of creation and the first appearance of the sun god. Like the capstone of a pyramid, *pyramidion* was sheathed in glittering *electrum* (an alloy of gold and silver) symbolically and visually connecting the sun god with the divine-like royalty whose name is on the piercing obelisk. Egyptian obelisks were models for the *Black obelisk* of Assyrian ruler Shalmaneser III (r. 858–824 BCE), Byzantine *Masonry obelisk* in Constantinople, modern-day Istanbul, and 19th-century Washington Monument.

NEFERTITI

Nefertiti (r. 1370–1330 BCE) is perhaps best remembered for her painted limestone bust, now in the Egyptian Museum in Berlin. When German archeologist Ludwig Borchardt found the bust in the workshop of the sculptor Thutmose at Amarna, he wrote: "Description is useless; see for yourself." Evidence suggests that the bust was modeled on the queen herself. Though slightly damaged, the bust shows a beautiful woman with a soft, gently curved face. Her graceful elongated neck balances a tall flat-top crown, which adorns her sleek, sophisticated head. Her full lips carved in bold relief and enhanced by bold red color, almond-shaped eyes and straight nose that seamlessly extends into forehead, create shadows that make the bust incredibly realistic. The Western concept of female beauty haunted by Nefertiti's timeless image is reflected in contemporary society, which can be exemplified by Angelina Jolie, a celebrity whose image populates media throughout the world.

Early-20th-century photo of the head-and-shoulders bust statue of Nefertiti, Queen of Egypt, 14th-century BCE. (Library of Congress)

After Akhenaton, Egyptians restored traditional religion and art forms even more conservatively. A single discovery of the tomb of Akhenaton's son but historically otherwise insignificant ruler, King Tutankhamen (r. 1332–1322 BCE), exposed unseen exquisite taste for objects that accompanied the ruler in the hereafter—from board games, boxes of writing implements, perfume jars, delicate jewelry, chairs covered with gold and inlay of silver, glass paste and semiprecious stones, statuettes of servants, to the famed funerary mask of King Tut found within three nested coffins. The innermost coffin, made of several hundred pounds of gold decorated with enamel work and incised designs with hieroglyphic inscriptions contain approximate $1.5 million worth of gold. Successive rulers such as Ramses II (r. 1279–1213 BCE) left numerous temples and objects that honored military exploits and festivals.

When in 332 BCE Alexander the Great (r. 336–23 BCE) conquered Egypt, its native Pharaonic rule, ended but not its culture (see Chapter 2). Works made for the Greeks, particularly in Alexandria, followed contemporary Hellenistic models, but works created for the Egyptians echoed local traditions. Two peoples, two languages, and two cultures coexisted side by side in Egypt, and after Alexander's death, Ptolomy I and his dynastic successors kept the Pharaonic artistic traditions alive. Roman Emperor Augustus (r. 27–14 BCE) conquered Egypt in 30 BCE and continued the tradition of building Egyptian-style temples establishing himself as the rightful heir of the pharaohs. Augustus exported obelisks and other monuments

They funerary mask of King Tutankhamun. (AP Photo/Tara Todras-Whitehill)

CLEOPATRA

The Hellenistic sculpture of the last Ptolemaic ruler Cleopatra VII (r. 51–30 BCE) now in Berlin is a rare surviving image of this legendary woman of formidable intellect and ambition. Praised by some and reviled by other ancient historians, Cleopatra was famous for her incomparable beauty and irresistible charm, sweet voice, and knowledge of many languages (see Chapter 2). Despite her powerful political figure, Cleopatra gained her fame in popular culture due to her femme fatale image of great seductress who commissioned a suicide.

---

to Rome. Emperor Hadrian (r. 117–138) recreated his vision of Egypt at his villa at Tivoli. Back in Egypt, artists continued Pharaonic tradition, marked by funerary masks with idealized panel portraits done in encaustic, a colored beeswax technique. Most surviving examples are from the Faiyum region, hence known as "Faiyum portraits," and are precursors of Christian icon painting in encaustic and tempera.

Indeed, Egypt is important for the development of various Christian practices. According to tradition, Mark the Evangelist established the first churches among the Greek-speaking upper class in Alexandria and introduced Christianity in Egypt in the first century (see Chapter 5). Because Emperor Constantine I (d. 337) directed Egypt's wheat taxes to Constantinople immediately after its foundation in 330, Egypt was tied to the Byzantine world both economically and culturally. This cultural contact with the Byzantine and Orthodox world is manifest in the art of Christian communities in Egypt.

Among the oldest Coptic accomplishments are the desert monasteries and hermitages such as oratories at Kellia, monastic complex at Abu Mina east of Alexandria, and White and Red monasteries (Deir el-Abyad and Deir el-Ahmar) near Sohag.

COPTIC ICON—CHRIST AND MENAS

Icons are the most distinctive form of Coptic art. One of the oldest and best-preserved Coptic icons, *Christ and Menas* is the small-scale panel originally from Bawit and dated to the late sixth or early seventh centuries. The icon shows strikingly lighthearted friendship between Christ and Menas, an Egyptian early Christian abbot and martyr who was decapitated during the persecutions under Emperor Diocletian in the third century. Christ wraps his right arm around Menas' shoulder in a familial gesture of unity and compassion. The importance of St. Menas and his allegiance to Christ transcended the Alexandrian desert as he was often represented in Coptic and Byzantine churches in the Eastern Mediterranean.

ONE PLACE SACRED TO ALL THREE MAJOR RELIGIONS: MOUNT SINAI

Wedged between Africa and Asia and overseeing Europe, the triangular Sinai Peninsula houses intercultural art. Sinai's rocky desert attracts people because of its location, natural resources, and Biblical history. On Mount Sinai God spoke and delivered his Ten Commandments to Moses, which are sacred to the followers of all three monotheistic religions. Empress Helena, mother of Constantine I (d. 337), founded a church dedicated to Virgin Mary near the traditional site of the Burning Bush. By the sixth century the site became a monastery. Today, it is known as St. Catherine's monastery after a third-century martyr, whose body was buried in the church. St. Catherine's monastery remains the longest living Christian Orthodox monastery in the world. Its collection includes 2,000 icons and a library, second only to the Vatican library, with some 3,000 manuscripts written in Greek, Arabic, Syrian, Georgian, Armenian, Coptic, Ethiopian, and Old Church Slavonic, a showcase of the cross-cultural world *par excellence.*

Coptic churches are usually domed three-aisled basilicas with three apses in the east, each with an altar. Changing liturgical needs probably resulted in the development of an additional space before the sanctuary, which is unique to Coptic churches and is known as *khurus.* The production of Coptic Christian art—woodwork, manuscripts, textiles, ceramics, bone and ivory carving, icons, and wall paintings—continued after the Arab conquest of 642. Dated to the seventh and eight centuries and subsequently restored are the Church of St. Sergius (Abu Serga), built on the site where according to belief the Holy Family stayed in Egypt, and the so-called Hanging Church (al-Mu'allaqa), which rests on the remains of the Roman fortress of Babylon in Old Cairo. These churches are renowned for their preserved medieval liturgical furnishing and tall sanctuary screens intricately done in marquetry technique—wood inlaid with ivory.

Islamic art and architecture in Egypt is associated with the successive and often competing religious dynasties—the Umayyads, Abbasids, Fatimids, Ayyubids, Mamluks, and Ottoman Turks—each ruling Egypt for a prolonged period of time (see Chapter 2). These dynasties created religious and secular objects by combining their native and local artistic practices in their accomplishments, which are, hence, often stylistic hybrids. The first mosque in Africa was built in 641 (21 AH) by Amr ibn al-As, the commander of conquering Arab troops, in their garrison city and later capital, al-Fustat ("encampment"), today part of Old Cairo (see sidebar Saving the Mosque Chapter 2). The mosque has been heavily altered throughout its long history of an active congregation place, but remains an important landmark of Islamic and Arab presence in Egypt. Architecture of the Egyptian province of the Abbasid caliphate shows combinations of royal style in Samarra with Coptic, Syrian, and Byzantine influences.

St. Catherine's Monastery seen from one of the mountains neighboring Mount Sinai in Egypt. (AP Photo/Rina Castelnuovo, File)

IBN TULUN MOSQUE

The mosque of Egyptian governor Ahmad ibn Tulun is one of the oldest surviving and the best-preserved mosques in Cairo. Dedicatory Kufic inscription dates the building to 879 (265 AH). This hypostyle Arab-type mosque exemplifies cultural hegemony of the Abbasids. Ibn Tulun, a native of Sammara, razed Jewish and Christian cemeteries on the top of the hill Jabal Yashkur, where he built his ceremonial mosque originally connected to a palace, now lost. The mosque is the third largest mosque in the world, covering approximately 6.5 acres or half-area of the Great Pyramid. Built by a Coptic architect, the mosque is associated with both Sammaran and Byzantine building traditions. Mud-brick construction, carved stucco decoration, and spiral stone minaret evoke stylistic features of al-Mutawakkil's mosque in Sammara. Preserved marble columns flanking prayer niche are Byzantine *spolia*, whereas the original ablution fountain, later restored under the Mamluks, was domed in both cases, a feature associated with Byzantine and Syrian building traditions.

When the Fatimids conquered Egypt in 969, they moved capital from Fustat just to the north and named it Cairo, via al-Qahira "the Victorious." The Fatimids built Cairo's enclosure walls, colonnaded streets, lavish mosques, shrines, bazaars, palaces, and residences. Although Fatimid Egypt was often at war with its neighbors, including Umayyad Spain and Abbasid Baghdad, commercial and diplomatic ties made Cairo a metropolitan cultural hub of the Arabic-speaking Muslim world as well as an important artistic center of the Mediterranean. Muslim, Christian, and Jewish communities lived side by side and exchanged products of the east and west. Egyptian luxury goods, particularly luster ceramics, rock crystals, and textiles were exported abroad.

The Ayyubids, a dynasty formed by famous Sultan Salah al-Din (Saladin) who fought against the Crusaders in the Holy Land, are acclaimed for their remarkable military and fortification architecture. The Ayyubids used massive stones from the Pyramids at Giza to build palaces and the Citadel, whose ruins still dominate the skyline of Cairo. From the 13th to the 16th centuries, the Mamluks, aquasi-Turkish dynasty comprised of elite warriors, originally slaves of various nationalities, extensively developed medieval city of Cairo. Mamluk art is extremely conservative and stylistically often indistinguishable from the earlier Fatimid art. The Mamluks densely populated Egyptian cities and built numerous religious, funerary, charitable and residential buildings. Elaborate, honey-comb-looking *muqarnas* portals, slender multistoried minarets and intricately carved stone domes marked the cityscapes. Although early Mamluks decorated secular portable artworks done in enameled glass, inlaid metalwork and marquetry with figural and narrative scenes, people recognize Mamluk art and architectural decoration by elegant calligraphic inscriptions and repetitive, nonfigurative vegetal and geometric motifs of unprecedented luxuriousness and complexity. Emblems, in the beginning pictorial and later epigraphic including official titles, often identified the household and the owner of these objects.

The Ottoman governors, who succeeded the Mamluks, continued essentially medieval art projects, until the rule of an Ottoman viceroy of Egypt, Muhammad Ali (1769–1849), who is often considered the "founder of modern Egypt." An Albanian, born in Kavala, town in Macedonian part of modern-day Greece, Muhammad Ali,

---

BEN-EZRA SYNAGOGUE

From before the time of the Hebrew Exile in approximately the 15th century BCE, a Jewish population existed in Egypt. Among Jewish sacred places is the Synagogue of Ben Ezra in Old Cairo, located on the site where according to local tradition baby Moses was found. The Romans destroyed the synagogue and the Copts built the church dedicated to St. Michael. In the ninth century, Abraham Ben-Ezra, the rabbi of Jerusalem purchased the church. Traveler Benjamin of Tudela (d. 1173) recorded that the synagogue kept the Torah of Ezra the Scribe. Indeed, during 1892 restoration a hoard of ancient and medieval manuscripts was found in the geniza (store room). Hence, the synagogue's other name El-Geniza Synagogue. This basilica with a gallery for women in its layout resembles Coptic and Early Christian churches. In the center is a marble bema, platform for Torah reading. Famous rabbi and philosopher Moses Maimonides (d. 1204) worshipped in the synagogue when he lived in Cairo.

TRADITIONAL RESIDENCE ARCHITECTURE

Historically the principles for residential buildings are similar for both rich and poor, the differences being in scale and decoration. Environmentally sound, adobe and stone houses are multistoried with flat roofs, vertical recesses, narrow openings on the street façade often with latticework *mashrabiya* wooden screens and monumental portals, which stretch upward but not higher than the top of the façade, emphasizing its verticality. A courtyard in a typical Arab house, uncovered or partially roofed *qa'a* became a living hall to which various dependences attached for a unit. These living units would be added vertically rather than horizontally, to form either duplex and triplex apartments or commercial rental architecture, frequently built as real-estate investments. Rental buildings—variously known as *khans, wikalas, fonduqs, qaysariya*—had commercial space. Middle- and upper-class units were lavishly decorated. Latrines in medieval palaces had seats of marble and mosaic floors. Pharaonic Egypt may have provided the prototype of such architecture, which was widely used in pre-modern Egypt.

THE FATIMID AND MAMLUK DOMES

In contrast to typical Islamic mosques, the Fatimids did not use minarets in their mosques. Instead, they opted for the use of masonry and ribbed domes in their religious and funerary architecture. Generally, orthodox Muslims use only simple stone slabs for tombs, but the Shi'ite rulers introduced *mausolea* for pious individuals and shrines to the descendents of the Prophet Muhammad. These *mausolea* are square in plan and surmounted by a dome. Often monumental in scale, reaching sophisticated proportions, and lavishly carved in zigzag, starburst and arabesque motifs, and calligraphic inscriptions, these royal sepulchers influenced the development of huge funerary complexes of great artistic value, unique to the Muslim world. The Sunni Mamluks continued to incorporate domes in their architecture; however, it disappeared after the Ottoman conquest.

following brief occupations by the French and then the British, initiated pro-European influences in Egypt. To support the modernization and economic prosperity, Muhammad Ali not only encouraged industrialization and influx of foreigners, but also sent best of the Egyptian students of various ethnicities to study in Europe. Although his domed mosque in Cairo replicates medieval the Blue Mosque and Hagia Sophia in Istanbul, the Ottoman capital, Muhammad Ali's expansions of Cairo, Alexandria, and other Egyptian cities included leveling off medieval structures and planting city parks. By giving away free land to those who would build in modern style, Muhammad Ali and later his grandson Ismail encouraged the development of modern architecture further. Egyptian cities acquired network of wide boulevards, railway stations, regulated city-blocks, and new types of buildings such as clubs and theaters, following Baron Haussmann's urban redesign of Paris. Builders introduced new materials associated with the industrialization such as cast-iron and glass panes. On the exterior, but not necessarily in the interior, buildings resembled concurrent European counterparts. They had rectangular windows instead of traditional *mashrabiyas*, which Muhammad Ali outlawed. The neoclassical stucco-decoration was limited to pillars and vases, however, without figurative statues prominent in Europe.

In the early 20th century, art appreciation and development of arts in Egypt resulted from the art education curricula in primary and secondary schools, formation of the first fine arts schools and museums, as well as from their sanction by the governmental and religious institutions, which allowed figurative art. In 1904, German art dealer Edward Friedham donated 210 paintings to the city of Alexandria for the first Egyptian Museum of Fine Arts. The museum was originally housed in a private villa and after 1952 the new government approved the museum's national status. In 1908, Prince Youssef Kamal financially supported the foundation of the first Egyptian School of Fine Arts in Cairo, which offered free education to talented students. In the beginning the artists were trained by European artists in European styles and techniques. The best students received scholarship for further studies in Europe, mostly Paris and Rome. These students participated in various artistic trends that challenged academic styles—Impressionism, Surrealism, Cubism, Dadaism, social-realism, and abstraction—and investigated international, regional, and national identities in their work.

The new social mobility in increasingly modernizing Egypt enabled talented artists of modest background and means to acquire their positions through energy, creativity, and renewed interest in national patrimony, often glorified through neo-Pharaonic art, detached from contemporary ethnic and religious nuances. Upon his return from studies in Paris Muhammad Mukhtar joined nationalists and intellectuals who questioned socio-political reality of still predominantly agrarian Egypt. Mukhtar's sculpture *Egypt's Awakening* parallels the end of the British rule of Egypt and discovery of King Tut's tomb in 1922. This granite sculpture, prominently displayed originally at Ramses railway station and today at the gate of Cairo University, shows a rising sphinx next a women standing unveiled. *Egypt's Awakening* represents an iconic image of the Egyptian quest for political independence, liberating modernity, and women's emancipation (see Chapter 5).

Mukhtar belonged to the "Pioneers" (*al-ruwwad*), the first graduate artists of the Cairo School of Fine Arts (1911) who initiated the development of a national art. In addition to combining the Pharaonic past and the artists' own present, the *Pioneers* often employed folk art to develop their own individual styles that captured Egyptian societal complexities. Yusuf Kamil painted impressionist Egyptian landscapes and Raghib Ayad portrayed familial life of peasants, folk dancers, and Coptic Church. Trained in both law and painting, Muhammad Naghi, an aristocrat and diplomat, was exposed to art not only in Western and Central Europe but also in Brazil and

Ethiopia. Naghi later became the first Egyptian director of the Cairo School of Fine Arts, Museum of Modern Art of Egypt, Egyptian Academy in Rome, and one of the pivotal figures for the relocation of the UNESCO heritage, Temple of Abu Simbel following its endangerment after the creation of the artificial Lake Nasser.

During the 1930–1950s the second generation of the Egyptian artists either combined global and local heritage or instilled covert Egyptian themes in their works. Often artists formed groups and societies to institutionalize and advocate their art and roles in society. The militant "Muslim Brotherhood" (1928) attracted artists with conservative Islamic and anti-Western values. The nationalist "Young Egypt" (1933) aimed at reviving glorified Arab-Pharaonic art. Pro-leftist revolutionary "Society for Artist Propaganda" and "Art and Freedom" group (Georges Hinayan, Ramsis Yunan, Mahmud Said, Kamal al-Mallakh, and Inji Aflatoun) proclaimed "Long Live Low Art" manifesto (1938). Husayn Yusuf Amin, Hamid Nada, Abd al-Hadi al-Gazzar, and Gazibiyya Sirry are artists of the "Contemporary Art Group" (1946) who challenged Western romanticized perception and academic styles. These artists believed in art education as a vehicle for societal activism. They investigated poverty (al-Gazzar, *Hunger*, 1949), superstition (al-Gazzar, *Green Fool*, 1951), child marriages and unanswered expectations for female rights (Amin, *The Wedding of Zulaykha*, 1948), and promoted social reform through visual symbolism borrowing from religious and folk traditions. Similarly, some architects considered environmental, economic, and cultural specifics in their designs.

The art scene changed after 1952 when Egypt became a republic (see Chapters 2 and 3). Elite art patronage was discontinued, and old governmental art scholarships were replaced by new ones. Al-Gazzar's *al-Mithaq* (*The Charter*, 1962) imbued with symbolism shows new Egypt ambiguously. A green-skinned towering figure crowned

---

HASAN FATHY

Hassan Fathy (1900–1989) is an internationally renowned Egyptian architect. In the late 1930s Fathy reestablished the use of traditional, inexpensive, and locally obtainable materials such as mud-brick and traditional building forms such as wind scoops that function as natural "air conditioners" to build affordable housing for the poor. For the village New Gourna (Qurna) in Qina province, Fathy revived Nubian traditional building techniques. Fathy described his work in *Gourna, A Tale of Two Villages* (republished as *Architecture for the Poor*), translated into 22 other languages. He designed more than 160 projects and was awarded numerous prizes including highly prestigious Aga Khan Prize for Islamic Architecture (1980). Yet his influence on architecture in Egypt remained relatively insignificant, whereas his contribution to world architecture has become more apparent only recently. Fathy's revival of environmentally sustainable adobe architecture precedes by more than a half a century trends in sustainable or green architecture within pressing economic and political issues of global world today.

with an emblem of the republic and leafless, a dead tree is simultaneously the God-dess of the Tree of Life, the resurrected Osiris, and the Great Mother, symbolizing Egypt. "Mother Egypt" holds the charter of the revolution flanked by kneeling fig-ures of a factory worker and farmer. The page with the chapter of The Thunder (Quran 13) is on the ground. In the background at the banks of the nationalized Suez Canal, miniaturized figures of imam and priest, religious leaders of Islamic and Coptic communities, are embracing each other.

After the Six Day War (see Chapter 2) that devastated Egyptian intellectuals and indeed all Arabs, some artists expressed their grief, some turned back to Islamic traditions of calligraphy and aniconism to convey political, territorial, and spiritual messages in their work. In 1966 artworks from the Cairo Museum of Modern Art done by native Egyptians and foreigners were separated into two distinct locations. In the process many works were lost. Many artists emigrated to the West and are returning to Egypt to exhibit or to teach, such as Liliane Karnouk, who in her instal-lations and art education emphasizes "tradition of assuming and integrating polari-ties" from ancient to contemporary Egyptian art.

Egypt under Mubarak emphasized art as the "living measure of civilization" by supporting state-of-the-art architectural projects as well as the development of the Museum of Modern Art and collections that now show artworks of unrecog-nized and previously unappreciated artists. After the Egyptian first prize (1995) at the prestigious Venice Biennale, which promotes innovative contemporary artistic trends, the international presence of contemporary Egyptian artists was enhanced. Simultaneously, these internationally recognized artists have become less concerned with cultural, national, or regional themes and more with their immediate environ-ment in increasingly globalized society.

Since the January 25 Revolution a whole new world of graffiti, caricature, and protest through art has emerged. We are just beginning to see this genre evolve. These images evoke both the disgust with the pace of change, the players, as well as the limits on changes that can take place. In an image circulating over Facebook after the December 2011 elections, a caricature of a male labeled as "the military" is about to kiss another male labeled as "the Muslim Brotherhood"—Fags, meaning

NEW LIBRARY IN ALEXANDRIA

The Bibliotheca Alexandrina (2002) exemplifies the alternating notions of glo-balized society and cultural identities in contemporary Egypt. An architectural marvel, the library revives the legendary ancient library built in Greek times and at the same time reasserts Egyptian international spirit for learning and cultural exchange. Global in physical appearance, as a tilting sun disk rising from the ground at the Alexandrian waterfront, and at the same time techno-logically and technically outstanding, the library received Aga Khan Award (2004) for its "crucial role in the progress of civilization."

that these two groups are proverbially in bed with one another. At the same time, there was hope that the revolution would bring rights to all groups, including gay rights; however, this caricature is meant to demonstrate both the political and moral perversion.

Production and Reception of Egyptian Art

Egypt is the oldest tourist destination in the world. People realized early that the finest Egyptian works of art rank among the best produced anywhere and at any time. Already in antiquity Greek tourists made guide books enlisting remarkable works in the Mediterranean to be seen, which resulted in the books *On the Seven Wonders.* The traditional list of the seven wonders included even two objects from ancient Egypt—the Great Pyramid of Giza and the Lighthouse of Alexandria. The Great Pyramid of Khufu (Cheops) at Giza is the only object from the list that still stands today, as all the other marvels, including the Lighthouse from Alexandria, were destroyed either by earthquakes or fire and suffered further from plundering.

Although not always accurate, the early and often firsthand testimonies about the ancient marvels record Western reception of ancient Egyptian art. In his *Account of Egypt* Greek traveler and historian Herodotus of Halicarnassus (fifth century BCE) described in detail not only the Great Pyramids of Giza, but also temples, ritual objects, and even the priestly clothes. Herodotus entertained the longstanding but false idea that the pyramids were built by slaves and propagated that Khufu forced his daughter into prostitution to obtain building material. Historian Diodorus Siculus (first century BCE) and geographer Strabo (63/64 BCE to 24 CE) described Egyptian pyramids as royal tombs. Other ancient thinkers like Plato (428/427–348/347 BCE) and Pliny (23–79 CE) were interested in major artistic concepts of ancient Egypt, such as proportions and visual illusions. Egyptian paintings and sculptures inspired ancient Greek and Roman artists. After the Roman conquest of Egypt, characteristically Egyptian plants, animals, and hybrid creatures populated the Pompeiian wall paintings. Later, people were interested in ancient Egyptian archeological remains and inscriptions to verify accounts from the Bible. Medieval accounts sometimes identified the pyramids with the granaries of Joseph, which Egypt possessed at the times of great famine (Genesis: 39–50).

When the Arabs conquered Egypt, they marveled at ancient pyramids and developed various legends about their function. One popular legend was that the Great Pyramids concealed literature and scientific knowledge and protected them from catastrophic Biblical flood and the annual inundation of the Nile. The Arabs explored Egyptian pyramids on-site and in-depth. In 820 in his *Universal History* historian Al-Ma'sudi recorded how Caliph Al-Ma'mun seized the pyramids in search for their immense treasures, and how passageways were open for the Khufu (Cheops) pyramid. By the 13th century, stone from pyramids were used as a building material for Islamic palaces and fortifications in Cairo.

Under the Fatimids Cairo emerged as a metropolitan center of arts of the Arab–Islamic civilization. The Fatimids attracted talented artists who often combined local with artistic traditions from wider region of the Mediterranean world, from Syria and Iran to Spain. Persian traveler, poet, and theologian Ismaili Nasir Khusraw (d. ca. 1074) visited Cairo and left first recorded evidence on its art and architecture which is not related to the Pharaonic period. Khusraw described Islamic Cairo and its mosques, gardens, and buildings.

Form the 13th century onwards, numerous visitors to Egypt, some of them traders and government officials, continued to explore and more or less accurately document rich artistic heritage of Egypt. With the rise of antiquarian interest in Europe huge amount of information was collected on the Egyptian monuments, the pyramids and ancient funerary objects but also on mosques, palaces, Fatimid luster pottery, or Coptic monasteries. With an increasing interest in all the arts of the Islamic lands, the art of Islamic Egypt gained growing scholarly and public interest. Mamluk artists produced some of the finest artworks in the Islamic world, which were highly popular in the 19th century and copied by Egyptian, French, Bohemian, and Russian artists, in particular. However, the interest in the arts of Pharaonic Egypt remained unsurpassed.

Egyptology and Egyptomania

The first large-scale archaeological expedition landed in Egypt with armies of Napoleon Bonaparte in 1798. Bonaparte intended to halt the British power in the East, including its colonial predominance in India. Despite the failure of Bonaparte's military campaign, the work of his savants was a turning point in the studies of Egyptian art. More than 150 scientists, engineers, and artists explored, excavated, described, measured, mapped, illustrated, and documented various aspects of Egyptian culture including the great temples and ancient tombs. Furthermore, the accidental archeological find of the Rosetta stone enabled the deciphering of hieroglyphic script used by ancient Egyptians. As a result of Bonaparte's campaign, the *Description de l'Égypte* was published beginning in 1809. This extraordinary scholarly achievement, comprised of 21 volumes and 837 engraved plates, marks the beginning of modern Egyptology. European travelers, treasure hunters, and resident diplomats started to collect archeological findings and to send them to their own countries, thus creating first Egyptian museum collections. The rivalry between European nations to build their own Egyptian collections resulted into colonial Egyptology, which branched in two trends. One, the development of the academic Egyptology and the foundations of appropriate school departments at the universities in Great Britain, Germany, France, Denmark, Italy, and elsewhere. Second, the development of the global cultural phenomenon, which may be called Egyptomania marked by overwhelming taste for everything inspired by Egyptian art.

The Egyptomania became closely intertwined with the cultural praise, profit-making entertainment extravaganzas and unleashed consumption of replicas of Egyptian architecture, fashion, jewelry, clothing, interior design, furniture, crockery, healing stones, dance moves, and even hairstyles. In the 19th century London houses were equipped with the Regency style settees in the form of sphinxes and crocodiles while Parisian salons were filled with the furniture in Empire style, which combined Greco-Roman and Egyptian motifs. Funerary architecture, gates to cemeteries, prisons, and medical schools were built in the Egyptian Revival style because of the massiveness of construction. When in 1823 John Foulston designed a library in Neo-Egyptian style for the Town Center of Devonport, Plymouth, England, set within other public buildings in a variety of historical styles, he justified his decision by educational and sublime reasons associated with the "picturesque effect."

The Freemasons also adopted Egyptian motifs as an exotic nod for their secret rites. Wolfgang Amadeus Mozart, himself a Freemason, set his last opera *The Magic Flute* (1791) in Egypt, at the time regarded as the birthplace of the Masonic fraternity, whose symbols and rituals are evident in the opera. Some productions, like Karl Friedrich Schinkel's from 1815, exemplify seemingly endless associations between Egyptian art and beliefs in its power to achieve immortality.

Egypt became the fascinating topic in literary salons and the subject matter of many novels exemplified by Théophile Gautier's *Romance of a Mummy* (1856). In 1849, just a year before he wrote the controversial *Madam Bovary*, Gustave Flaubert visited Egypt and vividly recorded the desert, mosques, pyramids, and the sphinx, but also the city life and various peoples he met—from sheikhs to whores, snake charmers, and acrobats—which fueled Western myths about exotic Egypt and the "sensual East." Bolesław Prus, however, immersed himself into studies of art, writings, and history of the New Kingdom, before he wrote historical novel *Pharaoh* (*Faraon*, 1895) which examines Egyptian polity and its social strata in order to offer global archetypical image of the struggle for power and knowledge. Similarly, Cairo-born Nobel Prize winner for literature (1988), Naguib Mahfouz, in his novels—*Old Cairo*, 1932; *Modern Cairo*,1954; *Cairo Trilogy*, 1956–1957; *Rhadopis of Nubia*, 1943; *Akhenaten, Dweller in Truth*, 1985—not only addresses complexities of Egyptian society, but also depicts its historical art and architecture (see section on literature in this chapter).

In the 21st century, graphic movies such as *The Mummy Returns* (Stephen Sommers 2001) or *The Last Pharaoh* (Randall Wallace 2010) remain big blockbusters, while museums in Europe and North America continue to routinely display striking luxury objects from the Egyptian past. The best-equipped museums often have entire sections dedicated to ancient Egyptian art, occasionally with segments of entire building complexes. (See appendix with the list with museums with permanent collections.)

The dazzling artifacts from the king Tutankhamun's tomb are the most traveling objects in the world. The world exhibition tour the *Treasures of Tutankhamun* (1972–1979), started at the British Museum in London and then traveled to other countries including USSR, Japan, France, Canada, and Western Germany. In the United States only, nearly 8 million visitors viewed the artifacts during sold-out tours at each of seven museums they were displayed. The "Tut-mania" became a trademark for Egyptomania. In 2002, the new King Tut's exhibition, *Tutankhamun and the Golden Age of the Pharaohs*, marked the addition of the new Egypt department at the Museum of Ancient Art in Basel, Switzerland. Organized by

National Geographic, the Anschutz Entertainment Group Exhibitions and Arts and Exhibitions International, with cooperation from the Supreme Council of Antiquities of Egypt, this exhibition with more than 130 artifacts has toured Europe and the United States, with the exception for Metropolitan Museum that refused to participate this time based on its policy on ticket charging. The Supreme Council of Antiquities of Egypt expects to gain money for the reconstruction of Egyptian monuments, building of a new museum and continual archeological excavations. Indeed, Egypt still has new discoveries to offer. Thus far, 118 ancient pyramids were discovered. In 2008, at Saqqara archeologists unearthed yet another, some 4,300-year-old pyramid, which was built several hundred years after the Great Pyramids of Giza. This pyramid most likely belonged to Queen Sesheshet from the sixth dynasty, the last dynasty of the Old Kingdom whose achievements are considered the peak of Pharaonic civilization.

Art Museums with Significant Collections of Egyptian Art

Museums in Egypt

Graeco-Roman Museum, Alexandria

Address: Mathaf El Romani Street, Alexandria, Egypt
Tel: 03-4865820; 03-4876434
Web site: http://www.grm.gov.eg/aboute.html
Opening hours: The museum is open eight hours per day, seven days per week, every day of the year from 9:00 A.M. to 5:00 P.M., with the exception of a brief closure for Friday prayers between 11:30 A.M. and 1:30 P.M. Closing time is brought forward one hour during the month of Ramadan.

Egyptian Museum, Cairo

Address: Egyptian Museum, Midan El Tahrir, Cairo 11557, Egypt
Museum Director Telephone No: (202) 5796948; (202) 5782450
Museum Telephone No: (202) 5782448; (202) 5782452
E-mail: egymu1@idsc.net.eg
Web site: http://www.egyptianmuseum.gov.eg/home.html
Opening hours: 9:00 A.M. to 2:00 P.M.

Islamic Museum, Cairo

Address: Bab El Khalk Square
Tel: 3901520
E-mail: islammusdirector@hotmail.com
Web site: http://www.islamicmuseum.gov.eg/
Opening Hours: The Museum is opened daily to the public from 9:00 A.M. to 4:00 P.M.

Coptic Museum, Cairo

Address: Fakhry Abd el Nour street No 4, Abbassia, Cairo, Egypt
Tel: 3639742 or 3628766
Web site: http://www.copticmuseum.gov.eg/english/default.htm
Opening Hours: Daily, from 9:00 A.M. to 5:00 P.M.

Egypt in the Museums of the World

Italy

Egyptian Museum, Turin

Address: Museo Egizio, V. Accademia delle Scienze, 6, 10123 Torino
Tel: 011 561 7776-fax 011 562 3157
E-mail: info@museoegizio.it
Web site: http://www.museoegizio.it/pages/hpen.jsp
Opening Hours:
Winter: 8:30 A.M. to 7:30 P.M. from Tuesday to Sunday (January 1 to June 10
and September 10 to December 31)
Summer: 9:30 A.M. to 8:30 P.M. from Tuesday to Sunday (June 11 to September 9)

Archeological Museum, Florence

Address: Archaeological Museum, Via della Colonna, 36
Tel: +39 055 23575; +39 055 294883
Fax: +39 055 264406
Web site: http://www.firenzemusei.it/00english/archeologico/index.html
Opening Hours: Monday: 2:00 to 7:00 P.M.; Tuesday and Thursday: 8:30 A.M.
to 7:00 P.M.; Wednesday, Friday, Saturday, and Sunday: 8.30 A.M. to 2:00 P.M.

The Vatican Museums-Museo Gregoriano Egzio

Address: 13 Viale del Vaticano, Rome, Italy
Tel: +39 0669883333
Web site: http://mv.vatican.va/2IT/pages/MEZ/MEZMain.html
Opening Hours: 8:30 A.M. to 6:00 P.M.

Germany

Egyptian Museum, Berlin

Address: AMP, Bode Str. 1-3, 10178 Berlin (corresponding address only)
Tel: +49-30-20 90 55 44
E-mail: aemp@smb.spk-berlin.de

Web site: http://www.egyptian-museum-berlin.com/a01.php?fs=0.5
Opening Hours: Daily 10.00 A.M. to 6:00 P.M., Thursdays 10:00 A.M. to 10:00 P.M. The Egyptian Museum will finally close the permanent exhibition in the 'Alte Museum' at 'Lustgarten' on Sunday February 22, 2009. The closure is necessary due to preparations for the move of the complete exhibition to the New Museum on Museum Island. There the exhibition will be reopened in the middle of October in 2009.

United States

Metropolitan Museum of Art, New York

Address: 1000 Fifth Avenue at 82nd Street, New York, New York 10028-0198
Tel: 212-535-7710
TTY Tel: 212-570-3828
Web site: http://www.metmuseum.org/
Opening Hours:
Monday: Closed (Except Holiday Mondays)
(Memorial Day, Labor Day, and Columbus Day are Met Holiday Mondays.)
Tuesday to Thursday: 9:30 A.M. to 5:30 P.M.
Friday and Saturday: 9:30 A.M. to 9:00 P.M.
Sunday: 9:30 A.M. to 5:30 P.M.
(Tuesdays to Sundays: galleries cleared 15 minutes before closing.)
(Closed Thanksgiving, Christmas, and New Year's Day)

The Brooklyn Museum, New York

Address: 200 Eastern Parkway, Brooklyn, NY 11238-6052
Tel: (718) 638-5000
TTY Tel: (718) 399-8440
Fax: (718) 501-6136
E-mail: information@brooklynmuseum.org
Web site: http://www.brooklynmuseum.org
Opening Hours: Wednesday to Friday: 10 A.M. to 5 P.M.; Saturday and Sunday: 11 A.M. to 6 P.M.

Museum of Fine Arts, Boston

Address: Avenue of the Arts, 465 Huntington Avenue, Boston, MA 02115-5523
Tel: 617-267-9300
TTY Tel: 617-267-9703
Web site: http://www.mfa.org/
Opening Hours: Monday and Tuesday: 10 A.M. to 4:45 P.M.
Wednesday to Friday: 10 A.M. to 9:45 P.M.
Saturday and Sunday: 10 A.M. to 4:45 P.M.

University of Pennsylvania Museum—Penn Museum

Address: 3260 South Street, Philadelphia, PA 19104
Tel: (215) 898-4000
E-mail: info@museum.upenn.edu
Web site: http://www.museum.upenn.edu/
Opening Hours: Tuesday through Saturday: 10 A.M. to 4:30 P.M.
Sunday: 1 to 5 P.M.

The Walters Art Museum

Address: 600 N. Charles Street, Baltimore, MD 21201
Tel: 410-547-9000 (24-hour infoline)
E-mail: info@thewalters.org
Web site: http://www.thewalters.org/
Opening Hours: Wednesday through Sunday: 10 A.M. to 5 P.M.

The Oriental Institute

Address: 1155 East 58th Street, Chicago, IL 60637
Tel: 773-702–9514—General Information
Tel: 773-702-9520—Museum Office
E-mail: oi-administration@uchicago.edu
E-mail: oi-museum@uchicago.edu
Web site: http://oi.uchicago.edu/
Opening Hours: Tuesday: 10:00 A.M. to 6:00 P.M.; Wednesday: 10:00 A.M.
to 8:30 P.M.; Thursday to Saturday: 10:00 A.M. to 6:00 P.M.;
Sunday noon to 6:00 P.M.

The Field Museum

Address: 1400 S. Lake Shore Drive, Chicago, IL 60605-2496
Tel: (312) 922–9410
Web site: http://www.fieldmuseum.org/
Opening Hours: Regular hours are 9 a.m to 5 P.M. daily. Last admission
at 4 P.M.;
Open every day except Christmas.

Cleveland Museum of Art

Address: 11150 East Boulevard, Cleveland, OH 44106
Tel: 216-421-7350 or 1-888-CMA-0033
E-mail: info@clevelandart.org
Web site: www.clevelandart.org
Opening Hours: Tuesday, Thursday, Saturday, Sunday: 10:00 A.M.
to 5:00 P.M.; Wednesday and Friday 10:00 A.M. to 9:00 P.M.

Detroit Institute of Arts

Address: 5200 Woodward Avenue, Detroit, MI 48202
Tel: 313-833-7900
Tel: 313-833-7530 (Weekend Hotline)
Web site: http://www.dia.org
Opening Hours:
Wednesdays and Thursdays: 10 A.M. to 5 P.M.
Fridays: 10 A.M.to 10 P.M.
Saturdays and Sundays: 10 A.M. to 6 P.M.
Closed on Mondays and Tuesdays

The Nelson-Atkins Museum of Art

Address: 4525 Oak Street, Kansas City, MO 64111-1873
Tel: 816-751-1ART
Web site: http://www.nelson-atkins.org/
Opening Hours: Wednesday: 10 A.M. to 4 P.M.
Thursday and Friday: 10 A.M. to 9 P.M.
Saturday: 10 A.M. to 5 P.M.
Sunday: Noon to 5 P.M.

New Haven Museum & Historical Society

Address: 114 Whitney Avenue, New Haven, CT 06510
Tel: 203-562-4183
Fax: 203-562-2002
Web site: http://www.newhavenmuseum.org/
Opening Hours: Tuesday to Friday: 10 A.M. to 5 P.M.
Saturday: 12:00 to 5:00 P.M.

Saint Louis Art Museum

Address: One Fine Arts Drive, Forest Park, St. Louis, MO 63110-1380
Tel: 314-721-0072
Fax: 314-721-6172
Web site: http://www.slam.org
Opening Hours: Tuesday to Sunday: 10:00 A.M. to 5:00 P.M.
Friday: 10:00 A.M. to 9:00 P.M.

United Kingdom

The British Museum

Address: Great Russell Street, London WC1B 3DG
Tel: +44 (0)20 7323 8299
E-mail: information@britishmuseum.org

Web site: http://www.britishmuseum.org/default.aspx
Opening Hours: The museum is open every day 10:00 A.M. to 5:30 P.M.

France

The Louvre Museum

Address: Musée du Louvre, 75058 Paris Cedex 01
Tel: +33 (0)1 40 20 51 77
Fax: +33 (0)1 40 20 84 58
Web site: http://www.louvre.fr/llv/commun/home.jsp?bmLocale=en
Opening Hours: The museum is open from 9:00 A.M. to 6:00 P.M. every day except Tuesday

Archaeological Museum Nantes

Address: BP 40415 44004 Nantes Cedex 1
Tel: +33 2 40 71 03 50
Fax: +33 2 40 73 29 40
E-mail: musee.dobree@cg44.fr
Opening Hours: Du mardi au vendredi 13h30 à 17h30
Samedi et dimanche 14h30 à 17h30

Museum Calvet, Avignon

Address: 63, Rue Joseph Vernet, 84000 Avignon, France
Tel: +33 4 90 86 33 84
Web site: www.musee-calvet.org
Opening Hours: Monday, Wednesday to Sunday: 10:00 A.M. to 1:00 P.M.,
2:00 to 6:00 P.M.

Musée de la Castre

Address: Place de la Castre, Le Suquet, 06400 Cannes
Tel: + 33 493385526
Fax: + 33 493388150
Opening Hours: 10:00 A.M. to 1:00 P.M. and 2:00 P.M. to 5:00 P.M.

Musée des Sciences Naturelles

Address: 2, Rue Marcel Proust, 45000 Orléans, France
Tel: +33 2 38 54 61 05
Fax: +33 2 38 53 19 67

Museum de Toulouse

Address: 35 Jules Guesde alleys, Toulouse
Tel: +33 5 67 73 84 84

Website: www.museum.toulouse.fr/
Opening Hours: 10:00 A.M. to 6:00 P.M. every day except Mondays

Czech Republic

National Museum/Národní muzeum

Address: Václavské náměstí 68, 115 79 Praha 1, Czech Republic
Tel: +420 224 497 111
E-mail: nm@nm.cz
Web site: http://www.nm.cz/?xSET=lang&xLANG=2
Opening Hours: Monday to Sunday: 9:00 A.M. to 5:00 P.M.
Closed every first Tuesday of the month.

Denmark

New Carlsberg Glyptotek (Ny Carlsberg Glyptotek)

Address: 7 Dantes Plads Copenhagen DK-1556, Denmark
Tel: 33-41-8141
E-mail: info@glyptoteket.dk
Web site: http://www.glyptoteket.dk
Opening Hours: Daily 10:00 A.M. to 4:00 P.M.
Closed on Mondays

The Netherlands

Allard Pierson Museum

Visiting Address: Oude Turfmarkt 127, Amsterdam
Postal Address: P.O. Box 94057, 1090GB Amsterdam
Tel: + 31 20 52 52 556
Fax: + 31 20 52 52 561
E-mail: allard.pierson.museum@uva.nl
Web site: http://www.allardpiersonmuseum.nl/english/
Opening Hours:
Tuesday to Friday: 10.00 A.M. to 5:00 P.M.
Saturday and Sunday: 1:00 to 5:00 P.M.
Monday: Closed

Rijksmuseum

Address: Postbus 74888, 1070 DN Amsterdam, The Netherlands
Tel: +31 20 6747000
E-mail: http://www.rijksmuseum.nl/contact?lang=en

Web site: http://www.rijksmuseum.nl/index.
jsp?lang=en&gclid=CKLQi-X8s5YCFQOaFQodyyWcLQ
Opening Hours: Every day from 9:00 A.M. to 6:00 P.M., on Fridays from
9:00 A.M. to 8:30 P.M.

Sweden

The Museum of the Mediterranean (Medeltidsmuseet)

Address: Medelhavsmuseet, Fredsgatan 2, Box 16008, 103 21 Stockholm
Tel: 08-519 550 50
Fax: 08-519 553 70
E-mail: info@medelhavsmuseet.se
Web site: www.medelhavsmuseet.se
Opening Hours:
Tuesday to Friday: 5:00 to 8:00 P.M.
Saturday and Sunday: 12:00 to 5:00 P.M.
Monday: Closed

Switzerland

Musée d'art et d'histoire

Address: MAH | Charles-Galland 2, Case postale 3432 PO Box 3432
CH-1211 Genève 3 CH-1211 Geneva 3
Tel: +41 22 418 26 00, +41 22 418 26 00
Fax: +41 22 418 26 01, +41 22 418 26 01
E-mail: mah@ville-ge.ch
Web site: http://mah.ville-ge.ch
Opening Hours: 10:00 A.M. to 5:00 P.M.
Closed on Monday

Portugal

Calouste Gulbenkian Museum, Portugal

Tel: 21 782 3461/3450 (the weekend: 21 782 3461)
Fax: 21 782 3032
E-mail: museu@gulbenkian.pt
Web site: www.museu.gulbenkian.pt
Opening Hours: Tuesday to Sunday from 10:00 A.M. to 6:00 P.M.

Russia

Pushkin Museum, Moscow Russia

Address: 121019, Russia, Moscow, Volkhonka st., 12
E-mail: Finearts@gmii.museum.ru

Web site: http://www.museum.ru/GMII/
Opening Hours: Daily 10 A.M. to 7 P.M. (entrance till 6 P.M.)
Closed on Mondays

Hermitage Museum

Address: Dvortsovaya Naberezhnaya, 34, 190000 St Petersburg, Russia
Tel: (812) 710-96-25
Tel: (812) 710-90-79
E-mail: visitorservices@hermitage.ru
Web site: www.hermitagemuseum.org/
Opening Hours:
Tuesdays to Saturdays 10:30 A.M. to 6:00 P.M.; Sundays 10:30 A.M. to 5:00 P.M.
Closed on Mondays

Japan

Kyoto National Museum

Address: 527 Chayamachi, Higashiyama-ku, Kyoto, Japan 605-0931
Tel: 075-541-1151
Fax: 075-531-0263
E-mail: welcome@kyohaku.go.jp
Web site: http://www.kyohaku.go.jp/eng
Opening Hours: Tuesday to Sunday: 9:30 A.M. to 5:00 P.M. (entry till 4:30 P.M.)

REFERENCES

Adal, Raja. 2009. *Nationalizing Aesthetics: Art Education in Japan and Egypt, 1872–1950.* Dissertation. Harvard University.

Al-Asad, Mohammad. "The Mosque of Muhammad 'Ali in Cairo." *Muqarnas* 9 (1992): 39–55.

Al-Asad, Mohammad. "The Mosque of al-Rifa'i in Cairo." *Muqarnas* 10 (1993): 108–24.

Al-Harithy, Howyda N. "The Complex of Sultan Hasan in Cairo: Reading between the Lines." *Muqarnas* 13 (1996): 68–79.

Al-Harithy, Howayda. "The Concept of Space in Mamluk Architecture." *Muqarnas* 18 (2001): 73–93.

Ali Ibrahim, Laila. "Residential Architecture in Mamluk Cairo." *Muqarnas* 2 (1984): 47–60.

Andrews, Carol, ed. 2005. *Ancient Egyptian Book of the Dead.* Translated by R. O. Faulkner, with an introduction by J. P. Allen, Curator, Department of Egyptian Art, Metropolitan Museum of Art. New York: Barnes and Noble.

Antipater on the *Seven Wonders of the World* in *the Greek Anthology,* book IX. London: Heinemann, 1916–.

Asante, Molefi K. 2002. *Culture and Customs of Egypt.* Westport, CT: Greenwood Press.

Bagnall, Roger S., ed. 2007. *Egypt in the Byzantine World, 300–700.* Cambridge, UK; New York: Cambridge University Press.

Behrens-Abouseif, Doris. 1989. *Islamic Architecture in Cairo: An Introduction.* Leiden; New York: E.J. Brill.

Behrens-Abouseif, Doris. "The Facade of the Aqmar Mosque in the Context of Fatimid Ceremonial." *Muqarnas* 9 (1992): 29–38.

Biffi, Nicola. 1999. *L'Africa di Strabone: libro XVII della Geografia.* Modugno: Edizioni dal Sud.

Bloom, Jonathan M. "The Mosque of al-Hakim in Cairo." *Muqarnas* 1 (1983): 15–36.

Bloom, Jonathan M. "The Origins of Fatimid Art." *Muqarnas* 3 (1985): 30–38.

Bloom, Jonathan M. "The Mosque of the Qarafa in Cairo." *Muqarnas* 4 (1987): 7–20.

Bloom, Jonathan M. "The Introduction of the Muqarnas into Egypt." *Muqarnas* 5 (1988): 21–28.

Bloom, Jonathan M. *Arts of the City Victorious: Islamic Art and Architecture in Fatimid North Africa and Egypt.* New Haven, CT: Yale University Press in association with the Institute of Ismaili Studies, 2007.

Bolman, Elizabeth S., ed. *Monastic Visions: Wall Paintings in the Monastery of St. Antony at the Red Sea.* Atlanta, GA: American Research Center in Egypt, Inc.; New Haven, CT: Yale University Press, 2002.

Brewer, Douglas J. and Emily Teeter. *Egypt and the Egyptians.* Cambridge, UK; New York: Cambridge University Press, 2007.

Cartocci, Alice and Gloria Rosati. *Egyptian Art: Masterpieces in Painting, Sculpture and Architecture.* New York: Barnes & Noble, 2007.

Cicero, Marcus Tullius. *Letters to Atticus.* D. R. Shackleton Bailey. (Translator) Loeb Classical Library. Cambridge, Mass.: Harvard University Press, 1999.

Creswell, K.A.C. *The Muslim Architecture of Egypt.* 2 vols. Oxford: Clarendon Press, 1952–1959.

Curran, B., Grafton, A., Decembrio A. "A Fifteenth-Century Site Report on the Vatican Obelisk." *Journal of the Warburg and Courtauld Institutes* 58 (1995): 234–48.

Davis, Whitney M. "Plato on Egyptian Art." *The Journal of Egyptian Archaeology* 65 (1979): 121–27.

Diodorus, Siculus. book I *Ancient Egypt,* Oldfather, C. H. (Translator). *Library of History: Loeb Classical Library.* Cambridge, MA: Harvard University Press, 1935.

Edwards, I.E.S. "Treasures of Tutankhamun." In *Philadelphia and the Countryside-Press Releases. GoPhila Online.* http://www.gophila.com/Go/PressRoom/pressreleases/tut/Tut ExhibitionRecap.aspx (accessed December 29, 2008).

Esposito, John, ed. *Oxford History of Islam.* New York: Oxford University Press, 1999.

Fathy, Hassan. *Architecture for the Poor: An Experiment in Rural Egypt.* Chicago: University of Chicago Press, 1973.

Faulkner, Raymond O., translator. Andrews, Carol, ed. *The Ancient Egyptian Book of the Dead.* Austin: University of Texas Press, 1990.

Frankfurter, D., ed. *Pilgrimage and Holy Space in Late Antique Egypt.* Leiden: Brill, 1998.

Geography of Strabo, The. Book 17. Horace Leonard Jones (translation based in part upon the unfinished version of John Robert Sitlington Sterrett). *Loeb Classical Library.* Cambridge, MA: Harvard University Press, 1923.

Goldschmidt, Arthur. *Biographical Dictionary of Modern Egypt.* Cairo: American University in Cairo Press, 2000.

Grossman, Peter. "The pilgrimage center of Abû Mînâ." In *Pilgrimage and Holy Space in Late Antique Egypt,* D. Frankfurter, ed. Leiden: Brill, 1998, 281–302.

Grossman, Peter. *Abû Mînâ.* Mainz am Rhein: P. von Zabern, 1989.

Herodotus. *History. Book 2.* Hertforshire: Bradda Books, 1979 (chapter on account of Egypt).

Hunt, Lucy-Anne, et al. "Coptic Art." In *Grove Art Online. Oxford Art Online.* http://www.oxfordartonline.com.jproxy.lib.ecu.edu/subscriber/article/grove/art/T019365.

Kalavrezou-Maxeiner, Ioli. "The Imperial Chamber at Luxor." *Dumbarton Oaks Papers* 29 (1975): 225–51.

Karnouk, Liliane. *Modern Egyptian Art. The Emergence of a National Style.* Cairo: American University in Cairo Press, 1988.

Karnouk, Liliane. *Modern Egyptian Art, 1910–2003.* New rev. ed. Cairo: American University in Cairo Press, 2005.

Kessler, Christel. *The Carved Masonry Domes of Mediaeval Cairo.* Cairo: American University in Cairo Press, 1976.

Kozma, C. "Dwarfs in Ancient Egypt." *American Journal of Medical Genetics Part A,* 140, no. 4 (2006): 303–11.

Kreiser, Klaus. "Public Monuments in Turkey and Egypt, 1840–1916." *Muqarnas* 14 (1997): 103–17.

Kuklick, Bruce. *Puritans in Babylon: The Ancient Near East and American Intellectual Life, 1880–1930.* Princeton, NJ: Princeton University Press, 1996.

Luberto, M. R. *The Pyramids (The Great Mysteries of Archeology).* New York: Metro Books, 2007.

Mikdadi, Salwa. "Egyptian Modern Art." In *Heilbrunn Timeline of Art History.* New York: The Metropolitan Museum of Art, 2000–. http://www.metmuseum.org/toah/hd/egma/hdegma.htm (October 2004).

Nabil, Swelim. "Imhotep." In *Grove Art Online. Oxford Art Online,* http://www.oxfordartonline.com.jproxy.lib.ecu.edu/subscriber/article/grove/art/T039994.

New Pyramid Found in Egypt. Discovery News. Discovery online. http://dsc.discovery.com/news/2008/11/11/pyramid-egypt.html.

Oakes, Lorna, and Lucia Gahlin. *Ancient Egypt: An Illustrated Reference to the Myths, Religions, Pyramids and Temples of the Land of the Pharaohs.* New York: Barnes & Noble, 2003.

Online article on the new pyramid found in Egypt: http://news.yahoo.com/s/ap/20081111/aponremiea/mlegyptnewpyramid.

Online article on the new pyramid found in Egypt: http://www.chicagotribune.com/news/nationworld/sns-ap-ml-egypt-new-pyramid,0,1347988.story?track=rss.

Pliny, the Elder. *The Elder Pliny on the Human Animal: Natural History,* book 7. Translated with Introduction and Historical Commentary by Mary Beagon. New York: Oxford University Press, 2005.

Plutarch. *Life of Antony,* ed. C.B.R. Pelling. Cambridge [Cambridgeshire] and New York: Cambridge University Press, 1988.

Puente, Maria. "King Tut Reigns Again." *USA Today Life. USA Today Online.* http://www.usatoday.com/life/2005-06-06-tut-mainx.htm.

Rabbat, Nasser O. *The Citadel of Cairo: A New Interpretation of Royal Mamluk Architecture.* Leiden, NY: E.J. Brill, 1995.

Rabbat, Nasser. "Al-Azhar Mosque: An Architectural Chronicle of Cairo's History." *Muqarnas* 13 (1996): 45–67.

Raymond, Andre. "The Rab': A Type of Collective Housing in Cairo during the Ottoman Period." In *Architecture as Symbol and Self-Identity.* Katz, Jonathan G. ed. Philadelphia, PA: Aga Khan Award for Architecture, 1980.

Raymond, Andre. "Cairo." In *The Modern Middle East: A Reader.* A. Hourani, P. Khoury & M. Wilson eds. Berkeley, CA: University of California Press, 1993: 311–37.

Ritner, Robert. "Funerary Literature." In *Ancient Egypt.* David P. Silverman, ed. London: Duncan Baird, 2003, 136–37.

Roehrig, Catharine H., ed. *Hatshepsut, from Queen to Pharaoh.* New York: The Metropolitan Museum of Art, 2005.

Roth, Leland M. *Understanding Architecture, Its Elements, History, and Meaning.* Boulder, CO: Westview Press, 2007.

Roukema, Riemer. "The Sphinx: Sculpture as a Theological Symbol in Plutarch and Clement of Alexandria." In *The Wisdom of Egypt: Jewish, Early Christian, and Gnostic Essays in Honour of Gerard P. Luttikhuizen.* Anthony Hilhorst and George H. van Kooten eds. Leiden; Boston: Brill, 2005, 285–311.

Russmann, Edna R. *Eternal Egypt: Masterworks of Ancient Art from the British Museum.* Berkeley, CA: University of California Press, 2001.

Sayyid-Marsot, Afaf Lutfi. *A Short History of Modern Egypt.* Cambridge: Cambridge University Press, 1985.

Silverman, David P., ed. *Ancient Egypt.* London: Duncan Baird, 2003.

Tamraz, Nihal S. *Nineteenth-Century Cairene Houses and Palaces.* Cairo: The American University in Cairo Press, 1994.

Taylor, Christopher S. "Reevaluating the Shi'i Role in the Development of Monumental Islamic Funerary Architecture: The Case of Egypt." *Muqarnas* 9 (1992): 1–10.

The Seven Wonders of the Ancient World. Written and directed by Rolf Forsberg. Video-recording. Questar Home Video, 1990.

Vernoit, Stephen. "Islamic Art and Architecture: An Overview of Scholarship and Collecting, c. 1850–c. 1950." In Stephen Vernoit, ed., *Discovering Islamic Art.* London: Taurus, 2000, 1–61.

Vernon, Jennifer. "King Tut Treasure to Return to U.S. in 2005." *National Geographic Daily News, 1/2005. National Geographic Online.* http://news.nationalgeographic.com/news/2004/12/1201041201kingtut.html.

Ward Perkins, J.B. "The Shrine of St. Menas in the Maryût" *Papers of the British School at Rome* 17, no. 4 (1949): 26–71.

Waxman, Sharon. *Loot: The Battle over the Stolen Treasures of the Ancient World.* New York: Times Books, 2008.

Williams, Caroline. "The Cult of the 'Alid Saints in the Fatimid Monuments of Cairo. Part I: The Mosque of al-Aqmar." *Muqarnas* 1 (1983): 37–52.

Williams, Caroline. "The Cult of the 'Alid Saints in the Fatimid Monuments of Cairo. Part II: The Mausolea." *Muqarnas* 3 (1985): 39–60.

Williams, Caroline, H. *Islamic Monuments in Cairo: A Practical Guide.* Cairo: American University in Cairo Press, 1993.

Williams, Caroline. "Twentieth-Century Egyptian Art: The Pioneers, 1950–52." In *Re-Envisioning Egypt, 1919–1952.* Arthur Goldschmidt, Amy J. Johnson, and Barak A. Salmoni, eds. Cairo: The American University in Cairo Press, 2005, 426–47.

Williams, John A. "Urbanization and Monument Construction in Mamluk Cairo." *Muqarnas* 2 (1984): 33–46.

Winegar, Jessica. *Creative Reckonings: The Politics of Art and Culture in Contemporary Egypt.* Stanford, CA: Stanford University Press, 2006.

EGYPTIAN MUSIC

Ancient Egyptian Music

Traditional music begins with the types of instruments that can be made with the resources of Egypt, for example, reeds, cane, animal hair, animal skins, and so on to form flutes, drums, harps, and simple woodwind instruments. Depictions on tombs demonstrate a multiplicity of such instruments and the application of their usage (religious, military, or celebratory). The *nayy* (flute) and the *tabla* (drum) are examples of Old Kingdom instruments that have been found on archeological digs and still exist in roughly the same form today. Ibis-headed Thoth, the same god that is responsible for language gave the ancient Egyptians music. Thoth's wife Hathor had connections to music and dance as well; however, she received more attention because of her relationship to fertility, thus connecting sexuality, music, and dance. Similarly, Egyptians worshipped the God Bes who kept away evil and brought music, sexual pleasure, and fertility. Nevertheless, aside from knowing the Gods associated with music and dance, we know little about the actual substance of the music beyond the capability of the instruments. Ethnomusicologists believe that the ancient Egyptians did not have a system of notation, thus it makes it harder for us to know what their music sounded like. Some speculate that Coptic music bears some similarity (see subsequently).

In ancient Egypt some percussion instruments were used specifically for religious purposes or rituals, and these include clappers, sistra, cymbals, and bells. Other percussion instruments were associated with social gatherings as well as military processionals and these included tambourines and drums. Most aerophones, for example, flutes, *zummara* (clarinet—single and double), oboes (single and double), trumpets, and bugles were used specifically for military processionals. Finally, stringed instruments, for example, harps, lyres, and lutes (*'ud*), served a variety of functions. Although some think of stringed instruments developing later, some appear as early as the Old Kingdom, and a sketch of a woman holding a lute appears from the 20th dynasty (New Kingdom).

*The ancient deity Bes had connections to music, children, fertility, and protection.
(Courtesy of Mona Russell)*

Coptic Music

Although it is purely ceremonial and it bears connections to the liturgies and chants
sung in the first churches in Syria, its instrumentation, pomp, and ritual connect it
to traditions that predate Christianity in Egypt. The early church most likely used
a large range of the small percussion instruments found in ancient Egypt including
the sistrum, drums, clarinets, flute, and harp. Egypt may have even introduced the
church bell, the *naqus*, clapped with an iron rod. By the modern era, in terms of instrumentation, the service became more oriented toward vocal music and only small
hand cymbals and the triangle remain. Many of the liturgies until quite recently
were unwritten, the words passing orally from generation to generation. Professional
training for cantors did not begin until the middle of the 19th century. A major project of transcribing and recording these liturgies has taken place since 1930 under the
leadership of Ragheb Mofteh (d. 2001), who indefatigably brought together people
and resources before passing away at the age of 103, including the recording of
24 hours of hymns himself!

There are some groups of scholars that trace a direct connection between the
music of the ancient Egyptians and Coptic liturgy; in their estimation it is the music
of the ancients simply adapted to the new religion of Christianity. Evidence seems
to suggest this connection, for example, the similarity of instrumentation and places

where several notes are jammed into a syllable. In other words, the lyrics were forced to fit the music. A new generation of scholars is examining different aspects of the music, for example, perception, reception, and context. Some scholars argue that the Coptic chant (or its ancient predecessor) with its loud reverberating sound in the soothing environment in proper body alignment has healing qualities that ward off both ancient and modern maladies, including depression, high blood pressure, and insomnia. To the newcomer, Coptic music's "soothing quality" may seem strange since most Westerners would equate healing with "upbeat" music and might find Coptic music sad, gloomy, or even lugubrious. Coptic music exists on a whole different plane than Western music, which depends on dualities of major and minor, high and low, whereas Coptic music utilizes color and scale, which are subject to interpretation. There are 10 major scales that can be interpreted in different ways by the performer, just as the color red could mean anger, victory, blood, roses, or fire depending upon mood.

Arab Music

The *rebab* or *rebaba* is a cousin to the lute, which some believe preceded the lute. Regardless of this, it was certainly more accessible to the common man since it was made from materials close at hand, whereas the lute was made almost entirely from wood, a nonindigenous substance. The *rebaba*, a stringed instrument made from animal skin, stretched over a gourd or wooden box with a long neck, no frets, and animal hair strings that can be bowed or plucked. After the rise of Islam, several cultural traditions were allowed to blend in Egypt centered around the playing of this instrument and the recitation of classical poetry, the epitome of Arab culture. This process involved the syncretic blending of Persian musical and literary traditions along with Hellenic and Byzantine influences to create melodious ballads of epic proportion. Much like improvisational jazz that creates and recreates on a basic theme, traditional Arab music is based upon melodic modes called *maqamat* often played on the *rebaba* and accompanied by drums, cymbals, clarinet, and/or flute. The *maqamat* scales have more tones, or perhaps more accurately microtones, than most Western forms of music (aside from jazz).

One of the most famous stories that continued to be musically performed in Egypt as well as North Africa, Greater Syria, and the Arabian Peninsula, is the epic of the Bani Hilal. This particular tribe did not migrate from the Arabian Peninsula and participate in the Islamic conquests in the seventh century. Instead, conditions three centuries later most likely necessitated its northward and westward migration. The tribe locked horns with the Fatimid caliph who then paid the nomads to regain lost territory in present-day Tunisia. Eventually, a Berber dynasty in present-day Morocco wiped them out, but vestiges of the tales that they told remained with survivors, to be sung in coffeehouses, weddings, and courts from Algiers to Cairo to Damascus. The entire "story" takes more than 100 hours to "tell," and professional storytellers spend 10 years or more learning the craft from senior members of their family. The key age for mastering the art of performance comes between 15 and 18 years of age.

Great poets not only know every detail of plot and can analyze each character with the finesse of a psychoanalyst, but they can also tailor a show to meet the needs of an audience, voicing loud booms, groans, grunts, bodily functions, crashes, or even the words "wake up" to arouse a sleepy audience member. Such craftsmanship creates an active performance environment as everyone looks around to see who the offender could be, and the audience becomes part of the show. An interactive audience will be a motif that carries into the modern period. To this day, an audience that sits without clapping, cheering, tapping, or encouraging traditional music is thought to be unappreciative or the musicians lacking.

Whereas the *Sirat Bani Hilal* is extremely complex and has no single hero, *Sirat Baibars* is relatively straightforward and contains the battles, exploits, and great deeds of the former mamluk Sultan, champion of Ayn Jalut, and slayer of Crusaders (see Chapter 2). The tales are filled with bawdy humor, cautionary moral lessons, and a dose of strangely told history. Poets and storytellers would utilize the coffeehouse as a forum for telling these and other tales all the way through the middle of the 20th century. As coffeehouses began to buy radios in the interwar period (available on installment) and later televisions, the need for itinerant poets declined. In addition, the spread of modern education meant that many storytellers would prefer to send their sons to school rather than keep them at home memorizing complex plots and details about characters for an obviously shrinking market. Thus, by the close of the 20th century, the numbers of men with storytelling skills had radically diminished and the telling of epic poems marginalized to folk theater. Thankfully, a few anthropologists and ethnomusicologists have recorded and/or transcribed the stories. Nevertheless, what appears on Egyptian television or in theaters is usually quite abbreviated.

Two other contexts for what might be termed "traditional" music or Arab music include *mulids* (saint celebrations) and Sufi rituals, both of which have received condemnation from mainstream or orthodox religious elements. First, Islam as a religion does not condone the notion of saints or intermediaries, and thus by its very definition, engaging in overly celebratory rituals on the birthday of the Prophet, Ali, Fatima, Hasan, or Husayn, which dates back to the Fatimids (see Chapter 2) would be considered offensive. Second, engaging in behavior that is unbecoming, unflattering, or unfitting those deserving of respect is problematic. Nevertheless, mainstream religious officials believed that celebrating the Prophet's birthday with simple Quranic recitation was permissible. This practice led to the creation of other types of celebratory poems that could be chanted, recited, or sung, and over time these came to be accompanied by music. Another controversial celebration is the birthday of the Moroccan-born founder of the Ahmadiyya Sufi order, Shaykh Ahmad Badawi (d. 1276), who had a vision to relocate in Egypt, where he was influenced by other great thinkers and mystics. Egypt was also facing numerous threats during this time (Crusades, Mongols), and he proved able to fight both internal and external demons, thus making him one of the most beloved figures of Egyptian history. The shrine and mosque built over his tomb are sites for pilgrimages, and his home of Tanta the location for the annual festival where a variety of music, chanting, and dancing that is common to Sufism takes place. The *mulid* is a booming marketplace for many things, among them cassette tapes, CDs, and now DVDs of Quranic chanting, Sufi music, and even popular music.

The goal of Sufism is to achieve a oneness with Allah. There are some parallels between Sufism and the goals of religious ecstasy desired by Catholic mystics, for example, Saint Teresa of Avila. Different Sufi brotherhoods have different paths for achieving the state of *tawhid* or unity with God, but one method is through chanting different verses of the Quran or different names of God (of which there are 99)—which can take a musical effect. The person who leads the group in song, the *munshid*, performs at *mulids*, but is also responsible at ordinary ceremonies of remembrance *dhikr* (pronounced zikr), in which believers are to achieve this state of unity with God. In the Delta, there are sometimes *munshidas*, or female singers who perform this role, but this is not usually the case in Upper Egypt where social values tend to be more conservative. Occasionally, people prefer to hire a *munshid* to sing at a wedding rather than an ordinary performer because this is seen as less corrupt than pop music and having some moral value, yet more "fun" than simple Quranic chanting. Obviously, audience participation and activation is key at *mulids* and *dhikrs*—the group has to be engaged.

Modern Music

The era of modern music began in the age of the Khedive Ismail (r. 1863–1879), when he introduced different instruments and contexts for performance into Egypt. His intent, his roots, and the outcome are all quite complex. Ismail was the son of Ibrahim Pasha and a concubine, which conveniently made him the cousin of the Ottoman Sultan (see Chapter 2). Although Turkish-speaking in origin, he was schooled in Vienna and Paris, where he developed a taste for European things. Nevertheless, his father had learned Arabic and left him with the impression that one must understand the people he is governing. It is under his rule that Arabic becomes the language of administration. Ismail had a strong desire to turn Cairo and parts of Egypt into a piece of Europe, nevertheless, the remainder of the country would remain as it had been for millennia: a center of production to support consumption in the city where the arts could flourish.

He built a huge rococo-styled opera house that he hoped to have finished by the grand opening of the Suez Canal in 1869. His European advisors helped him to complete this "Westernized" project with an Egyptian veneer. His opera advisor Draneth Bey passed a note to the famous Italian composer Verdi begging him to write what would become *Aida*, a "national" production that would involve collaboration with Mariette Bey, the curator of the Egyptian Museum and antiquities advisor. Unfortunately, *Aida* was not ready in time for the Suez festivities, and *Rigoletto* was performed instead. The Opera House was not yet finished, but it was far enough along to house the performance. When *Aida* came to the stage in late 1871 for the true grand opening, the product was precisely that to which Ismail aspired. Its form was European and its content glorified the Egyptian nation with a pharaonic theme. Audience members from European diplomats to royal ladies in their latticed boxes (to obscure them from view to others) all agreed that the show was a spectacular event.

The Opera House was not the only theater that housed musical performances. Various acting troupes, first foreign and later Syrian, Lebanese, and Egyptian staged musical and nonmusical productions in Cairo and Alexandria. The range of quality could vary quite significantly from that found in the finest theaters in Europe to what one European visitor described as something akin to screaming cats.

The other major change was that in these formal contexts, the violin replaced the *rebaba*. Ismail was also a huge sponsor of parks and other municipal improvements, the most important one being Azbakiyya Gardens in the center of Cairo. By the turn of the 20th century it was quite common for military bands to play at the park in the evenings alternating between Egyptian and English groups. Apart from formal groups and contexts, the open air cafés and restaurants in this district became a place where musicians could congregate. In this way musicians could establish their reputations by earning a particular seat in their favorite café, an honor conferred by one's peers.

With the turn of the 20th century came three important technologies for disseminating music to larger audiences: the record, the radio, and the talking movie. It was in 1909 that the United Kingdom's Gramophone Company created the first record label "His Master's Voice" and shortly thereafter began to seek both traditional and hybridized "modern" Arab artists to record. Typical of this new genre were people like Sayyed Darwish (1892–1923), a working-class Egyptian who spoke to the heart and the soul of the nation by utilizing some Western instrumentation to expand the horizons of Arab music. He worked with great theater troupes of the day, like those of Neguib al-Rihani and Ali al-Kassar. Perhaps his most poignant accomplishment was taking words from a Mustafa Kamel speech and setting them to music in order to create the Egyptian National Anthem. Sadly, his untimely death meant that he never got to hear it played when the great nationalist hero Saad Zaghlul returned from exile.

Mohamed Abdul Wahab (1907–1991) better represents the transitions made between the new technologies. Like Darwish, Abdul Wahab came from a humble background. At age 13 he made his first recording of "traditional" music. After the death of Sayyed Darwish, he had the opportunity to take over one of his musical theater projects that earned him greater recognition. He also started working on films and made the leap from silent to sound. He was a pioneer in the genre of Egyptian film generally, and the Egyptian musical, in particular. He helped to craft the figure of the romantic hero and introduce the singing romantic vixen, launching the career of numerous stars including Leila Murad (d. 1995). Abdul Wahab liked experimenting with the organization of sound and the effect of the "big band" with different (Western) instruments, as well as rhythms that could be syncopated or incorporated into a traditional sound, including samba, rhumba, tango, and mamba. Mohamed Abdul Wahab had a bizarre and competitive professional relationship with the great singer Umm Kulthum (d. 1975) (pronounced Kulsum).

Umm Kulthum, like Abdul Wahab and Darwish, came from a modest background. Her humble origins were part of her trademark appeal. Her father was an *imam*, and it was her training in proper classical Arabic that facilitated some of her

Egyptian singer Umm Kulthum performing to an audience of 2,200 at the Olympia Music Hall in France on November 14, 1967. (AP Photo/Jacques Marqueton)

poetic and musical abilities. She was even allowed to dress as a boy and go along with her father for various types of recitation jobs, including singing at weddings. Eventually a wealthy family took her in and gave her guidance in the ways of society so that she could advance in a musical career. Where Abdul Wahab tested and experimented, Umm Kulthum believed in the advantages of tradition. She preferred to recite classical poetry, and even when she starred in a musical film, her character was the "good girl," for example, the 1947 film *Fatma* in which she played a nurse who healed an ailing pasha, falling in love with another family member, who marries her, impregnates her, and leaves her. Umm Kulthum did not enjoy making films. The lights bothered her eyes, and she missed the interaction with the audience. After the revolution in 1952 Umm Kulthum was a key supporter of the new regime, and her Thursday night concerts meant that everyone was home by their radio waiting for the concert to begin like clockwork. Presidential addresses could easily be given beforehand to a waiting audience.

The relationship between Umm Kulthum and her audience was as intimate and intense as between lovers. In 1964 Mohamed Abdul Wahab ended the rivalry with her and wrote a special song *Inta Omri* (You Are My Life) especially for her. The performance of this song, which is roughly 40 minutes in length, could take several hours as the singer and audience interacted. Her technique was like that of the traditional storyteller—give a line and perhaps repeat it over and over again to the delight and frenzy of the group, cascading back and forth between the rhythms that it wanted to hear. Both the range and strength of her voice were remarkable, as is the staying power of her popularity; one can still hop in a cab and hear her anywhere in Egypt. When she died in 1975, the crowds thronging the streets for her funeral were certainly more intense and heartfelt than for any heads of state.

Other singers maintained popularity through film and radio recordings in Egypt including Syrian-born Egyptian residents Farid al-Atrache (d. 1971) and his extraordinarily beautiful and talented sister Asmahan, whose untimely death in a car accident in 1944 sparked tabloid-like controversies related to espionage and the war (both sides) and to her competition in the industry with Umm Kulthum. Like Umm Kulthum, Asmahan had an extraordinary range in her voice, and she combined the dynamics of Western operatic technique with the power and drama of traditional Arab music. Few singers could master both styles and no one but Asmahan could do both in the same song! Her brother's soulful voice and his talent with beautiful leading ladies like dancer Samia Gamal in splashy movie productions, for example, *Habib al-'Omr* (*Life's Love*) and *'Afrita Hanem* (*The Genie Lady*) characterized the post-World War II era.

A great actor and singer who came of age after the revolution was Abdel Halim Hafez (1929–1977). Apart from Asmahan and Farid al-Atrache who came from Druze nobility in Syria, although refugees from the French colonial government, most other singers came from quite modest backgrounds, and Abdel Halim was no exception. Like many poor Egyptian youngsters, he contracted bilharzia, a parasitic disease common in developing countries. Furthermore, he was orphaned at an early age. With so many strikes against him, it is hard to imagine that he would ever succeed. Born Abdel Halim Ali Ismail Shabana, Abdel Halim was the last-minute substitute for another singer on a live radio show celebrating the one-year anniversary of the 1952 revolution. The person who managed national radio programming, whose first name was Hafez, gave Abdel Halim the support he needed and Abdel Halim took his name as a gesture of thanks. Prior to this substitution, Abdel Halim already had a contract with Abdul Wahab for recording his music and working on some of his films. In the 1950s his career in film and recording blossomed. By the 1960s he had his own record label. Like other artists he experimented with change in various directions. On the one hand, he did more work with colloquial folk songs, and on the other, after watching the tremendous success of Elvis, the Beatles, and other English-speaking artists, he approached folks at the AUC to learn English. He was particularly keen on acquiring an American accent. A young American professor in the Department of Public Service (Adult Education) declined his offer to pay for private lessons much to the dismay of the professor's Egyptian niece. She was dumfounded that he (or anyone else) could refuse Abdel Halim, who was beloved by his many fans. Although Abdel Halim was doing well professionally, he still suffered with his illness until his premature death in 1977. As in the case of Umm Kulthum the crowds mobbed the streets and his body was interred in the Rafai mosque in Cairo, where some members of the former Egyptian royal family are buried.

A great nationalist and patriot of this era was Muhammad Fawzy, who liberated Egypt's recording industry from foreign control in the mid-1950s. A celebrated musician, composer, actor, and producer Fawzi created the first Arab-owned record company in the Middle East only to have his assets nationalized once his company became profitable. He had done all of the leg work and signed many of the major stars including Umm Kulthum. Interestingly enough, when Muhammad Abdel Wahab and Abdel Halim Hafez created their own label, the state did not perceive this as a threat nor as a big enough asset to consume (Frishkopf 2008).

The deaths of the "greats" by the late 1970s and the opening of the economy initiated a new era in music. The state that controlled television, radio, and record labels was no longer the sole arbiter of taste and function in society. Furthermore, where most musicians entered the music scene through the traditional gateway around the cafés of Muhammad Ali Street, now new types of music and means for entering the industry entered Egypt. More Western music arrived in Egypt, more Islamic critics began to discuss the "evils" of music and new forms of hybridized music emerged.

One trend since the 1970s has been the reemergence of *shaabi* or "folk" music. This is somewhat of a misnomer since modern alienation and problems overlay traditional forms and instruments, which are then amplified to new levels and accompanied by Western instruments. Working-class malaise, the continuing conflict in the Middle East (including those who experienced it first or secondhand in 1967 and 1973), and the rise of a new elite with infitah economics helped to fuel the new trends. Ahmed Adawiya paved the road for the new *shaabi* music in the 1970s and early 1980s before his tragic death due to heroin overdose. So talented and admired was this giant that others have literally taken his name.

One concert that helped to awaken Egyptian tastes to Western music was an appearance by the Grateful Dead. Imagine seeing the Grateful Dead by the Sphinx and pyramids in 1978. Apparently it was a typical "Dead" event complete with loud music and heavy partying. Despite some snafoos not uncommon to Egypt—delays, equipment problems, and so on—the show went on brilliantly with some selections featuring local *'ud* (lute) and *tabla* players. In fact, recently the group made the concert available on DVD. Nevertheless, from the perspective of a graduate student (Zahi Hawass) who would one day be responsible for all of Egypt's antiquities, the Sphinx looked "sad" and was in fact damaged, and there was general concern for the well-being of all the monuments given the level of noise and vibration.

Not surprisingly with 10,000 people attending the Dead concert, the relatively low cost of the transistor radio and the cassette tape, Western music spread rapidly into the infitah economy. At the same time, nonetheless, Islamic trends were on the rise, and critics for example, Shaykh Abd al-Hamid Kishk (1933–1996) raised their voice not to sing, but to warn against this dangerous pastime. Shaykh Kishk, born in a small village outside Alexandria, made his way to the pinnacle of traditional education at al-Azhar, after which he preached at the Ain al-Hayat mosque. His radical views earned him several years in prison under Nasser. He was a vocal critic of the Sadat administration as well; however, up until 1981 it was more routine for him to be arrested, detained, and released. He was among the 1,500 people in the mass arrest just before Sadat's assassination. In the period after his release from prison under Nasser up to his imprisonment under Sadat he grew enormously popular. His Friday sermons became so well received that his mosque in Kubri al-Ubba had to undergo continuous renovation to accommodate demand, and one of the major themes that he preached was the seduction of music and song based on the Quran (17:64). Ironically, Shaykh Kishk's words were like "music" to the ears of many and cassette tapes of his sermons spread like wildfire.

Despite the warnings of naysayers and Islamists, the popular music scene bloomed in the 1980s and 1990s with new faces and stars. Amr Diab (b. 1961) represents this generation influenced by Western rock and roll but interested in blending Arab rhythms and instruments. Unlike the previous generation that climbed their way up from poverty, Diab was a product of upper-middle-class privilege. His first hit *Ya Tareeq* came out in 1983, and since that time he has won the World Music Awards three times, 1998, 2002, and 2007. Like other innovative Egyptian artists he has incorporated other sounds, for example, Spanish guitar, and worked with other artists, namely, French-Algerian Khaled and Greek folk singer Angela Dimitrou to diversify his sound which has kept his career at the top of its game for the last quarter century. His most recent collaboration has been with Shakira. Ironically, as Diab's popularity has grown worldwide, his contact with his Egyptian base has diminished.

In 2001 Sting applied for permission to do what the Grateful Dead had done in 1978—sing at the pyramids. Pyramids shows are fairly rare. There had been a much maligned "millennium" concert, but that had been run by the Ministry of Culture; certainly the private sector could do better, or could it? The cast of characters was formidable and the intention grand, but the whole thing turned out as it only could in Egypt. Sting, legendary rock star formerly with the Police, was touting a new solo album and was going to share the stage with Cheb Mami, an Algerian Raï artist and Egyptian *shaabi* singer Hakim (b. 1962). Ten percent of the proceeds would benefit a Palestinian medical charity. A huge financier was backing the project, but this time the antiquities director was the starry-eyed graduate student from the Grateful Dead concert. He did not want to see the Sphinx suffer again. He wanted the show restricted to the arena where the Sound and Light show takes place, but it only seats 3,000, and 15,000 tickets had already been sold. Thus, once more Dr. Hawass would have to witness (though not personally) the desecration of the pyramids. He felt strongly that such shows were damaging, whereas he could tolerate periodically hosting the opera *Aida,* something in keeping with the "cultural dignity" of the area at noise and vibration levels that would not harm the structures. Nevertheless, the power of money and stardom won over that of culture and heritage. Attendees to the concert complained about transportation as people sat two hours in buses and cars waiting to get in while the concert was in progress. One report claimed that the final negotiated seating area had only 8,000 seats and the organizers sold 25,000 tickets. For those who actually made it into the venue, fans waited patiently for Sting to take the stage, and when he was about to—nearly a hour late—*shaabi* star Hakim who was not on time for his slot suddenly appeared and demanded to be heard, literally taking the stage and essentially ordering the audience to leave because he felt slighted: "Whoever is willing to accept the insult of an Egyptian in Egypt can stay!" After the tantrum, Sting performed with Cheb Mami.

Hakim's antics at the pyramids certainly did not cost him his career. Born in a small town in middle Egypt, Hakim had the opportunity to witness poverty, de-

Sting performs in front of the Sphinx at the Giza plateau, April 25, 2001. (AP Photo/ Enric Marti)

Hakim, of Egypt, performs at the annual Nobel Peace Prize concert in Oslo, Norway, Monday December 11, 2006. (AP Photo/John McConnico)

spair, and inequality all around him but still had the benefit of social status—his father was the mayor. His location in Mughagha no doubt placed him in the context of traditional storytellers and poets whose style mixed with modern woes and instrumentation to create a new blend. He started out with friends playing small local gigs as a youngster. His father encouraged him to continue his education, and he chose al-Azhar, where he perfected his mind by day and at night he hit the clubs on Muhammad Ali Street, where musicians and singers mingled and performed. A decade later, by the early-mid 1990s he was a household name. Like many other successful Egyptian artists he has done some interesting collaborations including Puerto Rican merengue artist Olga Tanon, American king of soul James Brown, and Puerto Rican rapper Don Omar. Like Amr Diab he remains popular by infusing traditional Arab sound with other compatible rhythms and singing songs that people want to hear. Hakim even toured the United States in 2000.

Shaaban Abd al-Rahim is a former *makwaggi* (professional clothes ironer and he comes from a family of ironers that uses the nearly obsolete traditional foot iron). The wedding singer turned pop star has taken the *shaabi* style pioneered by Ahmed Adewiya to a whole new level. He has tried to learn lessons from the great artists of the 20th century by forging Umm Kulthum's humility (although difficult to accept at times with his double-wristed watches, heavy gold chains, and garish clothing), Adewiya's *shaabi* artistry, Sayyed Darwish's nationalism, and believe it or not even Atrache and Wahab's romantic leading man. When he sang a ballad about how he quit smoking, large numbers of Egyptians suddenly quit smoking. In 2001 when he came out with "*Ana Bakrah Isra'il*" (*I hate Israel*), he zoomed from obscurity to fame. In the same year, *al-Muwatin, al-Mukhbir, wal-harami* (A Citizen, A Detective, and a Thief) came out in which he played the role of the thief, a role that vaguely parallels his rags to riches story. His songs have critiqued America's role in the Iraq War, (Egyptian) suspicions that the United States created 9/11, and the Danish cartoon controversy. Shaaban is quite comical and knows how to turn dollar or perhaps more accurately a guinea. After the meteoric rise of "*I hate Israel*," which coincided with Ariel Sharon's reemergence in politics, McDonalds of Egypt saw a loss in profits and hired Shaaban to sing the jingle for the McFalafel sandwich. Nevertheless, Jewish groups in the United States protested and Shaaban's jingle was quickly pulled. He thrives on controversy and takes it home to the bank. He goads people into viewing him as an oafish clown, which only energizes media coverage. Although many people consider Shaaban a voice of the people, what constitutes those people varies by class. While working-class and even some middle-class Egyptians find resonance in his voice, looking forward to his straight to video clip approach for dispersing his blatantly political message, well-heeled Egyptians often find him crass and vulgar. Furthermore, the more discriminating among them might point out his coziness with the former regime. There are songs and videos that praise Mubarak literally gushing out love for him, and even one in support of his election in 2005, for example, the song "*Kalimat al-haqq*" ("*A Word of Truth*").

Another source for contemporary music is the Nubian voice represented by Mohamed Mounir (b. 1954). Originally from a region sunk by Lake Nasser and relocated by the state, Mohamed was shaped by this experience as well as his compulsory military service where he first began performing for large groups. His music blends Egyptian, Nubian, various other African influences as well as Western influences. Indeed, he views himself as a cultural bridge, particularly in the wake of 9/11. He has worked tirelessly to seek some mediation between elements within his country as well as between the Middle East and the West. Part of this effort included making the *hajj* to better understand his own faith by taking part in one of its sacred rituals, to confront religious hypocrites, and to make the West aware of the true meaning of Islam. Shortly thereafter he put out *el-Ard . . . el-Salam* (*Earth . . . Peace*), a rather spiritual CD, whereas most of his other work is more about love, happiness, goals, and so on. Similar to some of the other great artists of this era he has appeared in or created the soundtrack for a number of films. Most of his work has been with legendary director Youssef Chahine. Mounir is a great contributor to charity, for example, benefits from a recent concert at the new opera house are slated to go to the reserve fund of the Red Crescent Society set aside for natural disasters in Egypt.

Finally, there is the upcoming generation of heavy metal rockers that Mark LeVine documents in his recent work on the interplay between Western music forms and resistance in the Middle East. Notable in this category are the sons of the recently released political dissident Ayman Nour (see Chapter 3). While their father spent four years of his life in prison on questionable charges, Shady and Nour ranted their version of an antiestablishment message with their group Bliss. It should be noted that the younger son, Shady, was still in his late teens at the time of his father's release in February 2009. Perhaps their age and their means (music) allowed Bliss (or its latest incarnation) to succeed where their father had failed—or have been impeded by the government. In other words, opposing the government through an organized opposition party, a newspaper, and registered media outlets created problems, whereas crooning to the new generation was not problematic. During the January 25 demonstrations, Nour was arrested and the police wanted to release him and thus release themselves of responsibility for a high-profile prisoner; however, it was later reported that he escaped.

The January 25 movement has not only inspired new music but also revived older music. Eskenderella plays original songs in addition to music popularized by working-class balladeer Shaykh Imam (1919–1995), which hits so close to home for many of the protestors that some have proclaimed this group "the band of the Revolution." Other sources of inspiration include Sayyid Darwish and Abdel Halim Hafez, whose older tunes combined with newer events inspire new songs and concerts that provide both continuity and change. Cairokee, Wust al-Balad (Downtown), and Tanboura are three other groups that fit into this genre of revivalist revolutionary.

Egypt, at the crossroads of many cultures has always served as a cultural melting pot. The popular music scene in Egypt, even in its *shaabi* or traditionalized form, has taken on a number of Westernized aspects. Many artists package themselves in Western forms, utilize the latest technology, and collaborate with various international stars and sounds to further enhance their careers. The most successful singers, the most sought-after at weddings, are accessible only to the most wealthy class of Egyptians. Ordinary folks can only listen to the radio or watch video clips on TV.

REFERENCES

Danielson, Virginia. *The Voice of Egypt: Umm Kulthum, Arabic Song, and Egyptian Society in the Twentieth Century.* Chicago: University of Chicago Press, 1998.

Fricke, David. "The Dead Rock the Pyramids." *Rolling Stone,* October 16, 2008.

Frishkopf, Michael. "Nationalism, Nationalization, and the Egyptian Music Industry: Muhammad Fawzy, Misrphone, and Sawt al-Qahira (SonoCairo)," *Asian Music* 39, no. 2 (2008): 28–58.

Frishkopf, Michael. *Music and Media in the Arab World.* Cairo: AUC Press, 2010.

Hawass, Zahi. "Sting and the Pyramids." http://www.guardians.net/hawass/StingandthePyramids.htm.

LeVine, Mark. *Heavy Metal Islam.* New York: Three Rivers, 2008.

Noshokaty, Amira and Sara Mourad. "Songs of Revival." *al-Ahram Weekly.* (Issue 1078) December 29, 2011 to January 4, 2012. https://sites.google.com/site/weeklyahramorgegissue1076/entertainment/the-enchanting-secrets-of-desert-oases.

Reynolds, Dwight. *Heroic Poets, Poetic Heroes: The Ethnography of Performance in an Arabic Oral Epic Tradition.* Ithaca: Cornell University Press, 1995.

"Sting Concert Not without Problems." http://www.cairolive.com/newcairolive/frontpic/stingcon.html.

"Sting Upstaged at Concert" *BBC News.* April 26, 2001.

FOOD

From Ancient to Modern

Sitting at the crossroads of Africa, Asia, and Europe, Egypt has been an entrepôt of various circuits of overland and sea trade since ancient times. Both as the subjects of conquest as well as conquerors of other nations, Egyptians have made contact with large numbers of people who helped them make sense of the commodities in their trading network. Certainly one of the most enduring of these contacts was the Ottoman Turks who ruled Egypt directly from the 16th to the 18th centuries and indirectly from the Muhammad Ali dynasty up until World War I. The Turks were notable because it was during their reign that New World products, for example, the tomato, a staple of many basic Egyptian dishes entered the country and many other New World goods improved due to the Turks' skills in botany and animal husbandry. Consider why Americans even call the New World bird that is eaten at Thanksgiving a "turkey." The Turks' skills in this area are legendary yet unappreciated by most of us in the 21st century.

Most "Egyptian" dishes that are shared across the Mediterranean still retain Arabic names, but can often be found in Greek or Turkish restaurants. Favorites, for example, *mousa'a* (eggplant casserole) and *ba'lawa* (nut-filled phyllo dessert) in Egypt are known as *mousaka* and *baklava* in Greece. Here in the United States, a youngster with a hybrid identity often learns from a young age that a "dish" belongs to his or her country, but it is not always that simple. *"Loukamades"* that translates into

English as Greek donuts, in Arabic is *lu'mat al-adi* (*luqmat al-qadi*), which translates into the "piece of the judge," meaning something so sweet and delicious one could bribe the judge with it. Does this connection really stress its true origin in an anecdote? As anyone who as ever witnessed two individuals debating the "true origins" of a dish, it is better to simply enjoy the food and know it is better for the great cultural blending than to stress cultural superiority.

The basic staff of life for Egyptians since ancient times has been bread, or as they call it *'aysh*, from the same root that connotes life. Elsewhere in the Middle East the word *khubz* is used for bread, from the root meaning to bake. The poor, historically and contemporarily, eat *'aysh baladi* (country or folk bread), referring to the pita bread made from whole wheat that has a course texture, whereas the elite eat *'aysh shami* (Syrian bread), referring to pita bread made with refined white flour. Since wood and other types of fuel have been scarce in Egypt, community ovens have been more common often run on animal dung. Even in ancient times there were many other types of breads with various shapes and loaves, but the enduring bread of the masses has been pita bread.

Wheat-growing in ancient times was important for making another staple, beer. Apparently, Osiris was the first brew master and passed his skills to the Egyptians who continued to pass them to Greeks, Romans, and others. Even after prohibitions against the consumption of alcohol in Islamic times, beer continued to be made in Egypt. In modern times, the al-Ahram brewing company was founded in 1897 before the creation of the Bank Misr group (see Chapters 2 and 4), and managed to suffer through nationalization in 1963. Stella (in the al-Ahram group) was reborn after privatization in 1997 and purchased by Heineken in 2002. Another product of the al-Ahram group is wine (also with ties to ancient Egypt) which is considered more taboo since it is explicitly forbidden in the Quran, whereas other alcohol is only forbidden by analogy according to those schools of Islamic law that allow analogy. Nonetheless, there is the market for both tourists and for Copts, who use it for church rituals and have no restrictions on ordinary consumption. Prior to the era of nationalization the winery had been a family business (since 1882) and it was purchased by the al-Ahram group in the era of privatization. According to the company's marketing, the Gianclis family had found a place for its vineyards where the ground was free of salt similar to the famed Champagne region of France.

What other foods did the ancient Egyptians eat and what did they value? We learn an enormous amount from what was left behind in tombs, what was written on papyri, as well as what was documented by visitors and conquerors. They raised cattle, goats, ducks, quails, pigeons—not to mention the abundance of protein provided by the eggs and dairy products produced by some of these animals, and by the fish so abundant in the Mediterranean, the Nile, and lakes around oases, for example, Lake Qaroun in Fayyum. These foods are still consumed by Egyptians today.

Although used in the original context with incense, Prof. Tom Parker of NCSU once said, "The ancient world was a really stinky place." This statement probably applied to ancient Egyptian food (in the days before refrigeration), which is why the ancients became skilled at using seasonings, for example, salt, pepper, cumin, dill, coriander, fenugreek, fennel, sesame, caraway seeds, anise, hibiscus, ginger, and after the arrival of the Greeks, mint. One can still get teas made from hibiscus (*karkady*), caraway (*karawya*), anise (*yansoon*), fenugreek (*ḥelba*), or mint (*na'na'*). The Egyptians enjoyed eating foods with strong flavors since their belief systems acknowledged a connection between pungent flavors, physical health, and spiritual well-being. Some of these foods included onions, leeks, garlic, salted fish, bitter greens, and tart vinegar. The main aspect of eating involved what was available, what could be grown, or what was easily traded. The most common foods were fava beans (*ful maddamas*), peas, lettuce, and cucumbers. Fava beans are still eaten today, both as *ful maddammas*, prepared in a variety of fashions (see Recipe Appendix), as well as the main ingredient in *ta'amiyya*, the Egyptian version of *falafel*, which elsewhere in the Middle East is made of chick peas.

The main sweetening ingredient in ancient Egypt agent was honey and fruits, such as figs, which have actually been found in tombs. Ancient Egyptians stayed away from pork, believing that their fatty skin carried disease. Both Judaism and Islam explicitly forbid the eating of pork. It is hard to determine when specific foods arrived in Egypt, but among other (main dish) favorites that are traditional, but perhaps not "ancient" are *molokhiyya* (a green leafy vegetable) and *ul'ass* (a root vegetable). Whenever an Egyptian tries to describe these items or translate them for a visitor he or she is at a complete loss, and dictionaries are not much help either. *Molokhiyya* is usually translated as "Jew's mallow," which is not particularly enlightening. Some claim that it dates back to the time of the Pharaohs, hence the translation of "Jew's mallow" as it was one of the foods perhaps eaten by the Jews. Egyptians love it, but some Westerners find its consistency and pungent flavor odd. *Ul'ass* (see Recipe Appendix) is known as the cocoyam or taro in English.

Today's Table

One of the most common dishes in Egypt is rice, served alongside just about any meal, which usually consists of a vegetable stew (sometimes with meat in it), some type of meat, salad, and seasonal fruit(s) for dessert. Rice is the main component of *maḥshi* (stuffing) (see Recipe Appendix) that can be used to fill grapeleaves (*wara'a 'anab*), cabbage (*crumb*), green peppers (*filfil*), zucchinis (*kosa*), tomatoes (*ota*), small eggplants (*bitangan*), or just about any vegetable that can be hollowed or wrapped.

Ordinary breakfast in Egypt, that is, breakfast that is not during the month of Ramadan, consists of cheese, bread, jams, olives, or yogurt, along with tea or juice. The most common types of cheeses that are eaten are *gibna bayḍa* (white cheese), similar in taste and texture to feta cheese, and *gibna rumi*, a hard, sharp yellow cheese, similar to parmesan cheese. Both cheeses are eaten either on ordinary pita bread or *'aysh fino*, small thin sandwich rolls. Fried, scrambled, or hard boiled eggs might accompany breakfast. The abundance of various regional fruits means that most people have jam in their homes even though it is now usually store-bought rather than homemade. Honey and cream are also popular spreads for a quick breakfast in the morning. Egyptians love sweet and salty combinations, hence various olives and pickles are extremely popular sides to accompany breakfast. The olives found in Egypt are similar to those in Greece. *Ṭurshi* or pickles are not just cucumbers, but consist of a wide variety of vegetables and include green peppers, celery, okra, cauliflower, turnips, carrots, and other treats often spiced up with hot peppers. For Egyptians who are not students, office workers, or stay-at-home mothers, and therefore need a more substantial breakfast, that is, the peasant or the day laborer, *ful and ṭa'amiyya* remain the staples of the diet. A day laborer may not get another meal until his or her work is complete, so he or she needs something that will stick to his or her ribs. On the weekends, middle- and upper-class Egyptians are more likely to eat larger breakfasts consisting of *ful maddamas*, eggs, or other special dishes. One such dish is *shakshuka*, also known as *beeḍiskandarani* or Alexandrian-style eggs (see Recipe Appendix). Hot cereals made of rice, wheat, barley, or couscous are popular, sweetened with milk, cream, sugar, nuts, honey, and/or raisins.

Lunch is the big meal of the day. Taking a mid-day break in a country where summer temperatures can easily exceed 100 or even 110 degrees Fahrenheit should not be surprising. Often temperature "averages" are below actual temperatures because public-sector employees are released from work when temperatures exceed a specified level, thus one finds the "recorded" daily temperature lower than actual temperatures. Given the heat, historically people would seek shelter during the heat of the day, eat, take a rest, and then work the rest of the day. Even after the rise of new urban professions in the early 20th century, traditional customs remained. Early 20th-century advertisements for doctors and clinics reflect hours in the morning and late afternoon or early evening. After the Egyptian revolution and the creation of the public sector, most Egyptians either went home for lunch or postponed lunch until after returning home at the end of the day. The creation of multiple positions and rotating jobs and shifts in the 1980s and beyond means the amount of time that one spends in a public-sector job allows one to eat lunch before or after his or her public sector work. For example, a teacher or a physical therapist working a morning shift in a school or a hospital would be home by early afternoon, and his or her counterpart would eat before taking the next shift at the school or hospital. Day laborers, taxi drivers, and skilled workers, often stop and eat a quick sandwich again, as there are places to get other favorites, for example, brain, tongue, liver, and other various organs or the Egyptian equivalent of a Greek gyro, *shawarma* (various types of meat cooked on a large flame, sliced and seasoned to order) at small stands in every city. Another quick, inexpensive, high-protein treat is *kusheri*, a blend of lentils, rice, pasta, and spicy tomato sauce topped with crunchy fried onions, also available as a fast food (see Recipe Appendix).

Between lunch and dinner, Egyptians usually drink afternoon tea or coffee (see Recipe Appendix). If one is a guest in someone's home, tea or coffee might come with some type of dessert or sweet, for example, a traditional semolina cake (*basbusa*) or other desserts *ba'lawa*, *kinafa* (pastry with nuts), cheese, or *miḥallabiyya* (rice pudding). These are easier to purchase elsewhere than to make. Egyptians enjoy desserts for special occasions: birthdays, holidays, weddings, births, or simply as a gift for the hostess when visiting.

Dinner is a simple meal much like breakfast. Often families munch on any leftovers from lunch, along with simple sandwiches of cheese and bread or tuna and bread, olives, yogurt, and so on. Egyptian yogurt is not like American yogurt, it is the full-fat creamy yogurt. The abundance of fresh produce, for example, strawberries, prickly pears, figs, dates, watermelon, mangoes, guavas, bananas, apples, oranges, peaches, and grapes—all of which are much sweeter and tastier than those that ripen through shipping as in the United States—make fruit-eating a delight. There are stands that provide fresh fruit juice, but again the traveler should be aware that the fruit may not be clean and the glasses may not be washed under the most sanitary of conditions. Long-term residents learn the places to go or at least the shifts they trust.

Holiday Foods

Holidays provide a time for special eating. Muslims break their fast at Ramadan with a fruit compote, usually composed of dates, apricots, raisins, nuts, and rosewater, but various family ingredients vary. The purpose of the compote is to help fasters quickly raise their blood sugar and help to settle their stomachs in readiness for a heavy meal after a long day of fasting. Evenings during Ramadan are a time when families entertain relatives and friends. One favorite component of a number of side dishes is a *beshamel* sauce that can be combined with macaroni (and ground beef) for a standard side dish or used to top vegetable combinations. During Ramadan rice dishes that are normally made with water are more likely to be made with some type of meat or chicken stock to be extra tasty and provide more calories. Tables are generally filled end to end with an enormous quantity and variety of foods. The traditional dessert of fresh fruit is likely to be replaced by (or at least accompanied by) a variety of sweet dishes, for example, *kinafa*, *basbusa*, *ba'lawa*, or *Umm Ali* (phyllo pastry pudding with cream, nuts, and raisins) (see Recipe Appendix). After having eaten a huge "breakfast," the faster often has a second invitation (especially) on Thursday or Friday for *suḥur*, a late night meal meant to tide the faster over until morning. Technically, according to the traditions established by the Prophet one has until about and one hour and 25 minutes before the dawn call to prayer to eat. According to these traditions, this is supposed to mean getting up and taking a sip of water and eating something like a date. Long ago and faraway, families used to live in multigenerational family dwellings or even separate homes located in one part of the city in a single town. In modern times given the dispersal of families to different parts of the city (or even different cities) and the creation of new networks of friends through work, practice has evolved into eating a large second meal late at night to accommodate visiting and entertaining. Ironically, food consumption usually rises during the month of Ramadan.

In 2008, severe inflation and shortages marked the period. While the wealthy and upper middle class could sustain ordinary levels of consumption, even the middle class could not deal with the 30 percent spike in fuel costs that triggered major increases in food costs. Egypt is a major food importer, and even for locally produced goods, there are major transportation and distribution costs. The cost of butter increased by 71 percent, dairy products by 38.5 percent, and pasta by 32.8 percent, making 2008 Ramadan season among the most difficult in recent memory. Traditionally, food tables outside of mosques, restaurants, or even homes have been set up to offer the poor sanctuary during Ramadan. In light of the desperate situation, the former first lady Suzanne Mubarak instead created an initiative to provide food bags directly to the needy in the poorest governates of Egypt. Whether or not the food reached those in need is unknown at the time of writing.

A cookie that is exchanged at the end of Ramadan during the Eid al-Fitr and eaten during Coptic Christmas is *kahk*. Another beloved dish at Coptic Christmas that is eaten year-round in Egypt is *fata*. It is a casserole made of lamb, rice, onion, garlic, butter, and toasted bread. It involves multiples steps, far more than the average American would choose to prepare on an ordinary day, so do not turn down an invitation for *fata* because it is delicious!

Another festive dish, *fatir*, is one that most Egyptians prefer to buy at stands rather than to make themselves. Sources of culinary information usually describe it as a pancake or flatbread that can be filled with fruits, nuts, or any other type of filling; but if one travels to Egypt and gets a *fatir* at a stand at the beach or a *mulid* (celebration of a saint's birth) or any type of celebration, it is more likely to remind him or her of getting fried dough at the fair, or perhaps a beignet in New Orleans.

The feast of the sacrifice provides another opportunity for both charity and good eating. To this day, people still buy lamb, sheep, goats, and other traditional animals to sacrifice just as Abraham (Ibrahim) did instead of son Ishmael (Ismail)—even in large cities—and then a portion of the meat is donated to charity. The traditional method for cooking is lamb kebabs or *kofta* (ground skewered meat) cooked over a grill (see Recipe Appendix).

Recipe Appendix

Ful Madammas, Salata Baladi

Most Middle Eastern grocery stores as well as some progressive organic and vegetarian markets carry fava beans in cans. There are a wide variety of bean types from smaller imported Egyptian ones to larger ones grown in California. Some are packed in water and salt, whereas others have pre-added garlic or oil. Egyptians eat *ful* with hard-boiled eggs, *tahina* salad, or *salata baladi* along with pita bread. Lemon, olive oil, garlic, salt, and pepper are nice additions.

Dried fava beans can also be found in grocery stores in many parts of the country, but not everywhere. Egyptians traditionally cooked them in a clay pot for long periods of time—instead, try a slow cooker. Simply sort through the beans, rinse, and place in a slow cooker with enough diluted broth to cover the beans by several inches. If cooking a whole bag of beans, use six to eight cups of water, with four to six bouillon cubes and a few cloves of garlic, some freshly ground pepper, cooking on low heat for 10–12 hours. Egyptians say it is a good idea to add a spoon of lentils or rice to the pot.

A *salata baladi* is a traditional salad that consists of tomato, cucumber, onion, and parsley dressed with lemon, olive oil, salt, and pepper. Variations include dressings with vinegar. The salad can also contain romaine lettuce. The ingredients are all chopped in small squares.

QULQAS (PRONOUNCED UL'ASS) TARO

½–1 pound beef cubed (the higher the quality, the better)

2–2½ pounds taro (peeled and sliced, one inch pieces)

Cooking oil

2 small onions or one large onion

2–4 cloves garlic (depending on size)

2 c tomato juice (or even V-8)

1 t white vinegar

Salt and pepper to taste

White rice

Add enough oil to fry the taro until golden brown, remove and drain on paper towels. Clean pan out. Add enough oil to sauté garlic and onion, and then add meat with some salt and pepper. Remove excess oil. Add tomato juice, vinegar, and adjust seasonings. Bring to boil, reduce heat and cook for 20 minutes. Add taro and cook for another 10 minutes. Serve with rice.

MAḤSHI

Compared to Greek version of filling, the Egyptian version is much more rice-filled.

1 small onion

2–3 cloves garlic, minced

Olive oil

½–1 pound ground beef or lamb (the higher the quality, the better)

1½ c rice

8 oz. can tomato sauce

1 can diced tomatoes (drain and save juice) or one large tomato skinned seeded and diced (for liquid substitute 1 cup water with chicken bouillon cube)

Salt and pepper

¼ c fresh coriander (1 T + 1 t dry coriander leaves)

1 T fresh or 1 t dry mint

1 T butter

Sauté onion and garlic in a small amount of oil. Add ground meat, salt, and pepper to taste. Drain fat. In a bowl combine rice, tomato sauce, meat, diced tomatoes, coriander, and mint.

For grapeleaves: These are widely available even in many regular supermarkets in either the pickled foods area or in the ethnic foods area, and certainly in Middle Eastern grocery stores. Before stuffing with rice mixture, bring a pot of water to boiling and boil a few leaves at a time for a few seconds and remove with tongs or gently with a fork. This step removes the saltiness of the brining solution, and if not done the grapeleaves will taste like the brine and not the *maḥshi.* To stuff the grape leaves take a small amount of rice in the center of each leaf and wrap it burrito-style. Do not wrap too tightly since the rice will need to expand, nor too loosely since the product fall apart—it is a delicate balance. The Middle Eastern ideal is smaller finger-shaped ones, but this could take a lifetime with a large quantity of *maḥshi.*

For cabbage: Rinse cabbage head and throw away the outer leaves. Put the entire head in 10–12 cups of boiling water and cut away the leaves with a knife. The hot water will make it easier to separate the leaves. Remove the head of separated leaves. Add lemon juice to water. Add juice of one lemon to the boiling water, and boil leaves six at a time for a minute and place leaves in a colander. Cut off stem, and cut large leaves into halves lengthwise along stem. When stuffing cabbage leaves, unlike grapeleaves, they are not sealed or closed on the ends, but simply rolled. The same issue of rice expansion applies.

For vegetables: For green peppers, zucchini, small eggplants, tomatoes, first wash, cut off the top and hollow out all vegetables carefully. For tomatoes, make an aluminum foil cradle since they are so delicate, but other vegetables are hearty enough to withstand the cooking. Stuff the vegetables loosely with the rice mixture. Do not pack or stuff to the top because the rice will expand.

For cooking all Maḥshi: Place one tablespoon of butter and the reserved tomato liquid (or chicken stock) in the bottom of a large heavy pot or Dutch oven. Carefully layer all of the items to be cooked (grapeleaves, cabbage, stuffed vegetables, etc.). If you need to add a bit more water or liquid to make sure that there is about two inches of liquid in the bottom of the pan, then do so. The items will be cooked by boiling or steaming. Bring the liquid to a boil then simmer for about an hour for grapeleaves. The cabbage may take a bit longer. The vegetables may take less time, perhaps 40–45 minutes depending on which vegetables used.

If you have leftover maḥshi it may be cooked by itself and served as a dish.

SHAKSHUKA

1 small onion very finely chopped

Clarified butter (unsalted butter will work) or extra virgin olive oil

3 large tomatoes, skinned, seeded, and sliced half inch thick

6 hard boiled eggs, shelled

Salt and pepper

Heat enough clarified butter or oil to sauté onions and add onions. Sauté until softened, add tomatoes, and cook over medium heat for about 10 minutes. Place hard-boiled eggs into tomato mixture. Season with salt and pepper to taste. Before serving, slice eggs in half and place on platter.

KUSHERI

Kusheri is available at many little restaurants and stands all over Egypt. For decades, the longstanding favorite of tourists is Lux on 26th of July Street near Falaki square in Cairo, but rumor has it that its title as king of kusheri has been taken by Abou Tarek on Champollion Street, complete with a webpage and Shaaban singing his praises (www.aboutarek.com). A pint-sized bucket costs less than a quarter. Although it is quite cheap for Americans, one needs to consider what the average starting salary for a public-sector employee in Egypt is, and realize that eating *kusheri* daily, while nutritionally sound (protein, fiber, and folic acid in lentils), could eat up a significant portion of someone's salary. Nevertheless, relative to McDonald's of Egypt where one can easily spend as much as the United States (without nearly the comparable nutritional value), traditional foods, for example, *kusheri* and *ful* are still bargains. There is a recipe found at the previous link as well as one provided subsequently. It can easily be doubled to make an enormous quantity, enough to give every student in a classroom of 30–35 a Dixie-cup size sample at a very small cost.

1 c lentils (brown)

2 c water

2 cloves garlic, minced

1 small onion quartered

½ t salt

Freshly ground pepper

1 t extra virgin olive oil (substitute regular olive oil or canola oil to lower cost)

½ c rice (feel free to substitute brown for a healthier version—this helps vegetarians)

8 oz. small elbow macaroni or ditilini pasta (feel free to substitute a multi-grain pasta to go even healthier)

3–4 T extra virgin olive oil (see earlier note)

1–2 t salt

2–4 cloves garlic, minced

¼ c vinegar (white or cidar)

Large can crushed tomatoes

1–3 t crushed red pepper

Sort through lentils (even if the package says pre-sorted) to make sure that there are no small stones or pieces of dirt and rinse. Place lentils and the next six ingredients in a medium-sized saucepan and bring to boil, then add the rice, bring to a boil again stir, reduce heat, cover, and simmer for 30–40 minutes. While lentils are cooking prepare pasta according to instructions on package.

Rinse and drain pasta so that it does not continue to cook. Occasionally check on lentils to make sure there is enough liquid for rice and lentils, there should not be a need to add more than a little. Next, make the spicy sauce. Heat olive oil and sauté garlic. Carefully add vinegar and crushed tomatoes. Season with salt and crushed red peppers. When the lentils are cooked, all the water will be absorbed. Mix the pasta and the lentil mixture. Serve lentils and sauce separately or mix together. Serve with additional hot sauce if desired.

UMM ALI

Although a number of the other Middle Eastern sweets are frequently available at Middle Eastern grocery stores, and share a heritage with a number of other countries, Umm Ali is distinctly Egyptian. Experiment with different nuts, raisin combinations, and so on. This dish can also be put into individual custard cups. It is a delightful, rich dessert that will enchant visitors when you recount the history told in Chapter 2 about one of the only women to rule Egypt, the brave Shajarat al-Durr who briefly ruled in her own name, then coruled with a husband, whom she forced to divorce his first wife (Umm Ali). Shajarat al-Durr later killed her husband and was killed by her own retinue, the dessert created by Umm Ali in celebration of her death. Oddly enough, one variant of the Umm Ali story is that the dish was not created until the Turks arrived—under Selim (the Grim)—and in an effort to please him as he was touring a small Delta village, the best cook around (Ali's Mom) threw everything she had that was good for a dessert into a casserole and baked it in the community oven. Even better, and pluckier, by the Brits, is that an English nurse named O'Malley is responsible, which is almost laughable. Chefs have questioned the existence of coconut, both in the original recipe and in Egypt. It is plausible given that coconut was grown on the Arabian Peninsula (Oman) by the travels of Ibn Battuta just a short time later, and the household of Umm Ali was an elite one; she would have access to goods acquired from Red Sea trade. It is equally possible that the original version may not have had coconut.

10 oz. cooked puff pastry (to cook puff pastry bake phyllo leaves at 400 degree Fahrenheit for about 15 minutes in a preheated oven until puffed and golden).

⅓ c pistachio nuts chopped

⅓ c flaked almonds toasted (just a few minutes in toaster oven is fine)

¼ c golden raisins (optional)

2 T sweetened coconut flakes (optional)

2 T lemon juice

1 c milk

¾ c sugar

Pinch of cinnamon

1 egg, beaten

2 t rosewater

1 c light cream

Preheat oven to 375 degrees. Mix puff pastry, nuts (raisins and coconut if desired), and lemon juice. If you are planning to dole out in individual custard dishes, it should make about six portions. Grease dishes first and divide mixture, or grease a large round baking dish or a 9 × 12 baking dish and place the pastry nut mixture on bottom. Next, heat milk, sugar, and cinnamon almost to boiling, then shut off the stove. Add a small amount of heated milk to beaten egg to heat it (so that the egg does not cook), then add the rest of the egg to the milk mixture. Pour this over the nut mixture and sprinkle with rose water. Gently top with cream. Bake for 30 minutes until golden brown. To make it look really nice, broil it for the last one to two minutes of cooking so that it is truly bubbly and golden grown on top.

KAHK

1 c unsalted butter

2–2 ¼ c all-purpose flour (or a mix of ½ white and ½ wheat all purpose flours)

½ t cinnamon

½ t ground cloves

½ t ground ginger

¼ c milk

½ t instant yeast

1 t sugar

Sprinkle rose water

Filling: Egyptians make a filling of dates—make it easy on yourself and buy date jam. Also buy some good nuts, for example, filberts, hazelnuts, or pistachios—chop them and mix with sugar—the cookies have no sugar, therefore the filling and the coating are the sugar.

Powdered sugar.

Melt butter completely on stove or in microwave. While butter is melting, whisk flour and spices together. Combine flour and butter; allow this mixture to cool to warm. Blend yeast and sugar, soften with milk and rose water. Add to dough. Knead, place in a warm spot, and let rise for one hour. When ready to work with the dough, preheat oven to 350 degrees. Using a small cookie scooper, or a melon baller, or just guestimating, shape dough into equally sized balls, then flatten and fill with fruit/jam, nuts, honey and gently reclose; many leave an opening so that one can see what the filling is. A true Egyptian would let the cookies sit again, but if you have preheated the oven, go ahead and bake for about 15 minutes. Remove from cookie sheet and cool on wire rack completely before dipping in powdered sugar. Also note that a true Egyptian would probably double or triple this recipe, because she would be making enough cookies to share with a lot of people.

KOFTA

2 pounds ground lamb (or ½ lamb ½ beef or just high quality beef)

3–4 cloves minced garlic

2 T dried parsley

1–2 T minced onion (on finest setting on grater) include liquid

1 t salt or more to taste

Freshly ground pepper

Mix all ingredients and allow to sit in fridge for at least two to three hours before cooking. If using wooden skewers, soak in water while meat is sitting; this keeps the ends from burning during the grilling. Take meat and wrap around skewers in a log-like fashion. Grill to taste. Serve with *tahina* and *salata baladi* on pita bread.

REFERENCES

Fassone, Alessia, and Enrico Ferraris. *Egypt: Pharaonic Period.* Translated by Jay Hyams. Dictionaries of Civilization Series. Berkeley: University of California Press, 2007.

Mehdawy, Magda. *My Grandmother's Kitchen: Traditional Dishes Sweet & Savory.* Cairo: AUC Press, 2006.

Parker, S. Thomas. "A Possible Early Church in Jordan." Lecture given at ECU, November 28, 2007.

Riolo, Amy. *Nile Style: Egyptian Cuisine & Culture, Ancient Festivals, Significant Ceremonies, and Modern Celebrations.* New York: Hippocrene Books, 2009.

Tise, Larry. "Why Is Our Thanksgiving Bird Called a Turkey." H-Net Discussion Networks. http://h-net.msu.edu/cgi-bin/logbrowse.pl?trx=vx&list=H-SHEAR&month=0811&week=d&msg=pw0yWRRlI104Sju09HN5Jw&user=&pw=.

SPORTS AND LEISURE

Introduction

Are you Ahly or Zamalek? This is one of the first questions that a visitor or long-term resident is likely to be asked, and unlike his or her country of origin, religion, marital status, and whether or he or she has children it may not be as simple to answer if one does not follow soccer (football), the beloved national sport. Ahly refers to the national team, whose home field is Cairo International Stadium (but whose home club is actually in Zamalek) and Zamalek refers to another local team whose home field is also Cairo International Stadium (but whose Club resides in Mohandiseen and Zamalek).

Like many things in Egypt, the British often take or receive credit for creating the first sporting clubs in Egypt; however, Egyptian nationalists are quick to point out that various forms of fitness and sport had their origin in Egypt. Where does the truth lie? It is probably somewhere between the two extremes. Pictorial and written evidence suggest that ancient Egyptians participated in a variety of competitive and noncompetitive sports that we might classify today as track or field, gymnastics, hockey, squash, swimming, fishing, equestrian events, archery, and martial arts. Some of these games even included written regulations, uniforms, and a neutral referee to negotiate disputes. A culture of "fitness" dates back at least as far as the

Egyptian Hasan Zaki, left, fights for the ball with Mahmoud Makluk of Libya during the African Nations Cup soccer match Group A at Cairo football Stadium, January 20, 2006. (AP Photo/Ariel Schalit)

reign of Djoser (d. ca. 2613 BCE), who himself is depicted in one of the oldest documents pertaining to sport dating back nearly 5,000 years. In medieval times, we know that polo, martial arts, and other "fighting skills" were popular with the mamluks. What was common to both ancient and medieval times was that these pastimes were pursued by people who had the leisure to do so or were sponsored by people who had the leisure to do so. There is even some speculation that ancient Egyptians had some precursor to the Olympics.

Other leisure-time activities pursued by ordinary Egyptians did not necessarily involve fancy equipment or regulated competition. Chess (*shaṭarang*) has long been played in the Middle East. In fact, the English term "checkmate" comes from the Arabic "*al-shaykh mat*" or the ruler has died. Traditional Egyptian chess pieces tended to be simpler than ornate, carved Western pieces, owing to Islamic traditions shunning human representation and idolatry. The game of checkers dates back to ancient Egyptian times and is known by its old name *dama.* In contrast to both checkers and chess, backgammon (ṭawla) and dominoes require not just strategy, but a certain amount of luck from the player. In other words, both of these are technically games of chance that merit some warning under the dictates of Islam.

Another game played in Egypt is one that is common to many of its African neighbors and it has ancient roots: Mankala. The board for Mankala has six pits (*buyut*) in each side. Egyptians play with either four or six ḥaṣa (pebbles) in each pit for a total of 48 or 64. Play begins by one player taking his or her pebbles from one pit and dropping them one by one in a counter-clockwise direction in each pit. If the last pit into which the player places a pebble has only one pebble, then the player stops, and his or her opponent begins play. If the pit contains two or four pebbles, then he or she captures those pebbles and those of the pit opposite to it, in addition to any preceding pits (from the starting point) that contain only two or four pebbles and their partners on the other side (as long as there are no pits intervening that have a different number). If the last pit contains three, five, or more pebbles then the player must redistribute them in ordinary play fashion in a counter-clockwise direction.

GAREED (PALMS)

In his early-19th-century observation of modern Egyptians, Edward Lane noted that the game of *Gareed*, was played in mamluks times, but that Egyptian peasants continued to play it usually in times of celebration, such as marriage or circumcision in the family of a notable. This game of Bedouin origin was adopted in Upper and Lower Egypt, differing only in the length of the jousting palm branch. Deltans tended to use smaller branches and their counterparts further south used playing sticks up to six feet in length. Each team consists of 12 to 20 people mounted on horseback with a handful of freshly cut palm branches (*gareeds*), which are wielded at the opposing team. The only way to ward off the attack is by catching the *gareeds* or cutting them with a sword. Obviously, the game could result in serious injuries or even fatalities.

The round ends when there are no pebbles left in any of the pits, and the winner is the person with the most pebbles. The game ends when one player wins successively until he or she reaches 60 (pebbles). A variation of the game involves more variable distribution of the pebbles, but relatively the same rules. A game similar to the ancient game of Senet is Seega, and it can be played either on a board or outdoors using holes in the ground. The game is played on a grid of five by five, seven by seven, or nine by nine. To set up play, game pieces, "dogs," are placed on alternate squares or holes of the board. Thus, for a grid of 25, 12 dogs are used. The objective of each player is to capture the opponent's dogs between two of one's own. Play advances one square or hole at a time, and diagonal moves are not allowed. Cards (*kotchina*) along with dominoes and board games form the activity of coffeehouses. Common practice with many games in the coffeehouse is that the loser should buy beverages not only for himself and his opponent, but also for any spectators who happen to take an interest in the game.

SENET OR ṬAB

Some games that existed in ancient Egypt are still played today, perhaps with some modification. The ancient Egyptian game of Hounds and Jackals, or Senet, was played on a grid of three rows of ten, and turns determined by throwing knucklebones. Game boards have been found in pre-dynastic burial sites. *Ṭab*, discussed in Lane's *Manners and Customs of the Modern Egyptians* describes a variant of the game played in the 19th century in which *Naṣara* (Christian) dogs are moved and become Muslim dogs once they achieve a "privileged" position. The modern board has four squares by 7, 9, 11, 13, or 15 squares and the object of the game is to move across the board and capture the opponent's pieces before he or she does the same. The game is still played by throwing traditional sticks that determine each move.

BAṢ RA

Deal each player four cards and lay four cards on the ground, and if any jacks are laid down, reshuffle in deck. The object of the game is to collect as many cards from the floor as possible with like cards or with cards of equal value, for example, queen takes a queen, or 7 takes 3+4. If a player "eats" all the remaining card(s), then he or she gets a "Baṣra" which is worth 10 extra points. Jacks are able to "eat" all of the cards on the ground, but this move is not counted as a "Baṣra." The 7 of diamonds behaves like a jack, and is scored like one. After the entire deck has been played, players score their cards. Three points are given for the most cards, one point for each jack, one point for each ace, two points for the 2 of clubs, and three points for the 10 of diamonds. Players agree to play to a determined point value, usually 100 or 200.

Coffee, Tea, and Coffeehouses

While many might associate tea with the British, Muslim merchants brought the beverage to the Middle East centuries before the British occupation in 1882. Nevertheless, tea time for the middle and upper classes and the rituals surrounding it were certainly influenced by decades of British occupation. Egyptian tea, made with loose tea leaves, tends to be much stronger than tea made from teabags. Coffee, on the other hand, was an African discovery, that found perfection in the Middle East. First discovered in Ethiopia, the bitter drink made its way to the Middle East around the 12th century when it started to be grown in the southern part of the Arabian Peninsula (present-day Yemen). Coffee began to be incorporated into Sufi rituals (see Chapter 5) as a means of keeping participants awake. Since most schools of Islamic law allow the concept of analogy, coffee became the topic of debate and discussion as to whether it should become a forbidden substance, along with other intoxicants and drugs. Thankfully, for imbibers, most judges have ruled in favor of the drink. Nevertheless, centralizing states, for example, the Ottomans, deemed coffeehouses to be problematic, since much like pubs and taverns in colonial American times, these were places that malcontents and revolutionaries organized.

The coffeehouse is a predominantly male space where stories are told, games played, and the traditional waterpipe smoked. In Egypt the water pipe is called the *sheesha*, which usually evokes thoughts of illicit drugs in the minds of Westerners, but it is simply used for tobacco, often flavored with fruit, for example, apples or grapes. The coffee, *ahwa*, or *ahwa 'arabiyya* (Arab coffee) (Egyptians are likely to be angered if one calls it "Turkish coffee") is stronger and sweeter than regular coffee, even if unsweetened, because it has cardamom added. The traditional vessel for making the coffee is an *ibrik*, which one can still get from the copperwares market *suq al-nahhaseen* in Cairo or made from stainless steel, and can be purchased on either side of the Atlantic or Mediterranean.

PERFECT ARABIC COFFEE AND A FORTUNE

One cup very cold water

One tablespoon extremely finely ground coffee (even if it is not Arab coffee it is OK)

Cardamom—one pod or one-eighth teaspoon ground

Sugar—try half teaspoon and go with more, less, or none at all.

Bring water and sugar to a boil in the *ibrik*. Take off the heat. Add the coffee and cardamom. Stir as it goes back on the heat. Allow it to rise up to a foam, lift up off the heat, place back on the heat and allow to foam once more. Do not stir. Pour slowly into small cups.

While men were at coffeehouses drinking, women as well, made coffee part of their visiting rituals. Reading the grounds in the bottom of one's coffee cup, which is a type of fortune-telling, is still a skill that some Egyptian women claim to possess.

Traditional Celebrations

From at least Fatimid (969–1171) times onward there are chronicles of urban street fairs that went along with various types of secular and religious celebrations (see section on religion and thought in Chapter 5). People would gather near the center of town to watch performers play music, perform gymnastics, juggle, and (later) release fireworks. Another form of street performance was the shadow play, originally from China, which most likely made it to Egypt via the mamluks (1250–1517). In other parts of the Middle East, Mongols were the transmitters of this art form that involves using ornate opaque flat puppets on sticks in front of an illuminated backdrop, providing a larger image, as well as the illusion of movement. Through shadow plays, authors could critique society, or even rulers, in ways that would not be possible directly, and many of these manuscripts still exist. The ability to allow ordinary Egyptians to release pent-up frustrations through fun, games, and critiques of their authoritarianism enabled various rulers to continue to exercise that authority (see the section on performing arts in this chapter).

Less Time for Fun and Games, New Venues for Play

Prior to the era of Muhammad Ali (r. 1805–1848) when agricultural cultivation became more intensive, the average peasant only worked about 150 days a year compared to about 250 afterwards. The increased pace of work and intensification of capitalist agricultural production restricted the peasant's ability to engage in many traditional leisure-time activities. As discussed, peasants enjoyed playing various incarnations of board, chance, and ball games many of which had been played in Egypt since ancient times. By the late-19th century when the British occupation began, there was little time for the Egyptian peasant to "play."

The British occupation did bring formal sporting clubs to Egypt, introduce physical education into the curriculum into the government schools for boys and girls, and these changes permanently affected the sports and sport choices that Egyptians currently play. Egyptian nationalists would likely point out that some of the games that made their way to Europe via the Greco-Roman civilization were originally "Egyptian." Nevertheless, other games were merely similar; it is human nature to pick, prod, and throw what is available. In Egypt, local trees, for example, palms provided material for balls and bats, and the like.

Even before the arrival of the British, basic types of military drills and other types of physical drills existed in the schools for boys. These had long been staples of the military curriculum. As any devout Muslim will explain, praying five times a day is actually an exercise, both spiritual and physical, as the body goes through its ritualized movements. Furthermore, the agility needed to go through the movements and the proper ablutions helps to maintain flexibility. Thus, for those not attending school or even those attending traditional schools, maintaining religious standards has helped maintain fitness for practicing Muslims for centuries. Although some girls' schools prior to the British occupation had various practical home economics that involved physical labor, for example, doing the cooking and laundry of the school, there was no sports per se in government schools until after the arrival of the British; and it was a heated topic in the press usually based upon the argument that girls were not suited to such exertions. In fact, even the introduction of physical education into boys' schools attracted media attention, since it took hours away from other subjects; but within a few years, the sports pages would become a regular feature of the press, as would journals dedicated to sports (Rizq 1999). In other words, the urban reading public of Egypt would become converted to the culture of sports in a relatively short span of time.

In the late-19th century Europeans first established sporting clubs to create elite havens within Cairo and Alexandria, and at first only Europeans were allowed admittance. Attaining skills in the Anglicized sports of golf, tennis, and the like were signs of "civilization" much in the same way that speaking with a proper French or English accent was a sign that one attended the right school. By the turn of the 20th century some elite Egyptians began to be allowed into the clubs, but the British upheld rigorous entrance procedures by maintaining ridiculously high membership fees, annual dues, and often times one had to join under the patronship of an existing member. The Gezira Sporting Club is perhaps one of the most famous of these establishments where the elite continue to play golf, tennis, swim, enjoy a martial arts class, skateboard, take in a game of squash or table tennis, go to a horse race, dine in one of the eating areas (depending upon season), or simply walk in the gardens (previously the Khedivial Botanical gardens). While it is a shabby shell or what it once was, it is still a delightful piece of green in an otherwise concrete jungle on the island of Gezira in the neighborhood of Zamalek. During the height of Nasser's nationalizations, he seized portions of the club's land (golf courses) to give to the Ahly soccer team.

Conflicting accounts of what the Gezira club was like for non-European members and guests vary significantly. Britons themselves record stories of being ashamed by the behavior of their compatriots as they brought Egyptians as tennis or golf partners. Edward Said (1935–2003), the Palestinian-American scholar who spent his formative years in Cairo, vividly remembers being scolded by the officer in charge in the 1940s simply because he was an Arab. Nevertheless, Chafika Soliman Hamamsy, an upper-class Zamalekite, has nothing but positive memories because she was able to follow the seemingly endless list of rules that applied to ALL children (regardless of ethnicity) and that the club had a great liberating effect on socializing, game-playing, and indirectly on appearance (for girls) since a person cannot play tennis or swim without the proper clothing. Regardless, prior to the Egyptian Revolution clubs were places of distinction with little access for the masses.

In the face of such discrimination, elite Egyptians began to form their own clubs. In 1907 a group of Egyptian pashas and beys, that is, men with titles, land and political connections, along with one token Englishman, met to discuss the formation of what would eventually become the National Club (*al-Nadi al-Ahly*). Abd al-Khaleq Tharwat, one of the club's founders, and a leading politician of the time (see Chapter 3), discussed the importance of the club in 1919 on the eve of nationalist demonstrations. He saw the club as a networking zone for students after graduation, a place to congregate rather than the traditional coffeehouse. It would be a place that would inculcate the proper nationalist values and fitness in its citizens.

The Zamalek Club started under the auspices of several different names and different types of organizations as evidenced by one of its original names, the Mixed Club (*al-Nadi al-Mukhtalat*), where Egyptians and Europeans socialized and played sports. It had several locations before settling in Zamalek. Both the Ahly and Mukhtalat were active in playing in the first Anglo-Egyptian cup series that pitted Egyptian teams against those sponsored by British army units. The Mukhtalat Club eventually became the Faruq Club (Royal Club), receiving royal sponsorship. The king and his father had become avid fans, and they worked to sponsor various national competitions, culminating in the creation of a national league and a Faruq Cup in 1948, that would become the Egypt Cup after the Revolution. The Faruq Club would then receive its more familiar name, the Zamalek Club.

Other individuals involved in the nationalist movement and in the royal family connected the notion of physical fitness and the overall health of the nation. Egypt sent a delegation to the Stockholm Olympics in 1912, but it was not until Prince Umar Tusun took over the project that an Egyptian Olympic Committee (EOC) was formed over the period between 1912 and 1914. It consisted of members from the Ministries of War and Public Instruction, as was the procedure at the time. Within ten years Egypt was able to send a team able to advance beyond the first round of competition. At the Paris Olympics of 1924, the Egyptian delegation was small and interest was highest in soccer, particularly among the Egyptian correspondents sent to Europe to cover the events (Lopez 2008). While Egypt did not have an outstanding performance, it did go beyond the first and second rounds of play defeating France and Hungary, only to be defeated by Sweden in the quarter-finals. Most of the delegation consisted of single members in his particular event, for example, boxing, track and field, cycling, and so on. They had been given relatively little training and poor equipment, such that the wrestler, Ibrahim Mustafa, did not even have shoes designed for his sport and spent most of his match holding together his uniform (Jacob 2005).

Societal trends in body-building and other forms of masculine, physical sport led to greater Egyptian participation in these events, as well as greater recognition by the EOC of their potential. By 1928 at the Amsterdam Olympics, Egypt received two gold medals, one in wrestling and one in weightlifting, as well as a silver and a bronze in diving. Considering that the Egyptian team consisted of 32 men, bringing home four medals in three of the five events in which it participated demonstrated great progress. The soccer team, while not overwhelmingly successful, did inflict a humiliating loss on its former overlord Turkey, and managed a close win over Portugal, but lost to Argentina and Italy. These international successes buoyed the enthusiasm of nationalists and King Fuad. They organized pan-African games, first slated to be held in 1927, then postponed until 1929. Evidence suggests that both the British and the French feared a rallying of their colonial subjects under the mantle of sports. This view was contrary to the original intention when the games were first discussed in 1924, and it was thought that the games could instill proper values in colonial subjects (Lopez 2008).

Over the course of the 1930s and 1940s Egypt would continue to perfect its weight-lifting and soccer teams for international competition; however internal and international crises, for example, the controversy surrounding 1936 Olympics, and the cancellation of the 1940 and 1944 Olympics due to World War II, interrupted or marred Egypt's participation. In fact, Egypt pulled out of the 1932 Olympics because its own organizational committee had fallen apart. Nevertheless, during this period, Egypt continued to produce gold medalists, notably at the 1936 Olympics, weight-lifter Khidr al-Tuni lifted 854 pounds (387.5 kilograms) or more than 77 pounds (35 kilograms) than the silver medalist, a record that would last more than a de-cade. Egypt continued winning gold medals in weightlifting, wrestling, and boxing up until 1948. Soccer did not fare as well in competition during the 1930s and 1940s; nevertheless, the Egyptians proved capable of international competition. By the 1952 summer Olympics, which straddled the era of monarchy and revolution, Egypt re-ceived only one bronze medal in wrestling. Egypt's age of gold was over until 2004 (Lopez 2008).

Societal attitudes were changing during the interwar era as well, and not just for men. Health, beauty, and fitness received wider attention among the urban upper-middle and upper classes. Previously girth for a man or being proportionately pleas-ingly plump for a woman were signs that a person had the means to consume the food that he or she desired and the leisure to not burn extra calories through manual labor. By the 1930s and 1940s new standards of fitness and beauty were in evidence through the various sports that could be followed in the press, the arrival of Holly-wood and Egyptian films in cinemas, and an expanding literate, urban public that was following these changes, both through specialized journals as well as ordinary ones. Advertising reflected the new body image, particularly for women, and there were numerous advertisements for weight-loss centers, gyms, self-defense courses, and various weight-management supplements. As discussed in Chapter 3, for men the fitness and weightlifting craze even filtered down into the ranks of the lower-middle class, where the line between gym and thug hangout was often quite thin.

Leveling the Playing Field

After the Egyptian Revolution, Nasser tried to expand and replicate the experience of the wealthy by creating various types of clubs (on a less extravagant scale) for a much wider audience usually grouped according to occupation, for example, offi-cers, teachers, faculty, journalists, and so on based on one's professional syndicate. Membership rates would be accessible to those within that group and all members of an individual's family would be given membership. Such clubs usually include swim-ming, tennis, squash, handball, basketball, volleyball, various forms of martial arts, table tennis, and some might have more extensive programs. Previously, only a small portion of the population had access to what had been considered elite pastimes, but now with the expansion of education and the creation of mass syndicates to contain and constrain the masses, sporting clubs were a potential outlet for the citizens' pent-up frustrations. The officers themselves, having gone through military training and discipline, shared the philosophy of politician Abd al-Khalaq Tharwat, who believed in inculcating citizens with good habits. Physical education remained an important component of the school curriculum. Healthy citizens equal a healthy nation.

With respect to Olympic training, the new regime chose to boycott the 1956 Olympics in Melbourne, Australia since it was part of the British Commonwealth and Egypt was in the midst of the Suez Crisis. During the 1960s the teams Egypt fielded, even after the breakup of the UAR, were combined with Syria; however, only a handful of Syrians were on any of the teams. Compared to the teams of the 1940s, those of the 1960s and 1970s began to shrink with respect to the number of participants, the number of events, and the number of sports, which given the numbers of citizens with access to gyms, fitness, and training appears odd. Perhaps without monarchical prestige and large patron sponsorship, the games could literally not go on.

After the opening of the economy and the rise of new patrons, as well as the change of regime with Mubarak a new interest in the Olympics took place in 1984. Egypt fielded a team of 114 participants, with its first women ever, participating in 74 events in 15 sports. In comparison, the 1976 team had only 26 players slated to participate in seven events in four sports. Ultimately the 1976 team boycotted the games as part of a larger African boycott targeted against South Africa's allies, and the 1980 games were boycotted as well based on the U.S.-led complaint against the Soviet invasion of Afghanistan. Thus, it is clear that Egypt developed its team during the years of infitah and boycott. It was also in 1984 that Egypt fielded its only winter team (one person one event) at Sarajevo.

With respect to women's participation, there had actually been Egyptian women that made the team in 1960, but were not allowed to participate, even though they made their qualifying events. Some believe it was because the government was under pressure not to have women participate due to conservative attitudes regarding women in the male domain of sports and concerns for female modesty. Another of the concerns with respect to one of the 1960 participants was that she was the daughter of feminist Doria Shafik, who was then under house arrest (see Chapter 5). In other words, the matter was personal rather than sports-related. Finally, there was speculation that the matter was procedural.

After the opening of the Olympics to women, participation has still been fraught with difficulties regarding recognition, funding, and conservative attitudes. In 1984 the women competed in synchronized swimming, swimming, and diving. Since then they have also competed in table tennis, judo, taekwondo, fencing, shooting, gymnastics, archery, track and field, modern pentathalon, rowing, weightlifting, wrestling, and badminton. Women that choose sports involving less modest clothing have had to overcome more obstacles, as well as Egypt's lady wrestler, Hayat Farag, who has few Egyptian competitors and has had to wrestle men in order to keep in shape, drawing criticism from conservatives. This woman is somewhat of an enigma in that she is veiled and admits to breaking her own code of modesty in order to compete at the sport she loves.

The renewed interest in the Olympics has led to results. The 2004 team was the most successful since the interwar period, finally bringing back the gold with wrestler Karam Ibrahim. He was greeted personally at the airport by Gamal Mubarak, son of then President Mubarak and thought to be the "heir" to the presidency (see Chapter 7), perhaps signaling a link between the Olympics and "monarchical" prestige. Ibrahim's teammates included three bronze medalists, two in boxing and one in taekwondo, as well as the silver medalist boxer with the name of dual significance in Egypt,

Muhammad Ali. The 2008 Olympics brought only a bronze in judo; however, Egypt still fielded a 100 person team (74 men, 26 women) in 68 events representing 19 sports.

The heightened athleticism represented in the Olympics mirrored other trends since the opening of the economy. While most middle- and upper-class families have kept their membership at the "club" associated with their syndicate or one of the large soccer clubs (which are all-encompassing health clubs), many new types of fitness, dance, and weightlifting gyms have opened over the last few decades. The major cities in Egypt have followed Western fitness trends regarding dance-exercise, step, pilates, spinning, kick-boxing, salsa, yoga, and so on to meet demand. Samia Allouba's Gym, Dance, and Fitness Center in Maadi caters to an expatriot crowd, as well as upper class Egyptians, and in addition to a large number of fitness classes one would find at any club in the United States, it offers a highly popular belly-dancing class taught by renowned dancer Fufa al-Faransawi. A number of western chain gyms have also relocated in Egypt, including Gold's Gym. It has five branches, the premier one operating out of a giant luxury boat moored on the Nile off of Giza. All the major hotels have health clubs, and there are a growing number of "women's only" clubs to meet the demand of women who want to stay in shape, but choose not to exercise in front of men. Women who follow Islamic dress codes are relieved not to have the extra heat of head coverings, full sleeves, and long pants while they work out. Not surprisingly, Curves has been a huge success. Its first franchise premiered in 2007, and by 2009 there were already nine branches.

Soccer: The Great Rivalry and International Competition

While tennis, handball, squash, and track and field have remained popular and Cairo has hosted both regional and continental events related to these sports, soccer remains the country's obsession. As indicated in the introduction, the fiercest loyalties belong to Ahly and Zamalek, although the Egyptian League contains fourteen other teams. Each year the two popular teams have two rounds of traditional games in the league championship. Cairo Stadium is filled to capacity and must have riot police on hand to keep the 74,000+ crowd in hand. There is a bit of a class component to the rivalry given the history of the clubs. Although both were started by wealthy landowning Egyptians, the Zamalek club was tinged by its association of mixing with foreigners, the elitism of its location, and its patronage by the monarchy. Nevertheless "monarchy" is back in style and the club remains popular despite the fact that its record lags behind that of Ahly. *Ahlawis*, as its fans are known, praise their team for having won the Egypt Cup 35 times; the Arab Cup Winner's Cup in 1995; the Africa or CAF Cups in 1982, 1984, 1985, 1986, 1987, 1993, 2001, 2005, 2006, and 2008; CAF Super Cup in 2002, 2006, 2007, and 2009; and the prestigious intercontinental FIFA bronze medal in 2006. *Zamalkawis* still faithfully support their club despite the fact that its record is not as stellar: it has won the Egypt Cup 21 times; the Arab Cup in 2003; the Afro-Asian Cup in 1988 and 1997, a CAF Super Cup in 1994, 1997, and 2003; and Africa or CAF Cups in 1984, 1986, 1993, 1996, 2000, 2002. In May 2009, after weeks of telephoning member rosters on a daily basis, the Zamalek Club held historic elections, in which

27,000 members participated in electing businessman Mamdouh Abbas over lawyer Mortada Mansour. The board reorganization brought several former players into the organization with the hope of bringing the club up to fan expectations.

All fans of Egyptian soccer had their expectations crushed when they found out that their country had failed in its bid for the 2010 World Cup. As South Africa claimed the bid over Egypt, politicians, journalists, fans, and sportswriters all bemoaned the loss. The announcement came around the same time as the return of the victorious 2004 Olympic athletes. Dr. Fathi Surur, speaker of the People's Assembly charged with awarding the medalists the parliamentary Gold Medal, used the occasion to compensate the loss of 2010 and to connect the athlete and athletic success to the success of the nation. Other commentators noted that South Africa was successful specifically for reasons unrelated to the sport, namely a delegation of high-power South Africans including Nelson Mandela, Bishop Desmond Tutu, and Charlize Theron, while Egypt had only Omar Sharif speaking on its behalf. In other words, there was a cultural-psychological dimension to the loss that questioned the nation's modernity and fitness for the event (Jacob 2005; Lopez 2008). The country had already undergone strategic modifications to facilitate the event, including an incomplete five stadium project. El-Borg Stadium outside Alexandria stands as a monument of what could have been. It is an 80,000 seat mammoth, which is about four times larger than what the local clubs require, and therefore it sits mostly unused.

Vacations and Leisure

Historically, the notion of the division between "work" and "life" did not exist. People worked hard and played hard, but they did not punch time clocks or conceive of life as divided between these poles. In Egypt, they simply did what they needed to do in order to survive, pay taxes, and submit to state orders for community labor. When they were not doing these things, they had fun. The wealthy had the means to escape Cairo, whether because of heat, crowding, or other reasons and locate their families in cooler and/or cleaner venues. In the 19th century revolutions in the organization of work as well as transportation and communication changed the way in which Egyptians managed their lives. The railroad, the steamship, and better roads all meant that there were greater opportunities to move people and goods both within the country and outside the country. What began in the mid-19th century as larger numbers of European tourists coming to Egypt and greater movement of Egyptians within Egypt to take advantage of educational opportunities, changed by the early 20th century.

Elite Egyptians began vacationing in larger numbers, internally, regionally, as well as in Europe, by the turn of the 20th century. Egypt's beaches have provided a natural retreat, and are currently accessible by car, rail, and numerous bus lines. Egypt's royal family took the lead in these matters, and Alexandria's Montazah palace constructed during the reign of Abbas II (r. 1892–1914) provides a monumental case in point of the new types of vacation homes. By the inter-revolutionary period (1919–1952) Cairene families would pack up and go to the beach or return to the family estate in the country, with or without the family patriarch. The family head might have to stay in the city working (at least part of the time), while his family escaped the heat. Visiting mosques, shrines, and saints' tombs en route were part of some family traditions, unless traveling by the ever-expanding train routes, which advertised regularly in mainstream, specialized, and women's journals. Reasonably priced vacations were becoming more accessible with the development of vacation locations targeted at the middle class, for example, Ras el-Bar, located on the Mediterranean, on the Damietta branch of the Nile. During this period, Egypt's Red Sea coast was relatively undeveloped from both the mainland and Sinai coasts. Egyptian college students of the 1940s recollect staying in simple bunk-like pensions in Hurghada, which were about the only option at the time. With respect to regional travel, Lebanon was a popular spot for summer vacations, particularly for the wealthy. Both the steamship and the airplane made European travel accessible, and advertising reflected changing tastes of elite Egyptians.

The rise of beach-going created the bathing suit as an item of apparel, particularly in the 1940s as the custom began to spread further into the middle class. Conservative critic Shaykh Abul Ayun offered numerous negative commentaries regarding the new beach ware, and cartoons reflected the new debate. One discussing both the social and political climate of 1946 depicted an Amazonian beach beauty that caused men to fall in her wake. The cartoon compared the new suits to the testing of new bombs. Women of the middle and upper classes began to wear bathing suits, shorts, and even sleeveless shirts or dresses. The styles that began as vacation or beachwear began to make their way into sporting clubs, and less modest styles became more acceptable clothing in general. Elite women had long been following European fashion trends, but wore modesty garments over the clothing (see Chapter 5).

After the Egyptian Revolution, Nasser helped to make vacations more accessible for the working classes by making vacation homes available by syndicate and providing vacation outings (day trips) for various factories, groups, and cooperatives. The vacation homes for university professors, officers, journalists, and so on were not luxurious chalets, but functional beach apartments that contained the necessities for the average family: zero to two bedrooms, sitting room, small kitchen, and bathroom. Certainly among elite officers, better opportunities prevailed, and vacationing provided a time for social and political networking (Abaza 2006). The coastline west of Alexandria up to Marsa Matruh became more developed, as did the Red Sea coast, but none spectacularly so. After the rise of Sadat and infitah a huge change took place in Egypt's tourist economy that was more fully developed under his successor Mubarak (see Chapter 4). In particular, the Sinai has become an internationally recognized location for various water sports, of which many Egyptians take advantage. Even within the Sinai development is uneven. Sharm el-Sheikh at the bottom tip of the Sinai is known for its high-end luxury hotels, restaurants, and trendy bars, whereas Dahab further to the north has a reputation of being a "hippie" hangout. A browse through any hotel search engine will confirm that the former has many more high-end hotels, but Dahab and some of the smaller cities have more family-owned places. Some allege that the government has "given" Dahab its reputation since it fears competition through its tourism monopolies.

More and more exclusive beaches and vacation clubs have opened in recent years. The rise of the extremely wealthy, along with the Islamic trends, has led the elite to have more private beaches and clubs. For women who choose to wear Islamic swimsuits or modified bathing coverings or who value their privacy, swimming at an exclusive beach or pool are a greater assurance that no one will photograph them in their "revealing" outfits. Conservative women will not swim at the beach or the pool during times of the day when men are likely to see them. Some may not swim at all. Others may choose to go to a women's club, swim in the women's pool or during women's hours, or at the beach they may swim early or late in the day when it is unlikely that they will be seen clearly by anyone outside their family.

Most middle-class Egyptian families take between one and four *masyafs* (summer outings) a year. Many lower middle-class Egyptians that have relocated to large urban centers simply return home to their village for a visit rather than taking a fancy vacation, and even some wealthy Egyptians enjoy a visit to the country as one of their vacations. For the less wealthy, the extensive railroad network with three classes of service provides the means of transportation, whereas the wealthy simply drive. For the elite, trips to Europe and the United States are also typical summer vacation spots. Popular year round are the trips to the holy land for pilgrimage or *'umra* (see Chapter 5). During the fall and winter, hunting is particularly good in Egypt's Faiyum oasis. King Faruq's former hunting lodge has been converted into a lovely hotel, where well-heeled Egyptians and tourists can relive the luxury. Upper-middle-class Egyptians can practice their skills at the *Nadi Tersana* (shooting club) in Cairo, but hunting for game has been an age-old necessity for Egyptian peasants.

Ironically, few Egyptians take advantage of sightseeing in their own country. Even those who can afford to spend the money on such vacations do not. As school children, they participate in a range of trips to museums, pyramids, and the like; however, it is not atypical for an eager foreign tourist or businessman to tell an Egyptian acquaintance about the latest ancient ruin, museum, or sight he has seen only to be told by the Egyptian, "I have never gone there before . . . what is it like?"

REFERENCES

Decker, Wolfgang. *Sports and Games of Ancient Egyptians.* Trans. Allen Guttmann. New Haven, CT: Yale University Press, 1992.

Jacob, Wilson Chacko. "Working Out Egypt: Masculinity and Subject formation Between Colonial Modernity and Nationalism, 1870–1940." Ph.D. Dissertation, NYU, 2005.

Hamamsy, Chafika Soliman. *Zamalek: The Changing Life of a Cairo Elite, 1850–1945.* Cairo: AUC Press, 2005.

http://www.sports-reference.com/olympics/countries/EGY/. Consulted years 1920, 1924, 1928, 1936, 1948, 1952, 1960, 1964, 1968, 1972, 1976, 1984, 1988, 1992, 1996, 2004, and 2008.

http://www.zamalek-sc.com/. Official site of the Zamalek club.

Lane, Edward. *An Account of the Manners and the Customs of the Modern Egyptians.* Cairo: AUC Press, 2004.

Lopez, Shaun. "Football as National Allegory: *al-Ahram* and the Olympics in 1920s Egypt." *History Compass* 7 (1) (2008): 282–305.

Rizq, Yunan Labib. "A Diwan of Contemporary Life: The Sports Page." *al-Ahram Weekly.* September 23–29, 1999. http://weekly.ahram.org.eg/1999/448/chrncls.htm.

Said, Edward. *Out of Place: A Memoir.* New York: Vintage, 2000.

el-Sayed, Mohamed. "Egypt Bid: Love at First Sight." *al-Ahram Weekly.* http://weekly.ahram.org.eg/2004/2010/sc82.htm.

POPULAR, YOUTH, AND CONSUMER CULTURE

Consuming Desires

The ancient Egyptians and their magnificent tombs filled with splendid jewelry, luxury foods, musical instruments, intriguing games, and ornate furniture were the ultimate "conspicuous" consumers, preparing themselves for a comfortable life in the hereafter. Historically, Egypt, at the crossroads of Mediterranean, African, and Asian trading routes received a large variety of goods coming from all parts of the known world. By the medieval and Ottoman periods, Egypt's market areas had extensive units for housing both merchandise and merchants, known as *wikalas* (*khans*, *caravanserais*). The ultimate in efficient space usage, these buildings had vaults for goods and animals on the lower floors and apartments on the higher levels. Since Egypt's merchants came from around the (old) world, large *wikalas* often housed inhabitants by spoken language. According to the early-19th-century traveler Edward Lane, there were still 200 such buildings operating in greater Cairo.

Male and female traders could come to the market to buy goods; however, historically from the medieval period onward, most elite women were secluded. Ordinary women could also come to the market, but they did not have the means to buy anything other than subsistence goods. Traders could access secluded women by sending female traders, *dallalas*, to peddle their goods. Many women were in business for themselves or with their husbands. Additionally, *dallalas* served as social networkers, information disseminators (gossipers), fashion consultants, and informal matchmakers. A conversation between a potential customer and a *dallala* might begin by discussing the last client, her family, and her purchases, all in an effort to convince the second woman to make a similar purchase or perhaps consider the first woman's son as a potential suitor for her daughter. In the 18th century, French traders began utilizing local Syrian traders, both men and women to access local markets. They needed women with access to other women, and they needed men with language skills to survey local tastes with respect to textile patterns, which could then be copied. The Syrian Christian community in Egypt served as a link between the two groups.

In the 19th century after the reforms of Muhammad Ali and the *tanzimat* reforms (see Chapter 2), many more European merchants and bankers came to Egypt with the dream of establishing profitable trade. During the age of Ismail (r. 1863–1879) the ruler set a new standard of consumption that was emulated by the elite. Having studied in Paris and revisited for the *Exposition Universelle* in 1867, he was inspired to rebuild the heart of Cairo in the fashion of Paris. The new capital would have wide, logically ordered streets, leading to orderly squares. Ismail hired French botanist and gardener Barillet-Deschamps to help with Azbakiyya Park and Gardens in the heart of what would become the city's new central shopping district. This neighborhood contained a number of foreign consulates, hotels, and restaurants, as well as the Cairo Stock Exchange.

By the turn of the 20th century, both European and Middle Eastern entrepreneurs had opened department stores and boutiques that advertised in the mainstream and women's presses. For example, Au Bon Marché and Printemps were like their French counterparts, whereas Sednaoui was started by two relocated Syrian brothers and organized along Western lines. The change from private to public consumption was gradual, and *dallalas* continued to function into the 20th century, despite their reputation for rumor-mongering and high prices. Even the reorganization of stores was gradual for Middle Eastern businessmen. A dramatic instance of this transition is the Sednaoui brothers who began as peddlers from a cart. Indeed, the new shopping district literally, in some cases, grew out of the old bazaar district.

New Shopping Districts

While driving through Cairo today, one can still see the distinctive architecture that emerged with the new department stores. Fantastic cupolas, huge windows, and neo-baroque style characterize the department stores best exemplified by the old Tiring building with its giant dome supporting four "Hercules" figures of the main branch of Sednaoui with its old-fashioned elevators installed by Gustav Eiffal for an elegant vista of the store. The neighborhood surrounding Azbakiyya Park and Gardens, which formed the nucleus of the modern shopping district, resembled a triangle laid out by Qasr al-Nil, Sulayman Pasha, and Fuad Streets, known today as Qasr al-Nil, Talaat Harb, and 26th of July Streets. In Alexandria, the neighborhood around Sharif Street evolved into the same role, and similarly smaller areas in cities, for example, Mansura, Port Said, and Damietta served the same function. Traditional shopping districts did not cease to exist, but rather continued to operate and serve a different set of customers.

The modern district catered to an elite and/or foreign clientele and although the group with access would expand over the course over of the 20th century, before the 1952 revolution it would only reach a small segment of the population. The ability to shop in such stores, measured by the ownership of a suit(s) for a man, was the sign that one belonged to this class. A cartoon from the 1940s demonstrates this notion of status. A mother tells her daughter that a man is a real catch because he has four suits. A decade or so earlier simply having a suit or a good suit might have been a sufficient measure, but to have four meant that a person would not be wearing the same one until it was worn to shreds. Not only did one have to have the right clothes, one had to have the right look to appear downtown. According to one former store worker, a prerequisite for men was a clean-shaven face (Kerboeuf 2005).

The Jewish bourgeoisie started many of Egypt's old department stores, and the clerking class was quite diverse and multicultural before the revolution. Indeed, most department stores required more than one language from their staff to meet the demand of the clientele, with French being the most common second language. After the 1948 Arab–Israeli War and after the revolution the stores continued to thrive. It was only after the Suez Crisis and the nationalizations that followed in the 1960s that the stores came under the purview of the state and lost much of their distinctive flavor.

From Nationalization to Infitah

Mona Abaza, who has written extensively on department stores, and also grew up in Egypt, writes nostalgically that children of the 1960s and 1970s remember the nationalized stores as the place where one purchased school uniforms and other sundry items for the home, for example, cheap cloth, linens, and appliances. Interestingly enough, the government chose to leave the stores with their original names, in contrast to everything related to the monarchy. Streets, buildings, bridges, and schools with monarchical names all acquired names with nationalistic or liberational themes. Egyptians associated department stores with quality, therefore keeping names was a sound idea, so Sednaoui, Omar Effendi, Rivoli, and Hannaux remained. The culture of dazzling service, panache, and style slowly faded, although some of the tailors and dressmakers who worked in these stores continued to offer their services for those able to pay for them. According to Abaza, even talented shoemakers still rendered services to maintain the "well-heeled" men and women of Cairo and Alexandria (Abaza 2006).

The newly nationalized stores served as showcases for the public-sector companies, where growing numbers of families could access refrigerators, radios, and televisions, as well as more practical items for example, tables, chairs, and desks. The stores offered these items on installment so that only a small fraction, about one-fifth to one-fourth of the price, would be necessary in advance. Those who could afford to shop in Paris, London, Rome, or Beirut (before 1975) chose to do so rather than continue to suffer the deteriorating quality of Egyptian fashion. Furthermore, a black market existed in consumer goods that were in high demand, but not produced (well) by the public sector, for example, bras, bathing suits, makeup, and the newer technology in small appliances. The latter included smaller radios, new cassette recorders as well as any other small kitchen appliance that could easily fit in a suitcase (Abaza 2006).

Most Egyptians (due to age or class) had not been part of the great prerevolutionary departmental store culture, but as education and incomes expanded so too did the desire for more goods and appliances. There were three inter-related prongs to this process. One strand of consuming desires came from the many Egyptians, particularly officers, sent abroad on missions to study first largely in the Eastern Bloc, but later in the United States where they witnessed firsthand different foods, goods, and varieties of appliances. By the missions of the 1970s in the United States, those individuals had the opportunity to actually purchase (small) items that they could bring back home. Some could even visit relatives that had immigrated to the United States, literally living the American dream.

By the 1970s changes in the economy and changes in the way in which the government distributed its subsidized, rationed goods, reduced the ability of even the "wealthy" to afford a complete staff of domestic servants. The decline of domestic service meant that more Egyptians who previously relied on servants to wash clothing and dishes required better machines and soap to do that work. Laundry in most upper-class households was done weekly by someone coming from outside, whereas other domestic chores were done by a household staff that might include maid, cook, serving boy or man (perhaps several), doorman, and gardener. With the opening of the economy in the 1970s, more Egyptians began seeking the larger appliances that became available in greater numbers of brands with increasing quality.

Abaza points out that Egyptians used to keep large quantities of dry goods, for example, rice, sugar, and tea, in a pantry, kept under lock and key. They stockpiled in fear of government shortages, and they were concerned about servant pilfering. In the 1960s, mothers who had been convinced of the utility of store-bought formula hoarded this largely imported dry good when it became available at the local pharmacy. By the 1980s these shortages did not exist and new types of foods as well as new means for storage and cooking became available. Middle- and upper-class Egyptians began purchasing more than one refrigerator as well as a "deeb (deep) freezer" to store such items. Those working in the Gulf or simply going on pilgrimage were among the first to bring back microwave ovens before they became readily available. Gulf remittances also enabled Egypt's lower middle class and peasants to experience the consumer dream for the first time in the 20th century as workers sent their families money to purchase the first televisions, refrigerators, and semi-automatic washing machines.

Infitah also brought American television shows to Egypt, which in turn created new consuming desires. One of the early and highly successful series in Egypt was *Dallas*. The antics of the wealthy Texas clan kept Egyptians glued to their new television sets, even though some of the racier scenes had been edited. Everyone wanted to know who shot JR; but before they could find out, the government deemed the series morally deficient and pulled it from the air. Nevertheless, Dallas opened the door for other dramas, for example, *Dynasty*, *Knot's Landing*, and *The Bold & the Beautiful*. The popularity of the American series inspired new boutiques in keeping with the trend, for example, "Dallas" and "Sue Ellen." The stores were not Texas-themed, nor were they necessarily Western, but they evoked the style and the consumption of the wealthy classes represented by the women of Dallas. Just as the wealth and the consumerism of infitah began to dominate the streets of the cities, an equally powerful counter-message arose in Islamic trends. In the 1970s tank tops, bikinis, miniskirts, and sleeveless dresses were all common among urban women, but progressively through the 1980s, sleeves, hemlines, and the acceptability of ordinary bathing suits for adult woman all declined.

The Rise of the Mall and New Fashion Trends

As women's fashions changed and Islamic trends took hold, a new fashion of Islamic chic did not replace the old styles but emerged alongside them. There still existed many conservative women who saw dressing in overtly colorful or decorated clothes as subverting the requirements for modesty dictated by the Quran. Other women continued to dress as they always had, perhaps moderating sleeve and hemlines. Still other women accustomed to a lifetime of fashion, but now choosing to cover everything other than their face and hands, wanted to do so with style. New stores, for example, Huda lil-Muḥaggibat (Huda for the Veiled Ones) opened to meet the demand with special clothing for work, leisure, and special occasions. Women could now even purchase an Islamic bathing suit.

While people might still go downtown for shopping, by the late 1980s or early 1990s the once glorious downtown had deteriorated and Azbakiyya Gardens was in a long, slow process of redevelopment. New forms of shopping were emerging. In 1989 the Yamama Center, Egypt's first shopping mall, opened on the island of Zamalek, an elite neighborhood in Cairo. Abaza describes the process of mall development in Egypt as one bringing together foreign capital (often Saudi), foreign expertise, as well as local capital. In the past three decades more than two dozen malls have been built. Some, for example, the World Trade Center lie barren, whereas competitors Nile City and Arcadia thrive just a short walk up the Corniche in the neighborhood of Bulaq. Beginning in the 1960s, the government began a renewal process of this historic quarter. On the waterfront, Bulaq had been a major port and marketplace housing the previously discussed *wikalas* as well as other important forms of urban architecture, such as mosques, bathhouses, fountains, and schools. The government built the TV station, the foreign ministry, and the National Library/Archives along this corridor, which is close to Liberation Square downtown (Midan Tahrir). Sadat even relocated thousands of families as some of the new buildings went up. As the process continued under Mubarak, the hotels, malls, and offices have literally sucked the water pressure away from the working-class neighborhood surrounding the high-rent, Nile-front complexes. The unsuccessful World Trade Center stands as an odd skeleton in the hybridized neighborhood. Zamalek's Yamama Center, once a rare and popular gem in the Cairo landscape is now largely abandoned aside from the high season for Gulf visitors in the summer.

The City Stars Mall between Heliopolis and Medinat Nasr embodies the latest mall model adopted from the Gulf. Unlike shopping downtown or in crowded Zamalek, up to 6,000 cars can park at the City Stars garage. The shopping complex contains residential and hotel space, a food court, entertainment pavilion, international designers, for example, Tommy Hilfiger, Givenchy, and Calvin Klein, and successful local retailers, for example, Baraka Optics. There is even a *suq* (market) area where tourists can buy trinkets without the noise, smell, pollution, and bargaining associated with Khan al-Khalili (traditional bazaar area). Relatively few Egyptians can afford to eat at the food court, let alone shop at the wide range of stores offered by the mall, but as long as one dresses neatly and comports himself or herself properly, he or she can enjoy the air conditioning and window shopping free of charge. As such the mall becomes a place to see and be seen. It has become the locus for short stories and novels, for example, *Being Abbas al-Abd* (see Literature).

According to Abaza, all of Cairo's malls have a flavor, personality, or client base. The newer malls in Heliopolis, Medinat Nasr, and the satellite cities attract an upper-middle-class clientele. Initially, at the early malls, those in traditional clothing were not allowed entrance, that is, only those in clean, Western clothes were permitted entrance. Nevertheless, this requirement disenfranchised Gulf Arabs with a great deal of buying power. Although some Gulf women and men shed their conservatism and traditions in Cairo, a broad spectrum of clothing exists. Mall security, often retired military personnel, are quite able to distinguish between the peasant or working-class

Egyptian and the Gulf tourist in traditional garb. Even in the suburbs, malls can garner a reputation. The Wonderland Mall became known as a pickup spot, and many families stopped patronizing it in favor of more "decent" malls. Ironically, the connection between consumerism and social networking has remained throughout the centuries. Despite its amusement park, six-screen cinema, discotheque, eateries, internet café, upscale coffee shops, and restaurants, Wonderland has struggled to survive. Some scholars speculate that the existence of so many abandoned malls, alongside the continued creation of new malls, is linked to their relationship with organized crime or money-laundering; however, such theories have yet to be proven.

In the past few years, downtown Cairo has seen a bit of renewal. While Azbakiyya Park is not the enormous, city-center garden it once was, it has been restored as a pedestrian greenway. As well al-Azhar park opened in 2005 as a 74-acre park. It is a bastion of green bringing people back to the city. Several other urban renewal projects have taken place both to add more green to Cairo, as well as to renew landmarks, particularly after the 1992 earthquake. Some of the projects include Café Riche, Groppi's tearoom, the Cairo Stock Exchange, some chancelleries, and a few of the grand department store buildings. Some malls have opened downtown, and even a few former department stores have become mini-malls themselves. The Talaat Harb Mall and the Bustan Center downtown attract a middle- to lower-middle-class youthful clientele. The Tiring building, the original Chemla branch, and the Abdin Square Omar Effendi have been subdivided into a series of smaller stalls, pushcarts, and/or smaller stores.

The New Coffeehouse Culture

A major socializing trend among youth has been the new coffee shops that have emerged all over Cairo, its suburbs, Alexandria, the major tourist cities of the Sinai, and generally in urban areas. These new coffee shops are distinct culturally from those discussed in Sports and Leisure section of this chapter. The latter are masculine spaces that traditionally served coffee and tea. In recent times soft drinks have been added to some menus. Nevertheless, the mainstay of the menu was Arab (Turkish) coffee and tea, the space was generally masculine, and there was no food served. Men and women patronize the new coffee shops, and the menus are trendy and creative, including sandwiches, salads, soups, and even some entrees. The serving staff is multilingual—almost a hearkening back to the days of yesteryear in department stores—and they wear a uniform in conformity with the décor of the venue. Rather than French being the shared language of the elite, English is the domain of the coffee shop and distinguishes those patrons who have studied at the "right" schools, for even the workers must speak passable English.

The new coffeehouse is a bit more than a Starbucks-i-zation of Egypt. In his recent book on the Starbucks phenomenon, Bryant Simon argues that the Starbucks model creates isolation in which individuals remain wrapped up in their own little laptop-ensconced worlds rather than becoming community-focused, socially enabled citizens who desire to engage with the world around them. While Starbucks exists in

Egypt, its association with the United States, its demonization by talk-show clerics, and perhaps its lack of social organization have made it one of the less popular of the new coffee shops—which are known as just that—"coffee shops" in English. The new breed of coffee shops cost many times more than a traditional beverage. According to a recent study by de Koning, this exclusivity keeps out "unqualified" guests. If the simple cost—which could be as much as 15 times more for a designer coffee beverage, for example, a frappuccino—does not keep out the patron, managers have door policies that do, based upon appearance: clothing, behavior (overly flirtatious), or even perceived potential for trouble. This exclusion is applied to male and female alike. Both rambunctious men and gold-digging women are excluded, that is, anyone perceived to be crossing behavioral or class boundaries (2006).

Whereas young men have greater leeway and options for socializing, the number of respectable options for women is limited. Men are able to congregate in a wide variety of inexpensive or free public spaces, for example, movie houses, the zoo, parks, traditional coffeehouses, or even on the streets. Before the 1990s, the only public place where unmarried women could congregate was at sporting clubs. The new coffee shops created a mixed gender space where women could come after work or on weekends to socialize. Since Islamic culture frowns upon drinking, bars and discotheques are not permissible for most unmarried girls. Thus, for upper-middle-class women, the coffee shop is a safe place to mix and mingle with friends and potentially a place to meet others of the opposite sex, who are of the same social class. The type of coffee shop and the willingness of women to cross those boundaries is created within the space of the shop. Some have music blasting out from one (or more) of Egypt's Arabic music video channels. As Simon argues in his work on Starbucks, the layout of tables and chairs impacts how clientele interact with one another. Some of the coffeehouses have both quiet areas as well as larger group areas, and still other shops have more open seating areas that promote what de Koning terms "chance encounters." Décor ranges from stainless steel modern to warm and comfortable. Women with concerns about their reputation do not frequent shops with completely open layouts, opting for the privacy of more closed settings (de Konig 2006).

According to de Koning, conversations in mixed group settings at these coffee shops is frank, bold, and deals with issues of respectability, virtue, and reputation as well as topics of current interest. She argues that unlike the closed Starbucks world, they create community and codes of normality for the upper-middle class (2006). *Enigma* magazine represents the voice of upper-class concerns and Amy Mowafi's FeMail column and her Facebook link to her magazine and radio show is evidence of the kinds of conversations that take place among young, well-to-do Egyptians. The following are some recent topics: the honesty equation, how much do we tell our partners—is it ever OK to lie?; celebration of singledom; do bad guys and girls have more fun?; what's love got to do with it: what are our priorities in a relationship?; what is a number: does age matter in a relationship?; should housework be divided 50/50 if both the man and the woman in a marriage work? In other words, conversations are not particularly different than in the United States, but there is a greater concern for women's reputation. Even among the most Westernized and elite of Egyptians, opinions reflect a melding of indigenous and Western values. In a rant in her FeMail column, Mowafi pondered the topic of going "Dutch" on dates. The subheading of the title reflected her basically Islamic orientation—"what is mine is mine." Although most of the piece discussed her willingness to spend money on her friends and various beauty rituals, her bottom line is she will not split costs with her man. She never comes out and states her reason, but according to Islam, a woman's property is all her own and a man must provide for her at the level to which she is accustomed—hence, the "what is hers is hers."

Internet Culture

The new coffee shops are generally wireless hot zones where people can bring laptops and connect to the internet. The internet first arrived to Egypt in the early 1990s and became available to the public in the mid-1990s. Nevertheless, it was only after 2002 when the monopoly on subscriptions owned by Telecom Egypt ended and competition made the internet more available both to individual users as well as to entrepreneurs. Now one can find Wi-Fi technology everywhere from the new coffee shops to McDonalds as well as specialized internet cafés.

Internet cafés have blossomed not only in wealthy districts, but in middle- and working-class neighborhoods as well. While peasants, working class, and many adults over the age of 45 or 50 do not know how to use the internet proficiently, someone in their family or social circle probably does. Certainly by class, the statistics change, only the most elderly of elite Egyptians refuse to become computer literate. Children, teenagers, and the younger generation tend to be computer savvy, and their families depend upon them to keep in touch with family members who are working in the Gulf or have relocated in the West. In addition, internet cafés provide a wide variety of games that would otherwise be inaccessible to middle- and lower-middle-class children. Hourly fees, which vary according to neighborhood, allow children to spend their pocket money or their *eidiyya* (holiday gift money) on an activity that they enjoy. Children often pool their money to play these games together sharing the hourly fee of one computer.

The internet has also created a new set of panic and fears for the state. After the de-monopolization of the internet, the chief justice of the Cairo Criminal Court urged the state to take strong action regarding the regulation of the internet, and the state responded to this request with vigor establishing a unit within the Ministry of the Interior to monitor its use. This monitoring fluctuates in waves of greater and lesser restrictions of civil liberties, and it targets enemies of the state using hot-button issues of public morals, perversion, and immorality. Accusations of entrapment have been laid against the government. Even the casual tourist in Egypt will notice that one day he or she will visit the internet café and simply pay a fee, and during the next few visits he or she will have to register his or her passport number, along with every Egyptian who must sign in with his or her national identification card, because the state is suddenly taking an interest in who is using each and every computer. Under Mubarak the state took a high profile in its crackdown on homosexuality and what it deemed as perversion, while overlooking other breaches of the Islamic moral order, which it claimed to be maintaining, for example, adultery, prostitution, and so on, which were also taking place over the internet.

Egypt and Tunisia have repeatedly appeared on Reporters without Borders list of "Enemies of the Internet" due to the two governments' heavy-handed treatment of individuals who freely express their opinions. After the Jasmine Revolution and January 25 movement the groups removed both offenders; however, it remains to be seen, particularly in Egypt with the military in control whether or not intellectual freedom will reign.

Nightlife: Bars, Clubs, and Discotheques

Since Egypt was home to some of the earliest brewers and winemakers, it should not surprise the reader that such ancient traditions do not easily fade away despite the fact that alcohol consumption is forbidden in Islam. While still permitted among the Coptic population, the vast majority of Muslims follow codes of law that utilize analogy, thus prohibiting all forms of alcoholic beverages. Historically, it is clear that all Muslims did not follow these dictates. Muslims and Christians celebrated Coptic festivals publicly up until the 15th century. These rituals frequently involved the consumption of alcohol. The Fatimid ruler al-Hakim (r. 996–1021), who was known for his eccentricity, outlawed alcohol not only for Muslims (who were obviously partaking), but also for Christians and Jews who used wine in religious services. He dumped large quantities of the beverage into the Nile to prevent its consumption. At other times the state tried to profit from its consumption by taxing the product in the Ayyubid period (1171–1250) as reported by the chronicler al-Maqrizi.

Taverns as we know them in the West existed during Greco-Roman period (fourth century BCE to seventh century AD), but did not appear again until after the French invasion (Lewicka 2005). Some coffeehouses, particularly in areas where mixed populations lived, may have discretely served a variety of beverages. Goitein's research on the Jewish community indicates that the medieval Jewish community did not sponsor taverns of any sort, despite lack of prohibition on drinking, sales, or consumption. Mario Ruiz's research, based on court records from the 19th century, indicate that Alexandrian coffeehouses (which only date back to the 16th century) served more than coffee and more than men.

Chroniclers refer to wine houses and wine cellars and sites that produced fermented barley, but it is not clear if these are places where people actually gathered to enjoy drinking or whether these were simply sites of production and/or sales. The linkage between drinking and illicit activities for example, prostitution, drugs, and gambling certainly existed at particular locales, for example, the Nilometer and the Hakimi canal, where people were known to gather and partake of immoral activities during Fatimid, Ayyubid, and mamluk times (10th to 15th centuries) (Lewicka 2005). Thus, it is not surprising that when various forms of drinking establishments and dance halls opened in the period after the French occupation (1798–1801), people would associate these venues with dangerous behavior. Muhammad al-Muwaylihi wrote a Rip van Winkle-like story about someone from the early 19th century who awakens in the late 19th century, and he critiques these establishments, seeing them as a dangerous mingling of the sexes and the classes. In reality, barriers existed with respect to class; however, women could enter. There still existed the notion that only a disreputable woman would enter such an establishment. During the age of Ismail (r. 1863–1879), who systematically developed downtown Cairo, and after the British occupation (1882), the number taverns and dance halls in the capital increased. These were male-dominated spaces and generally only foreign women and Egyptian women of ill-repute could be found there.

In the liberal period (1922–1952), among the elite, casinos, nightclubs, bars, and other forums for drinking, dancing, and socializing multiplied. King Faruq himself became a regular on the pyramids road circuit. In other words, such establishments were no longer connected with vice. A range of quality existed, and the best bands learned the latest Western dance rhythms to play at elite clubs, interspersed with indigenous dance that (as is the case today) may or may not have been performed by Egyptian dancers. Egyptian film glamorized love scenes toasted by champagne, seduced by accomplished ballroom dance, and accompanied by both Western and Arab music. As it became more acceptable for women to be out in public generally, the quantity and quality of the places increased as did their acceptability. In the semi-autobiographical *Love is Like Water*, Samia Serageldin tells how her uncle and aunt fell in love and of their attraction to one another as documented in a society column interview. Their love of music, dance, and nightlife was a decisive factor in their initial compatibility. The ease with which the upper class danced, drank, and listened to Western music was not necessarily shared by all Egyptians even of the middle class. In the 1947 movie *Fatma*, the middle-class nurse played by Umm Kulthum is appalled by the bar in the home of Anwar Wagdi, unlike his former cocktail-sipping girlfriend played by Zouzou Chakib. A woman from the lower middle class who worked her way up to the middle class by education would not approve of violating the dictates of Islam, especially by setting up a permanent temple to this violation in one's home.

The period of the 1960s and 1970s was an era of more openness and less restrictions as the habits of the elite trickled down to the middle class. As discussed in section Egyptian Music of this chapter, both the Egyptian music industry and Western music boomed in Egypt. After the defeat of 1967 and the Iranian Revolution, the resurgence of Islamic trends put forth in motion a critique of Western culture and its negative influences, including drinking, dancing, and music. Most luxury hotels and even many four-star hotels kept their discotheques and numerous drinking establishments to service not just the tourists, but also the large numbers of foreigners resident in Egypt. Egyptians who wanted to drink could continue to drink. The Stella brewing company and the Gianclis winery both survived nationalization and return to the private sector, despite criticism and attack from Islamists.

Egyptian film celebrates both closet and public drinkers identifying class distinctions and providing a barometer for public opinion. The main character, played by Adel Imam, in *Terrorism and Kabob* (1992) is meant to represent the average Egyptian suffering from all the problems and frustrations of the middle class. In one hysterically funny scene of the movie, he comes home on Thursday night (the equivalent of the American Friday), ready to celebrate the weekend with a special sexual foreplay ritual in which his wife dons a wig and they plan to split a Stella beer. Stella locals are about the size of a beer and half (4.5 percent alcohol and 500 milliliters), and the couple conveniently keeps one hidden in their refrigerator in a large envelope. Unfortunately, the couple's romantic interlude is interrupted, and the husband ends up with an earful of complaint for spilling beer on the clean floor. In other words, there are still average folks who do drink on occasion, but not necessarily to excess. In the aforementioned movie scene, although the children "caught" the parents either in or on the verge of a variety of suspicious acts, the only problem that the wife seemed to have was that her floor got dirty. While one could interpret the husband as metaphorically sullying her with the beer, there was no stated criticism.

In *A Citizen, A Detective, and A Thief* (2001), Selim is a worldly individual who drinks, dances, writes, and engages in premarital sex. Over the course of the film he becomes even more successful. He represents the class that (re)emerged with the privatization policies that started under Sadat but blossomed under Mubarak and brought forth a whole new level of wealth, as Amy Mowafi calls them, the "haves" and the "have yachts". Meeting the entertainment demand for this class as well as visitors and investors from the Gulf who come to Cairo to have fun, is an enterprise in and of itself. Downtown Cairo, the hotels, Mohandiseen, Maadi, the satellite cities, Alexandria, the Red Sea beach resorts, and even Luxor and Aswan have thriving night spots to meet this demand. Particularly in and around Cairo there is more variety: sports bars, piano bars, a jazz club, discotheques, and clubs catering to different ages and sexual orientations, whereas at resorts one is more likely to find bars and music geared toward the 20-something generation. Before visiting Egypt, the traveler should read recent reviews because hotspots change quickly. Compare several different reviews carefully checking dates to make sure that the reviews are recent. Clubbing in Egypt can be quite an experience where one can meet people from all over the world, including unveiled Gulf women in sleeveless clothing. Whereas Western tourists come to see the pyramids, relics, monuments, and museums, many Gulf tourists come to Egypt for the nightlife and clubbing. In the summer, they are lazily making their way back to their rooms between 4:00 and 6:00 A.M. just when the most zealous Western tourists are getting up to beat the heat (Wynn 2007).

REFERENCES

Abaza, Mona. *Changing Consumer Cultures of Modern Egypt: Cairo's Urban Reshaping.* Leiden: Brill, 2006.

Bahgat, Hosam. "Egypt's Virtual Protection of Morality." *Middle East Report,* No. 230 (Spring 2004): 22–25.

Kerboeuf, Ann-Claire. "The Cairo Fire of 26 January 1952 and Interpretations of History." In *Re-envisioning Egypt, 1919–1952.* Goldschmidt, Arthur, et al., ed. Cairo: AUC Press, 2005, 194–216.

de Koning, Anouk. "Café Latte and Caesar Salad: Cosmopolitan Belonging in Cairo's Coffee Shops." In *Cairo Cosmopolitan: Politics, Culture, and Urban Space in the New Globalized Middle East.*

Kupferschmidt, Uri. "Who Needed Department Stores in Egypt?: From Orosdi-Back to Omar Effendi." *Middle Eastern Studies* 43 (2007): 175–92.

Lewicka, Paulina. "Restaurants, Inns, and Taverns that Never Were: Some Reflections on Public Consumption in Medieval Cairo." *Journal of the Economic and Social History of the Orient* 48 (1) (2005): 40–91.

Ruiz, Mario. "Rethinking Cosmopolitanism in Middle East Studies: Case of Alexandria." Roundtable discussion paper. Annual Meeting of the Middle East Studies Association, 2006.

Singerman, Diane, and Amar, Paul, eds. *Cairo Cosmipolitan: Politics, Culture, and Urban Space in the New Globalized Middle East.* Cairo: AUC Press, 2006.

Simon, Bryant. *Everything but the Coffee: Learning about America from Starbucks.* Berkeley, CA: University of California Press, 2009.

Wynn, L. L. *Pyramids and Nightclubs.* Austin, TX: University of Texas Press, 2007.

PERFORMING ARTS: THEATER, DANCE, FILM

Theater: The Beginnings

Like most things in Egypt, the history of theater dates back to ancient times. While there may not have been specially constructed buildings for productions (theaters), evidence of specific types of performance dates back to the third millennia BCE. Recordings of passion plays regarding the myth of Osirus (see Chapter 2) are recorded on stone stela referred to as Ikhnernefert or Ikhernofert. These performances often took place at the temple of Edfu, as well as other locations and coincided with the festival of Horus. Two key players in such celebrations were Hathor, the goddess of music, dance, and the arts and Bes, another god associated with music, song, and dance. In these performances Osirus's evil brother Seth, represented by a live hippopotamus, might actually be killed on stage. Such plays would end with the resurrection of Osirus (Gunnels 2002).

With the Ptolemies, Greek forms of production arrived, as well as the theater as a venue for performance. Even in provincial towns a theater could hold as many as 10,000 spectators. Greek theater was part of the cult of Dionysus, the god of wine, sexuality, fertility, and agriculture. While the Greeks were unconcerned about incorporating Egyptian elements into their productions, the cult of Dionysus shared a number of similarities with that of Hathor, who also had connections to fertility, festivity, refreshment, and the arts. Papyri indicate that there were performances of classic Greek comedies and tragedies from authors such as Euripides, Aristophanes, Aeschylos, and Menander. As was typical of Greek theater, most scholars believe that all parts were performed by men wearing masks.

In Roman times spectacle marked theatrical performance. While many Westerners are familiar with the blood and gore aspects of gladiator fights, animal sacrifice, and killing Christians for sport, the Romans also practiced pantomime and other forms of drama that do not easily make their way into the historical record. Nevertheless, a short Roman play, *Charition* written sometime before 200 CE was found in Egypt at the Oxyrhynchus Theater (near present-day al-Bahnasa). Even though Byzantine era Christianity looked down upon the theater for its lack of morals, productions continued. In particular, mime, distinct from silent pantomime of today, was quite popular. Unlike previous forms of theater it had a wide-ranging audience with respect to class, and its content was varied. The third-century CE author Herodas (sometimes spelled Herondas) authored a number of Iambic mimes (*mimiambi*) discovered in the 19th century. Their bawdy content so shook the Europeans, who discovered them, that until recently they have received little attention. They are quite interesting not only for their blatant sexuality, but also for the prominent role given to women, slaves, and ordinary folks. A few titles bear witness to their content: "The Go-Between," "The Whoremonger," "The Cobbler," and "The Schoolmaster" (Herondas 1921).

Shadow Theater

Since religious authorities frowned upon theater, some scholars speculate that most theater, apart from mime and comedy, had died out by the time that the Muslim conquerors arrived in the seventh century. Monotheism, be it the Christianity of the Byzantines or Islam of the Arabs, would be unaccepting of Greek drama, which relied on the conflict between the individual and divine forces (in the plural). The history of theater in Egypt usually jumps from the Greeks to the French invasion (1798) or to the shadow theater of the Middle Ages.

Shadow theater known as *karagöz* (the name of the main character whose name literally means "black-eyed" in Turkish) or *khayal al-zill* (Arabic for "shadows of fancy") used both Turkish and Egyptian colloquial dialect, and it dates back to at least Fatimid times (10th to 12th centuries). A well-appointed shadow theater might have several musicians, for example, tambourine, flute, and drum, as well as assistant puppeteers. The only necessity is a single performer, the shadow-master, who uses a stand similar to a puppet theater, which is lit from behind. The projection of light on to a white backing creates the shadow imagery and a world of illusion that helped writers push boundaries in terms of content, which could be sexual, comical, political, or all of the above. The puppets are translucent leather or material or paper placed on sticks or rods controlled by the master, who provided the movement and voices (with a special voice distortion instrument for Karagöz). Learning the skill of a shadow-master requires one to memorize a repertoire of performances (at least enough to last the month of Ramadan); the ability to manipulate multiple pieces simultaneously; the dynamism to create and sustain characters; and the charisma to engage the audience with sound effects, bodily humor, and the like.

The shadow theater required other professionals as well. A special cutter cut camel leather or other material (e.g., fish skin) to make the puppets using special knives or scissors. After cutting, the character would then be carefully stitched. Animating was another occupation, that of the *megariz*, the person who pierced and rodded the puppet in readiness for performance. Finally, no shadow performance would be complete without a good script (Feeney 1999). The most famous shadow playwright, some of whose manuscripts are still in existence, is Ibn Danyal (1248–1311). The overall structure of a play tends to follow the same format: two-part prologue whereby God, Muhammad, and his descendents are thanked followed by those who made the production possible, including the master, the writer, the puppet makers, and even the audience. Smart masters usually know that the government should be praised as well, particularly if it is to be mocked later in the production. The play begins in earnest with some kind of song or dance, and the narrator introduces the audience to the characters. Common plot themes include disguise, mistaken identity, cross-dressing, slapstick humor, ethnic humor, violence, and sexual innuendo. Plays often conclude in song, and the narrator urges the audience to return.

In addition to shadow plays, prior to the introduction of European theater, Egypt had a guild for entertainers which included *ḥabaẓiya* or *moḥabbazeen*, male actors who performed satirical or farcical comedies. Often these troupes traveled and performed in front of generally male audiences, which 19th-century travelers remarked as having been observed (at a distance) by women. Apparently, the genre was so enjoyed by the royal women that Ellen Chennells, governess to the Khedive Ismail's daughter Zeinab, reports that the women themselves put on their own shows. Ironically, the ruling class was usually a target of this group and taxation a major issue, as were corruption, servant–master relations, religious minorities, and sexuality. The plays were short and did not allow for significant character or plot development, but the genre itself had stock characters, themes, and issues recognizable to the audience: the corrupt official, the clever slave, the gullible master, and so on.

From the French Invasion to the British Occupation

When the French arrived in 1798, they began organizing familiar entertainment in and around Azbakiyya. In addition to the dance halls, restaurants, bars, brothels, and gaming quarters, Napoleon made arrangements for a theater to be built and sent for a small professional troupe of comedians, some ballet dancers, marionette puppeteers, women, and some distillers; all of these people would make Egypt more entertaining for the troops. Amateur groups entertained in the meantime, and not surprisingly the first theater was a target of public hatred and it burned in a revolt in the spring of 1800. Although he left Egypt, Napoleon made good on his promise to send professionals; however, the troupe was on board a ship captured by English cruisers, and General Menou negotiated their return to France (Sadgrove 1996).

The large number of European advisors to the royal family, the burgeoning cosmopolitan commercial community in Alexandria, new forms of education and philanthropy, as well as the advent of journalism as a profession all worked together to create theater in Egypt over the course of the 19th century. A small European community, first in Alexandria, and later in Cairo began sponsoring amateur theatrical and operatic groups. These began in the days of Muhammad Ali (r. 1805–1848), and by the 1840s the Europeans, plus the ruling and commercial elite who understood European languages could actually sustain a short opera season that traveled to the imperial capital (Istanbul) as well.

By the 1840s European travelers wrote regularly about the "Teatro del Cairo" which appeared to have both amateur and professional troupes. Writers usually described the cosmopolitan nature of the audience, which included Egyptians, Syrians, Greeks, Armenians, and Jews. Furthermore, there was a connection between philanthropy and performance since travelers often commented on the charitable destination of proceeds, for example, the poor or the blind of the city. Guidebooks for Egypt indicate the ability of travelers to attain tickets at major hotels without cost.

By the 1850s and 1860s, theater culture became more entrenched in Egypt with the arrival of larger numbers of Europeans, as businessmen, missionaries, and bankers took advantage of the changes in laws regarding land and finance (see Chapter 2). In Alexandria, the European, Zizinia, Alfieri, and Rossini theaters all opened. In Cairo, much of the theater activity was more informal in cafés and bars, up until the opening of French Comedy Theater (Théâtre de Comédie), which was sponsored by subventions from Ismail (r. 1863–1879) and opened in conjunction with the Suez Canal festivities of 1869. While much more is made of the opening of the Cairo Opera House (see also Chapter 2), the theater was part of Ismail's renovations to Azbakiyya Park and Gardens, the type of place where Europeans or Eurpeanized Egyptians could ride in boats, buy food from vendors, listen to military bands, venture to indoor or outdoor theater, watch street performers, or even have their picture taken. In 1869 Azbakiyya was also the site of Egypt's first standing circus sponsored as well by the Khedive Ismail. The circus would move to Alexandria during the sweltering heat of the summer. Finally, never content with the minimum, Ismail built an open-air hippodrome near the circus, designed to hold 8,000 spectators of equestrian performances.

Built on land confiscated from tenants opposite the French Comedy Theater, the Opera House had a pre-opening in 1869 and an official opening in 1871. Not only did Ismail sponsor the theater and opera out of his own pocket, he apparently made sure that pashas subscribe to the opera and that they sustain a certain number of performers. Royal patronage was so significant that when the Khedive's daughter

POVERTY, CHARITY, AND PERFORMANCE

Egypt's upper class consisted of Muslims, Christians, and Jews who were actively engaged in a variety of charitable organizations in the 19th and early 20th centuries. The nascent press served as a reminder of their duties as members of their various faiths and increasingly as citizens to help the "deserving poor" of the nation. The blind, the deaf, and certain categories of poor, like widows or children, needed assistance, as opposed to healthy men who could help themselves. In the late-19th century these organizations would be significant in raising money to build schools, orphanages, and asylums. By the early 20th century, photography would become a key element in documenting this work for the press and in advertising fund-raising events, such as plays put on for charitable causes.

CIRCUS AND HIPPODROME

The Hippodrome opened just two years after the Circus in 1871 on nearby Gamil Street. It was an oval-shaped, open-air stadium built to seat 8,000 spectators. The arena contained special curtained boxes for upper-class women that concealed them from others. From press advertisements, it appears that performances were generally on Fridays and Sundays. By 1872, the Circus closed and was demolished, which allowed the Opera House to expand. The Hippodrome was presumed to be a better venue for the Circus anyway. An ice-skating rink opened on the former site of the Circus in 1877. With bankruptcy, the Hippodrome was sold in 1879, but it appears to have remained in the family as it became a royal stable by 1880.

Zeinab (b. 1859) died in August 1875 and the entire family and entourage (employees included) went into deep mourning for several months, an economic slump devastated the performing community. A delegation of artistes visited the court to explain the circumstances, and on January 10, 1876 the Khedive himself, accompanied by a number of his sons, went to the theater to restore the cultural economy.

The opera and comedy theaters were new enough in 1869 that newspaper announcements necessitated explanations to readers of the "gestures" and "performances" contained in each venue. In his study of 19th-century theater, P. C. Sadgrove notes private Egyptian schools were becoming increasingly aware of theater. They advertised performances, awards, and writing contests in the burgeoning press. He remarks that nationalist or proto-nationalist writers saw in the theater its didactic potential, first realized under the direction of Yaqub Sanua (1839–1912), an Egyptian Jew perhaps more famous for his political and satirical writings and cartoons. Sanua, conversant in several languages, including Arabic, Italian, and French, believed that Egyptians should have access to theater in their mother tongue. His first play (*A One Act Operetta in Colloquial Dialect*) was boldly based on a rumor regarding a breach of the harem of princess Nazli, a daughter of Muhammad Ali, by an Italian gentleman, using the artifice of women's dress. Playing on local capital (gossip), using easily understood language, and some of the leitmotifs of shadow theater, for example, cross-dressing, Sanua captured the hearts of his audience, including the Khedive himself. Although his original troupe was all male, he later found Christian, Jewish, and poor girls willing to work as actresses much to the delight of audiences. Sanua's real intent was political and didactic as told through a *karagöz*-like character in another play, who informed the audience that theater is civilization, progress, and refining manners. As Sanua became more critical of the Khedive's government in his art, he found his theater shutdown, only to continue publishing his message first in Egypt and later from exile in Paris. Interestingly enough, Sanua's famous political journal, *The Man with Blue Glasses*, often contained theatrical dialogue critiquing Ismail and governmental mismanagement.

The next burst in activity of Arab theater came with the arrival of Syrian journalists in Egypt. Both the sectarian conflict of the 1860s in Syria (note that Syria in this time period means Greater Syria and includes what we now refer to as Lebanon) as well as greater censorship elsewhere in the Ottoman empire led many journalists generally, and Syrian Christians in particular to Egypt. In the absence of political parties, newspapers would come to serve the function of political parties. Many of the individuals arriving in this period would establish important and longstanding papers, the most significant of which is *al-Ahram*, founded in 1876 by the Taqla brothers. In the mid-1870s, Salim al-Naqqash, a Syrian journalist with family roots in Syrian theater, convinced the Khedive Ismail to renew an Arab theater in Egypt with a Syrian troupe, which included men and women. By 1877, Naqqash had begun collaborating with another talented Syrian, Adib al-Ishaq, and by 1878 when the theater business was no longer profitable the two turned to journalism. Other scholars have suggested that it was activist and Islamic reformer Jamal al-Din al-Afghani (see Chapter 2) who urged the men to turn their talents to journalism. Both theories suggest a link between theater, politics, and nationalist agendas. In any case, the Arab theater fell into the hands of its leading actor Yusuf al-Khayyat, who returned to the Khedive for patronage.

Khayyat appears to have had some success by moving his troupe about the delta, giving performances in Alexandria, Damietta, Zagazig, and Cairo. Comedy and farce seemed to have been the preferred genres, and performances were sometimes given for charitable societies. Spreading the medium, an actor, formerly in Naqqash and Khayyat's troupes, al-Qardashi loaned his expertise to productions in his wife's private school in Alexandria beginning in 1877. While 1878 saw blossoming productions in Cairo and Alexandria from these groups, the following year marked decline for the theater since the Khedive Ismail was deposed and with his deposition went support for Khayyat's troupe, and reduced governmental support for the comedy theater and the Opera House.

AL-AHRAM

al-Ahram is the oldest continuously running newspaper in the Middle East. It began as a weekly newspaper operating out of Alexandria with the Taqla brothers, Salim and Bishara, in 1876; and by 1881 it became a daily. In 1900 it moved to the capital city and to its current offices on al-Galaa St. in 1968. Many famous writers have contributed to the paper over the years, representing a broad spectrum of philosophies: lawyer-politician Ahmad Lutfi-Sayyid, poet Ahmad Shawqi, playwright Tawfiq al-Hakim, litterateur Taha Hussein, feminist author Bint Shati, nobel laureate Naguib Mahfouz, Muslim Brotherhood ideologue Sayyid Qutb actually worked for the paper, and Anglophone authors Ahdaf Soueif and Edward Said. A legacy of the Nassert era (see Chapters 2 and 3) is that the state currently owns controlling interests in the paper.

In 1879, Abdullah Nadim (1843–1896) (see Chapter 2) having met Naqqash and Ishaq became convinced of the theater as a means of articulating with the masses. His experience as a telegraph operator in the palace of the Queen Mother gave him the opportunity to view a number of productions and hear a substantial amount of hard fact as well as gossip. In other words, he had both creative and practical experience for the theater. He was also part of the circle of Jamal al-Din al-Afghani, who pushed his disciples toward publication and activism. His first performance had a classical format, it began with a *qaṣida* (poem) praising the Khedive Tawfiq as well as his ministers. The play centered upon a male embodiment of Egypt, which is odd, because Egypt is almost universally depicted as a woman. Due to many factors, at this point in time it would have been difficult to portray Egypt as a woman. Having the fatherland figure dialogue with the various people of his country to discuss its decline served Nadim's purpose well. The play's first showing was a benefit to raise money for his charitable organization. His intent was to highlight the problems of misrule and to indicate where solutions lay. He then had to praise the ruler again at the end to smooth over the criticism. The language of the play is significant since the Nation (Egypt) spoke in classical Arabic, as did the Bedouin; however, everyone else spoke in Egyptian dialect.

Due to the lack of funding and the increasingly difficult political environment, theater (both European and Arab) fell on hard times in the 1880s. The rallying cry of the Urabi Revolt (1881–1882) was "Egypt for the Egyptians!" (see Chapter 2). All non-Egyptians, including Syrians, felt the bitterness, even as some of them wrote in support of making the government accountable. Among the many people to leave Egypt were prominent figures in the theatrical community, including Qardashi, Naqqash, and Ishaq. Egyptian Nadim would focus his talent on journalism. Nevertheless, his writings were often in dialogues, and even his more formal writings were in a combination of classical and colloquial Arabic so that they could be understood when read aloud, that is, "performed" in homes, on street corners, and in coffeehouse for the illiterate masses.

The Pinnacle of Egyptian Theater, 1882–1952

Between the British Occupation (1882) and World War I, theater continued to develop, but with less state finance and more political motivation. Furthermore, the link that existed between theater and the new educational system as well as philanthropy, served the cause of dramatizing the problems of the occupation and solving the country's social and welfare problems. In her *Nurturing the Nation*, Lisa Pollard discusses the (re)opening of the Arab Theater in 1908 and a speech given by an editor of a children's journal, who linked the theater to nationalism as a place where children learn morals and apply them in their roles uplifting the nation. A key player in this process was Salama Higazi, trained as prayer caller and *munshid*, he opened an Arab Theater in Azbakiyya that combined theater with singing. Many other singers, performers, actors and actors turned directors got their start in his theater. Higazi toured his troupe throughout the delta and North Africa.

New Syrian troupes moved into Egypt and new Egyptian troupes formed, particularly out of the branch formed by Higazi. George Abyad (1880–1959), a Syrian who received practical, royal, and professional training came out of this generation. Having done some acting in his native Beirut, he traveled to Cairo where he worked at the train station in Alexandria (always a locus for theatrical material) and received khedivial support to study theater in Paris, later forming his own company in Egypt in 1910, which continued to be successful in the increasingly competitive market for another two decades. Perhaps the two most famous names that emerge in this era were Egyptians Neguib al-Rihani (1889–1949) and Ali al-Kassar (d. 1957); indeed, they are arguably Egypt's most famous and beloved stage actors of any age.

Neguib al-Rihani got his start in the theater of Aziz al-'Id. The two men, 'Id and Rihani worked in the Franco-Arab theater, which adapted French vaudeville to Egyptian theater, in addition to some of the basic staple farce that had been part of Egyptian productions since the times of the *ḥabaziya* and shadow theater. During World War I the Franco-Arab theater was popular since many European actors had left the country. Also, Arab actors had become part of *faṣl muḍḥik*, funny skits between larger European productions, in which they told jokes, poked fun at government officials, and did impersonations of characters found in the older forms of Arab theater. As one might expect, with frustrations high, the theater offered both a means of criticism of the occupation as well as a safety valve for releasing the tension.

By 1916, as the Franco-Arab Theater came into its own, Rihani and 'Id came to have serious disagreements over *how* French vaudeville should be adapted to the stage. For Rihani, he felt it should be more than just a literal translation, but a cultural and metaphorical translation that created Egyptian characters in Egyptian

---

ENTREPRENEURIALISM, LOVE, THEATRE, AND JOURNALISM: A TALE OF TWO FATIMAS

Egyptian Fatima Rushdi (1908–1996) was a student of Syrian Aziz al-'Id, creator of the first entirely colloquial theatre. Although she had previously done some acting, she was illiterate, and learning how to read advanced her professionally. She married her mentor, and later they created a new troupe under her name. She was (in)famous for both innovations in theatre and her offstage affairs, repeatedly reported in the press.

Fatima "Rose" el-Youssef (d. 1958), came to Egypt from Tripoli (now Lebanon) as a child and learned acting from Iskandar Farah, another Syrian in Egypt. Rose married famous theater names, Mohamed Abd al-Qaddus and Zaki Tulaymat (founder of the Institute of Dramatic Arts in 1930), with whom she had children. She put aside her acting career for that of journalism, creating *Rose el-Youssef* (see Chapters 3 and 5) in 1925. Her son Ihsan Abd al-Qaddus (1919–1990) became a famous writer, and edited her magazine; and her daughter Amal Tulaymat (b. 1924) became a successful businesswoman in the world of art.

circumstances. The format and construction was French farce: character-driven scenes, French songs, accompanied by Western music. The dialogue was a combination of colloquial Egyptian dialect and French, and the humor tapped into indigenous elements of shadow theater and farce. Rihani's signature character, *Kishkish Bey*, was a bumbling village chief with an eye for beautiful, especially Western, women and all things modern, despite his inability to understand them. Ironically, Rihani had no formal theater training other than the two years he spent under the direction of 'Id—his former profession had been as a bank teller. He would spend the rest of his life writing, acting, and directing. As many other actors would (and still continue to) do, Rihani made the transition to screen acting, making about a dozen films before his death. Westerners will often remark that acting in Egyptian film is "so over-the-top" or "too dramatic," perhaps owing to the stage origins of the actors (Abou-Saif 1973).

Ali al-Kassar got his start in Neguib al-Rihani's troupe around 1916 and owes his success as well to the socio-political climate of the time. Kassar's trademark character was *Osman Abd al-Basit*, the staple Nubian character of stage and later film. Much in the same way that child actors on long-running American television series find it difficult to escape their image in a typecast role, Rihani and Kassar could never stray far from *Kishkish Bey* or *Osman*-like roles. According to Eve Troutt Powell, actors were simply expected to reanimate these time-honored personae that were in the cultural understanding of the audience. *Osman* was the "one and only Nubian of Egypt," and in black face on stage he bore striking similarities to the Nubian servant characters created in the scripts of Yaqub Sanua in the 1870s. *Osman* became the conduit through which Egyptians could mock the British occupation, yet he was the vehicle for off-color humor and the dynamics of servant–master relations. Furthermore, the character's half-Nubian, half Sudanese origins were used as a means of expressing Egypt's domination over the Sudan. Like Rihani, Kassar transitioned to film; however, he never used black face in film. The expression of his Nubian-ness was achieved on screen by surrounding him with Nubians. Almost symbolically, with Kassar's retirement and death came the final retirement of his character and the independence of the Sudan in 1956 (Powell, 2008).

Egyptian theater in Egyptian dialect became a huge money-making venture. According to Ziad Fahmy, Rihani made 28,500 Egyptian pounds in 1918 alone, and after seven years on his own, Kassar had earned approximately 47,000 Egyptian pounds. Not surprisingly, the theater district around Emad el-Din Street blossomed. At the same time, theater was relatively accessible for the urban middle classes at five piastres a ticket for an ordinary seat in this time period, with double and triple price tickets for special seats. To encourage women who could not afford private boxes to attend, special days and times were set aside for women and/or families. A parallel entertainment quarter developed in Rod el-Farag, a district in Shubra along the Nile, made more accessible by the building of the tramway at the turn of the 20th century. Open-air theaters and more inexpensive performances could be seen here, and even big names, for example, Ali al-Kassar made investments, gave appearances, and scouted for new talent in the casinos famous for singing, dancing (see subsequently), and comedic performances.

In the period between Egyptian independence and the revolution (1922–1952), competition between new theater troupes flourished, as well as between theater and the emerging medium of cinema (see subsequently). Despite depression and war, the ranks of the urban middle classes grew significantly. Competing for audiences were the Ramses Theater dominated by the troupe of actor Yusuf Wahbi, the Fatima Rushdi troupe, Munira Mahdiyya's troupe, the Ukasha troupe, the Neguib al-Rihani troupe, Ali al-Kassar's troupe, and a National troupe formed in 1935, with the Azbakiyya Theater as its base. Poet Ahmad Shawqi (1868–1932) and playwright Tawfiq al-Hakim (1898–1987) expanded the repertoire of theater beyond comedy to include poetic drama (Shawqi), and a range of translations of great works from around the world as well as entering the realm of social realism.

Theater after the 1952 Revolution

Hakim's writing blossomed after the revolution with social criticism about the new regime. With the arrival of television in 1960, the heavy censorship, and lack of state sponsorship, many of the old theater troupes withered away with the death or sequestration of the holdings of their owners. The Free Officers had initially co-opted actors, for example, Yusuf Wahbi into the regime's Ministry of Culture and National Guidance, but after the 1956 Suez Crisis, such figures were replaced with a newer, younger generation more tightly allied to the regime, for example, Lutfi al Khuli (b. 1929) and Ali Salem (b. 1936). Depicting Egypt in all its glory throughout history and shaping Arab Socialist realism into theatrical form fell into the hands of this new group of artists. Nasser was a man of simplicity who preferred a quick afternoon at the cinema over the leisurely lingering, bourgeois evenings at the theater or opera. In 1971, a year after Nasser died, the Opera House burned to the ground, not to be replaced until 1988.

Theater by the 1960s and 1970s became either state-sponsored theater, espousing a bland version of the state's propaganda, with little thought to costumes, lighting,

---

NEW OPERA HOUSE

After the 1971 fire, the preeminent site of culture for a century was replaced by a different marker of modernity, a garage. In the first year of his presidency, Sadat was not in the position of rebuilding a new Opera House, a bastion of Western culture. It was not until 1988, under Mubarak, that Egypt built a new Opera House, in conjunction with the Japanese government. Authorities chose the island of Gezira, and selected an updated Islamic-modern style. The current Opera House contains a Museum of Contemporary Art and an extensive Music Library. The facility houses regular (Western and Arab) music, ballet, choral, stage, and other performances. There is even a planetarium on site. It also serves as an umbrella organization for other major theatres in the country and for advancing the cause of music and art among the younger generation.

or scenery; or the theater of the absurd, a mocking of the growing authoritarianism of the government. The great writers of the latter genre are Hakim, Mahmud Diyab (1932–1983), and Alfred Farag (b. 1929). Because criticizing directly was too threatening, it was easier to use sophisticated allegory or metaphors, for example, making the ruler a cockroach or placing him in a distant place or time (see Hakim's *Fate of a Cockroach* or *Sultan's Dilemma*). After the 1967 war and after the rise of Sadat (see Chapter 3), fundamentalist trends turned sharp criticism toward the theater.

The production of "Rod el-Farag" and its short run at the Mohamed Farid Theater before the building's "accidental" burning are telling of the trends in the early 1980s. The play, actually written *before* the assassination of Sadat became much more highly charged when it was performed in 1982, after the president's death. The plot had nothing to do with the death of a political leader, nor was it part of the theater of the absurd from the previous decades. Its inspiration was more classical in nature, telling an age-old story, the Greek myth of Phaedra, with a plot line similar to the story of Potiphar and Joseph in Genesis and retold somewhat differently in Sura 12 of the Quran. In fact, author Sarhan originally named the play "*Imra't al-Aziz*" ("Wife of the Ruler") using the same phrase as the Quran; however, this terminology did not pass government censors and the new name came with the location of the first scene, where the leading lady sings in a cabaret and a British officer gets shot by the adopted son of Aziz Pasha. Given the rise in fundamentalist trends, a number of the racier scenes and monologues had also been cut from the script.

EARLY CRITICS OF THEATRE, RECENTLY RETIRED ACTRESSES, AND NEW CONCERNS

The opening of the Institute of Dramatic Arts in 1930 created a flurry of criticism in the press. The new coeducational facility offered a select number of positions in free classes between five and eight in the evenings, so that individuals with day jobs could attend. The curriculum included both practical and theoretical classes taught by scholars, including Taha Hussein, and actors, for example, Zaki Tulaymat. Even fencing, music, dancing, and physical education were in the curriculum, which sparked the ire of conservative Muslims, who bristled at the thought of women performing indecent movements.

In recent years a number of actresses have donned the headscarf, some even disavowing the profession. This group includes Suheir el-Babli, Suheir Ramzi, Hanan Turk, and Sabreen. Consequently, this has forced them into a form of retirement either by choice because they no longer want to put themselves in compromising positions or because the Mubarak government did not as a general rule allow newscasters or actresses to wear veils of any sort. Since Mubarak's fall there has been a high-profile case against a comedian Adel Imam for "offending Islam" in which two different courts came to two different judgments in April 2012.

Egypt is a land of conspiracy theory, and many believe that supporters of Sadat and/or the government were behind the burning of the theater after only 18 performances, even though the official cause of the fire was faulty wiring, particularly since the director froze or paused on the assassination scene. Others believe that disgruntled fundamentalists set the fire. Regardless, by 1982 the real Rod el-Farag was no longer a great stepping stone to the theater district around Emad el-Din St., and the latter was only a shell of its former self. Today a new Cultural Center graces Rod el-Farag, and new theaters dot new neighborhoods and districts.

Comedy, farce, and political satire still form the backbone of Cairo's stage. In other words, the things that made Egyptians laugh in the earliest days of vernacular theater, still make Egyptians laugh today. Bill Clinton's antics inspired not one, but two productions: "Me, My Wife, and Monica" and "Monica and the Blue Dress." After the invasion of Iraq, America bashing inspired a spate of productions on stage and film (see subsequently). One of the more enduring critiques of American culture and policy was a play entitled "Messing with the Mind" at the Hanagir theater performed by the Movement troupe. It opened with the audience literally being stormed by the actors, dressed as U.S. soldiers, cursing and yelling to turn off their mobiles (cell phones). A major figure was General Tommy Fox, so named after the broadcast network. His character played a stooge defending American policies. Not to be left out, CNN appeared as a network always trying to present "happy" news, for example, the distribution of McDonalds' food to the children of Iraq after its invasion. The production had commercials with "real people" products, for example, Condoleeza Margerine, oozing with potential to solve problems, and the empowering, masculine Colin Powell steroid drink. Multilingual songs spiced up the show, such as "No to Intifada" performed by General Fox. Controversial elements included an attempt on Fox's life by a suicide bomber, which the director defended by pointing out that only military personnel were on stage when the event took place. The production demonstrated consistency in elements of Egyptian theater: comedy, political satire, multiple skits, and music. Not all theater is political, much of the stage while remaining true to older forms of comedy has also adapted to new sources, for example, television. Down the street from an experimental theater one might find a musical that is more likely to emulate a comedic soap opera.

Dance

Just as theater has a long history in Egypt, so too does dance—perhaps even longer and more celebrated, at least among the many tourists who visit the country. They come to watch the shows (now dominated by foreign dancers) and examine inscriptions on ancient tombs depicting fertility cults, celebrations, and sacred rites. Once again we have to look back to the goddess Hathor, who was associated with music, dance, and fertility to understand the origins of the *raqs sharqi* or Eastern Dance. On carefully examining the inscriptions of tombs, one can see that it was not only women who were involved in dance. Rows of men can also be seen in dance rituals wearing the characteristic sash cinched around the hips.

Female Egyptian musicians play music and dance at a banquet in this fresco from the tomb of Nakht. (Corel)

Many trace the *raqs sharqi*, which can be seen all over the Middle East, North Africa, and parts of the Balkans, to Egypt. While the "high form" can be quite complicated and elaborate, attending any celebratory function (assuming the participants have no religious prohibitions against dance), one can find young and old, male and female, performing the *raqs baladi* or the country (folk) dance, involving a rhythmic movement of the torso and hips. The Western term "belly" dance does not accurately describe it, since the hips, shoulders, and small steps of the feet are far more important than anything the belly does. With respect to regional variation, there is some distinction in the dances done in the south (Nubia), near the oases, in Alexandria, and around the Suez Canal cities. Generally, the unity of the Nile valley has left a cultural imprint in terms of folk dance.

Historians, anthropologists, dancers, and ethnomusicologists seem to be united in the notion that female performance for other females was historically an honorable profession. These women, referred to as *'awalim (s. 'alma)*, were literally known as scholars, who were distinct from singers and dancers who performed in front of men and might also engage in prostitution, as well as prostitutes who were registered in another guild, and taxed as such. After the French occupation and the rise of Muhammad Ali, the number of performing women increased. With venereal disease rampant in the army, as part of an 1834 prohibition on prostitution, Muhammad Ali put a blanket ban on all female performers in Cairo. This ban had the effect of cheapening female performers of all sorts by placing them in the same category. The women simply moved outside of Cairo, where ironically many who were not previously engaged in prostitution turned to the profession in order to make ends meet. The law did not affect male dancers, the *khawal*, who according to 19th-century observer Edward Lane, were much appreciated even before 1834, particularly by those who felt women should not be public dancers. *Khawals* wore vests, pantaloons, petticoats, makeup, and long hair, performed at various functions, for example, weddings, births, circumcisions, and festivals. During the prohibition on women's performance their popularity undoubtedly increased.

Around 1850 the ban on prostitution was lifted and female performers returned to the capital. With the development of downtown Cairo during the age of Ismail, a host of new venues appeared culminating in the creation of nightclubs, dancehalls, and casinos by the late 19th century. Such locales had existed since the time of the French occupation but had not necessarily been frequented by Egyptians. As discussed in Egyptian Music, Muhammad Ali Street was an area where performers congregated including singers and dancers. Two not necessarily mutually exclusive career paths existed for dancers: (1) dancing at traditional venues, for example, weddings, births, and festivals, which still might have a certain degree of gender segregation at the turn of the 20th century or (2) dancing in clubs, cabarets, and casinos that were developing downtown, in Rod el-Farag, and other points along the Nile. The more traditional career path would nearly evaporate by the mid-20th century as wedding and social practices changed and new technologies emerged.

After the British occupation in 1882, the nightclub business grew and prostitution expanded, and the colonizers assumed responsibility for licensing establishments. To escape taxation and stigma, many prostitutes sought cover under the shadow of singing, dancing, waitressing, and hostessing, thus bringing further stigma to the entertainment industry. The line between the two was often blurred, particularly in the minds of club owners, whose chief profit came from the practice of "opening." After an enjoyable performance, a patron could invite a performer to sit at his table and "open" bottles of champagne, liquor, or beer.

The technologies of the 20th century brought new opportunities for performers with the invention of recording and film, and the expansion of the middle class created larger audiences for urban clubs. Movies (see subsequently) relied heavily on music and dancing, and the clubs and theaters, some of which have already been discussed also depended upon the talents of female entertainers, especially dancers.

The most famous entertainer whose casino showcased the talented dancers of stage and cinema was Badia Masabni (1894–1975), the wife of Neguib al-Rihani. Syrian-born Badia had been molested as a child causing her family to live in exile for a number of years in Argentina (to avoid the shame that had been brought upon the family). Eventually, Badia moved to Cairo where she took up singing and dancing in the theater of George Abyad and Neguib al-Rihani, whom she later married. Masabni learned an extraordinary amount about the theater and its organization from her talented husband. In 1926 Badia left her turbulent, on-again/off-again marriage to start her own business, Casino Badia on Emad el-Din Street. Like many famous

"OPENING" AND THE RED LIGHT DISTRICT

Women's groups successfully petitioned the government to end legal prostitution in 1949, and the time-honored tradition of "opening" was officially forbidden in 1951. Nevertheless, implementing the law would be difficult. Red lights and bells would mark the beginning of a vice-squad raid. In 1973 a new system emerged that put a close on "opening": government licensing of entertainers through a process of examination. As well, the beginnings of more fundamentalist trends meant restrictions on costumes, including covering the belly (even if only with meshed fabric), closing slits in skirts, and ending the fraternization with the customers. Rather than performers, now other workers would do the schmoozing with the clients, and the work was not restricted to women. In a recent article in the *NY Times* on the return of male belly dancing, a young Egyptian reported that he gets paid by nightclubs on pyramids row to dance, but if owners are questioned, he merely appears as an enthusiastic customer.

couples today there were rampant rumors of infidelity on both sides and severe disagreements over money management.

Badia was the modern-day *'alma.* She was a singer, dancer, innovator, entrepreneur, and mentor. Many dancers attribute certain movements or even modern belly dancing to Badia's style, when in reality she hired Western and Arab choreographers to help her adapt the *raqs sharqi* to the stage, with traveling movements, larger arm motions, and undulations that would be more easily seen by an audience. Like her husband, Badia set aside special times for women and families, which also promoted her club as something other than a cheap brothel, where women could see for themselves what lay inside her four walls or on her terrace. She frequently changed the program to keep patrons interested. Badia opened second and third locations in Opera Square and in Giza, where the Sheraton hotel currently stands, just beyond el-Galaa (Evacuation) Bridge—what used to be the English Bridge more commonly called Kubry Badia—or Badia's bridge. It was at this latter location on the Nile during World War II that a German officer went head to head with the dancer. One version of the story has the German taking offence to a Hitler comedy routine, while most seem to center on her lack of receptivity to German propaganda. The outcome was to accuse Badia of being a British agent. Certainly the clubs and the houseboats moored on the Nile between Pont Anglais and Midan Kit Kat down the Nile in Imbaba were filled with spies, agents, double-agents, and low lives of various sorts. Badia was more suited to scouting talent than scouting for information. She would find two of the most beloved dancers of Egyptian stage and film, Tahia Carioca and Samia Gamal (see subsequently). Ironically, Badia's relationship with the state would not be a happy one. Although many assume it was the Free Officers who gave her a hard time, it was about two years before the 1952 revolution that she began to have problems regarding back taxes. She had already sold her Emad el-Din location to competitor Beba 'Izz el-Din (1910–1950), before purchasing the Opera location. With the state breathing down her neck, she decided to liquidate her assets for a portion of their value and return to Lebanon rather than pay the taxes in a literally "fly by night" operation. Beba bought the Opera location as well, notorious for being the spot that sparked the Cairo fire of January 1952 (see Chapter 2). Ironically, by then, Badia had settled on a chicken farm outside of Beirut, and Beba (a.k.a. Safia Helmi) tinged with her association as a Nazi spy (or praised as an Egyptian patriot for her anti-British stance) had passed away in a car accident (Dougherty 2000).

Badia's legacy lived on in her two most famous dancers, Tahia Carioca (d. 1999) and Samia Gamal (d. 1994), whose lives and careers bore remarkable similarities. Both women have conflicting birth dates, so it is uncertain whether they lied about their age to avoid difficulties as youngsters advancing their careers or scaled down as their popularity increased when they approached middle age. Tahia's birth date is variously given as 1915 and 1919, and Samia's as 1922 and 1924. Both women were non-Cairenes, discovered by Badia, given new stage names, were known as innovators on stage and screen, and were favored by the palace with frequent invitations for performances. Badawiyya Muhammad Karim took the stage name Tahia (on Badia's recommendation) and later worked some Latin rhythms into her dance routine and encouraged her drummer to tap out Latin beats. This was after the global success of Fred Astaire and Ginger Rogers appearance in *Flying down to Rio* in 1933, hence the appellation Carioca (for the Brazilian Carioca dance). Indeed, the "latin" high step would become one of her many signature steps. Tahia's charisma, smile, artistry, ornate costumes, and connection to her audience are especially evident on video clips from live performances. In comparison, her performances in movies are magnificent but less connected. Tahia made 200 films in a career spanning six decades, although it was briefly interrupted by the Free Officers. Tahia's association with the monarchy and an issue of back taxes landed her in prison as would her political opinions under both Nasser and Sadat.

Fresh-faced Samia Gamal was like a younger sister or girl next door to Tahia's worldly charm; however, both women managed multiple and tabloid marriages in their lifetimes. Born Zeinab Ibrahim Mahfuz, she was dubbed Samia Gamal (literally Highness of Beauty) by her mentor, Badia. She added more variation to the *raqs sharqi*, including ballet steps and Latin rhythms. Dancers frequently credit her with being the first to wear high heels and adding veils to her dance. After a wardrobe malfunction in the 1950s, she apparently was the reason that the dancers of Cairo all began taking off their shoes for a period of time. Samia had taken private lessons before learning from both Badia and Tahia as well as lesser-known performers at Casino Masabni. The great love of her life was her on-stage and on-screen lover Farid al-Atrache who never married her. Some accounts point to his noble Druze heritage and inability to marry an actress and dancer, whereas others claim he simply could not commit as he never married. Like Tahia, Samia made numerous movies, and she still made some dance appearances as late as the 1980s.

While Tahia and Samia had enormous popularity after the 1952 revolution, the era of the cabaret or casino had come to an end. There would be other great soloists, for example, Fifi Abdou (b. 1953), showcased on stage and film, but the bourgeois lifestyle of the elite was drawing to a close. The 1952 revolution was more suited to a new, hybrid form of dance that celebrated both modernity and the essence of Egyptian folklore. Its creator was Mahmoud Reda (b. 1930), who formed his own dance troupe in 1959 based on the discipline, organization, and template of models found in the Soviet Union and the West (Shay 2002). Reda was actually a gymnast from the 1952 Egyptian Olympic team, consumed with a passion for dancing á la Fred Astaire or Gene Kelly. He and his brother Ali were part of the cabaret and ballroom dance scene of the interwar years, and it was Ali who actually began doing choreography. When unable to do a job, Mahmoud replaced him and was later selected to go to the Soviet Union for a youth festival in 1957. Reda chose another member of the Heliolido Sporting Club, dancer Farida Fahmy to be his female lead. She was not only active in sports, but was also a participant in the club's amateur theater group. Athleticism, popular culture, and opportunity all blended together to create this new dance form.

Reda's "folk" dance had a number of distinctive characteristics. First and foremost, his dances would be cleansed of the sexually suggestive moves associated with the *raqs sharqi* and his dancers would be modestly dressed. Second, his group was an ensemble that did not showcase talent like Carioca or Gamal among the dancers. Although Farida Fahmy would be the lead female dancer, the notion of a soloist would not exist. Third, Reda would look nostalgically to life in Egypt to draw upon images, myths, icons, and movements, to incorporate into his dances: the stick dance, licorice drink seller, water well, sugar doll, port workers in Suez, and so on. Egyptians everywhere, male and female, young and old, rich and poor, would recognize these symbols, elements, and postures as part of their own childhood, history, religion, village, and so on, that is, they could connect to them. Nevertheless, the training, organization, and discipline were all what one would find in a modern dance troupe in the West or in the Soviet Union. As for the costumes, while there were symbolic elements within them, the ruffles, the lace, and the bell-bottom Lycra pants were anything but Egyptian (Shay 2002).

Initially the government did not sponsor the troupe; however, by 1961 Nasser saw its utility. Along the Giza side of the Nile in Agouza, the Balloon Theater was constructed to house the Reda troupe and other groups supported by the state. The Reda troupe also received funding to make two movies, *Holiday at Mid-Year* (1961) and *Love at Karnak* (1965), which showcase the ensemble and demonstrate the difficulties of creating a national dance troupe. Ali Reda, who by then had married Farida Fahmy, directed the movies making the effort a family affair, in which Fahmy and Mahmoud played leads. These movies popularized the idea of folk dance, raised awareness, and connected the troupe to Egyptian national identity as they placed the dancers in colorful local contexts, epitomizing Reda's philosophies of dance. Memorable scenes in *Love at Karnak* include a splashy opening scene at the train station where the group is literally and metaphorically trying to take off, Fahmy pronouncing that the ensemble makes the company not the lead dancer, male dancers crooning about being in the temple of Hatsheptsut, and a dream sequence that connects the present to pharaonic past—all of which builds to a closing number in high-Reda style. As depicted in the film, low wages, hard work, and numerous strategic obstacles encumber the dancer; the female dancer in particular also suffers from the stigma on her character. Folk dancers, like Farida Fahmy, generally have a more wholesome image, but in recent years all public dancing has come into question with Islamist trends.

Although the Egyptian government gave the Reda troupe sponsorship, it created its own National Folk (Folkloric) Troupe in 1961, under the direction of Boris Ramazin a former Moiseyev dancer provided by the Soviets. They share space in the Balloon Theater with the Reda Troupe, and provide a distinctly different brand of "Egyptian" dance. Egyptians often criticize this troupe for doing nonnative line dances, for example, the *dabka* that are more familiar to Syria and Palestine or dances from the Balkans that appear Slavic in nature. A more authentic group of musicians and dancers is the Nile Folkloric Troup, also housed at the Balloon Theater. This group has gone through various incarnations with respect to name and leadership; however, its basic mission since 1956 has been the same: preserve traditional forms of music, song, and dance from all parts of Egypt. Interestingly enough, during the U.S. bicentennial, when Egypt wanted to send the Reda troupe to perform on the mall, the folklorists at the Smithsonian insisted upon this group. The Tannoura Egyptian Heritage Folklore Troup, founded in 1988, uses the Mausoleum of al-Ghuri near Khan al-Khalili as its headquarters. This all-male ensemble performs something similar to a Sufi ceremonial dance, in a flowing, spinning skirt-like garment that actually raises above the head—for about 20 minutes—accompanied by traditional instruments, *rababa*, *ney*, *mizmar*, and the *darbuka* (goblet drum).

Despite the prohibitions waged by Islamists, the economics of infitah, the tourist market, and the wedding market have all re-sparked the demand for traditional dancers. The torch has been passed to a new generation, which is mostly foreign but includes a few Egyptians, for example, Dina. Older Egyptians shake their heads and say these women cannot dance like Samia or Tahia, they are all costume and no substance. Dancing still carries negative connotations for women. While folk dancers insist that they are more respectable than those doing the *raqs sharqi*, dancers judge each others' costumes and worry how others are holding them in judgment.

Film

Egypt has an incredibly rich film industry based upon its local traditions in music, dance, comedy, and theater; however, up until the 1930s there was little truly Egyptian enterprise and even up until the time of the 1952 revolution, the flagship company Studio Misr still could not produce enough films to fill its one movie house in Cairo (Vitalis 2000). The first movie screenings took place in 1896 in Cairo and Alexandria, not long after the first audiences viewed them in Europe; the first cinema opened about a decade later. Since there would be dependence on foreign films, Hollywood in particular, dubbing and translation began in 1912. Cinema was much more accessible to the masses than the theater. Even for first-class seats, tickets were still about half price as those of a live performance.

During the colonial period Egypt was the only country in the region to develop a film industry, and thus it would play an important role spreading the medium throughout Africa and Asia. There are a number of landmark events in the history of Egyptian cinematography. It was in 1925 that Talaat Harb, the founder of the Bank Misr group, founded the Egypt Company for Cinema & Performance. Rather than being an artsy film studio, it would be intended for advertising and informational films. The nationalist press touted the potential benefits of film, which were demonstrated in the recording of the funeral procession of Mustapha Kamil (d. 1907) and the return of Saad Zaghlul from exile in 1922. Most specialists agree that *Layla* (1927) is the first significant feature film made in the country; however, some Egyptian nationalists will point out that the original director was Turkish (Orfi) only to be replaced by an Egyptian of Austrian extraction (Rosti). It was also in 1927 that religious scholars at al-Azhar University rallied together to protest the decision of actor and director Yusuf Wahbi to portray the Prophet Muhammad on film, a position that would be defended and clarified to include all the Orthodox caliphs in 1930 (and upheld since that time). In 1934, Talaat Harb built Studio Misr, and the company sent a number of promising young Egyptian directors to Europe to study, including Ahmad Badrakhan (d. 1969) and Niyazi Mustafa (d. 1986), both of whom would go on to have long and productive careers.

Among early successes in Egyptian cinema were comedies and musicals. The Egyptian film industry demonstrated great synergy with the performing arts, as well as the large number of American films that were becoming increasing popular in the country. Individuals who were active in the theater community, for example, Yusuf Wahbi, Neguib al-Rihani, Ali al-Kassar, and Fatima Rushdi aimed their talents toward the new medium, writing, acting, directing, and producing. Rihani's *Kishkish Bey* and the ditties produced for stage and screen, worked with the burgeoning music industry to produce smash sensations. *His Excellency Kishkish Bey* was so popular that it was not only an early silent film (1931), but it also returned just three years later with a sound track. Ultimately, as Rihani traveled more to Europe and watched American films, for example, Chaplin and the Marx brothers, his leading man roles turned more Westernized, but still interested in the beautiful, young girls. Ali al-Kassar played his standard character Osman in a series of Togo Mizrahi films of the 1930s and 1940s, exemplified by his performance in *Seven o'Clock* (1937), which includes a number of staples of Egyptian theater farce: mistaken identity, cross-dressing, and ethnic stereotyping. A true pioneer, Fatima Rushdi directed *The Wedding* in 1933, and she attended its Paris premier; however, she apparently later destroyed all copies of the film.

The real money in early film-making came with musicals, which combined a variety of indigenous and Western dance styles, with plots centered upon entertainers or building various forms of celebration into the storyline. According to Viola Shafik, more than one-third of the films produced between 1931 and 1961 were musicals, and that number increased to about 50 percent between 1944 and 1946 (2007). Along with music came dancing, and Badia Masabni was an innovator here, appearing either herself or showcasing her dancers, for example, Tahia Carioca, who was a little known background dancer in Togo Mizrahi's *Dr. Farhat* in 1935. By 1942 Tahia took centerstage in *I Love the Wrong One* and in 1946 opposite Badia's ex-husband Neguib al-Rihani in *Ladies' Games*. Similarly, Samia Gamal demonstrated her talent

---

TOGO MIZRAHI LEGEND OF EGYPTIAN CINEMA, 1905–1986

Togo Mizrahi, an Italian Jew raised in Alexandria earned a European Ph.D. in economics, and exemplified the cosmopolitanism of the film industry. His early works dealt with social criticism and then he began a string of comedies in the mid-1930s based on ethnic humor starring the Jewish comedian *Shalom* and pseudo-"Nubian" Ali al-Kassar. Mizrahi also acted in a number of his own films under the stage name Ahmad al-Mashriqi, and he was known to have had facility in all aspects of production. He is perhaps most beloved for his *Layla* series of movies, in which he directed singer Leila Murad. His final movie was a historical film, *Sallama* (1946), starring singing legend Umm Kulthum. Mizrahi left Egypt for Italy in 1948. Some feel that he was coming under suspicion of Zionism, whereas others simply cite health issues. His Alexandria and Giza studios fell under the direction of his nephew until the early 1960s, when they were sequestered by the government.

---

with her offstage lover Farid al-Attrache in *The Love of My Life* (1947), *The Genie Lady* (1947), and *The Last Lie* (1950).

Big names in music, for example, Muhammad Abdul Wahab, Umm Kulthum, and Leila Murad all had successful box-office careers, albeit typecast in particular roles. Muhammad Abdul Wahab was the dashing, crooning leading man, while Umm Kulthum appeared as a poor servant or slave who falls in love with her master in three of her six films. Even in *Fatma* (1947), where she had earned her way into the middle class with a degree as a nurse, she fell in love with the son of her wealthy patient, thus reproducing the conflicts of her previous films. So beloved was the singer in her career and in this role that Nobel laureate Neguib Mahfouz named his two daughters, Umm Kulthum and Fatma.

Leila Murad, daughter of the famous musician Zaki Murad, began her career in the Casino Badia and was later discovered by Abdul Wahab who invited her to star with him in *Long Live Love* (1938). Between 1939 and 1944 she worked with Togo Mizrahi on the first of the *Layla* films that catapulted her to fame and earned her the Cinderella image: *Layla Country Girl, Layla Lady of the Camelias, Layla Schoolgirl,* and *Layla in the Shadows.* She continued her work on the *Layla* films with off- and on-screen love Anwar Wagdi between 1944 and 1947: *Layla Daughter of the Poor* and *Layla Daughter of the Rich.*

Egyptian film audiences love irony, inside jokes, and double entendres. *The Flirtation of Girls* (1949) is an excellent example of Egyptian cinema at its prerevolutionary height. The plot centered upon Layla Murad's character, a delinquent, rich school girl who could not even master her native tongue (see Language for a discussion of this problem). At 31 years, Murad was a bit old to continue playing the school girl, but Egyptians love characters in predictable roles. To remedy her poor Arabic, her father hired tutor Neguib al-Rihani for the summer. The Arabic tutor is full of songs and lines with double meanings, hearkening back to Rihani's work in the

Franco-Arab theater. Not surprisingly, the old teacher falls in love with the flirty young girl, who has eyes for a sleazy club owner. Eventually, she would be reunited with a distant relative who is a handsome young pilot (Anwar Wagdi), with whom the actress Murad had an off-screen relationship. In the movie, actor Yusuf Wahbi and singer Muhammad Abdul Wahab play themselves. The songs and the lines are all parodies of previous roles and movies of the actors and their relationships to one another. The final scene of the movie has the tutor, the pilot, and the girl driving off in an army jeep. Indeed, it was the last scene that Rihani would ever film. He died of typhoid in May 1949 and the film was released in October (Armbrust 2000).

The cast of *The Flirtation of Girls* was also evident of the cosmopolitanism of the Egyptian film industry. Neguib al-Rihani was the son of an Iraqi Christian and an Egyptian Copt. Leila Murad was the daughter of a famous Egyptian Jewish cantor and musician and Polish mother. She had converted to Islam to marry Anwar Wagdi, the Muslim costar of the film. Filmed in 1948 during the crisis and war with Israel, it demonstrated the unity of the national family (Armbrust 2000). Interestingly enough, the unity would later be tested as Murad's marriage with Wagdi fell apart, and he apparently reported her as a spy for Israel shortly after the 1952 revolution claiming that she had funneled money to the Israeli military. Beloved by the people, Murad had already been chosen as the official singer of the revolution over Umm Kulthum. After investigating the claims, Murad was found innocent of these charges, but her last movie appearance was in 1953. Apart from some isolated, brief public appearances, her career ended abruptly at this time. She had proclaimed herself a Muslim and an Egyptian and remained in Egypt until her death in 1995.

The cosmopolitan unity of the 1940s appeared in a theater script in which Rihani collaborated, entitled *Hassan, Marcos, and Cohen.* It was a takeoff on Tristan Bernard's *Le Petit Café*; instead of being a light-hearted comedy it struck at the heart of basic class struggles in Egypt while simultaneously engaging in popular ethnic stereotyping typical of classical theatrical farce. Its purpose was to demonstrate that people get along for the sake of self-interest in business and that everyone can learn from the strengths (and weaknesses) of one another. Although the script was written for theater in 1943, the movie about three interdenominational owners (Muslim, Christian, and Jew) of a pharmacy who want to cheat their Muslim employee out of his inheritance came about some 11 years later, starring comic geniuses Stephane Rosti and Hassan Fayeq. 1954 marks an interesting year politically since it was the year that Nasser came to full power and the year that the Lavon Affair implicated a handful of Egyptian Jews working for the Israeli government to undermine the negotiations for the Suez Pact (see Chapters 2 and 3). Typical of many of the great Jewish stars of the screen, Zeinat Sedki (1913–1978), costarred in *Hassan, Marcos, and Cohen.* She would scarcely be seen after 1958, making only as many films the rest of her life as she made in her most productive year.

The prerevolutionary years of Egyptian cinema also saw the first attempts at symbolism and realism, as well as depicting struggles between the classes. *The White Rose* (1933/1934), directed by Muhammad Karim, was the first musical starring Muhammad Abdul Wahhab. He received a rose in a garden from the daughter of his employer, after helping her collect the pearls from her broken necklace. Despite his deep love for her, he could not marry her because of the difference in social status. The color of the rose and the pearls symbolized the purity of their love. Set in a working-class neighborhood, in *Determination* (1939), director Kamal Selim finds love for his protagonist, a butcher's son, but not without a great deal of trial and tribulation and some assistance by influential individuals from a higher social class. While the fairy godparent element existed, the basic backdrop to the movie was the alley setting, inhabited by earthy, working-class folks. By the late 1940s, the monarchy found realistic depictions threatening, and the Ministry of Social Affairs issued a censorship code aimed at suppressing leftist and overly realist trends, including images of soiled alleys, donkey carts, women in certain types of traditional garb, demonstrations and strikes, approval of crimes, or anything resembling the spirit of revolt (Shafik 2007).

The movie business generated popular protest as well. The Muslim Brotherhood, Young Egypt, and other groups across the political spectrum pointed out the connections between Hollywood and Egypt. MGM and Twentieth Century Fox both owned theaters in Cairo and Alexandria. This economic strength generated grist for the political rumor mill. Actor Yusuf Wahbi criticized the American film industry as aiding in the cause of Zionism. The critique came as an effort to promote local industry and to lobby for government subsidies, which began in the 1940s but was not achieved until several years after the revolution (Vitalis 2000).

The Egyptian Revolution was not initially a monumental event in the history of cinema. While Nasser enjoyed going to the movies with his family, he did not believe that film was a medium that could revolutionize society in the way that Lenin envisioned for the Soviet Union. After the Suez Crisis and particularly after the nationalizations of the 1960s, the film industry eventually fell under the jurisdiction of the Ministry of National Guidance. A new generation of directors came of age in the 1950s and 1960s under the aegis of state sponsorship. According to Viola Shafik, this period brought about only a temporary and incomplete rise in standards that would be ended with the partial reprivitization under Sadat. Nevertheless, the efforts Tharwat Ukasha during his tenure as Minister of Culture are notable (1958–1962 and 1969–1970).

Although his earliest work was pre-1952, the most significant director in the post-revolutionary era is undoubtedly Youssef Chahine (1926–2008). A supporter of the new regime, in *Blazing Sun* (1954), Chahine depicted an interclass romance between a pasha's daughter and the overseer's son. It was in this film that he introduced Egyptian audiences to fellow Victoria College alumnus Omar Sharif. Chahine also received training in the United States as an actor, and only later turned to directing. He continued to follow Hollywood trends, adapting Panavision and Cinemascope to location filming all over Egypt, literally changing the way audiences saw the country. Indeed he claims to have been the first to film in Upper Egypt in *Nile Boy* (1951) and again in *You're My Lover* (1957). His masterpiece *Cairo Station* (1958) invokes the trials and tribulations of Nasserist Egypt set against the backdrop of the main railway station at Ramses Square. Chahine himself appears in the psycho-drama as a crippled deviant who longs for the sexy soda girl (Hanuma) played by Hind Rostam. Hanuma has her mind on her upcoming marriage to overbearing Abu Siri, the porter who is trying to organize a workers' union. Meanwhile, the station is also the venue for a feminist rally, the rendezvous of secret lovers, a gay pickup scene (silent and only a few seconds on camera), and the killing of an innocent girl. The movie even has a brief appearance by a rockabilly band, "Mike and the Rockets" featuring Asaad Kelaada, director of American hits, such as *Rhoda* and *Everybody Loves Raymond.* Although many random elements appear in *Cairo Station*, its thrilling climax helped to popularize the genre of police crime drama that would continue through the 1960s, 1970s, and 1980s (Cairo Station 2006).

Chahine's autobiographical quartet, *Alexandria Why* (1978), *An Egyptian Story* (1982), *Alexandria Again and Forever* (1990), and *Alexandria . . . New York* (2004) begins his life journey as young student Yahia (Chahine) in cosmopolitan, yet fragile, war-torn Alexandria dreaming of becoming a star and moving to Hollywood. The next segment picks up with Yehia in mid-life crisis as he faces open-heart surgery and examines his life, career, and world cinema critically. The third segment can be considered an "all about Chahine" as he writes, directs, and plays Yehia falling in love with an actor (who coincidentally used to play Yehia), until he meets a new young actress who inspires him in new directions. The star-studded cast includes Tahia Carioca playing herself. The final chapter has Yehia dealing with the repercussions of an affair with his first love, Ginger, from drama school in the United States. He finds out about a son, Iskander (Alexander), a ballet dancer in post-9/11 New York, who wants nothing to do with his Arab heritage.

More famous than his autobiographies are Chahine's epic films, for example, *Saladin the Victorious* (1963). Rather than realistically portraying the Kurdish leader of the Middle Ages it was more a homage to Nasser and contemporary Arab unity. However, after Nasser's defeat in the 1967 war, Chahine's work became more critical as seen in *The Sparrow* (1972).

Another generation of great directors came of age with the merger of infitah economics and a more open political climate after the death of Sadat. This group known as the new realists includes Atef al-Tayeb, Bashir al-Dik, Mohamed Khan, Khairy Beshara, and Daoud Abd al-Sayyed (Shafik 2007). The economic and social climate created by infitah and oil wealth created the potential for new story lines, heroes, and settings. An excellent example is Daoud Abd al-Sayyed's (b. 1946) smash hit *al-Kitkat* (1991) based on an Ibrahim Aslan novel (see Literature). The setting is the Imbaba, a working-class neighborhood, often known for its sectarian conflicts. The main character is a blind, hashish-smoking shaykh (Husni) who has pawned his dwelling in exchange for his supply. Meanwhile, his son is looking to sell the place to finance his own dreams of emigration. While this film tackled some of the real social problems with its quirky hero, it conformed to staples of Egyptian cinema with slapstick, physical humor including the blind leading the blind, Shaykh Husni driving a motorbike with his son's assistance, and a toe-tapping soundtrack. Also from 1991, Khairy Beshara's (b. 1947) movie about a boxer, *Crab* starring Ahmed Zaki, similarly used music to spice up the story line, which was so successful that for several years thereafter "the crab" haircut worn by the protagonist became the fashion for hip, young men. Crab hair salons even emerged in the stylish suburbs.

Mohamed Khan (b. 1942), son of an Italian and Punjabi immigrants in Egypt, studied film-making in the UK and is known for his "rebel" style, which is not neces-

---

AHMED ZAKI (1949–2005): AN ACTOR FOR ANY ROLE

Ahmed Zaki was known for his complete absorption in his roles, the most famous of which were his portrayals of two presidents, Nasser (*Nasser 56*) (1996) and Sadat (*Days of Sadat*) (2001). A dark-skinned boy from Zagazig with a great sense of humor would normally hope to be cast in supporting side-kick roles, but ever since his stunning small-screen performance as litterateur Taha Hussein in 1974, Zaki enchanted Egyptian audiences. He was known as "King of Third Class"—in reference to cheap theatre seats—for his ability to connect with audiences, a title formerly held by Farid Shawki. Diagnosed with lung cancer in 2004, Zaki was still working on one of his dream projects, a movie treatment of the life of entertainer Abdul Halim Hafiz. He apparently gave permission to edit his own funeral procession into the movie; however, the project was only 70 percent complete at the time of his death.

A STAR IS BORN

When filming movies or miniseries, Egyptian directors routinely send their assistants to hotels and tourist areas to round up foreigners as extras, particularly for party scenes or crowds. Long before Cate Blanchett was Elizabeth, she was a boxer's bimbo in *Crab* (1990), discovered by someone on the crew at her hotel. She was hired to cheer on the (losing) American and to appear in the party scene. Ms. Blanchett does not list this film on her credits.

---

sarily as acknowledged in Egypt as it is abroad. Several of his works are as acclaimed at home as they in international festivals, and they include his collaboration with great Egyptian actors, for example, Adel Imam (b. 1940) in *Street Player* (1983) or Ahmed Zaki in *Wife of an Important Man* (1987) and *Days of Sadat* (2001).

Poking fun at the West generally or America specifically has become a cottage industry in recent Egyptian film-making. *The Sa'idi at the American University* (1998) delighted audiences with its back-handed criticism of Cairo's Westernized elite. The story centers around Khalaf, a *Sa'idi* from Sohag who receives a scholarship to study political science at AUC. Always the target of jokes themselves (see Etiquette), *Sa'idis* are also authentic Egyptians. Khalaf, brilliantly played by comedian Mohammed Hineidy, who at 36 was more than double the age of many AUC students, who often enter before the age of 18. Sold-out Egyptian audiences loved his garish clothing, folksy wisdom, and traditional ways in the face of his snobbish, Westernized, immoral peers in their jeans and polo shirts. Neither AUC nor Israel took kindly to the movie, in which a demonstration carried out an Israeli flag-burning. Indeed much of the filming took place at the Russian embassy where the buildings bear a remarkable resemblance to the old campus since AUC at times sought legal action against the film makers for use of its name. In the end, the *Sa'idi* finds success in school and condemns those who find "us" (authentic Egyptians) backwards—in reference to Americans and their supporters.

As the Palestinian–Israeli conflict escalated, the Western critique of America via film continued even before 9/11, the invasion of Afghanistan, or the invasion of Iraq. Prior to its filming as a video around 2000, *Mama America* had been an extremely successful theatrical production in which the various children of the Arab world, including "son" Egypt and a latecomer cousin Israel squabble over Mama's inheritance—not without lengthy commentary on what it means to be tied to Mama America and that for which she stands. The movie begins and ends with the statue of liberty, and, in the end, lady liberty is blown up and the Egyptian arrested because he looks like a terrorist. In *Hello America* (2000), an Egyptian goes to the United States to study, only to be hit by a presidential candidate's daughter. The Americans try to buy the Egyptian's silence, and he demands change in foreign policy. The viewings of this film brought about audience response and participation, particularly after the protagonist tells the United States what it can do with its foreign aid.

Some actors and film makers of the old school long for the cosmopolitanism of yesteryear, and the remake of *Hassan, Marcos, and Cohen* (1954) (see earlier) as *Hassan and Marcos* (2008) is an attempt to demonstrate the potential for Egypt to overcome sectarian struggles and religious extremism. It brings together two living legends of Egyptian cinema, Omar Sharif and Adel Imam. Although his parents were Syrian, and Sharif had made a career in the west with hits, such as *Lawrence of Arabia* (1962), *Dr. Zhivago* (1965), and *Monsieur Ibrahim* (2003), he still considers Egypt home. Adel Imam is the Egyptian "every man" who can usually guarantee box office success with his name alone, as evidenced in hits, such as *Terrorism and Kebob* (1992) (see Popular, Youth, and Consumer Culture), *Hello America* (2000), and *The Yacoubian Building* (2006) (see Literature). In the new script, there is no Cohen since Egypt of 2008 has almost no Jews, and the Jewish population is nearly all female. Interestingly enough, Sharif, who was born Christian, converted to Islam to marry film star Faten Hamama (married 1955–1974). He plays the role of Mahmoud, a Muslim Shaykh who due to religious fanaticism and violence gets put in a witness protection program and receives a new identity as Marcos, the Christian. Imam plays a Coptic clergyman, who similarly gets relocated in the same building as a Muslim, Hassan. The two develop a friendship and their children fall in love. Rather than bringing about harmony, the film and even its promotional materials caused such controversy that some groups called for a boycott of Imam's movies.

Female directors have been less common; however in recent years, the work of Kamla Abou Zekry has been notable. Her *One-Zero* (2009), with its largely female cast and crew presents a tableau of class, gender, and religion in Egypt through a narrative of interwoven stories set against the backdrop of an important soccer match that the whole nation is watching, reminiscent of the Egypt–Algeria Africa Cup game of the same year. The various stories of relationship struggles all climax with the soccer game, and as the post-game mayhem commences the strands of the individuals tales are lost in the fray. An upbeat soundtrack and a storyline with an aspiring

---

FATEN HAMAMA, THE LADY OF THE ARAB SCREEN

Faten Hamama (b. 1931) became a star at age eight after her father sent a photograph to a director, which landed her a small role in an Abdul Wahab film. During the 1940s, she achieved leading lady status and married actor and director Izz al-Din Zulficar in 1947. By 1954, Hamama divorced Zulficar and married Omar Sharif the following year. The couple starred in several romantic films together. Hamama is famous for playing roles highlighting the plight of women in Egypt. At first a strong supporter of the revolution, she later became a critic and lived in exile from 1966 until 1971. Although she made her last film in 1993, she returned to the small screen in a highly touted miniseries, *Face of the Moon*, in 2000; and in the same year she was chosen star of the century by the Egyptian Writers and Critics Organization. So beloved is this actress that there is a Faten Hamama metro station, bus stop, and neighborhood.

---

pop star allow for the musical element adored by Egyptian audiences without forced or artificial means.

It is this high quality that has made Egyptian cinema a regional leader since the interwar period. Egypt had something that Hollywood did not—a language understood by the masses of the Middle East. Although North Africa, the *maghrib*, and the Arab east, the *mashriq*, have distinct dialects, the Egyptian dialect is easily understood. This is partially because of its decades long position as a leader in mass media, but also simply because of its medial location. With the development of oil wealth and new technologies, Egypt has shifted to producing videos (and later DVDs) for consumption in the Gulf. Excessive heat, air-conditioning, and VCRs, all helped to popularize staying home to watch movies, whereas the *maghrib* and to a lesser degree the *mashriq*, developed their own film industries. By the 1970s and 1980s, Saudi investors contributed to Egyptian films, helping to defray the enormous cost of actors' salaries, which could potentially take as much as half of the budget of a film. In the 1990s a trend toward European coproduction emerged as Egypt's film industry went into crisis with the advent of satellite television and a concomitant shortage of studios, technicians, and equipment. Throughout its century-long history, cinema in Egypt has weathered the storm due to its connection with older forms of the performing arts and adaptation to new technologies.

REFERENCES

Abou-Saif, L. "Najib al-Rihani: From Buffoonery to Social Comedy." *Journal of Arabic Literature* 4 (1973): 1–17.

Armbrust, Walter, ed. *Mass Mediations: New Approaches to Popular Culture in the Middle East and Beyond.* Berkeley, CA: University of California Press, 2000.

Armbrust, Walter, ed. "The Golden Age before the Golden Age: Commercial Egyptian Film before the 1960s." In *Mass Mediations: New Approaches to Popular Culture in the Middle East and Beyond*, 292–328. Berkeley, CA: University of California Press, 2000.

Cairo Station: Re-Winding a Classic Film. Panel Presented at the Middle East Studies Association Conference in Boston 2006, with papers by Elliott Colla, Joel Gordon, and Ted Swedenburg.

Dougherty, Roberta. "Badi'a Masabnia: The Egyptian Print Media's Carnival of National Identity." In *Mass Mediations: New Approaches to Popular Culture in the Middle East and Beyond*, 243–68. Walter Armbrust, ed. Berkeley, CA: University of California Press .

Ener, Mine. *Managing Egypt's Poor and the Politics of Benevolence, 1800–1952.* Princeton, NJ: Princeton University Press, 2003.

Fahmy, Ziad, "Media Capitalism: Colloquial Mass Culture and Nationalism, 1908–1918." *International Journal of Middle East Studies* 42 (2010): 83–103.

Feeney, John. "Shadows of Fancy." *Saudi ARAMCO World,* March–April 1999. http://www.saudiaramcoworld.com/issue/199902/shadows.of.fancy.htm.

Gunnels, Naomi. "The Ikhernofret Stela as Theater: A Cross-Cultural Comparisson." *Studia Antiqua, Journal of the BYU Student Society for Ancient Studies* 2 (2) (2002): 3–16.

Herondas. *The Mimes of Herondas.* Translated by M. S. Buck. New York, 1921. http://elfin spell.com/Mimes.html.

Lane, Edward. *Manners and Customs of the Modern Egyptians Written during a Stay between 1833–1835.* Cairo: AUC Press, 2004.

National Cultural Center. "Cairo Opera House." http://www.cairoopera.org/index.aspx.

Pollard, Lisa. *Nurturing the Nation: The Family Politics of Modernizing, Colonizing, and Liberating Egypt, 1805–1923.* Berkeley, CA: University of California Press, 2005.

Powell, Eve Troutt. "Burnt-Cork Nationalism." In *The Colors of Enchantment: Theater, Dance, Music, and the Visual Arts of the Middle East.* Sherifa Zuhur, ed. Cairo: AUC Press. Cairo: AUC Press, 2008, 27–38.

Rizq, Yunan Labib. "Dramatic Beginnings: Diwan of Contemporary Life" *al-Ahram,* November 21–27, 2002. http://weekly.ahram.org.eg/2002/613/chrncls.htm.

Sadgrove, P.C. *The Egyptian Theater in the Nineteenth Century, 1799–1882.* Reading, NY: Ithaca Press, 1996.

Shafik, Viola. *Arab Cinema: Culture and Identity.* Cairo: AUC Press, 2007.

Shay, Anthony. *Choreographic Politics: State Folk Dance Companies, Representation, and Power.* Middletown, CT: Wesleyan University Press, 2002.

Vitalis, Robert. "American Ambassador in Technicolor and Cinemascope: Hollywood and Revolution on the Nile." In *Mass Mediations: New Approaches to Popular Culture in the Middle East and Beyond*, 269–91. Walter Armbrust, ed. Berkeley, CA: University of California Press .

Williams, Daniel. "Making a Comeback: Male Belly Dancers in Egypt." *NY Times,* January 2, 2008. http://www.nytimes.com/2008/01/02/world/africa/02iht-letter.1.8984242.html?r=2.

Zuhur, Sherifa, ed. *Images of Enchantment: Visual and Performing Arts of the Middle East.* Cairo: AUC Press, 1998.

CHAPTER 7

Contemporary Issues

BEFORE AND AFTER THE REVOLUTION

After nearly 30 years of putting up with the Emergency Law that was put into place after the assassination of Anwar Sadat (1981) and the façade of democracy that has existed since the 1952 revolution, the people of Egypt proclaimed an end to their toleration and forced the resignation of President Mubarak. What were the long- and short-term factors that forced his exodus in February 2011? What will come of the movements that started?

As discussed in Chapter 3, Mubarak was able to retain solid control of Egypt since 1981 by regularly renewing the Emergency Law and silencing any opposition or unflattering rumors. Even as the president aged and became ill, it was illegal to speak of his health. In 2007, several reporters received sentences for indicating that he was not well. Although Mubarak later pardoned the individuals in question, no one dared speak about the his health again until he continued to refuse to comment in 2010 about whether he would be running for president in what should have been the upcoming 2011 presidential elections. While Egyptian sources were understandably mute, Western sources indicated that he was terminally ill with some form of cancer, pancreatic or stomach. He received treatment in Europe a number of times for various ailments, some disclosed and others unspecified. In order to make meetings and speaking engagements, he was apparently receiving large doses of medication so that he could perform before visitors and cameras for short periods of time. Several Arab papers reported that he collapsed twice before taping his non-resignation speech to the country (February 10, 2011), and *al-Masry al-Youm* indicated that he had an argument with his son (Gamal) in which he blamed both him and his (own) wife for ruining his legacy in Egypt.

Mubarak was a key ally for the West in general and the United States in particular; he upheld the uneasy peace with Israel established by his predecessor Anwar Sadat. Nevertheless, Mubarak overplayed his hand in his bid to establish a hereditary presidency. The first step in this procedure and to consolidate his position was to have no immediate successor. Thus, Mubarak had no vice president since 1989. Throughout his presidency, particularly after an assassination attempt in 1995 and an assault in 1999, observers inside and outside Egypt asked why he had no vice president. Mubarak casually dismissed these queries, explaining other constitutional contingencies and stating that the existence of a vice president does not guarantee a smooth transition of power. Meanwhile, he carefully and slowly put in place, the mechanisms that would allow his son Gamal (b. 1963) to become president, without realizing he was sowing the seeds for his own destruction.

Since 2000, the year that Bashar al-Assad succeeded his father in the presidency of Syria, both Mubaraks were attempting to make the right moves personally and professionally to maneuver Gamal into the presidency. Gamal became a member of the general secretariat of the ruling party (NDP). He left his private-sector job and established an NGO for helping unemployed Egyptians find housing and work. In a country riddled by underemployment, unemployment, and obstacles to marriage created by real and artificial housing shortages, a young, articulate, powerful individual addressing these problems could have a promising political future, especially someone with name and face recognition. Gamal gave more interviews, at first voicing his opinion on banking and finance, areas in which he studied and

---

MUBARAK TRIALS

On August 3, 2011, trials for Mubarak, his sons, the former Minister of Interior Adly, other regime officials, and insider Hussein Salem began in a police academy building that once bore Mubarak's name. The trial started as a media circus with the spectacle of Mubarak in a hospital bed inside a cage, broadcast on national television, until the court decided that lawyers were posturing for the media. Questions were raised regarding bias in the three-man panel after the testimony of Field Marshal Tantawi in late September, thus leading to at least two postponements in the hearings. Nevertheless, the large number of plaintiffs, lawyers, and jurisdictions complicated matters in addition to the fact that Mubarak and Adly were originally being tried separately for the same charge against the killing of the protestors in the demonstrations leading up to Mubarak's ouster. Mubarak's charges, as well as those of his sons and a colleague also dealt with corruption. Mubarak was acquitted on the corruption charges; however, his sons face separate charges in another trial. In June 2012, Mubarak and Adly received life sentences on charges of killing the protestors. The judges ruled that lower level officials were not culpable.

worked, gradually branching out into all arenas of life in Egypt. His face became a regular feature of the press, and there was talk of a new party, *al-Mustaqbal* (the future), with the same name as his organization. Instead, in 2002 his father gave him a powerful position within the party (NDP), as General Secretary of the Policy Committee, the third most powerful position in the organization. By 2004 Gamal's cabinet was in place chosen from his Policy Committee. Rather than being stodgy old-schoolers, now it would include younger technocrats and academics, some of whom had advanced degrees from Western universities. In short, people who would support his presidency. This faction in the years to come would lean toward neoliberalist capitalism in its most decadent, self-serving form, much to the dismay of the military and nationalist capitalists who would come to be cut out of the pie.

Meanwhile, opposition groups in Egypt across the political spectrum banded together to oppose the continuation of the Emergency Law, the hereditary succession of power, and presidential elections by referendum (see Chapter 3) ; Kefaya is notable in this regard. Some individuals questioned Gamal's credentials. For example, he had no military experience, unlike Nasser, Sadat, and his father. Many still believe that a military candidate will always have the edge. While some argued Gamal would never be accepted by the military (and he was not), the traditional backbone of the regime, others dismissed military experience as an outdated prerequisite that even presidents Clinton and Obama of the United States did not fulfill. In other words, 21st-century Egypt, at peace with Israel, does not need a seasoned military veteran as president. Gamal had other assets: considerable charm, enthusiasm, and

MILITARY IN GOVERNMENT

The army as part of the ruling elite has been a long-established trend in Egyptian history. Perhaps most spectacularly the army reaffirmed its importance in the revolution of 1952, which restored government to native Egyptians for the first time since the days of the pharaohs. More recently, in the heady days of the demonstrations in January and February 2011, the army appeared to be the "protector" of the people, and it began to shepherd the process of transition to civilian rule. Nevertheless, in the months that followed, SCAF delayed ending the Emergency Law, it used extreme force on continuing demonstrations, and in the wake of the first round of elections in late 2011 it appeared unable and unwilling to give up its power or its accountability with respect to the vast resources it has historically received in foreign aid. Even after ending the Emergency Law in early 2012, loopholes allow for its reimposition. In the buildup to the 2012 presidential run-off during which the courts invalidated the new parliament, SCAF announced far-reaching powers for itself as the Muslim Brotherhood's candidate Mursi was ready to claim victory: a legislative role, control over the budget, control over who writes the new constitution, lack of presidential control over SCAF, and appointment for life for SCAF.

intelligence—not to mention the fact that he could speak English with greater ease than any past Egyptian president.

While the elder Mubarak handily won the 2005 election (see Chapter 3), opposition to the notion of hereditary succession did not end, nor did the Mubaraks' maneuvering. In 2007, on his father's 79th birthday, Gamal ended his 44 years of bachelorhood and married 24-year-old Khadiga "Moni" El-Gamal, AUC graduate and daughter of a wealthy businessman. The profile of a single politician would not bode well in a country where the family anchors society. Kefaya organized demonstrations all over Egypt on the wedding day because the opposition group connected the pending nuptials to the younger Mubarak's political future. In March 2010, while he was recovering from gall bladder surgery in Germany, the senior Mubarak received the blessed news that Khadiga gave birth to his first granddaughter, Farida, thus completing the family unit. Prior to the 2011 revolution, given the previous restrictions on presidential candidates, if the senior Mubarak did not run, it would have been difficult for anyone else to emerge as a viable candidate. By this point Gamal had given his first U.S. interview to Fareed Zakaria of CNN (March 2009), where one of the early footers in the lengthy conversation read "expected to be next Egyptian president."

The last serious presidential candidate Aymon Nour was arrested for not filing his papers properly, released briefly to run in 2005, imprisoned, and then released early (for health reasons) just prior to Obama's visit in 2009. After his release he and his wife Gamila Ismail mysteriously divorced, and talk of her run for the 2011 presidency ended. Perhaps this was an object lesson of what could happen to individuals who opposed the Mubaraks? Not surprisingly, initially Nour's papers for a run in 2011 were rejected by party committee. New or branch-out parties were still dominated (or infiltrated) by NDP old guard members and having served in prison

---

MUBARAK THE FAMILY MAN

M. Hosni Mubarak has been married for many years—although few sources say how long to Suzanne Saleh Sabet, daughter of an Egyptian doctor and a Welsh nurse. Mrs. Mubarak, unlike most Egyptian women, takes her husband's name in deference to Western political tradition. She has a BA and an MA from the American University in Cairo in Political Science and Educational Sociology, respectively. The Mubaraks have raised two sons, Alaa and Gamal. While the world knows a great deal about younger son Gamal, one is hard-pressed to find many details about Alaa aside from the names of his wife and children. He is a businessman, and it is sometimes alleged that while his family was in power he forced his way into lucrative partnerships. In May 2009, Alaa's son Muhammad, whose age was variously given as 12 or 13 years, died suddenly in France of a mysterious heart ailment. President Mubarak was so close to the young man, but in such fragile condition himself that he did not attend the funeral.

would be an obstacle. Nevertheless, in the summer of 2010 when a committee to support Gamal was plastering Cairo with his pictures, Nour threatened to do the same with his own pictures. After the revolution, by the fall of 2011 Nour was back in campaign mode. No longer just the Tomorrow party, Nour created the Revolution Tomorrow party.

Ayman Nour has been at the forefront of demonstrations aimed at ending military rule. As for Gamila Ismail, she ran for parliament in the Qasr al-Nil district as an independent. Like most women who ran as independents she was not successful in the first round of results announced in early December 2011.

In early 2010, Mohamed ElBaradei, Nobel laureate and former director of the International Atomic Energy Agency initiated meetings with various opposition leaders in Egypt, including Nour, hinting that he might run in what was expected to be the upcoming 2011 presidential election. Egypt watchers worldwide speculated as ElBaradei gave interviews and speeches, fueling hope for a new direction in Egyptian politics. He moved outside his own comfort zone into the world of Facebook and Twitter, in order to network with his 21st century supporters. At this point in time, no one could predict the revolution or that the presidential elections would be

Mohamed ElBaradei, shown here in his position as director general of the International Atomic Energy Agency, helped to spark a movement for reform in Egypt. (AP Photo)

delayed until June 2012. ElBaradei began his mission by trying to unite the opposition in Egypt including various strands of the left on the one hand and the Muslim Brotherhood on the other. The Muslim Brotherhood has been extremely successful in gaining independent seats in parliament and working as a bloc, but political liberals and leftists do not necessarily see eye to eye with the Brotherhood on women's issues, minority affairs, and other civil rights matters. Perhaps we can see this networking as a precursor to the January 25 movement, particularly in the desire to unite against Mubarak. Once the demonstrations began in late January 2011, he appeared in the square, which helped to galvanize support. Shortly thereafter there were reports that ElBaradei was under house arrest; however, he later denied those reports. He has maintained an independent stance, unaffiliated with any of the old, new, or reworked parties. Nevertheless, he has created a National Association for Change, and his message has remained focused on the need for constitutional reform and to transition away from military rule. Forces inside and outside the government see him as an honest broker and a mediator. When the transitional government of Essam Sharaf resigned just days before the late November 2011 elections, due to its inability to either keep order or keep the military in check, *al-Jazeera English* reported that ElBaradei offered to resist running for election and step up to the plate as interim prime minister, engaging in negotiations with SCAF. Nevertheless, SCAF's initial choice Kamal el-Ganzouri took office in early December 2011.

JANUARY 25 MOVEMENT

Not long after the 2010 parliamentary elections, the Jasmine Revolution of Tunisia broke out; and Mubarak took preemptory measures, for example, reducing the price of staples. Indeed, poverty, Egypt's struggling economy, and lack of hope for young people entering the job market regardless of education or skill set was but one of the major complaints that would emerge in the weeks to come, along with the hereditary presidency and the Emergency Law. Inspired by events in Tunisia, between January 17 and 20 at least five Egyptians tried to set themselves on fire, mostly in front of the public buildings in the capital. Simultaneously, activist Egyptians sponsored protests. The new medium of social networking served as a call to battle. Wael Ghonim of Google Middle East, set up "We are all Khaled Saeed" to invite people to protest on January 25, 2011. Saeed was a young man who had been beaten to death by Egyptian police outside an Alexandria internet café in June 2010. Police brutality and torture were among the chief complaints of demonstrators. Asma Mahfouz, an Egyptian woman in her mid-20s, made a YouTube video encouraging her friends and countrymen not to burn themselves, but rather stand proudly with her in Tahrir Square regardless of the treatment they might face by riot police. She claimed they must demand their human rights from the corrupt administration. This demand was the single most important claim of the protestors; however, to earn it, Mubarak had to leave. Tens of thousands of young Egyptians turned out for the demonstrations, not only in Tahrir but all over Egypt in the days that followed.

A massive crowd gathers in Tahrir, or Liberation, Square in Cairo, Egypt, on February 1, 2011. Tens of thousands of people flooded into the heart of Cairo, filling the city's main square as a call for a million protesters was answered by the largest demonstration up to that time of continuing demands for President Hosni Mubarak to leave after nearly 30 years in power. (AP Photo)

Mubarak's response to the demonstrations was calculated and swift. While sending out riot police and army units, there were relatively few major confrontations with the protestors in the early days. In a speech delivered shortly after midnight on January 29, Mubarak forced the resignation of his entire cabinet, but did not step down himself. In making this choice, Mubarak quickly sacrificed the Minister of the Interior Adly, and eventually he would sacrifice his own son Gamal, who reportedly left Egypt on January 26 aboard a private jet. Adly represented the hated brutality and repression portrayed by the mangled face of Khaled Saeed as well as ridiculous tactics, such as the release of prisoners on January 28. Meanwhile, Gamal stood for just about everything that was wrong with the administration. First, he stood for nepotism in its most outlandish form. Second, and in a related matter, he stood for corruption at the highest levels of government. Estimates of Mubarak family's accumulated wealth is somewhere between $40 billion and $70 billion. Third, Gamal represented a neoliberal faction within the government that was willing to sell Egypt's assets to the highest bidder, be it Persian Gulf princes, the West, or the Chinese. Thus, he alienated nationalist capitalists, for example, the Sawiris family, who traditionally monopolized Egyptian wealth in the infitah era (see Chapters 4 and 5). On January 31, Naguib Sawaris even joined the demonstrations. Fourth, Gamal threatened the military's traditional power base with his power base of technocrats (Amar 2011). At the same time, Hosni Mubarak steadfastly refused to step down. At best on February 1 he agreed not to run for another term, but insisted to remain in power until a smooth transition could take place, and he placed Vice President Omar Suleiman, former head of the Intelligence Services, a branch of the military, in charge of the day-to-day operations of the government.

Mubarak took a few more precautions. He arranged curfews, allowed the automated teller machines (ATMs) to run out of money, and stores to run short of needed supplies. He jammed internet and wireless signals to thwart mobile communications. Many Egyptians in Tahrir had even lifted passphrases on their wireless routers so that demonstrators could pick up signals. Social networking or no social networking, Egyptians continued to demonstrate. They did so in an organized, peaceful, and tasteful manner, even cleaning up after themselves. Mubarak wanted Egyptians to grow tired, angry, frustrated, hungry, and moneyless. Then he sent out the thugs, the horses, and the camels on February 2 to bully the crowds. According to AUC Professor and activist Khaled Fahmy, the pro-government thugs were clearly identifiable as they came across the 6 October Bridge. Some did not even know which direction to turn (non-Cairenes), yet they had banners, flags, and printed pamphlets—items that took the antigovernment groups days to prepare on site. His idea was that he could "restore order" and indeed there were segments of the population growing frustrated by the interruption to daily life that the new order was bringing. Amidst all the demonstrations Christians held mass on Sunday and Muslims prayed at regular intervals in Tahrir Square. There was unity of agreement that Mubarak must go. The U.S. administration that had supported Mubarak on day one of the demonstrations, by February 10 agreed that he must go. In Mubarak's rambling speech he promised to amend the most grievous parts of the constitution (those affecting the presidency) and to have judicial supervision of elections, yet mostly it was a patriarchal rant that connected him to the most significant events of the 20th century at the end of which he stated he would part with Egypt only in death. Confused reporters in the United States repeatedly asked for translations of Mubarak's statement, refusing to believe that he was not resigning. The following day, amidst another Friday of demonstrations, Vice President Suleiman announced Mubarak's resignation and the transfer of power to SCAF. By the time Mubarak departed, 800 Egyptians perished in the riots and nearly 6,000 were reported wounded.

On one hand, Egyptians' prayers were answered, and Mubarak was out of power. Nevertheless, on the other hand, by returning power to the army, Egypt was in many ways put back to the status quo minus Mubarak. Many of the activists and reformers have been disappointed in the initial direction of the revolution. The committee to amend the constitution contained no women, and a Constitutional Referendum was hurriedly packaged and passed on March 19, 2011. About 41 percent of those eligible to vote turned out, many of whom were first-time voters, and the referendum passed with just over 77 percent voting in favor of the packaged restructuring. The "la'" movement or "no" campaign included groups who felt that the entire constitution should be scrapped immediately as some articles were offensive and that the changes were not far-reaching enough. Further constitutional change would await the election of a new assembly.

Egypt's ex-President Hosni Mubarak lays on a gurney inside a barred cage in the police academy courthouse in Cairo, Egypt, June, 2012. (AP Photo, File)

Between March and the parliamentary elections (November 2011–January 2012) there were three trends: continued party formation, continued demonstrations, and the bizarre feeling of status quo minus the stability. New parties emerged and old ones are regrouped. For example, the oldest party in Egypt, the Wafd, continues to sell itself as a liberal, secular party. Nevertheless, during its long history it has tainted itself by association with the regime (both the British and Mubarak) as well as the Muslim Brotherhood. Due to its financial backing and its media connections, in addition to the better aspects of its history, it was able to gain a few seats in parliament. Similarly, hoping to buy influence, billionaire financier Naguib Sawaris, a Copt, launched the Free Egyptians party; however, his intent was not to run for office. The NPUP, better known as Tagammu, the left-leaning branch of the ASU that grew into its own party, has joined forces with the Free Egyptians and the Egyptian Social Democratic party to form the Egyptian Bloc, a secular political alliance to counter the influence of the Muslim Brotherhood. Another party that was expected to join this group was the Egyptian Tahrir party, formed in large part by Sufis, but many of whose organizers and candidates are non-Sufis including Copts and women. The Egyptian Bloc's overtly secular message has been construed by many as antireligious and some initial enthusiasm has dwindled. Nevertheless, it did manage to finish in third behind two religion-oriented parties.

The Muslim Brotherhood appears to be splintering into a number of parties dividing along generational and ideological lines. Americans often speak of "the Brotherhood" as though it were one party and one political strategy. Mainstream brothers flocked to the Freedom and Justice party, which garnered about 40 percent of the seats in the first stage of the 2011 elections. The Freedom and Justice party is considered centrist since it joined an alliance with other moderate groups, most notably Ayman Nour's Revolution Tomorrow and *al-Karama* to form the Democratic Alliance for Egypt, which is committed to "the good of all Egypt" rather than "Islam as a solution" (Jadaliyya). The more conservative *salafis* created the Nour party, and received about 25 percent of the vote. It should be noted that the Nour party is in an alliance with two smaller *salafi* parties, known as the Alliance for Egypt.

There are more moderate and more radical politicians who at one time or another were associated with the Muslim Brotherhood. As for the former, they created the *Wasaṭ* or Center party. Although it existed before the revolution (1996), its role as a mouthpiece for the opposition to the government meant that it never had an official existence until after the fall of Mubarak. The Wasaṭ party did not do as well as either Freedom and Justice or Nour, and not surprisingly shortly after the first round of elections there were allegations of vote-buying (with food) laid against Freedom and Justice by Wasaṭ. At the other end of the Brotherhood's spectrum is the Gama'a al-Islamiyya, the group best known for assassinating Sadat. This group won two districts in Assiut. Next there are parties affiliated with youth. The Justice party was started by younger, disenchanted members of the Muslim Brotherhood. It sees itself as an option between the religious parties and the liberal ones. It is difficult for a small party to gather enough votes by itself to get elected, which is why the Revolution Continues Alliance contains a younger generation of disheartened Muslim Brothers, socialists, Islamo-socialists, and even some liberals: the Socialist Popular Alliance, the Egyptian Socialist party, the Egyptian Current party, the Equality and Development party, Revolutionary Youth Coalition, and the Egyptian Alliance party. They received about 4 percent of the vote.

Even as campaigning was taking place for the multiphase elections in late 2011 and early 2012, demonstrations in Egypt did not stop. Among the most noteworthy incidents is the Maspero massacre on October 9, 2011 in which Coptic Christian protestors marched from Shubra to Maspero to express their outrage over a church burning in Aswan as well as lack of government response to such occurrences. Video and eyewitness testimony tell the story of armored personnel carriers running into peaceful protestors. Twenty-eight people died and more than 300 were injured in this incident, which SCAF claims was incited by the protestors. Similarly, in the wake of demonstrations, beatings, and tortures following the first round of parliamentary elections, SCAF accused protestors of initiating the violence. Notable here was the presence of women in the demonstrations on December 20, 2011 after the circulation of a video and photographs of a woman in a blue bra, who had been stripped and beaten by a soldier. Gen. Adel Emera of SCAF while cleverly stating remorse for the incident did not actually express responsibility.

Egyptians in late 2011 felt less safe than they did in late 2010. The military appeared to have supreme control over various spheres of their life, and at the same time their day-to-day security was not what it used to be. During the early weeks of the revolution, the world heard heart-warming stories of neighborhood watches; however, it was never clear if the coverage was complete or if it continued. Burglaries, street crime, carjacking, and assault—things about which most Egyptians rarely concerned themselves in prerevolutionary days, by 2011 became ordinary incidents. In the early weeks of the revolution police stations were ransacked, many officers stopped reporting for duty, weapons were looted, and prisoners released. Both the reality and the fear perpetuated by stories (true and false) has changed the nature of how Egyptians view their world. Despite these problems, according to Scott Macleod, the overwhelming majority of them still have an optimistic view of the future, with 67 percent seeing Egypt as having a brighter economic future and 63 percent as seeing their family's condition improving (2011). Much will depend upon the military's willingness to cede power to a civilian government and demonstrate transparency in its accounts. While there was hope in the removal of the Emergency Law in January 2012, the existence of clauses to invoke it in cases of "thuggery" make most Egyptians wary. The presidential elections also gave Egyptians cause for hope in completing the cycle for reform; however, a number of events just prior to the second round of presidential elections in June 2012 increased uncertainty: the SCC dissolving the newly elected parliament (see Chapter 3) and approving former regime figure Ahmed Shafiq to run in those elections, SCAF announcing new powers to "ease" the balance of power, the end of the Mubarak trial (see sidebar), and the specter of Mubarak hovering between life and death, and close election results (see subsequently).

The most high-profile presidential candidates, particularly for Westerners, ended up choosing not to run (ElBaradei), having difficulty filing papers (Ayman Nour), or in the case of the former secretary-general of the Arab-League Amr Moussa, running as an independent and receiving fewer votes than other major candidates

---

LIFE, DEATH, AND CONSPIRACY THEORY

Among Middle East watchers, there is an old expression: there are no conspiracy theories, just conspiracies. The state of Mubarak's health has certainly provided grist for the rumor mill. While he was president, discussion of his health could end in a prison sentence, as he appeared to cover some sort of ailment(s). After his imprisonment, opposition groups accused the former president of using his fragile health to receive special treatment. For someone lying in a hospital bed in a cage, he looked remarkably robust; and Egyptians complained that when the cameras were not directly on him he would move about with ease. At the conclusion of his trial, he was sent to the Tora prison hospital. Days later reports surfaced of stroke, heart attack, and even "clinical death." Mubarak was transferred to the military hospital in Maadi, and rumors ranged from those claiming he wanted greater comfort to those stating that he might fake his own death so that he can live out the rest of his days abroad. Interestingly enough, the "death scare" of Mubarak came in the week between the elections and the announcement of a winner in the June 2012 presidential race. Most Egyptians were more concerned about this outcome.

(11 percent). The first round was extremely close between the top four candidates: Mohamed Mursi of the Islamist Freedom and Justice Party (25 percent); Mubarak's former prime minister, Ahmed Shafiq, running as an independent (24 percent); Hamdeen Sabahi of the (Nasserist) Dignity Party (22 percent); and Abdel Moneim Fotouh, who ran as an independent, supported by *salafi* Nour Party, Wasat, and the Egyptian Current Party (18 percent) (Jadaliyya). Only the top two candidates could participate in the run-off election, which initially called Mursi as the winner. Shortly thereafter the Presidential Election Commission announced that the vote was too close to call, and each side claimed victory. More than a week after the run-off election, on June 24, 2012, Mursi was proclaimed the victor with just under 52 percent of the vote. Wael Ghonim tweeted [in English], "1st elected civilian in modern history of Egypt as President. Critical milestone. Revolution isn't an event, it's a process so it continues." (@Ghonim) Echoing the sentiment that history had been made and struggle might follow, activist Hossam Bahgat tweeted [in Arabic], "Today is a sublime day. Tomorrow opposition to the new president begins. Mubarak is the vanquished of the fallen." (@hossambahgat) As for Shafiq, rumors quickly spread of his supporters blocking the streets in Medinat Nasr, and as both tweets and news reports indicated, the human shield was not observed by passersby and cars (Khazbak 2012).

PEACE WITH ISRAEL AND THE GAZA BORDER

Although Egypt has had peace with Israel officially since 1979, the conflict between the Palestinians and Israelis lingers in the hearts of most Egyptians, despite the fact that most have never been to the land in question. There are a number of factors contributing to Egyptian concerns for the Palestinian cause. Whether one is a Muslim or a Copt, Jerusalem is a holy land and its occupation by (perceived) foreigners is a crime. Second, although it has been several decades since the 1948, 1967, and 1973 wars, family members still recount the stories of experiences in and/or loved ones lost in those conflicts. Third, until recently the government has allowed the Palestine problem to be a political football to be passed around and played in the media in hopes that people will forget their own problems and focus on an external enemy. By allowing "freedom" of the press on this issue, the former regime appeared magnanimous and advanced. While censoring many other topics, the government even after 1979 continued to stoke the flames of hatred and excess. Events of the past few years, in which HAMAS has taken control of the Gaza Strip, reduced the Egyptian presence therein, and empowered Mubarak's biggest opposition bloc (the Muslim Brotherhood), call into question the strategy of cold peace and open press.

Cold peace has meant that both parties sent diplomatic missions; however, Israel was always far more eager in sending governmental, business, cultural, educational, and other contacts to Egypt. Rare were the individuals like playwright Ali Salem, who actually waited until after the Oslo accords (1993), and in 1994 drove his car across the Rafah border in a gesture of goodwill and friendship, much to the dismay of friends and family, documented in his *A Drive to Israel: An Egyptian Meets His Neighbors.* Mubarak made only a single state visit to Israel on the occasion of Yitzhak

The Muslim Brotherhood, once part of the opposition as in this 2005 rally, now has links to the Freedom and Justice party, which won the 2012 presidential election. (AP Photo)

Rabin's funeral in 1995. The Egyptian government maintains its embassy in Tel Aviv and consulate in Eilat, closing them only under the most difficult of circumstances, for example, after the Sabra and Shatila Camp massacres in 1982 or heated moments of the intifadas. Evidence of the strain between the countries is the sanction on an Egyptian citizen who marries an Israeli—loss of citizenship. While the Coptic church has strict rules regarding marrying within the church, and Muslim women can only marry Muslim men, a Muslim man can marry any monotheist including a Jew. Regarding loss of citizenship, in a recent decision the Supreme Administrative Court upheld a previous ruling to this effect; however, the judge added that each case should be investigated separately. Many believe that there might be distinctions between Arab Israelis and non-Arab Israelis in this matter since nearly 20 percent of the population is Muslim, Christian, or Druze, that is, Palestinian Arab, not to be confused with Jews who come from the Arab world. Regardless, it seems an extreme measure to take against a citizen when a state of peace has existed between the two countries for decades.

Egypt shares a history with Gaza as it was the administrator of the territory between the 1948 and 1967 wars (see Chapter 2). Israel pulled out of the Gaza Strip in 2005, and Egypt's significance as a mediator has returned since there is no other third party acceptable to both the Palestinians and Israel. When Ariel Sharon unilaterally decided on this evacuation, we cannot be certain of what his motives were; he suffered a debilitative stroke just a few months later. The effect of isolating Gaza only hardened the parties involved, which helped bring HAMAS to power in 2007 (see Chapter 1). The Gaza Strip is like a cage that Israel can shut off and close at any moment—by air, land, and sea, as well as with supplies, power, food, and medicine. Egypt's Rafah border offers a single doorway (outside of Israel) into that locked cage. Egypt hoped that once in power, HAMAS leaders would soften as did the PLO after the Lebanese Civil War. HAMAS did not back down. Rather than listening to Egyptian representatives, HAMAS flexed its muscles with the Muslim Brotherhood, its parent organization. The Muslim Brotherhood, while not an official party in Egypt, represented the most successful bloc of independent candidates prior to Mubarak's fall (see Chapter 3); since Mubarak's fall, Brotherhood-affiliated parties were the most successful in the earliest round of elections. Relations with Israel and international pressure dictated Mubarak's decision to close the Rafah border to commercial traffic after the rise of HAMAS; but after HAMAS squeezed Mubarak through his opposition (the Muslim Brotherhood), he was forced to relax security on illegal tunnels. Weapons from Iran and other sources seeped through the porous border, and rocket fire from Gaza into Israel between 2007 and 2008, particularly in Sderot and its environs increased. There was no severe finger-pointing at Egypt, because the United States, Israel, and the EU realized its predicament and simply urged Mubarak to mediate. Egypt attempted to moderate between the two sides, negotiating a lull in the hostilities in 2008, which would bind HAMAS to a ceasefire, end Israel's embargo on the strip, and also require Egypt to police its borders more carefully. Neither Israel nor HAMAS felt the other side lived up to the spirit of the agreement. Israel responded with airstrikes beginning in late December 2008 and a ground assault in early January 2009, known as the Gaza War. After the Gaza War, Egypt moved back toward its closed door position on Rafah. Egypt received assistance and training from U.S. troops to better police the border.

Nevertheless, as Israel maintained its blockade and Palestinian suffering mounted, various groups attempted to reach Gaza, including a flotilla of six ships organized by international humanitarians flying under the Turkish flag in late May 2010. Israeli commandos stormed the lead ship and intercepted the flotilla, leaving nine dead and many more wounded. This action led to a severe rupture in Israel's relations with Turkey, its strongest Muslim supporter. As a result, Egypt once again was in a difficult position of both enforcing safety on the border, but needing to open Rafah to assure humanitarian assistance. Ironically, the policies pursued by the United States and Israel aimed at punishing HAMAS have only strengthened it. The world cannot cast its eyes aside as the people inside the strip continue to suffer, yet it is HAMAS that controls the strip and all materials moving inside it. Israel might like to cut the strip away like an ugly scab and leave Egypt responsible for Gaza's economic well-being, but Egypt will not accept this potential menace or the underlying acknowledgement that it would not be part of a future Palestinian state. In other words, its physical separation would contribute to its ultimate political fate. Egypt, taking a chapter out of the Israeli playbook, has also decided to build a fortification on the border, which would end much of the illegal tunnel smuggling and strengthen Egyptian security. Palestinians have complained vociferously that whatever else might go through the tunnels, in the wake of frequent blockades and closures, these openings are the only dependable means of getting food, cooking oil, and other basic supplies. With the Rafah gate open, Egypt has been diligent in making aid-givers conform to specific guidelines. A Jordanian aid group, consisting of activists, academics, and unionists was denied entry in July 2010 while presumably carrying supplies and materials to start a children's hospital. Whether their union orientation, their Islamist bent, or the stated reason of lack of sufficient notice was the actual reason is unknown, but it is an indication that Egypt is watching. Shortly thereafter, Egypt denied entry to Gaza-bound Iranian parliamentarians. This denial came about a month after the Iranian Red Crescent gave up on sending aid into Gaza. Given that Iranian president Ahmedinejad has repeatedly forecast the end of the Israeli state, as well as connections between HAMAS and Iran, it would seem that Egypt is erring on the side of caution.

Since the January 25 movement there has been a great deal of discussion about the future of the Egyptian–Israeli peace. While meeting with German Chancellor Merkel on January 31, 2011, Israeli prime minister Netanyahu eerily warned that the Egyptian Revolution could relive the Iranian experience of 1979. Most observers point out the absence of anti-Israeli rhetoric in the demonstrations, with the focus being on ridding Egypt of Mubarak and getting civil rights for all Egyptian citizens. With the passage of time, most experts inside and outside of Egypt seem to forecast the continuation of a cold peace that may turn chillier, but no major change in relations despite the initial concerns of the Israelis. As for the Rafah passage, the transitional government in Egypt has made it easier for Gazans to pass over the border, with only visa restrictions on men between the ages of 18 and 40. Egypt also regulates the bus companies that cross the border.

HIV AND AIDS

Egypt currently spends about $3 million on AIDS programs annually, and for the past two decades, with greater or lesser energy, it has devoted some effort to public awareness. Nevertheless, these attempts have been inconsistent and not necessarily focused in the most at-risk populations. While the recorded prevalence of HIV is rather low in the country, prostitution, child prostitution, intravenous drug use, male-to-male sexual contact, and the gay tourism industry are all stable if not increasing. Little information is available on the incidence of infected blood since the government is reluctant to admit wrongdoing at any level. There is a tendency to dismiss HIV and AIDS as a foreign issue because of its association with drugs or illicit sex, and this myth has been furthered through government policy and the media. Long-term visitors seeking more than a traveler's visa, for example, students on Study Abroad or business people must submit a negative HIV test along with other paperwork. Movies, for example, *Love in Taba* (1992) demonstrate the power of Israeli women carrying the lethal virus into Egypt and into the unsuspecting bodies of Egyptian men. While director Ahmed Fouad's tale is more telling of his views on peace with Israel, it demonstrates the overall lack of knowledge about the virus's transmission. Thus, at the popular and governmental level, HIV belongs to the foreigner, to the enemy, to someone else—not to the healthy Egyptian.

Whether the program is related to the government, a Muslim association, or a Coptic charity, abstinence and marital fidelity have been the foundation of all HIV and AIDS education. There is a huge amount of stigma associated with the disease, and one might read figures as low as 2,500 for the official number of HIV-positive individuals in Egypt. In a country where the newspapers have been known to publish the names of HIV-positive individuals, people lose jobs, travel restrictions ensue, there is little incentive to be tested for the virus. The UN estimates that there are some 11,000 individuals who are HIV-positive and that the number is increasing exponentially. Compared to sub-Saharan Africa, the numbers out of a population of more than 83 million seem small; however, without a national plan the country faces a rapidly growing problem.

Egypt needs to bring together all the ministries, NGOs, and other interested parties in combating the disease. Currently, without an all-encompassing plan it is difficult for NGOs to reach sex workers, street children, drug users, and other groups that are outside the purview of the law without some sort of agreement with the government and the police. Without educating and reaching the most at-risk groups the HIV-positive population will continue to grow. A 2009 survey conducted by the WHO indicated that condom use among this population was well below 15 percent, as well as for men having sex with other men. The need for outreach and education is quite clear.

Another area that needs to be addressed with respect to HIV and AIDS has been with medications and living conditions. Antiretroviral drugs have been extremely successful in slowing the progress and morbidity of the disease, and in the mid-2000s Egypt began producing its own drugs to reduce the previously prohibitive cost to patients. Nevertheless, there are still access problems for some patients. Moreover, many HIV-positive patients do not die from AIDS; they suffer from various other ailments and secondary infections. They are often refused medical care, and even if they receive medical care they do not get proper follow-up. Lack of proper nutrition, not taking medicine as instructed, and poor living conditions all contribute to a shortened lifespan of the HIV-positive population in Egypt.

WOMEN, POPULATION, AND THE CONTROVERSY OVER FEMALE GENITAL MUTILATION (FGM)

In September 1994 Cairo had the honor of hosting the International Conference on Population and Development. Thousands of participants from nearly 200 countries converged on the city victorious to discuss pertinent population planning issues, such as birth control, infant mortality, immigration, education, and reproductive rights with a goal of achieving consensus on a variety of quantitative and qualitative goals. As the world spotlight was shining on Egypt, CNN aired a clip of a young, adolescent girl undergoing an FGM procedure (also known as female circumcision) at the hands of a barber. While the country's first instinct was to lash out at the news agency (a failed $500 million lawsuit aimed at proving CNN's intent to destroy Egypt's image) slowly new programs emerged and the government broke its silence on the issue. Rather than ending the practice, it has become more professionalized, which is now done by medical practitioners rather than barbers or homegrown midwives. While this might seem to be an improvement, it also appears to give sanction to the practice.

The Egyptian Demographic Health Survey (EDHS) in 2008 indicated that 75 percent of all FGMs were performed by medical practitioners, and that while the number of women between 15 and 17 who have undergone the procedure is declining, it was still about 75 percent, compared to more than 90 percent for women between 15 and 49 who were or ever had been married. Adhering to the motto, it takes a village to raise a child, various women's organizations, NGOs, and government ministries have worked together to create FGM-free villages. There are now approximately 120 FGM-free villages, and the National Council for Childhood and Motherhood has worked to criminalize FGM; however, enforcing this law is another matter. The former government received support from the religious establishment. Al-Azhar's Supreme Council, Dar al-Ifta, and the Coptic Church have condemned the practice and attempted to separate it from any perceived tradition, but these endorsements do not mean that all mainstream clergymen support these views. One of the biggest obstacles has been women, who insist on getting the procedure for themselves or their daughters. A 2005 EDHS indicates that the overwhelming reason that women give for FGM is maintaining tradition (57 percent), followed by reducing sexual desire (32 percent), hygiene or cleanliness (29 percent), and seeking religious approval (12 percent). Given the prevalence of the practice in Upper Egypt, it is clear that these concerns cross religious lines.

Another major issue with respect to women and control of their bodies is abortion. Egyptian law prohibits abortion except in matters where a woman's life is in danger. Women's rights groups have been trying to change the law so that victims of rape can abort the fetus of these unwanted unions and in doing so, reduce the number of homeless street children—both runaway girls and abandoned children. The law, proposed before the revolution, would require that a woman immediately present herself to a police station, where she would testify, be subject to forensic testing, and open to herself to humiliation and re-victimization as she relives the crime. Unmarried women would even have to prove that their virginity had been compromised. The law technically passed through parliament, but since all legislation must be in conformity with the *sharia* there must be approval from the Islamic Research Academy, where scholars are split on the issue. Some completely dismiss abortion, whereas others are willing to work within a 120-day window, the point at which Muslims believe life begins, and even within this group there are still divisions. Regardless of the legislation, there is already the morning-after pill available to women with access to a doctor willing to phone-in the prescription. Additionally, many pharmacists discreetly render the drug without prescription. Rape is a problem that is faced by women of all classes, and the morning-after pill works well for those who know it is available, those who can afford it, and those who are able to get to it in time. Poor, uneducated, and young women, may not know about the morning-after pill, or have the means to get it in the 24- to 48-hour timeframe within which it is most effective.

Birth control is yet another major reproductive issue that has dominated discourses by, about, and for women since the 1930s. The earliest debates about limiting family size came from bourgeois Egyptians toying with the idea of improving the quality of national life by reducing the number of citizens competing for limited resources. After the 1952 revolution, the Free Officers looked at the masses as an untapped resource rather than a nuisance, but after the 1960 census it was clear that something needed to be done. The total fertility rate per Egyptian woman was higher than seven children. By the mid-1960s Egypt had a National Family Planning Program and made birth control, usually the pill, widely available through clinics staffed by women. At the time, the discourse in the press reflected the anxieties of many, including those who were against birth control, and in particular, those who felt that birth control would give women sexual license. Nevertheless, as historian Laura Bier has pointed out, in distinction to the United States and Western Europe, the movement toward birth control in Egypt was framed in different terms. It was not about sexual freedom and ownership of one's body, but rather it was the maternal obligation of a good citizen (2008).

Initially there was not a great deal of success in these family planning efforts; however, decades later, demographers and sociologists can look at population trends and see Egypt's decline in total fertility rate. By the late 1990s, the total fertility rate had dropped to 3.8, and by 2009, it was estimated to be 2.66. Projections for the future estimate that by 2025, it could be 2. It is clear that sexually active women in Egypt have knowledge of existing and accessible methods of birth control; however, many do not routinely or effectively use those methods. Recent EDHS indicates that more than 95 percent of married women between the ages of 15 and 49 know about available methods of birth control, but only 60 percent regularly practice. Many female non-birth-control users state a desire to limit family size, that is, there is a gulf between practice and ideal. Another matter related to birth control is both political and religious. While most Muslim theologians historically have supported the use of birth control, some have recently spoken out against it. In particular, in Egypt some men and women have objected to the use of birth control on the grounds that it is a Western and/or Zionist plot to reduce the number of Muslims in the world.

Even though Egypt has managed to reduce its growth rate, since much of the population is in its fertile age-bearing years (approximately 40 percent), it is still critical to manage the situation. Furthermore, there are regional gaps between urban and rural areas as well as upper and lower Egypt, with rural and Upper Egypt having the highest fertility rates and the closest spacing between children. The implications for continued high birth rates in these areas put strains on already stressed resources including water, food, education, and employment. One of Egypt's biggest problems is feeding its population. In recent years demand for meat coupled with reduced internal meat production has led to increased prices offset slightly by imports. The country is not self-sufficient in cereals, sugar, or oils and necessitates imports of these items, two of which it used to export earlier (see Chapter 2). While there is theoretically enough water in Egypt, maintenance of pipelines, equipment, and fittings, along with the unequal distribution of the population create waste and inefficiency.

By 2030 the country might reach 103 million inhabitants. Many peasants have left the countryside in search of a better life in Cairo. The city designed for a population of 2 million, holds more than eight times that many, plus many more unofficial squatters. It is estimated that somewhere between 500,000 to 5 million people live in the City of the Dead. The layout of large family tombs includes a receiving room before entering the separate areas where male and female bodies are buried. It is in this area that squatter families make their home. The government has acknowledged this population, dating back to Nasserist period when sewage and water lines extended to this district. Other squatters' quarters are not as fortunate. Even if there is electricity, marginal populations often have to walk long distances to acquire potable water, and lack of sewage leaves them at risk for disease.

THE CITY OF GARBAGE, SWINE FLU, AND THE CULLING OF THE PIGS

In the Muqattam Hills on the outskirts of Cairo is another city of squatters, which has been rendered into a formal quarter: the city of Garbage Collectors, Manshiyat Nasr. Tens of thousands inhabitants have churches (they are largely Copts), shops, schools, houses, and live amongst heaps of garbage. For years the *zabbaleen* (garbage collectors) created garbage fiefdoms for themselves in neighborhoods where they would clear away the trash for a monthly tip. In other words, the government did not (in most cases) pay their salary, but they were paid by those to whom they rendered their services. The enterprising, established "kings" of garbage carved out their fiefs in the most exclusive neighborhoods, where the "best" garbage lay—one man's trash is another man's treasure. Long before the green movement, the *zabbaleen* would skillfully recycle and remove all usable items to clean and prepare for resale, fix broken ones, separate organic waste, which they would compost or feed to their own pigs or to *zabbaleen* who specialized in raising swine for the small Coptic population of Egypt, and burn the remainder utilizing the heat for fuel. Thus, their salary would come from hard work and efficient use of resources, and the reselling of materials collected, for example, glass, plastic, and steel. Even before the culling of the pigs (see subsequently), municipal authorities in Cairo had been trying to replace the *zabbaleen* with paid garbage collectors, but they could not reach anywhere near the 80–90 percent recycling rate that the *zabbaleen* achieve. Since 2003 the government has been outsourcing some garbage collection to international companies, but they have not been as widely accepted. For example, in a middle-class building in Mohandiseen, where the *zabbaleen* formerly came once a week for a pick up to a single drop with the regularity of a clock, the new municipal collectors are supposed to come twice a week and have the advantage coming to each door on the three-story building. Nevertheless, the municipal collectors often miss several scheduled days in a row. Theoretically, the new system was an improvement for the elderly, third-floor inhabitants of the building, but in the summer of 2009, they bemoaned the loss of the *zabbaleen*. When questioned about various absences the municipal collector

---

DR. GALIL, A KIND-HEARTED SOUL

Dr. Galil is a talented surgeon, who has turned over most of his practice to plastic surgery. With respect to his clientele, about 50 percent are either ex-patriots or "cosmetic" tourists, seeking a better deal on breast augmentations, liposuction, Botox injections, or eye lifts; and about 50 percent are Egyptians from the highest to the lowest classes. Cosmetic procedures in Egypt cost about half what they do in Europe or the United States. Dr. Galil works with various Coptic charities that help pay for the operating room and other costs, and about 15 percent of his work is pro bono, much of it with the *zabbaleen*. The children often wear loose-fitting *galabiyyas,* which are not flame-retardant and sometimes suffer from severe burns. With Dr. Galil's expert care, they receive world-class care at no cost. A Copt, Dr. Galil feels fortunate to have been born into privilege, given the gift of surgical aptitude, and to have studied at good schools in Egypt and the United Kingdom, so he enjoys giving something back.

---

complained about the need to attend a wedding or a funeral back home in the village with no one to cover the shift. This never happened with the *zabbaleen.* Currently, there are NGOs trying to mediate between the government and the *zabbaleen* to replace the international companies when their contracts run out in 2015. The *zabbaleen* still run much of the garbage business, especially since the companies have not been reliable or efficient.

When swine flu broke out in 2009, Egypt took a proactive response—in many ways much more proactive than the United States. All visitors entering the country had their temperature scanned, and anyone with a fever was quarantined and tested. While all documented cases of swine flu were passed by humans, the government of Egypt went one step further and lashed out at the country's pigs. The overwhelming majority of the population is Muslim and does not eat pork, and as a result many correlate pigs with filth and disease. Thus, there was no outcry of support for 70,000 people affected. In May 2009 the government culled some 400,000 animals without compensation to their owners, some of whom earned as much as 20,000 Egyptian pounds annually from meat sales. Soon there were other concerns too. Many Egyptians do not trust their government, and they wondered what happened to the meat, which was supposedly returned to the owners. The cost of chicken and seafood skyrocketed because people did not trust beef, especially ground beef, to be pure, that is, pork-free. Furthermore, everyone expected the streets to be filled with refuse in the absence of the garbage-eating pigs. While the gloom and doom scenarios did not play out, the event did leave the already-sensitive Muslim and Coptic communities divided.

SECTARIAN CONFLICT

Religious extremism from both Egypt's Muslim and Christian communities has led to bitter sectarian conflict. An incident on Coptic Christmas Eve 2010 and response to it by the government and media is symptomatic of the problem and why it has not been properly addressed. Upper Egypt has been particularly challenging because of the higher proportion of Christians to Muslims compared to the rest of the country. Whether real or perceived, the region is also (in)famous for its "blood" feuds—killing in retribution for another killing or honor crime. On January 6, 2010, six Copts and one Muslim guard were killed in a drive-by shooting outside a Nag Hammadi Church just after mass, apparently in retribution for the alleged rape of a 12-year-old Muslim girl by a Christian man. The *majlis al-shura* was quick to denounce the incident and some members even denied its connection to sectarian violence seeing it only as a criminal offence. In other words, some in government, tried to dismiss it as an isolated, random crime. Critics of the government say it has not done enough to heal the rift between the two communities. Writer Alaa al-Aswany (see Chapter 6) in an editorial shortly after the incident, highlighted three major problems: (1) a climate of poverty and oppression in the country; (2) Islamic extremism, namely of the variety that encourages supremacist movements; and (3) Coptic fundamentalism, which has encouraged separatism, particularly from Diaspora Copts (2010).

The recent battle between the Coptic Church, secular Copts, and the state over the issue of divorce is yet another microcosm of problems between the church and the state. In theory, Egypt is a secular, democratic state, but as discussed in Chapter 3, Islam guides the law in Egypt. Historically, personal status issues, for example, marriage, inheritance, and divorce, were under the purview of the church and only in modern times came under the jurisdiction of the state. The state has only reluctantly violated conventions of the Coptic Church, which include no divorce (except in cases of adultery) and therefore no remarriage or second marriage. The only loopholes for Egyptian Copts have been conversion to Islam to resort to Islamic law. For example, a man could convert to Islam and marry a second wife, with or without divorcing his first wife. Islamic law prevails unless both non-Muslim parties are from the same sect. Secular Copts and women's rights activists would like to see uniform marriage and divorce laws for the entire country, whereas Coptic fundamentalists bristle at the thought of state interference in the sacred institution of the family. A new personal status law would impact all non-Muslims in Egypt. Pope Shenouda (d. 2012), the late Coptic Patriarch, spoke out vigorously in June 2010 against the draft law. It remains to be seen what impact if any the revolution will have on these debates.

At Coptic Christmas 2011 there were scenes of both violence and unity among the Muslim and Christian populations. In response to the violence of previous years, Muslims all over the country served as human shields around Coptic churches to insure that there would be no bloodshed against their Christian brethren; however, there was still a Church bombing in Alexandria on January 1, 2011, that served as an ugly reminder of the violence.

Due to the marginalization of the Copts, sectarian violence, and a *modus vivendi* with the former regime, initially Pope Shenouda urged restraint on the part of Coptic youth when demonstrations broke out across Egypt in late January 2011. Nevertheless, when the movement proved its nonviolent means for change and Mubarak stepped aside, the head of the Coptic Church revised his opinion praising youth, the army, and the people in mid-February. In the wake of the demonstrations, many police failed to return to active duty thus leaving the streets of Egypt generally, and its major cities in particular without order. In this vacuum sectarian violence spiked again; however, some critics of the old regime claim these were elements of the old order fomenting unrest. Since the beginning of the 2011 revolution, during outbreaks of sectarian violence, some cynics have alleged that it is plain-clothed police or soldiers who are the instigators as a means of keeping the military in power. In other words, they allege that the military is creating a job for itself in keeping order and stability.

With the death of Pope Shenouda in March 2012, it remains to be seen who will fill his shoes. At times, Shenouda was known as a maverick for standing up to the rise of Islamic extremism during his early years in office; however, at the same time he was also known for restraint, accommodation, and peaceful means of resolution. The Copts of Egypt, like all other citizens, desire full rights in post-revolutionary Egypt.

DEATH OF SHAYKH TANTAWI, A VOICE OF MEDIATION

About a year before the 2011 revolution, Pope Shenouda lost one of his long-time supporters and someone who tried to work to mediate rifts between Egypt's Muslim and Coptic communities. Nevertheless, Tantawi's frequent remark that Copts must and do enjoy equal citizenship also reflects a certain amount of denial of sectarian strife. In March 2010, Grand Shaykh al-Azhar Mohamed Sayed Tantawi (b. 1928) passed away while on a state visit to Saudi Arabia. Since 1996 Tantawi had served in this role as the highest ranking imam at al-Azhar University. While this is a presidentially appointed position, it is considered a more independent role than Tantawi's previous position (1986–1996) as Grand Mufti at Dar al-Ifta (literally the house of *fatwas*), which assists the government in issuing position statements on contemporary issues.

The religious establishment in the Middle East generally, and in Egypt in particular, has served as a bridge between the rulers and the ruled. Tantawi had the difficult position of serving in high-ranking positions, mediating between the authoritarian, American-sponsored government on the one hand and the people, who have turned increasingly toward their religion, on the other. Although fundamentalists criticized him for being a bland spokesman for the establishment and liberals for wavering on vital points, he paved a moderate path with clearly articulated reasoning. His detractors have often used his alleged hesitation as a reason to disparage his views; however, his opinions often require detailed research. Many of his decisions have come at critical moments.

While at Dar al-Ifta, he ruled that interest on government bonds was not usury, but rather profit, allowing the government to develop a mortgage industry. In using the same type of analogical reasoning and adding a few twists, with the advent of satellite TV, he could get around restrictions on games of chance and usury paving the way for various types of game shows, including *Who Wants to be a Millionaire* and *Deal or No Deal*.

Tantawi was a moderate supporter of women's rights, and he spoke out against FGM (see earlier), receiving criticism from some of his colleagues. Much to the dismay of fundamentalists and advocates of free choice, he was a staunch opponent of the *niqab*, the full-face head-covering. In 2009, during a visit to a secondary school where he saw a girl wearing the garment, he asked her to remove it and when she did not, he did so for her. He informed her that she should never wear it again and that he would see to it that a *fatwa* be issued regarding the (non)wearing of the *niqab* in public schools. Some Muslims defended his right to define proper tradition, since there is absolutely nothing in the Quran that calls for covering the face. Others, on the left and the right, saw it as an invasion on individual choice. Tantawi, as Shaykh al-Azhar, was in a position of authority for Muslims worldwide. After France banned headscarves in public schools in 2003, Tantawi advised women to accept the restriction and issued a *fatwa* allowing them to go uncovered. With respect to other women's issues, Tantawi supported a woman's right to abortion in the case of rape (see earlier). He also accepted the practice of artificial insemination, but only with a woman's living husband as the donor. In a more conservative vein, he ruled against women leading community prayers; however, he found nothing problematic about women leading women in prayer.

Tantawi gave critical support to both Egypt and the United States with respect to foreign policy and the war on terror. He was extremely strong in his condemnation of bin Laden and the 9/11 attacks, and it was neither the first nor the last time that he would be asked to specify the difference between legitimate jihad and outright killing. Tantawi pointed out that jihad was a defensive action and that the killing of innocents was wrong. At various points in time he seemed to waver on this position with respect to suicide bombings in Israel; however, a careful reading of his opinion sheds light on his views, perhaps seeing parts of the holy land and Palestinians under attack as an exception. After being hounded by reporters on the issue, he reportedly took off his shoes and threw them at the offending journalists. Nevertheless, he has issued statements regarding the value and safety of Israeli lives. With respect to the war in Iraq, in 2003, he dismissed officials who promulgated anti-American *fatwas*, and released a decision in August of that year stating that it is not al-Azhar's position to become involved in the politics of other nations. Even so, in 2006 he did offer to go to Iraq to mediate between factions of Muslims that were fighting. He repeatedly encouraged Iraqis to participate in the democratic process.

Perhaps Tantawi's greatest legacy was as an interfaith leader. In 2002 he met with the Archbishop of Canterbury and signed an agreement to promote interfaith dialogue. In 2008, at another such meeting sponsored by the UN in New York, Tantawi was captured on film shaking hands with former Israeli prime minister Shimon Peres. The picture created a media storm in the Egyptian press, and there were even calls for his dismissal. While the populace expects Mubarak and government officials to demonstrate this type of behavior, the religious establishment is held to a different standard. Rather than accepting the photograph, Tantawi first denied it and later feigned ignorance. Ironically, he and Mr. Peres would cochair a session in Kazakhstan at yet another interfaith meeting in July 2009. Perhaps, Mr. Mubarak told him he would have to learn how to work with his allies.

Although Tantawi's days of leadership had their moments of controversy, he was generally an eloquent, thoughtful individual who served as a bridge between the people and the government as well as the government and the world. Tantawi was born in 1928, the same year that the Muslim Brotherhood was founded, and he journeyed through the years of British occupation, fascism, war, revolution, infitah, and American hegemony. The life experience of his successor Dr. Ahmed el-Tayeb, who, born in 1946, was just a child when the Free Officers took power, is significantly different. Nevertheless, observers believe that the Sorbonne-educated imam will be more of a free thinker than his predecessor. Just days before the outbreak of the Egyptian revolution el-Tayeb announced that he would not attend an interfaith meeting sponsored by Pope Benedict, stating that these sorts of meetings do little good for the Eastern world.

JIHAD, THE U.S.–EGYPTIAN RELATIONS, AND HOPE IN OBAMANIA

A U.S. visitor to Egypt in the summer of 1991 might have been shocked to get into a cab and find a smiling driver giving the thumbs-up saying, "Bush Good," referring to George H. W. Bush, architect of Desert Storm—and repeating the same experience over and over again. While Egyptian cab drivers are notorious for chatting up foreigners in hopes of getting a high fare, the first Gulf War did split families into pro- and anti-coalition factions. A decade or so later the same U.S. visitor would be hard-pressed to find a driver willing to say anything approaching positive about the United States or its president, George W. Bush. In fact, a cab ride could become a captive audience defense (willingly or unwillingly) of U.S. foreign policy or simply icy silence. What changed in a decade was not merely the policy in the United States, but circumstances in the Palestinian–Arab–Israeli conflict and the nature of Islamic radicalism worldwide. Understanding the nature and goals of jihadists in the post-1967 era generally and after Sadat's assassination and the Gulf War in particular helps set the context for these different receptions.

Jihadists represent a small minority even if their actions might be supported by a larger group of individuals due to political climate or circumstances. According to political scientist Fawaz Gerges, in the post-1967 era there emerged two sets of enemies in fighting the jihad, the near and the far. The alienation and humiliation of losing to Israel was devastating, but there was still a sense that something needed to be done to battle enemies of the faith. Fighting Israel was no longer a realistic possibility, but fighting corrupt Muslim rulers was a more attainable objective, that is, the near enemy, and it would be an objective that would facilitate longer term goals, for example, living in an Islamic state. Politically, Sadat's signing of the peace treaty with Israel and the Soviet invasion of Afghanistan mobilized the Egyptian jihadists in a particular way, and Sadat paid with his life. Lack of support for Sadat's foreign policy on the one hand and the perception of crushing attacks on the *umma* (community of believers) on the other helped to mobilize a range of support for jihadists from outright funding or joining the cause to simply feigning ignorance of their internal activities to generalized apathy from others (what we do does not matter). One of the people arrested in the wake of Sadat's assassination was a young physician, Ayman al-Zawahiri, who would later become second in command of al-Qaeda, but not before fighting the Soviets in Afghanistan. One of his associates, Shaykh Omar Abdel-Rahman was in prison at the time of Sadat's assassination, and after he was acquitted of conspiracy in the assassination, he moved on to Afghanistan and later to the United States where he would later be convicted of conspiracy in the World Trade Center bombing (1993) (Gerges 2007).

The first Gulf War (1990–1991) raised the stakes in Egypt as jihadists saw how to hit their government—by ruining its tourism dollars. At this time, however, Egyptians were still divided over what was the greater evil, and perhaps a slight majority seemed to believe that Saddam Hussein was the looming threat even if they did not heartily support the coalition. For jihadists, fighting the near enemy became quite easy, with the potential of getting the attention of the far enemy in tourist attacks. The climax came during the 1997 massacre of tourists at the Valley of the Kings after which jihadists reached a *modus vivendi* with the Egyptian government. At this point more radical transnational factions began to form with the goal of hitting the far enemy, the United States, the enabler of Israel and the corrupt Muslim regimes. Without U.S. dollars these governments could not function. Such transnational groups bombed the U.S. embassies in Kenya and Tanzania (1998), and attacked the USS Cole in 2000. (Egyptian) Islamic Jihad claimed responsibility for the former and al-Qaeda for the latter. Jihadists and their fans in the Egypt could support these actions because they represented fighting in the way of Islam, hitting American military and quasi-military outposts (American embassies abroad resemble fortresses) after grievous injustices against the world of Islam. The CIA had been essentially competing with Muslim operatives in Albania and Bulgaria, and rendered them back to Egypt where they were tortured and in some cases hung. This competition as well as the struggle in Bosnia added to the perception of the persecuted *umma*. For jihadists and many non-jihadists, the U.S. government had stepped beyond reasonable bounds. Although many associate this activity (rendering of prisoners) with 9/11, it began with the instability in the Balkans under Clinton. Later, with the war on terror, such activities would grow worldwide. In the meantime, Egyptians watched and read news reports about the Chechen war and wondered why Americans did nothing to protect them. Why Americans cared about Kuwaitis but not about Chechens was a popular theme in op-ed pieces of the mid-1990s. As one might imagine, the answer usually had dollar signs and oil without mention of history or interest in the region.

In the immediate aftermath of 9/11 there was great sympathy and concern about the attacks because of the targeting of civilian populations. Certainly the response from the Egyptian government and all of its organs was swift. Then president Mubarak, then Shaykh al-Azhar Tantawi (see earlier), and the president's son all quickly stepped into the limelight to condemn the attacks. Since Sadat's rapprochement with the West, there was always a divide between the face of government and the face of the people—popular opinion—reflected in TV shows, longstanding news columns, op-ed pieces, and quite literally the voice on the street. In the period that followed, Arab media coverage of the U.S. invasion of Afghanistan, the build-up to the invasion of Iraq, and the on-the-ground coverage of anti-Arab or anti-Muslim sentiment in the United States, as well as the Israeli reoccupation of portions of the West Bank, highlighted certain aspects of the war on terror. Unfortunately, the beautiful sights of people going to mosques in the United States to learn more about Islam did not make their way to Egypt or receive equal coverage; and even if they did, they were certainly muted by images of Muslims being slaughtered in Afghanistan, Iraq, the West Bank, and later the Gaza Strip, not to mention coverage of a second Chechen war. The image or perception of a persecuted *umma* dramatically rose to new heights as did the image of the United States as an imperialist power, which was reinforced by popular culture (see Chapter 6).

The uneasy peace established by jihadists and the government was symbolically broken in the Sinai in 2005 and 2006. On Revolution Day a group linked to al-Qaeda Syria claimed responsibility for a suicide bombing that killed 88 people, the majority of whom were Egyptians, and only 10 percent of the fatalities were international visitors. Similarly, the following year on the Egyptian holiday of Sham el-Nassim, 23 people were killed and 80 wounded in an attack on Dahab. Although there had been a few isolated smaller incidents, for example, at Taba, which gets mainly Israeli tourists, the timing and location of these incidents suggests that the groups were sending the message that they were targeting the government (the near enemy) and its Westernized, bourgeois supporters, by hitting on dates when large numbers of Egyptians would be on holiday.

The political climate has changed, and more people are politicized through a variety of media—the spread of satellite television with its 24-hour news cycles, religious programming, not to mention grassroots prayer and study groups as well as social networks. It is in this environment that conspiracy theories abound. A recent World Public Opinion Poll indicates that Middle Easterners generally, and Egyptians in particular, believe that Israel is behind the 9/11 attacks (43 percent), whereas those who believe al-Qaeda is responsible, those who believe the United States is responsible, and those who do not know or would not commit to answer, were fairly close at 16 percent, 12 percent, and 18 percent, respectively. Anecdotally, these numbers appear conservative. In the summers of 2008 and 2009, few Egyptians expressed the belief that al-Qaeda was responsible, and frequently responded "don't you know that no Jews died in the attacks?" It was this bias that President Barack Obama had to overcome in his historic speech at Cairo University in June 2009.

Obamania hit the streets of Cairo as the city prepared to receive the 44th president of the United States on a state visit. During his 55-minute speech Obama discussed toleration and confrontation in a world of extremism, the Palestinian–Arab–Israeli conflict, nuclear weapons, democracy, and women's rights. In a city that stops for nothing 24/7, virtually everything came to a standstill. Even the university's rigorous exam schedule ground to a halt. Cab drivers, workers, intellectuals, housewives, and professionals all geared up for his speech. Afterwards, three octogenarians were supremely impressed by his Quranic recitations, and the workers in the National Library chatted with ease about his good looks and facility with words. Universally throughout Egypt, among all classes and educational levels, there seemed to be a general level of concern. There was a man who could speak clearly and eloquently. For English speakers, whether minimal or masterful, his speech hit concise points. For non-English speakers, the captioned translation captured the essence of his meaning. Everyone wanted to know whether his actions could live up to the beauty of his words. No U.S. ex-patriot in the country could answer that question.

EGYPT: SOLVING PROBLEMS AND THE LITTLE CAR THAT COULD

In a country where large problems seem too overwhelming to tackle all at once, Egyptians find suitable patches to meet their needs. With the government falling short on many services, for example, roads and transportation, unemployment, crowding, and education, people work to fill in the missing niches. A prime example is a *tok tok*. A *tok tok* is a strange hybridized vehicle that is something between a motorized tricycle and a rickshaw, covered with open sides, a front seat for a driver and a two-person back seat. It is extremely common in Southeast Asia. U.S. movie watchers may have seen one in *The Other End of the Line* (2008); as the climax of the film approaches, the protagonist ditches his cab and makes his way through the crowded streets of Mumbai in a *tok tok* to get to his beloved quickly.

An enterprising Egyptian who had worked in Pakistan brought some of the earliest vehicles to Mansura in the mid-late 1990s. After first importing them, later he began to produce them himself by hiring the unemployed youth of the city. The low operating cost of the vehicle and its ability to maneuver down narrow pathways made it a popular form of transportation and a useful farm vehicle too. The main obstacle his venture encountered was in the licensing of the *tok tok* as it was neither a motorcycle nor a car. Egyptian bureaucrats are notoriously rigid and the obvious concern was about the safety standards of the vehicle, which did not preclude creating a new category. In the meantime the number of *tok toks* continued to multiply, and their small size allowed smaller—read younger—drivers to use them. While the *tok toks* added a great supplemental income to many families, they were contributing to other problems, namely underage and inexperienced drivers on the road, perhaps giving youth another reason not to stay in school.

Good ideas are difficult to keep muted and thus the *tok tok* spread without registration, well beyond Mansura to other cities of the delta up to the outskirts of Cairo and into the capital. The vehicles have had great versatility, whether as farm vehicles, cheap taxis, or as open-air cabs in tourist venues. Some enterprising Egyptians began fabricating licenses for the vehicles to make them look more official and gain a profit at the same time. Others found it confounding that the government could ban the *tok tok*, yet benefit by selling it at government-owned stores for example, Omar Effendi (prior to its re-privatization in 2007). In particular, the densely populated governates of Cairo and Giza took extremely hard lines on the issue and insisted that not only would there be no licensing, but also these venues would be *tok tok*-free. Meanwhile, other jurisdictions, for example, Kafr al-Sheikh, basked in the glory of the *tok tok*, which provided citizens with a much cheaper means of getting to work than the taxi and was more reliable than public transportation—not to mention it provided work for the unemployed.

In 2008, the People's Assembly Legislative Committee passed a new law to improve transportation flow in the country that would ultimately impact the *tok tok* as well as the country's fleet of aging taxis. The new law cracked down on a whole series of violations including driving without a license, prohibiting the licensing of a cab more than 10 years old, and driving one more than 20 years old. As for the *tok toks*, they would be classified as motorcycles, which would eliminate their undetermined status; however, from the literature it would appear that they were to remain outside the capital. One article estimated some 750,000 in the capital at the time of the new law. Nevertheless, the numbers of *tok toks* in and around Cairo and Giza continued to increase. One commonly sees *tok toks* both in highly urban settings, for example, around the tight streets surrounding Cairo University where it is difficult to get around or in the working-class neighborhood of Bulaq al-Dakrur, where residents simply cannot afford taxis. Unfortunately, the longstanding situation of unregistered *tok toks* and illegally licensed *tok toks* has meant that the vehicles are the means for a variety of crimes, for example, the abduction of girls. Citizens feel as threatened by them as by the bicycle thieves of an earlier generation. The police have begun to fight back by cracking down on unlicensed drivers and unregistered *tok toks*, which often come in pairs. In Beni Abid, a small town in the Daqahliya governate, a Mansura man, clearly unaware of the crackdown, picked up two officers right in front of the police station, only to be returned to his starting point. Instead of simply receiving a fine, the man was beaten, tortured, and allegedly thrown from the fourth-floor balcony of the station; however, the police maintain that the man jumped after excusing himself to go to the bathroom. Is the warning from the highly publicized story meant to be about the brutality of the Egyptian police or an object lesson for illegal *tok tok* operators?

The saga of the *tok tok* is a microcosm of citizen–government response to problems in Egypt. The vehicle was never a major solution to the country's transportation, unemployment, or any other problem, but it was a creative response to a situation. Nevertheless, it created its own set of problems, which in turn created new entrepreneurs inside and outside of government. The illegal license industry boomed, new *tok tok* importers emerged, local producers expanded, and people with a vested interest in the *tok tok* to lobby government officials multiplied. Just as the *tok tok* was never the answer for the country's transportation woes it was neither the original source. In 2008 when the debate in the People's Assembly tackled legislation over traffic flow and safety, the members of parliament had to acknowledge the *tok tok*. Much of the debate centered on reformers who wanted more rules and legislation for safety versus those who felt that the poor suffered the most from heavy-handed regulation. The lag time between the arrival of the vehicle and the legislation allowed it to multiply unregulated at such a pace that the government found it difficult to contain without severe repression. This is the cycle of creative response, replication, new problem, and repression that has endlessly repeated itself in the country.

KICK BACK, RELAX, AND WATCH

Egyptians look forward to Ramadan as a time when they can gather with family and friends, but it is also a special time for television miniseries. According to *al-Masry al-Youm*, 52 new programs were scheduled for the 2010 season, including a mixture of comedy, historical events, and romance. One of the controversial highlights was a series on the Muslim Brotherhood, entitled *The Group*, which did not get script approval from the son of Hassan al-Banna (d. 1949) (see Chapter 2), who founded the organization. The Muslim Brotherhood, as previously mentioned, has a strong standing in public. Its constituency has a vested interest in how *The Group* is portrayed, and it appears as though the script may have had a more violent flare than the brothers would like. They may produce a counter-version of the story. Following along the historical theme, and on the coat tails of the 2007 success of the series on Faruq, there was one detailing the life of his mother Nazli in exile (see Chapters 2 and 3). Yet another "Egyptian" queen profiled for Ramadan was Cleopatra; however, she was portrayed by a Syrian actress. In the midst of the monarchy-mania and passion for religion, a series entitled *Downfall of the Caliphate* focused on the last 20 years of the Ottoman Empire (Ramadan 2010).

Viewers looking for something lighter returned to the hit (in its seventh Ramadan season) *One Man, Six Women.* Copying the successful formula, but perhaps with a more dramatic tone, Dina Abdel Raziq, portrayed a savvy woman at various stages of life, married to different men in *Zahra and Her Five Husbands.* Tunisian-born beauty Hind Sabri, famous for her various roles in Egyptian movies, played the lead in best-seller turned comedy, *I Want to Get Married.* Another screen actor who returned to television Ahmad Mekki played three roles simultaneously of a father and twin sons in *The Very Big One.* Other new comedies included *Not Friends* and *My Mother's Husband* (Ramadan 2010).

Some Egyptians opt for their Ramadan miniseries by actor or actress or personality. Beloved actress Yousra portrayed a forensics doctor in a CSI-type series. Nour el-Sherif returned to play businessman Saad al-Dali for the third season, while Yahya al-Fakharani donned the garb of an upper Egyptian tribal chieftain to portray legendary *Shaykh al-Arab Hammam.* Singer Mohamed Fuad played an average guy trying to take care of his four sisters in *More Precious than My Life* (Ramadan 2010).

What does this sampling of the Ramadan lineup tell us about Egypt today? The obsession with monarchy is dual-pronged. First, it is related to the nostalgic perception regarding the days before the 1952 revolution when life was simpler, government functioned as a democracy, and the British could be blamed for most evils. Second, it is related to preoccupation and concerns with the notion of hereditary presidency and concerns about the arrival of the Mubarak dynasty. By focusing on queens rather than kings, directors stand less chance of drawing censure from the government, yet at the same time it is perhaps telling of the emasculated position of Mubarak in his weakened state. Regarding nonhistorical programming, family concerns are central.

Egyptian President Mohammed Morsi speaks to reporters during a joint news conference with Tunisian President Moncef Marzouki, unseen, at the Presidential palace in Cairo, Egypt, Friday, July 13, 2012. (AP Photo/Maya Alleruzzo)

As is the case with Egyptian society, few adult main characters are single, and those that are, remain deeply embedded in family webs of relationships to which audiences can relate, yet at the same time, particularly in comedies, there are aspects that border on the farcical, which take audiences back to the roots of performing arts in the country. As the prices for all the fixings for a traditional Ramadan *iftar* or *suhur* (see Chapter 6) skyrocket, Egyptians need something to laugh about as they foot the bill to entertain friends and family.

REFERENCES

"13 February 2011 Statement." www.copticpope.com.

Abul Gheit, Zeinab. "Death on Wheels." *Egypt Today*, August 2008.

Amar, Paul. "Why Mubarak Is Out." *Jadaliyya*, February 1, 2011. http://www.jadaliyya.com/pages/index/516/why-mubarak-is-out.

Associated Press. "Egypt Restricts Marriage to Israelis." *Jerusalem Post,* June 6, 2010.

Aswany, Alaa. "Who Killed Egyptian Copts on Their Feast Day?" *The Globe and Mail*, January 15, 2010.

Attalah, Lina. "UN HIV/AIDS Envoy: Egypt Needs Consistent Policy," *al-Masry al-Youm,* February 21, 2010. http://www.almasryalyoum.com/en/news/un-hivaids-un-envoy-egypt-needs-consistent-policies.

Ayoub, Dina. "El-Toktok." *Cairo My Love: All About Cairo*, April 23, 2007. http://cairomy love.blogspot.com/2007/04/i-find-it-rather-hard-to-find-formal.html.

Bier, Laura. "From Birth Control to Family Planning: Population, Gender, and the Politics of Reproduction in Egypt." In *Family in the Middle East: Ideational Change in Egypt, Iran, and Tunisia.* Kathryn Yount and Hoda Rashad, eds. New York: Routledge, 2008, 55–79.

Carrigan, Peter. "Khawaga's Tale: Plastic Surgery." *Daily News Egypt*, December 10, 2006.

"Egypt Elections Watch." http://www.jadaliyya.com/pages/index/Egypt%20Elections% 20Watch.

Fahmy, Amal. "Declare No to FGM/C." *al-Masry al-Youm*, February 7, 2010. http://www. almasryalyoum.com/en/news/declare-zero-tolerance-fgmc.

Fleishman, Jeffrey. "In Egypt All Eyes on Mubarak's Health." *L.A. Times,* March 27, 2010.

Gerges, Fawaz. *Journey of a Jihadist: Inside Muslim Militancy.* Orlando: First Harvest, 2007.

Khazbak, Rana. "Shafiq Campaigners in Disbelief, Hysteria Following Election Loss." *Egyptian Independent* (June 24, 2012).http://www.egyptindependent.com/news/shafiq-campaigners-disbelief-hysteria-following-election-loss.

Macleod, Scott. "Egyptian Democracy," *Huffington Post*, November 30, 2011. http://www. huffingtonpost.com/scott-macleod/egyptian-electionsb1121953.html.

"Mubarak in Delicate Health." *al-Masry al-Youm*, February 14, 2011. http://www.almasry alyoum.com/en/node/318581.

Natter, Katharina. "Egypt's Zabbaleen Reclaim Their Share in Garbage Collection." *Daily News Egypt*, July 28, 2010.

Ramadan, Ahmed. "Ramadan TV: An Overloaded Schedule." *al-Masry al-Youm*, August 11, 2010. http://www.almasryalyoum.com/en/news/ramadan-tv-overloaded-schedule.

Reuters and Barak Ravid. "Netanyahu Warns Outcome of Egyptian Revolution Could Be Like Iran's." January 31, 2011. www.haaretz.com.

Salem, Ali. *A Drive to Israel: An Egyptian Meets His Neighbors.* Trans. Robert Silverman. Tel Aviv: Tel Aviv University Press, 2001 (1994).

Sheahan, Lauren. "Battling AIDS Stigma in Egypt." http://crs.org/egypt/shame-silence-stigma/.

Slackman, Michael. "Mohamed Sayed Tantawi Dies at Age 81." *New York Times*, March 10, 2010.

World Health Organization. "Percentage of Condom Use as Reported by Male Injecting Drug Users, Street Children, Female Sex Workers, and Men Who Have Sex With Men." PowerPoint provided drawn from Shawky, et al. "HIV Surveillance and Epidemic Profile in the Middle East and North Africa." *Journal of Acquired Immune Deficiency Syndrome* 51 (2009).

World Public Opinion. "Who Was behind September 11th." http://www.worldpublicopinion. org/pipa/pdf/sep08/WPO911Sep08quaire.pdf.

Glossary and Abbreviations

'amma: the masses, ordinary folks, people of the working classes.

Arab Republic of Egypt (ARE): the current official title for Egypt.

Arab Socialist Union (ASU): mass political organization created by Nasser as a substitute for political parties. Dissolved in 1978 after Sadat allowed the creation of platforms within the ASU to turn into parties.

AUC: American University in Cairo.

Ayyubids: dynasty that ruled Egypt between 1171 and 1250.

ba: according to the ancient Egyptians, the nonphysical aspect of one's being, akin to our modern notion of personality.

baladi: country or folk style, meaning traditional (often with negative connotation) in contemporary terms.

Bar-Lev line: a chain of fortifications built by the Israelis on the eastern coast of the Sinai Peninsula during the War of Attrition (1967–1970).

Baṣra: in addition to being a city in Iraq, it is the name of a Middle Eastern card game.

Beylicate: Bey refers to the title conferred by the Ottomans and could be held by anyone, mamluk or non-mamluk, who held a powerful position in the military, commerce, or land administration; however, the beylicate refers more explicitly to the wielding of that power by mamluks. Over the course of the 17th century the mamluks vacillated in power with central administration; but by the 18th century the "beylicate" was more fully in control.

BMI: Business Monitor International.

CAPMAS: the Central Agency for Mobilization and Statistics is the central warehouse for gathering data for the Egyptian government.

Copt: an Egyptian Christian. Origin of the word comes from the ancient Egyptian *hikaptah* or house of the spirit of Ptah.

dallala: a female trader.

Delta: refers to the northern, or lower part of Egypt, where the Nile branches into several veins and empties into the Mediterranean Sea. Cairo sits at the base of the Delta.

dhikr: a Sufi ceremony of remembrance (of Allah).

dhimmi: a non-Muslim who pays taxes, including an extra poll tax (*jizya*), in an Islamic state, for example, medieval Egypt or the Ottoman Empire.

EDHS: Egyptian Demographic Health Survey.

Egyptian Feminist Union (EFU): Western-style feminist organization founded by Huda Shaarawi in 1923.

Egyptian Olympics Committee (EOC): formed in the early 20th century to facilitate Egypt's participation in the Olympics.

ETUC: Egyptian Trade Union Confederation.

EU: European Union.

Fatimids: ruled Egypt from 969 to 1171.

fatwa: legal opinion rendered by a recognized scholar or imam.

FDI: foreign direct investments.

felool: remnants, refers to the members of the old regime trying to reenter government service after 2011 revolution.

FGM: female genital mutilation, also known as female circumcision or female genital cutting. Practice of cutting some portion of the female genitalia with the desired outcome of upholding tradition, reducing sexual desire, or maintaining hygiene. While many believe it to be an Islamic tradition, it predates the religion.

fiqh: Islamic jurisprudence.

fonduq: historically, see definition of *wikala;* currently hotel.

Fustat: city founded by the Arab conquerors near present-day Cairo.

futuwwat: urban groups organizing around the concept of youthful masculinity, historically involved in urban protest, as well as neighborhood "protection."

Gareed: jousting-like game of Bedouin origin played on horseback.

GCC: Gulf Cooperation Council.

GDP: gross domestic product.

General Secondary Exam (GSE): test taken by graduating seniors in Egypt to determine suitability for university-level studies. Scores determine what an individual can study.

ḥajj: pilgrimage to Mecca; it is one of the five pillars of Islam.

ḥalaqa: circle, as in a circle of study.

HAMAS: *ḥarakat al-muqawimat al-islamiyya.* The Islamic Resistance Movement was founded in 1987 as a Palestinian branch of the Muslim Brotherhood and a resistance movement in its own right.

ḥijab: headscarf. Refers to the head covering that many women have adopted in the past three decades. It differs from traditional modesty garments, which covered the face and body.

Horus: ancient Egyptian god, son of Osirus and Isis, god of the sky.

ibrik: vessel for making Arabic coffee.

ifṭar: breakfast, or the breaking of the fast, during the month of Ramadan it is the first meal eaten after sunset.

ijara: concept in Islamic finance that allows for leasing a property with the option to buy, with the consideration of gain due to repair and management.

iltizam (multazim): tax farm in which the tax farmer purchases the right to collect taxes over a certain area of land. The multazim is then responsible for the land's irrigation and general upkeep; but he or she does not own the land and this right does not interfere with the right of others to farm the land.

Infitah: economic and political policy of Sadat; literally means "opening." It refers to an economy more open to outside investment and a political system consisting of more than one party.

intifaḍa: uprising. The first *intifaḍa* refers to the spontaneous uprising that began in the occupied territories (West Bank and Gaza Strip), beginning in late 1987 and continuing with greater or lesser severity until 1993. It was notable for its grassroots organization. The second *intifaḍa* began in September 2000, marked by the reentry of Ariel Sharon in Israel politics, and it ended in 2005.

Isis: ancient Egyptian goddess; wife or sister of Osiris, mother of Horus; goddess of fertility and motherhood.

iqṭa: military land grant that allows the possessor to collect taxes and remit a portion to the central treasury. For example, in the ninth century, the Abbasids turned Egypt into an *iqṭa'*.

jihad: from the Arabic root meaning to struggle or exert effort, the third form verbal noun means the struggle that all Muslims put forth to do the right thing. It is often translated as "holy war" because in some contexts in the Quran it refers to a defensive struggle for the faith. Interestingly enough, the words, killing in the way of God, are used for more aggressive actions [*qatilu fi sabil Allah*]. Thus, the word has been "hijacked" by both radical Islamists, as well as those describing their actions.

ka: according to the ancient Egyptians, this concept represents the life force of an individual, differentiating the living from the dead.

Kefaya: political movement in response to the idea of inherited presidency in Egypt, the longstanding Emergency Law, and the general lack of democracy under Mubarak.

khan: see definition for *wikala.*

khaṣṣa: the elite; the upper classes.

Khedive: Persian title for ruler adopted unofficially by the Muhammad Ali dynasty before the age of Ismail and officially thereafter, until the reign of Husayn Kamil, when the ruler's title changed to Sultan.

khurus: area within a Coptic Church before the sanctuary; space unique to Coptic Churches.

kuttab: (small) elementary school, usually attached to a mosque.

Liberation Rally (LR): mass political organization created by Nasser as a stand-in for political parties from 1953 to 1958.

Lower Egypt: northern Egypt; the region of the Nile Delta.

ma'at: philosophy of the ancient Egyptians relating to divine cosmological unity and order and personified in the Goddess Ma'at.

madrasa: school. The *madrasa* is more advanced than a *kuttab,* and may also be attached to a mosque or it may be a freestanding institution.

mahr: bride-price.

Majlis al-sha'ab: People's Assembly, which traditionally (prior to 2011) has consisted of 454 seats, of which 10 are appointed by the president. Members serve five-year terms. Currently the number of seats is 508.

Majlis al-shura: Advisory council, upper house of the Egyptian parliament, with a largely consultative role. Traditionally, 264 seats and after 2011 270, and in both cases one-third are appointed by the president and two-thirds are elected for staggered six-year terms.

mamluk: literally he who is owned; a slave—refers to elite caste of slaves owned by Caliph and other petty rulers throughout the Middle East. The slaves often came to hold power in their own right.

mamluk, baḥri: ruled Egypt from 1250 to 1383, so named because they were housed on the island of Roda (*bahr* = sea and the Nile is as vast as a sea).

mamluk, burgi: ruled Egypt from 1383 to 1517, so named because they were housed at the Citadel (*burg* = tower).

Mankala: ancient game common to the region and continent.

mashrabiya: latticed wooden screen common to traditional architecture in Egypt.

mastaba: from the Arabic for bench, it is a mud-brick, flat-topped Old Kingdom monumental tomb with slanted walls erected above an underground burial site.

MENA: Middle East and North Africa.

Miṣr: Arabic name for Egypt, pronounced *maṣr;* civilized.

Modern Standard Arabic (MSA): An updated form of classical Arabic that appears in newspapers and media broadcasts.

Monophysitism: Form of Christianity adopted in Egypt that emphasizes the single, divine nature of Christ formed by a fusion of its human and divine aspects.

mulid: celebration of a saint's birth.

Munshid(a): person who leads the group in song at a *mulid* or a *dhikr,* or other traditional celebration. Sometimes *munshids* are hired in place of singers at weddings.

murabaḥa: Concept in Islamic law that allows for resale with the specification of gain.

musharaka: Concept in Islamic law and finance that allows for joint ventures whereby all parties share gains and losses according to terms specified in initial contract.

Muslim Brotherhood (*al-Ikhwan al-Muslimeen*): Organization founded in 1928 by Hasan al-Banna aimed originally at founding an Islamic state in Egypt. Currently works within the framework of the existing state. After the 2011 Revolution, it has been under the threat of splitting along generational and ideological lines.

Mutamiṣrun: "those who become Egyptian," referring to Greeks, Italians, and other Southern Europeans who came to Egypt in the mid-late 19th century and established roots there.

National Council for Women (NCW): Established by presidential decree in 2000, this organization under the umbrella of the NDP promoted the enhancement of women's rights socially, politically, and economically. After the 2011 Revolution it fell under sharp criticism of women's groups since its titular head was Mrs. Mubarak.

National Democratic Party (NDP): it was the ruling party of Egypt; the party of Hosni Mubarak.

National Progressive Unionist Party (NPUP): Left of center political party that considers itself a defender of the principles of the 1952 Revolution. Also known as *hizb al-tagammu'.*

National Union (NU): mass political organization created by Nasser as a substitute for political parties. The NU served this function during Egypt's Union with Syria.

naqus: church bell.

niqab: head-covering or veil for women that covers both the face and the head. This type of veil is more commonly found in the Gulf than in Egypt. In 2003 France banned the *niqab* for its citizens in public schools and in 2010 extended the ban to all public spaces.

Osiris: ancient Egyptian god; father of Horus, husband of Isis; god of the underworld.

Ottomans: ruled Egypt from 1517 until the outbreak of World War I.

Palestine Liberation Organization (PLO): Created by Nasser in 1964 as an umbrella organization for various Palestinian groups operating under his domain (Gaza Strip).

Pharaoh: title for ancient Egyptian kingship; literally means "big house" this individual is the physical incarnation of Horus.

People's Assembly (PA): (see also *majlis al-sha'ab*); name for the lower house of parliament in Egypt.

qadi: judge.

al-Qahira: Arabic word for Cairo, it means "the victorious."

qaysariya: see definition for *wikala.*

rakah: section of Islamic prayer.

raqs baladi: country or folk dance.

raqs sharqi: eastern dance, better known in the West as belly dancing.

rebaba: stringed instrument.

Revolutionary Command Council (RCC): Small circle of Free Officers who served as the executive branch of the Egyptian government after the Revolution up until 1956.

Sabra and Shatila: Palestinian refugee camps, (in)famous for being attacked by Christian Phalangist forces under the protection of the Israeli Defense Force during the Lebanese Civil War in September 1982. The Kahan Commission in Israel found the state indirectly responsible and Defense Minister Ariel Sharon personally responsible.

sa'id: upper Egypt.

sa'idi: person from upper Egypt.

ṣalat: prayer; one of the five pillars of Islam.

ṣawm: fasting during the month of Ramadan; one of the five pillars of Islam.

SCAF: Supreme Council of the Armed Forces.

Seega: Egyptian game similar to ancient game of Senet in which the objective is to capture the opponent's dogs.

serdab: Old Kingdom burial chamber with a slit or hole so that the *ka* of the deceased could move easily and offerings could pass into the chamber that housed the *ka* statue.

Set or Seth: ancient Egyptian god; brother of Osiris and Isis; god of the desert.

Senet: ancient Egyptian board game played on a grid of 3 by 10.

shabka: gift of jewelry given to a bride by the groom and/or his family.

shahada: testimony of faith; one of the five pillars of Islam; believer professes "There is no God but God, and Muhammad is His Prophet."

Shari'a: Islamic law.

Shaykh al-Balad: title of the leading mamluk during Ottoman times.

sheesha: water pipe, known elsewhere as *narghile* or *hookah.*

Socialist Labor Party (SLP):   Islamo-Socialist party founded in the late 1970s.

Sufism: Islamic mysticism.

suhur: late-night meal eaten during the month of Ramadan that allows for socializing and to tide faster over for the long day ahead.

Supreme Constitutional Court (SCC):   highest court in Egypt.

takaful: Islamic finance concept whereby a pool of investors puts money into a holding company that invests in a local venture. Thereafter dividends are divided among investors periodically.

Tanzimat: period of reform in the Ottoman Empire from 1839 to 1876.

tawhid: unity; goal of Sufism is to achieve unity with Allah.

tok tok: vehicle built from the engine and wheels of a motorized tricycle, but covered with a front and back seat, and open on the sides.

tujjar: wealthy, long-distance trader.

Tulunids: ruled Egypt from 868 to 905.

'ud: lute.

'ulama' (sing. 'alim):   the religious establishment; men who are learned in religious studies.

Umayyads: ruled Egypt from 661 to 750 and controlled the caliphate during the same time period.

umma: Islamic concept for the community of believers.

Umm Walad: legal term in Islamic law for a slave that has conceived a child.

'umra: pilgrimage made to Mecca at any time other than the official pilgrimage period in *dhul al-hijja* is considered an *'umra* rather than a *hajj.*

United Arab Republic (UAR):   official title for the country of Egypt between 1958 and 1971.

UNEF: United Nations Emergency Forces.

UNESCO: United Nations Educational, Scientific, and Cultural Organization.

United Nations Special Committee on Palestine (UNSCOP):   created a plan to partition Palestine in 1947.

Upper Egypt: region of Egypt below the Nile delta.

'urfi: customary, as in marriage according to customary law.

USAID: United States Agency for International Development.

Wafd: party founded in 1919, based on the refusal of the British occupiers to allow Egyptian nationalists to attend Versailles Peace conference after World War I.

Wafdist Women's Central Committee (WWCC):   organized protests and boycotts during the 1919 Revolution in Egypt.

waqf: charitable endowment.

wikala **(a.k.a caravanserai, fonduq, khan):** building that historically had areas for housing goods and pack animals on lower floors, with apartments for merchants above.

wuḍu: ablution for prayer.

Young Egypt (Islamic Socialist Party): party founded by Ahmad Husayn in 1933.

Zabbaleen: garbage collectors of Cairo, known for their efficiency and recycling of materials.

zakat: mandatory almsgiving; one of the five pillars of Islam.

zar: ritual ceremony for placating spirits.

zummara: clarinet-like instrument.

Facts and Figures

	Country Info
Location:	Far northwest Africa, bounded by the Mediterranean Sea to the north, Israel and the Palestinian Autonomous Region to the east, Sudan to the south, and Libya to the west.
Official Name:	Jumhuriyat Miṣr al-Arabiyah (Arab Republic of Egypt)
Local Name:	Miṣr
Government:	Republic
Capital:	Cairo
Weights and Measures:	Metric system, with traditional units for landholdings
Time Zone:	6–7 hours ahead of U.S. Eastern Standard
Currency:	Egyptian pound
Head of State:	Vacant
Head of Government:	Mohammed Morsi
Legislature:	Majlis al-Sha'ab (People's Assembly)
Major Political Parties:	Wafd, Free Egyptians, NPUP, Egyptian Social Democratic Party, Egyptian Tahrir Party, Freedom and Justice Party, Revolution Tomorrow Party, Karama, Nour, Wasaṭ, Gama'a al-Islamiyya

TABLE A-2 Basic Facts and Figures

	Demographics
Population:	83,688,164 (2012 est.)
Population by age:	(2011 est.)
0–14	32.7%
15–64	62.8%
65+	4.5%
Median Age:	(2011 est.)
Total	24.3 years
Males	24.0 years
Females	24.6 years
Population Growth Rate:	1.992% (2012 est.)
Population Density:	217 people per sq. mile (2012 est.)
Infant Mortality Rate:	24.2 deaths per 1,000 live births (2012 est.)
Ethnic Groups:	Egyptian (99.6%), Other (0.4%)
Religions:	Muslim (90%), Christian (10%)
Majority Language:	Arabic
Other Languages:	English and French are common second languages
Life Expectancy (Average):	72.9 years (2012 est.)
Fertility Rate:	2.94 children per woman (2012 est.)

TABLE A-3 Basic Facts and Figures

	Geography
Land Area:	385,229 sq. miles
Arable Land:	2.9%
Irrigated Land:	13,629 sq.miles (2008)
Coastline:	1,522 miles
Natural Hazards:	Drought, flash flooding, earthquakes, landslides, sand and dust storms, wind storms known as khamsin
Environmental Problems:	Desertification, water pollution, coastal oil pollution, soil salination, urban pollution
Major Agricultural Products:	Cottonseed, wheat, *corn,* rice, tomatoes, potatoes, oranges, sugar cane, sorghum, dates, grapes, onions
Natural Resources:	Petroleum, natural gas, iron, phosphates, manganese, limestone, gypsum, talc, asbestos, lead, zinc, rare earth elements
Land Use:	0.5% cropland, 2.9% arable land, 96.6% other
Climate:	Desert, with hot, dry summers and moderate winters

TABLE A-4 Basic Facts and Figures

	Economy
GDP:	$231.9 billion (2011 est.)
GDP Per Capita:	$2,898 (2011 est.)
GDP By Sector:	Agriculture - 14.4%; industry - 39.5%; services - 45.8% (2011 est.)
Exchange Rate:	5.94 Egyptian pounds = $1 USD (2011)
Labor Force:	Agriculture - 32%; industry - 17%; services - 51% (2001 est.)
Unemployment:	12.2% (2011 est.)
Major Industries:	Textiles, food processing, tourism, chemicals, pharmaceuticals, petroleum, construction, cement, metals, light manufacturing
Leading Companies:	Orascom Group, Suez Cement, Delta
	Textiles, National Bank of Egypt, Bank of Alexandria, Banque du Caire, Banque Misr, Cairo Amman Bank, Egyptian American Bank, Egyptian Natural Gas Holding Company, Egyptian General Petroleum Corporation, Misr Petroleum, Nile Valley Gas Company, MobilNil
Electricity Production:	123.9 billion kWh (2008 est.)
Electricity Consumption:	109.1 billion kWh (2008 est.)
Exports:	$27.96 billion (2011 est.)
Export Goods:	Crude oil, petroleum products, cotton, textiles, metal products, chemicals, processed food
Imports:	$57.41 billion (2011 est.)
Import Goods:	Machinery and equipment, food, chemicals, textiles, wood products, fuel
Current Account Balance	$-8.609 billion (2011 est.)

TABLE A-5 Basic Facts and Figures

	Communications and Transportation
Telephone Lines:	9.618 million (2010)
Mobile Phones:	70.66 million (2010)
Internet Users:	20.14 million (2009)
Roads:	40,420 miles (2009)
Railroads:	3,418 miles (2010)
Airports:	86 (2010)

TABLE A-6   Basic Facts and Figures

	Military
Defense Spending (% of GDP):	3.4% (2005 est.)
Active Armed Forces:	468,500 (2010)
Manpower Fit for Military Service:	18,060,543 males; 17,244,838 females (2010 est.)
Military Service:	1–3 years mandatory service for males ages 18–30, followed by 9 months of reserve duty

TABLE A-7   Basic Facts and Figures

	Education
School System:	Students begin their education with six years of primary school, beginning at the age of six. Students then continue to early secondary school, which lasts for three years, and then choose either a three-year or five-year technical program or a three-year academic program.
Education Expenditures (% of GDP):	3.8% (2008)
Average Years Spent in School:	11.0 (2004)
Students per Teacher, Primary School:	27.0 (2009)
Primary School–age Children Enrolled in Primary School:	9,988,181 (2008)
Enrollment in Tertiary Education:	2,488,434 (2008)
Literacy:	72.7% (2009 est.)

Sources: ABC-CLIO World Geography database; CIA *The World Factbook* (https://www.cia.gov/library/publications/the-world-factbook); UNESCO

TABLE B   Climate

TABLE B-1   Temperature

Month	Type	Cairo Min/Max	Alexandria Min/Max	Luxor Min/Max	Aswan Min/Max	Hurghada Air/Water Average	Sharm Air/Water Average
		Forecast	Forecast	Forecast	Forecast	Forecast	Forecast
Jan	F	47/66	49/65	42/74	46/75	75/64	75/64
Feb	F	48/69	49/67	44/78	49/79	77/64	77/64
March	F	52/75	52/70	51/84	54/86	79/68	79/68

(Continued)

TABLE B

TABLE **B-1** *(Continued)*

Month	Type	Cairo Min/Max	Alexandria Min/Max	Luxor Min/Max	Aswan Min/Max	Hurghada Air/Water Average	Sharm Air/Water Average
April	F	56/83	58/75	60/95	63/97	88/77	88/77
May	F	63/90	62/80	69/103	71/101	95/79	95/79
June	F	68/95	69/83	72/107	76/108	99/82	99/82
July	F	71/96	73/86	74/106	76/108	107/82	107/82
Aug	F	71/95	73/87	74/107	76/107	108/84	108/84
Sept	F	68/89	71/85	71/101	72/103	100/81	100/81
Oct	F	64/86	64/82	64/95	66/99	90/77	90/77
Nov	F	54/75	59/76	54/85	58/86	79/73	79/73
Dec	F	51/69	52/69	45/76	50/69	79/66	79/66

Source: http://www.touregypt.net/climate.htm

TABLE **B-2** Average Monthly Rainfall

Month	Average Rainfall in Millimeters
January	4
February	4
March	3
April	1
May	2
June	0.5
July	0
August	0
September	0.5
October	1
November	3
December	7

Source: http://www.climatetemp.info/egypt/

TABLE C   Population

TABLE C-1   Population by Age, Religion, Ethnicity (2011)

Total Population	82,079,636
0–14	32.7% (13,725,282 male; 13,112,157 female)
5–64	62.8% (26,287,921 male; 25,383, 947 female)
65 and over	4.5% (1,669,313 male; 2, 013,016 female)
Muslims	90%
Copts	9%
Jews	Statistically insignificant
Other Christian	<1%
Egyptian	99.6%
Other (ethnicity)	0.4%

Source: CIA *The World Factbook*

TABLE C-2   Population by Marital Status

Marital status

Single: 13,659,314 (29.33%)

Married: 29,189,966 (62.69%)

Widowed: 2,942,709 (6.32%)

Divorced: 437,953

Source: http://egypt.usaid.gov/en/aboutus/Pages/egyptfactsandfigures.aspx

TABLE C-3   Life Expectancy (2011)

Country		**Male**	**Female**
Egypt	72.66%	70.07%	75.38%
US	78.37%	75.92%	80.93%

http://www.sis.gov.eg/VR/egyptinnumber/egyptinfigures/englishtables/46.pdf **See chart in state information service that goes from 1960 to 2008—add point for 2011**
Sources: State Information Service and CIA *The World Factbook*

TABLE C-3   Literacy (2011)—age 15 and over who can read and write

Total	71.4%
Men	83%
Women	59.4%

Source: CIA *The World Factbook*

TABLE D   Education

TABLE D-1   Schools, Classrooms, Students, in Governmental and Private Sector 2008–2009

Educational Stage	Private Students	Sector Classrooms	Schools	Government Students	Sector Classrooms	Schools
Pre-Primary	206,972	6,873	1,514	543,471	161,124	6,401
Primary	760,601	22,973	1,584	844,6722	189,111	15,282
Preparatory	224,834	7,435	1,185	374,0114	844,6722	8,470
General Secondary	63,389	2551	602	734,322	21,817	1,730
Industrial Secondary	2074	77	10	663,415	19,980	854
Agricultural Secondary	0	0	0	123,482	3,706	177
Commercial Secondary	68,163	1,863	204	395,297	11,136	545
Single Class (mixed)	0	0	0	70,039	3,229	3,229
Improved Crafts for Girls	0	0	0	20,457	777	777
Handi-capped Education	663	88	19	37,195	4,131	840
Total	1,326,696	41,860	5,118	14,774,514	358,461	38,305

Source: Ministry of Education, as cited by CAPMAS, *Egypt in Figures 2010*

TABLE D-2   Students Enrolled in Governmental Universities by Sex and Percentage

University	Total	Females	Males
Cairo	293,425 (15.4%)	135,935 (14.6%)	157,490 (16.2%)
Alexandria*	175,230 (9.2%)	94,106 (10.1%)	81,124 (8.3%)
Ain Shams	212,799 (11.2%)	118,382 (12.7%)	94,417 (9.7%)
Assiut	72,560 (3.8%)	33,408 (3.6%)	39,152 (4.0%)
Tanta	93,526 (4.9%)	47,686 (5.1%)	45,840 (4.7%)
Mansura	124,743 (6.5%)	71,924 (7.7%)	52,819 (5.4%)
Zagazig	105,181 (5.5%)	57,331 (6.2%)	47,850 (4.9%)
Minya	48,697 (2.6%)	25,350 (2.7%)	23,347 (2.4%)
Minufiyya	75,470 (4.0%)	36,838 (4.0%)	38,632 (4.0%)
Suez Canal	48,132 (2.5%)	25,225 (2.7%)	22,907 (2.3%)
Ganub al-Wadi	45,060 (2.4%)	26,239 (2.8%)	18,821 (1.9%)
Helwan	98,689 (5.2%)	51,516 (5.5%)	47,173 (4.8%)
Azhar	322,809 (16.9%)	112,713 (12.1%)	210,096 (21.5%)
Fayum	23,742 (1.2%)	13,603 (1.5%)	10,139 (1.0%)
Beni-Suef	44,367 (2.3%)	18,860 (2.0%)	25,507 (2.6%)
Banha	59,428 (3.1%)	29,110 (3.1%)	30,318 (3.1%)
Sohag	29,584 (1.6%)	16,852 (1.8%)	12,732 (1.3%)
Kafr al-Shaykh	25,342 (1.3%)	14,861 (1.6%)	10,481 (1.1%)
Mubarak Police Academy	6,167 (0.3%)	0 (0)	6,167 (0.6%)
Total	1,904,951 (100%)	929,939 (100%)	975,012 (100%)

*Excludes data for distance learning at Alexandria University.
Source: Ministry of Higher Education and al-Azhar University as cited by CAPMAS, *Egypt in Figures 2010*

Table D-3   Graduates of Higher Institutes Following the Ministry of Higher Education

Division	Total	Females	Males
Engineering	6,786 (7.49%)	1,176 (17.32%)	5,610 (82.68%)
Computers	14,254 (15.74%)	4,228 (29.66%)	10,026 (70.34%)
Commerce	26,508 (29.28%)	9,963 (37.58%)	16,545 (62.42%)
Agriculture	2,127 (2.34%)	740 (34.79%)	1,387 (65.21%)
Social Services	33,482 (36.98%)	18,108 (54.08%)	15,374 (45.92%)
Language or Translation	1,073 (1.18)	610 (56.84%)	463 (43.16%)
Tourism and Hotels	4,471 (4.93%)	1,143 (25.56)	3,328 (74.44%)
Information	695 (0.76%)	335 (48.20%)	360 (51.8%)
Literature	1,131 (1.24%)	478 (42.26%)	653 (57.74%)
Total	**90,527 (100%)**	**36,781 (40.62%)**	**53,746 (59.38%)**

Table E   Labor

Table E-1   Quarterly Estimates of Unemployment of 15- to 64-year-olds (2006–2009)

Item	First Quarter	Second Quarter	Third Quarter	Fourth Quarter
2006				
Male	7.72	6.90	7.20	6.00
Female	25.08	24.90	25.40	18.90
Total	**10.00**	**10.90**	**11.10**	**8.99**
2007				
Male	5.99	5.83	5.89	5.86
Female	20.87	19.56	19.40	19.41
Total	**9.06**	**8.86**	**8.91**	**9.12**
2008				
Male	5.63	5.41	5.82	5.63
Female	20.50	18.76	18.27	19.69
Total	**9.04**	**8.37**	**8.55**	**8.84**
2009				
Male	5.19	5.20	5.26	5.27
Female	22.90	23.17	22.80	22.85
Total	**9.37**	**9.42**	**9.36**	**9.40**

Source: CAPMAS

Table E-2   Estimates of Labor Force by Sex and Governorate (15 and over) 2008 (by the thousand)

Governorate	Percent Female of Total	Total	Female	Male
Cairo	21.0	2,535	534	2,001
Alexandria	17.9	1,291	231	1,061
Port Said	32.3	234	76	158
Suez	26.2	186	49	137
Damietta	18.4	370	68	302
Daqahlia	23.5	1,814	427	1,387
Sharqiyya	18.1	1,737	314	1,423
Qalyubiyya	16.7	1,327	221	1,106
Kafr al-Shaykh	21.1	960	203	758
Gharbiyya	25.0	1,430	358	1,072
Minufiyya	26.3	1,247	328	919
Buhayra	38.1	2,173	827	1,346

(*Continued*)

TABLE E–2   (*Continued*)

Governorate	Percent Female of Total	Total	Female	Male
Ismailiyya	25.2	344	87	257
Giza	13.7	1,882	259	1623
Beni Suef	36.6	921	338	584
Fayum	15.2	784	119	664
Minya	28.0	1,541	431	1,110
Assiut	15.6	1,001	156	845
Sohag	15.7	986	154	832
Qena	18.8	893	168	725
Aswan	18.2	412	75	337
Luxor	19.8	142	28	114
Red Sea	8.3	101	8	93
al-Wadi al-Gadid	44.2	87	38	49
Matruh	10.2	94	10	85
North Sinai	17.6	102	18	84
South Sinai	16.2	59	10	50
Total	22.4	24,652	5532	19,120

Source: CAPMAS, *Egypt in Figures 2010*

TABLE E-3   Civilian Employees in the Public Sector and Public Business Sector by Economic Activity and Sex (2009)

Economic Activity	Percentage	Total	Female	Male
Agriculture, Public Works, and Water Resources	3.5	27,591	6,268	21,323
Industry, Petroleum, and Mineral Abundance	28.7	224,192	19,859	204,334
Electricity and Energy	14.4	112,651	12,933	99,718
Transportation	7.3	57,152	4,531	52,621
Supply and Internal Trade	5.0	39,507	7,238	32,269
Money and Economy	8.0	62,480	13,460	49,020
Housing and Construction	20.4	159,740	13,154	146,586
Health, Social, and Religious Services	3.5	27,191	10,183	17,008
Culture and Information	0.2	1,930	303	1,627
Tourism and Aviation	5.3	41,140	6,590	34,550
Defense, Security, and Justice	3.7	28,874	2,177	26,697
Total	**100**	**782,448**	**96,695**	**685,753**

TABLE F   Rulers, Viceroys, Governors, & Presidents of Egypt

TABLE F-1   Ancient Egyptian Dynasties

Predynastic Period (4500–3150 BCE)

1st Dynasty (3150–2700 BCE)

> Narmer 3150–3125
>
> Aha, 3125–3100
>
> Djer, 3100–3055
>
> Uadji, 3055– 3050
>
> Den, 3050–2995
>
> Adjib, 2995–?
>
> Semerkhet, ?–2960
>
> Qaa, 2960–2925

2nd Dynasty (2925–2700 BCE)

> Hetepsekhemwy
>
> Nebra
>
> Nynetjer
>
> Weneg
>
> Sened
>
> Peribsen
>
> Khasekhemuy

Ancient Kingdom (2700–2200 BCE)

3rd Dynasty (2700–2625 BCE)

> Nebka
>
> Djoser
>
> Khaba
>
> Sekhemkhet
>
> Neferkara
>
> Huni

4th Dynasty (2625–2510 BCE)

> Snefru
>
> Khufru
>
> Djedefra
>
> Khafre
>
> Baefre

(Continued)

Table F-1   (*Continued*)

Menkure

Shepsekaf

5th Dynasty (2510–2460 BCE)

Userkaf

Sahura

Neferirkara

Shepseskara

Raneferef

Menekauhor

Djedkara Isesi

Unas

6th Dynasty (2460–2200 BCE)

Teti

Userkara

Pepi I

Merenre

Pepi II

Merenre II

Nitocris

First Intermediate Period (2200–2061 BCE)

7th and 8th Dynasty (ca. 2200–2160 BCE)

9th and 10th Dynasty (ca. 2160–2040 BCE)

11th Dynasty-first part-(2160–2061)

Mentuhotep I

Intef I

Intef II

Intef III

Middle Kingdom (2061–1785 BCE)

11th Dynasty-second part-(2061–1991)

Mentuhotop II (2061–2009)

Mentuhotep III (2009–1998)

Mentuhotep IV (1998–1991)

(*Continued*)

Table **F–1**   (*Continued*)

Second Intermediate Period (1785–1552 BCE)

13th and 14th Dynasty (1785–1633 BCE)

15th and 16th Dynasty (ca. 1730–1530 BCE)

17th Dynasty (1650–1552 BCE)

Principal Theban rulers:

>Rahotep

>Intep V

>Sobekemsaf II

>Gehuty

>Mentuhotep VII

>Nebiryau I

>Taa I

>Taa II

>Kamose

New Kingdom (1552–1069 BCE)

18th Dynasty (1552–1295 BCE)

>Ahmose, 1552–1526

>Amenhotep I, 1526–1506

>Thutmose I, 1506–1493

>Thutmose II, 1493–1478

>Hatshepsut, 1478–1458

>Thutmose III, 1458–1425

>Amenhotep II, 1425–1401

>Thutmose IV, 1401–1390

>Amenhotep III, 1390–1352

>Amenhotep IV/Akhenaten, 1352–1338

>Smenkhkara, 1338–1336

>Tutankhamen, 1336–1327

>Ay, 1327–1323

>Horemheb, 1323–1295

19th Dynasty (1295–1188 BCE)

>Ramses I, 1295–1294

>Seti, 1294–1279

>Ramses II, 1279–1213

(*Continued*)

TABLE F–1 (*Continued*)

Merenptah, 1213–1202

Amenemes, 1202–1199

Seti II, 1199–1196

Saptah, 1196–1190

Tausret, 1196–1188

20th Dynasty (1188–1069 BCE)

Sethnakht, 1188–1186

Ramses III, 1186–1154

Ramses IV, 1154–1148

Ramses V, 1148–1144

Ramses VI, 1144–1136

Ramses VII, 1136–1128

Ramses VIII, 1128–1125

Ramses IX, 1125–1107

Ramses X, 1107–1098

Ramses XI, 1098–1069

Third Intermediate Period (1069–664 BCE)

21st Dynasty (1069–945 BCE)

Smendes I, 1069–1043 BCE

Amenemnisu, 1043–1040

Psusennes I, 1040–993

Amenemope, 993–984

Osorkon the Elder, 984–978

Siamon, 978–959

Psusennes II, 959–945

22nd Dynasty (945–715 BCE)

Sheshonk I, 945–924

Osorkon, I 924–890

Sheshonk, II, 890–889

Takelot I, 889–774

Harsiesis, 870–860

Osorkon II, 874–850

Takelot II, 850–825

(*Continued*)

TABLE F–1 (*Continued*)

        Sheshonk III, 825–773

        Pimay, 773–767

        Shehonk V, 767–730

        Osorkon IV, 730–715

23rd Dynasty (818–715 BCE)

        Osorkon III, 787–759

        Takelot III, 764–757

        Rudamon, 757–754

        Iuput II, 754–754

24th Dynasty (727–715 BCE)

        Tefnakht, 727–716

        Bakenrenef, 716–715

25th Dynasty (ca. 774 –656)

        Alara

        Kashta

        Piankhi, 747–716

        Shabaka 716–702

        Shabataka, 702–690

        Taharqa, 690–664

        Tanutamani, 664–656

Late Period (672–332 BCE)

26th Dynasty (672–525 BCE)

        Neccho I, 672–664

        Psamtik I, 664–610

        Necho, 610–595

        Psamtik II, 595–589

        Apries, 589–570

        Ahmose II, 570–526

        Psamtik III, 526–525

27th Dynasty, 1st Persian Period (525–404 BCE)

        Cambyses, 525–522

        Darius I, 522–486

(*Continued*)

TABLE F–1 (*Continued*)

    Xerxes I, 486—465

    Artaxerxes I, 465–424

    Darius II, 424–404

    Artaxerxes II, 404

28th Dynasty (404–399 BCE)

    Amertaeus, 404–399

29th Dynasty (399–380 BCE)

    Nepherites I, 399–394

    Psammuthis, 394–393

    Achoris, 393–380

    Nepherites II, 380

30th Dynasty (380–342 BCE)

    Nectanebo I, 380–362

    Tachos, 362–360

    Nectanebo II, 360–343

2nd Persian Period (343–332 BCE)

    Artaxerxes III Ochus, 343–338

    Arses, 338–336

    Darius III, 336–332

TABLE F-2 Alexandrian and Ptolemaic Rulers

Alexander, 332–323

Perdiccas, regent to Philip III of Macedon 323 and Philip IV; Ptolemy appointed satrap

Philip III Macedon, 323–317

Philip IV Macedon, 323–309

Ptolemy I Soter, 305 founds dynasty (305–283)

Ptolemy II Philadelphus, 283–246

Ptolemy III Euergetes, 246–222

Ptolemy IV Philopator, 222–205

Ptolemy V Epiphanes, 204–181

(*Continued*)

TABLE F–2 (*Continued*)

Ptolemy VI Philometor, 180–145 (with Cleopatra I until 176) (with Cleopatra II and Ptolemy VIII Physcon between 169 and 164) (with Ptolemy Eupator in 152)

Ptolemy VII Neo Philopator, 145–ca.132/131 (with Cleopatra II)

Ptolemy VII Physcon and Cleopatra II ca. 132/131–127

Cleopatra II, 130–127 and with Ptolemy VIII and Cleopatra III, 127–116

Ptolemy IX Lathyros and Cleopatra III (later Cleopatra IV), 116–110

Ptolemy X Alexander and Cleopatra III, 110–109

Ptolemy IX, 109–107

Ptolemy X and Cleopatra III (later Berenice III), 107–88

Berenice III, 88–80

tolemy XI Alexander II and Berenice III, 80

Ptolemy XII Auletes and Cleopatra V, 80–58

Cleopatra VI and Berenice IV, 58–55

Ptolemy XII and Cleopatra VII, 55–51

Ptolemy XIII and Cleopatra VII, 51–47

Ptolemy XIV and Cleopatra VII, 47–44

Cleopatra regent to Caesarion, 44–30

TABLE F-3   Islamic Dynasties and Medieval Government in Egypt

Conquest of Egypt—Rashidun "Orthodox Caliphate" Umar 639 AD

      Umar (d. 644)

      Uthman (644–656)

      Ali (656–661)

Umayyad Dynasty (661–750)

Abbasid Dynasty (750–1258)

      Tulunids (868–905)

      Ikhshid-Kafurid regime (935–968)

Fatimid Dynasty-competing with Abbasids (969–1171)

Ayyubid Dynasty (1171–1248)

Baḥri Mamluks (1250–1382)

Burgi Mamluks (1382–1517)

Ottoman Rule (1517–1914)

TABLE F-4 Muhammad Ali Dynasty 1805–1952

Muhammad Ali (r. 1805–1848)

ii

Ibrahim (r. 1848) = Ahmad Tusun = Said (r. 1854–1863) = Abdul Halim

ii   ii

Ismail (r. 1863–1879) Abbas Hilmi I (r. 1848–1854)

ii

Muhammad Tawfiq (r. 1879–1892) = Husayn Kamil (r. 1914–1917) = (Ahmad) Fuad
                                                                    (r. 1917–1936)

ii   ii

Abbas Hilmi II (r. 1892–1914)   Faruq
                                                                    (r. 1936–1952)

                                                                    ii

                                                                    (Ahmad)
                                                                    Fuad II (r. 1952)

TABLE F-5 Presidents of the Republic

General Muhammad Neguib 1952–1954

Gamal Abd al-Nasser 1954–1970

Anwar Sadat 1970–1981

Muhammad Hosni Mubarak 1981–2011

TABLE G Agriculture and Land Use

TABLE G-1 Planted Area (1961–2008) (thousands of Feddans)

Year	Planted Area	Year	Planted Area
1961	5605	1985	5943
1962	5454	1986	6019
1963	5343	1987	6063
1964	5388	1988	6183
1965	5549	1989	6270
1966	5688	1990	6918
1967	5623	1991	7023
1968	5723	1992	7134
1969	5710	1993	7179
1970	5785	1994	7173
1971	5756	1995	7813

(Continued)

TABLE **G-1**   (*Continued*)

Year	Planted Area	Year	Planted Area
1972	5747	1996	7563
1973	5772	1997	7726
1974	5785	1998	7761
1975	5781	1999	7848
1976	5874	2000	7833
1977	5796	2001	7946
1978	5838	2002	8148
1979	5826	2003	8113
1980	5820	2004	8279
1981	5876	2005	8385
1982	5822	2006	8411
1983	5797	2007	8547
1984	5853	2008	8432

Source: Ministry of Agriculture as cited by CAPMAS

TABLE **G-2**   Development of Reclaimed Land (thousands of Feddans)

Year	2002/2003	2003/2004	2004/2005	2005/2006	2006/2007	2007/2008	2008/2009
Item	18.0	23.5	14.5	7.8	2.2	2.1	0.67

Source: General Authority of Projects and Agricultural Development as cited by CAPMAS, *Egypt in Figures 2010*

TABLE **G-3**   Production of Some Agricultural Products 2007–2008

Type		2007	2008
Wheat	8.1	7379	7977
Barley	−16.3	178	149
Maize	6.8	6930	7401
Sorghum	2.7	844	867
Rice	5.5	6877	7253
Beans	−17.8	428	352
Lentils	−50.0	2	1

(*Continued*)

TABLE **G-3** (*Continued*)

Type		2007	2008
Linen	−5.4	92	87
Peanuts	−4.1	218	209
Sesame	−11.9	42	37
Soybeans	11.5	26	29
Sunflower	−27.6	29	21
Sugar Beets	−6.0	5458	5133
Onions	12.3	1817	2040
Citrus	3.2	3134	3233
Fruits*	−3.3	10582	10236

*Fruits include all sorts in addition to watermelon, melon, and nuts.

Source: CAPMAS, *Egypt in Figures 2010*

TABLE **H**   Trade, Aid, and Economic Indicators

TABLE **H-1**   Suez Canal Traffic

Statement	January 2007	January 2008
Total number of Ships	1511	1676
Oil tankers	274	280
No. of other passing ships	1237	1396
Loading of passing ships (million ton)	63.4	72.9

Source: http://www.sis.gov.eg/En/LastPage.aspx?CategoryID=345

TABLE **H-2**   Total US Assistance 1975–2009, Support by Sector

Environment	1%
Health and Population	3%
Education and Training	4%
Democracy and Governance	4%
Agriculture	4%
Other Economic Growth	6%
Food Aid (PL 48404)	13%
Policy Reform Cash Transfers	17%
Infrastructure Projects	20%
Commodity Import Program	28%
Total: $28.6 Billion	

Source: http://egypt.usaid.gov/en/aboutus/Pages/budgetinformation.aspx

TABLE H-3   Total US Economic Support by Sector, Obligation of FY 2009

Environment	2%
Health and Population	8%
Democracy and Governance	8%
Education and Training	15%
Supplemental for Sinai	20%
Economic Growth	22%
Policy Reform Cash Transfers	25%
Total $250 million	

Source: http://egypt.usaid.gov/en/aboutus/Pages/budgetinformation.aspx

TABLE H-4   Remittances of Egyptians Working Abroad by country July 2006 to September 2008 (million US$)

Countries	2006/2007 %	2006/2007 Value	2007/2008 %	2007/2008 Value	2008/2009 %	2008/2009 Value
Saudi Arabia	13.6	859.4	11.2	959.4	12.5	976.1
Kuwait	17.5	1106.0	21.0	1797.1	20.4	1594.0
U.A.E.	15.7	989.6	16.3	1392.9	17.7	1380.3
Qatar	1.6	102.1	1.5	131.0	1.8	140.7
Bahrain	0.3	21.9	0.9	77.6	0.5	36.4
Oman	0.3	17.7	0.4	31.6	0.4	27.5
Libya	0.1	5.5	0.4	33.2	0.3	20.5
Lebanon	0.4	24.6	0.2	18.0	0.3	22.0
USA	32.9	2080.3	32.3	2762.9	29.1	2269.1
France	0.8	53.5	0.7	61.1	0.6	50.2
Germany	3.3	209.6	0.7	61.1	0.6	50.2
Italy	0.7	42.0	0.8	71.1	0.9	72.3
Netherlands	0.5	32.5	0.2	17.7	0.2	19.4
UK	3.7	235.5	3.1	267.5	6.2	481.8
Greece	0.2	14.1	0.2	16.7	0.2	22.4
Spain	0.2	10.4	0.1	8.4	0.1	6.5
Switzerland	4.1	261.0	3.0	255.5	2.7	213.1
Japan	=	3.0	=	4.1	0.1	5.1
Canada	0.2	13.2	0.3	28.7	0.3	26.5
Other countries	3.0	233.6	4.6	395.4	3.8	239.1
Total	100	7805.7	100	8559.2	100	6321.0

Source: CAPMAS, *Egypt in Figures 2010*

TABLE **H-5** Domestic Debt August 2007 to September 2008 Value: LE by millions

Item	Percent Change	2008	2009
Gross Domestic Budget Sector Debt	16.7	599603	699667
Budget Sector Deposits	13.6	120904	137341
Net Domestic Budget Sector Debt	17.5	562326	478699
Gross General Gov't Domestic Debt	19.3	478699	562326
General Gov't Deposits	13.6	131043	148811
Net Domestic General Gov't Debt	21.3	381965	463363
Gross Domestic Public Debt	19.0	537559	639953
Public Sector Deposits	11.4	150501	167733
Net Domestic Public Debt	22.0	387058	472220
Indicators as Percent of GDP		**2008**	**2009**
Gross Domestic Budget Sector		67.0%	67.4%
Net Domestic Budget Sector Debt		53.5%	54.1%
Gross General Gov't Domestic Debt		57.3%	58.9%
Net Domestic General Gov't Debt		42.7%	44.6%
Gross Domestic Public Debt		61.6%	60.0%
Net Domestic Public Debt		43.2%	45.5%

Source: Ministry of Finance as cited by CAPMAS, *Egypt in Figures 2010*

TABLE **I** Communication & Information Technology

TABLE **I-1** Mobile Phone Subscriptions per 100 people

Place	2006	2007	2008	2009
Egypt	23	38	51	67
United States	81	87	89	97

Source: www.usaid.gov

TABLE **I-2** Participants in Telephone Services

2007	2008
11.2 million	11.3 million

Source: http://www.sis.gov.eg/En/LastPage.
aspx?CategoryID=345

TABLE I-3   Post Office Services by Governate and Type of Office

Governate	Mobile Lines	Agencies of Post Services	Domestic Offices	Governmental Post Offices
Cairo	—	176	1	205
Alexandria	9	78	—	136
Port Said	1	4	1	34
Damietta	31	13	5	52
Daqaliyya	146	53	50	223
Sharqiyya	272	46	2	298
Qalyubiyya	72	60	6	191
Kafr al-Shaykh	147	17	4	123
Gharbiyya	70	41	6	243
Minufiyya	109	66	22	219
Buhayra	270	58	12	172
Ismailia	31	—	—	52
Giza	39	52	3	128
Helwan	14	8	2	93
6 October	—	6	—	66
Beni Suef	99	17	4	105
Fayum	122	28	13	90
Minya	175	36	43	162
Assiut	72	38	2	188
Sohag	106	17	11	264
Qena	106	16	7	214
Aswan	63	26	—	159
Luxor City	52	6	2	50
Red Sea	—	11	—	24
al-Wadi al-Gadid	—	4	1	48
Matruh	7	6	4	25
North Sinai	—	3	1	46
South Sinai	—	6	—	20
Total	**2017**	**916**	**202**	**3669**

Source: CAPMAS, *Egypt in Figures 2010*

Major Holidays in Egyptian Culture

Holiday	Date
Coptic Christmas	January 7
Mother's Day/Family's Day	March 21
Sinai Liberation Day	April 25
Labor Day	May 1
Revolution Day	July 23
Armed Forces Day	October 6
Victory Day	December 23
Islamic New Year	Varies, Based on Islamic Lunar Calendar
'Ashura	Varies, Based on Islamic Lunar Calendar
Mulad al-Nabi	Varies, Based on Islamic Lunar Calendar
Coptic Easter	Varies, Based on Coptic Calendar
Sham al-Nassim	Varies, Based on Islamic Lunar Calendar
Ramadan	Varies, Based on Islamic Lunar Calendar
'Eid al-Fiṭr	Varies, Based on Islamic Lunar Calendar
'Eid al-aḍha	Varies, Based on Islamic Lunar Calendar
Nawruz	Varies, Based on Coptic Calendar

SECULAR HOLIDAYS

Mother's Day: This event is not a major holiday, nor a consumerist frenzy as it is in the United States; in fact, many Egyptians would not even know that it is traditionally observed on the vernal equinox. Now it is more generically known as Family Day.

Sinai Liberation Day: Sinai Liberation Day commemorates the withdrawal of all Israeli troops from the Sinai Peninsula on April 25, 1982, and the return of the peninsula to Egyptian control. Israel occupied the peninsula during the Six Day War of 1967. The signing of the Camp David Accords in 1979 paved the road for diplomatic recognition between the countries and Israel's complete evacuation of the Sinai in 1982. The president of Egypt usually makes a television appearance addressing Egyptian citizens and praising peace. Egyptians who live in the Sinai Peninsula stage celebrations.

Labor Day: Egyptian Labor Day falls on May 1 each year, when the Egyptian president gives a speech praising the role that Egyptian workers played in the development of Egypt as an industrialized nation. It is not coincidental that Nasser chose Labor Day to fall on May Day, the recognized International Workers' Day. Traditionally, the wide observation of this national holiday has made it hard for outsiders to conduct business, as most Egyptian workers receive the day off. However, with the creation of the internet, globalization, the widening of multinationals and the service sector, this is less of a problem.

Revolution Day: Revolution Day is a celebration of the birth of Egypt as a Republic after the military coup on 23 July 1952. The celebration has traditionally occurred each year on that date, in recognition of the day a group of officers led by General Muhammad Neguib and Colonel Gamal Abd al-Nasser overthrew King Faruq and the Egyptian Monarchy. The president of Egypt and the minister of defense usually address the country praising the "July Revolution".

Armed Forces Day: The observance of Armed Forces Day occurs on October 6 of each year. This day commemorates the crossing of the Suez Canal by Egyptian forces in 1973 in an effort to retake the Sinai Peninsula, which Israel occupied in the Six Day War of 1967. The surprise attack ordered by Egyptian president Anwar Sadat marked the advent of the October or Yom Kippur War, or as it is known in Egypt "the War of the Crossing." Celebrations, parades, military exercises, fireworks, and signs of Egyptian patriotism usually mark the day. Ironically, Celebration of the October War is carried to such an extreme, including a spectacular memorial that many younger Egyptians erroneously believe that it was at this point that the Sinai was seized from Israel leading to its evacuation.

Victory Day: This day, December 23, marks the ending of the hostilities between Egypt on the one hand, and the United Kingdom and France, on the other, during the Suez Crisis in 1956. It marks the arrival of the United Nation's Emergency Forces which evacuated the combatants and later remained in the

Sinai until the 1967 June War as a peacekeeping force. Celebrations usually take place in Port Said where the evacuation took place.

RELIGIOUS HOLIDAYS

Islamic New Year: The Islamic New Year commemorates the Prophet's immigration to Medina. Because this holiday falls on the first day in the Islamic Lunar Calendar (1 Dhul-Hijjah), its date changes each year, depending on the sighting of the New Moon.

'Ashura: It is hard to determine what percentage of Muslims celebrate this holiday usually associated with Shiites, since it commemorates the martyrdom of Husayn, the grandson of the Prophet Muhammad. On 10 Muḥarram people fast to commemorate this day, which also has linkages to the Old Testament. On the same day Moses fasted to thank God for liberating his people from the tyrannical rule of the pharaoh of Egypt. Others observe the day by visiting the mosque of Husayn, believed to contain its namesake's head and other important relics, and participating in remembrances (*dhikrs*), poetry recitations, parades, music, dancing, and even carnival games.

Mulid al-Nabi: This holiday is a celebration of the birthday of the Muslim Prophet Mohammad. Although Shia Muslims and Sunni Muslims celebrations fall five days apart, most Egyptians are Sunnis, and they celebrate *mulid al-Nabi* on the 12th day of Rabi' al-Awwal, the third month in the Islamic Calendar. Muhammad's birth is usually marked by acts of charity and kindness across the country. The celebration of this holiday in Egypt dates back to the Fatimid era, although extreme religious conservatives frown upon its celebration. Whereas the public aspects of *mulid Husayn* celebrations are focused around his mosque, the *mulid al-Nabi* celebrations are more widely observed but are diffused all over the country.

Mulid Ahmad al-Badawi: Like the *mulid al-Nabi*, this holiday celebrates the birth of an important figure, in this case a 13th-century Sufi mystic. Many mainstream Muslims frown upon the notion of what some might view as "saint worship," thus it is not considered a major holiday by most Egyptians. Nevertheless, the celebration of his birth in October draws thousands of visitors to Tanta annually for healings, circumcisions, music, poetry, and fireworks.

Coptic Easter: Some Muslims confuse *Sham al-Nassim* (in the following text) with Easter, but it is a different holiday with religious origins. Copts use their own calendar to calculate the arrival of Coptic Easter, which arrives after Latin Easter. Devout Copts follow a vegan diet in the 55 days preceding Easter. Special services begin the week before Holy Saturday and continue through Easter Sunday. Those familiar with Western Protestant or even Catholic services would find Coptic services a bit longer and more complicated, filled with psalms, hymns, incense, and celebration. The festivities continue and blend in with those of *Sham al-Nassim*, including picnics and colored eggs. The return to eating meat is celebrated with roast leg of lamb, turkey, meat pies, as well as the traditional foods of *Sham al-Nassim.*

Sham al-Nassim: This holiday, which literally celebrates the breath of life, is enjoyed by a diverse group of Egyptians regardless of religion at the beginning of spring. Its origins span all the way back to pharaonic times. *Sham al-Nassim* falls on the Monday after Coptic Easter. The holiday bears striking similarities with the pagan forbears of Easter and Passover, as well as its Iranian cousin *Nawruz* (see the following text) celebrated a month earlier. Traditional foods include eggs, greens, fish, and onions. Traditionally, families enjoy picnics along the Nile, but in modern times this has been modified to include outings to parks and the zoo.

Ramadan: Ramadan is the ninth month of the Islamic Calendar, commemorating revelation of the Quran to the Muslim Prophet Mohammad. Most Muslims observe Ramadan by fasting from dawn until sunset. Government offices and many workplaces reduce working hours during the month of Ramadan. The holiest day of Ramadan is *laylat al-qadr*, the day in which the Quran was first revealed to the Prophet Muhammad. It occurs on an odd-numbered night in the last 10 days of the month.

'Eid al-Fitr: Also known as the lesser Bairam Feast or *'Eid al-Ṣugghayir*, this Muslim holiday means Festival of the Breaking of the Fast. It is a three-day celebration at the conclusion of the holy month of Ramadan. It commences after the sighting of a new moon, marking the beginning of Shawaal (the next month). People celebrate with large meals, cookies, and other sweets. Egyptians generally buy new clothing, at least for their children. The new clothes consist of an entire outfit, including underwear and socks. Elders give children a gift of money known as an eidiyya. Historically, eidiyyas were also given to dependents in a household or on an estate.

'Eid al-Adha: Also known as the Greater Bairam Feast or the *'Eid al-Kabir*, the name of this Muslim holiday means Festival of the Sacrifice. The holiday is in remembrance God's forgiveness of Abraham (Ibrahim), for his vow to sacrifice his son Ishmael (Ismail) in a story from the Quran. Lasting for four days, this celebration occurs seventy days after 'Eid al-Fitr, on the tenth day of Dhul al-Ḥijjah, and includes an official three day holiday. People commemorate it by making the same ritual sacrifice, usually a lamb and donating some portion of its meat to charity. Given the restrictions of urban life, fewer people in the city sacrifice their own animal, but the emphasis on charity and eating this particular meat (usually grilled) remains.

Nawruz (Nayruz): Iranian *Nawruz* is celebrated at the vernal equinox (see also Sham al-Nassim and Mother's Day). There seem to be indications that some segments of the population celebrated Nawruz at the same time as their Iranian cousins and in a similar, but perhaps more restrained manner. While celebrations during this month among Muslims seem to have waxed and waned historically, the Copts appear to have picked up the celebration and moved it to the Coptic New Year (1 Tout), which usually falls on 11 September, except on a leap year when it falls on September 12. The celebration of Nawruz includes a feast, and is celebrated across Egypt as a time of rebirth and new beginnings. It is also possible that Arabs confused the holiday with a pre-existing Coptic holiday, the feast of the rivers, which bore striking similarities to the old Zoroastrian festival. The commonalities between all of these festivals demonstrate the importance of peasants' relationship to the land and the need for people to release tensions against overbearing ruling authorities.

Coptic Christmas: In December 2002 then President Mubarak marked January 7 each year as an official holiday for all Egyptians. Coptic Christians remember this day as the birthday of Jesus Christ. Many Muslims, due to the position of Jesus as a prophet of God in Islam, also observe the holiday. As well, there is the desire among many segments of the Muslim population to share holidays with all segments of the population in an effort toward national unity, where previously there had been "Muslim" or "Coptic" holidays. This was particularly poignant in 2011 a few weeks before the Revolution, where despite one Alexandria Church bombing, throughout much of the country Muslims helped to form human shields around Coptic Churches (see Chapter 7).

Coptic Christmas is not celebrated as it is in the West. There are no flashy decorations, lavish gift exchanges, or endless strings of parties. It comes after 40 days of restricted eating. Copts go to Church at midnight on Christmas Eve, called to service with bells in the glorious tradition of the Coptic Church. Afterward, people return to their relatives' homes to eat a traditional meal of *fata* (see Chapter 6). *Kahk*, traditional cookies, are served for dessert. During Egypt's old "liberal" era between 1922 and 1952, many department stores, owned by the Jewish bourgeoisie, decorated for the Christmas/New Year season and encouraged the exchange of gifts. These stores were nationalized in the era after the Suez Crisis. The practice of Christmas decoration stopped in most places other than large hotels, and only in the era after the reopening of the economy has the practice of New Year's Eve celebration returned among the elite.

Egypt-Related Organizations

GOVERNMENT ORGANIZATIONS

Embassy

Chancery

3521 International Ct. NW
Washington, DC 20008
Tel: 202-895-5400
Fax: 202-244-4319 or 202-244-5131
Email: Embassy@egyptembassy.net

Consular Section

Tel: 202-966-6342
Fax: 202-244-4319
Email: Consulate@egyptembassy.net

Agricultural Office

5322 International Court NW
Washington, DC 20008
Tel: 202-966-2080
Fax: 202-895-5493

Cultural and Educational Office

1303 New Hampshire Ave. NW
Washington, DC 20036
Tel: 202-296-3888
Fax: 202-296-3891

Defense Office

2590 L St.
Washington, DC 20037
Tel: 202-333-1283
Fax: 202-333-7240

Economic and Commercial Office—San Francisco

1255 Post Street Suite 910
San Francisco, CA 94109
Tel: 415-771-1995
Fax: 415-771-1293

Economic and Commercial Office—Washington, DC

2232 Massachusetts Ave. NW
Washington, DC 20008
Tel: 202-265-9111
Fax: 202-328-4517

Medical Office

2033 M St. Suite 402 NW
Washington, DC 20036-3301
Tel: 202-296-5286
Fax: 202-296-5288

Press and Information Office—San Francisco

1255 Post Street Suite 1034
San Francisco, CA 94109
Tel: 415-346-3427
Fax: 415-346-3420

Press and Information Office—Washington, DC

1666 Connecticut Ave. Suite 400 NW
Washington, DC 20009
Tel: 202-667-3402
Fax: 202-234-6827

Procurement Office

5500 16th St. NW
Washington, DC 20011
Tel: 202-726-8006
Fax: 202-829-4909 or 202-829-5530

Consulates General of Egypt

Chicago

500 N. Michigan Ave. Suite 1900
Chicago, IL 60611
Tel: 312-828-9162
Fax: 312-828-9167
Web: http://egypt.embassy-online.net/Egypt-Consulate-General-Chicago.php

Houston

1990 Post Oak Boulevard Suite 2180
Houston, TX 77056
Tel: 713-961-4915
Web: http://egypt.embassy-online.net/Egypt-Consulate-General-Houston.php

New York

1110 Second Avenue
New York, NY 10022
Tel: 212-759-7120 or 212-759-7121 or 212-759-7122
Web: http://egypt.embassy-online.net/Egypt-Consulate-General-Houston.php

San Francisco

3001 Pacific Avenue
San Francisco, CA 94115
Tel: 415-346-9700
Web: http://egypt.embassy-online.net/Egypt-Consulate-General-San-Francisco.php

United Nations

Egyptian Mission to the UN

304 East 44th St. New York, NY 10017
Tel: 212-503-0300
Fax: 212-949-5999

General Information

Egypt State Information Service

3 al-Estad al-Bahary St.
Nasr City, Cairo
Egypt
Tel: 2-02-2261-7304 or 2-02-2261-7308
Email: Feedback@sis.gov.eg
website: www.sis.gov.eg/En/

Egypt's State Information Service is the main agency for public relations, media awareness, and statistics. The Web site provides a large variety of information for the public on news, government, culture, and tourism. It has a live streaming TV and Radio broadcast, as well as a link to publications by the government on its achievements and developments in fields including politics, economy, society, sports, and women's issues.

BUSINESS ORGANIZATIONS

American Chamber of Commerce in Egypt

33 Soliman Abaza St.
Dokki, 12311, Giza
Egypt
Tel: 20-2-3338-1050
Fax: 20-2-3338-1060
website: www.amcham.org.eg

The American Chamber of Commerce in Egypt (AmCham Egypt), established in 1982, works to enhance economic and investment opportunities for U.S. companies operating in Egypt. With 1,700 members it is one of the most active affiliates of the U.S. Chamber of Commerce abroad. Its Web site provides business services, education and training, trade services, resources, publications, and a number of online services such as a recruitment center and a web advertising function.

Bank Misr (Egypt Bank)

Cairo Branch
151 Mohamed Farid St.

Cairo, Egypt
Tel: 20-2-3912711
Fax: 20-2-3919779
website: www.banquemisr.com/English/Home.aspx

Bank Misr has played an important role in Egypt's history since 1920. It provided capital to create Egypt's national industries including spinning and weaving, insurance, transportation, aviation, and cinema. After the reorganization of the economy in 1960, Bank Misr has continued to play an important role in supporting Egyptian finance and industry. Bank Misr operates worldwide and utilizes state-of-the-art technology for banking systems and services in Egypt. Its computing center is one of the largest in the Middle East, and it connects to a network of branches that extends throughout the most of the branches in the country. In addition, Bank Misr has a large number of Automatic Teller Machines throughout the country. The Web site includes services for retail banking, corporate banking, and Islamic banking, while also providing a variety of investment services.

National Bank of Egypt

24 Sherif St.
Cairo, Egypt
Tel: 2-02-2390-4011
Fax: 2-02-2393-5599
website: www.nbe.com.eg/en/main.aspx

The National Bank of Egypt (NBE) advertises itself as the oldest commercial bank in Egypt, dating back to 1898. Its functions have changed with the political climate in the country: for a period in the 1950s, it served as a central bank, after the nationalizations of the 1960s, it served as both a commercial bank and a central bank. Furthermore, since the since mid-1960s, it has been responsible for issuing and managing saving certificates on behalf of the government. There are more than 400 banking units nationwide, as well as an international presence through the National Bank of Egypt (UK) Limited, NBE—New York Branch and Shanghai Branch plus two representative offices in Johannesburg—South Africa and Dubai—UAE. The Web site has many features, allowing prospective clients to obtain information, pay bills, contact the bank, and open an account.

Egyptian National Science and Technology Information Network

101 Kasr al-Ainy St.
Cairo 11516
Tel: 2-02-795-7253
Fax: 2-02-794-7807
website: www.sti.sci.eg
Email: info@enstinet.eg.net

The Egyptian Academy of Scientific Research & Technology began in 1980 as a bilateral agreement with the U.S. government to establish a nationwide system of information services to ensure availability and utilization of global recorded knowledge for the socioeconomic development of Egypt. Multiphase efforts of design and implementation were undertaken and completed by 1986 with the Egyptian National Scientific and Technical Information Network (ENSTINET), the first national information service in the region. One outcome of ENSTINET was to plan for Egypt-wide access to the world's resources of recorded information by playing a significant role in the formulation of a national data communication network with access via the internet. Currently, ENSTINET operates as a public information services organization. Its mission is to assist Egyptian problem solvers and decision makers in accessing and applying quality data and relevant information for development. ENSTINET provides the Egyptian research community with 24/7 online and onsite access to global information. Locally, ENSTINET has been developing and maintaining databases that contain both the literature published in Egypt in the field of science and technology and directories to assist researchers.

Egyptian Association for International Medical Studies

Kasr al-Aini Medical Faculty
Cairo, Egypt
Email: info@eams.net
Web: www.eaims.net

The Egyptian Association for International Medical Studies (EAIMS) an official, medical, independent, nonprofit, nongovernmental and nonpolitical organization founded in June 2003 in cooperation with the Medical Education Development Center (MEDC), Kasr al-Aini Medical Faculty at Cairo University. Its mission is sharing international medical experience in the fields of Human Medicine, Dentistry, Pharmacy, Physiotherapy, and Nursing. It is licensed by the Egyptian Ministry of Social Affairs as an international medical organization according to the National Egyptian Law of Non-Profit & Non-Governmental Organizations. EAIMS has a highly selected board of trustees that consists of a large number of professors and doctors in the Faculty of Medicine, Kasr al-Aini Hospitals at Cairo University. Consistently, EAIMS is now considered as one of the most active specialized medical sciences organizations not only in Egypt, but also in Africa and the Middle East. EAIMS provides international candidates opportunities to join Egyptian programs such as medical electives, clinical clerkships, and research projects through an online registration process.

EDUCATIONAL ORGANIZATIONS

American Research Center in Egypt

2 Midan Simon Bolivar
Garden City, Cairo 11461

Egypt
Tel: 2-02-2794-8239
Email: cairo@arce.org
website: www.arce.org

Since 1948 the American Research Center in Egypt (ARCE) has been active in supporting scholarship, training, and conservation efforts in Egypt. ARCE maintains a solid working relationship with the Supreme Council of Antiquities within the Egyptian Ministry of Culture. The Web site has a variety of opportunities for scholarship and education in Egypt, including grants, events, summer language programs, publications, and information on its library.

American University in Cairo

P.O. Box 74
New Cairo, 11835
Egypt
Tel: 2-02-2615-1000
website: www.aucegypt.edu/Pages/default.aspx

After nearly 90 years in its "temporary" location in downtown Cairo, the American University in Cairo (AUC) moved to its new, state-of-the art $400 million campus in New Cairo in Fall 2008. Founded in 1919, its first president charted a course of scholarship, discipline, and research in an English language environment with an eye toward creating future leaders, not only for Egypt, but also for the region. Currently, the AUC has undergraduate and graduate studies in a large spectrum of areas including business, physical sciences, engineering, liberal arts, and social sciences; and it has a well-developed continuing education program. AUC also has a vibrant and extensive Study Abroad program that accepts students from all over North America and around the world.

Bibliotheca Alexandria (Library of Alexandria)

P.O. Box 138
al-Shatby, Alexandria 21526
Egypt
Tel: 2-03-4839999
Email: secretariat@bibalex.org
website: http://www.bibalex.org/Home/DefaultEN.aspx

The breathtaking architectural wonder sets high standards for itself: "The Library of Alexandria aims to be a center of excellence in the production and dissemination of knowledge and to be a place of dialogue, learning and understanding between cultures and peoples." The new library hopes to bring back the spirit of the original library, highlighting Egypt's contributions to the world, allowing Egypt to access the world's knowledge, serving as a premier center for digital information, and creating an environment of tolerance and understanding through learning. It consists of three museums, a planetarium, and four art galleries, in addition to its vast holdings in multiple languages.

Cairo University

Building 1
University City
Giza, Egypt
Tel: 20-2-567-6282
Web: www.cu.edu.eg/english/

Originally named the Egyptian University, then Fuad I University, this nationalist project started in 1908. After operating briefly in the downtown location where AUC would soon locate, the University nearly went bankrupt were it not for the largesse of a princess who sold off estates in the delta for funding, provided land and a palace for operations, and even hawked her jewelry when monies continued to run short. Her brother and temporary namesake of the school was one of its early rectors; and while he was king it grew into a major institution of higher learning, incorporating older schools of law and engineering into the existing faculty of arts. The curriculum has expanded significantly since that time to include engineering, communications, nursing, education, medicine, and veterinary medicine. The University views itself as committed to change. It is preparing students for the 21st century globalized marketplace with a developing curriculum, interactive learning, and new information technologies. Cairo University has 17 colleges and 6 institutes in Cairo, as well as branch campuses in Fayyum, Bani Suef, and Khartoum.

TOURISM ORGANIZATIONS

Egypt Air

720 Fifth Ave.
New York, NY 19919-4168
Tel: 212-581-5600
(212) 586-6599
Web: http://egyptair.com/

Egypt Air has domestic flights to eight different cities, including Cairo, Luxor, Alexandria, and Sharm al-Sheikh. As a member of the Star Alliance it has destinations in more than 100 different international cities in 59 different countries on four different continents.

Egyptian Hotels Association

8 al-Sadd al-Aaly St
Dokki, 11312, Giza
Egypt
Tel: 2-02-3337-9883 or 2-02-3748-8468
Fax: 2-02-3761-1333 or 2-02-3760-8956
Email: eha@link.net
Web: http://www.eha-redsea.org/en/index.php

The objectives of the Egyptian Hotels Association (EHA) are to participate positively in studying and issuing legislation related to the hotel industry, promote tourism marketing plans, as well as to assist the two or three star hotels in getting fair market share of these plans during international trade fairs, to establish a pricing policy with the aim of ensuring a fair market share to all hotel categories, to prepare detailed feasibility studies to determine investment opportunities in the hotel industry, and to define growth rates and expansion in hotel capacity, to play a more active role in reconciling members, to participate in evaluating training programs, and to play an active role in cooperation with the Egyptian Tourism Federation in the implementation of these programs, to establish and implement local media plans in order to generate a supportive public opinion toward the obstacles and requirements of the hotel industry, and finally to solve urgent hotel problems that require solutions. The EHA also puts on a variety of international tourism events each year. As of the writing, the general webpage link was broken, but the Red Sea branch was intact; the EHA also provides information through the State Information Service tourism portal (see preceding text).

Egyptian Tourism Federation

8 al-Sadd al-Aaly St.
Dokki, 11312, Giza
Egypt
Tel: 2-02-3748-3313
Fax: 2-02-3761-4286
Web: www.etf.org.eg

The Egyptian Tourism Federation promotes itself well: "The Egyptian Tourism Federation (ETF) seeks to establish the ultimate climate for sustainable growth of Egypt's tourism industry and enhance its workforce at the highest international standards." The ETF has established close relations with connected associations, for example, EHA, Egyptian Travel Agents Association, Egyptian Chamber of Tourist Establishments, the Egyptian Chamber of Tourist Commodities, Egyptian Chamber of Diving and Water Sports, and the Ministry of Tourism, in order to further its aims. The ETF is a liaison between governmental and nongovernmental entities associated with tourism, and it serves as an advocate for legislation. Indeed, the ETF by law, must solicit public opinion before going to parliament to discuss any measure. The Egyptian Tourism Federation's Web site has helpful links for travelers, employers, and possible employees, while also providing a news source in the travel industry via its free newsletter.

Egyptian Tourist Authority

630 5th Ave.
Suite # 1706
New York, NY 10111
Tel: 212-332-2570
Fax: 212-956-6439
website: www.egypt.travel/

The Egyptian Tourist Authority (ETA) provides information for visitors to Egypt. The ETA facilitates trip-planning by providing information on where to stay, what places to see, and information on culture. The future traveler can go to the Web site to learn how to write his or her name in hieroglyphs, pronounce a few Arabic phrases, download some brochures, watch a commercial, or take an online aerial tour of the country. There is also information for professionals in the Egyptian tourism industry and members of the press.

EGYPTIAN–AMERICAN ORGANIZATIONS

Egyptian American Professional Society, Inc.

1781 Dogwood Dr.
Yorktown Heights, NY 10598

Created in 1977 this organization fosters links between professionals in Egypt and the United States working on similar types of projects in the arts and sciences. In doing so, it helps Egyptian Americans retain contact with their cultural heritage; and the bridge serves as a synergistic link that promotes awareness of projects, resources, discoveries, and developments on both sides of the Atlantic.

Egyptian American Medical Society

30-60 Crescent St.
Suite A
Astoria, NY
Tel: 718-545-7570
website: http://www.theeams.com/

Founded in 1987 this organization focuses on domestic and international humanitarian assistance. Among its significant achievements has been its aid to Egypt during natural disasters, for example, floods and the 1992 Earthquake.

The Egyptian American Group

324 Central Ave.
Jersey City, NJ 07307
Tel: 201-656-0505

The Egyptian American Community Foundation

200 Park Ave.
Suite 4514
NY, NY 10166
Tel: 212-822-3255
Tel: 212-822-3277
Fax: 212-858-7750
Email: info@eacfoundation.org
website: http://www.eacfoundation.org/

This nonprofit charitable organization with a diverse board of directors solicits funds from the Egyptian American community in an effort to sustain various humanitarian and social initiatives. The focus has been on children, education, health, and families, both in Egypt and among new immigrant families in the United States. Building these networks helps Egyptian Americans maintain links with their heritage and insure that the Egyptians remember that heritage in the years to come with pride. The grants from the organization also work on this side of the Atlantic, providing scholarships for the study of the Middle East at American universities as well. The Web site contains useful information about its officers, its charitable causes, and information on donation.

Association of Egyptian American Scholars

website: http://aeascholars.org
Email: info@eascholars.org

After 60 years of Fulbright exchanges, Egyptian government missions or simply at their own initiative, numerous Egyptians scholars have come to North America to study or work, and many have settled here permanently. Dr. Mohamed "Bill" El-Wakil of Wisconsin and Dr. Ahmed Shouman of New Mexico brainstormed the idea of creating an Egyptian American scholars association in 1968, and by 1974 the group was formalized with support from both the Egyptian government and the Society of Friends of Egyptian Scholars Abroad. Through the years close to 600 scholars have joined the Association, and many are still active and supportive.

The Association of Egyptian American Scholars has American, Canadian, and Egyptian chapters in an attempt to encourage partnerships and promote scholarly dialogue across international boundaries.

American Egyptian Cooperation Foundation

235 East 40th St., Suite 22A
New York, NY 10016
Tel: 212-867-2323
Fax: 212-697-0465
Web: www.americanegyptiancoop.org
Email: aecf32@verizon.net

According to its mission statement: "The American Egyptian Cooperation Foundation (AECF) is an independent, non-profit American organization dedicated to improve and broaden cooperation, understanding, dialogue, and bonds of friendship between the American people and the people of Egypt." The efforts of AECF work at both the individual and institutional levels, bringing together human and institutional resources from both countries. Since 1987 the AECF's mission supports the unique relationship that binds the United States and Egypt, and provides the means to sustain and supplement government efforts in all fields of cooperation. The scope of AECF programs and activities includes cultural, educational, scientific, public relations, and economic affairs aimed at generating greater mutual understanding. The AECF has branches in New York, Washington, DC, San Francisco, Chicago, Houston, and Cairo. In addition to its numerous programs, it produces a quarterly newsletter designed to educate its members on the latest developments and government policies in Egypt.

The Council on Egyptian-American Relations

1002 23rd St. NW
Washington, DC 20037
Tel: 202-413-8384
Fax: 301-933-2211

This nonprofit organization began in 1999 as a means for forging stronger ties between Egypt and the United States through strategic, economic, and cultural interests of mutual benefit.

Egyptian American Cultural Association

P.O. Box 9551
Washington, DC 20016
Web: www.eacaonline.org
Email: info@eacaonline.org

Founded in the early 1970s and located in the U.S. capital, the Egyptian American Cultural Association (EACA) is a nonprofit, nonpolitical and nonreligious association that seeks to both celebrate Egyptian cultural heritage by allowing a forum for interaction, but also to promote outreach in the community and build tolerance through understanding. A major component of the EACA is engaging youth and providing a venue for acceptance, pride, celebration, and education. Over 30 years of its establishment, EACA's main entity and mission remain the same as it was in the early 1970s. The EACA's Web site has links to different news and arts resources, streaming radio and television, and other information celebrating the cultural achievements of Egypt.

Egyptian-American Society (of Chicago)

Tel: 312-362-8332
Fax: 312-362-5923
Email: info@egyptianamericansociaty.com
website: http://egyptianamericansociety.com/

The Egyptian American Organization

P.O. Box 5194
Palos.Verdes, CA 90274
Tel: 310-356-3500
website: www.eaous.com
Email: info@eaoUS.com

Founded in 1984 the Egyptian American Organization (EAO) describes its mission as follows: "to provide a forum for Egyptian Americans to serve their interests and preserve their rich cultural traditions so they and their children would take pride in their unique heritage, their knowledge of the Arabic language, and their bicultural experience." A major focus of the organization is forging relations between the Egyptian American community and the larger population within which it resides. Furthermore, the group monitors developments within Egypt and encourages progress. This organization is a nonprofit tax-exempt California corporation, and therefore it is heavily dependent upon the unremunerated work of its members. The Web site is packed with information on activities, charitable efforts, scholarships, membership information, and back issues of the newsletter.

The Egyptian American Society

10075 Tuzza Ct.
Elk Grove, CA 95757
Tel: 408-391-4025

Fax: 408-273-6679
Email: eascafe@gmail.com
Web: www.egyptianamericansociety.org

The Egyptian American Society (EAS) is a San Francisco Greater Bay area organization dedicated "to build strong intercultural understanding among the immigrant Egyptian community . . . and the larger local mainstream American community." Although its mission statement emphasizes its cultural rather than religious or political orientation, the webpage since the Revolution has displayed a more political edge. It has been serving the San Francisco Bay area as state tax-exempt since the early 1970s, providing a variety of community-based services and outreach programs. The large number of volunteers that create and run the organization's man programs are its most important asset. The mission of the group is to serve the community and to enhance multicultural understanding.

HUMAN RIGHTS ORGANIZATIONS

Center for Egyptian Women's Legal Assistance

El Hegaz Tower, Eng. Abdul-Hady Rady St.
Ard-el-Lewa, Bulaq, al-Dakrur,
Giza, Egypt
Tel: 20-2-7316585
Fax: 20-2- 3266088
Email: info@cewla.org
Web: http://www.cewla.org/index.php

The Center for Egyptian Women Legal Assistance (CEWLA Foundation) works to empower women by making them aware of their legal rights, providing assistance to these women, and working to change laws that discriminate against women. Founded in 1995, this NGO is one of the most active organizations in the field of women's human rights. CEWLA operates in a poor, densely populated urban area (Bulaq al-Dakrur) in Giza. Another set of goals involves training women through legal, social, and literacy classes in order to enable them to become better workers and citizens. CEWLA also works towards drawing the attention of government officials into the realm of oppressive and discriminatory laws so that Egypt remains in step with the full implementation of international conventions in the realm of women's human rights. Another major area of work for the center is combating the cultural and social heritage that discriminates against women and working to modify views that embrace stereotypical roles of women as inferior to men. CEWLA believes that women must be empowered politically and economically to combat violence against other women. Finally, CEWLA trains NGO cadres on human rights and legal awareness to spread such awareness among other organizations.

UNICEF—Egypt

87 Misr Helwan Agricultural Road
Maadi
Cairo, Egypt
Tel: 20-2-2526-5083 (ext. 87)
Fax: 20-2-2526-4218
Email: cairo@unicef.org
website: http://www.unicef.org/egypt/index.html

According to its Web site, "[T]he United Nations Children's Fund (UNICEF) is a global program working for children's survival, development, and protection." UNICEF, in partnership with the under its Program of Cooperation with the Government of Egypt (2007–2011), places children and women's rights at the forefront of a broad range of development issues. As in its aims worldwide, UNICEF places a high value on protecting children from violence, abuse, and exploitation. Second, UNICEF addresses a range of educational and occupational issues aimed at enhancing the knowledge and life skills of Egyptian adolescents while also addressing gender inequalities and enhancing young people's participation. With respect to children, it focuses on improving the quality of education, increasing retention, and improving achievement rates. Third, UNICEF appeals to policymakers with the goal of improving the political, economic, and social environment for children. Fourth, with respect to health, UNICEF seeks to use the platform of the Unite for Children, Unite Against AIDS campaign, to prevent the spread of HIV and AIDS among young people and fight the stigma against people living with HIV. Generally speaking with respect to health, UNICEF aims to ensure that children under five years receive the highest standards of health via improved nutrition, quality immunization services, and are encouraged through the promotion of healthier lifestyles.

The Egyptian Organization for Human Rights

8/10 Mathaf al-Manial St., 10th Floor
Manyal al-Roda
Cairo, Egypt
Tel: 2-02-3636811 or 2-02-3620467
Fax: 2-02-3621613
Web: www.en.eohr.org

Although it is less than 30 years old, The Egyptian Organization for Human Rights (EOHR) is one of the oldest and premier NGOs and its headquarters are in Cairo. EOHR has a national membership of 2,300 and has 17 provincial branches located throughout Egypt. EOHR is a nonprofit, NGO working within the framework of the principles established in Universal Declaration of Human Rights and all other international human rights instruments regardless of the identity or the affiliation of the victim(s) or of the violator(s). It acts against both governmental and nongovernmental human rights violations. This organization is part of the International and Arab human rights movement, cooperating with the UN and its affiliates concerned with human rights. EOHR is a constant and reliable source on different human rights issues and news in Egypt. It produces a lengthy annual report documenting and covering various human rights abuses. Recently, it appears that the NGO sold most of the space on its webpage to an online pharmacy, which may cause confusion to someone who has not previously visited the site.

ENGLISH LANGUAGE EGYPTIAN MEDIA

Al-Ahram Newspaper

Galaa St.
Cairo, Egypt
Tel: 2-02-7704781
Fax: 2-02-7704781
Email: weeklymail1@ahram.org.eg
Web: http://weekly.ahram.org.eg/

Al-Akhbar Newspaper

P.O Box 1034
Glendora, California 91740
Tel: 626-852-2722
Fax: 626-914-1544
Web: www.alakhbar-usa.com

Egypt Today Magazine

3A Road 199
IBA Media Building
Degla, Maadi,
Cairo, Egypt
Tel: 20-2-2755-5000
Fax: 20-2-2755-5050 or 20-2-2755-5155
Web: www.egypttoday.com

Annotated Bibliography

This bibliography is not meant to be a complete or exhaustive discussion of sources, but simply a start to give readers an idea about what is written and who is writing in English on Egypt-related topics. Aside from statistical information, which is best gathered from electronic resources, the bibliography is weighted toward books rather than articles, with a few exceptions. Using the cited authors' names should generate further sources.

GEOGRAPHY

The best sources for statistical information are CIA, *The World Factbook*, which is updated regularly (https://www.cia.gov/library/publications/the-world-factbook/geos/eg.html), or the World Bank's Development indicators (http://data.worldbank.org/country/egypt-arab-republic). The State Information Services portal to land and people, http://www.sis.gov.eg/En/Cover01.aspx?CategoryID=10, has further links to maps, administrative districts, climate and weather, and other useful information. Four general reference works that place Egypt in its regional context are Ewan Anderson's, *The Middle East: Geography and Geopolitics* (New York: Routledge, 2000), Alasdair Drysdale and Gerald Blake's *The Middle East and North Africa, A Political Geography* (New York: Oxford University Press, 1985), Colbert Held's *Middle East Patterns: Places, People, and Politics* (Boulder, CO: Westview Press, 2005), and Dona Stewart's *The Middle East Today: Political, Geographical, and Cultural Perspectives* (New York: Routledge, 2008). Mark Tessler's *A History of the Israel-Palestinian Conflict* provides a thorough analysis of geopolitical issues between Israel and Egypt (Bloomington: Indiana University Press, 1994). For a reference guide to maps of Egypt's past, see Bill Manley's *The Penguin Historical Atlas of Ancient Egypt* (New York: Penguin, 1997).

HISTORY

Broad Overviews

One of the oldest, standard histories of Egypt is by the late Professor Emeritus at the London School of Oriental and African Studies, P.J. Vatikiotis. His *The History of Modern Egypt from Muhammad Ali to Mubarak* is strongest on the Nasser period about which Professor Vatikiotis did most of his publication and at 560 pages it provides the most detail on the modern period (Baltimore: Johns Hopkins University Press, 1991 [4th edition]). James Jankowski's *A Short History: Egypt* (Boston: OneWorld, 2000) takes the reader all the way back to Pharaonic times; however, its strongest point is the early 20th century up to the Revolution, the period in which Jankowski has done the most primary source research. Arthur Goldschmidt Jr., Afaf Marsot, and Robert Tignor all have relatively short monographs, informed by their own lengthy careers, as well as years mentoring other scholars. Now in its second edition Goldschmidt's *Modern Egypt: The Formation of a Nation State* gives a brief synopsis of ancient history, before focusing on the period in the title (Boulder, CO: Westview, 2004). Goldschmidt also edited a *Biographical Dictionary of Modern Egypt* that is a useful reference tool (Boulder, CO: L. Rienner, 2000). Marsot revised her *Short History* and renamed it *A History of Egypt from the Arab Conquest to the Present Time* (Cambridge, MA: Cambridge University Press, 2007). The strongest aspect of Tignor's *Egypt: A Short History* (Princeton, NJ: Princeton University Press, 2010) is his ability to explain complex concepts in layman's terms; however, peasants and women receive little attention. Jason Thompson's *A History of Egypt from Earliest Times to the Present* (Garden City: Anchor, 2009), is especially strong on the Pharaonic and Greco-Roman periods that are often missing in the other histories. Political scientist Glenn Perry contributes with *The History of Egypt* (Westport, CT: Greenwood, 2004), which is not as strong as any of the aforementioned volumes except in the arena of recent history.

Ancient to Graeco-Roman

Douglas Brewer and Emily Teeter's *Egypt and the Egyptians* is a readable source for beginners on Ancient Egypt (Cambridge, MA: Cambridge University Press, 2007), and is now in its second edition. Alessia Fassone and Enrico Ferraris's contribution to the *Dictionaries of Civilizations Series—Egypt: Pharaonic Period* (Berkeley, CA: University of California Press, 2007), is beautifully illustrated and deals topics by subject, also easy for novices. Egypt's former Director of Antiquities, Zahi Hawass, who received his Ph.D. from the University of Pennsylvania, has published a number of books written to reach wide audiences on popular topics. Some of his titles include *Pyramids: Treasures, Mysteries, and New Discoveries in Egypt* (Boston: White Star, 2007); *Tutankhamun: The Golden King and the Great Pharaohs* (Washington, DC: National Geographic Society, 2008); *Mountains of the Pharaohs: the Untold Story of the Pyramid Builders* (New York: Doubleday, 2006).

On the more scholarly level, Bruce Trigger's *Ancient Egypt: A Social History,* first published in 1983, remains a standard in the field (Cambridge, MA: Cambridge University Press, 2001). The scholarly debates first stirred by Martin Bernal's *Black Athena* in the 1970s are carried to new levels in Troy Allen's *The Ancient Egyptian Family: Kinship and Social Structure* (New York: Routledge, 2008); however, it falls short of meeting some expected historical standards in the field. Dog lovers and academics alike will enjoy Douglas Brewer, Terence Clark, and Adrian Philips, *Dogs in Antiquity: From Anubis to Cerberus, the Origins of the Domestic Dog.* Egyptology Series (Warminster: Aris & Phillips, 2001). Lisa Minniche's work, *Sacred Luxuries: Fragrance, Aromatherapy, and Cosmetics in Ancient Egypt* (Ithaca, NY: Cornell University Press, 1999) is a lavishly illustrated text that details Egypt's trade and use of these luxury products. It is not quite as scholarly as her previous work, *An Ancient Egyptian Herbal*, first published in 1986 and reissued in 2006 (Austin, TX: University of Texas Press). Ian Shaw's *Oxford History of Ancient Egypt* is a comprehensive general history (Oxford: Oxford University Press, 2000).

A standard study for the post-Pharaonic period is Bell's *Egypt from Alexander the Great to the Arab Conquest: a Study in the Diffusion and Decay of Hellenism* (Westport, CT: Greenwood, 1977). Although comprehensive, Bell's study is a bit outdated, since it was first published in 1946. Amelie Kuhrt's study of *The Persian Empire* covers its dominion over Egypt, see Volume One (New York: Routledge, 2007). Walter Ellis's study of *Ptolemy of Egypt* gives important information on the man who assisted Alexander and created the ruling institutions for the dynasty that would bear his name (New York: Routledge, 1994). Another interesting chapter in this period of history is *The Reign of Cleopatra*, written by Stanley Mayer Burnstein (Westport, CT: Greenwood, 2004). For an urban history of Egypt, see Richard Alston's *The City in Roman and Byzantine Egypt* (New York: Routledge, 2002).

Arab Conquest to Ottoman Conquest

One of the few monographs that cover the Islamic expansion in Egypt is Alfred Butler's *The Arab Conquest of Egypt* (London: Darf Publishers, 1988). Based on the large cache of documents held by the Jewish community at Fustat, the multivolume series by S. D. Goitein, *A Mediterranean Society*, tells much more than simply the life of Jews or religion, but gives a complete picture of commercial and economic life of medieval Cairo, Six Volumes (Berkeley, CA: University of California Press, 1999). Adam A. Sabra's *Poverty and Charity in Medieval Islam: Mamluk Egypt* uses *waqf* documents to trace urban charitable institutions (Cambridge, MA: Cambridge University Press, 2001). A great way for understanding another culture and for bridging Egypt's various eras is by studying its celebrations, see Boaz Shoshan's *Popular Culture in Medieval Cairo* (Cambridge, MA: Cambridge University Press, 1993). The institution of the family and its dissolution studied across time is a fascinating topic, and Yossef Rappoport has done this in *Marriage, Money, and Divorce in Medieval Islamic Society* (Cambridge, MA: Cambridge University Press, 2005), which deals specifically with mamluk Egypt and Syria.

Ottoman to 19th Century

The inspiration for the thematic portion of my history came from reading the dissertation of Alan Mikhail, "The Nature of Ottoman Egypt: Irrigation, Environment, and Bureaucracy, in the Long Eighteenth Century," (Ph.D.: University of California Berkeley, 2008), now revised and updated as *Nature and Environment in Ottoman Egypt: An Environmental Study* (Cambridge: Cambridge University Press, 2011). Nelly Hanna is perhaps one of the greatest historians of this period, with works published in English, French, and Arabic. Among my favorites are *In Praise of Books: A Cultural History of Cairo's Middle Class* (Syracuse, NY: Syracuse University Press, 2003) and *Making Money Big in 1600: the Life and Times of Ismail Abu Taqiyya* (Syracuse, NY: Syracuse University Press, 1998). Along with the late Raouf Abbas (Hamid) she edited an anthology dedicated to another eminent historian of Egypt, André Raymond, *Society and Economy in Egypt and the Eastern Mediterranean, 1600–1900* (Cairo: AUC Press, 2005). Jane Hathaway is another established authority on this period, and her *The Politics of Households in Ottoman Egypt* is particularly useful for understanding power dynamics (Cambridge, MA: Cambridge University Press, 2002). Afaf Marsot's *Women and Men in Late Eighteenth Century Egypt* explains the political instability of the period and examines how it allowed women to gain from it financially. It also sets the context for the conditions in Egypt at the time of the French invasion. The work done by Napoleon's team in *Description de L'Égypte* is the most comprehensive view of Egypt at the time of the invasion; however, it is filtered through the lens of the invaders. This multivolume work is now available digitally, http://descegy.bibalex.org/. There is now a whole series of books written about the invasion, including a translation of Egyptian chronicler al-Jabarti done by Shmuel Moreh (Princeton, NJ: M. Wiener, 1993); Juan Cole's *Napoleon's Egypt: Invading the Middle East* (New York: Palgrave, 2007); Paul Strathern's *Napoleon in Egypt* (New York: Bantam, 2007); and although a fictional account, Samia Serageldin's *The Naqib's Daughter* was written using primary source material (Fourth Estate, 2008).

Nineteenth and Twentieth Centuries

The reign of Muhammad Ali has been the subject of a number of excellent monographs including those written by Khaled Fahmy, Afaf Marsot, Helen Rivlin, and Letitia Ufford: *All the Pasha's Men: Mehmed Ali, His Army, and the Making of Modern Egypt* (Cambridge: Cambridge University Press, 1997); *Egypt in the Reign of Muhammad Ali* (Cambridge: Cambridge University Press, 1985); *The Agricultural Policy of Muhammad Ali in Egypt* (Cambridge: Harvard University Press, 1961); *The Pasha: How Mehmet Ali Defied the West, 1839–1841* (Jefferson: Mcfarland,

2007), respectively. Ehud Toledano's *State and Society in Mid-Nineteenth Century Egypt* is a revisionist account of the much maligned ruler Abbas, as well as a more general social history of the period, now available in paperback (Cambridge: Cambridge University Press, 2003). F. Robert Hunter's *Egypt Under the Khedives: From Household Government to Modern Bureaucracy* is one of the best books for learning about the workings of government in the nineteenth century (Pittsburgh, PA: University of Pittsburgh, 1984). Lisa Pollard's *Nurturing the Nation: the Family Politics of Modernizing, Colonizing, and Liberating Egypt, 1805–1923* begins its narrative in the time of Muhammad Ali and takes the reader up to Egypt's independence, covering a wide range of topics beyond those suggested in the title including education and the press. Mine Ener's *Managing Egypt's Poor and the Politics of Benevolence, 1800–1952* (Princeton, NJ: Princeton University Press, 2003) is another study that begins in the age of Muhammad Ali and tracks government (mis) management of its neediest citizens up to the time of the 1952 Revolution. Andrew McGregor traces *A Military History of Modern Egypt: From the Ottoman Conquest to the Ramadan War* (Westport, CT: Praeger, 2006).

Juan Cole's study of the Urabi Revolution, Ami Ayalon's study of the press, and Irene Gendzier's biography of Yacub Sanua help situate the social and intellectual climate of the late nineteenth century: *Colonialism and Revolution in the Middle East: Social and Cultural Origins of Egypt's Urabi Movement* (Cairo: AUC Press, 1999); *The Press in the Middle East* (Oxford: Oxford University Press, 1994); *The Practical Visions of Yacub Sanu'* (Boston, MA: Harvard University Press, 1966), respectively. With respect to the British occupation, Afaf Marsot's *Egypt and Cromer* remains a classic (London: Murray, 1968). Eve Troutt Powell's *A Different Shade of Colonialism: Egypt, Great Britain, and the Sudan* gives another piece of the puzzle as it depicts Egypt's role as both occupied and occupier. Recent dissertations by Mario Ruiz, Shane Minkin, and Will Henley shed light on the interplay between the state, the individual, the multiplicity of ethnic communities in Egypt generally and Alexandria in particular in the late 19th century (University of Michigan, 2004; NYU, 2009; Princeton, 2007; respectively). The research of Jennifer Derr is particularly exciting because it takes the focus away from the delta and turns to the much neglected, *sa'id*, see her 2009 dissertation from Stanford. It covers the multi-directional pull between the government under British occupation, multinational capitalists, and upper Egyptian peasants between 1868 and 1931. Similarly, Zeinab Abul Magd's research on Qina demonstrates how assumptions regarding empire do not work, see "Rebellion in the Time of Cholera: Failed Empire, Unfinished Nation in Egypt," *Journal of World History* 21 (4) (2010): 691–719.

Amira Sonbol's edited edition of Abbas Hilmi II's memoirs, gives the reader a firsthand account of the Egyptian monarchy (Reading, NY: Ithaca, 2003). Another recent royal account is Prince Hassan Hassan's *In the House of Muhammad Ali: A Family Album, 1805–1952* (Cairo: AUC Press, 2000), which is a delightful collection of photographs, memories, art, and architecture.

Studies of Egyptian nationalism and its development during the so-called liberal era have multiplied in recent years. James Jankowski and Israel Gershoni's numerous collaborations in this area have set a standard for the field, their most recent works include *Redefining the Egyptian Nation, 1930–1945* (Cambridge: Cambridge University Press, 2002) and *Confronting Fascism in Egypt: Dictatorship versus Democracy in the 1930s* (Stanford: Stanford University Press, 2010). Others have argued that national identity was a process that took longer to develop, along with institutions of nineteenth century, see e.g. my *Creating the New Egyptian Woman: Consumerism, Education, and National Identity, 1863–1922* (New York: Palgrave, 2004). Similarly, Michael Gasper argues that this identity emerged from representations drawn from the peasantry by a new intelligentsia between the mid-1870s to the mid-1910s, see his *The Power of Representation: Publics, Peasants, and Islam in Egypt* (Stanford: Stanford University Press, 2008).

Afaf Marsot's *Egypt's Liberal Experiment, 1922–1936* (Berkeley, CA: University of California Press, 1977) remains enlightening. Michael Doran's *Pan-Arabism before Nasser: Egyptian Power Politics and the Palestine Question* examines foreign policy from the same period (New York: Oxford University Press, 1999). Beth Baron's *Egypt as a Woman: Nationalism, Gender, and Politics* does much more than the title suggests (Berkeley, CA: University of California Press, 2005). She examines how slavery ended in Egypt and describes the activities of politically active women of different stripes between 1919 and 1940. Magda Baraka's *The Egyptian Upper Class between Revolutions* highlights bourgeois life between the 1919 and 1952 revolutions (Reading, NY: Ithaca, 1998). Amy Johnson's monograph on the liberal era reformer Ahmed Hussein demonstrates that there was some progress on rural reform even before the Revolution, see her *Reconstructing Rural Egypt: Ahmed Hussein and the History of Egyptian Development* (Syracuse, NY: Syracuse University Press, 2003). The volume that Johnson edited with Barak Salmoni and Arthur Goldschmidt Jr. on the inter-revolutionary era, *Re-Envisioning Egypt*, contains some of the cutting edge research in the field (Cairo: AUC Press, 2005).

Joel Gordon's *Nasser's Blessed Movement: The Free Officers and the July Revolution* focuses on the period just before and after the Revolution (Oxford: Oxford University Press, 1991), while Kirk Beattie's *Egypt during the Nasser Years: Ideology, Politics, and Civil Society* (Boulder, CO: Westview, 1994) covers the period up until Nasser's death. Beattie follows up on the struggle for hegemony in Egyptian politics with his *Egypt During the Sadat Years* (New York: Palgrave, 2000). John Waterbury's *The Egypt of Nasser and Sadat: The Political Economy of Two Regimes* remains a standard (Princeton, NJ: Princeton University Press, 1983). The literature dealing with the Suez Crisis constitutes its own genre; however, for understanding the roots of American aid to Egypt, read Jon Alterman's *Egypt and American Foreign Assistance 1952–1956: Hopes Dashed* (New York: Palgrave, 2002). For anything beyond Sadat, refer to Government and Politics section.

GOVERNMENT AND POLITICS

In addition to the previously cited CIA *The World Factbook* (geography), the Egyptian government's agency for collecting data, CAPMAS, has useful information about the nature of the country, http://www.capmas.gov.eg/. As well, the State Information Service portal to Politics provides links for topics including parties, reform, the constitution, and the various branches of government http://www.sis.gov.eg/En/Editpolitics.aspx?CategoryID=28.

Derek Hopwood's *Egypt: Politics & Society: 1945–1990,* revised, is now in its third edition (New York: Harper Collins, 1991); while it is a classic in the field, it is still not up to date. Enid Hill's *Mahkama: Studies in the Egyptian Legal System: Courts, Crimes, Law, and Society* (Reading, NY: Ithaca Press, 1979) lays out the structure of the modern system of justice. Nathan Brown's *The Rule of Law in the Arab World: Courts in Egypt and the Gulf* examines the development of the judiciary over time (Cambridge: Cambridge University Press, 1997). Ibrahim Oweiss, ed. *The Political Economy of Contemporary Egypt* is an anthology with contributors including Denis Sullivan, Afaf Marsot, Robert Bianchi, Raymond Hinnebusch, and Charles Issawi, and although written in 1990 contains extremely useful information for understanding contemporary society.

Maye Kassem's *Egyptian Politics the Dynamics of the Authoritarian Rule* sees continuity since the time of the 1952 revolution between the powerful executive branch and other elements of society, e.g. parties, reform movements, and other branches of government (Boulder, CO: L. Rienner, 2004). Hesham al-Awadi's *In Pursuit of Legitimacy: the Muslim Brothers and Mubarak, 1982–2000* (New York: Tauris, 2004) follows the rebirth of the Brotherhood above ground over the course of Mubarak's presidency and in doing so, its eventual challenge to the regime. In *Egypt After Mubarak: Liberalism, Islam, and Democracy in the Arab World* Bruce Rutherford looks at competing centers of power, for example, the Muslim Brotherhood, the judiciary, and the private sector (Princeton, NJ: Princeton University Press, 2008). To write *Shop Floor Culture and Politics in Egypt* political scientist Samir Shehata lived as a worker for a year to understand the factory as a microcosm of Egyptian society and identity (Albany, NY: SUNY, 2009).

ECONOMICS

The State Information Service's portal to the Economy, http://www.sis.gov.eg/En/FourStTemplate.aspx?CategoryID=337, has further links for information relating to economic indicators, banking and finance, foreign trade, investment, agriculture, and more. For background on Egypt's economic challenges, see Charles Issawi's chapter on Egypt in his *An Economic History of the Middle East and North Africa* (New York: Routledge, 2006). Noha el-Mikawy and Heba Handoussa's *Institutional Reform and Economic Development in Egypt* (Cairo: AUC Press, 2004) examines the relationship between politics and economics, focusing on changes in the 1990s. A recent study by the World Bank analyzes its policy studying various programs in *Egypt: Positive Results from Knowledge Sharing and Modest Lending an IEG Assistance Evaluation, 1997–2007* (Washington, DC: World Bank Press, 2009). Although relatively little space is dedicated to Egypt specifically, Waleed Hazbun's *Beaches, Ruins, Resorts: Politics of Tourism in the Arab World* raises interesting questions regarding one of Egypt's major sources of income (Minneapolis, MN: University of Minnesota Press, 2008).

SOCIETY

Religion and Thought

Most Westerners find Abdullah Yusuf Ali's translation of *The Holy Qur'an* to be the easiest to read and Arabic-readers will agree that it remains a faithful rendition of the meaning (London: Wordsworth, 2000). For many years, Richard Mitchell's *Society of Muslim Brothers* (Oxford: Oxford University Press, 1993 [1969]) was the classic on the subject until Norwegian scholar Brynjar Lia's *The Rise of the Muslim Brothers: the Rise of an Islamic Mass Movement, 1928–1942* was published in 2006 (Reading, NY: Ithaca). Sayyid Qutb was the ideologue for the Muslim Brotherhood and William Shepard has translated and edited his some of his writings under the title of *Sayyid Qutb and Islamic Activism: A Translation and Critical Analysis of Social Justice in Islam* (Leiden: Brill, 1996). Raymond Baker's *Islam without Fear: Egypt and the New Islamists* (Boston, MA: Harvard University Press, 2003) situates contemporary politics within the realm of the resurgent Islam. Carrie Rosefsky Wickham's *Mobilizing Islam: Religion, Activism, and Political Change in Egypt* is a highly readable explanation of the rise in Islamic activism in Egypt (New York: Columbia University Press, 2002).

A general history of the Copts, including beliefs and struggles during various historical periods, is Christian Cannuyer's *Coptic Egypt: The Christians of the Nile* (New York: Harry Abrams, 2001). Similarly, Jill Kamil's *Christianity in the Land of the Pharaohs: The Coptic Orthodox Church* (Cairo: AUC Press, 2002) is a comprehensive history of the church. Sana Hassan's *Christians versus Muslims in Modern Egypt: The Century Long Struggle for Coptic Equality* (New York: Oxford University Press, 2003) takes a more polemical view of the relationship between the communities. While not focused on belief, Joel Beinin's *The Dispersion of Egyptian Jewry: Culture, Politics, and the Formation of a Modern Diaspora* details the history and dissolution of Egypt's Jewish community, explaining its different communities (Berkeley, CA: University of California Press, 1998). The previously cited study by S. D. Goitein, *A Mediterranean Society*, is the most complete picture of Jewish life in medieval Cairo (see History-Arab Conquest to Ottoman Conquest). Gudrun Kramer's *The Jews of Modern Egypt, 1914–1952* is another informative source on the recent history of Jews in Egypt (Seattle, WA: University of Washington Press, 1989).

Social Classes and Ethnicity

Barry Kemp's *Ancient Egypt: Anatomy of a Civilization* uses archeological evidence (material culture) to understand what gave Egyptian society its distinctive characteristics, including social stratification (New York: Routledge, 2005 [2nd edition]). In terms of statistics, see the citation given for the CIA *The World Factbook* or the State Information Service's portal to land and people (geography). Amira Sonbol's *The New Mamluks: Egyptian Society and Modern Feudalism* is an attempt to see continuity in Egypt's history by drawing a distinction between the elite and the masses, with change occurring as a shift in the elite (Syracuse, NY: Syracuse

University Press, 2000). Nasser tried to explain what Egyptian ethnicity meant in his *Philosophy of the Revolution* (Washington, DC: Public Affairs Press, 1955), which many believe to be ghost-written by his friend Muhammad Hasanayn Heikal.

Women

The *Oxford History of Ancient Egypt* (cited in history) provides a complete picture of women and covers their contributions through the Roman period, often through the use of primary sources. See Jane Rowlandson's *Women and Society in Greek and Roman Egypt: A Sourcebook* for a more detailed view of this period (Cambridge: Cambridge University Press, 1998).

As we move into the medieval period, a number of the essays in Nikki Keddie and Beth Baron, eds. *Women in Middle East History: Shifting Boundaries in Sex and Gender* (New Haven, CT: Yale University Press, 1993) deal with Egypt or have authors that have made significant contributions to the field including Huda Lutfi, Carl Petry, Jonathan Berkey, and Paula Sanders. Leila Ahmed's *Women and Gender in Islam* is a more general text, but draws many examples from Egypt, taking the reader from pre-Islamic times up to the modern period (New Haven, CT: Yale University Press, 1993). Mary Ann Fay has written extensively on mamluk women, see her contribution in her edited volume on *Autobiography and the Construction of Gender and Identity in the Middle East* (New York: Palgrave, 2001) or her chapter in Madeline Zilfi, ed. *Women in the Ottoman Empire: Women in the Early Modern Era* (Leiden: Brill, 1997).

Margot Badran's interest in feminist Huda Shaarawi and the feminist movement in Egypt, led to her editing, translating, and publishing Shaarawi's memoirs *Harem Years: The Memoirs of an Egyptian Feminist, 1879–1924* (New York: The Feminist Press, 1987), as well as writing a monograph on the relationship between the feminist movement and nationalism, *Feminists, Islam, and Nation: Gender and the Making of Modern Egypt* (Princeton, NJ: Princeton University Press, 1995). She has also co-edited (with Miriam Cooke) a volume of work by Arab feminist authors in translation, making them available to English reading audiences for the first time. Her *Opening the Gates: A Century of Arab Feminist Writing* is now in its second edition (Bloomington, IN: Indiana University Press, 2004 [1990]). Judith Tucker's *Women in Nineteenth- Century Egypt* paved the way for scholars to begin applying methods used generally in social history to the history of women and gender (Cambridge: Cambridge University Press, 1985). Marilyn Booth has translated a significant number of works, published scholarly articles, and wrote *May her Likes be Multiplied: Biography and Gender Politics in Egypt* (Berkeley, CA: University of California Press, 2001). Badran, Tucker, and Booth charted new ground in writing about and generating interest in Egyptian women.

Beth Baron's work on the women's press, *Women's Awakening in Egypt: Culture, Society, and Press* (New Haven, CT: Yale University Press, 1994) and the previously cited (see history) *Egypt as a Women* added to the understanding of elite and middle class women. Similarly, Cynthia Nelson's biography of *Doria Shafik: Egyptian Feminist, A Woman Apart* (Gainsville, FL: University of Florida, 1996) reinforced this foundation. My own previously cited *Creating the New Egyptian Woman* falls into this category and adds the dimension of consumer studies. Researchers wanted more answers about the experience of ordinary women, and the work of Evelyn Early, Andrea Rugh, as well as Diane Singerman and Homa Hoodfar addresses these shortcomings: *The Baladi Women of Cairo* (Boulder, CO: L. Rienner, 1993); *The Family in Contemporary Egypt* (Syracuse, NY: Syracuse University Press, 1984) and *Reveal and Conceal: Dress in Egypt* (Syracuse, NY: Syracuse University Press, 1986); *Development, Change, and Gender: A View from the Household* (Bloomington, IN: Indiana University Press, 1996), respectively. While these scholars focused on urban experiences, Lila Abu-Lughod studied the Bedouin of the Western desert to understand gender relations as expressed in poetry, see her *Veiled Sentiments: Honor and Poetry in Bedouin Society* (Berkeley, CA: University of California Press, 2000 [2nd edition, updated]). Her anthology *Remaking Women: Feminism and Modernity in the Middle East*, with contributors, e.g. Khaled Fahmy, Mervat Hatem, Omnia Shakry, and Marilyn Booth is heavily tilted toward Egypt (Princeton, NJ: Princeton University Press, 1998) and has added significantly to the field. Hanan Kholoussy's *For Better or Worse: The Marriage Crisis that Made Modern Egypt* (Stanford: Stanford University Press, 2010), while situated in early twentieth century Egypt helps contextualize the current crisis that couples face today.

The return of the veil has generated a great deal of interest in the garment. Written at the time that many were still unveiled, Sherifa Zuhur's *Revealing, Reveiling: Islamist Gender Ideology in Egypt* is still a much-cited publication (Albany, NY: SUNY, 1992). Rather than focusing on the garment, Saba Mahmood has penetrated the world of women's religiousity, see her *Politics of Piety: The Islamic Revival, The Feminist Subject* (Princeton, NJ: Princeton University Press, 2005).

With respect to lesbianism, see Brian Whitaker *Unspeakable Love: Gay and Lesbian Life in the Middle East* (Berkeley, CA: University of California Press, 2006) for the contemporary period, and Saher Amer for the medieval period, in her article in the *Journal of Sexuality* 18 (2) (2009).

Education

James Heyworthe-Dunne's institutional study remains the most thorough study in English, *An Introduction to the History of Education in Modern Egypt* (London: Cass, 1968). Previously published author, Judith Cochran situates Egypt's current problems within a larger developmental framework in rooted in education, see *Educational Roots of a Political Crisis in Egypt* (Lanham: Lexington, 2008). Gregory Starett's *Putting Islam to Work: Education, Politics, and Religious Transformation in Egypt* contextualizes Islamic resurgence, as well as its appearance in schools and mass media (Berkeley, CA: University of California Press, 1998). Donald Malcolm Reid's *Cairo University and the Making of Modern Egypt* (Cambridge: Cambridge University Press, 2002) tells the story of the creation of the first national university. Similarly, his *Whose Pharaohs: Archeology, Museums, and National Identity from Napoleon to World War I* explains how Egyptians regained control of their antiquities through the study of Egyptology. There are two studies of student movements in Egypt that are useful for understanding their role in history, see Ahmed Abdallah, *The Student Movement and National Politics in Egypt, 1923–1973* (London: al-Saqi, 1985) and Haggai Erlich, *Students and the University in 20th Century Egyptian Politics* (London: F. Cass, 1989). For those interested in women and education, see Beth Baron's previously cited work on the press or my *Creating the New Egyptian Woman* (see women).

CULTURE

Language

The most indispensable tool for anyone learning the Egyptian dialect is the dictionary by Martin Hinds and el-Said Badawi, *A Dictionary of Egyptian Arabic* (Beirut: International Book Center, 1986); however, it is a costly text and requires some knowledge of the language. For those eager to learn how to write Arabic, Kristen Brusted, Mahmoud al-Batal, and Abbas al-Tonsi's *Alif Baa: an Introduction to the Arabic Language and Sounds* (Washington, DC: Georgetown University Press, 2010) now has an online component. It is easy to follow, and the learner can work at his/her own pace. These authors also have a series of texts for learning Modern Standard Arabic. If Egyptian dialect is the objective, then Ahmed Tahir Hassanein and Mona Kamel's *Yalla Ndardish bil-Arabi, Let's Chat in Arabic A Practical Introduction to the Spoken Arabic of Cairo* (Cairo, 1990) is recommended and was published in two versions, one for readers of Arabic and one for non-Arabic readers; however, it appears that it may be out of print. As a replacement, *Kullu Tamam*, written by two professors from the University of Amsterdam, appears to be an adequate substitute (Cairo: AUC Press, 2004).

Etiquette

While it is painfully out of date, Edward Lane's *Manners and Customs of the Modern Egyptians Written During the Years 1833–1835* is a good starting point for understanding traditions (Cairo: AUC Press, 2004). Obviously many things have changed in the nearly 200 years since Lane roamed the streets of Cairo; however, there are still many kernels of truth and residual customs. Published collections of Egyptian proverbs, tend to focus on those that are ancient rather than modern, while modern collections include all Arabic proverbs without distinguishing Egyptian from others, Stephen McGrane's *Trust in God, but Tie Your Camel* is a notable recent effort (Tamarac, FL: Llumina, 2009). At one time Veronica Seton-Williams and Peter Stocks's *Blue Guide Egypt* was the one of the most detailed, comprehensive travel guides with important cultural tips; however, it was last published in 1993 and is a bit out of date (New York: W. W. Norton, & Co.). Lonely Planet, maintains a staff of writers who travel regularly and update this information, see Benanev, et al., *Egypt* (Oakland, CA: Lonely Planet, 2010 [10th edition]).

Literature

The chapter on literature itself has many suggestions for authors and titles of modern literature; additionally, more information can be found at the government's State Information Service portal to Egyptian literature past and present: http://www. sis.gov.eg/En/FourStTemplate.aspx?CategoryID=543. This section is meant more for commentary or reference, or in the case of ancient literature, edited or annotated versions of texts, e.g., William Kelly Simpson, et al., *The Literature of Ancient Egypt: An Anthology of Stories, Instructions, Stelae, Autobiographies, and Poetry* (New Haven, CT: Yale University Press, 2003 [3rd edition]). Although not specifically about Egypt, Roger Allen and D. S. Richard's *Arabic Literature in the Post-Classical Period* (Cambridge: Cambridge University Press, 2006) covers general trends and Egypt is well-represented. Hoda Elsadda's chapter on "Egypt" in Radwa Ashour's, et al., *Arab Women Writers: A Critical Reference Guide, 1873–1999* (Cairo: AUC, 2004) is a useful resource.

Art and Architecture

Two general reference books that include particularly rich sections on art are Oakes and Gahlins's *Ancient Egypt: An Illustrated Reference to the Myths, Religions, Pyramids, and Temples of the lands of the Pharaohs* (New York: Barnes & Noble, 2003), which takes the reader up to the Ottoman period and David Silverman, ed., *Ancient Egypt* (London: Duncan Baird, 2003), which includes material from renowned Egyptologists on the global legacy of ancient Egypt. Alice Cartocci and Gloria Rosatti's *Egyptian Art: Masterpieces in Painting, Sculpture and Architecture* is geared toward beginners and covers a time span from pre-historic to Ptolemaic, with subjects including architecture, sculpture, paintings, pottery, clothing, and jewelry (New York: Barnes and Noble, 2007). A general work on Coptic Art and architecture is Gawdat Gabra's *Coptic Monasteries: Egypt's Monasteries: Egypt's Monastic Art and Architecture* (Cairo: AUC Press, 2002). Elizabeth Bolman and Patrick Godeau's (eds.) *Monastic Visions: Wall Paintings in the Monastery of St. Anthony at the Red Sea* (New Haven, CT: Yale University Press, 2002) is unique because it represents the most complete and best-preserved collection of monastic art, only recently having been restored. Moving into the Islamic period, Caroline Williams's *Islamic Monuments in Cairo: A Practical Guide* offers a meticulous and concise overview of 200 objects, as well as two introductory chapters (Cairo: AUC Press, 2004, [5th edition]). Written by a contemporary artist, Liliane Karnouk's *Modern Egyptian Art, 1910–2003*, is an overview of modern Egyptian art and artists in the context of global trends (Cairo: AUC Press, 2003 [1995]). Anthropologist Jessica Winegar interviews contemporary artists with the aim of understanding how they create their art and cultural identity through institutions where art is produced, sold, and collected: *Creative Reckonings: The Politics of Art and Culture in Contemporary Egypt* (Stanford: Stanford University Press, 2006).

Music

For information on recitation of epic poems, see Dwight Reynolds, *Heroic Poets, Poetic Heroes: The Ethnography of Performance in an Arabic Oral Epic Tradition* (Ithaca, NY: Cornell University Press, 1995). On traditional Arabic music generally, see Michael Frishkopf's chapter on music in *The Islamic World*, edited by Andrew Rippin (New York: Routledge, 2008), and his article on the nationalization of the Egyptian music industry in *Asian Music* 39 (2) (2008) outlines the key players. Virginia Danielson's biography of *Umm Kulthum* presents a nuanced picture of both 20th century Egyptian history as well as the recording industry, *The Voice of Egypt* (Chicago, IL: University of Chicago Press, 1998). Sherifa Zuhur, who has published numerous works on the visual and performing arts, also has an excellent biography of *Asmahan: Women, War, and Song* (Austin, TX: University of Texas Press, 2000). One of the best ways of learning about Egyptian music is by listening to it: http://www.6arab.com/index.php, which is available in English or Arabic; however, the English does not always work well. Click on the icon for Middle with the pyramids for Egyptian artists; even if the English is not functioning, the menu is picture driven and the tool bar's translator may help. This site is great because it includes artists from the past as well as the present.

Food

Undoubtedly the best source for Egyptian food is an Egyptian grandmother, the older the better since the newer types of appliances and cookware have changed the way traditional dishes are prepared. In such a spirit, Magda Medawy's *My Grandmother's Kitchen: Traditional Dishes Sweet & Savory* fits the bill (Cairo: AUC Press, 2006). Amy Riolo's *Nile Style: Egyptian Cuisine & Culture, Ancient Festivals, Significant Ceremonies, and Modern Celebrations* places Egyptian food in its historical and cultural context (New York: Hippocrene Books, 2009).

Leisure and Sports

For an introduction to the history of Egyptian sport, see Wolfgang Decker, *Sports and Games of the Ancient Egyptians*, translated by Allen Guttmann (New Haven, CT: Yale University Press). Lane's *Manners and Customs of the Modern Egyptians* (cited in etiquette), has detailed information on games of all sorts, including rules. Although not specific to Egypt, Ralph Hattox's monograph *Coffee and Coffeehouses: The Origins of a Social Beverage in the Medieval Near East* delivers on the promise of its title (Seattle, WA: University of Washington Press, 1985). Relli Shechter's monograph on *Smoking, Culture, and Economy in the Middle East: The Egyptian Tobacco Market 1800–2000* outlines the history of one the coffeehouse's standard products and how it was marketed and remodeled into a new one (London: Tauris, 2006). Recent research by Wilson Chacko Jacobs and Shaun Lopez helps situate the context for the rise of competitive sports in the monarchical period, see Jacobs's "Working Out Egypt: Masculinity and Subject Formation Between Modernity and Nationalism, 1870–1940" (Ph.D. diss, NYU, 2005), updated and revised as *Working Out Egypt: Effendi Masculinity and Subject Formation in Colonial Modernity, 1870–1940* (Durham, NC: Duke University Press, 2011), and Lopez's article on football (soccer) in *History Compass* 7 (1) (2008). For the official Web sites of the biggest football clubs, see http://www.ahlyegypt.com/ and http://www.zamalek-sc.com/forum/index.php. Interestingly enough, the Zamalek Club's site appears to be based in English, but branches out into forums in Arabic, whereas the Ahly site is in Arabic, but can be accessed by non-readers using the translator bar. On women and sport, see Yoav Di-Capua's contribution to the *Encyclopedia of Women in Islamic Cultures*, Joseph and Najmabadi, eds., entitled "Sports—Arab States" (Vol. 3, Leiden: Brill, 2005). Magda Baraka's work on the *Egyptian Upper Classes between Revolutions* (cited in history) and Mona Abaza's *Changing Consumer Cultures of Modern Egypt: Cairo's Urban Reshaping* (Leiden: Brill, 2006) address the rise in leisure culture and vacationing.

Popular Culture

Mona Abaza's volume (see preceding text) on *Changing Consumer Cultures of Modern Egypt* details the shift from traditional shopping patterns to the rise of mega-malls and gated neighborhoods. Uri Kupferschmidt's monograph on *European Department Stores, Middle Eastern Consumers: the Orosdi Back Saga* is difficult to find, but tells the story of one of the most important entrepreneurial families in Egypt (Istanbul: Ottoman Bank Archives & Research Center, 2007). Singerman and Amar's (eds.) *Cairo Cosmopolitan* is an anthology that covers urban renewal, coffee shops, pop music, sufism, racism, the internet, youth, and the places where young people congregate (Cairo: AUC Press, 2006). Singerman (ed.) has followed up with a companion volume *Cairo Contested: Governance, Urban Space, and Global Modernity* (Cairo: AUC, 2009). For a historical/nostalgic view of Cairo and its development, see Samir Raafat, *Cairo: The Glory Years* (Cairo: AUC Press, 2004). Lila Abu-Lughod's *Dramas of Nationhood: The Politics of Television in Egypt* deconstructs the soap opera as a reflection of political and social issues in the country (Chicago, IL: University of Chicago Press, 2005). Samia Mehrez's *Egypt's Culture Wars: Politics and Practice* questions the secular state as she interrogates literature, film, and mass media, as well as its perception and reception by the public (New York: Routledge, 2008). Walter Armbrust's *Mass Culture and Modernism in Egypt* takes up the issue of audience reception of music, television, and mass media, in addition to its impact on national identity (Cambridge: Cambridge University Press, 1996).

Performing Arts: Theatre, Dance, Film

Naomi Gunnels's article on the Ikhernofret is a good introduction into the earliest theatre in Egypt (*Studia Antiqua, Journal of the BYU Student Society for*

Ancient Studies 2 (2), Fall 2002). P. C. Sadgrove's *The Egyptian Theatre in the Nineteenth Century, 1799–1882* does much more than the title suggests, discussing ancient and medieval precedents to modern theatre (Reading, NY: Ithaca Press, 1996). Sherifa Zuhur has published several books on visual and performing arts in the Middle East, two include *Images of Enchantment* and *Colors of Enchantment* (Cairo: AUC Press, 1998) and (Cairo: AUC Press, 2001); and a large number of the chapters deal with Egypt. Walter Armbrust (cited in popular culture) is one of the leading Anglophone authorities on Egyptian film, see also his *Mass Mediation: New Approaches to Popular Culture in the Middle East and Beyond* (Berkeley, CA: University of California Press, 2000). Viola Shafik's *Popular Egyptian Cinema: Gender, Class, and Nation* (Cairo: AUC Press, 2007) deals specifically with Egyptian film, while her *Arab Cinema: Culture and Identity* addresses the link between film and other forms of performance (Cairo: AUC Press, 2007 [revised edition]). Many Egyptian films are available with subtitles from Arab Film Distributors, and one can watch endless clips of dancers and films discussed in chapter 6 on YouTube.

CONTEMPORARY ISSUES

A good place for background on contemporary issues is *MERIP Reports* (Middle East Research Information Project), www.merip.org, currently under the directorship of Chris Toensing, an Egypt specialist. The online version allows search by subject; however, older issues are available only in libraries. A superb online publication *Jadaliyya* devotes a section to Egypt: http://egypt.jadaliyya.com/. A magazine that is specific to Egypt and updated daily is *al-Masry al-Youm*, which comes in an Arabic and an English version, the link for the latter: http://www.almasryalyoum.com/en. The oldest continuously operating newspaper in the country provides an English language weekly, accessible online as well: http://weekly.ahram.org.eg/. The previously cited CIA *The World Factbook,* World Bank Development indicators, CAPMAS, and State Information Service all provide up to date information on various aspects of contemporary life.

Thematic Index

Index